DEEPER INTO DIVING

by

John Lippmann

AN IN-DEPTH REVIEW OF DECOMPRESSION PROCEDURES AND OF THE PHYSICAL AND PHYSIOLOGICAL ASPECTS OF DEEPER DIVING

An essential reference for divemasters, instructors and other diving professionals

Deeper Into Diving

DEEPER INTO DIVING

ISBN 0 9590306 3 8

Published by **J.L. Publications**, P.O. Box 381, Carnegie, Victoria, Australia, 3163.

First edition, July 1980
Reprinted December 1991
Reprinted November 1992
Reprinted June 1993
Reprinted February 1994
Reprinted September 1995
Reprinted March 1996

Cover photo by Max Gleeson
Desktop Publishing by Waverley Desktop Publishing Pty. Ltd.

Deeper Into Diving

Foreword

Once again John Lippmann has done a significant service for the diver. His previous books **The DAN (Diving) Emergency Handbook** and **The Essentials of Deeper Diving** are tributes to his skills of sifting through the widely spread and sometimes complex available information and rewriting it in simple, readable form. Be it in relation to diving accidents and how to provide first aid, to the knowledge necessary before a diver decides to dive deep to 100 ft (30 m), or more, his books provide a wealth of information. This vital data was made available to divers to markedly add to their safety, and ensure well informed planning before getting into a situation where special knowledge over and beyond that provided to new, or even quite experienced, divers is a must.

Now he has done it again with **Deeper Into Diving**, aimed at diving instructors. This book enables him in the first section to go further into the physiology and pathophysiology of so many problems engendered for the human body when diving deep. Problems of which many divers are ignorant, or at best ill-informed, and, so, often choose to ignore! But deep diving with SCUBA is **NOT** just like diving to 60 ft (18 m) or so. It requires additional training and problem considerations to dive to 100 ft, or more, with the same degree of safety as shallower dives. To do so requires a better knowledge of the physiological effects of deep diving on the body, including factors such as nitrogen narcosis, respiration and CO_2 retention, gas uptake and elimination, decompression, temperature effects, equipment problems, etc. All instructors should be well versed in this information.

Above all is the knowledge that tables and computers hold no specific guarantees as to the occurrence of decompression sickness. Section two, therefore, is devoted especially to decompression tables. Besides a brief and lucid history, he gives very readable comparative backgrounds and examples of diverse tables used today under a wide range of circumstances, including the U.S. Navy Tables, the Huggins Tables, The Bassett Table, DCIEM Tables, the Buehlmann Tables, the BS-AC Tables and the PADI Recreational Dive Planner. The instructor, after reading about so many variations, will soon realize we have still a lot to learn about decompression! However, better informed, divers should, with this book, be able to pick their way through the complexities, clearly explained, to a safer dive profile than those who have not been exposed to this data!

I heartily endorse this volume, not only for instructors, but for all those contemplating, or who are, deep divers. Much of this knowledge is also relevant for all kinds of diving, not just deep diving.

Indeed, I would hope that many divers will obtain and read all three books to date. It would be very worth their while and materially add to their diving safety and enjoyment.

Peter B. Bennett, Ph.D., D.Sc.
Professor of Anesthesiology
Executive Director, National Divers Alert Network (DAN)
Senior Director, F.G. Hall Hypo-Hyperbaric Center
Duke University Medical Center
Durham, NC 27710, USA

About the Author

John Lippmann is a Statistician and Mathematics Lecturer at a College of Technical and Further Education. He has been SCUBA diving for the past 18 years and instructing for the past 9 years. He holds SCUBA Instructor qualifications with a number of agencies which include the Federation of Australian Underwater Instructors (FAUI Advanced Divemaster Instructor), the National Association of Underwater Instructors (NAUI Master SCUBA Instructor), the Confederation Mondiale Des Activities Subaquatiques (CMAS Three Star SCUBA instructor and the British Sub-Aqua Club (BS-AC Advanced Instructor). He is also an instructor and examiner in Advanced Resuscitation (Oxygen Administration) and Sub-Aqua with the Royal Life-Saving Society of Australia and is currently the Co-ordinator of the Mechanical Oxygen Panel of the Royal Life-Saving Society - Victoria.

John Specializes in teaching Diver Rescue and Deep Diving courses. He has written articles about accident management and decompression for a variety of diving magazines and journals, and is often called upon to present lectures on these topics.

John is the co-author of **The Diving Emergency Handbook** which is released as specific editions in Australia, the USA, Germany, the United Kingdom and, soon Japan. The U.S. edition is titled **The DAN Emergency Handbook.** He is also the author of **The Essentials of Deeper Diving** which is released in Australia, the USA and Germany.

Acknowledgements

The author gratefully acknowledges the assistance provided by the Department of the Arts, Sport, the Environment, Tourism and Territories to the Australian Underwater Federation, which has enabled this book to be published in Australia.

I wish to acknowledge the substantial contribution by Dr. John Knight, without whose friendship and encouragement this book might never have got off the ground. Thanks also to Dr. Peter Mosse for his assistance with the chapter on Respiration and Circulation and to Dr. Cheryl Bass and Dr. Peter Rogers for their contributions towards the section on Women and Diving.

Very special thanks go to Surgeon Commander Des Gorman (RNZN), Professor Peter Bennett, Dr. Carl Edmonds and Dr. David Parsons for their continued encouragement, support and assistance with my projects, and for the many hours they have devoted to editing various sections of the draft of this book.

I also wish to acknowledge and thank the following people for reviewing various chapters of the draft and for their support and constructive suggestions:

Professor Dr. Albert Buehlmann, Karl Huggins, Ron Nishi, Dr. Tom Hennessy, Commander Paul Weathersby (USN), Major Marc Moody (RAOC), Drew Richardson, Dr. Max Hahn, Dr. George Lewbel, Dr. Janene Mannerheim, Dr. Susan Bangasser, Dr. Bruce Bassett, Dr. Michael Powell, Mike Busuttili, Ari Nikkola, Professor Brian Hills, Dr. Peter Wilmshurst, Dr. Ian Millar, Dr. Chris Acott, Gain Wong, Charlie Leeman, Beat Mueller, Dennis Graver and Gary Hatton.

Thanks are also due to Wayne Rolley, Peter Stone and Dr. Peter Wilmshurst for photographs supplied by them, to the various individuals and organizations who allowed me to reprint their tables and to Dr. Mark Fajgman for his continued support.

Finally I want to thank my wife Angela for her encouragement and patience while I spent the seemingly endless hours battling with the draft of this book. The book is dedicated to our son Michael.

DISCLAIMER

The contents of this book represents the author's view of current learning on this subject as at July1990. However, the reader is warned that hyperbaric medicine and decompression theory are relatively new and dynamic fields. As our understanding and knowledge increases, certain currently held beliefs (some of which are subject to some conjecture) may be disproved or modified. The reader is strongly advised to read new literature as it is released and, if necessary, to reassess appropriate areas of the text of this work accordingly.

Neither the author nor publisher accept responsibility for the accuracy of any examples or interpretations of the workings of the decompression tables included in this work, nor for the accuracy of the comparative tables. Whilst all care and skill have been taken in the preparation of these technical aspects, the reader should be aware of these limitations.

DEEPER INTO DIVING

- CONTENTS -

Page

PREFACE

SECTION 1: PHYSICAL, SENSORY, PHYSIOLOGICAL AND PSYCHOLOGICAL CONSIDERATIONS

1. Physical, sensory, physiological and psychological problems associated with depth. 3

2. Physiology.

   2.1 Respiration and circulation. 9
   2.2 Effect of SCUBA diving on respiration and circulation. 36

3. Nitrogen uptake and elimination. 41

4. Bubble formation. 47

5. Decompression sickness.

   5.1 Cause, manifestations, management and after-effects. 59
   5.2 Prevention. 93

6. Nitrogen Narcosis. 117

7. Carbon dioxide and diving. 123

8. Heat loss. 131

9. Dysbaric osteonecrosis. 145

10. Women and diving. 153

11. Drug use and the diver. 167

Page

SECTION 2: DECOMPRESSION TABLES

12. History of decompression tables. 177

13. U.S. Navy Tables.

13.1 History and design. 185
13.2 Using the U.S. Navy Tables. 195
13.3 Adapting the U.S. Navy Tables to sport diving 215

14. More conservative alternatives based on the U.S. Navy Tables.

14.1 The Huggins Tables. 225
14.2 The Bassett Table. 229
14.3 The NAUI Dive Tables. 237

15. New U.S. Navy Tables. 239

16. Swiss/German Tables.

16.1 The ZH-L System 247
16.2 The Buehlmann Tables. 253
16.3 The Buehlmann/Hahn Tables. 265

17. DCIEM Tables. 279

18. The BS-AC Tables.

18.1 The RNPL/BS-AC Table. 303
18.2 The BS-AC '88 Tables. 325

19. The PADI Recreational Dive Planner. 347

SECTION 3: ALTITUDE CONSIDERATIONS AND DIVING

20. Flying after diving. 381

21. Diving at altitude. 393

SECTION 4: MULTI-LEVEL DIVING

22. Multi-level diving using tables. 423

23. Dive computers. 443

Page

SECTION 5: DECOMPRESSION STOP DIVING

24. Decompression stop diving. 477

25. Omitted decompression. 485

SECTION 6: ADMINISTRATION OF OXYGEN TO DIVERS

26. Oxygen. 499

27. Emergency in-water recompression using oxygen. 517

SECTION 7: OTHER CONSIDERATIONS

28. Some equipment considerations.

28.1 Regulator performance at depth. 525
28.2 Buoyancy considerations. 527

29. Air supply calculations. 531

APPENDICES 549

INDEX 606

Preface

In 1838, William Newton first filed a patent for a diaphragm-actuated, twin-hose demand valve for divers. The first SCUBA system appears to have been developed and patented in 1918 by Ohgushi, a Japanese. This system could either be operated with a surface supply of air or as a self-contained system with an air supply carried on the diver's back. The diver used his teeth to trigger air flow into his mask. In 1943, Cousteau and Gagnon developed the first SCUBA system incorporating a demand valve to release air as the diver inhaled.

These early milestones marked the beginnings of what has now become an enormous industry - the recreational diving industry. Many millions of people throughout the world have now enjoyed the wonders of the underwater world with the aid of SCUBA. Recent figures indicate that there *may* currently be between two and three million active SCUBA divers (i.e. doing one or more dives in 12 months) in the USA alone (although some argue that this figure is a vast overestimate).

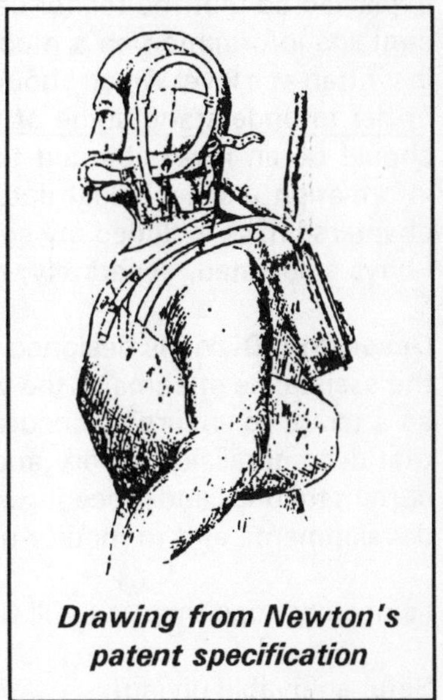

Drawing from Newton's patent specification

There is presently quite an animated debate about whether or not diving has become safer or more hazardous over recent years. Some critics have suggested that safety has at times been compromised in the pursuit of the commercial dollar. There has certainly been an increase in the number of reported diving accidents, both fatal and non-fatal, but this does not necessarily mean that the accident *rate* has increased. The increased number of reported accidents may be a result of a combination of a better understanding of the signs and symptoms of various diving accidents, better reporting of accidents and a greatly increased number of active divers. However, the fact remains that far too many divers have accidents and it is essential that all divers become well-versed in the essential aspects of safe diving, accident prevention and accident management.

The type of diving undertaken by recreational divers has changed dramatically over the years. Whereas the early divers mainly did relatively shallow, shore-based dives, the improvement of diving equipment, the ready access to a multitude of dive charter boats, and the discovery and lure of new wrecks and reefs in deeper water has encouraged many divers to venture deeper into the sea. Although these deeper dives may at times offer a certain challenge and excitement, the greater depth introduces new problems which make deeper dives potentially far more hazardous than dives conducted in shallower water.

A U.S. Navy report of their diving accidents between 1968 and 1981 showed that the accident rate for dives to 100 ft (30 m) or more was more than twice the rate for dives between 50 ft (15 m) and 100 ft, and nine times that for dives shallower than 50 ft. More recent DAN statistics indicate that more than 70% of the bends cases reported in the U.S.A in 1988 were divers who had dived deeper than 80 ft (24 m). BS-AC figures indicate that 47% of British sport divers who had contracted bends in 1988 had undertaken deep dives. So it is obvious that deeper diving is more dangerous than remaining in shallower water.

A diver, especially one who tends to dive in deeper water, must be aware of and must understand the potential problems associated with depth, so that he or she can minimize the risks associated with this type of diving.

My book titled **The Essentials of Deeper Diving** was written to provide the essential information to such divers, and presents the information at a level which should be easily understood by the average diver.

This book, however, is for the more experienced diver, especially the diving educator. Here much of the information introduced in **The Essentials of Deeper Diving** is expanded and explained so that the reader can gain a far greater insight into the subject. This book also contains information on a much wider variety of decompression tables and procedures. It is written at a level which should be understood by the diving educator, and should help him or her to understand some of the more technical texts and reports which are available. It should be an invaluable aid to diving instructors as it provides a lot of the background information and technical data that is not always easily obtainable. At the end of most chapters I have included my sources so that readers can further their knowledge if desired. I have also listed, separately, references which I believe are particularly suitable.

Deeper Into Diving is designed to be a thorough and accurate reference, and I have enlisted the assistance of some of the world's authorities on decompression and diving medicine in an attempt to ensure its accuracy at the time of writing. However, the reader must realize that decompression theory and diving medicine are both dynamic areas, and some of the current theories and procedures may change with time. It is important to keep abreast of new developments and to modify our practices accordingly.

I sincerely hope that you will find this book to be a valuable addition to your diving library.

Safe, enjoyable diving,

JOHN LIPPMANN

NOTE:

Diving is a sport for both sexes. For the sake of grammatical ease I have only written in one gender.

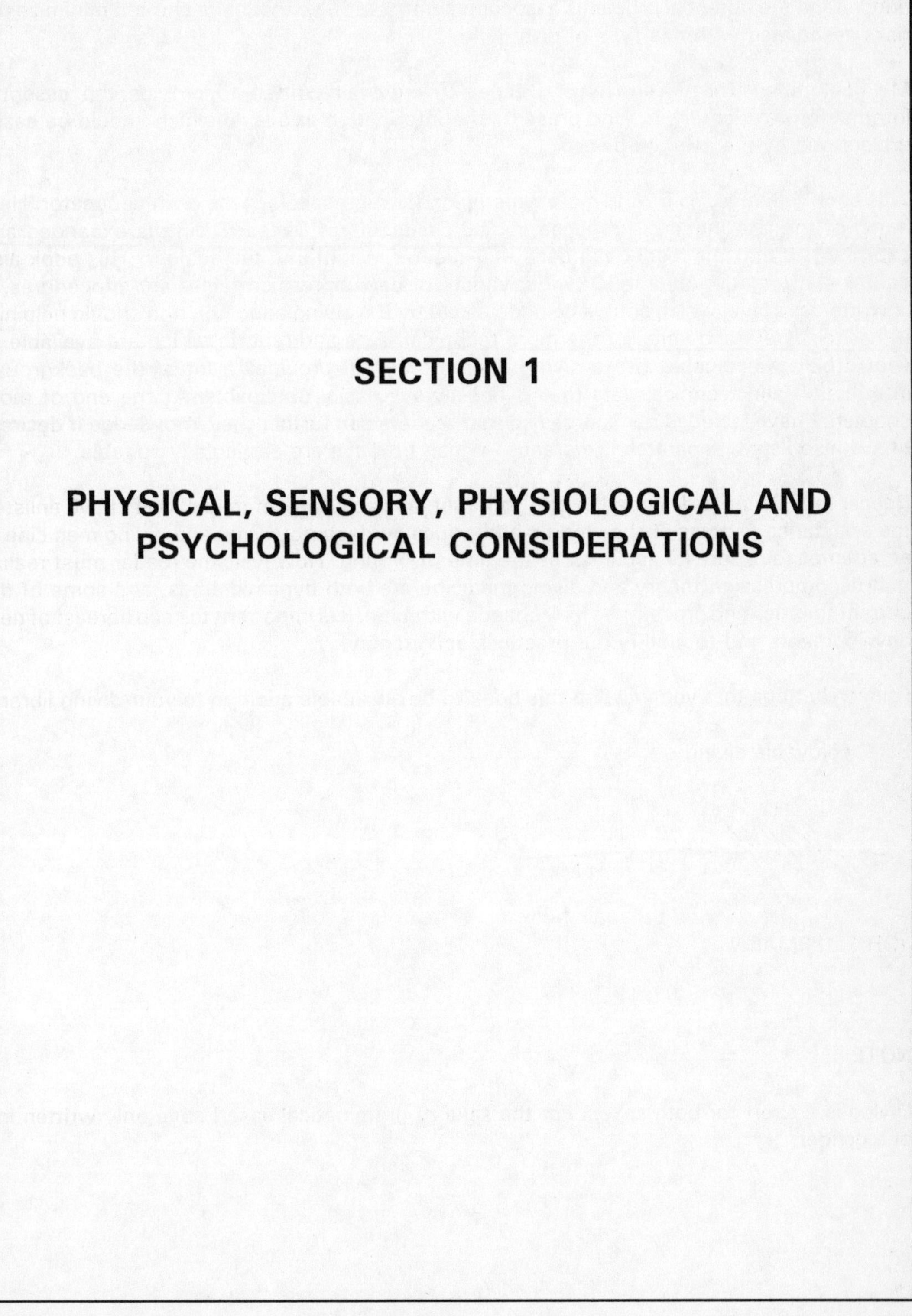

SECTION 1

PHYSICAL, SENSORY, PHYSIOLOGICAL AND PSYCHOLOGICAL CONSIDERATIONS

CHAPTER 1

SENSORY, PHYSICAL, PHYSIOLOGICAL AND PSYCHOLOGICAL CHANGES DUE TO IMMERSION

Wrapped up in a wetsuit, wearing gloves and floating neutrally buoyant, the diver is not exposed to the multitude of stimuli that we get on the surface. Gravity is hardly felt except where the weight-belt is. The hands are insulated from the outside world by gloves. The main stimuli to reach the diver come from the eyes, and they are peering into the murk through a facemask which reduces the field of view to a few degrees. No wonder that divers in nil visibility become disorientated! Add to this the effects of cold, interfering with the sense of touch, muscular movement, nerve transmission and logical thought, and the effects of nitrogen narcosis interfering with brain function. The deep diver is exposed to a hostile environment and at the same time heavily handicapped.

The human has evolved as an animal adapted to living in an air environment and eating, drinking, walking, talking and (usually) reproducing on land. Our physiology and responses are geared to an air environment at an ambient pressure of one atmosphere.

When we choose to leave our normal environment and plunge into the sea, we must suddenly learn to adapt to a foreign environment. Masks help us to see in this new environment, fins help to push us along, SCUBA allows us to breathe, wetsuits keep us warm, but the functioning of most of our senses is altered and/or reduced. We suffer from **sensory deprivation**. To add to this, the effects of the increasing pressure cause physiological changes within our bodies, and the relative unfamiliarity with the environment may cause psychological changes within us.

Diving requires that we learn to adapt to the physical, sensory, physiological and psychological changes, however we are unable to adapt completely, only partially, and as divers we must learn to allow for the changes. Most of the problems and changes are inherent to all dives but some problems are magnified, and some new problems arise, as the depth of diving increases. Unless adequately compensated for, these may become potentially hazardous.

This chapter introduces some of the changes that we must accommodate when we decide to gear up and slip into the "silent world" that we have grown to love. The physiological changes will be dealt with in depth in the following chapters.

Vision

To most of us vision is the most important sense both on land and underwater. Diving masks generally cut out the peripheral vision on which we are normally quite reliant and which is one of the most sensitive areas of our vision. Some masks also have blind spots in the plane of vision. For example, masks with two lenses introduce a central blind spot, while those with extra side lenses do increase peripheral vision but also introduce extra blind spots and, at times, double images. Therefore, our **field of vision is normally greatly reduced when we dive.** We cannot often see as far underwater as we can on land due to particles in the water, so the **depth of vision is usually greatly reduced** while diving.

The greater refraction (bending) of light in water **alters the size and perspective of what we see.** Objects appear to be closer (by about 25%) and thus larger (by about 30%) than they really are. This magnification or displacement effect can actually be an advantage to some short-sighted divers. The effect is shown in Figure 1.1 and explained in Figure 1.2.

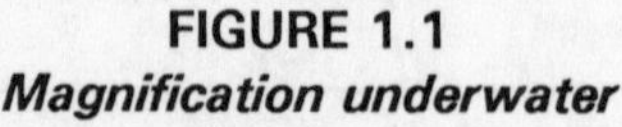

FIGURE 1.1
Magnification underwater

FIGURE 1.2
Displacement of image in water

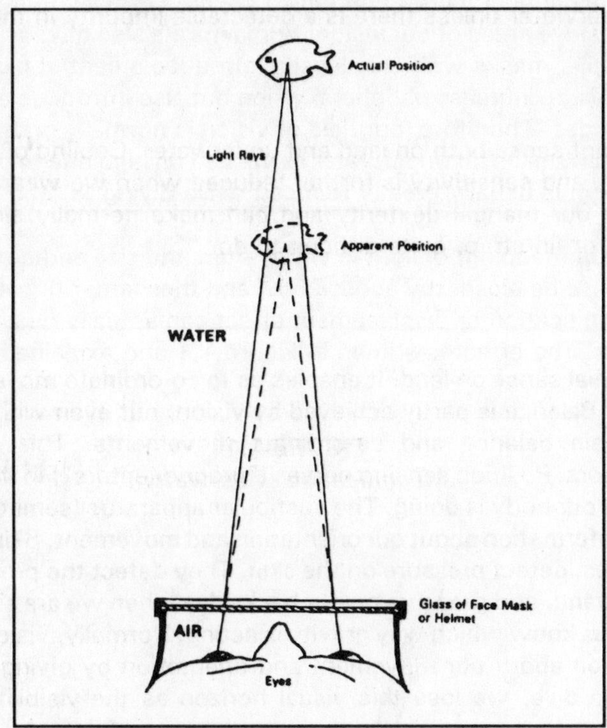

Reprinted with permission from R. Thomas and B. McKenzie

If the water is fairly murky or if we are quite deep, most of the red, orange and yellow light is absorbed or reflected and the predominent color becomes blue. The eye is not very sensitive to blue light or to the lower light levels at depth, or in murky water. **Colors of objects seen at depth are often not the true colors of the objects.**

Sound

Sound is greatly affected when transmitted through the water. **Sound originating from above the surface is greatly reduced** when transmitted into the water, as many sound waves are reflected at the surface. When we are underwater our **hearing is reduced** to some degree by the effect of water on the eardrum, and some frequencies are affected more than others, causing the **sound to be distorted**. The wearing of a hood further decreases the hearing. Sound travels much faster in water than in air (about four times the speed) and this, together with the fact that sound is transmitted to us through our skull bones rather than our eardrums, makes it **far more difficult to detect the direction of the source of the sound.**

Smell and Taste

Smell and taste are usually important senses to us when we are landbound but they usually are not utilized underwater unless there is a detectable impurity in the breathing air.

Touch

Touch is an important sense both on land and underwater. Cooling of the skin reduces the sensitivity to touch, and sensitivity is further reduced when we wear gloves. Cooling and gloves also reduce our manual dexterity and can make normally simple tasks, such as readjusting a mask or fin strap, quite difficult to do.

Balance

Balance is an essential sense on land. It enables us to co-ordinate movements and orientate our body correctly. Balance is partly achieved by vision, but even with our eyes closed we can usually maintain balance and co-ordinate movements. This is achieved by the combination of factors. Position sensing nerves ("proprioceptors") in the muscles and joints tell us exactly what our body is doing. The vestibular apparatus (semi-circular canals) in our inner ears provide information about our orientation and movement. Skin pressure receptors, as their name implies, detect pressure on the skin. They detect the pressure on the soles of our feet when we stand, and pressure on our backsides when we are sitting. In other words these receptors let us know which way gravity is acting. Normally, vision provides our major source of information about our movement and orientation by giving us a visual horizon. However, when we dive, we lose this visual horizon as the visibility is reduced. Thus, underwater, we become more reliant on the other sources of determining position and this can introduce certain problems. If cold water suddenly enters one ear, the vestibular apparatus' receive conflicting information about orientation and we suffer from vertigo. When we are underwater, the pressure is equal on all parts of our body, so we lose the ability to feel gravity (except at our weight-belt) and, hence, to determine which way is down and, more importantly, which way is up. The result of the combination of these factors is that **underwater there is no inherent sense of the vertical or of balance.** Without visual cues it is difficult tell if we are laying horizontally or vertically, or whether we are facing the surface or the sea bed. Divers who operate in zero visibility can very easily become disorientated.

Weightlessness

A neutrally buoyant diver is essentially weightless. Weightlessness is one of the delights of diving in that it gives us the ability to move freely in three dimensions. However, **it can make normally simple tasks a little more difficult.** If we push on an object underwater we get forced back in the opposite direction, unless we are sufficiently anchored. This must be compensated for if certain tasks are to be done. Professional divers often overweight themselves in order to gain sufficient anchorage. For safety these divers are attached to a rope from the surface ("life-line"). Free-swimming divers should never be overweighted and must compensate for the weightlessness in other ways.

Temperature Loss

Water conducts heat about twenty-five times faster than does air, so, unless we are adequately insulated, **we lose heat rapidly when underwater.** As we dive deeper the water gets cooler, our wetsuit compresses, the air we breathe becomes denser and these all combine to cause us to lose body heat more rapidly. Hypothermia becomes a greater potential threat as we begin to dive deeper. The **cold slows down our thinking and our reflexes, it makes manual tasks more difficult and depletes our energy.**

Effects on Ventilation

Being immersed means that we must work **harder to breathe.** Immersion forces extra blood into lung blood vessels, making the lungs stiffer and making breathing more of an effort. Breathing from a regulator increases this effort due to the breathing resistance within the regulator. Wearing a tight wetsuit top further increases the effort of breathing. As we go deeper the air becomes denser and breathing requires more and more effort. The increased effort of breathing causes an **increase in carbon dioxide levels** in our blood, which in turn increases our breathing rate, further increasing the effort of breathing. High carbon dioxide levels potentiate other diving ailments and may, in itself, cause us to become unconscious underwater. At depth, the denser air does not diffuse with alveolar air as easily, further **reducing ventilation efficiency.**

Our maximum breathing capacity at 100 ft (30 m) is about one half that at the surface. The ventilation requirements of a 1-2 knot swim at 100 ft may approach, or exceed, our maximum breathing capacity. **If we exercise at depth we may require more air than some regulators can supply us with.** It would be unlikely that we could "outbreathe" one of the newer, higher performance regulators as long as it is functioning correctly, however, a poorly adjusted high performance regulator can quite easily be outbreathed.

Psychological Effects

Little is known about the psychological effects of diving, but there is evidence to suggest that psychological factors often contribute to diving accidents. Unless we are confident in our own diving ability and also confident in our equipment, when under stress our anxiety can turn to **panic.** Panic can, and does, cause serious incidents to occur. Our training is designed to teach us strict procedures to adopt in the event of an emergency, so that we may avoid the tendancy to panic.

At times, when a diver is in clear, deep water and loses sight of familiar objects, a **fear of isolation in the vastness of the sea develops and panic may ensue.** Occassionally, after ascending from depth up a long anchor line and temporarily forgetting that his buddy was nearby, divers have reported feeling very alone in a strange world and surrounded by a hell of a lot of water. This is known as the **Blue Orb Syndrome** and it can be overcome by focusing on familiar objects or people; such as focusing on your gauges or on your buddy.

Physiological Effects

Physiological abnormalities such as nitrogen narcosis, hypoxia and carbon dioxide toxicity can cause variable psychological reactions, depending on the personality of the diver, the environment and the severity of the physiological effect. Nitrogen narcosis distorts our thinking, narrows our attention and may allow us to do stupid things.

It becomes obvious that we must do a lot of adapting, whether we realize it or not, in order to safely continue our sojourns into the underwater world. Many of the potential problems mentioned will be discussed more fully in the following chapters.

SUMMARY

* **The human has evolved as a land animal and is not naturally equipped to cope with the underwater environment.**
* **The underwater environment introduces many potential problems to which a diver must learn to adapt.**
* **Various physical, sensory, physiological and psychological changes occur when we dive.**

  Some of these changes are:

  - **reduced vision**
  - **loss of color**
  - **sound distortion**
  - **reduced input from smell and taste**
  - **reduced sense of touch**
  - **loss of balance and orientation cues**
  - **weightlessness**
  - **temperature loss**
  - **impaired ventilation**
  - **anxiety**
  - **nitrogen narcosis**
  - **high carbon dioxide levels**

CHAPTER 2

PHYSIOLOGY

2.1 Respiration and Circulation

The functions of the respiratory and circulatory systems are intimately related; so much so that it is appropriate to consider them together. The respiratory system provides a mechanism to bring blood and air close together (without actually allowing physical mixing) so that gas exchange can occur. Gas exchange is the uptake of oxygen from the lungs and removal of carbon dioxide from the blood. The circulatory system then circulates the oxygen to all the tissues of the body where another round of gas exchange occurs: this time oxygen passes from the blood to the tissues and carbon dioxide from the working tissues to the blood. Both systems are also involved in the control of acid-base balance within the body.

THE RESPIRATORY SYSTEM

The respiratory system consists of the ribs, intercostal muscles, diaphragm, lungs, mouth and nose, and a series of pipes connecting the mouth and nose with the lungs (Figure 2.1.1).

FIGURE 2.1.1

The respiratory system

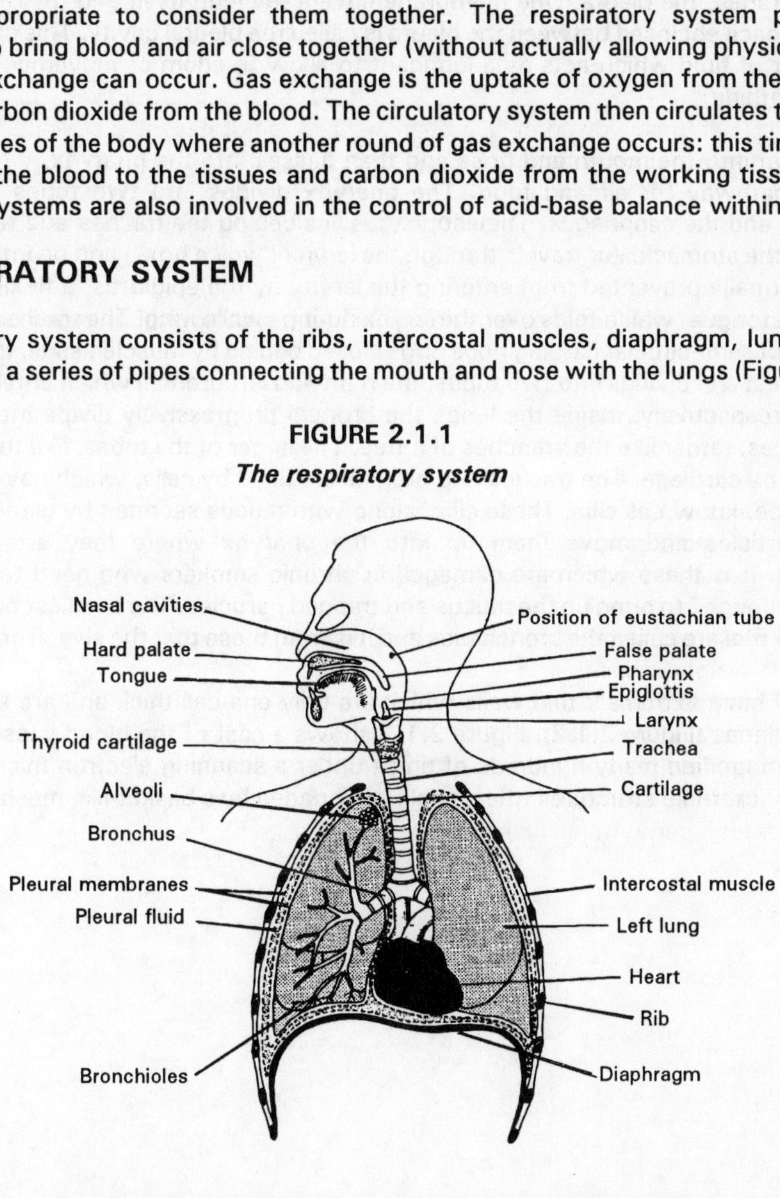

Reprinted with permission of P. Gadd and Macmillan Publishers Ltd.

The two lungs are roughly cone-shaped and are situated in the thorax. The thorax consists of the ribs, sternum and thoracic vertebrae and is separated from the abdomen by the diaphragm, a dome-shaped muscle attached to the vertebrae and lower ribs. All the ribs are attached to the vertebral column, however, only the first seven ribs on each side are attached directly to the sternum. The next three are attached to the ribs just above, while the front ends of the last two are free. Between the ribs lie the intercostal muscles, which help in the action of breathing. The diaphragm is composed of muscle and strong fibrous tissue. The thorax also serves to protect the heart and largest blood vessels.

The lungs themselves are composed of elastic tissue and each is surrounded by two very thin membranes, the pleura. One membrane covers the lung itself and the other the chest wall. The space enclosed between the pleura is called the pleural cavity. This cavity contains a thin layer of fluid which acts as a lubricant to allow freedom of movement of the lungs during breathing.

Air is drawn into the mouth and nose and then passes into the pharynx, which is a short common pathway for air and food. The pharynx divides into two tubes - the trachea (windpipe) and the esophagus. The esophagus lies behind the trachea and takes food and fluids into the stomach. Air travels through the larynx ("voice box") and on into the trachea. Food is normally prevented from entering the larynx by the epiglottis, a flexible flap at the back of the tongue, which folds over the larynx during swallowing. The trachea is composed of a series of semi-circular cartilaginous rings closed behind by muscle tissue. It passes down into the chest and divides into two tubes, the right and left bronchi which enter the right and left lungs respectively. Inside the lungs the bronchi progressively divide into smaller and smaller tubes, rather like the branches of a tree. The larger of the tubes, like the trachea, are supported by cartilage. The trachea and bronchi are lined by cells, which have tiny hairs on their surface, known as cilia. These cilia, along with mucus secreted by glands, act to trap foreign particles and move them up into the pharynx where they are subsequently swallowed. It is these which are damaged in chronic smokers who need to resort to the "smoker's cough" to bring up the mucus and trapped particles. The smallest branches of the respiratory tree are called the bronchioles and it is from these that the alveoli or air sacs arise.

The alveoli have extremely thin walls which are only one cell thick and are surrounded by many capillaries (Figure 2.1.2). Figure 2.1.2 shows a cast of the blood vessels making up the lungs magnified many hundreds of times under a scanning electron microscope. Note the small pocket-like structures (the alveoli) surrounded by a basket-like mesh of capillaries.

FIGURE 2.1.2
Cast of a lung

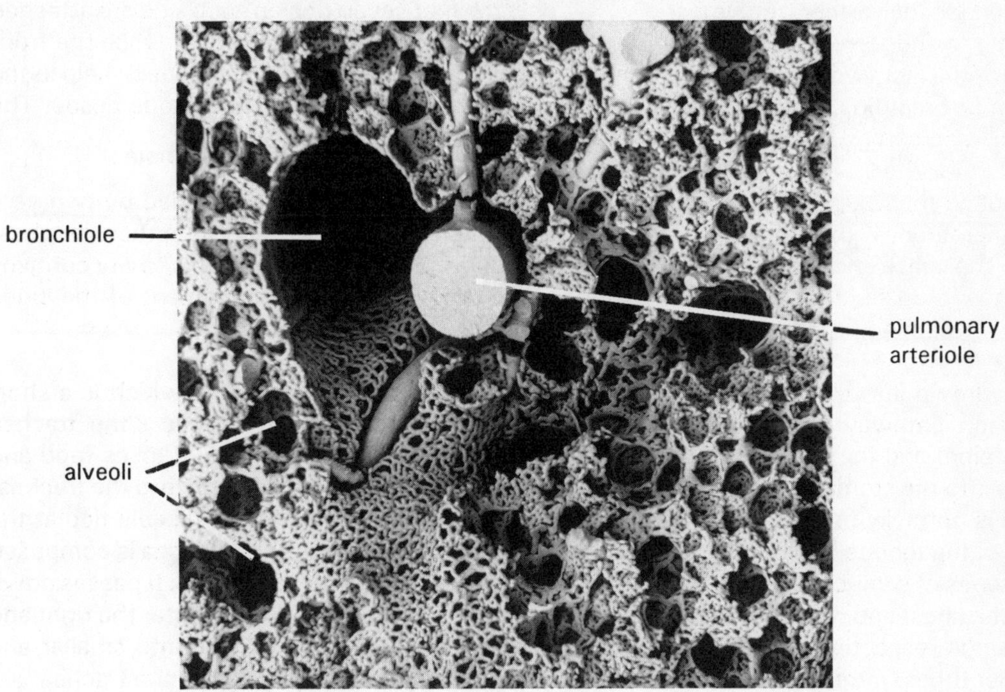

The alveoli can be likened to tiny balloons with a basket of fine blood vessels wrapped around (Figure 2.1.3). The inner surfaces of the alveoli are coated with a soapy substance known as surfactant. Surfactant acts to decrease the surface tension of the alveoli, thereby reducing their tendency to collapse. If this surfactant is washed off, as for example may occur during drowning, the alveoli may collapse. The distance separating the gas in the alveoli from the blood in the capillary is approximately 1 μm (very roughly 1/20 of the thickness of this page). The barrier between gas and blood is called the alveolar-capillary membrane. If the alveolar capillary membrane is torn and air enters the blood, an air embolism results.

FIGURE 2.1.3
An alveolus surrounded by capillaries

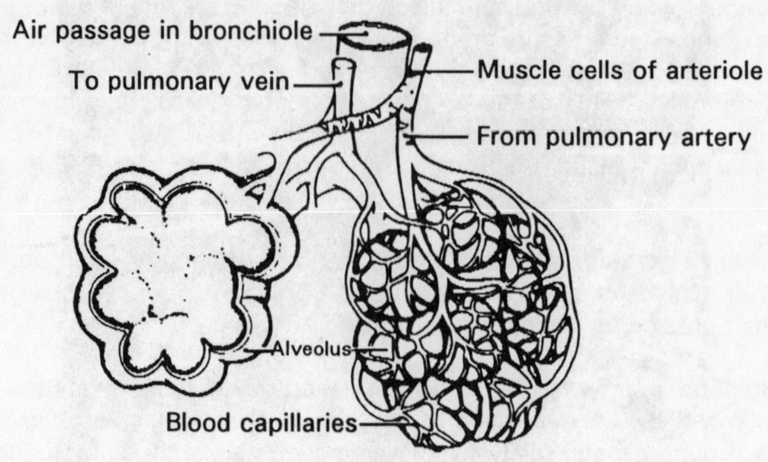

There are approximately 300 million alveoli (in both lungs). If all the alveoli were opened out and laid flat they would cover an area of about 1090 ft^2 (100 m^2), which is approximately the area of a tennis court.

The respiratory tract can be divided into two portions, the Conducting and the Respiratory portions. The "Conducting portion" connects the external environment with the gas exchange area of the lung. It consists of the nose, nasal passages, pharynx, larynx, trachea, bronchi and bronchioles. It is responsible for warming or cooling of inspired air, humidifying inspired air and filtering particles from it. Speech is also made possible by the flow of air over the vocal cords which form part of the conducting portion. The "Respiratory portion" is the area where actual gas exchange occurs - the alveolar sacs.

At birth, the lungs and thoracic cavity are the same size. After birth the thorax grows more rapidly than the lungs so that a negative pressure is established within the intrapleural space, bringing about a stretching of the lungs. This is the reason the lungs collapse if the pleural membrane is damaged as, for example, in a pneumothorax.

MECHANISM OF BREATHING

Inspiration and expiration are brought about by the up and down movement of the diaphragm and the elevation and depression of the ribs by the intercostal muscles. This causes changes in the volume of the chest cavity and, therefore, the pressure.

Inspiration occurs when the pressure inside the chest is less than the pressure outside. As the thorax expands, the pressure in the thorax becomes less than that in the atmosphere, creating a pressure gradient, and so air begins to flow through the nose and/or mouth into the lungs. During expansion of the lungs, the pulmonary capillaries adjacent to the alveoli are "pulled open", resulting in an increase in blood flow through them during inspiration and producing ideal conditions for the transfer of gases between the alveoli and the blood in the capillaries.

Expiration occurs when the pressure inside the chest is greater than outside. When the diaphragm relaxes, the chest cavity decreases in size and so the pressure is now higher in the lungs than outside, causing air to rush out.

Normal ventilation is achieved by *active* movement of the diaphragm and the intercostal muscles, followed by *passive* recoil of the elastic chest walls and diaphragm. At rest, breathing is brought about solely by the action of the diaphragm. During exercise, the inspiratory intercostal muscles also become involved, actively expanding the thorax and the expiratory muscles actively squeezing the chest to force the air out of the lungs.

Figure 2.1.4 shows the physiological volumes and capacities which make up the total lung volume.

FIGURE 2.1.4
Respiratory volumes and capacities
(Figures for a young adult male)

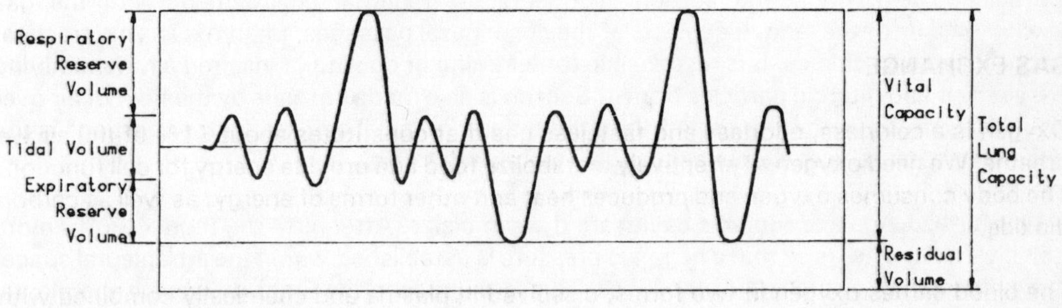

The Tidal Volume (TV), approximately 500ml, is the volume breathed in each breath.

The Inspiratory Reserve Volume, (IRV), approximately 3000ml, is the volume which can still be inspired after a normal tidal volume inspiration.

The Expiratory Reserve Volume (ERV), approximately 1100ml, is the volume which can still be exhaled after a normal tidal volume expiration.

The Residual Volume (RV), approximately 1200ml, is the volume which remains in the lungs after a forced exhalation.

The Vital Capacity (VC) is the sum of the IRV, the TV and the ERV.

The Total Lung Capacity (TLC) is the sum of the VC and the RV.

At rest the tidal volume is around 500ml. The tidal volume increases with exercise intensity. Thus since the vital capacity is constant for an individual, a greater proportion of the IRV and ERV are used during exercise.

The Respiratory Minute Volume (RMV) is the amount of air moved into the respiratory system each minute. It is the product of the tidal volume and respiratory rate and is approximately 6 liters/minute at rest (i.e. 500ml/breath x 12 breaths/minute).

A related physiological volume of importance to divers is the FEV_1 (The Forced Expiratory Volume in the first second). This is the proportion of the vital capacity which can be exhaled forcefully in the first second. For divers it should normally be in excess of 75%. Values below this may indicate significant trapping of air in the lungs, which may predispose a diver to pulmonary barotrauma.

The volume of air not involved in gas exchange is known as "dead space". It is important to realize that most of the air in the respiratory tract is not available for exchange. Thus the air that fills the respiratory passages (approx. 150ml) makes up what is known as the "anatomical dead space".

GAS EXCHANGE

Oxygen is a colorless, odorless and tasteless gas that constitutes about 21% of the air we breathe. We need oxygen to effectively metabolize food and provide energy for cell function. The body consumes oxygen and produces heat and other forms of energy, as well as carbon dioxide.

The blood carries oxygen in two forms: dissolved in plasma and chemically combined with hemoglobin (called oxyhemoglobin).

Oxygen is not very soluble in plasma at normal temperatures and pressures, so very little is normally dissolved in plasma. The vast majority of oxygen is chemically combined with hemoglobin.

When breathing air at normal atmospheric pressures the hemoglobin is 97.5% saturated with oxygen. As the oxygen rich blood reaches the tissues, the hemoglobin releases some oxygen but still remains about 75% saturated. The oxygen is released from the hemoglobin because the partial pressure of oxygen in the tissues is lower than in the blood. The greater acidity of the blood in the tissues also promotes unloading of the oxygen from the hemoglobin.

Carbon dioxide is a waste product of our metabolism. It combines with water in the body to form carbonic acid, a weak acid which breaks down readily to form bicarbonate. Carbon dioxide is carried in our blood in three ways. A small amount (8%) is dissolved in the plasma, another small amount (11%) is bonded to hemoglobin or plasma proteins, but most of the carbon dioxide (81%) in our blood is carried as bicarbonate. As the carbon dioxide diffuses from the tissues into the blood, the acidity of the blood increases.

Composition Of Alveolar Air

Alveolar air differs quite markedly from atmospheric air (Table 2.1.1) because:

(i) Alveolar air is only partially replaced by atmospheric air each breath, due to mixing of fresh air with what remains in the anatomical dead space, and

(ii) Air is humidified as it travels to the lungs, thereby changing the percentage composition of the gas.

TABLE 2.1.1
Composition of air (mmHg)

	Atmospheric air	Air in alveoli	Expired air
Nitrogen	597	569	566
Oxygen	159	104	120
Carbon dioixide	0.3	40	27
Water vapor	3.7	47	47

The partial pressure of oxygen is increased and the partial pressure of carbon dioxide is decreased in expired air due to dilution with dead space air.

(Note that the partial pressure of oxygen in expired air is quite high. This is why Expired Air Resuscitation is possible).

At all times the partial pressure of oxygen in the alveoli is higher than that in the blood of the lung capillaries while the partial pressure of carbon dioxide in the blood is higher than in the alveolar air. Thus, there is a continuous gradient for the diffusion of oxygen from the alveoli into the blood and carbon dioxide out of the blood into the alveoli. Similarly, in the tissues, after the oxygen unloads from the hemoglobin it diffuses along a concentration gradient to the tissues. **Diffusion is the movement of substances (including gases) from areas of high concentration to areas of lower concentration.**

FIGURE 2.1.5

The exchange of gases across the alveolar-capillary membrane

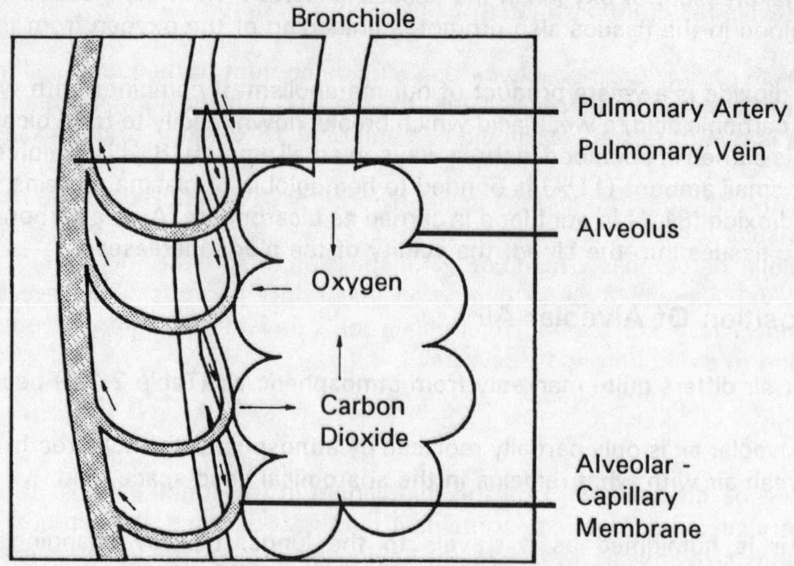

Note: the shaded area in the pulmonary blood vessels represents oxygenated blood whereas the unshaded area represents deoxygenated blood.

CONTROL OF RESPIRATION

The partial pressure of carbon dioxide in the arterial blood (normally about 40mmHg or 0.053ats) **and the acidity (pH) of this blood are the fundamental factors regulating breathing.**

The respiratory center, located in the medulla (in the brain stem), contains groups of nerve cells, called chemoreceptors, sensitive to carbon dioxide. In addition, carbon dioxide and acidity levels may act through chemoreceptors in the major arteries.

When blood rich in carbon dioxide reaches the brain the medulla sends nerve impulses to the diaphragm and other respiratory muscles, making them contract, causing inspiration and the subsequent removal of carbon dioxide with expiration. The depth and frequency of breathing is adjusted so that carbon dioxide is discharged in the expired gas at the same rate as it is produced in the tissues (about 200ml/min). This ensures that the carbon dioxide and acidity levels of the blood return to normal.

The rate of breathing set by the regulatory action of carbon dioxide ensures that ventilation is more than adequate to supply the oxygen needed by the body. The resting body needs around 250ml of oxygen per minute. Exercise can increase this to as much as 3000ml a minute. During exercise, production of carbon dioxide increases and the body responds, via the chemoreceptors, by increasing the rate and depth of respiration to maintain constant oxygen and carbon dioxide levels. The increased acidity is detected by receptors in the brain, and the rate and depth of breathing is increased until the acidity is reduced to normal levels.

Lack of oxygen does not normally stimulate breathing significantly unless the arterial oxygen levels fall to dangerously low levels. There are chemoreceptors sensitive to low arterial oxygen in the walls of the aorta and the carotid arteries. These stimulate the breathing if oxygen levels fall dramatically (i.e. below about 0.10atm).

An increase of only 0.3% in the carbon dioxide content of the blood will normally result in the doubling of the volume of air breathed in and out. In normal breathing, 85% of the stimulus is due to raised carbon dioxide and only 15% is due to depressed oxygen levels.

Finally, stretch receptors located in the pleura transmit impulses to the respiratory center. During inspiration these are stretched and send messages to the brain, leading to an inhibition of particular nerve cells which control inspiration (inspiratory neurons), and activation of other nerve cells which cause expiration (expiratory neurons). The reverse occurs during expiration. These act to limit overinspiration but add additional impetus to swap from inspiration to expiration and vice versa.

BLOOD

Blood can be considered to be the middleman in the functioning of the respiratory and circulatory systems. The body contains 4 to 6 liters of blood, the actual amount depending on the body size and sex, with females having lower blood volume than males. Figure 2.1.6 shows the composition of blood and a brief description of what the constituents are.

FIGURE 2.1.6
Composition of blood

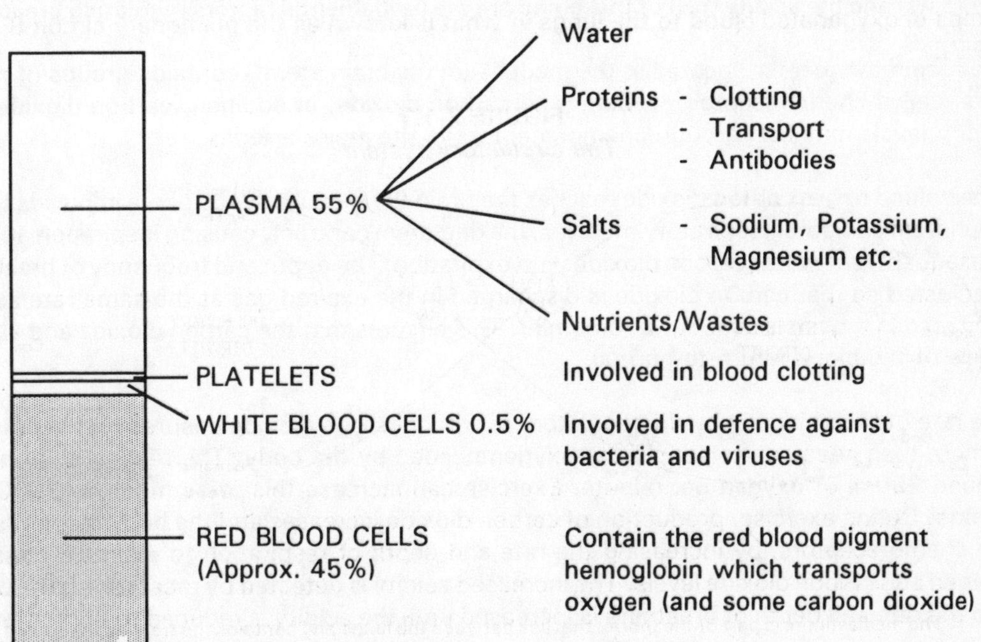

Blood cells are formed in the bone marrow. Red blood cells, called erythrocytes, live for approximately 120 days and are then removed by the spleen. White blood cells, called leukocytes, live from six hours, to two weeks, to a year, depending on the type of cell. Red blood cell formation is controlled by a hormone erythropoietin which is produced by the kidneys. Reduced oxygen levels increase the amount of erythropoietin, thus producing more red blood cells.

THE CIRCULATORY SYSTEM

The circulatory system consists of the heart and blood vessels.

THE HEART

The heart is a hollow muscular organ situated in the mediastinum* of the thoracic cavity, surrounded by a thin connective tissue sac, the pericardium which, in a manner similar to the pleural membranes of the lungs, allows the heart to beat independently and without friction. The heart is placed obliquely in the chest, one third to the right and two thirds to the left of the sternum.

The heart is a strong muscular pump which, in the average adult, beats about 70 times/minute. Every minute about six liters of blood is pumped around the body. When we exercise this output doubles, or triples, depending on how hard we work. The heart consists of two separate pumps, one on the left side of the heart and one on the right side. Each pump has two chambers. The upper chamber, or atrium, receives blood from the body or lungs and the lower one, the ventricle, is filled with blood from the atrium. The pumps work by muscular contraction, squeezing the blood out of the chambers. The left ventricle pumps oxygenated blood throughout the body in what is known as the systemic circuit, and the right ventricle pumps deoxygenated blood to the lungs in what is known as the pulmonary circuit (Figure 2.1.7).

FIGURE 2.1.7
The circulatory system

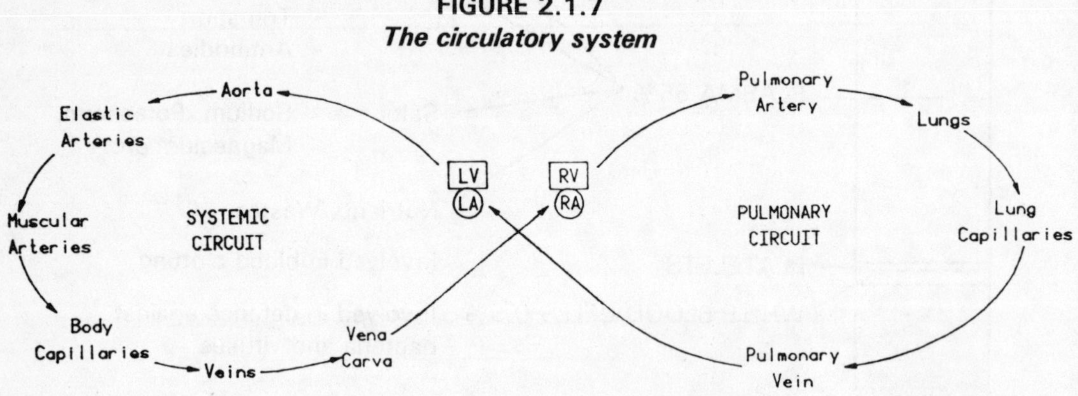

* The mediastinum is part of the thorax that lies between the lungs and contains the trachea, heart and major blood vessels and the esophagus. It is sealed off from the abdomen by the diaphragm and is continuous with the neck above.

The systemic circuit is a high resistance circuit, which means that the left ventricle has to work hard to circulate the blood. Like any muscle which is forced to work hard, it gets bigger. In contrast, the pulmonary circuit is a low resistance circuit as the resistance to blood flow through the lungs is much less than that to blood flow to the, much larger, rest of the body. Thus, the right ventricle does not have to work as hard as the left ventricle and, so, has a thinner wall.

Special one-way valves, which work simply on pressure differences, prevent back flow from the ventricles to the atria during ventricular contraction (tricuspid and mitral valves in Figure 2.1.8), and prevent back flow from the pulmonary arteries and aorta into the ventricles during relaxation of the ventricles (semilunar valves in Figure 2.1.8).

FIGURE 2.1.8
The heart - internal structure

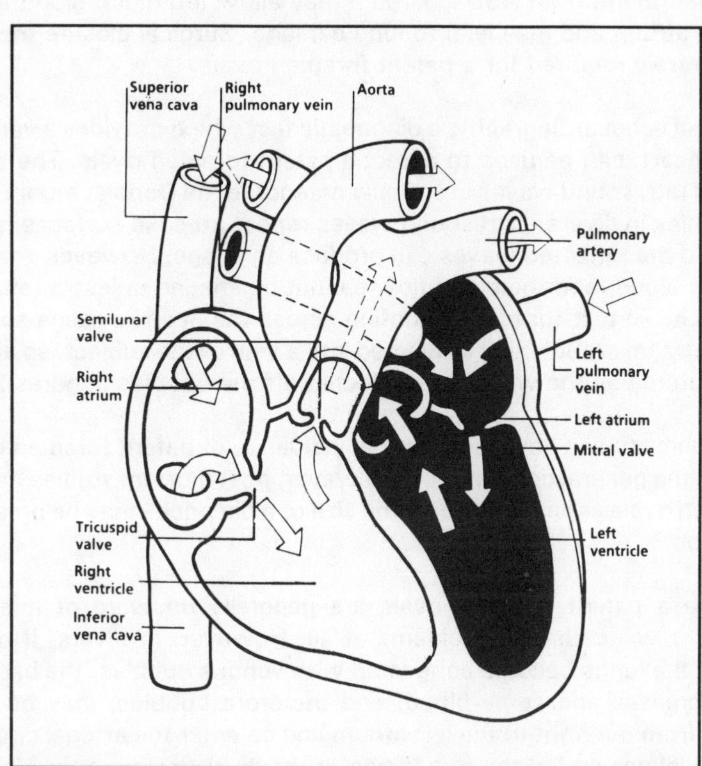

Reprinted courtesy of The Royal Life-Saving Society of Australia

The heart goes through cycles of ventricular relaxation and filling (diastole) and ventricular contraction and emptying (systole).

Foramen Ovale

The "foramen ovale" (oval window) is an opening between the right and left atria of the heart. In the developing fetus the lungs are not functional so the blood bypasses the lungs, the majority passing directly from the right atrium to the left atrium through the foramen ovale. When the baby is born and begins to breathe, the foramen ovale closes, allowing the blood to be pumped through the lungs for oxygenation.

Initially the foramen ovale is closed by means of a "flap" valve, which remains closed as the pressure in the left atrium is slightly higher than that in the right atrium. In most people the valve eventually seals over and the foramen ovale disappears. However, in some individuals, the valve fails to seal completely and they have what is known as a Patent Foramen Ovale. Occasionally, the foramen ovale remains open, or it may adhere at the edges but have holes in it, and the individual is said to have an Atrial Septal Defect (ASD). This situation allows blood to flow from the left to the right atrium or vice versa, depending on the pressure gradient between them. If an ASD is large it may allow too much blood to shunt from the left to the right atrium and may lead to lung damage. Surgical closure may be required for an ASD but is rarely required for a patent foramen ovale.

Two-dimensional echocardiography, a diagnostic test which provides a very accurate image of the beating heart, can be used to detect a patent foramen ovale. The technique utilizes the reflection of ultrasound waves in a similar manner to the Doppler monitors used to detect circulating bubbles in divers. Ultrasound waves reflect off solid surfaces, such as the walls of the heart, and the reflected waves can produce an image. However, the waves will pass directly through blood, and the blood flow cannot be imaged unless a reflecting medium is introduced into it. To test for blood shunting across the heart, a saline solution containing minute air bubbles (microbubbles) is injected into a vein of the subject, so allowing the blood flow to be monitored as the waves are reflected off the bubbles (Figures 2.1.9 to 2.1.11).

Echocardiographic studies have indicated an incidence of patent foramen ovale of between 5% and 24% in the general population.[1,2] However, post mortem studies have indicated that a patent foramen ovale - sometimes only the size of a pin prick - may be present in up to 30% of the population.[3]

Individuals with a patent foramen ovale are generally unaware of it as, under normal circumstances, it will cause no problems at all. However, in divers, if decompression is inadequate and the lungs become congested with venous bubbles, the back pressure in the right atrium increases and some blood, and therefore bubbles, may be allowed to pass directly across from the right to the left atrium and so enter the arterial circulation, possibly causing an arterial gas embolism. In addition, if the diver performs the Valsalva maneuver, right-to-left shunting may be precipitated, or enhanced, during the release phase of the maneuver.[2]

Some individuals have a defect in the septum between the ventricles (ventricular septal defect) which will also allow blood to follow an abnormal pathway through the heart, and may lead to a similar problem to that described above.

FIGURE 2.1.9
Echocardiogram before contrast injection

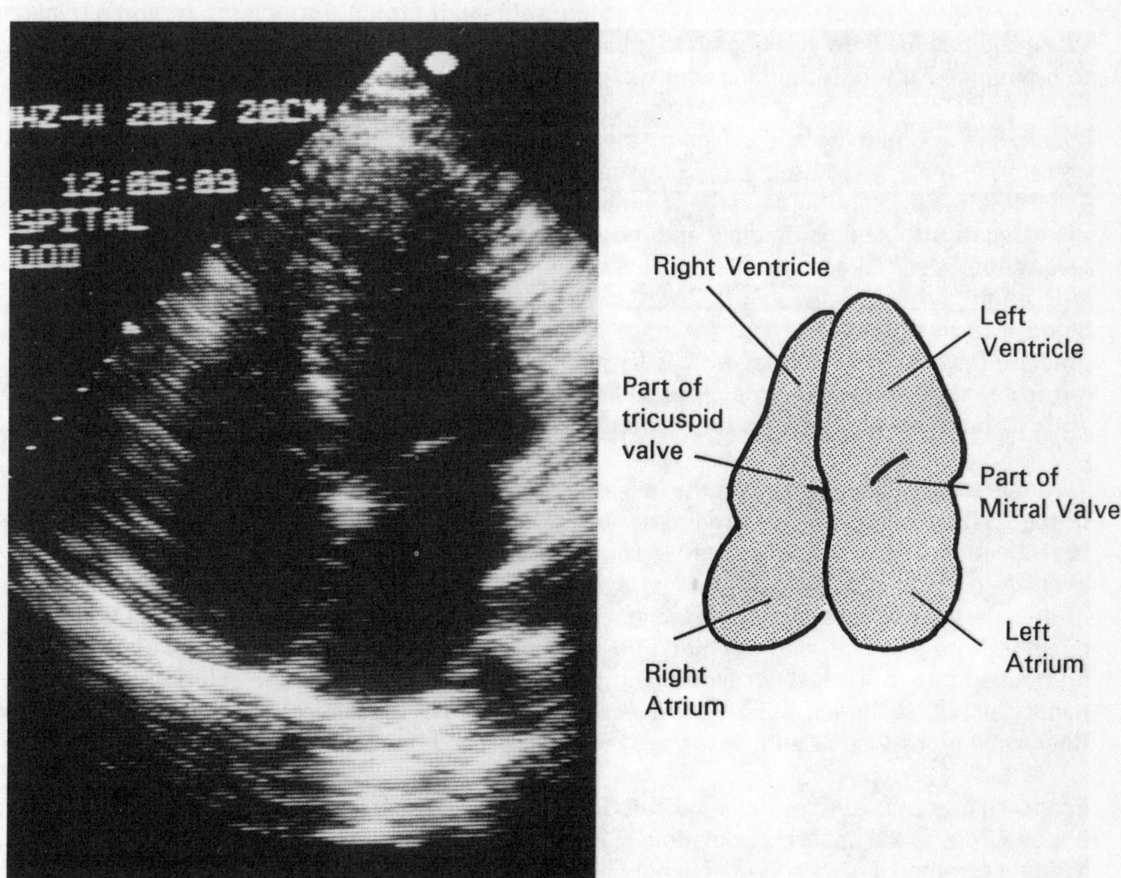

The photograph shows the four chambers of the heart viewed from the apex of the heart at top.

FIGURE 2.1.10
Contrast bubbles entering right side of heart.

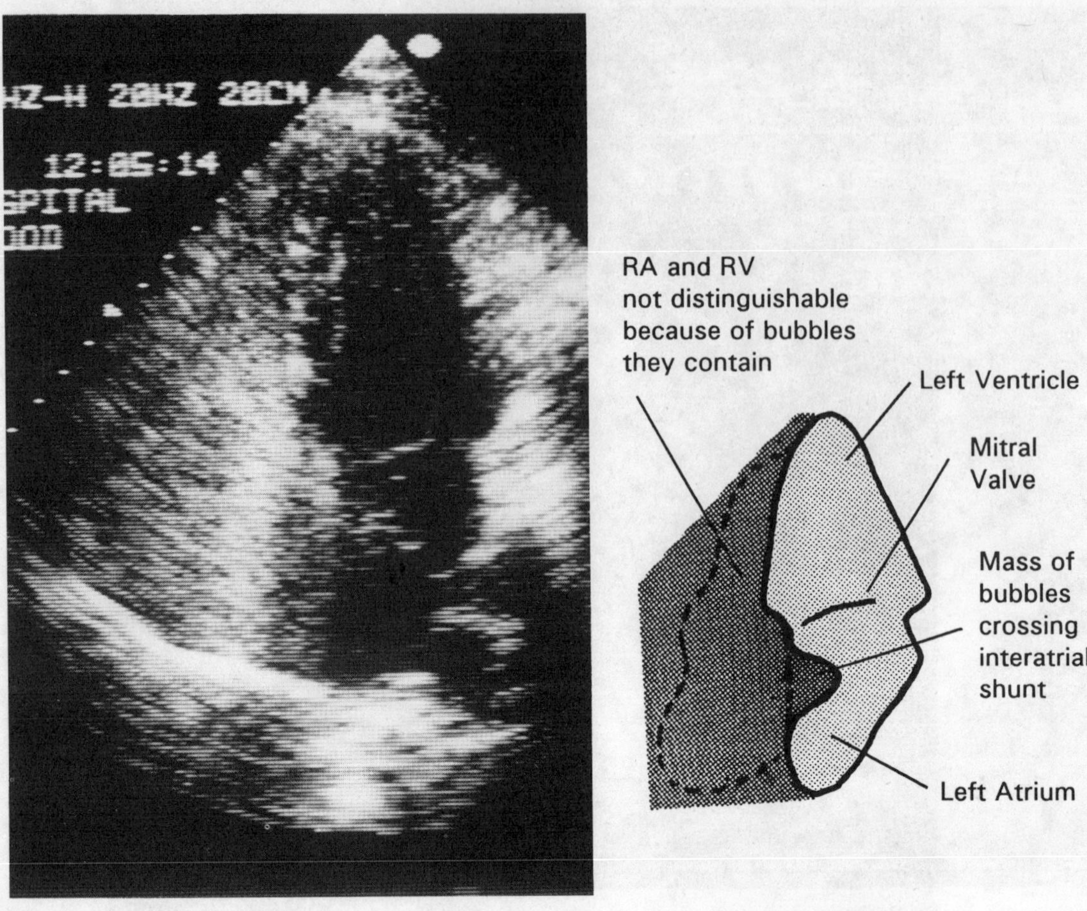

Taken immediately after the contrast enters the heart and fills the right atrium and ventricle (which appear white).

FIGURE 2.1.11
Contrast bubbles passing into left side of heart.

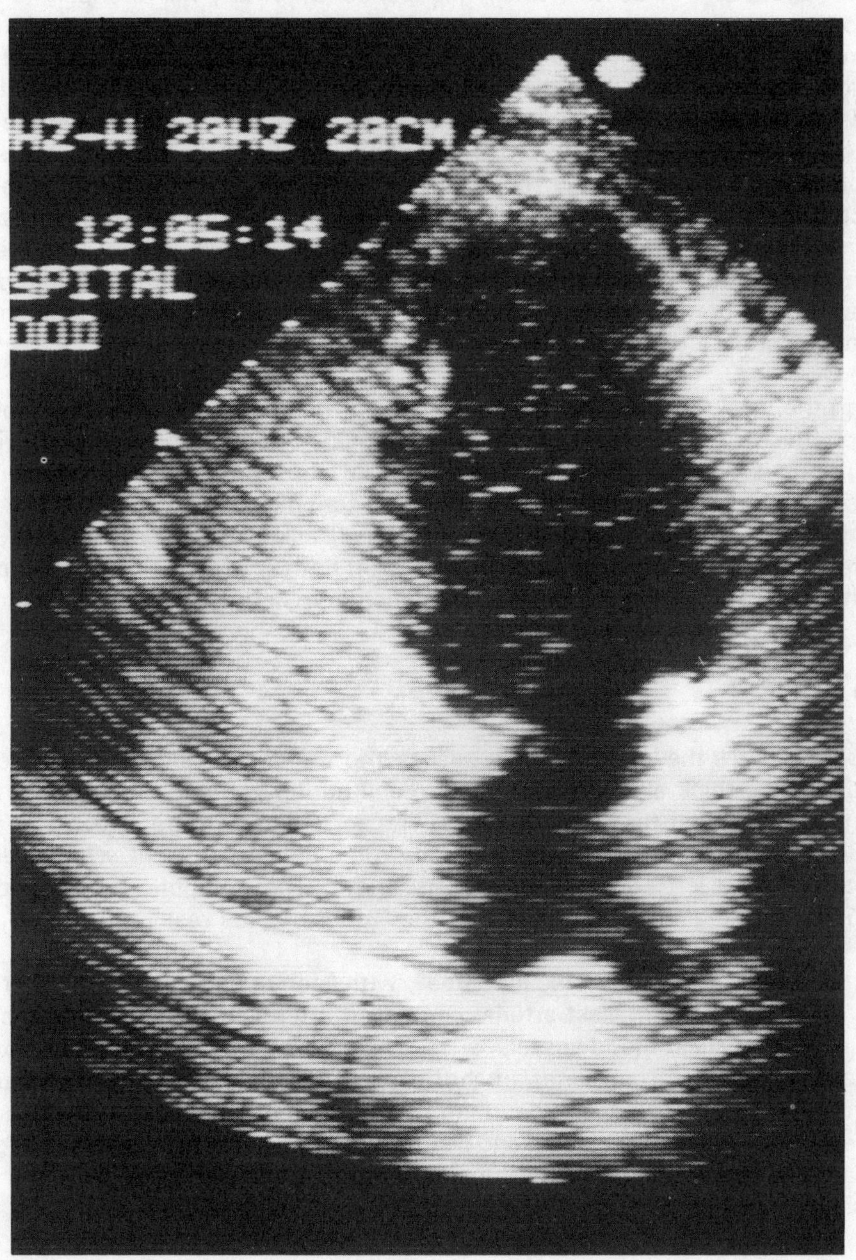

Bubbles pass through the mitral valve and disperse in the left ventricle (lots of bright dots in left ventricle).

Photographs courtesy Dr. Peter Wilmshurst, St. Thomas' Hospital, London.

Control of the Beating Heart

The heart is capable of beating totally independently of any nerve supply (a fact readily attested to by any heart transplant patient). The individual muscle cells which make up the heart are capable of beating by themselves. When they are in contact with each other they beat at the rate of the fastest beating cell, the so-called "pacemaker". In the wall of the right atrium is a small specialized region which is in fact the pacemaker for the entire heart since it's cells beat the fastest. In the normal functioning of the heart the atria contract first and then, following a brief pause, the ventricles contract. Clearly, if both the atria and ventricles contracted together, inefficient pumping would result. To ensure that this does not occur the atria and ventricles are separated by an insulating material, and a special relay system conducts an electrical message from the atria to the ventricles, with a built in delay. Thus, the atria contract first, expelling the blood into the ventricles which, when full, then contract and expel blood into the main arteries.

Although the heart can contract in the absence of nerves, in the normal person nerves of the autonomic nervous system supply the pacemaker region in the wall of the right atrium. The Autonomic Nervous System is that part of the body's nervous system which is responsible for controlling the body's involuntary activities. As such there are two parts, the sympathetic and parasympathetic divisions which generally have opposite effects. Sympathetic nerve activity (resembling the effects of adrenalin) both speeds the heart up and makes the beats more forceful, while the Parasympathetic nerve activity has the opposite effect.

BLOOD VESSELS

When blood leaves the left ventricle it passes into the aorta, which is the largest artery in the body. It has thick elastic walls which recoil during ventricular relaxation to maintain arterial pressure whilst the ventricle refills. The aorta gives off branches to all parts of the body. Blood leaving the right ventricle passes into a pulmonary trunk which divides almost immediately into a left and right pulmonary artery. These supply the left and right lung respectively and in general run parallel to the "tubes" of the respiratory tract.

The blood vessels make up a vascular "tree", with each branch giving rise to progressively smaller branches. The smallest arteries are called arterioles and it is from these that the capillaries, the smallest blood vessels, arise. The arterioles have the job of controlling flow to the capillary beds. The capillaries are the business end of the entire cardiovascular system. It is through their thin walls that gas (and nutrient) exchange occurs. The heart and large blood vessels are really only a pump and distribution system for the capillaries. Figure 2.1.12 shows a cross section of a capillary running through a muscle tissue. Note the thin wall of the capillary (marked "C").

FIGURE 2.1.12
Cross section of capillary

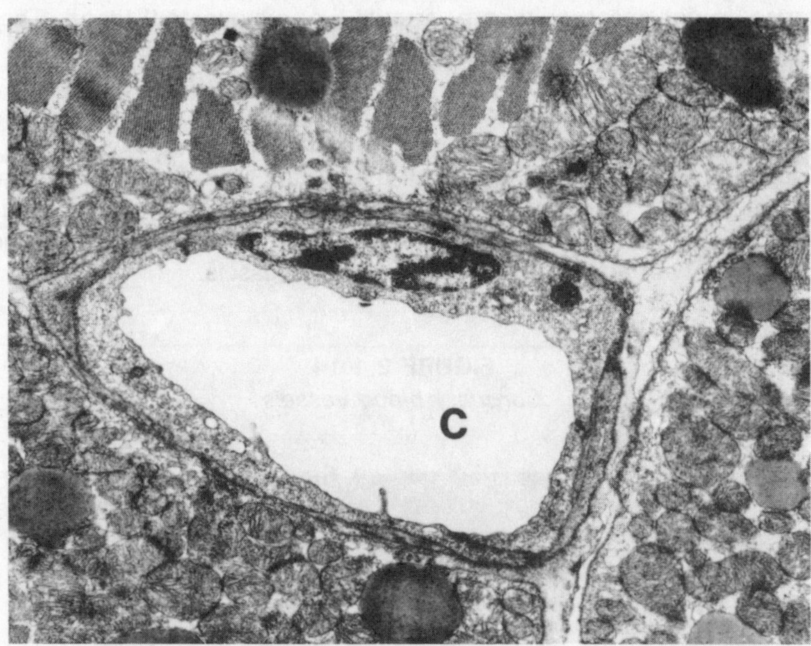

From capillaries, the blood is gathered into small thin-walled veins and finally returned to the atria of the heart (Figure 2.1.13). Most veins direct the blood flow by means of one-way valves which prevent the blood travelling in the wrong direction.

FIGURE 2.1.13
Blood vessels

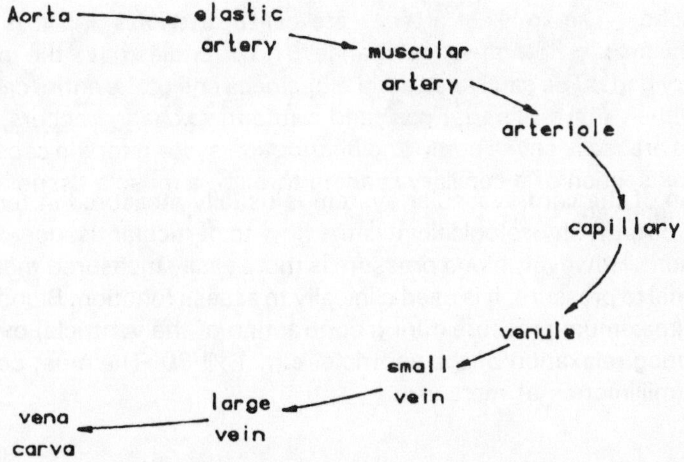

Arteries are thick-walled vessels which, by definition, carry blood away from the heart. Veins generally have thinner walls and may be somewhat flattened. Veins carry blood towards the heart. A common source of confusion is that oxygenated blood is referred to as arterial blood and yet arteries do not necessarily carry arterial (i.e. oxygenated) blood. The pulmonary arteries actually carry deoxygenated or venous blood. Similarly, the pulmonary veins carry oxygenated or arterial blood.

Heart muscle is very active and requires a constant supply of oxygenated blood. The coronary blood vessels arise from the base of the aorta. Figure 2.1.14 shows a cast of the coronary blood vessels magnified many hundreds of times by a scanning electron microscope, and the dense mass of capillaries surrounding the muscle cells. The tissue has been digested away with acid to just show the blood vessels.

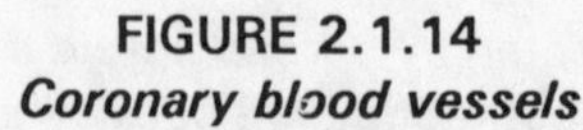
FIGURE 2.1.14
Coronary blood vessels

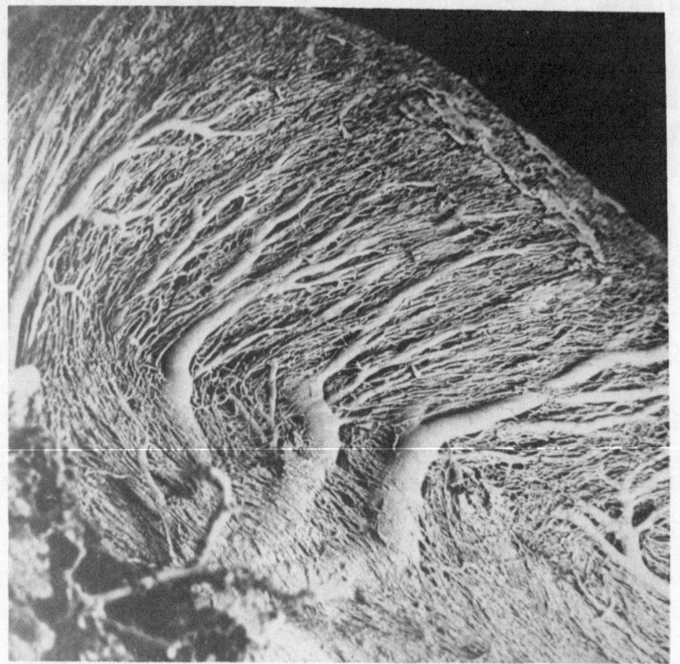

The function of the cardiovascular system is usually measured in terms of blood pressure and cardiac output. Physiologically it is the flow to particular tissues which is important, not blood pressure. However, blood pressure is more easily measured than flow and, since flow is proportional to pressure, it is used clinically to assess function. Blood pressure is measured as systolic (maximum pressure during contraction of the ventricle) over diastolic (minimum pressure during relaxation of the ventricle) e.g. 130/80. The most common pressure units are mmHg (millimetres of mercury).

Small changes in the diameter of the arterioles effectively control the flow and, therefore, the distribution of blood. The arterioles can be thought of as "taps" controlling blood flow into the capillary beds. Arterioles are also responsible for the overall resistance of the circulation which in turn affects blood pressure. As arterioles constrict the resistance to blood flow increases and the blood pressure rises. In addition, flow beyond the point of constriction is reduced. Dilation of arterioles reduces resistance and causes the blood pressure to drop, at the same time increasing flow to the tissues beyond the point of dilation.

The diameter of arterioles is controlled by local and reflex controls. Local controls serve the metabolic needs of the tissue in which they occur. During increased muscular activity changes in the local levels of oxygen, carbon dioxide and acidity act on the muscles making up the blood vessels, causing the vessels to dilate and increase blood flow. The diameter of arterioles is also controlled by the Autonomic Nervous System.

If blood pressure is high, it is detected by baroreceptors in the major arteries and relayed to the brain. As a result of parasympathetic nerve activity and reduced sympathetic activity, the heart rate decreases, arterioles dilate and cause a reduction in both heart output and the resistance to blood flow, returning blood pressure toward normal. The dizziness one feels upon standing up quickly after having been laying down is due to pooling of blood in the veins, due to gravity, thereby causing a drop in blood pressure to the brain. The body then responds in the opposite way to that described above, to restore blood pressure. The time it takes for the dizziness to pass is the time it takes blood pressure to be restored.

CIRCULATORY FAILURE

Circulatory failure takes two main forms, shock and fainting.

Shock can be defined as a loss of effective circulating blood volume. This may be an actual physical loss of blood or other body fluid, or a physiological loss where, although there is no actual blood loss, a redistribution of blood or a leaking of plasma into the tissues leads to the same overall response as if it were lost. The net result of this loss of circulating blood volume is that blood supply to the tissues is insufficient to meet the oxygen demands of the cells, thereby depressing cellular metabolism.

In the broadest sense, shock may result from any condition that decreases the heart's ability to pump effectively or decreases the return of blood from the veins to the heart.

Shock is classified according to the event which causes it. The resultant physiological changes, however, are the same in each case.

Hypovolemic Shock (Reduced blood volume)

Hypovolemic shock can be caused by:

hemorrhage - such as trauma (accidental or surgical), childbirth or internal (crushing) injuries. It is often very difficult to know how much blood is lost in crushing injuries. e.g. a thigh muscle can accommodate 1 litre of blood with only approximately $^{5}/_{16}$ inch (1 cm) increase in diameter.

plasma loss - from burns or decompression sickness

dehydration - due to heat exhaustion, heat stroke, diarrhoea, diuresis (excess urinary output)

Neurogenic Shock (Nervous System generated)

The cause in this case is a generalized vasodilation due to decreased tensions in the muscles that make up the walls of the blood vessels (decreased vasomotor tone). Blood volume is not changed but the capacity of the blood vessels is increased. The increased diameter of the small arteries reduces the resistance to blood flow and leads to a reduction in blood pressure. Because the veins have dilated and the blood pressure has dropped, blood pools in the veins. The result is a decreased return of blood from the veins to the heart leading to a decreased cardiac output.

Conditions such as spinal anesthesia, spinal cord injury, damage to the brain stem, low blood glucose (insulin shock), severe pain, action of tranquilizer, narcotic or sedative drugs, bad fright or grief can all cause Neurogenic Shock.

Vasogenic Shock (Blood vessels generated)

Vasogenic Shock is quite rare. The commonest form is the so-called Anaphylactic Shock which results from a very severe form of allergic reaction (antigen-antibody reaction). This leads to the release of histamine and several other potent chemicals which lead to vasodilation and increased capillary permeability (i.e. a widening of the gaps between the cells of the walls of the capillaries) which greatly increases the normal leakage of plasma from the capillaries. The result is equivalent to losing blood from the circulatory system.

Cardiogenic Shock (Heart generated)

Any condition which reduces cardiac function leading to a decreased cardiac output can cause signs and symptoms of shock. Conditions such as a heart attack, heart surgery, prolonged arrythmias and other heart diseases are included in this category.

Septic or Endotoxic Shock

This is caused by any widespread overwhelming infection. Persons at risk include those with peritonitis, burns, post partum (post childbirth) infection, as well as those who have undergone gastrointestinal surgery or surgery on their kidneys and/or urinary tract, and those taking medication to suppress their immune system.

The Effects of Shock

Regardless of the cause of shock the effects are essentially the same.

The immediate effect is a decrease in the cardiac output which leads to a decrease in arterial blood pressure (hypotension) which is responsible for the reduced blood flow to the tissues. The reduced blood pressure is detected by the arterial baroreceptors and the body tries to compensate in the following way:

Compensatory Reactions

Activation of the sympathetic nervous system in response to the reduced blood pressure leads to both an increased heart rate and an increased force of contraction, which both increase the cardiac output. In addition, constriction of blood vessels occurs to increase peripheral resistance and increase the return of blood to the heart. Constriction only occurs in non-essential vascular beds (areas of blood supply), such as the skin and gastrointestinal tract and, therefore, blood is directed to the essential vascular beds of the brain and heart.

The decrease in blood pressure also activates mechanisms which act on the kidneys to reduce urine production, so retaining fluid. This assists in maintaining blood pressure, but at the expense of renal damage if the shock continues for too long.

The signs and symptoms at this stage are the familiar ones of:

- rapid, weak, thready pulse (due to the reduced blood volume) cold, pale and clammy skin dry mouth and throat (all due to generalized stimulation of sympathetic nerves. e.g. the pale, cold skin is due to blood being prevented from entering the skin by the shutting down of skin arterioles)

- nausea
  restlessness
  apprehension
  (all due to stimulation of the brain associated with the general sympathetic response)

- rapid respiration
  (due to increasing accumulation of lactic acid and other metabolites (metabolic acidosis))

If the underlying cause is not treated or corrected, there is a further decrease in cardiac output and decreased tissue perfusion. This is the so-called decompensatory phase.

Progressive Shock leading to Decompensated Shock (The Killer!)

Maintained constriction of arterioles results in decreased blood flow to the capillary circulation (microcirculation) of most organs. This has a variety of effects which include:

- damage to tissues due to lack of oxygen (ischemic hypoxia), and a continuing increase in lactic acid and other metabolites produced by anaerobic (without oxygen) metabolism, leading to changes in the acid-base balance of the blood
- local vasodilation of arterioles (and to a lesser degree venules) from the accumulation of lactic acid, carbon dioxide and other metabolites
- pooling of blood in the capillaries, due to the poor blood flow, causing a loss of fluid and plasma proteins from the circulating blood

Eventually, metabolism may cease and organ systems may fail.

In the brain (where vasoconstriction does not occur) severe ischemia and hypoxia lead to depressed function. When the regions of the brain responsible for control of heart and blood vessels (cardio-vascular center) are affected, sympathetic stimulation of the heart and blood vessels is reduced resulting in a further decrease in blood flow to the brain.

In the heart, as the blood pressure drops, coronary blood flow is reduced despite vasodilation. The increased acidity of the blood (acidosis) further depresses cardiac function.

Thus in summary:

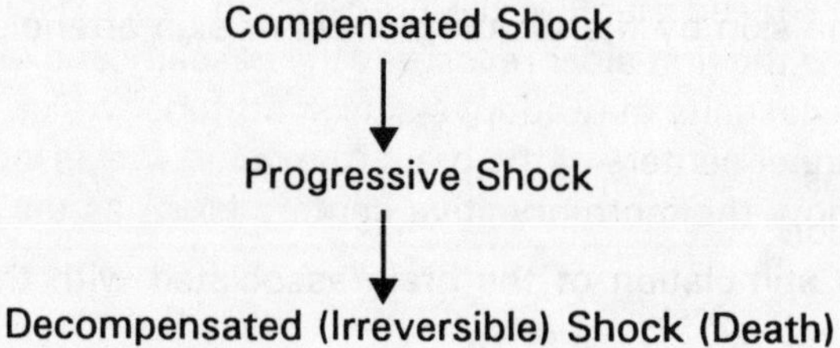

First Aid for Shock

The aim of first aid in the case of shock is to ensure that compensated shock is not allowed to progress to decompensated shock. The first aid steps, which should be familiar to all divers are as follows:

- Act to prevent further shock. Look for *arterial bleeding* and, if present, stop it. Except for arterial blood loss, the particular cause of the shock is often of little importance to the first-aider as the first aid is the same for all types of shock.
- Lay the patient down and raise the legs
- Oxygen
- Reassurance
- No fluids (as an operation and anesthetic may be required)

- Protect from extremes of temperature (i.e. hot or cold). Overheating causes vasodilation which will worsen the condition
- No sedatives or alcohol
- Monitor the airway, breathing and pulse
- Medical advice

The rationale behind this first aid is possibly not so well known but a little reflection on the physiology of shock should reveal the reasons.

Since the primary problem is decreased delivery of oxygen to the tissues because of the reduced blood supply, breathing 100% oxygen will allow the remaining blood to carry more oxygen and so maximize tissue oxygenation. This will allow more aerobic (oxygen-using) metabolism and reduce the amount of acidification of the tissues (from anaerobic metabolism).

As mentioned earlier, in the upright position blood tends to pool in the legs. So by laying the casualty down and raising his legs, the blood can run "downhill" in the leg veins and assist return of blood to the heart, thereby improving cardiac output and so blood pressure.

Alcohol and sedatives depress central nervous system function and, in addition, alcohol causes dilation of peripheral blood vessels, leading blood away from where it is needed most.

Similarly, overwarming causes opening up of peripheral blood vessels in much the same way as alcohol. A first aider should aim to keep the patient at a "comfortable" temperature, neither too hot nor too cold.

Reassurance is also extremely important in stopping the progression from compensated to decompensated shock. Indeed much of the progression in the degree of shock is probably mediated via the brain. If the first aider reassures the casualty and exudes confidence (often contrary to reality), the casualty may adopt a similar attitude, which can be vitally important in their survival. The higher centers of the brain (the points we associate with being human) can greatly influence how the more primitive centers (such as the cardiac and respiratory control centers) work.

Finally a shock victim should not be moved except to avoid immediate danger to life. Moving the patient often provokes a deterioration in the patient's condition. In past years many victims of shark attack, who were in compensated shock on the beach after the bleeding had been stopped, died in the ambulance while being moved to medical care. The South Africans, in the 1960s, introduced the idea of restoring the blood volume to normal with intravenous fluids (blood or plasma) on the beach, before moving the patient. The results were spectactularly good and this routine is now standard practice throughout the world.[4]

Where at all possible arrange for medical aid to come to the patient, rather than moving the patient. Transport of a patient during compensated shock can rapidly lead to decompensated shock. However, in a remote location transport of the patient may be unavoidable. In this situation, the patient should be transported laying down with his legs elevated if possible. It is absolutely essential to ensure the patient is stabilized before moving him, no matter how long this may take. This can be taken as the time when all of the initial signs and symptoms have been reversed. Should these return during transport, stop immediately and restabilize the patient before proceeding.

The commonest form of circulatory failure is a faint (known to doctors as a vago-vasal attack). Although the mechanism causing it is the same as that outlined under neurogenic shock, it is self-curing. In most faints, which are commoner in the warmer months, the precipitating cause is lack of movement in the legs allowing a lot of blood to pool, due to gravity, in the legs. This reduces the venous return to the heart. As there is less blood returned to the heart there is less to pump out and the cardiac output is reduced. The sudden drop in cardiac output causes a drop in blood pressure to below that required to pump blood upwards (in the standing person) from the heart to the brain, resulting in a failure of blood supply to the brain and subsequent loss of consciousness. When the unconscious person falls over, the heart no longer has to pump the blood against gravity and the blood pressure is then adequate to supply the brain with enough blood to enable the person to regain consciousness.

THE LYMPHATIC SYSTEM

Closely associated with the functions of the circulatory system is the the lymphatic system. The capillaries of the cardiovascular system are specialized for gas and nutrient exchange. As such their walls are thin and relatively "leaky", thereby allowing most substances, including waste, to cross. In fact the only things that do not leak out of the blood are the blood proteins and blood cells. Some of the water is later drawn back into the blood vessels by the trapped blood proteins. However, a total of about three liters every 24 hours is not. If this were not returned to the circulation the blood would effectively "run out". Clearly this does not happen. The role of the lymphatic system is to return the leaked fluid to the circulatory system.

The lymphatic system consists of a series of lymphatic vessels and lymph nodes. Lymphatic vessels originate as microscopic blind-ending lymph capillaries which progressively join one another to form larger vessels. The two largest lymph vessels then empty into the great veins of the chest, just near their entry into the right atrium. Along the way lymph vessels pass through lymph nodes - small bean-shaped structures packed with lymphocytes - specialized cells - which are involved in filtering the lymph and attacking foreign bacteria. The lymph nodes tend to be aggregated in the groin, armpit and lower jaw (Figure 2.1.15). These areas tend to become swollen and tender when you have an infection. What is actually happening is that the lymphocytes are busily trying to destroy the foreign bacteria and the lymph nodes become swollen and sensitive to pressure as a result of this.

FIGURE 2.1.15
The lymphatic system

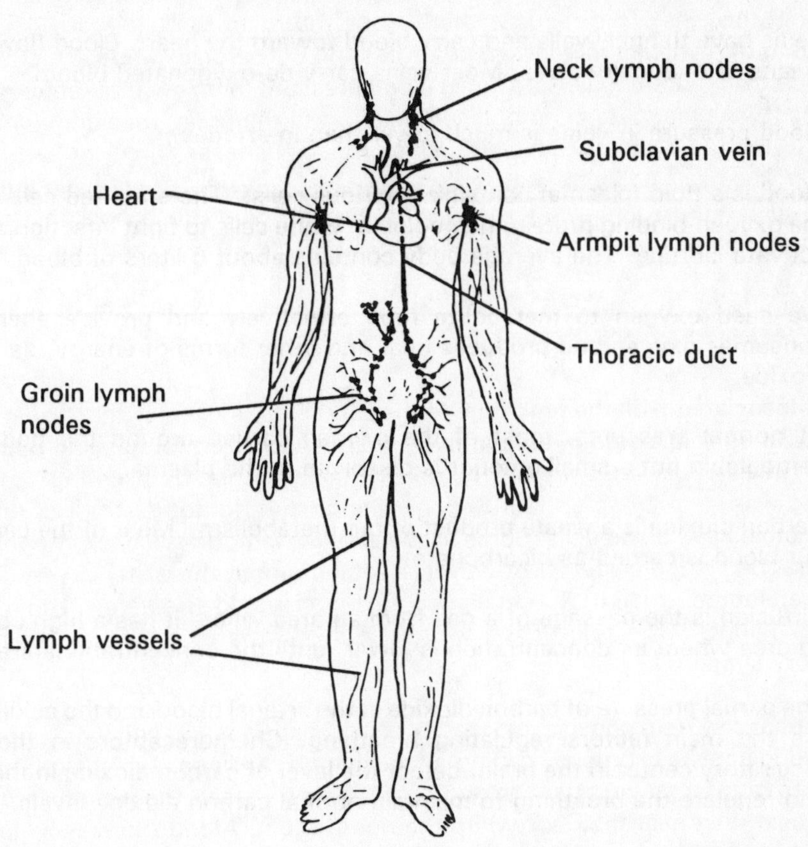

Flow of fluid in the lymph vesssels is largely determined by the action of skeletal muscles (muscles attached to bone) which, when they contract, put pressure on the lymph vessels and squeeze the fluid through them. Small one-way valves prevent back flow. Thus, in people who are confined to wheel chairs or forced to stand or sit still for long periods, fluid builds up, particularly around the ankles.

Apart from its important accessory role to the cardiovascular system, the lymphatic system is important to divers for another reason. It has been shown that toxins delivered by many of our dangerous marine animals (and terrestrial animals for that matter) are transported through the lymphatics. Hence, the basis of the pressure-immobilization technique. The wide pressure bandage applied from above the wound to below it collapses the lymph capillaries and so halts the flow of toxin towards the heart. Since muscular activity is needed to make the lymph flow, immobilizing the affected limb prevents that process.

SUMMARY

* Arteries have thick, elastic walls and carry blood away from the heart. Most arteries carry oxygenated blood.

* Veins have thinner walls and carry blood toward the heart. Blood flow is directed by means of one-way valves. Most veins carry de-oxygenated blood.

* Blood pressure in veins is much lower than in arteries.

* Blood is a fluid (plasma) containing various cells. There are red cells which contain the oxygen-binding protein, hemoglobin, white cells to fight infection and platelets to activate clotting. The average body contains about 6 liters of blood.

* We need oxygen to metabolize food effectively and provide energy. The body consumes oxygen and produces heat and other forms of energy, as well as carbon dioxide.

* At normal pressures, most of the oxygen carried around the body is bound to hemoglobin but a small amount is dissolved in the plasma.

* Carbon dioxide is a waste product of our metabolism. Most of the carbon dioxide in our blood is carried as bicarbonate.

* Diffusion is the passage of a gas from an area where it has a high concentration to an area where its concentration is lower, until the concentrations are equal.

* The partial pressure of carbon dioxide in the arterial blood and the acidity of this blood are the main factors regulating breathing. Chemoreceptors in the medulla (the respiratory center in the brain) detect the level of carbon dioxide in the arterial blood and regulate the breathing to maintain normal carbon dioxide levels.

* Lack of oxygen does not normally stimulate breathing significantly unless the arterial oxygen levels fall dangerously low.

* Shock can be defined as a loss of circulating blood volume resulting in an inadequate supply of oxygen to the tissues. This may be caused by an actual physical loss of blood, or other body fluid, or a physiological loss where a redistribution of blood, or a leaking of plasma into the tissues, leads to the same overall response as if it were lost.

* The signs and symptoms of shock include rapid, weak, thready pulse, cold, pale , clammy skin, dry mouth and throat, weakness, nausea, restlessness, apprehension, and rapid respiration.

* The first aid for shock includes action to prevent further shock (e.g. stopping severe bleeding immediately), laying the patient down and raising his legs, giving high concentrations of oxygen, reassurance, protection from extremes of temperature, monitoring ABC, medical advice.

* The lymphatic system consists of a series of lymphatic vessels and lymph nodes. Its role is to remove foreign material and to return leaked fluid to the circulatory system.

REFERENCES

1. Lynch, J. et al (1984), "Prevalence of right-to-left atrial shunting in a healthy population: detection by Valsalva maneuver contast echocardiography". *Am. J. Cardiol.*; 53: 1478-80.

2. Wilmshurst, P. et al (1989), "Relation between interatrial shunting and decompression sickness in divers". *The Lancet*; 8675: 1302-1306.

3. Hagen, P. (1984), "Incidence and size of patent foramen ovale during the first 10 decades of life: an autopsy study of 965 normal hearts". *Mayo Clin Proc;* 59: 17-20.

4. Struik, C. (1983), "Shark Attack in Southern African Waters and the Treatment of Victims". Tim Wallett, Capetown.

RECOMMENDED FURTHER READING

Tortora, G. and Anagnostakos, N. (1987), "Principles of Anatomy and Physiology", 5th edition, Harper and Row, New York.

Vander, A. et al (1985), "Human Physiology: The Mechanisms of Body Function", McGraw-Hill, Sydney.

2.2 Effects of SCUBA diving on respiration and circulation

RESPIRATION

The Effort of Breathing Underwater

Normally, the main work of breathing is done to overcome the elastic forces resisting the expansion of the lungs during inspiration. Work is also done to overcome the frictional resistance to air flowing through the air passages. At normal pressures and breathing rates, far less energy is required to overcome the frictional resistance than the elastic forces.

As the breathing rate increases the proportion of work done in overcoming the resistance to air flow increases. This resistance increases even more as the breathing gas becomes more dense, as it does when breathed under pressure.

The resistance to air flow at 100 ft (30 m) in a chamber has been shown to be twice that at the surface. The maximum breathing capacity (the maximum volume of air which can be breathed in and out over a given time) was shown to be halved.[1] These tests were performed on subjects who were at rest and were using equipment that is far more efficient than SCUBA equipment.

While using SCUBA, the resistance to air flow through the regulator makes breathing even more of an effort. Most of the resistance underwater to depths of 100 ft (30 m) is due to the regulator. In addition, the effort of pushing water away as the chest expands during inspiration is more than that required in air and increases with depth. If we exert ourselves and breathe more rapidly, the effort of breathing becomes greater still. Wearing a tight wetsuit, buoyancy compensator and weight belt restricts chest and abdomen movement and exacerbates the problem. So the diver swimming against a current at 100 ft (30 m) will be working very hard indeed.

Impaired Ventilation

Because of the increased dead space with SCUBA and the greater airway resistance, a diver must breathe deeper and faster to adequately ventilate his lungs. Consequently, far more effort must be put into breathing and this may lead to an earlier onset of fatigue than would occur for the same work done on land. If, due to exertion at depth and/or poor equipment function, ventilation is reduced enough to markedly decrease the transfer of oxygen to, and carbon dioxide from, the blood in the lungs, the resultant high carbon dioxide levels (hypercapnia) and/or low oxygen levels (hypoxia) may be potentially dangerous. Either could ultimately cause the diver to lose consciousness.

In SCUBA diving hypoxia rarely develops as a result of this reduced ventilation, since the reduced ventilation is offset by the rise in the partial pressures of oxygen in the high pressure air. Carbon dioxide build-up can and does cause a number of problems which are discussed in Chapter 7.

Adaptation

A few studies have been done to determine whether or not SCUBA divers adapt to breathing underwater. Some studies have indicated that SCUBA divers may develop a reduced responsiveness to carbon dioxide and a higher resting carbon dioxide level than non-divers.[2] This is more pronounced in certain individuals.

Respiratory adaptation to carbon dioxide can affect both state of consciousness and heart rhythm. If a diver were insensitive to carbon dioxide, breathing would not be stimulated as readily, higher blood carbon dioxide levels would result and the diver would be more likely to lose consciousness.

CIRCULATION

Upon immersion, with the body vertical, the veins of the legs and abdomen are squeezed by the higher hydrostatic pressure around the legs and abdomen, causing the blood to be pushed to regions of lower pressure. As a result, immersion increases the amount of blood in the lungs, heart and great veins (central blood volume).

The veins in the chest sense the increase in central blood volume and the kidneys are prompted to remove water from the circulation in an attempt to return blood volume to normal. Thus, there is an increase in urine output leading to thickening of the blood (hemoconcentration) and dehydration, as well as an urge to empty the bladder.

However, in SCUBA diving, circulatory changes are not usually marked as the diver is usually not vertical. No consistent pattern has been demonstrated in either pulse or blood pressure, however, the rate of urine production increases and dehydration therefore occurs. The main factor operating in normal SCUBA diving is cold, which causes peripheral vasoconstriction (constriction of blood vessels supplying the skin and extremities), leading to an increase in central blood volume.

Diving Reflex

Cardiovascular changes occur with breath-hold diving. Diving animals such as seals, whales and ducks can hold their breath for very long periods of time. Whales can hold their breath for up to two hours and seals for over 20 minutes. These animals have a higher blood capacity for oxygen than humans and also utilize oxygen more efficiently.

When these animals dive, the blood vessels supplying organs such as the skin, kidneys and intestines constict, reducing blood supply to these organs and permitting a selective supply to the vital organs; the heart, brain and lungs. This vasoconstriction is accompanied by a dramatic reduction in the heart rate (bradycardia). This combination of effects maintains normal arterial blood pressure, reduces heat loss and conserves oxygen.

Although this "diving reflex" is not as well developed in humans, similar changes have been observed in some breath-hold divers. The pulse rate may decrease by up to 50%, briefly.[3] However, when man is immersed in cold water, the reduced heart output is often insufficient to compensate for the intense vasoconstriction of the peripheral vessels, and blood pressure may rise significantly.

Diving bradycardia in humans appears to result from the combination of breath-holding and facial cooling. Although the bradycardia and vasoconstriction reduce oxygen consumption in diving animals, some experiments have shown that cardiovascular changes due to breath-hold diving do not appear to reduce oxygen consumption in man.[4] However, the diving reflex is believed to have contributed to the survival of certain individuals who were successfully resuscitated after periods of immersion of up to 60 minutes in cold water.

A number of deaths have occurred in divers (mainly older divers) who surfaced after a dive, put their face down in the water to snorkel back to the boat, and then suddenly died. It has been suggested that the divers may have had previous cardiovascular damage, or electrical instability in the heart, that normally caused no problems but, with the bradycardia brought on by facial immersion, caused ventricular fibrillation and subsequent death.

SUMMARY

* When we SCUBA dive the resistance to air flow through our airways and regulator increases the effort of breathing. The problem is magnified by increased depth, a tight wetsuit, buoyancy compensator and/or weight-belt.

* The increased breathing effort at depth may reduce ventilation markedly and result in high carbon dioxde (and occasionally low oxygen) levels in the blood.

* Some studies have indicated that SCUBA divers may develop a reduced responsiveness to carbon dioxide, making the diver more subject to loss of consciousness.

* Circulatory changes are not usually marked in the SCUBA diver.

REFERENCES

1. Marshall, R. et al (1956), "Resistance to Breathing in Normal Subjects During Simulated Diving". *Journal of Applied Physiology*; 9: 5-10.

2. Florio, J. et al (1979), "Breathing Pattern and Ventilatory Response to Carbon Dioxide in Divers". *Journal of Applied Physiology*; 46: 1076-80.

3. Hong, S. and Rahn, H. (1967), "The Diving Women of Korea and Japan". *Scientific American*; 216: 34-43.

4. Craig, A. and Medd, W. (1968), "Man's Responses to Breath- Hold Exercise in Air and Water". *Journal of Applied Physiology*; 24: 773-777.

OTHER SOURCES

Dueker, C. (1985), "SCUBA Diving in Safety and Health". Madison Publishing Associates, California.

Edmonds, C. et al (1981), "Diving and Subaquatic Medicine", 2nd edition. Diving Medical Center, Sydney.

Lanphier, E. and Camporesi, E. (1982), "Respiration and Exercise". In: *The Physiology and Medicine of Diving,* 3rd edition, Bennett, B. and Elliott, D. (eds), Best Publishing Co., California.

McAniff, J. (1986), "U.S. Underwater Diving Fatality Statistics, 1983-1984". National Underwater Accident Data Center, Report No. URI-SSR-86-18, University of Rhode Island.

RECOMMENDED FURTHER READING

Dueker, C. (1985), "SCUBA Diving in Safety and Health". Madison Publishing Associates, California.

Edmonds, C. et al (1981), "Diving and Subaquatic Medicine", 2nd edition. Diving Medical Center, Sydney.

Lanphier, E. and Camporesi, E. (1982), "Respiration and Exercise". In: *The Physiology and Medicine of Diving,* 3rd edition, Bennett, B and Elliott, D. (eds), Best Publishing Co., California.

CHAPTER 3

NITROGEN UPTAKE AND ELIMINATION

REVISION OF SOME GAS LAWS

Dalton's Law

The partial pressure of a gas in a gas mixture is the part of the total pressure of the gases in the mixture that is contributed to by that gas.

For example, air is composed of a mixture of gases, being approximately 21% oxygen and 79% nitrogen. So, whatever the pressure acting on a given volume of air, the partial pressure of oxygen will be 21% of the total pressure and the partial pressure of nitrogen will be 79% of the total pressure exerted by the air.

Dalton's Law puts it the other way round.

The total pressure exerted by a mixture of gases is the sum of the partial pressures that would be exerted by each of the gases if it alone occupied the total volume.

Henry's Law

At a constant temperature, the amount of gas that will dissolve into a liquid is proportional to the partial pressure of the gas over the liquid.

Doubling the partial pressure will double the amount (number of molecules) of gas that will dissolve into the liquid. Another influence on gases dissolving in liquids is temperature.

NITROGEN ABSORPTION

At at sea level, the average human body contains about one liter of dissolved nitrogen. All of the body tissues are saturated with the gas, which means that the partial pressure of the nitrogen dissolved in the body tissues ("**nitrogen tension**" in the tissues) is equal to the partial pressure of nitrogen in the alveoli (nitrogen tension in the alveoli) - about 570 mmHg (0.75 ATA). We are said to be in a state of "**saturation**" or "**equilibrium**", and our body cannot absorb any more nitrogen unless the partial pressure of the nitrogen inthe breathing gas is increased. If the partial pressure of inspired nitrogen should change because of a change in the pressure (or the composition) of the breathing mixture, the pressure of the nitrogen dissolved in the body will eventually attain a matching level. Additional quantities will be absorbed, or some of the gas will be eliminated, until the nitrogen tensions in the lungs and in the tissues are again in balance. At this time we will again be in equilibrium or "saturated", although the actual gas pressures will be different to those of equilibrium at sea level.

If we descend in the sea to a depth of 33 ft (10 m) where the ambient pressure is 2 ATA, since our regulator supplies air at ambient pressure, the partial pressure of nitrogen in our lungs increases to 1.58 ATA. In accordance with Henry's Law, the amount of nitrogen which will be absorbed or released is almost directly proportional to the change in partial pressure. If one liter of nitrogen is absorbed at a pressure of one atmosphere, then two liters will be absorbed at two atmospheres (33 ft or 10 m depth), and three liters at three atmospheres (66 ft or 20 m depth). The additional nitrogen in the lungs is quickly dissolved into the blood and carried throughout the body. Wherever the blood passes tissues that are not saturated, where the nitrogen tension of the tissue is lower than that presently in the blood, some of the gas will diffuse into those tissues. The partial pressure in the blood will therefore be somewhat reduced and, as it once again passes through the lungs, it will absorb more nitrogen which will then be carried on to the still-unsaturated tissues. This cycle will continue until all of the tissues of the body, and the blood as well, reach equilibrium with the partial pressure of the nitrogen in the lungs.

Some body tissues absorb (and release) nitrogen far more rapidly than others and, therefore, become saturated sooner. The differing rate of nitrogen absorption depends on the fat content of the tissue and the amount of blood flow (perfusion) to the tissue.

Nitrogen is five times more soluble (i.e. more will dissolve) in fat than in water and, since body tissues contain various amounts of fat, they are capable of holding various amounts of nitrogen.

Some tissues are well-perfused by a large blood flow and thus receive a greater supply of nitrogen. Other tissues have a poor blood flow so they will take longer to become saturated with nitrogen. Capillaries, the smallest blood vessels, are found throughout the body. They are closer together in tissues, like muscle, which have high oxygen requirements, than in fat or tendon which use less oxygen. Capillaries open and close, so the blood flow through them is intermittent, influenced by the demands of the tissue for oxygen.

Some other important factors which affect the absorption (and elimination) of nitrogen are temperature and exercise.

Nitrogen becomes more soluble as temperature decreases so, **if a diver becomes cold during a dive, more nitrogen may dissolve in his peripheral tissues**. This amount will also be affected by the constricting of blood vessels, which will reduce the circulation to various tissues. As temperature increases the nitrogen becomes less soluble and may come out of solution as gas bubbles. (Thus, when a cold diver is rewarmed, decompression sickness has at times thought to be precipitated).

If a diver "exercises" during a dive the respiratory rate increases and the blood supply to the muscles is increased in order to deliver more oxygen. With this extra oxygen comes extra nitrogen which is absorbed by the tissues.

Tissues with a low fat content and large blood supply will saturate very quickly, whereas those with a high fat content and poor perfusion will saturate very slowly. Tissues which become saturated rapidly are sometimes called "fast tissues" (e.g. brain, heart, kidney, muscle), and those which become saturated slowly are called "slow tissues" (e.g. cartilage, tendon and fat stores).

It can take up to 3 or 4 days before all body tissues become saturated with nitrogen at a particular ambient pressure, although we are virtually saturated after 24 hours at pressure. The length of time seems to be independent of the quantity of nitrogen involved in the process. It will take the same time for the body to absorb 2 liters at a pressure of 2 ATA, or 4 liters at 4 ATA. Although SCUBA divers never become fully saturated with nitrogen, occasionally some of their tissues can.

Nitrogen will be absorbed more rapidly at the beginning of the dive due to the large difference in nitrogen partial pressures (**"nitrogen pressure gradient"**) in the lungs and in the body tissues. The absorption rate decreases as the partial pressures in the lungs and the tissues approach equilibrium.

NITROGEN ELIMINATION (Off-gassing or out-gassing)

When we ascend the reverse of the in-gassing process occurs. As the ambient pressure is reduced the partial pressure of the nitrogen in the lungs decreases. The blood now has a higher nitrogen tension than the air in the lungs, so nitrogen passes from the blood into the lungs, and leaves the body in the expired breath, leaving the blood with a lower nitrogen tension. When this blood again circulates through the tissues, nitrogen passes from the tissues into the blood and, so, the process continues. Some parts of the body will release the nitrogen more slowly than other parts for the same reasons that they absorb it more slowly - poor blood supply or a greater capacity to absorb the gas.

If we ascend slowly enough to prevent the nitrogen tension in the tissues and the blood from exceeding the ambient pressure, the nitrogen remains dissolved and passes to, and from, the lungs efficiently and safely. **However, if we ascend too rapidly the partial pressure of nitrogen in some tissues, or in the blood, may exceed the ambient pressure. When this occurs the blood or particular tissues are said to be "supersaturated" with nitrogen.**

If the blood or tissues are supersaturated, dissolved gas will begin to come out of solution and bubbles of nitrogen gas may form in the tissues or in the blood.

Many of the bubbles that are detected in the blood may not have formed there as the blood desaturates rapidly. Some scientists believe that many of the bubbles form between capillaries and are forced into the capillaries by the pressure of the nitrogen in the tissues, damaging the capillaries in the process. Once in the capillaries, **most of the bubbles are swept to the lungs where they are generally trapped in the lung capillaries. The nitrogen diffuses from the bubbles into the lungs and is eventually exhaled. However, these bubbles reduce the circulation through the lungs and, consequently, slow down the process of nitrogen elimination. In addition, bubbles can distort and damage delicate tissue, block the supply of blood to organs and cause various biochemical reactions in the body**. Biochemical changes in the blood can complicate the process of gas elimination, as can the opening and closing of the capillaries, temperature changes (which affect the solubility of nitrogen and perfusion) and exercise (which affects the perfusion and carbon dioxide levels).

Most of the current decompression tables and dive computers assume that gas uptake and elimination occur at identical rates. However, this is often not the case as many factors can alter the rates. Gas elimination often appears to be slower than uptake, especially when bubbles are present.

SUMMARY

* A diver is said to be "saturated" when the partial pressure of nitrogen in all of his body tissues is the same as the partial pressure of nitrogen in his lungs.

* Some body tissues absorb (and release) nitrogen far more rapidly than others and thus become saturated sooner. The differing rate of nitrogen absorption depends on the fat content of the tissue and the amount of blood flow (perfusion) to the tissue.

* The opening and closing of capillaries affects the rate of nitrogen uptake and release, as do temperature, exercise and various other factors.

* Complete saturation can take up to 3-4 days.

* When the partial pressure of nitrogen in a tissue is greater than that in the lungs, the tissue is said to be "supersaturated".

* If the blood or tissues become supersaturated, bubbles will begin to form.

* Most of the bubbles become trapped in the lungs, where they eventually resolve.

* Nitrogen elimination is slowed down when bubbles are present.

* Most current decompression tables and dive computers assume gas uptake and elimination occur at identical rates. However, gas elimination often appears to be slower than uptake.

* Bubbles can damage body tissues.

SOURCES

Buehlmann, A. (1984), "Decompression - Decompression Sickness", Springer-Verlag, Berlin.

Hills, B. (1977), "Decompression Sickness", Vol 1, John Wiley and Sons, London.

U.S. Navy (1985), "U.S. Navy Diving Manual", Vol. 1., Air Diving, U.S. Government Printing Office, Washington.

Vann, R. (1982), "Decompression Theory and Application". In: *The Physiology and Medicine of Diving*, Bennett, P. and Elliott, D. (eds), Best Publishing Co., California.

FURTHER READING

PADI (1988), "The Encyclopedia of Recreational Diving", PADI, California.

Vann, R. (1982), "Decompression Theory and Application". In: *The Physiology and Medicine of Diving*, Bennett, P. and Elliott, D. (eds), Best Publishing Co., California.

CHAPTER 4
BUBBLE FORMATION

It has been known for a long time that decompression sickness is an illness related to bubbles in the blood and tissues, but it still remains uncertain exactly when, and where, these bubbles begin to form.

Most traditional theorists believe that the partial pressure of inert gas dissolved in a tissue has to exceed the ambient pressure (i.e. the tissue is **supersaturated***) by some critical amount before gas bubbles form. Some believe that this critical amount is best described as a ratio, while others suggest that there is a critical pressure difference that should not be exceeded if bubbles are to be prevented from forming.

Most of the commonly available diving tables are based on the concept of a critical difference. They range from the U.S. Navy schedules, where the difference changes for each tissue at each depth, to the Royal Navy schedules where a constant difference is used. *All of these tables assume that the partial pressure of inert gas in a tissue can exceed ambient pressure by some amount before bubbles begin to form.*

In the 1960s, the Doppler ultrasonic bubble detection system was developed. It has since been used to detect the presence of bubbles in both animals and humans. This technique, together with X-ray studies, electrical resistance studies and pressure-volume change studies, has provided indisputable evidence that bubbles do form without the proposed ratios or differences having been exceeded.

Some modern theorists believe that bubbles will form whenever the partial pressure of the inert gas in a tissue exceeds the ambient pressure by any amount.

An important concept that is used to explain why bubble formation appears to be avoided after many dives, is the concept of "inherent unsaturation".

INHERENT UNSATURATION

As the blood is transported throughout the body, oxygen is unloaded into various tissues. The body uses more oxygen than it produces carbon dioxide and, because the carbon dioxide produced is more soluble than the oxygen, more of it remains dissolved. The result is that the total pressure (tension) of the gas in the tissues and in the venous blood is less than the ambient pressure. Therefore, the venous blood and tissues are said to be "unsaturated" and the amount of this unsaturation can be shown to be about 60 mmHg (0.08 Ats). This unsaturation provides an inherent safety margin during decompression. It appears that one can ascend a distance which is equivalent to a pressure reduction of 60mmHg (i.e. 2.6 fsw or 0.8 msw) before the inert gas tension in the tissue begins to exceed the ambient pressure, possibly causing bubbles to form.

* **A tissue is said to be supersaturated when the pressure of inert gas in the tissue (tissue tension) is greater than the ambient pressure.**

This unsaturation of the venous blood and tissues provides a carrying capacity for excess nitrogen during decompression. Also, since any bubbles formed are at ambient pressure (which is higher than the tissue or venous pressure), gas will tend to move from the bubbles into the venous blood, helping to resolve the bubbles.

THE PHYSICS OF THE BUBBLE

For a bubble to exist the total gaseous pressure within the bubble (P_{bubble}) must be equal to or greater than the crushing pressures exerted on it. These crushing pressures are:

1. The ambient pressure (P_{amb})
2. The pressure that the tissue exerts in resistance to deformation by the bubble (P_{tissue}). Localized falls in this tissue pressure may result from areas of turbulence and from tissue movements.
3. The pressure due to the surface tension of the bubble ($P_{tension}$). This pressure due to surface tension increases as the radius of the bubble decreases. Hence, smaller bubbles have greater surface tensions and vice versa. Very small bubbles are subjected to extremely high crushing pressures and tend to collapse, whereas large bubbles have negligible surface tensions.

Hence, for a bubble to exist:

$$P_{bubble} \geqslant P_{amb} + P_{tissue} + P_{tension}$$

($\geqslant$: equal to or greater than)

FIGURE 4.1

The forces acting on a bubble

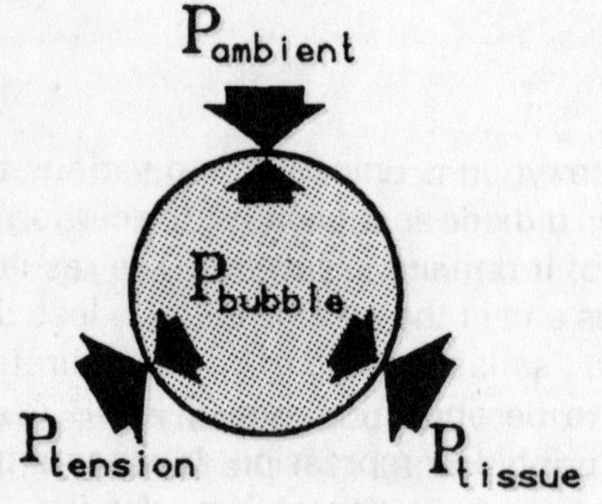

If P_{bubble} is greater than the crushing pressures, the bubble expands.

If P_{bubble} is equal to the crushing pressures, the bubble remains stable.

If P_{bubble} is less than the crushing pressures, the bubble is reduced in volume.

THEORIES OF BUBBLE (GAS PHASE) FORMATION

There are a number of theories which attempt to describe bubble formation, however, to date, no theory has been indisputably proven. The truth may lie in a combination of varies aspects of these theories.

One theory supposes that bubbles form afresh (de novo - i.e. where none existed before) within the fluid between the cells due to local reductions in pressure induced by some kind of mechanical stress. The stress creates tiny cavities within the tissues and, if excess gas is present, it will enter into and expand these cavities, thereby forming bubbles. When you pull a finger and the knuckle pops, the pop is thought to be due to gas suddenly entering the vacuum created by the pulling.

Bubbles do actually form afresh when there is enough turbulence (e.g. a beer is shaken) but, in the absence of turbulence, huge pressures (i.e. 100-1,000 ATA) are required before bubbles begin to form afresh. Exercise generates cavitation forces along muscles and tendons, thereby producing bubbles.

Sophisticated mathematical equations have been developed to determine exactly when bubbles should form. Enormous surface tensions must *normally* be overcome before a bubble can form afresh, and no equation to date has predicted the fact that bubbles can, and at times do, form when a diver ascends to the surface from depths as shallow as 23 ft (7 m), or possibly shallower. To explain how these initial surface tensions are avoided, theorists developed the concept of a bubble "nucleus", which is the basis of another theory.

This theory supposes that tiny bubble "nuclei" (microscopic pockets of gas) are present within our bodies, and that excess gas diffuses into these nuclei, expanding them and creating bubbles. Some theorists suggest that the nuclei are created by gas diffusing into low-pressure areas created by either the movement of surfaces over one another (tribonucleation), turbulence in the blood (Reynold's cavitation) or muscle activity.

Imagine that you are looking into a glass of beer, coca- cola or some other carbonated drink. The bubbles in the drink consist of carbon dioxide gas. While the lid was on the bottle the drink was held under pressure. Although a lot of excess carbon dioxide was dissolved in the liquid (i.e. the liquid was supersaturated) bubbles could not form as the ambient pressure was very high (i.e. the bottle was closed while the gas was under pressure). When the lid was removed, the ambient pressure dropped and the carbon dioxide could come out of solution to form bubbles (Henry's Law). Similarly, a diver is subjected to a high ambient pressure at depth, but, if he ascends rapidly, the supersaturated nitrogen gas can come out of solution and form bubbles.

Looking closely at the bubbling drink, you might notice that bubbles only arise from the bottom or the sides of the glass. If a solid object is submerged into the drink, bubbles will also form on its surface. This is true as long as the drink is held still, but if the drink is shaken, new bubbles form from within the liquid itself, rather than only at points of contact with the glass.

In the still drink, bubbles only form at tiny cracks or imperfections in the glass. It is argued that a small "nucleus" of gas is trapped in each of these cracks, and this nucleus resists being crushed. When the lid is removed and the excess dissolved gas begins to come out of solution, some gas diffuses into the bubble nucleus and expands its volume. Eventually, a bubble will form, break away, and leave the nucleus free to create another bubble. This process is shown in Figure 4.2.

FIGURE 4.2

Bubbles forming at a small crack in the wall of a container

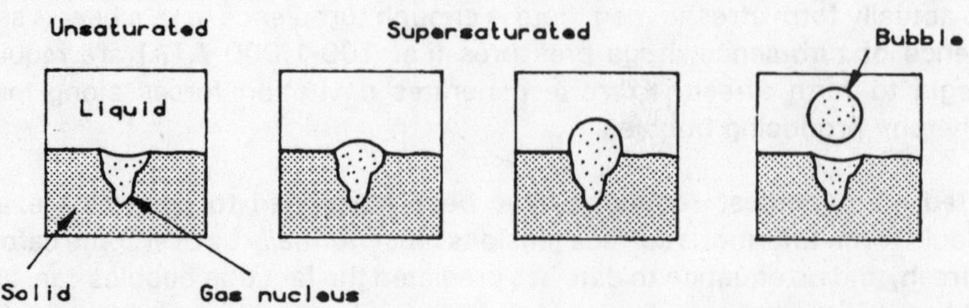

It has been proposed that the vessel walls, or other body tissues, may retain small pockets of gas which act as nuclei for bubble growth. Other researchers believe that spherical bubble nuclei are circulating continuously, stabilized by elastic, organic skins (Varying Permeability Model). These nuclei are small enough to remain in solution via Brownian motion, and strong enough to resist collapse from surface tension. The "skin" is composed of surface active molecules (like those in soaps and detergents) which reduce surface tension. It is suggested that gas can diffuse across these skins at pressures normally encountered by divers, but they become impermeable when subjected to pressures of about 8 ATA or more.

It has also been suggested that they can be crushed by high pressures and reformed within a few hours.

Experimental evidence in support of this theory first emerged when it was noted that the number of bubbles formed in water during decompression could be reduced by applying much greater pressures to the water before decompression. Pre-pressurizing the water was thought to crush the nuclei, forcing gas into solution and, hence, reducing the number of nuclei available to form bubbles. A similar procedure was tried on shrimps, which are transparent so bubbles are clearly seen, and on rats, and the pre-pressurization seemed to reduce the number of bubbles. In Hawaii, in 1985, a variation of the procedure was used in a reasonably successful attempt to rid a diver of a severe case of decompression sickness.[1] The diver was repeatedly compressed to a pressure of almost 8 ATA, in an attempt to crush any nuclei in which bubbles were growing.

The existence of bubble nuclei is still only very theoretical, since theorists cannot describe with certainty their size, constituents, location or their origin.

The "crack" explanation seems inadequate in itself to explain why bubbles form at less rigid surfaces, such as those within the human body. Bubbles form readily around paraffin when it is submerged in soda water, no matter how well the paraffin has been cleaned (Figure 4.3). Bubbles also form at the interface between fat and certain solutions. Fat and paraffin are both non-wettable (hydrophobic) substances, as they resist water upon their surfaces. *A non-wettable interface appears to facilitate the growth of bubbles, as it seems that less energy is required for bubbles to form at such an interface. Some experts now believe the non-wettable nature of the surface of the blood vessels may play an important part in allowing bubbles to form and grow.*[2]

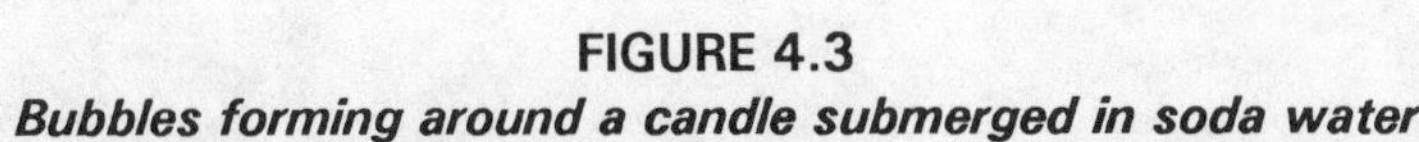

FIGURE 4.3

Bubbles forming around a candle submerged in soda water

THE EFFECTS OF BUBBLE FORMATION

Once bubbles form some may join together (coalesce) to form larger pockets of gas. Many of the resulting pockets may not be spherical and may, instead, become elongated (Figure 4.4). This increases the contact area with a tissue, increases resistance to movement and, at times, causes the bubble to become trapped in the tissue or vessel. If bubbles do lodge in tissue, or in blood vessels, they can put pressure on nerves, damage delicate tissue and block the supply of blood to vital organs. The bubbles themselves have been shown to permanently distort the shape of tissue.

FIGURE 4.4

Gas bubbles in the cerebral circulation of a rabbit

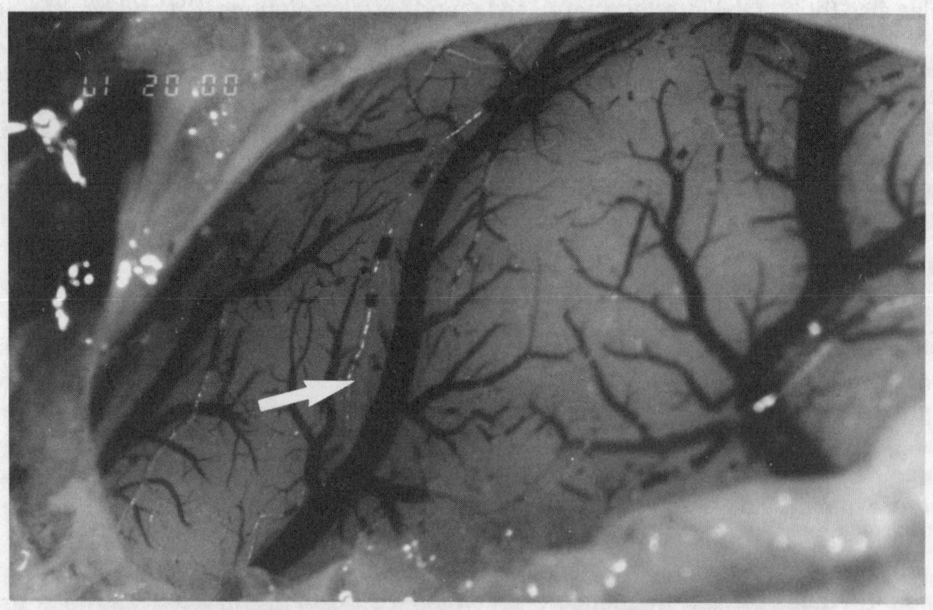

Photo courtesy Dr. D. Gorman.

Note how the bubbles have adopted the shape of the blood vessels and the large contact surface with the walls of the vessels.

Once a bubble exists, a reduction in the ambient pressure will cause further growth as the bubble will expand according to Boyle's law. This expansion reduces the partial pressures of the gases within the bubble, causing them to be lower than the partial pressures of the gases in the tissues surrounding the bubble. This pressure gradient will encourage more gas to diffuse from the tissues into the bubble, further expanding bubble size.

The presence of bubbles in the blood and tissues causes complex biochemical reactions within the body. The clotting mechanisms are activated and blood platelets become sticky and begin to stick to the bubbles and to each other.

Recent experiments have indicated that the presence of gas bubbles in the blood activates certain proteins (i.e. complement proteins), which appear to play an important role in the development of decompression sickness. An individual's susceptibility to bends appears to depend on how readily these proteins are activated. Experiments on rabbits indicated that decompression sickness could be avoided if the complement system was rendered inactive.[3,4]

The activation of complement proteins promotes the release of certain chemicals (mediators, such as histamine) which cause the capillaries to leak fluid from the blood into the tissue spaces, thereby reducing the blood volume and thickening the blood. The thicker blood is stickier, slows down the circulation, and allows more clotting. Red blood cells sludge together in clumps. Eventually, the reduced circulation causes shock, which may become severe.

As previously mentioned, **the presence of bubbles slows down nitrogen elimination.** This may be due to both the reduction in circulation though the lungs due to the bubbles blocking lung capillaries, and the changes in the blood, precipitated by the bubbles. **It now appears that bubbles can, at times, remain in a diver's body for days and even weeks after diving.***

DETECTION OF BUBBLES

Bubble formation (the gas phase) is difficult to study in biological systems as tissue is optically opaque. Various methods of detecting gas phase formation have been introduced over the years. Electrical conductance studies have proved successful in detecting gas trapped in tissues. If gas bubbles form, or accumulate, in a tissue the electrical resistance through the tissue increases. X-ray studies can detect pockets of gas, and the measurement of cerebrospinal fluid volume can also indicate the presence of gas.

The most common method used in decompression studies is ultrasonic monitoring. Ultrasound waves have a frequency of between 20,000 Hz and 10^9 Hz. Those used for bubble detection normally have a frequency of around 10^6 Hz. The waves are highly directional, easily focused and are strongly reflected at a gas-liquid interface. The waves travel in nearly straight lines in blood and most soft body tissues. The average body tissue has a high water content and ultrasound travels easily through it, but is readily reflected from bone and air.

Ultrasonic diagnostic equipment consists of transmitters to generate the sound waves, tranducers to convert the waves to, and from, electrical impulses, receivers to amplify the reflected wave and displays to present the results. One such device, the precordial probe, is designed to be placed on the chest and to receive signals scattered back from blood and gas emboli in the pulmonary artery or the right ventricle of the heart. Other veins, such as the subclavian or the inferior vena cava can also be monitored with these units.

* In Australia, a diver presented for a routine operation which required a general anesthetic. He had not been diving for about 4 weeks and had not noticed any manifestations of decompression sickness after his last dive. The anesthetist used nitrous oxide. Shortly after the diver awoke he complained of joint pains and other bends-like symptoms which all resolved rapidly when he was treated in a recompression chamber. It appears that there were asymptomatic bubbles remaining from his last dive and, it seems, the nitrous oxide diffused into and expanded these bubbles which grew large enough to cause symptoms.[5]

FIGURE 4.5

Diver being monitored for bubbles with a Precordial Doppler Monitor

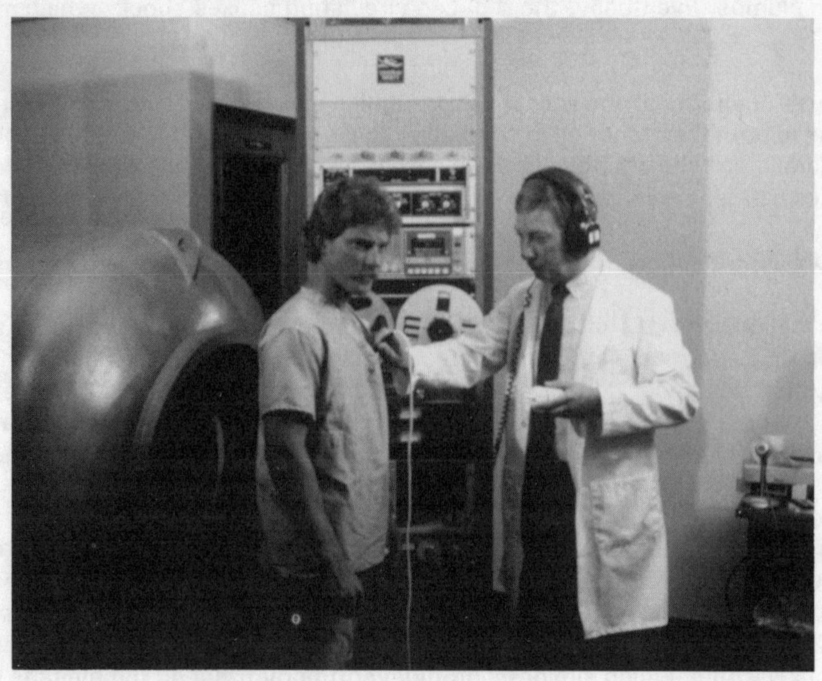

Photo courtesy Dr. M. Powell.

The Doppler Effect is the change in the frequency of a wave when the transmitter, receiver or scatterer are moving with respect to each other. Reflections from moving blood cells or gas bubbles have a different frequency from that transmitted. **Ultrasonic Doppler flowmeters respond only to reflection from moving bubbles and cannot detect reflections from stationary bubbles. Therefore, these devices can only detect bubbles that are circulating and not those trapped in the tissues.**

The signals that are picked up by the receiver are usually presented as sounds. A bubble in the blood is portrayed as a "chirp", "whistle" or a "clicking" sound which is superimposed on a background blood flow signal. The noise produced by the motion of the heart walls can make accurate bubble detection difficult, especially when a diver is active, shivering or cold. Normally, bubbles are dectected by listening to the signals from a bubble monitor through headphones. The listener(s) must be extremely well-trained and skilled to ensure a consistent and reliable result. The sounds can also be recorded on an audio tape. The bubbles are then classified into various grades of bubbles according to some classification scheme, such as that developed by Spencer (Table 4.1) or by Kisman and Masurel (Appendix F).

TABLE 4.1

The Spencer Scale for Classifying Bubbles

0	=	complete lack of bubble signals.
1	=	occasional bubble signal with the great majority of heart cycles free of bubbles.
2	=	many, but less than half, of the heart cycles contain bubble signals.
3	=	all heart cycles contain showers of single bubble signals, but not dominating the heart cycle signals.
4	=	gas bubbles present continuously, gas bubble signals louder than normal heart cycle signals.

Whether or not a bubble will be detected will depend on a number of factors, the primary one being the size of the bubble. The smallest bubbles detected by reflection alone appear to be about 20-25 *u*m in radius.

It has been shown that the larger the amount of Doppler-detectable bubbles the greater the likelihood of decompression sickness.[6] **However, the fact that no bubbles can be detected by a Doppler flowmeter does not necessarily mean that no bubbles are present. The monitor will only detect moving bubbles of a sufficient size passing through the area at which the probe is aimed. If the probe is incorrectly positioned or aimed, bubbles may be missed. Most importantly, stationary bubbles trapped in tissues will not be detected by Doppler systems.**

The gas phase detected by Doppler devices is probably generated in, or near, the capillaries of muscle or fat. As this gas phase grows, small bubbles may break off and get swept into the veins (intravascular bubbles) where they may, eventually, be detected by Doppler. The bubbles which cause pain at, or near, joints are thought to be located in the tendons and/or ligaments around the joints, and it is unlikely that the bubbles are located in the capillaries themselves (they are extravascular bubbles). Hence, there is no exact correspondence between the number of Doppler-detectable bubbles and the amount of gas phase formation in the tendons and ligaments. For this reason, Doppler detectors are poor predictors of joint pain. However, it is generally assumed that decompression profiles that cause few detectable bubbles (from muscle and fat) would normally cause few bubbles to be formed in ligament and tendon. Statistically this has been found to be true, and as a result Doppler monitors have been used extensively in the development and testing of decompression tables.

SUMMARY

* A tissue is said to be "supersaturated" when the pressure of inert gas in the tissue is greater than the ambient pressure.

* All of the commonly available tables assume that the partial pressure of inert gas in a tissue can exceed ambient pressure by some amount before bubbles form.

* Some experts now believe that bubbles will form whenever the partial pressure of inert gas in a tissue exceeds the ambient pressure by any amount.

* For a bubble to exist the total gaseous pressure within the bubble must be equal to, or greater than, the crushing pressures exerted on it.

* There are a number of theories describing bubble formation in the body. However, no theory has as yet been indisputably proven.

* It appears that bubbles may form readily at the interface of the blood and blood vessels.

* Bubbles can block and/or damage blood vessels, put pressure on nerves and distort and damage tissue.

* Bubbles activate various biochemical reactions in the body, which have been shown to play an important role in the development of bends.

* It is important to realize that bubbles do not need to create a mechanical blockage to cause damage. The physiological effects can be equally or more dangerous and can last for long periods of time.

* The presence of bubbles slows down nitrogen elimination.

* Doppler ultrasonic bubble detectors can only detect circulating bubbles and not those trapped in the tissues.

REFERENCES

1. Sands, B. (1985), "Radical Bends Treatment". *SCUBA Diver,* Dec 1985/Jan 1986: 22-25.

2. Hills, B. (1990), "Bubble Growth in Biological Systems". *SPUMS Journal*; 20 (1): 65-70.

3. Ward, C. et al (1987), "Complement Proteins Mediate Decompression Sickness in Rabbits". *Undersea Biomedical Research*, Supplement to 14 (2), March: 16.

4. Ward, C. et al (1990), "Complement activation involvement in decompression sickness in rabbits". *Undersea Biomedical Research*; 17 (1): 51-66.

5. Acott, C., personal communication.

6. Powell, M. and Johanson, D. (1978), "Ultrasound monitoring and decompression sickness". *6th Symp on Underwater Physiology*, Shilling, C. and Beckett, M. eds, Bethesda.

OTHER SOURCES

DeDecker, H. (1986), "Beer Bubbles and Bends: The Biophysics of Bubble Formation in Decompression Sickness". *SPUMS Journal*; 16 (4): 143-146.

Edmonds, C. et al (1981), "Diving and Subaquatic Medicine", 2nd edition. Diving Medical Centre, Sydney.

Hemmingsten, E. and Hemmingsten, B. (1990), "Bubble formation properties of hydrophobic particles in water and cells of Tetrahymena". *Undersea Biomedical Research*; 17 (1): 67-78.

Hills, B. (1977), "Decompression Sickness", Vol 1. John Wiley and Sons, London.

Hills, B., personal communications.

Nishi, R. and Eatock, B. (1987), "The Role of Ultrasonic Bubble Detection in Table Validation". *Proceedings of the UHMS Workshop on Validation of Decompression Schedules*, 13-14 Feb, Bethesda, MD.

Powell, M. et al (1982), "Ultrasonic Surveillance of Decompression", In: *The Physiology and Medicine of Diving,* 3rd edition, Bennett, P. and Elliott, D. (eds), Best Publishing Co., California.

Powell, M. et al (1988), "Doppler Ultrasound Monitoring of Gas Phase Formation Following Decompression in Repetitive Dives". PADI, California.

Powell, M., personal communication.

Spencer, M. (1976), "Decompression limits for compressed air determined by ultrasonically detected blood bubbles". *J Appl Physiol;* 40 (2): 229-235.

Vann, R. (1982), "Decompression Theory and Applications", In: *The Physiology and Medicine of Diving,* 3rd edition, Bennett, P. and Elliot, D. (eds), Best Publishing Co., California.

RECOMMENDED FURTHER READING

Hills, B. (1977), "Decompression Sickness", Vol 1. John Wiley and Sons, London.

Nishi, R. and Eatock, B. (1987), "The Role of Ultrasonic Bubble Detection in Table Validation". *Proceedings of the UHMS Workshop on Validation of Decompression Schedules,* 13-14 Feb, Bethesda, MD.

PADI (1988), "The Encyclopedia of Recreational Diving", PADI, California: 2.22-2.23.

Powell, M. et al (1982), "Ultrasonic Surveillance of Decompression", in *Physiology and Medicine of Diving,* 3rd edition, Bennett, P. and Elliott, D. (eds), Best Publishing Co., California: 404-434., 1982.

Vann, R. (1982), "Decompression Theory and Application". In: *The Physiology and Medicine of Diving*, 3rd edition, Bennett, P. and Elliott, D. (eds), Best Publishing Co., California: 352-382.

CHAPTER 5

DECOMPRESSION SICKNESS

5.1 Cause, manifestations, management and after-effects

HISTORICAL BACKGROUND

In 1650 the first effective air pump was developed and, and 20 years later, Robert Boyle used a pump to reduce the pressure within a vessel which contained a viper. The viper writhed in pain and Boyle noticed that a bubble had formed within the fluid of the viper's eye. He also noticed that bubbles had developed within other parts of the viper's body and concluded that they had been caused by decompression.

In 1841 decompression sickness was observed in caisson workers who worked in tunnels dug through wet soil. The pressure of the air in the tunnels had been raised in order to prevent the water entering into, and filling, the tunnels. These workers would spend many hours breathing the compressed air within the tunnel and would often suffer pains and other disorders after returning to normal environmental pressure.

In the later part of the 19th century similar symptoms were exhibited by sponge divers who had dived using compressed air and, early this century, by aviators who had flown to great heights in unpressurized aircraft.

What these sufferers all had incommon was that they had developed symptoms after their environmental pressure had been reduced, that is, after decompression. This ailment was initially called the "bends" as sufferers would often adopt a bent gait because of pain in the hips and knees.

Cause

Decompression sickness (DCS) results from the development of bubbles within the body. Excess gas is dissolved in our blood and body tissues when we dive, due to the higher partial pressure of the gases in our lungs. When we dive using air, the extra gases are oxygen and nitrogen. The oxygen is easily used up by the body functions and, generally, does not create bubble problems, but the extra nitrogen is not used and much of it is stored in the tissues. When we ascend, the excess gas is released from our tissues and, if the ascent is slow enough, this excess gas will stay dissolved and will leave our body in a safe and orderly way. If, however, we ascend too quickly, bubbles of excess gas will form in some of our tissues (where supersaturation is highest) and, at times, in our blood, during or following the ascent. These bubbles can distort and disrupt tissues, block and/or damage blood vessels and precipitate biochemical reactions within the body. When the bubbles, or their effects, cause symptoms it is called decompression sickness.

Bubbles can occur without creating symptoms or causing any damage to our body. Bubbles which do not cause symptoms are called "asymptomatic" or "silent" bubbles. Some experts fear that at times some silent bubbles can still cause damage. A 1988 study, in which 64 recreational divers were monitored by Doppler during 214 dives, found asymptomatic bubbles in approximately 18% of the divers. The bubble incidence was higher in those divers who dived to 80 ft (24 m) or deeper.[1]

There is growing evidence that bubbles are probably present in the blood of many divers who have dived to some of the No-Decompression Limits of the U.S. Navy Tables (and to similar limits on other tables). However, only a relatively small percentage of these divers display signs or feel symptoms of decompression sickness. (Although some experiments have put the rate as high as 5-8%[2,3]). The reason for this is explained as follows:

Bubbles form in various tissues throughout the body and within the blood itself. Some of the bubbles formed within the tissues will remain in the tissues, but those forming near capillaries may be forced through the pores of the capillaries. Once inside the capillaries, bubbles are swept along by the venous blood which takes them through the right side of the heart to the lungs. **The lungs act as a fairly effective bubble trap as most bubbles are trapped in the lung capillaries.** The gas gradually diffuses from the bubbles, across into the alveoli, and the bubbles eventually disappear. A diver usually will not feel any symptoms from the bubbles trapped in the lungs until between 25% to 60% of the lung circulation is blocked.

Manifestations (Signs and symptoms)

Table 5.1.1 summarizes the wide variety of manifestations of decompression sickness. The reasons why the various signs and symptoms occur are given in the paragraphs following.

TABLE 5.1.1

Signs and symptoms of DCS

Common:	Other:
Chest, torso or back pain,	Blood in stools,
Difficulty passing urine	Blotchy skin
Dizziness	Confusion
Inco-ordination	Convulsions
Lethargy and fatigue	Coughing
Loss of balance	Death
Loss of bladder/bowel control	Diarrhoea
Malaise	Headaches
Numbness	Hearing loss
Pain/discomfort at or near a joint	Itch
Paralysis	Nausea
Tingling sensations	Rash
Weakness	Ringing in ears
	Shortness of breath
	Swelling
	Stomach cramps
	Unconsciousness
	Visual disturbances
(Listed in alphabetical order)	Vomiting blood

The dive profile influences, to some extent, where bubbles form and, therefore, the type of symptoms which might occur. A short, deep dive produces a high nitrogen load within the "fast" tissues but a smaller load within the "slow" tissues, which need more time to saturate. If bubbles form during, or after, the ascent from a short, deep dive they will more likely form in the "fast" tissues such as blood and the central nervous system (brain and spinal cord). Symptoms such as paralysis, numbness, loss of bladder function and mental changes may occur. At times, difficulty in breathing, which is a symptom of a bubble overload in the lungs, occurs. **Rapid ascent makes bubble formation in the blood even more likely since there is less time for the lungs to rid the blood of its nitrogen load.**

Divers who develop decompression sickness after a long, shallow dive tend to complain of pain at or near a joint(s). However, clinical examination shows that they often have neurological signs and/or symptoms as well. This type of dive profile tends to produce pain at, or near, joints because the tissues around joints are poorly supplied with blood vessels making it is difficult for the large amount of nitrogen dissolved in these slow tissues to be carried away during the relatively short ascent time.

Most divers suffering from decompression sickness will feel symptoms within six hours of having dived, the majority showing some symptoms within the first hour. However, some divers have become symptomatic as long as one to three days, or even longer, after the dive, especially if there is a delayed altitude exposure. As a general rule, the earlier the onset of symptoms of any kind in decompression sickness, the more serious the illness is likely to be.

Pain can be a symptom of both mild and serious decompression sickness. It is often at, or near, a joint, but can be due to damage to nerves (spinal decompression sickness). When bubbles interrupt pain fibres in the spinal cord, pain is felt wherever the fibres originate. This is often the back and abdomen. Bubbles can cause pain with, or without, doing much damage. Bubbles affecting the inner ear can cause hearing loss, ringing, balance problems and nausea; which are all painless. Bubbles lodged within the brain can cause symtoms similar to stroke, again painless. Bubbles blocking vessels within various large organs cause no pain and often cause no damage if there are other blood vessels supplying the organ which can provide enough oxygenated blood to replace the supply from the blocked vessels. If blood does not get through, part of the organ may be damaged.

The most common signs and symptoms of decompression sickness are malaise (feeling unwell) and lethargy (extreme fatigue). It is not yet clear exactly what causes these symptoms but some doctors have suggested that they may be due to bubbles in the central nervous system and/or a general body stress reaction precipitated by the presence of bubbles. Although the symptoms often disappear, it is feared that at times they may have serious implications, especially if untreated.

We are often tired after the dive due to the effort of lugging the gear around and, at times, due to a hard swim. *The fatigue of decompression sickness is fatigue beyond what you would expect from the amount of exertion done.*

The location and volume of the bubbles determines the type of symptoms and the severity of decompression sickness.

Type 1 and Type 2 DCS

Decompression sickness is sometimes classified into *Type 1* or *Type 2* according to the symptoms present. Type 1 decompression sickness is when pain is the only symptom present. The pain can be around a joint, in the muscles, and can migrate up or down to an extremity. When neurological symptoms are present it is classified as Type 2 decompression sickness.

LUNG INVOLVEMENT

It was mentioned earlier that the lungs act as a fairly effective bubble filter. If, however, the lung capillaries become overloaded with bubbles, serious problems can develop. Because the bubbles are blocking a large portion of the lung capillary network, there is an increased resistance to blood flow through the lungs. Blood flow through the lungs is reduced so oxygen intake is also reduced. Symptoms such as *tightness across the chest, chest pain, shortness of breath, coughing* and *cyanosis* may result. This malady has often been called "the chokes" and it may be brought on by smoking after diving.

The resistance to blood flow through the lungs builds up a back pressure in the pulmonary arteries, and the right ventricle must work harder to pump the blood it receives from the systemic veins through the lungs. When it cannot maintain the pace, the circulation slows down and back pressure builds up in the systemic veins. Nitrogen delivery from the tissues to the lungs is reduced and more bubbles may form. The capillaries begin to leak fluid, which results in a reduced blood volume. This reduced blood volume precipitates shock, which is often associated with decompression sickness.

SPINAL DECOMPRESSION SICKNESS

Spinal decompression sickness is caused by bubbles forming in the fatty tissues which act as insulators around the nerves in the spinal cord and, either pressing directly on the nerves and affecting the transmission of impulses, or pressing on blood vessels and blocking them, so depriving the nerves of oxygen. Another mechanism is by bubbles in the venous sinuses surrounding the spinal cord blocking the flow of blood through the spinal cord capillaries, which again deprives the nerves of oxygen.

Most of our veins have one-way valves which prevent the back flow of blood. The veins which drain the spinal cord do not have one-way valves and, if the pressure inside the chest increases, a temporary back flow of blood can occur. When the lung capillaries are overloaded with bubbles and the pressure builds up in the veins which drain the spinal cord, the blood flow can temporarily reverse direction, pushing bubbles back into the venous sinuses. Coughing can exacerbate this problem by further increasing the backflow.

Spinal decompression sickness often follows in divers who show pulmonary symptoms ("the chokes").

Symptoms of spinal decompression sickness can also result when an artery which supplies blood to the spinal cord is blocked or damaged by a bubble. This type of decompression sickness, caused by an arterial gas embolism, is discussed later in the chapter.

Spinal decompression sickness can cause *tingling sensations or loss of feeling and movement in a limb,* or can even cause *paralysis of the lower half or both sides of the body.* It may be preceded by *back pain or abdominal pain or cramps.* There may also be *difficulty in passing urine* which produces greater abdominal pain due to urine retention in the bladder, or complete *loss of bladder or bowel control.* Unless treated rapidly and effectively, spinal decompression sickness may leave the diver with a severe and permanent handicap. Spinal symptoms can take a while to develop. What sometimes happens is that a diver feels really weak and tired after the dive, goes to sleep and wakes up paralysed. Spinal symptoms often occur after deeper dives.

CEREBRAL DECOMPRESSION SICKNESS

Bubbles may form directly in brain tissue and may distort and damage the tissue. Bubbles may also form in a blood vessel supplying part of the brain. If circulation is obstructed, damage can result. The resulting symptoms will depend on which tissue the obstructed vessel was previously supplying. Possible symptoms include *personality changes, severe headache, confusion, visual disturbances, staggering, speech disturbances, unconsciousness, convulsions and inability to move one side of the body. Death* can occur in some cases unless prompt action is taken.

Until quite recently it was believed that cerebral decompression sickness was rare, but it is now seen to occur quite commonly as many people who present for "pain only" decompression sickness display neurological signs when carefully examined. Many spontaneously report that they "feel themselves again" after recompression. Cerebral decompression sickness has often been seen to occur in divers who have not exceeded their No-Decompression Limits, as well as in those who have overstayed the limits.

ARTERIAL GAS EMBOLISM

Bubbles usually do not form in the arterial blood. However, a very rapid ascent from depth can, at times, cause bubbles to form directly in arterial blood.[4]

Venous bubbles can enter the arterial circulation when they pass through, or bypass, the pulmonary bubble trap.

The lungs have shunts which will open and allow blood to bypass the lung capillary beds when they become overloaded with bubbles. Bubbles in this blood enter the arterial circulation and can block small blood vessels supplying various tissues. The bubbles may also damage the lining of blood vessels they pass through, so reducing blood flow through the vessel. If they block or damage vessels supplying the spinal cord then spinal symptoms might occur, if they block vessels supplying the brain cerebral symptoms might occur, and if they block or damage vessels supplying the heart symptoms of a heart attack might result.

An unborn baby has a hole (called the *foramen ovale)* in the wall between the atria of the heart, so that blood can pass directly across the heart and bypass the non-functioning lungs. This hole is supposed to close after birth when the lungs begin to function. Initially, the foramen ovale is closed by means of a "flap" valve, which remains closed as the pressure in the left atrium is slightly higher than that in the right atrium. In most people the valve eventually seals over and the foramen ovale disappears. However, in some individuals, the valve fails to seal completely and they have what is known as a *patent foramen ovale*. Various studies have indicated that a small defect may remain in somewhere between 5% and 30% of adults.[5,6,7] A patent foramen ovale normally creates no problems but, in divers, if the lungs are congested with venous bubbles and the back pressure in the right atrium increases, some blood and, therefore, bubbles which would normally be filtered by the lungs, can pass through the hole and enter the arterial circulation. These bubbles may block or damage blood vessels, causing hypoxia and subsequent damage to the tissues supply supplied by the vessels.

In a study at Duke University, the hearts of 30 divers, who suffered from DCS, were examined by two-dimensional echocardiography, a sonar-like technique for imaging the heart. Eleven of these divers were found to have a patent foramen ovale which allowed blood to flow directly across from the right to the left side of the heart. These 11 divers were among the 18 divers who had the more serious, neurological symptoms of DCS.[8] A British study detected shunts in 28 of 43 divers (65%) who had suffered neurological decompression sickness within 30 minutes of surfacing.[9] This suggests that a patent foramen ovale may often be associated with a rapid onset of neurological decompression sickness. The researchers also suggested that *the presence of a patent foramen ovale might explain why certain divers have been bent after what should have been relatively safe profiles, where no other obvious risk factors were present*. The combined results of both studies seem to indicate that the presence of a patent foramen ovale may, at times, predispose a diver to severe decompression sickness. In addition, it has been theorized that the turbulence caused by blood passing through a patent foramen ovale may create low pressure "eddys" into which excess nitrogen gas may diffuse, causing (de novo) bubble formation within the heart.

There is currently debate in some Countries about the desirability, and feasability, of testing for a patent foramen ovale during a diving medical examination. The test is costly and there is a small risk associated with it. Since the test involves injecting microbubbles into the circulation, in individuals with a patent formaen ovale, some of these bubbles pass into the arterial circulation where, it is feared, some may occasionally cause subtle damage. In addition, the condition is often difficult to detect unless repeated tests are conducted.

When repetitive dives are done, some venous bubbles (resulting from the initial dive) which are trapped in the lungs may be compressed enough to pass through into the arterial circulation, where they will eventually become trapped. Extra gas may enter into and expand these bubbles during, and after, the repetitive dive, and damage may result.

The above are all examples of an **arterial gas embolism** resulting from decompression sickness.*

Cerebral symptoms can be detected in many cases of decompression sickness and it is feared that subtle brain damage is more common among sufferers of decompression sickness than was previously believed. Some diving physicians believe that the micro bubbles passing through the lungs may block tiny blood vessels in scattered areas of the brain, causing subtle brain damage.

PAIN AT OR NEAR A JOINT

The exact location of the bubbles that cause pain at or around a joint is still not known for certain. Joints contain, or are surrounded by, tissues such as cartilage, ligament, tendon and periosteum, all of which have a poor blood supply. Bubbles have been seen in tendons, which contain small areas of fat and which have poor circulation, a structural pattern that a bubble would deform and also pain nerves. Many tendons have intermittent blood flow through the capillaries which encourages bubbles to form in the parts where the blood flow ceases towards the end of, or after, the dive. Exercise, which predisposes to bends, will create a relative vacuum within areas of tendon and will also generate shear forces, both of which encourage bubbling.

At first there may be an area of *discomfort or numbness at or around the joint or its surrounding muscles*. Over the next hour or so a *deep, dull ache* may develop and at times a *sharp, stabbing pain, or a throbbing pain* may occur. The pain often increases over the next 12 to 24 hours and, if untreated, might take several days to abate. Occasionally, the area around the joint may become red and swollen.

The shoulder is the most commonly affected joint but other joints such as the elbows, knees, hips, wrists, hands and ankles can also be affected.

* The symptoms of an arterial gas embolism caused by decompression sickness are similar to those caused by an air embolism resulting from a lung overpressure injury. However, in the latter case, the gas involved in air, rather than nitrogen. In fact, an air embolism is a type of arterial gas embolism.

This type of decompression sickness is common among caisson workers and abalone divers who spend long periods underwater. It was initially believed to be the most common form of decompression sickness amongst sport divers but **the more serious neurological manifestations of decompression sickness now predominate**. The increase in frequency of neurological signs/symptoms may partly be due to the fact that recreational divers now tend to dive more deeply and frequently than before, and partly due to an increased knowledge of, and ability to test for, the more subtle manifestations of DCS.

SKIN MANIFESTATIONS

Skin manifestations can range from a *mild itch with a measle-like rash*, to an *angry red rash* or to a *bluish marble-like mottling* of the skin. The itch is relatively rare in SCUBA divers and is usually due to gas diffusing and out of the skin during decompression in a chamber.

The mottling of the skin is due to bubbles blocking the blood vessels of the skin, and is associated with severe decompression sickness.

The rashes tend to be on the upper body and thighs.

GASTROINTESTINAL DECOMPRESSION SICKNESS

The intestines can be damaged by the presence of bubbles within their walls or within the blood vessels supplying them. Symptoms of gastrointestinal decompression sickness include *nausea, vomiting (sometimes of blood), stomach cramps and diarrhoea (at times blood stained).*

INNER EAR DECOMPRESSION SICKNESS

When bubbles form in the vessels supplying the inner ear, or within the tissues of the inner ear, balance can become affected, at times permanently. Symptoms such as *dizziness, nausea, vomiting, staggering, ringing* and *hearing loss* may occur.

Sport divers rarely complain of inner ear symptoms as the only manifestation of decompression sickness. However, it often occurs as an isolated event in helium-oxygen diving.

CHANGES WITHIN THE BLOOD

The presence of bubbles in the blood causes complex changes to occur within it. These very important changes are described in detail in Chapter 4.

PREVALENCE OF THE VARIOUS SYMPTOMS OF DCS

The Divers Alert Network (DAN) documented accident cases for 1987 showed that only 23% of the divers displayed joint and/or muscle pain (Type 1 DCS), compared to 60% who displayed more serious (Type 2) symptoms of decompression sickness (the balance of the reported cases suffered from arterial gas embolism). In 1988 these proportions were 26% and 56% respectively.[10,11]

Table 5.1.2, which is based on figures from DAN's "Report on 1988 Diving Accidents", indicates the relative occurrence of Type 1 and Type 2 DCS in the USA in 1987 and 1988.

TABLE 5.1.2

Relative occurrence of "types" of DCS in 1987 and 1988

	Percentage of cases	
	1987	1988
Type 1 DCS	28	32
Type 2 DCS	72	68

81% (81/100) of the divers treated for decompression sickness at the Alfred Hospital in Melbourne, Australia, in 1988 and 1989, had neurological signs/symptoms.[12]

FACTORS WHICH INCREASE THE CHANCE OF DECOMPRESSION SICKNESS (PREDISPOSING FACTORS)

Some factors increase the likelihood of a diver getting decompression sickness. Factors influencing the occurrence of DCS include:

Time underwater

The shorter the time the lower the risk. Obviously, (ignoring depth considerations) shorter dives allow less time for nitrogen uptake. The risk of bends appears to be substantially less for dives with bottom times shorter than about 45 minutes.[13]

Rate and frequency of ascent: In general, the slower the ascent rate the lower the risk. During a slower ascent the "fast" tissues are allowed to desaturate far more safely as the large differences between the nitrogen tensions in the tissues and the ambient pressure are avoided. Therefore, there is less chance that bubbles will form in the blood and neural tissues, possibly causing severe DCS during, or after, a slow ascent. Multiple ascents within a dive appear to increase bubble formation by increasing the opportunity for bubble formation and altering the rate of gas uptake and elimination during the remainder of the dive, or during following dives.

Repetitive diving: Repetitive dives are associated with far more decompression sickness than are single dives. Approximately 65% of the recreational divers treated for DCS in the USA in both 1987 and 1988 became ill after repetitive dives.[10,11] British figures for 1989 indicate that 28% (39/137) of British divers treated for DCS had undertaken repetitive dives.[14]* The high DCS rate for repetitive dives is not surprising as the mathematics of gas elimination in all tables are known to be only vague approximations to what happens in the body. So a diver starts a repetitive dive with an unknown load of extra nitrogen in his body.

When we begin a repetitive dive, we already have excess nitrogen in our tissues. This nitrogen must be considered when calculating the profile for the dive. This is difficult to do properly as gas elimination during the surface interval will depend on the amount of bubbling resulting from the first dive. The greater the bubbling, the slower the off-gassing. Re-descending will add gas to any existing bubbles and may also increase the rate of nitrogen uptake. Re-descending might also allow some bubbles, trapped in the lung capillaries, to pass into the arterial circulation.

Almost all current decompression tables and dive computers assume that the same mechanisms of gas uptake, elimination and bubble formation that apply to a single dive also apply to a repetitive dive. This has been shown to be often untrue. The same overpressure ratios used to avoid symptoms on the first dive often do not apply to subsequent dives. Bubbling occurs far sooner. Almost all current tables and all current dive computers fail to accommodate this fact (the BS-AC '88 Tables attempt to).

Previous exposure to pressure: This is a major influence. It often takes far longer than the 12 hours allowed by the U.S. Navy Tables or the 24 hours allowed by the British and Australian Naval Tables to get all the extra gas out of a diver, especially if bubbles have formed. So, even if a dive is not classified as a repetitive dive, there may be residual nitrogen in a diver's body that should be accounted for, but is not.

Cold: Cold environmental temperature has been shown to predispose to the bends.

Nitrogen is more soluble at lower temperatures so more can be dissolved in the peripheral tissues of a cold diver. Cold also slows down the diffusion of gases within the body, and by causing peripheral blood vessels to constrict, alters the distribution of nitrogen throughout the body. The vasconstriction causes cold diuresis so, when the diver rewarms, he is significantly dehydrated and, therefore, more susceptible to decompression sickness. In addition, when the diver rewarms, the nitrogen becomes less soluble which encourages bubble formation.

Obesity: Fat has a high affinity for nitrogen and a poor circulation. After a long dive fat will hold a lot of nitrogen and needs quite some time to unload it. If given insufficient time to unload, bubbles can form in the fat. This may cause problems if it occurs in the fat in the bone marrow or spinal chord. Overweight people often have higher blood lipid (fat) levels, and it has been claimed, but not proven, that this may predispose to the activation of the blood chemical changes involved in decompression sickness. Fatty meals temporarily raise blood lipids and, hence, theoretically, could contribute to this.

* The more conservative no-decompression stop repetitive dive times allowed by the British tables may partly explain the vast difference between the British and U.S. figures. In addition, it is possible that the British do less repetitive diving than their U.S. counterparts.

A study involving 932 compressed air workers (mainly miners) found a significantly higher rate of DCS in obese men than in those with less body fat.[15] These subjects would have had long pressure exposures during which large amounts of inert gas was absorbed in the body fat. On the other hand, another study involving 376 male military divers, none of whom were obese, found that percentage body fat was not associated with an increased incidence of DCS.[16] However, it must be stressed that none of these divers were obese and many of the pressure exposures were probably relatively short.

High carbon dioxide levels (Hypercapnia): Excess carbon dioxide causes the blood vessels to dilate, which increases the delivery of nitrogen to various tissues. Once bubbles have formed, excess carbon dioxide will diffuse into and, so, enlarge the bubbles.

Exercise: Exercise during the dive increases the demands for oxygen. The breathing rate and circulation increase and more nitrogen is delivered to the tissues. Exercise also raises carbon dioxide levels in the blood. Exercise after the dive increases turbulence and agitation of blood and tissues, creating areas of low pressure for gas to diffuse into and, so, and favouring bubbling. Exercise immediately before the dive may influence nitrogen uptake at the start of the dive if the increased circulation has not yet returned to normal. Pre-dive exercise may also create new gas nuclei from which additional bubbles can form. 48.8% (131/268) of the recreational divers who suffered from decompression sickness or arterial gas embolism in the USA in 1988 reported having undertaken strenous exercise before, during or after the dive.[11]

Exercise during decompression stops may increase or decrease the likelihood of DCS depending on the degree of exercise. Heavy exercise will promote bubble formation, but some work has shown that mild exercise may increase gas elimination, possibly by increasing the blood supply to the various tissues. Because of the difficulty of defining mild exercise, divers are discouraged from exercising during safety or decompression stops. However, gently moving and stretching will prevent divers adopting a fixed posture which could restrict circulation to and, hence, off-gassing from, one particular area.

Deep diving: U.S. Navy experience, between 1968 and 1981 was that the accident rate for dives of 50 ft (15 m) or less was 0.06%. The accident rate for dives to between 51-100 ft (15.5-30 m) was 0.23%, nearly four times the rate for shallow fives. The accident rate for dives between 101-200 ft (30-61 m) was 0.54%, more than double the 50-100ft rate and nine times the rate for shallower dives.[17]

Approximately 68% of the recreational divers treated for DCS in the USA in 1987 had dived deeper than 80 ft (24 m)[10], however, this increased to 72% (160/222) in 1988.[11] In 1988, in Britain, 47% (42/89) of the divers treated for bends had undertaken deep dives (defined there as deeper than 100 ft/30 m) but, in 1989, this reduced to 35% (48/137).[18,14]

An extensive statistical analysis of a large number of dives indicates that for dives performed in accordance to conventional decompression schedules to depths shallower than 100 ft (30 m) and with bottom times shorter than about 45 minutes, the risk of DCS appears to be about 1%. Dives deeper than 100 ft and/or longer than about 45 minutes carry a substantially higher risk.[13]

Dehydration: Any reduction in the fluid content of the body reduces the blood volume and, so, reduces the cardiac output. Because of the effects of immersion, which increase cardiac output, this does not effect the uptake of nitrogen much. But, by the end of the dive, the effects of cold, decreasing the circulation to the limbs, and of dehydration, reducing the circulating blood volume and thickening the blood, combine to reduce the rate at which nitrogen can be removed from the tissues. In addition, the thicker blood is stickier and, therefore, more likely to clot around any bubbles that form.

Physical injury or previous decompression sickness: Damage to the circulation around the site of the injury may delay the release of nitrogen and predispose to bends. A study involving 932 compressed air workers (mainly miners) found a significantly higher rate of DCS in divers who had previously suffered from bends.[15]

Flying after diving: Flying, or otherwise ascending to a higher altitude, after having dived can predispose a diver to decompression sickness. The lower atmospheric pressure at altitude will allow any existing bubbles to expand and can also cause new bubbles to form. This is explained in detail in Chapter 20.

Diving at altitude: Most decompression tables apply to a diver who surfaces to the normal atmospheric pressure of 1 ATA. When we ascend from a dive at altitude, we ascend to an atmospheric pressure which is less than 1 ATA. If appropriate adjustments have not been made to the sea- level schedule, the chances of decompression sickness occurring will be greatly increased. This is explained in detail in Chapter 21.

Level of complement protein activity: The presence of high levels of complement proteins in the blood has been shown to be associated with an increased risk of DCS.[19] The activation of complement proteins promotes the release of certain chemicals (mediators, such as histamine) which cause the capillaries to leak fluid from the blood into the tissue spaces, thereby reducing the blood volume and thickening the blood. The thicker blood slows down the circulation and allows more clotting, together increasing the potential for, and the effects of, DCS.

Presence of a patent foramen ovale: Divers who have a patent foramen ovale (defect between the atria of the heart which allows some blood to flow directly from the right atrium to the left atrium) appear to have a higher risk of suffering severe decompression sickness.[8,9] Venous bubbles, which would normally be prevented from entering the arterial circulation by being filtered out by the lungs, may sometimes enter the arterial circulation through a patent foramen ovale.

Lack of fitness: Fitness is the ability to carry out strenuous physical exercise without distress. This requires a normal heart, lungs and circulation to provide oxygen in the appropriate amounts to the exercising muscles, and to carry away carbon dioxide. If one is not fit the circulation, driven by the heart, cannot do this adequately for very long. An inadequate circulation may not remove nitrogen from the tissues to the lungs fast enough during the ascent and, so, increase the risk of DCS. Navy decompression tables have been tested on reasonably fit and healthy sailors in various navies, and it is likely that the risk of DCS will be higher when such tables are used by a less fit diver.

Fatigue: Fatigue is associated with tiredness, which affects thought, and also with reduced cardiac performance which may give the same results as the lack of physical fitness. 31.7% (85/268) of the sport divers who suffered from decompression sickness or arterial gas embolism in the USA in 1988 reported fatigue or lack of sleep prior to the dive.[11]

Illness: Chronic illnesses often reduce one's fitness and, so, may be a bar to diving. Acute illnesses all decrease a person's fitness. The common ones are respiratory infections, which usually interfere with clearing one's ears. Since most divers refrain from diving when coughing and unable to clear their ears, full blown respiratory infections are not often linked with decompression sickness reports.

On the other hand the early stages of many illnesses are associated with circulatory changes. These usually include an increased heart rate which will result in a faster circulation. This leads to greater nitrogen uptake early in the dive. In addition, the effects of cold reduce the blood flow through the arms and legs later in the dive, so the extra nitrogen cannot always be got rid of easily and this increases the risk of DCS. Approximately 27% of the recreational divers who suffered from decompression sickness or arterial gas embolism in the USA in 1988 had dived while suffering from an illness that should have temporarily, or in some cases permanently, barred them from diving.[11]

Age: Predisposition to bends appears to increase as we age. The risk appears to increase sharply at middle age and beyond. Reduced circulation efficiency and increased body fat are possible reasons for this increase.

Anxiety: Anxiety results in an out-pouring of adrenaline, which increases the breathing rate, speeds up the heart, raises the blood pressure and increases the circulation. It also produces mental changes, which include both the inability to concentrate and inappropriate concentratiion on one aspect of a problem.

The first set of effects increase the uptake of nitrogen during the dive, while the second set increases the likelihood of diver error. The combination leads to an increased likelihood of DCS.

Alcohol: Alcohol depresses the brain. It changes people's thinking and, eventually, sends them to sleep. It interferes with clear-thinking and with manual dexterity. So, it is likely that divers who have been drinking will make more mistakes with decompression tables than others.

Alcohol is a diuretic (i.e. excretes water) and so dehydrates the diver. A dehydrated diver is more prone to DCS.

Alcohol is only slowly destroyed in the body and blood levels can still be above the legal limit for driving 24 hours after the last drink. So, the hung-over diver, who is dehydrated by the diuretic effects of alcohol, may also be still heavily affected by the depressant effects of alcohol.

Together these effects lead to changes in the circulation and in the diver's behaviour, and may lead to a higher risk of decompression sickness. In addition, since alcohol can reduce surface tension, which is one of the forces helping to prevent or limit the growth of bubbles, it is theoretically possible that drinking alcohol before or after diving may enhance bubble formation.[20] 44.7% (120/268) of the sport divers who suffered from decompression sickness or arterial gas embolism in the USA in 1988 reported drinking at least one alcoholic drink the night before diving or prior to entering the water on the dive day.[11] However, it has never been experimentally established that alcohol ingestion predisposes to bends.

Medications and other drugs: Little is known of the effects of drugs in preventing decompression sickness in man, and what is known of their activities in animals cannot be accurately transferred to man. So, there is no known wonder drug to prevent DCS. It has been suggested that aspirin, taken in large doses prior to diving, may reduce the risk of DCS, but there is no consistent evidence to support this.[21] In addition, since aspirin will prolong bleeding, can cause bleeding peptic ulcers, can cause severe allergic reactions in sensitive persons and may mask symptoms of DCS, divers are well advised to avoid using it in an attempt to prevent decompression sickness.

Drugs, a term which means any substance which affects physical and/or mental function, are seldom mentioned in reports of decompression sickness. Any drugs for the heart or for hypertension (high blood pressure) are likely to affect the heart's output, and so the circulation, producing the same changes as lack of fitness. Some of the illicit drugs affect the circulation and may alter nitrogen uptake and distribution, and the mental affects may cause the diver to make mistakes and compromise his decompression. A further complication is that pressure alters the effects of some drugs quite unpredictably.

Nitrogen narcosis: Nitrogen narcosis, by distorting a diver's thinking and causing deviations from the dive plan, increases the diver's chances of developing bends.

NOTE: Re women and decompression sickness

Women have a greater percentage of fatty tissue than men. Fatty tissue absorbs a lot of nitrogen and releases it slowly. Studies in which probes were inserted in muscles and subcutaneous tissue indicate that females do in fact absorb more nitrogen than males do. Hormonal changes during menstruation can result in fluid retention (edema) and fluid shifts. Also, some birth control pills can cause a microsludging or slowing of the circulation. All these factors theoretically suggest that women might be more prone to DCS than men are. Results of surveys comparing the relative DCS rates between men and women have been inconclusive and the results of experiments comparing the relative DCS rates between the sexes have often been contradictory. *The current consensus is that women are at no higher risk of decompression sickness than men are.*[22,23]

Figure 5.1.1, taken from DAN's "Report on 1988 Diving Accidents", shows the Decompression Sickness (DCS) Risk Profile for 222 of the divers who were treated for DCS in the USA in 1988.

FIGURE 5.1.1

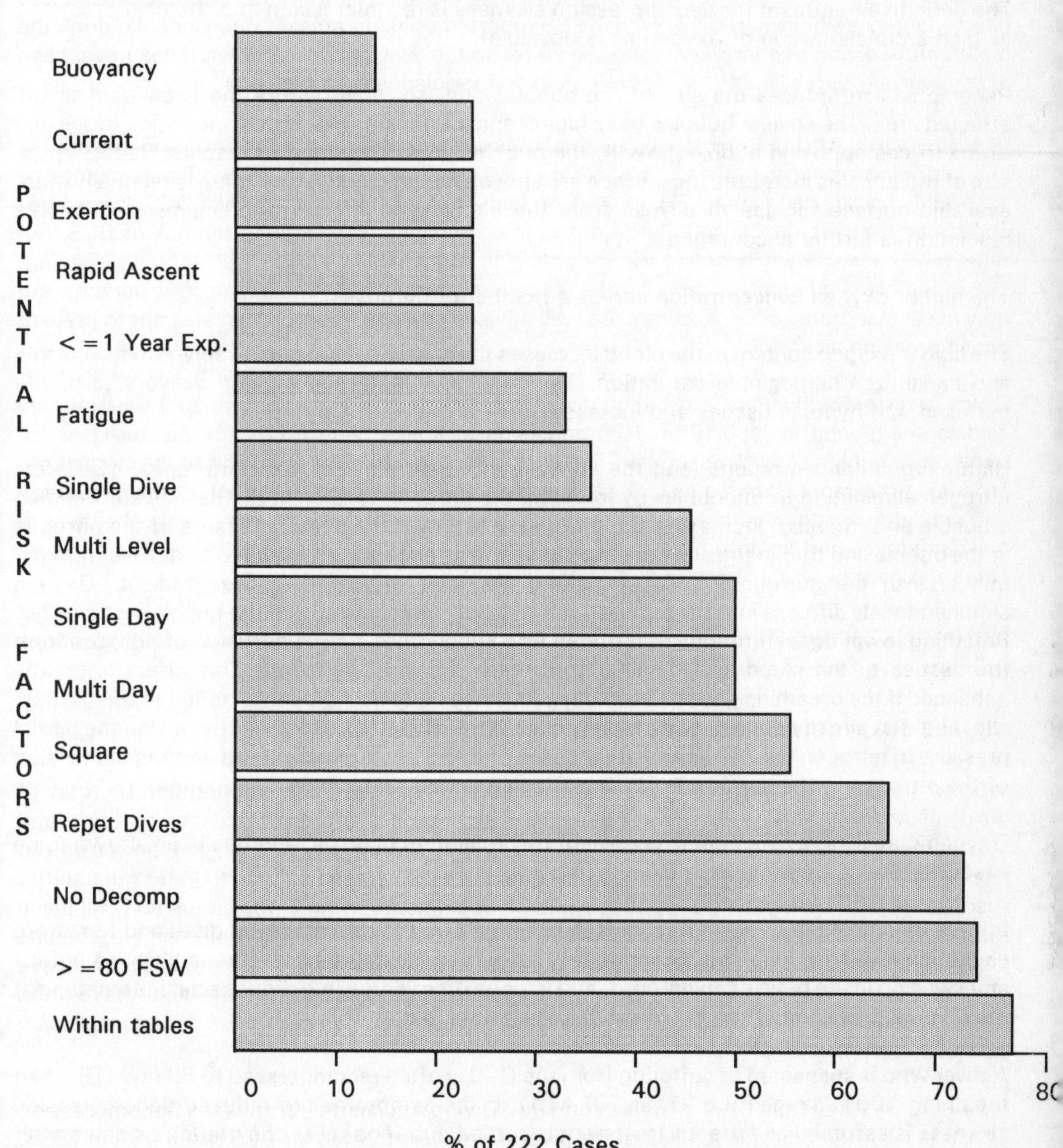

Reprinted courtesy Divers Alert Network (DAN).

Management of DCS

TREATMENT

The definitive treatment for decompression sickness is recompression in a chamber breathing as high a concentration of oxygen as is possible.

Recompression reduces the size of the bubbles and, so, may restore the circulation to the affected area. The smaller bubbles have higher surface tension pressures and, since this is one of the forces opposing bubble growth, the bubbles are encouraged to resolve. Reducing the size of the bubbles increases the surface area to volume ratio and, since there is relatively more available surface for gas to diffuse from the bubble into the surrounding tissues, bubble resolution is further encouraged.

The higher oxygen concentration serves a number of purposes:

The higher oxygen content in the blood increases the amount of oxygen dissolved in the plasma and maximizes hemoglobin saturation. This results in increased oxygen delivery to poorly perfused and hypoxic tissues and increases their chances of survival.

High oxygen concentrations (and the consequent lower nitrogen concentrations) accelerate nitrogen elimination from bubbles by lowering the nitrogen tension in the tissues surrounding a bubble and, thereby, increasing the difference between the partial pressure of the nitrogen in the bubble and that in the surrounding tissues. This encourages nitrogen to diffuse from the bubble into the surrounding tissues along the high to low pressure gradient. Oxygen simultaneously diffuses into the bubble but it is rapidly metabolized and the bubble gets smaller. Breathing lower concentrations of nitrogen also encourages a rapid diffusion of nitrogen from the tissues to the blood and, finally, from the blood into the lungs. This effect is greatly enhanced if the breathing gas is 100% oxygen, since no more nitrogen is added to the tissues, allowing that already present to be rapidly eliminated. Hyperbaric oxygen, by raising the partial pressure of nitrogen (as well as any other gases present) in a bubble without altering the tension of the nitrogen in the surrounding tissues, again enhances nitrogen elimination.

Oxygen may also reduce edema (swelling) by preventing hypoxia, and has been shown to be associated with a reduction in blood sludging.

Intravenous fluids (e.g. normal saline solution) are given to rehydrate the diver and to restore electolyte levels in the blood. Steroids (e.g. dexamethasone) are sometimes given to reduce any swelling in the brain or spinal cord, and various other drugs (e.g. lignocaine, indomethacin) may be used to combat the chemical changes in the blood.

A diver who is suspected of suffering from the DCS is often recompressed to 60 fsw (18 msw) breathing 100% oxygen (i.e. O_2 at 2.8 ATA). If the symptoms are reduced decompression sickness is assumed and the full treatment is carried out. If no relief of symptoms occurs after about 20 minutes at this pressure, the diagnosis of DCS may be questioned but the treatment is usually continued in the event that bubbles are present.

There are various treatment tables which are used to treat decompression sickness. A 2.8 ATA oxygen for 4.75 hours recompression regimen (USN 6/RN 62) is often successful in relieving symptoms of DCS[24,25] and, in SCUBA (air) divers where relief does not occur, compression to greater pressures breathing an oxygen-nitrogen mixture is rarely beneficial[25]. The 2.8 ATA regimens appear to produce an acceptably low frequency of overt central nervous system oxygen toxicity, are relatively short, are cheap, can be administered in almost any recompression chamber, and medical attendants are not incapacitated by narcosis and rarely develop DCS themselves as a result of the therapy. However, this large oxygen dose is toxic to both normal and injured brain and it appears that an oxygen dose between 1.0 to 1.5 ATA may be better to restore normal brain physiology.[26] A 2.8 ATA oxygen treatment appears to be a compromise between oxygen toxicity and ambient pressure and may not be ideal. It is possible that these regimens act primarily by reducing bubbles sufficiently to alleviate symptoms, rather than resolving the bubbles completely. A substantial number of divers who have been treated repeatedly at 2.8 ATA for decompression sickness still relapse with subsequent decompression to altitude, often as low as 1000 feet (300 metres) above sea-level.[27]

Many divers will relapse, or deteriorate, after an initial successful treatmentand experience has shown that repeated treatments with hyperbaric oxygen (HBO) often cause improvements in patients who are left with neurological problems after the initial treatment.[24] The repeated treatments are usually given 12-24 hours apart and may be similar, or at times identical, to the initial treatment.

Some alternative treatment regimens utilize pressures up to 6 ATA (165 fsw/50 msw). These procedures are often very time consuming, can be risky for the patient and for the medical attendant who is inside the chamber with the patient, and are often not very successful.[26] It has been suggested that oxygen-helium mixtures be used at the greater pressures for treating SCUBA (air) divers suffering from DCS but, to date, human data is too limited to determine the success of this procedure.[28] Animals have been successfully treated for decompression sickness by breathing hyperbaric oxygen in conjunction with injections of an emulsion of perflurocarbon.[29] Since nitrogen is far more soluble in perfluorcarbon than in blood, the nitrogen gas should diffuse rapidly from bubbles surrounded by such an emulsion. Further research is being conducted into this promising area.

FIGURE 5.1.2
Recompression chamber

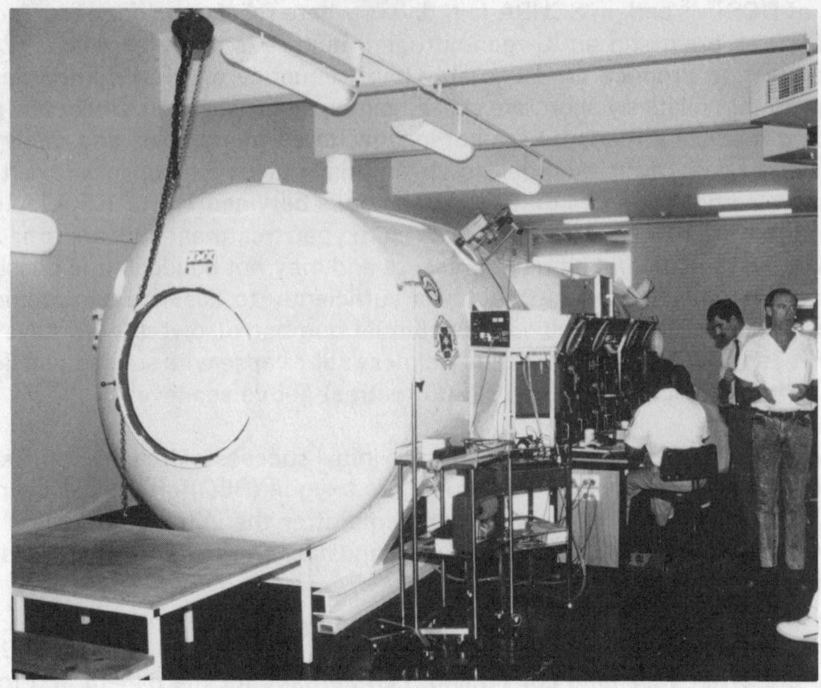

Photo courtesy Peter Stone

FIGURE 5.1.3
Diver being treated in a recompression chamber

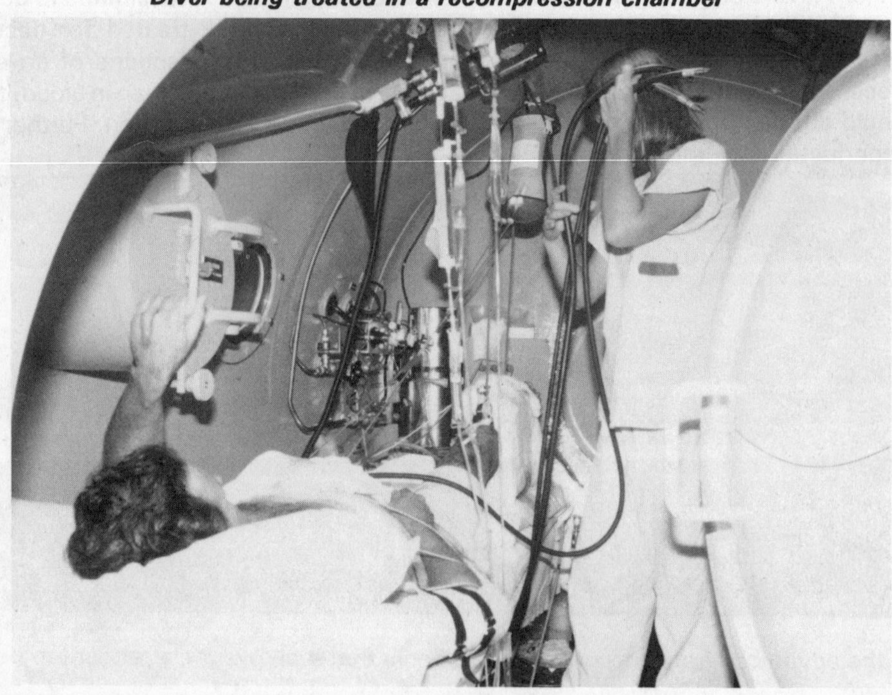

Photo courtesy Peter Stone

FIGURE 5.1.4
Drager Duocom portable recompression chamber used to transport a diver under pressure

FIGURE 5.1.5
Paracel portable recompression chamber used to transport a diver under pressure

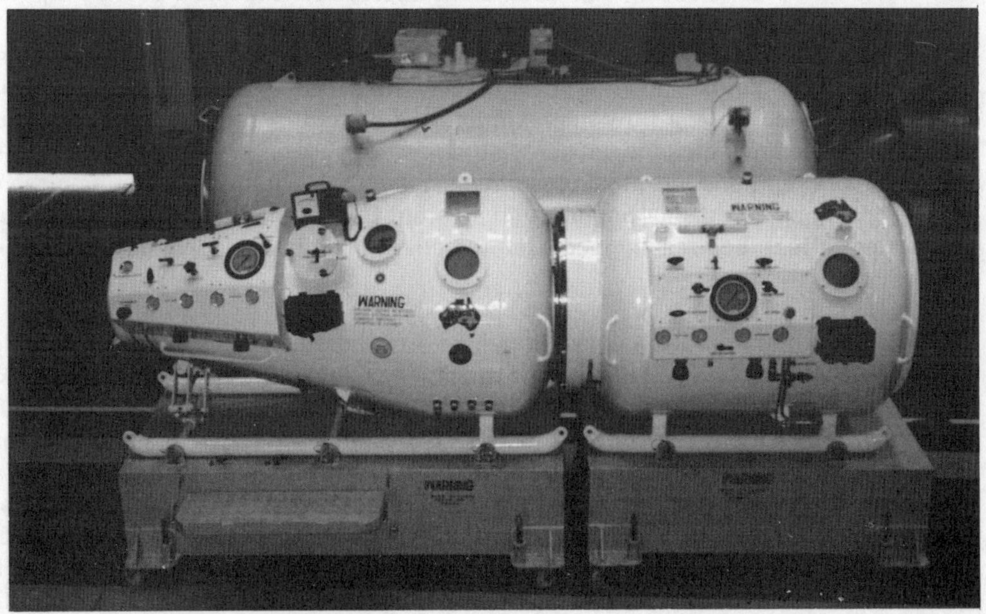

One of the advantages of this portable chamber is that it allows the attendant to perform CPR if required.

FIRST AID FOR DCS

The longer the interval between the onset of symptoms of decompression sickness and the commencement of hyperbaric oxygen treatment the more likely is the possibility of permanent damage. Therefore, it is essential to get a diver to a recompression chamber as soon as possible. The first aid procedure is designed to minimize the damage to the diver during this interval. The first aid procedure and its rationale is as follows:

* **MONITOR THE CONSCIOUSNESS, BREATHING AND PULSE AND RESUSCITATE IF NECESSARY**

  Supporting life is the most urgent requirement and, if resuscitation is indicated, it takes precedence over other first aid measures.

* **LAY THE CASUALTY DOWN**

  Although this is not essential with all types of decompression sickness, it serves a number of purposes:

  A diver suffering from decompression sickness is usually also suffering from shock. Blood delivery to the vital organs will be increased if the diver lies down.

  The diver should be laid flat and his airway maintained. Some work from Duke University has led some scientists to suggest that the raising of the legs may, at times, encourage circulating venous bubbles to by-pass the lungs and enter the arterial circulation in certain susceptible individuals, i.e. those with a patent foramen ovale.[8] Raising the legs is known to increase the pressure in the right side of the heart and the fear is that this may increase the blood flow across the heart in individulals with a patent foramen ovale. If these individuals are divers with venous bubbles, it is feared that raising of the legs may encourage these bubbles to enter the arterial circulation, possibly causing an arterial gas embolism. However, the flow across interatrial shunts is determined mainly, but not entirely, by the pressure gradient across the septum of the heart and, in most cases, leg-raising alters right and left atrial pressures similarly. A British study in which the effect of leg-raising on blood shunting through a patent formamen ovale was tested, found no consistent effect. Leg-raising increased the shunting in some individuals but reduced it in others.[6,9]

  If the diver suffers an arterial gas embolism (i.e. there is a rapid onset of neurological symptoms within about 20 minutes of the dive) as a result of decompression sickness, *slight* head-down position *may* be helpful for a short period of time (10 minutes maximum).[30,31] One researcher has described a slight head-down position to mean that the head is slightly lower than the chest, which is slightly lower than the abdomen, which is slightly lower than the pelvis, and the legs are horizontal.[32] This position is shown in Figure 5.1.6. The slight head-down position has been suggested as it may sometimes prevent more bubbles (from the lungs or trapped in the pulmonary vessels or heart) passing along the carotid arteries to the brain, possibly causing further embolization. If the head is lower than the chest, it is hoped that the buoyancy of the bubbles will discourage them from moving towards the brain, and may encourage the clearance of bubbles from the brain to higher parts of the body.

FIGURE 5.1.6

Slight head-down position for a conscious diver suspected of suffering from arterial gas embolism.

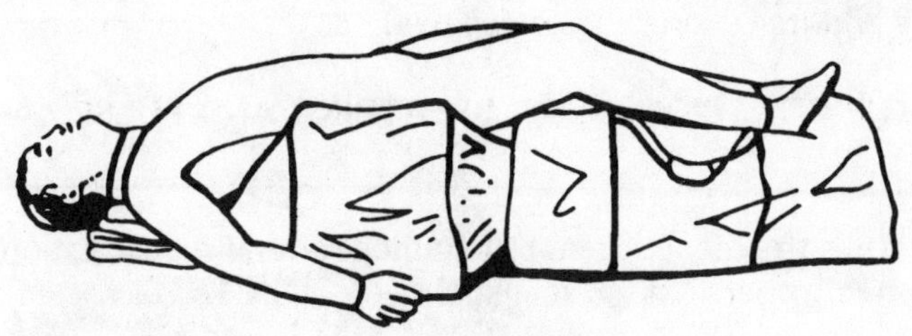

Note:

If a slight head-down position is used, it should only be used for a short period of time and then only if it can easily be maintained without impairing breathing or other resuscitative measures.

Unconscious or nauseous patients should be placed on the side to avoid aspiration of vomitus.

Certain animal experiments have supported this belief [33,34,35] but another animal study failed to offer support.[36] Anecdotal reports suggest that some divers, suffering from arterial gas embolism, have improved when placed in a head-down position. It has also been reported that some divers have rapidly deteriorated when changing from a head-down to a head-up posture.[32]

However, prolonged head-down position encourages cerebral edema (fluid build-up in the brain) which may be detrimental to the casualty.[37]

If a slight head-down position is used, it should only be used for a short period of time and then only if it can easily be maintained without impairing breathing or other resuscitative measures.

Unconscious or nauseous patients should be placed on the side to avoid aspiration of vomitus.

A patient suspected of suffering from arterial gas embolism must not be allowed to raise his head.

The left-side-head-low position has previously been suggested for bends sufferers, but is no longer recommended. Casualties placed in this position often find breathing difficult as the abdominal organs put pressure on the diaphragm and fluid may build up in the lungs and, in addition, the undesirable effect of cerebral edema is greatly encouraged when the head is down and the legs are raised. The leg-raising may, at times, precipitate blood flow across the heart in some casualties with a patent foramen ovale.

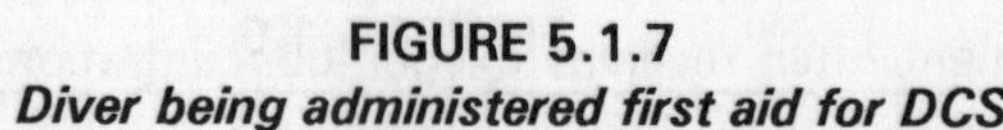

FIGURE 5.1.7
Diver being administered first aid for DCS

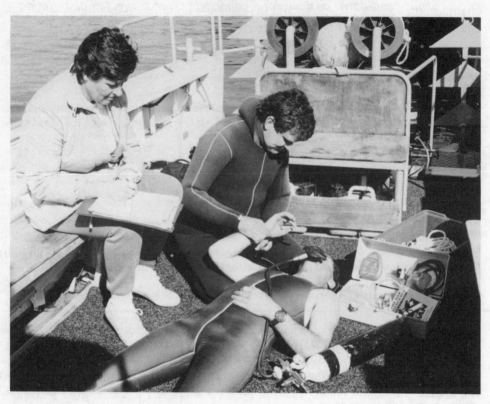

* **ADMINISTER OXYGEN**

Oxygen breathing will increase the oxygenation of any hypoxic body tissues and also help to flush out any dissolved nitrogen and nitrogen present in bubbles. The concentration of inhaled oxygen should be as near to 100% as can be reached in order to achieve the maximum benefit. (Oxygen administration is explained in detail in Chapter 26).

The periods of oxygen breathing should be recorded (i.e. time(s) put on oxygen and time(s) taken off oxygen) and the patient's response to oxygen should also be recorded. The doctor who will recompress the diver will then know how long the higher partial pressure of oxygen has been breathed for and will use this information to minimize the effects of pulmonary oxygen toxicity during the subsequent hyperbaric oxygen treatment. If a patient has had very long periods of breathing 100% oxygen without breaks, by the time he arrives at the chamber for recompression treatment options may have substantially diminished. Some treatment facilities prefer that the casualty breathes air for 5 minutes after each 25 minutes on oxygen while en route to the chamber. The air breaks minimize the toxic effects of the oxygen on the lungs. However, since the air breaks are generally unnecessary if the transport time is shorter than about four hours, and since the patient often receives oxygen concentrations well below 100%, many facilities prefer that oxygen breathing continues without breaks until arrival at the chamber. If air breaks are given and the patient's condition deteriorates when taken off oxygen, he should recommence oxygen breathing immediately.

If a bad response to oxygen occurs, the diver should breathe air for 15 minutes before oxygen is tried again.

The breathing of oxygen is a first aid measure and must never be substituted for the recompression required for decompression sickness and/or arterial gas embolism, regardless of the response.

* **TREAT FOR SHOCK**

The first aid for shock includes laying the patient down and administering oxygen and, hopefully, these will have been initiated already. The diver should be kept warm but not rewarmed rapidly, as rapid rewarming *may* encourage more bubbling. He should be reassured and kept still and quiet. This will maximize the blood supply to vital organs. Remaining still will discourage further bubble formation due to exercise.

* **ARRANGE RECOMPRESSION**

Contact the appropriate diving accident advisory service and/or the nearest recompression chamber.

They will give advice about any further first aid treatment that might be necessary, and will initiate the contacts necessary in order to transport the diver to a recompression facility.

* **SEEK MEDICAL AID**

The patient should be taken to the nearest competent medical facility as soon as possible so that proper medical treatment can be initiated. *Arrange for the attending medical person to contact a diving medical expert if this has not yet been done.*

Intravenous fluids will probably be given and the patient will be stabilized before being transported to the recompression chamber. If the patient is unable to urinate a urinary catheter might be inserted.

* **ENCOURAGE A CONSCIOUS AND STABLE PATIENT TO DRINK NON-ALCOHOLIC FLUIDS**

Drinking fluids will rehydrate the diver. This will reduce shock and thin the blood. The thinner blood is less likely to clot and sludge and obstruct the circulation. The ideal oral fluids are electrolyte type fluids such as one-half strength Gatorade, although virtually any non-alcoholic fluid will do the job. An easily obtainable and very suitable fluid is water. Alcohol should never be given as it will further dehydrate the diver. Acidic drinks should be avoided, if possible, as they could predispose to hemorrhaging of the stomach if gastrointestinal decompression sickness is present.

Allow oral fluids at the rate of four fluid ounces (approx. 110 ml) every 15 minutes, as comfortably tolerated by the patient, providing that the following conditions are met:

- *Fluids should not be given to a diver who is not fully conscious.* If the diver were to drink a lot of fluid and later became unconscious and required ventilation, he would be far more likely to regurgitate his stomach contents.

- *Fluids should not be given if the diver is suffering from stomach pain, urinary retention or paralysis* (unless a urinary catheter is used).

- *The amount and type of fluid given should be recorded, as well as the urinary output* (i.e. number of times and volume of urine passed). This will give the doctor an idea of how well the patient's bladder is functioning.

It is also important to check if the diver's bladder is getting larger. If it is, give no more fluids.

* **RECORD DETAILS OF THE DIVE PROFILE, FIRST AID GIVEN AND PATIENT'S RESPONSE TO FIRST AID.**

This information will be useful in confirming the nature of the injury and in its subsequent treatment.

Note:

Previously, it was commonly suggested that aspirin be given to a diver who is suffering from bends in the belief that it may reduce the blood clotting activated by the bubbles. Since there is no consistent evidence that aspirin, in normal doses, reduces clotting around bubbles,[21] and, since aspirin can cause a severe allergic reaction is sensitive people, will prolong bleeding, can cause bleeding peptic ulcers and may mask symptoms of bends, most hyperbaric physicians no longer recommend it in the first aid for bends.

DIVING AFTER DECOMPRESSION SICKNESS

The following advice is reprinted from Nichols, G., Dovenbarger, J. and Moon, R. (1990), "DAN's Top 10 Questions". *Alert Diver*; Tenth Anniversary Special Edition: 7.

"DCS is a contraindication for diving during the acute phase. There are numerous and differing medical opinions regarding returning to diving following a case of DCS. Unfortunately, there are no published guidelines for sport divers.

A conservative approach to symptoms which resolve after successful treatment would be to wait six weeks, then seek a physician's evaluation. Divers whose symptoms do not resolve after hyperbaric therapy should probably not return to diving.

There is also some disagreement about divers presenting with spinal cord symptoms. Some diving physicians feel that anyone with a history of spinal cord DCS should never dive again, even if their symptoms have completely cleared.

U.S. Navy Guidelines:

DCS-1 Divers should refrain from diving for at least seven days after successful recompression treatment.

DCS-2 Divers should refrain from diving for at least four weeks after successful recompression treatment."

The After-Effects of Decompression Sickness

Why worry about getting DCS?

Divers have been getting the bends for years. Traditionally the most commonly detected form was that of pain at or near a joint. Since the pain would usually disappear, even without treatment, and usually without leaving any obvious traces, most divers believed that no permanent or serious injury had been caused. It has been known for years that these types of DCS are at times followed by a gradual dying of bone tissue which can, eventually, permanently disable some divers. The incidence of bone necrosis in Australian abalone divers is believed to be higher than 30 percent,[38] so it is obviously not a problem to be ignored. Even today some divers put up with the symptoms until they disappear and believe that to be the end of the problem. Unfortunately, it may not be the case.

Many divers may feel that bone necrosis is an occupational hazard of the professional diver, and one that is impossible to avoid. This is not necessarily true. There is certainly a substantial number of commercial divers who have never felt symptoms of DCS and who show no evidence of bone decay. A skilled, knowledgable and careful diver can usually minimize the chances of getting bends and/or bone necrosis by planning and adhering to safe diving practices.

A British pilot study indicated that professional divers suffer progressive mental impairment, particularly loss of memory, throughout their diving career. The investigators suggested that a possible cause of this deterioration could be brain damage during decompression. They propose that micro-bubbles could be forming in the brain, producing many small areas of damage. The damage could build up in time and, eventually, cause symptoms. Further investigations are being carried out to validate, or disprove, this proposal.[39]

Many recreational divers believe (and some dive accordingly) that the threat of serious impairment is confined to commercial divers who dive often, and for long periods of time. Unfortunately, this is far from the truth as a substantial number of recreational divers have suffered permanent disability as a result of decompression sickness.

If the blood supply is cut off from some areas of the brain or spinal cord for a few minutes, nerve cells start to die off. Unless the blood supply is restored rapidly, serious long term neurological problems may result. These include weakness and paralysis in one or both legs, and commonly also involves problems with bladder control and sexual function. Paralysis down one side of the body also occurs. Speech may be affected, as may balance and various other functions. Rapid recompression is essential to minimize damage but, unfortunately, it often takes many hours before a diver is recompressed. Some nerve cells will be irrepairably damaged after only a few minutes. Oxygen given as a first aid measure will often help to reduce the damage but usually not to avoid it.

Despite oxygen breathing and rapid recompression some divers are left with serious neurological problems. Others, although relieved of their symptoms still show abnormalities in the activity of nerve cells when examined neurologically.

One British report describes post mortem studies of eight professional divers and three amateur divers who died sudden deaths, unrelated to diving. At post mortem, large areas of scarring in the brain and spinal cord, which corresponded to the areas of brain or spine involved in previous decompression accidents, were found in three of the professional divers. Changes of minor significance were seen in the remaining divers. The damage had not been clinically detected while the divers were alive. One such diver had suffered spinal decompression sickness, was treated successfully and followed up regularly by clinicians. There were some minor detectable neurological changes but these were hardly noticeable. He was murdered four years later and examination of his spinal cord revealed that about 40% of it was damaged, apparently as a result of his previous bend. The original treatment had relieved the obvious symptoms but permanent damage had still resulted.[40,41,42]

There is also evidence that some commercial divers who have never had symptoms of decompression sickness also have similar areas of scarring in the nervous system. There is a growing concern that "silent bubbles" may cause cumulative neurological damage in divers. The more frequently deep and long dives are performed, the greater the theoretical risk of neurological damage from silent bubbles.

Furthermore, it is possible that a relatively young diver may suffer decompression sickness and be treated without leaving obvious damage to the body functions, but still leaving scarring in the nervous system. As the diver grows older and the nervous system degenerates, the previous loss of nerve tissue might cause mental impairment and weakness to develop earlier than it otherwise would have. Some of the changes to our vision, hearing, memory and other functions that we put down to us growing older, may in fact have been caused by decompression problems of which we might or might not have been aware. However, at this stage this is still largely speculation.

A 1989 report describes a study in which the retinas of 80 divers of varying experience were examined. The researchers found evidence of damage in nearly half of the divers. All of the 26 professional divers studied had abnormal retinas. The changes were most marked in divers who had had the bends, although divers who had never had a bend also showed changes. In the divers who had never had the bends, the most severe changes occurred in those divers with the most experience. The researchers found clear evidence of obstruction to the capillaries supplying the retina, and proposed a number of possible causes - obstruction of the capillaries by bubbles or blood clots precipitated by bubble formation, or from the "stiffening" of white blood cells as a result of hyperbaric exposures in excess of around 4 ATA. (Some of these "stiffer" blood cells cannot pass through the walls of fine capillaries and, so, can form blood clots and obstruct circulation). Although none of the divers studied had visual problems as a result of their damaged retinas, the researchers believed visual problems could develop in some divers.[42]

It is true that a lot still remains to be proven, but there certainly is already enough evidence to make all divers reassess our diving practices. It is certainly well worthwhile avoiding the bends, and it also seems advisable to minimize the formation of the silent bubbles in our bodies. Neither will always be possible, but it is becoming more and more obvious that the effort is well worthwhile.

SUMMARY

* Decompression sickness (DCS or the bends) results from the development of bubbles within the body.
* These bubbles can distort and disrupt tissue and can block and damage blood vessels. Bubbles in the body precipitate various biochemical reactions which may themselves cause damage.
* Bubbles can occur without creating symptoms - "silent bubbles".
* The lungs act as filters and trap most of the bubbles in the bloodstream.
* The dive profile can influence where bubbles form and the type of symptoms which might occur.
* Rapid ascent makes bubbles more likely to form in the blood and the other "faster" tissues (e.g. brain)
* Symptoms usually occur within six hours of diving but can take as long as one to three days or more to show.
* The location and volume of the bubbles determines the type of symptoms and the severity.
* The most common signs and symptoms of DCS are malaise (feeling unwell) and lethargy (extreme fatigue).
* The vast majority of divers suffering from DCS display the more serious, neurological manifestations.
* Treatment for DCS includes recompression in a recompression chamber, hyperbaric oxygen and intravenous fluids. The recompression reduces the size of the bubbles and restores circulation. The hyperbaric oxygen provides greater oxygenation to hypoxic tissue and encourages nitrogen elimination from the bubbles, tissues and blood. The intravenous fluids rehydrate the diver and restore electrolyte levels in the blood.
* Despite oxygen breathing and rapid recompression some divers are left with serious neurological problems.
* It is possible that even though a treatment may appear to have been completely successful, damage may still have occurred and may show up later in the diver's life-time.
* It is also feared that "silent bubbles" may cause cumulative neurological damage in divers.

* The following are some of the factors which may predispose a diver to decompression sickness:

  Deep and/or long dives, rapid and/or multiple ascents, repetitive diving, cold water, obesity, excess carbon dioxide, exercise before, during, or after the dive, dehydration, level of complement protein activity, presence of a patent foramen ovale, lack of fitness, illness or injury, age, anxiety, ingestion of alcohol or various drugs and medications before diving, flying after diving, diving at altitude.

* The most common signs and symptoms of DCS are malaise (feeling unwell) and lethargy (extreme fatigue) but a large variety other manifestations occur, many of them neurological.

First Aid:

* Monitor consciousness, breathing and pulse and resuscitate if necessary.
* Lay the patient flat and maintain his airway.
* Administer 100% oxygen
* Treat for shock
* Seek medical aid (Arrange for them to confer with a Diving Medical Specialist)
* Arrange for transfer to a recompression chamber.
* Record details of dive profile, first aid given and response to first aid
* Encourage a conscious and stable patient to drink non-alcoholic fluids. Fluids are only given if the patient is not suffering from stomach pain, urinary retention or paralysis unless a urinary catheter is used.
* Record amount and type of fluid given. Record urinary output and check for bladder distension. If the bladder becomes distended give no more fluid until a urinary catheter is inserted.

REFERENCES

1. Dunford, R. et al (1988), "Ultrasonic Doppler Bubble Incidence Following Sport Dives". *Undersea Biomedical Research*; 15 (sup): 45-46.

2. Bassett, B. (1982), "The Safety of the U.S. Navy Decompression Tables and Recommendations for Sport Divers". SPUMS Journal; Oct-Dec: 16-25.

3. Spencer, M. (1976), "Decompression limits for compressed air determined by ultrasonically detected blood bubbles". *Journal of Applied Physiology*; 40 (2): 229-235.

4. Buehlmann, A. (1984), "Decompression - Decompression Sickness". Springer-Verlag, Berlin.

5. Lynch, J. et al (1984), "Prevalence of right-to-left atrial shunting in a healthy population: detection by Valsalva maneuver contast echocardiography". Am. J. Cardiol.; 53: 1478-80.

6. Wilmshurst, P. et al (1989), "Relation between interatrial shunting and decompression sickness in divers". The Lancet; 8675: 1302-1306.

7. Hagen, P. (1984), "Incidence and size of patent foramen ovale during the first 10 decades of life: an autopsy study of 965 normal hearts". Mayo Clin Proc; 59: 17-20.

8. Moon, R. and Camporesi, E. (1987), "Right-to-Left Shunting and Decompression Sickness". Undersea Biomedical Research, Supplement to Vol 15, Program and Abstracts, Annual Scientific Meet., UHMS, Bethesda.

9. Wilmshurst, P. (1990),"Cardiac Shunts and DCS". Diver; 35 (2): 13-16.

10. Divers Alert Network (1988), "Provisional Report on Diving Accidents". Divers Alert Network, North Carolina.

11. Divers Alert Network (1989), "Report on 1988 Diving Accidents". Divers Alert Network, North Carolina.

12. Weinmann, M. (in prep).

13. Weathersby, P. et al (1986), "Statistically Based Decompression Tables III: Comparative Risk Using U.S. Navy, British, and Canadian Standard Air Schedules" Naval Medical Research Institute Report No. 86-50, Naval Medical Research Institute, Bethesda.

14. Allen, C. (1989), "NDC Diving Incidents Report". *Diving Officers' Conference, 1989*, BS-AC, London.

15. Lam, T. and Yau, K. (1989), "Analysis of some individual risk factors for decompression sickness in Hong Kong". *Undersea Biomedical Research*; 16 (4): 283-292.

16. Curley, G. et al (1989), "Percent Bodyfat and Human Decompression Sickness". *Undersea Biomedical Research*; Supplement to 16, June: 29.

17. Blood, C. and Hoiberg, A. (1985), "Analyses of variables underlying U.S. Navy diving Accidents". *Undersea Biomedical Research*; 12 (3): 351-360.

18. Allen, C. (1988), "NDC Diving Incidents Report". *Diving Officers' Conference, 1988*, BS-AC, London.

19. Ward, C. et al (1987), "Complement Proteins Mediate Decompression Sickness in Rabbits". *Undersea Biomedical Research*; Supplement to 14 (2), March: 16.

20. Eckenhoff, R. (1989), "Alcohol and Bends". Undersea Biomedical Research; 16 (4): 269.

21. Philip, R. (1989), "Aspirin: The Making of a Myth". *Alert Diver*; 5 (1): 3.

22. Fife , W. ed (1987), "Women in Diving". *Proceedings of The Thirty-fifth Undersea and Hyperbaric Medical Society Workshop*; UHMS Publication No. 71 (WS-WD), Undersea and Hyperbaric Medical Society, Inc.

23. Bennett, P., personal communication.

24. Gorman, D. et al (1988), "Dysbaric illness treated at the Royal Adelaide Hospital 1987, a factorial analysis". SPUMS Journal; 18 (3): 95-101.

25. Green, R. and Leitch, D. (1987), "Twenty years of treating decompression sickness". *Aviation Space and Environmental Medicine*; 58: 362-366.

26. Holbach, K. and Caroli, A. (1974), "Oxygen tolerance and the oxygenation state of the injured human brain". In: Trapp, W. et al (eds), Fifth international hyperbaric congress proceedings. Simon Fraser University, Burnaby, Canada: 350-361.

27. Gorman, D. (in prep), "Principles of recompression treatment: recreational SCUBA-air diving".

28. Douglas, J. and Robinson, C. (1988). "Heliox treatment for spinal decompression sickness following air dives". Undersea Biomedical Research; 15: 315-320.

29. Lynch, P. et al (1989), "Effects of intravenous perfluorocarbon and oxygen breathing on acute decompression sickness in the hamster". Undersea Biomedical Research; 16 (4): 275-282.

30. Moon, R. and al (1989), "Dive Accident Positioning - Which End Is Up?". Alert Diver; 5 (3): 1,5.

31. Bennett, P. and Moon, R. (eds), Summary of Recommendations (draft) *UHMS/NOAA/ DAN Workshop in Diving Accident Management*. Duke University, Durham, North Carolina, 1990.

32. Gorman, D. and Helps, S. (1989), "Foramen Ovale, Decompression Sickness and Posture for Arterial Gas Embolism". *SPUMS Journal*; 19 (4): 150-151.

33. Van Allen, C. et al (1927), "Air Embolism from the Pulmonary Vein". *Arch Surg*; 19 (4): 567-599.

34. Gorman, D. et al (1987), "Distribution of arterial gas emboli in the pial circulation". *SPUMS Journal*; 17 (3): 101-115.

35. Atkinson, J. (1963), "Experimental Air Embolism". *Northwest Med*; 62: 699-703.

36. Butler, B. et al (1987), "Cerebral Decompression Sickness: Bubble Distribution in Dogs in the Trendelenberg Position". *Undersea Biomedical Research*; 14 (2) (Supp): 15.

37. Dutka, A. (1990), "Therapy for dysbaric central nervous ischemia". In: Bennett, P. and Moon, R. (eds), *UHMS/NOAA/DAN Workshop in Diving Accident Management*. Duke University, Durham, North Carolina.

38. Edmonds, C. (1986), "The Abalone Diver". National Safety Council of Australia, Melbourne.

39. Betts, J. (1987), "Brain Drain". *Diving Down Under*; July/Sept: 36.

40. Calder, I. (1987), "CNS Changes in Decompression Sickness". *Proceedings from the Diving Officers' Conference, 1987*, BS-AC, London.

41. Palmer, A. et al (1988), "Spinal cord damage in active divers". *Undersea Biom Res*; 15 (Sup): 70.

42. Newson, L. (1989), "Eye tests reveal dangers of diving". *New Scientist*; 21, Jan: 33.

OTHER SOURCES

Berghage, T. and Durman, D. (1980), "U.S. Navy Air Decompression Schedule Risk Analysis". Naval Medical Research Institute, Report No. 80-1, Department of the Navy.

Bove, A. (1982), "The Rationale for Drug Therapy in Decompression Sickness", *SPUMS Journal*; July-September:
7-99.

Bove, A. (1982), "The Treatment of Decompression Sickness", *SPUMS Journal*; July-September: 9-11.

Brown, C. (1979), "The Physiology of Decompression Sickness". In: *Decompression in Depth*, Graver, D. (ed), PADI, California.

Brubakk, A. (1984), "Decompression and Circulating Bubbles". *SPUMS Journal*; 14 (1): 28-29.

Buehlmann, A. et al (1967), "Saturation and desaturation with N2 and He at 4 ATA". Journal of Applied Physiology; 23: 458-462.

Davis, J. (1981), "Hyperbaric Oxygen Therapy: Applications in Clinical Practice". In: Hyperbaric and Undersea Medicine, Medical Seminars Inc.

Davis, J. and Elliott. D. (1983), "Treatment of the Decompression Disorders". In: The Physiology and Medicine of Diving, 3rd edition, Bennett, P. and Elliott. D. (eds), Best Publishing Co., California: 473-487.

Denison, D. (1988), "Bubbles". *Proceedings of Diving Officers' Conference*; BS-AC, London: 39-40.

Dueker, C. (1985), "SCUBA Diving in Safety and Health". Madison Publishing Associates, California.

Edmonds, C., Lowry, C. and Pennefather, J. (1981), "Diving and Subaquatic Medicine", 2nd edition. Diving Medical Centre, Sydney.

Edmonds, C. (1987), "Decompression Sickness - Its History and Physiology". *SCUBA Diver*; June: 22-26.

Elliott D. and Kindwall E. (1982), "Manifestations of the Decompression Disorders". In: *The Physiology and Medicine of Diving,* 3rd edition, Bennett, P. and Elliott, D. (eds), Best Publishing Co., California.

Gorman, D., "Decompression Theory", unpublished.

Gorman, D., "The Treatment of Decompression Sickness", unpublished.

Gorman, D. (1989), "Foramen-Ovale, Decompression Sickness, and Posture for Arterial Gas Embolism". *SPUMS Journal*; 19 (4): 150-151.

Hill, R. (1989), "Foramen Ovale Revisited". *NAUI News*; Jan/Feb: 39.

Hills, B. (1977), "Decompression Sickness", Vol 1. John Wiley and Sons.

Hills, B. (1984), "Decompression Physiology". *SPUMS Journal*; 14 (1): 3-18.

McKenzie B. (1984), "Decompression Sickness; an Overview". *SPUMS Journal*; 14 (3): 29-31.

Moon, R. (1989), "Patent Foramen Ovale: Are there any implications for SCUBA diving?". *Alert Diver*; 5 (2): 1,11.

Moon, R., personal communications.

Miller, J. (ed) (1979), "NOAA Diving Manual", 2nd edition. United States Department of Commerce.

Newson, L. (1989), "Hole in the heart brings on the bends". *New Scientist*, May: 12.

Popovic, P et al (1982), "Levodopa and Aspirin Pretreatment Beneficial in Experimental Decompression Sickness". Proceedings of the Soc. for Exptl. Biol. and Med.; 109: 1040-43.

Thomas R., and McKenzie, B. (1981), "The Diver's Medical Companion". Diving Medical Centre, Sydney.

U.S. Navy (1985), "U.S. Navy Diving Manual", Vol 1, Air Diving. U.S. Government Printing Office.

Vann, R. (1985), "Exercise and Decompression". *Alert Diver*; 2 (1): 3.

Wilmshurst, P. (1986), "Decompression Sickness: Some Areas of Concern". *NDC Bulletin*; 8: 6.

Wilmshurst, P. (1986), "The Pot Revisited". *Proceedings of the Diving Officers' Conference*, BS-AC, London.

Wilmshurst, P. et al (1989), "Neurological Decompression Sickness". *The Lancet*; April 1: 731.

Wilmshurst, P., personal communications.

Zhang, L. et al (1989), "Ethanol treatment for acute decompression sickness in rabbits". Undersea Biomedical Research; 16 (4): 271-274.

RECOMMENDED FURTHER READING

Buehlmann, A. (1984), "Decompression - Decompression Sickness". Springer-Verlag, Heidelberg.

Davis, J. and Elliott. D. (1983), "Treatment of the Decompression Disorders". In: *The Physiology and Medicine of Diving*, 3rd edition, Bennett, P. and Elliott. D. (eds), Best Publishing Co., California: 473-487.

Divers Alert Network (1988), "Provisional Report on Diving Accidents". Divers Alert Network.

Dueker, C. (1985), "SCUBA Diving in Safety and Health''. Madison Publishing Associates, California.

Edmonds, C., Lowry, C. and Pennefather, J. (1981), "Diving and Subaquatic Medicine", 2nd edition. Diving Medical Centre, Sydney.

Hills, B. (1984), "Decompression Physiology". *SPUMS Journal*; 14 (1): 3-18.

5.2 Prevention of decompression sickness

HOW CAN WE AVOID GETTING THE BENDS?

The simple answer to the question is that we cannot completely avoid getting bent. Some unlucky divers will get decompression sickness after diving very conservative and apparently safe dives. For example, in Australia during 1985, four divers were treated for decompression sickness after single dive profiles of 60 ft (18 m) for 30 minutes.[1] Two of these patients had severe symptoms. An Australian Navy diver was bent in a chamber after 10 minutes at 90 ft (27 m).[1] 58% of the bends cases treated in the USA in 1987 were divers who had dived "within" the U.S. Navy Tables (i.e. had completed sufficient decompression according to the tables) and this increased to 72% in 1988.[2] On the other hand, at times divers abuse the tables (e.g. do less than the recommended decompression) and show no signs of bends. Susceptibility to decompression sickness varies enormously from diver to diver and from dive to dive for a particular diver. A diver can dive one day without any incident and do exactly the same dive profile at another time and end up bent, for no apparent reason. It seems that the only way we can guarantee that we will not get bent is to give up diving (or flying!) and that seems a little too drastic for most of us. We can, however, modify the way in which we dive in order to minimize the likelihood of decompression sickness.

Over the years many practices which were designed to minimize bends risk have evolved. As the knowledge of diving medicine increases, some techniques which were previously believed to be safe have begun to cause concern. Ascent rates previously believed to be desirable and safe are now believed to be too fast in certain situations. No-Decompression Limits previously thought safe are now known to be too long.

Some of the practices that experienced divers have adopted over the years are now believed to be unsafe. Many divers refuse to accept this. They claim that they have never been bent during their diving career and, therefore, believe that their old diving practices must be safe. This might be true for some but it is very difficult to know for certain. When I sit back and wonder if I have ever been bent I cannot confidently say that I have not. I do know that I have never suffered from joint pain, difficulty breathing, numbness or from any other obvious symptom of decompression sickness, but I cannot be sure that I have not suffered from some of the more subtle effects. I have ascended rapidly, dived close to the limits of the tables and done repetitive dives afterwards. At the time I believed that it was all fairly safe diving practice. I have certainly suffered from extreme fatigue for a day or so after diving, especially after doing a series of deep dives. My eyesight is not as good as it used to be and my memory and concentration have deteriorated. I would like to believe that is due to the normal process of ageing (helped on a bit my my decadent past!), but just maybe the way that I used to dive has accelerated the process. Maybe those silent bubbles in my circulation have taken their toll. It is impossible to know for certain, but now I do not take any chances. I now try to avoid, or minimize, the bubbling within me when I dive. I avoid doing dives requiring mandatory decompression stops, I choose shorter No-Decompression Limits, I ascend slowly and do a precautionary stop for a while before surfacing and I plan repetitive dives conservatively. Some of these practices might be shown to be incorrect or unnecessary at a future time and will then need to be modified. However, in the light of the current available knowledge, I believe them to be both sound and sensible.

The rationale for these "safety factors" ("fudge factors") will be briefly explained in the following section.

1. CHOOSE CONSERVATIVE NO-DECOMPRESSION LIMITS

TABLE 5.2.1

No-Decompression Limits (bottom time) for various tables

ft	m	USN	RNPL/ BS-AC	Buehlmann (1986)	DCIEM	Bassett	Huggins	PADI RDP	BS-AC '88	Buehlmann Hahn
30	9	-	-	400	300	220	225	360	242	653
40	12	200	137	125	150	120	135	140	121	192
50	15	100	72	75	75	70	75	80	73	99
60	18	60	57	51	50	50	50	55	50	65
70	21	50	38	35	35	40	40	40	36	40
80	24	40	32	25	25	30	30	30	28	27
90	27	30	23	20	20	25	25	25	22	21
100	30	25	20	17	15	20	20	20	18	17
110	33	20	16	14	12	15	15	16	15	15
120	36	15	14	12	10	12	10	13	12	9
130	39	10	11	10	8	10	5	10	10	7
140	42	10	10	9	7	5	0	8	9	6
150	45	5	8	0	6	0	0	0	7	5
160	48	5	8	0	6	0	0	0	6	4
170	51	5	6	0	5	0	0	0	5	4
180	54	5	6	0	5	0	0	0	0	3
190	57	5	5	0	5	0	0	0	0	3
200	60	0	5	0	0	0	0	0	0	3

Notes:

1. The RNPL/BS-AC NDLs for 170-200 ft (51-60 m) are taken from the RNPL 1972 Tables.
2. The DCIEM NDLs beyond 150 ft (45 m) are taken from the imperial tables in Appendix B. Certain NDLs differ in the metric version.
3. The times shown for the PADI RDP are for the imperial tables.

If you look carefully through Table 5.2.1 and run along the rows for the various depths you will notice that, for the depths normally encountered in recreational diving, the U.S. Navy No-Decompression Limit (NDL) is almost always longer than the others.

The U.S. Navy Tables were created to avoid bends (not bubbles) in navy divers. At their acceptance trials in 1956, the standard decompression schedules produced an average bends rate of 4.6% (26/564).[3] Some statistics on the bends rate for U.S. Navy divers, published in 1981, quoted an incidence rate of about 0.04%.[4] Overall it appears that the U.S. Navy uses its tables quite safely, but it has been reported that the navy divers, unlike some sport divers, do not dive their tables to the limits.[5] Evidently they add various safety factors to the tables. Remember that over 70% of the civilian bends cases treated in the USA in 1988 were divers who had dived within the U.S. Navy Tables.

Various researchers have used ultrasound to monitor divers diving to the U.S. Navy No-Decompression Limits. Some (Bassett, Spencer)[5,6] have detected venous bubbles in about 30% of the divers tested and bends in up to 8% of the divers. Both of these studies had their shortcomings. Spencer used only a very small sample of divers and Bassett based his results on shorter exposures than the NDLs, followed by ascent to altitude. However, in contrast to these studies, in 1986 the U.S. Navy tested 197 man dives beyond the NDLs without any bends resulting.[7] Unfortunately, the tests did not include dives to the NDLs at 40 ft (12 m) and 50 ft (15 m) which are limits that may be expected to cause some problems.

The RNPL/BS-AC No-Decompression Limits are generally shorter than the U.S. Navy limits until depths beyond 120 ft (36 m). These tables were never tested beyond 100 ft (30 m) and I believe that they should not be used for deeper diving. These tables were designed to minimize bends, not bubbles.

The Buehlmann limits are taken from the 1986 Buehlmann Tables. These tables have evolved from years of experimentation and testing, and reportedly carry a very low incidence of bends.[8] *The maximum ascent rate is 33 ft/minute (10 m/minute)* and a safety stop of 1 minute at 10 ft (3 m) is required at the end of all dives to these limits. They have been designed to minimize both bends and bubbles. The BS-AC '88 limits are very similar to these. The Buehlmann/Hahn Tables are based on a similar system to the Buehlmann Tables but are generally less conservative.

The DCIEM No-Decompression Limits are the result of extensive experimentation and ultrasound monitoring. They were tested for hard work in cold water and, in most respects, should be quite suitable for the recreational diver. These tables are based on an ascent rate of 50-70 ft/minute (15-21 m/minute) and are designed to minimize bubbling.

The Bassett, Huggins and PADI RDP limits evolved from ultrasound studies of a few divers diving to the U.S. Navy NDLs. The bottom times were systematically reduced until no bubbles were detected after the divers ascended to the surface at 60 ft/minute (18 m/minute).

It becomes obvious that it may be unwise to dive the U.S. Navy Tables to the limit if bubbles, and possibly bends, are to be avoided. The RNPL/BS-AC times could also be expected to cause problems (and have done so) if used to the limit on certain deep dives. The NDLs of most of the other tables are generally quite similar, which seems to indicate that they might be suitable for a diver in good condition. Presumably, the divers on which the tables were tested were reasonably fit and well before, and during, the test dives, so it is still usually necessary to reduce these NDLs to allow for predisposing factors to bends.

2. SHORTEN YOUR ALLOWABLE BOTTOM TIME TO CATER FOR PREDISPOSING FACTORS TO DECOMPRESSION SICKNESS

Factors such as exercise, cold, excess fat and age predispose to bends. One reasonable suggestion is that **the No-Decompression Limits be reduced by at least 10% for each predisposing factor present.**[9]

It is suggested that you reduce the limit by 10% for every 22 pounds (10 kg) above normal weight. Reduce another 10% for every decade over the age of 40. Take off another 10% if you are cold, at least another 10% if you are exerting yourself during the dive, and so on. At times this will not leave much time to dive, but maybe these are just the times when we should not be diving at all!

Do not dive if you are unwell.
Ensure that you are well-hydrated before and after diving. Drink fluids (other than diuretics such as alcohol or coffee and other caffeine sources) whenever possible before, between and after diving.

3. ASCEND SLOWLY AND AVOID MULTIPLE ASCENTS

The very early U.S. Navy Tables used an ascent rate of 25 ft/minute (8 m/minute). These tables were used for "hard hat" diving so a faster ascent rate was difficult to achieve. With the introduction of SCUBA it became possible to increase the ascent rate and, when these tables were superseded in 1957, the ascent rate was increased to 60 ft/minute (18 m/minute). The RNPL tables, published in 1972, suggest an ascent rate of 50 ft/minute (15 m/minute). The Swiss tables, first published in 1976, suggest an ascent rate of 33 ft/minute (10 m/minute). You may wonder which ascent rate is generally the safest!

Slower ascent rates have become popular over the past few years. **There is an increasing amount of evidence indicating that decompression sickness, especially the more serious neurological DCS, is more likely to follow a rapid ascent, especially a rapid ascent from a deep dive.**

The blood and tissues with a large blood flow (e.g. neural tissues) absorb nitrogen rapidly and are soon saturated. A rapid ascent will create a large pressure difference between the nitrogen tension in these tissues and the ambient pressure. The deeper the dive, the greater the potential pressure difference and the greater the likelihood of bubbling.

During a slower ascent these "fast" tissues are allowed to desaturate far more safely as the large pressure differences are avoided. Therefore, there is less chance that bubbles will form in the blood and neural tissues, possibly causing severe DCS during, or after, a slow ascent.

Severe decompression sickness is less likely to follow a slow ascent. Slow ascents also reduce the likelihood of a lung overpressure injury and possible air embolism.

Many diving medical experts throughout the world are now recommending an ascent rate of about 30-33 ft/minute (9-10 m/minute). The Swiss have used this ascent rate for many years and have found it to be a "safe continuous decompression for saturated tissues in order to prevent bubble formation".[10] The Swiss (Buehlmann) tables are claimed to have a very low bends risk associated with them and this is believed to be partly due to the slow ascent rate.[8] It is claimed that this ascent rate enhances gas elimination for dives to depths of about 100 ft (30 m). However, some researchers recommend ascent rates of about 50-60 ft/minute (15-18 m/min) while deeper than about 100 ft (30 m), and then ascent at about 30 ft/minute (9 m/min) from 100 ft (30 m) to the surface.* This is suggested in order to avoid allowing the slower tissues to absorb too much extra gas during the early part of the ascent. These slower tissues do not absorb very much gas during a relatively short dive and may still absorb gas, while faster tissues are releasing it, during the ascent. However, computer simulations of gas uptake and elimination during ascent have shown that, over the range that could reasonably be done by a SCUBA diver, this effect is usually minimal.[11]

For recreational divers who generally dive shallower than 130 ft (39 m), a continuous ascent rate of 30-33 ft/minute (9-10 m/minute) seems reasonable although a faster ascent rate may sometimes be beneficial at depths greater than about 100 ft (30 m). ***The Divers Alert Network (DAN), PADI and NAUI strongly recommend ascending no faster than 60 ft/minute (18 m/minute).***

It is easy to suggest that you ascend at around 30 ft/minute but it is not so easy for you to do it unless some sort of ascent rate indicator is used. Some of the new dive computers are programmed for a continuous ascent rate of 33 ft (10 m)/minute and will let you know when you exceed this rate. Others allow faster ascents at depth and slow ascents nearer to the surface. *An ascent rate indicator set for a slow ascent rate towards the surface is an essential feature of a dive computer.* Digital depth gauges (e.g. the Uwatec "Digital") which incorporate an ascent rate warning are also available and are a tremendous asset to the diver.

Whenever possible, you should ascend up a line so that you have a point of reference. Always try to monitor your depth and time to control the rate of ascent.

If you ascend hand over hand up a straight shotline you will often ascend at something like the recommended rate. However, ascending up an angled ascent line reduces the vertical ascent rate and often provides better control as long as the line remains reasonably taut.

It is important to hang onto the BC exhaust valve during ascent so that buoyancy can be controlled instantly. Some divers find that holding the exhaust valve open at shoulder level allows them to easily maintain neutral buoyancy throughout the ascent. Others vent air periodically during the ascent. Both techniques require practice to achieve proficiency.

Make sure that you carefully observe your timer and your depth gauge on the way up. Each 30 ft (9 m) of ascent should take one minute. If you are beyond where you should be, then *slow down!* ***It is important to continue to practice your ascent technique so that you never ascend too rapidly.*** This essential aspect of diving is often ignored in diver training.

* Some dive computers (e.g. the Orca models) utilize a number of different ascent rates which depend on the depth range. The rates get slower as the diver gets closer to the surface.

A common misconception is that if you follow your smallest exhaust bubbles you will not exceed an ascent rate of 60 ft (18 m)/minute. Firstly, the rates of ascent of the bubbles increase dramatically as they expand and may be vastly different to 60 ft (18 m)/minute. Secondly, it is extremely difficult to follow the bubbles, especially when there are a number of divers, or if there is poor visibility or a substantial current. Thirdly, 60 ft (18 m)/minute may often be too fast anyway.

FIGURE 5.2.1
Diver controlling and monitoring rate of ascent by using ascent line and monitoring depth and time

Photo by Wayne Rolley.

Multiple ascents within a dive increase the risk of DCS by increasing the opportunity for bubble formation during the extra ascent(s) and by altering the rate of gas uptake and elimination during the portion of the dive following the previous ascent(s). This is also true for repetitive dives.

If bubbles form during an ascent and the diver re-descends, the bubbles will be compressed and, at times, gas may diffuse out of the bubbles. However, on other occasions, gas may be added to the bubbles and they will enlarge during the next ascent. Gas uptake may be more rapid when bubbles are present, and gas elimination is slower, both favoring bubble formation during, or after, the dive.

Additionally, it is known that equalizing the ears using the Valsalva maneuver can increase blood shunting across the heart of a diver with a patent foramen ovale (or similar defect). If such a diver performs the Valsalva maneuver while re-descending during a dive, bubbles formed during the initial ascent may be shunted into the arterial system.

If you have ascended prematurely during a dive and then re-descended, reduce the dive time considerably.

4. DO SAFETY STOPS

Over the past few years an increasing number of diving medical experts have been suggesting that divers do a precautionary stop at the end of all, or most, dives, even though the tables may not require it. The belief is that by spending some time off-gassing in the shallows before surfacing we will minimize bubbling within us.

Ultrasound (Doppler) studies have been done on divers after dive profiles of 100 ft (30 m)/25, 100 ft (30 m)/30 and 190 ft (57 m)/10. The subjects ascended at a controlled rate of 60 ft (18 m)/minute and, after surfacing, were monitored periodically using a Doppler bubble detector. No symptoms of DCS were seen, however, venous bubbles were detected to some degree in all divers after all dives. It was found that if short "safety stops" were added before surfacing, the number of detectable bubbles was greatly reduced. For example, in one series of tests, a diver dived to 100 ft (30 m) for a bottom time of 25 minutes (i.e. the U.S. Navy NDL) and ascended directly to the surface. When he was monitored, a lot of intravascular bubbles were detected. If he put in a stop of 2 minutes at 10 ft (3 m) it drastically reduced the degree of bubbling, and, if he put in a 1 minute stop at 20 ft (6 m) and another 4 minute stop at 10 ft (3 m) the bubbles were eliminated.[12] These results are shown graphically in Figure 5.2.2. Although these stop depths/times were only tested for a few specific exposures, it seems likely that the addition of similar stops may reduce bubbling after various other exposures.

FIGURE 5.2.2

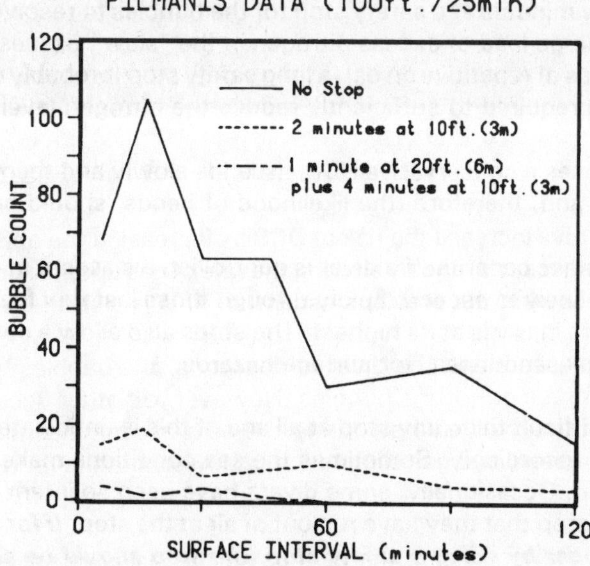

Note that the bubble count is highest in the first 30 minutes or so and then diminishes.

The standard U.S. Navy model predicts that off-gassing will be greatest at the surface and indicates that tissues will continue to load up with nitrogen during this shallow segment at the end of the dive.

However, more recently, one experiment indicated that nitrogen elimination at depths of 50 ft (15 m), or shallower, might be equal to or greater than at the surface.[13] The experimenters measured the off-gassing of nitrogen after exposures of 40 minutes at 4 ATA (100 ft/30 m). Nitrogen off-gassing was measured at depths of 100 ft (30 m), 50 ft (15 m) and 10 ft (3 m). The results indicated that nitrogen was removed most effectively at 50 ft (15 m). A couple of theories were offered to explain this. One theory supposed that the excess nitrogen will still be dissolved in the blood at these depths and will off-gas more efficiently in the absence of bubbles. Another theory suggested that a small amount of bubbling may have occurred and this will in fact enhance elimination by increasing the capacity for nitrogen to be transported to the lungs. If, however, the bubbles become large enough to block capillaries, the elimination of nitrogen will be reduced. However, these results were obtained after deep, long exposures and might not be applicable to many recreational dives.

The U.S. Navy has adopted the belief that off-gassing is better at 20 ft (6 m) than at the surface and has utilized it in its multiple level dive procedure which was published in 1983.[3] This procedure allows a diver to ascend to depths of 30 ft (9 m), or shallower, rather than surfacing to spend intervals between deeper dives. The procedure assumes that the diver will be at least as safe spending the interval in the shallows as he would be if he surfaced between the dives.

It seems reasonable to assume that a safety stop is a sensible precaution after most dives. It should reduce the amount of excess gas that we surface with and, thereby, reduce the number and/or size of any bubbles within us. However, *if substantial bubbling has occurred before reaching the stop, and/or if there is a large nitrogen load in some of the tissues, bends may still occur despite having done the stop.* If substantial gas formation is present it may take quite a while longer than a few minutes at a safety stop for the bubbles to resolve enough to prevent symptoms. If there is a large load of excess nitrogen in the "slow" tissues, as can occur after a very long dive (or a series of repetitive dives), a long safety stop (probably closer to 20 minutes than 5 minutes) may be required to sufficiently reduce the nitrogen levels.

I believe that if one chooses a conservative NDL, ascends slowly and then does a safety stop, the amount of bubbling and, therefore, the likelihood of bends, should be greatly reduced.

Safety stops also have other benefits. If a diver is controlling his ascent in order to stop before surfacing he will be less likely to ascend rapidly through those last few feet before the surface where the risk of pressure injury is at its highest. The stops also allow a diver to get organized, re-adjust gear and to look, and listen, for surface hazards.

In some situations it is difficult to do any stop at all and, if this is anticipated, the initial bottom time should be reduced accordingly. Sometimes the sea conditions make a stop difficult and possibly dangerous to do. Occasionally, some divers have been so intent on completing their planned time at a safety stop that they have run out of air at the stop. ***If for some reason a diver is placing himself in danger by doing a safety stop, the stop should be aborted*** as it is not a mandatory stop.

Over the past years many different depth-time combinations have been suggested for safety stops. The most desirable sequence is to some extent a matter of conjecture.

The question of safety stops and various other ascent procedures was addressed at a workshop convened by the American Academy of Underwater Sciences (AAUS) in September 1989. Participants included a number of recognized decompression experts. It was recommended that ***a safety stop be done somewhere between 10-30 ft (3-9 m) for 3-5 minutes at the end of every dive. The preferred depth range was 15-20 ft (4.5-6 m).***[14]

The Divers Alert Network (DAN) now recommend a safety stop at 15 ft (4.5 m) for 3 minutes, and both PADI and NAUI have included a 3 minute safety stop at 15 ft (5 m)* with their tables. The BS-AC '88 Tables tackle the problem by encouraging the diver to take one minute to ascend through the final 20 ft (6 m), although computer nitrogen uptake/elimination simulations seem to indicate that this may not be as effective in reducing the surfacing gas load as a safety stop would be.[15]

The exact depth of the safety stop(s) is not crucial as the stops are not mandatory, but the diver should try to maintain an even depth.

If there is a large swell shallow stops become difficult to do. If a diver is hanging onto an anchor line or shotline, or floating mid-water, he may be lifted up and down causing the stop depth to vary considerably. In these circumstances it is better to do the stop at around 20 ft (6 m) rather than in shallower water. After a dive deeper than about 100 ft (30 m) it may be better to do the stop around 20 ft (6 m) rather than shallower, as the smaller pressure difference between the maximum depth of the dive and the stop depth may reduce bubble formation.

Reef dives often provide shallow sections of reef where a diver can spend time at the end of a dive (Figure 5.2.3). Otherwise, an anchor line, or other ascent line, can provide a point of reference and stability when doing a safety stop (Figures 5.2.4 and 5.2.5).

* 15 ft has been rounded up to 5 m in the metric tables.

FIGURE 5.2.3
Diver doing a safety stop on shallow reef

Photo by Wayne Rolley.

FIGURE 5.2.4
Diver doing a safety stop on anchor line

Photo by Wayne Rolley.

FIGURE 5.2.5
Divers doing a stop on a decompression bar

Photo by Adrian Neumann.

If you have done a safety stop then use total dive time, rather than actual bottom time when calculating repetitive dives.

This is done to cater for any extra nitrogen that might have been absorbed in the slower tissues during the safety stop. Extra nitrogen may be absorbed if the nitrogen tension in some of the "slower" tissues, which may not have absorbed much extra gas during the dive, is lower than the partial pressure of nitrogen in the lungs at the depth of the stop. The resulting pressure gradient will encourage more nitrogen to diffuse into these tissues and they may end up with a slightly higher nitrogen load than if the safety stop had not been done. Although computer gas uptake simulations indicate that during a short stop this effect is minimal, and the experiments previously mentioned indicate that we may, at times, surface with less gas after doing the stop than we would have surfaced with had no stop been done, it is a wise precaution to use total dive time for repetitive dive calculations as it often adds a bit more conservatism to those calculations.

5. AVOID DEEP DIVES

There is no doubt that **deeper diving is associated with much more risk than shallow diving.** Sensory deprivation, nitrogen narcosis, cold and many other factors may combine to cause problems for a diver as he descends, especially beyond 100 ft (30 m) or so.

U.S. Navy experience, between 1968 and 1981 was that the accident rate for dives of 50 ft (15 m) or less was 0.06%. The accident rate for dives to between 51-100 ft (15.5-30 m) was 0.23%, nearly four times the rate for shallow dives. The accident rate for dives between 101-200 ft (30-61 m) was 0.54%, more than double the 50-100ft rate and nine times the rate for shallower dives.[16]

72% (160/222) of the recreational divers treated for bends in the USA in 1988 had dived deeper than 80 ft (24 m)[2]. In 1988, in Britain, 47% (42/89) of the divers treated for bends had undertaken deep dives (defined there as deeper than 100 ft/30 m).[17]

An extensive statistical analysis of a large number of dives indicates that for dives performed in accordance to conventional decompression schedules to depths shallower than 100 ft (30 m) and with bottom times shorter than about 45 minutes, the risk of bends appears to be about 1%. Dives deeper than 100 ft (30 m) and/or longer than about 45 minutes carry a substantially higher risk.[18]

If decompression sickness does occur after a deep dive it is more likely to have neurological manifestations.[19]

In addition, it has been reported that the architecture of white (and possibly red) blood cells alters when exposed to hyperbaric pressures in excess of about 4 ATA (equivalent to a depth of 100 ft/30 m). The blood cells become more rigid and this rigidity is not reversed on decompression. Since blood cells are larger than the spaces in the walls of capillaries, they must distort in order to pass through the capillary walls. It is feared that some of these stiffer blood cells may not be able to pass through the walls of fine capillaries and, so, may form blood clots which will obstruct circulation. This has been proposed as a possible cause of bone necrosis and eye damage in divers who have dived beyond 100 ft (30 m).[20]

Where possible, a recreational diver should restrict his diving to depths shallower than 100 ft (30 m).

6. AVOID EXCESSIVELY LONG DIVES

Excessively long dives carry a greater risk of decompression sickness. Most dive tables do not include half-times long enough to cater for the amount of gas dissolved in some of the very slow tissues after certain very long dives and the time required to release this excess gas. A series of repetitive dives can be similar to one long dive in this respect! Statistical analysis of a large number of dives has shown that the risk of bends increases substantially for dives longer than about 45 minutes.[18]

7. PLAN REPETITIVE DIVES CONSERVATIVELY AND MAXIMIZE SURFACE INTERVALS

Repetitive dives are often associated with decompression sickness. Approximately 65% of the recreational divers treated for bends in the USA in both 1987 and 1988 became ill after repetitive dives.[2]

Repetitive dive schedules must be calculated conservatively. This is especially true for multi-day repetitive dives.

Currently, relatively little is known about the effects of multi-day repetitive diving. However, PADI, in an attempt to assess the safety of the RDP in such situations, is conducting on-going experiments on multi-day repetitive diving. The results of the initial chamber tests, in which subjects simulated 4 dives a day for 6 consecutive days, were encouraging.[21] However, extensive testing still needs to be conducted in the ocean, where conditions are not as easily controlled as in the chamber. DAN statistics indicate that, in 1987, 55% of the recreational divers treated for bends in the USA had undertaken multi-day diving. In 1988, this figure was 50%.[2] In December 1989, DAN released some guidelines (probably based largely on the results of PADI's tests) suggesting that divers should restrict their diving to a maximum of 4 dives per day for 6 days, with preferably a no dive day on the 3rd or 4th day. DAN strongly recommended no more than 3 dives per day.[22]

Restrict repetitive diving to a maximum of 3 dives a day.

Restrict multi-day repetitive diving to a maximum of 6 days with a rest day on the 3rd or 4th day.

When repetitive dives are undertaken, the depths of the dives should become progressively shallower. This is important to minimize the pressure changes during the ascent from the later dives. During the later dives, the "slower" tissues will have a higher gas load as a result of the previous dives, and will be more likely to bubble if there is a large pressure difference during ascent. This may contribute to bubble formation in various other body tissues.

Repetitive bounce dives (short dives separated by short surface intervals) have a similar effect to multiple ascents and should also be avoided.

Maximize surface intervals and avoid having surface intervals shorter than 1 hour.

6. AVOID DECOMPRESSION STOP DIVES

By undertaking decompression stop dives, a diver places himself at risk of being unable to satisfactorily complete the required decompression. If the air supply runs out, or if other problems arise and the stops are not completed, the risk of decompression sickness is greatly increased. If the depths or times of the stops are incorrectly measured or adhered to, bends may result.

Because of the difficulty of doing a decompression stop dive correctly, and because of the amount of support equipment and personnel required to insure the safety of such dives, a recreational diver should not attempt decompression stop dives if they can be avoided.

7. ENSURE THAT YOUR DEPTH GAUGE IS ACCURATE

Depth gauges are often found to be inaccurate, at times very much so. While the digital gauges are generally more accurate, they too can become inaccurate.

If your gauge tells you that you are at 80 ft (24 m) and you are actually at 86 ft (26 m), you will be at least one schedule out with your decompression table calculations. I have personally found some expensive and reputable depth gauges and dive computers to be inaccurate by up to 30 ft (9 m) at at depth. This is a number of depth increments on the tables. **If a depth gauge or dive computer is reading shallower than the actual depth a diver can be in real trouble.**

Depth gauges should be tested and calibrated at least once a year. If a gauge has received a hard knock it should be tested before being used again. If a non zero-adjust depth gauge has been taken in an aircraft it should be checked again before being used.

Thoroughly wash your gauge with fresh warm water after every day of diving.

Check your gauge with your dive buddy's during the dive and *dive according to the gauge which is reading the deeper.*

It is a good idea to have a back-up gauge/computer in case your main unit fails. This is especially important if you are using a dive computer. If one unit fails and you have an identical unit (or one based on a similar model) you will still have access to your theoretical decompression status.

8. DIVING PROFILES

Some types of dive profile are more likely to produce bends than other types of profile.

Dive profiles which are less likely to produce bends are those which have a short time at the maximum depth during the early portion of the dive, and then gradually get shallower throughout the remainder of the dive. This is shown in Figures 5.2.6 and 5.2.7.

FIGURE 5.2.6

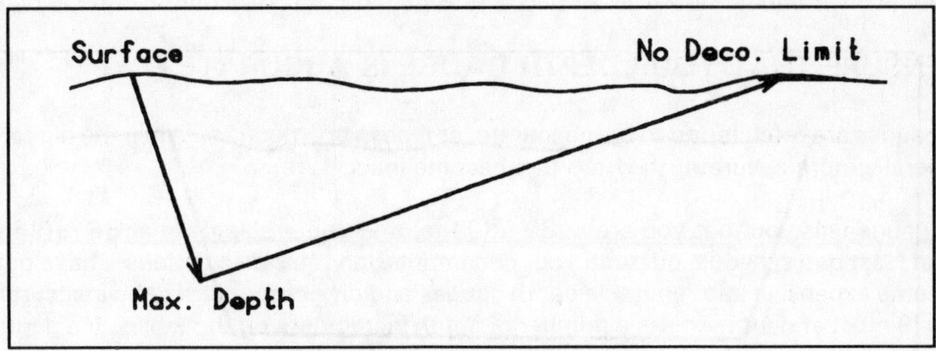

This profile is an ideal profile, especially for reef diving.

FIGURE 5.2.7

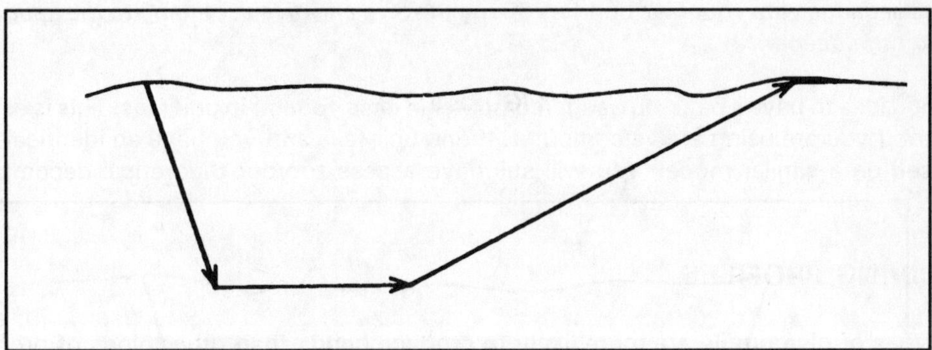

This, although not as good as the previous profile, is a quite a good profile. The time at the maximum depth should be less than half of the NDL.

Dive profiles which are more likely to produce bends are those of a "square wave" or "rectangular" form as shown in Figure 5.2.8, and those in which a diver redescends or works deeper, rather than shallower, throughout the dive.

FIGURE 5.2.8

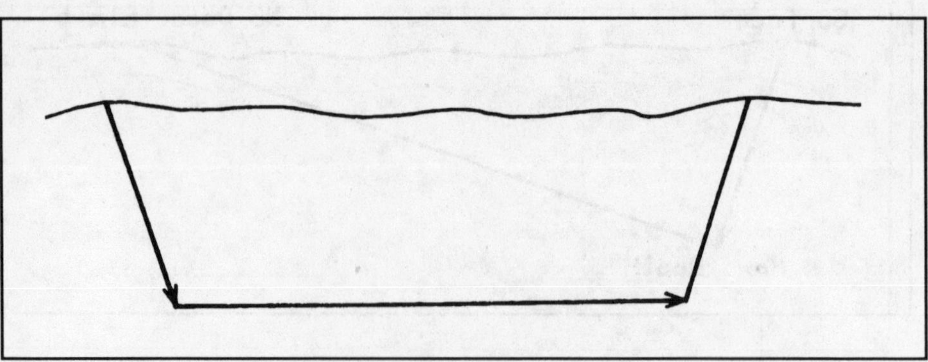

"Square wave" or "Rectangular" dive profile. This profile, often used in wreck diving, is conducive to bending. 90% of the divers treated for bends in the U.S.A. in 1987 are reported to have dived a square wave profile.[2]

FIGURE 5.2.9

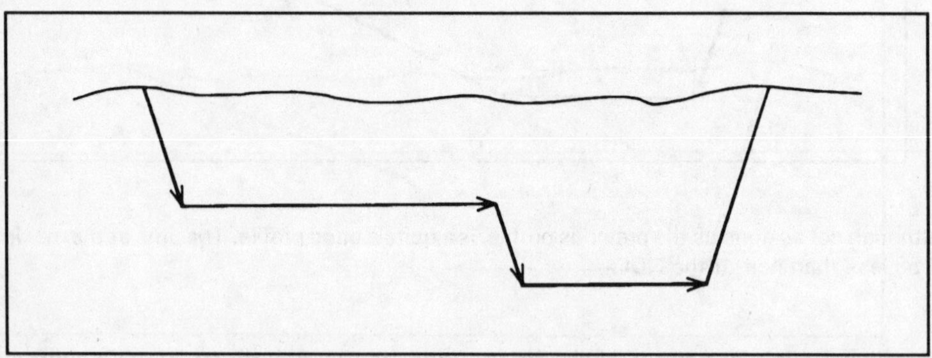

This type of profile, in which the diver descends to a deeper level, tends to cause bends.

FIGURE 5.2.10

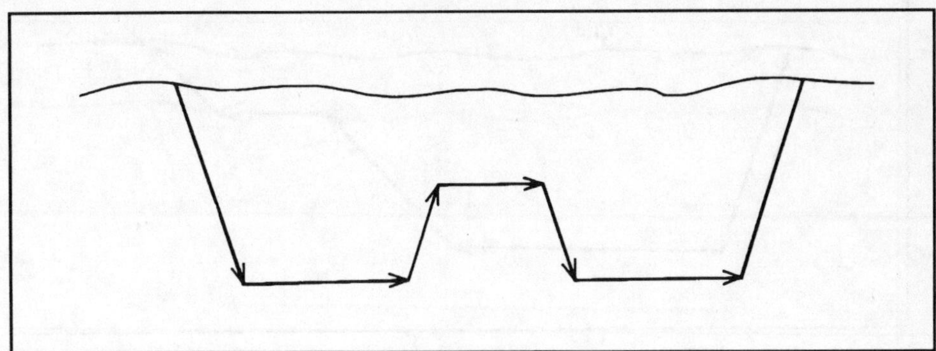

This profile, involving redescent to depth, has also proved to be rather hazardous.

FIGURE 5.2.11

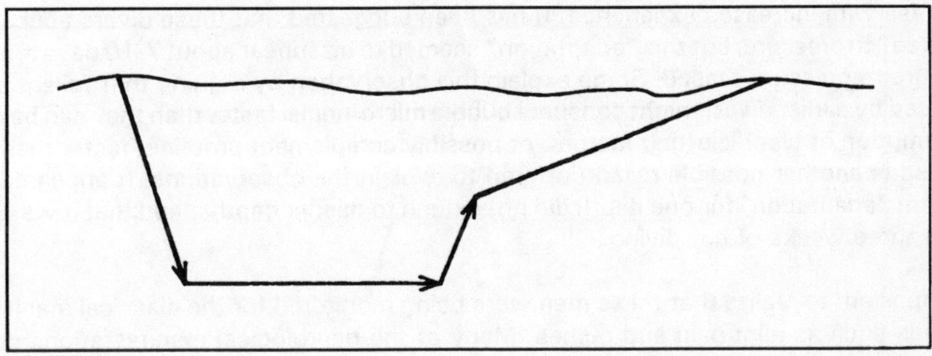

This type of profile often causes bends if the first big pressure change is too large.

FIGURE 5.2.12

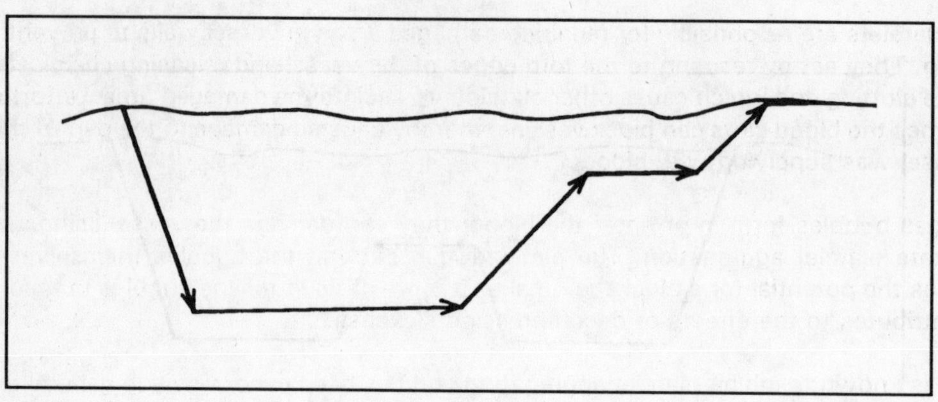

This type of profile can be used for wreck diving instead of the "square profile". It utilizes a slow ascent and a safety stop.

Frequent Diving

It has often been stated, somewhat carelessly, that divers who dive often are less likely to become bent. In the early 1950s it was observed that new caisson workers had a higher incidence of bends than those who had been regularly working in compressed air. In 1960 a study was undertaken on 22 British caisson workers to determine whether or not this observation could be confirmed.[23] The study reported that the incidence of bends in these divers fell with increased experience. It has been suggested that these divers appear to have "adapted" to pressure, but this "adaptation" seemed to disappear about 7-10 days after regular exposure to pressure ceased. Some explain this observation by arguing that "silent bubbles", produced by earlier dives, might consume bubble micro-nuclei faster than they can be replaced. Consumption of blood clotting factors, or possibly complement proteins, faster than they are replaced is another possible reason offered to explain the observations. It appeared that the apparent "adaptation" for one depth did not extend to deeper depths, and that it was lost after one to three weeks of not diving.

It is important to realize that these men were being monitored for the classical manifestations of bends such as joint pain and rashes. Many of the neurological manifestations commonly detected now were quite possibly overlooked at that time. It has been argued that perhaps these men were suffering gentle attacks of decompression sickness without feeling the pains they would have experienced if unadapted. These arguments have received considerable support from ultrasound studies, which often show considerable silent bubbles despite a lack of obvious symptoms of bends.

Adaptation has also been reported in certain professional divers and it has been argued that people who dive a lot acquire either an increased tolerance, or decreased sensitivity, to decompression sickness. **However, there is no evidence that adaptation has occurred in recreational SCUBA divers.**

Aspirin and DCS

Blood platelets are responsible for repairing damaged areas in vessel walls to prevent or stop bleeding. They act by reacting to the torn edges of the vessel and releasing chemicals which promote clotting and which cause other platelets to stick to the damaged area. Unfortunately, sometimes the blood clots can block vessels, thereby causing damage to the part of the organ the vessel was supplying with blood.

When gas bubbles form in or enter the blood, they can damage the vessel linings and, so, precipitate platelet aggregation. The platelets can stick to the bubbles themselves, which increases the potential for a blockage, makes it more difficult for the bubbles to resolve and, so, contributes to the effects of decompression sickness.

Aspirin is known to inhibit platelet aggregation and has been used widely in general medicine to reduce blood clotting. Consequently, it has been suggested that aspirin may help to prevent or reduce some of the effects of DCS. As a result, some divers began to take aspirin, prior to diving, in the hope that it would reduce the risk of bends. In addition, various organizations, worldwide, began to include aspirin in their first aid protocol for DCS. However, **despite repeated attempts, researchers have not consistently been able to show that aspirin prevents or reduces the platelet aggregation associated with DCS.**

Aspirin can cause gastrointestinal irritation and long term aspirin use can cause bleeding peptic ulcers. Aspirin, even taken in moderate doses, can cause severe allergic reactions in sensitive persons. It also prolongs bleeding and, if a diver who has taken sufficient aspirin before diving were to injure himself and begin to bleed, the aspirin could increase the severity of the bleeding. Since it is an analgesic, aspirin can mask some of the symptoms of DCS.

Given the known adverse effects of aspirin, and the lack of evidence that aspirin reduces the effects of DCS, most authorities now advise that divers refrain from taking aspirin in an attempt to avoid bends and as part of the first aid in the event of bends.

Contact (Corneal) Lenses and Decompression

A number of divers wear contact lenses when diving and there has been some concern whether this may predispose to bubble formation in, or near, the eyes.

A 1980 report describes an experiment designed to determine the effects of corneal contact lense wear during, or after, exposures to a depth of 150 ft (45.5 m) for 30 minutes.[24] Subjects wore either soft lenses, hard lenses with a small central hole, or hard lenses without a hole. No bubbles or symptoms arose in divers wearing the soft lenses or the hard lenses with a central hole. However, bubble formation was observed in the divers wearing hard lenses without a hole. Examination showed fluid accumulation (edema) in their cornea, giving it a cloudy appearance. These divers suffered soreness and reduced vision in their eyes which, eventually, resolved.

The researchers concluded that the bubbles resulted from nitrogen being trapped between the eyes and the hard lenses. Adding a small hole to the hard lenses seemed to allow the excess nitrogen to escape, and the soft lenses appeared to allow the nitrogen to diffuse through them. It was suggested that diving with soft lenses, hard lenses with a central hole, or preferably spectacles or an optical mask should not adversely affect the eyes.

Although there has been a report of a diver having similar problems to those described above after diving with soft contact lenses, the vast majority of divers who wear soft contact lenses while diving do so without problems.

Blood Donation and Diving

Blood volume returns to normal shortly after a blood donation, but the level of red blood cells will be lower than normal for up to two weeks. Consequently, it has been recommended that a diver waits two to three days before diving after having given blood.[25] Drinking plenty of non-alcoholic fluids during this time is also a wise precaution.

A donor should be well hydrated before giving blood. Since divers are often dehydrated after diving, especially after a number of repetitive dives, it is probably sensible to refrain from giving blood for a about two days after diving. Drinking plenty of non-alcoholic fluids will again assist rehydration.

There is no danger of giving someone excess nitrogen by way of a blood transfusion.

SUMMARY

* There will always be an incidence of bends as long as people continue to dive.
* Some divers get bent after extremely conservative dive profiles.
* The No-Decompression Limits of the more modern tables are generally shorter than the NDLs of the U.S. Navy Tables and many other conventional tables.
* It appears that if bubbling is to be minimized, the modern, shorter NDLs should be used in preference to the conventional NDLs.
* The allowable bottom time should be shortened to cater for predisposing factors to bends.
* Rapid ascents appear to produce more cases of neurological decompression sickness.
* Severe bends is less likely to follow a slow ascent.
* An ascent rate of about 30 ft/minute (9 m/minute) appears to be safe ascent rate for recreational diving although, at depths beyond about 100 ft (30 m) a faster rate may sometimes be beneficial. The ascent rate should not exceed 60 ft/minute (18 m/minute).

* It is often difficult to determine and control the rate of ascent. Using an ascent line and monitoring depth and time throughout the dive assists in controlling rate of ascent.

* Multiple ascents within a dive increase the risk of bends.

* A safety stop may reduce the amount of bubbling within us. A safety stop of 3-5 minutes at 10-30 ft (3-9 m) should be done at the end of every dive. The prefered depth is 15-20 ft (4.5-6 m).

* If you have done a safety stop use total dive time, rather than bottom time, when calculating repetitive dives as it often adds conservatism to the calculations.

* Deeper and/or long dives carry a higher risk of bends.

* DCS often occurs after repetitive dives so repetitive dive schedules must be calculated conservatively. This is especially true for multi-day repetitive dives.

* When repetitive dives are undertaken, the depths of the dives should become progressively shallower.

* A depth gauge which reads too shallow may cause a decompression accident.

* Certain dive profiles are less likely to cause bends. It seems desirable to go to the maximum depth early in the dive and then gradually work shallower throughout the rest of the dive.

* There is no evidence that frequent diving reduces the likelihood of decompression sickness in recreational divers.

* The vast majority of divers who wear soft contact lenses while diving do so without problems. Hard contact lenses may cause problems unless they have a small central hole.

REFERENCES

1. Gorman, D. (1985), "Guidelines for Safer Decompression for Sports and Scientific Divers". *Proceedings from "To Bend or Not to Bend" Symposium*, Adelaide.

2. Divers Alert Network (1989), "Report on 1988 Diving Accidents". Divers Alert Network, North Carolina.

3. Thalmann, E. and Butler, F. (1983), "A Procedure For Doing Multiple Level Dives on Air Using Repetitiv Groups". Navy Experimental Diving Unit, Report No. 13-83, U.S. Navy Experimental Diving Unit.

4. Dembert, M. et al (1984),"Health Risk Factors for the Development of Decompression Sickness Among U.S. Navy Divers". *Undersea Biomedical Research*; 11 (4): 395-406.

5. Bassett, B. (1982), "The Safety of the U.S. Navy Decompression Tables and Recommendations for Sport Divers". *SPUMS Journal*; Oct-Dec: 16-25.

6. Spencer, M. (1976), "Decompression limits for compressed air determined by ultrasonically detected blood bubbles". *Journal of Applied Physiology*; 40 (2): 229-235.

7. Thalmann, E. (1986), "Air-N_2O_2 Decompression Computer Algorithm Development". Navy Experimental Diving Unit Report No. 8-85, U.S. Navy Experimental Diving Unit.

8. Buehlmann, A. (1987), "Diving At Altitude and Flying After Diving". UHMS Symposium. *The Physiological Basis of Decompression*, Duke University Medical Centre.

9. Edmonds, C. (1987), "Decompression Sickness - Its History and Physiology". *SCUBA Diver;* June-July: 22-26.

10. Buehlmann, A. (1984), "Decompression - Decompression Sickness". Spinger-Verlag, Berlin.

11. Hamilton, R. (1990), Slow Ascent Rate: Beneficial But A Tradeoff. In: *Proceedings of the AAUS Biomechanics of Safe Ascent Workshop*, Lang, M. and Egstrom, G. (eds), American Academy of Underwater Sciences (AAUS) Diving Safety Publication AAUSDSP-BSA-01-90. AAUS, Costa Mesa, CA.

12. Pilmanis, A. (1975), "Intravenous Gas Emboli in Man After Compressed Air Ocean Diving". USN Office of Naval Research, Final Technical Report, Contract No. N00014-67-A-0269-0026, Nay 1, 1972 to June 30, 1975.

13. Kindwall, A. et al (1975), "Nitrogen Elimination in Man During Decompression". *Undersea Biomedical Research:* 2 (4): 285-297.

14. Lang, M. and Egstrom, G. (eds) (1990), "Proceedings of the AAUS Biomechanics of Safe Ascent Workshop". American Academy of Underwater Sciences (AAUS) Diving Safety Publication AAUSDSP-BSA-01-90. AAUS, Costa Mesa, CA.

15. Lewis, J. (1990), "A Review of Ascent Procedures for Scientific and Recreational Divers". In: *Proceedings of the AAUS Biomechanics of Safe Ascent Workshop*, Lang, M. and Egstrom, G. (eds), American Academy of Underwater Sciences (AAUS) Diving Safety Publication AAUSDSP-BSA-01-90. AAUS, Costa Mesa, CA.

16. Blood, C. and Hoiberg, A. (1985), "Analyses of variables underlying U.S. Navy diving Accidents". *Undersea Biomedical Research*; 12 (3): 351-360.

17. Allen, C. (1988), "NDC Diving Incidents Report". *Diving Officers' Conference, 1988*, BS-AC, London.

18. Weathersby, P. et al (1986), "Statistically Based Decompression Tables III: Comparative Risk Using U.S. Navy, British, and Canadian Standard Air Schedules". Naval Medical Research Institute Report No. 86-50, Naval Medical Research Institute, Bethesda.

19. Lehner, C. (1990), "Ascent Rate Experiments and Diver Safety". In: *Proceedings of the AAUS Biomechanics of Safe Ascent Workshop*, Lang, M. and Egstrom, G. (eds), American Academy of Underwater Sciences (AAUS) Diving Safety Publication AAUSDSP-BSA-01-90. AAUS, Costa Mesa, CA.

20. Newson, L. (1989), "Eye tests reveal dangers of diving". *New Scientist*; 21, Jan: 33.

21. Rogers, R. and Powell, M. (1989), "Controlled Hyperbaric Chamber Tests of Multi-Day, Repetitive Dives". (Presented at UHMS Meeting, June 9, 1989).

22. DAN Recreational Diver Decompression Advisory Board (1990). Recommendations for Recreational Divers.

23. Golding, F. et al (1960), "Decompression Sickness During Construction of the Dartford Tunnel'. *British Journal of Industrial Medicine*; 17: 167-86.

24. Simon, D. and Bradley, M. (1980), "Adverse Effects of Contact Lens Wear During Decompression". *JAMA*; 244: 1213-1214.

25. Hickey, D. (1984), "Medical Standards for Divers". *Undersea Biomed. Res.*; 11 (4): 413.

OTHER SOURCES

Berghage, T. and Durman, D. (1980), "U.S. Navy Air Decompression Schedule Risk Analysis". Naval Medical Research Institute, Report No. 80-1, Department of the Navy.

Buehlmann, A., personal communications.

Divers Alert Network (1988), "Blood Donation and Diving". *Alert Diver*; 4 (4): 5.

Dueker, C. (1985), "SCUBA Diving in Safety and Health". Madison Publishing Associates, California.

Hills, B. (1984), "Decompression Physiology". *SPUMS Journal*; 14 (1): 3-18.

Miller, J. (ed) (1979), "NOAA Diving Manual", 2nd edition. United States Department of Commerce.

Philip, R., (1989), "Aspirin: The Making of a Myth". *Alert Diver*; 5 (1): 3.

Pilmanis, A. (1987), "Decompression Tables and Dive Computers". *SPUMS Journal;* 17 (2): 71-72.

U.S. Navy (1985), "U.S. Navy Diving Manual", Vol 1, Air Diving. U.S. Government Printing Office.

RECOMMENDED FURTHER READING

Bassett, B. (1982), "The Safety of the U.S. Navy Decompression Tables and Recommendations for Sport Divers". *SPUMS Journal*; Oct-Dec: 16-25.

Divers Alert Network (1988), "Provisional Report on Diving Accidents". Divers Alert Network, North Carolina.

Dueker, C. (1985), "SCUBA Diving in Safety and Health". Madison Publishing Associates, California.

Lang, M. and Egstrom, G. (eds) (1990), "Proceedings of the AAUS Biomechanics of Safe Ascent Workshop". American Academy of Underwater Sciences (AAUS) Diving Safety Publication AAUSDSP-BSA-01-90. AAUS, Costa Mesa, CA.

CHAPTER 6

NITROGEN NARCOSIS

"I am personally quite receptive to nitrogen rapture. I like it and fear it like doom. It destroys the instincts of life. Tough individuals are not overcome as soon as neurasthenic persons like me, but they have difficulty extricating themselves. Intellectuals get drunk early and suffer acute attacks on all the senses, which demand hard fighting to overcome" .... Jacques Cousteau

More than 150 years ago it was first noted that individuals exposed to hyperbaric air behaved as if intoxicated. It is now widely accepted that divers breathing raised pressures of air exhibit signs and symptoms of narcosis and intoxication.

Nitrogen narcosis will affect all divers breathing air at depths in excess of 100 ft (30 m), although some will notice the effects at shallower depths while others may not notice them until deeper. The effects increase progressively with increasing depth. They appear on arrival at a particular depth and, generally, will not worsen as exposure continues at this depth. The effects are readily reversible on ascent to shallower depths.

The exact process that produces narcosis is complex. In recent years there have been two major theories as to the cause of this narcosis. One relates to the increased nitrogen partial pressure, while the other relates to carbon dioxide retention. There has been a substantial amount of experimental evidence refuting carbon dioxide build-up (hypercapnia) as the cause of narcosis, although hypercapnia does appear to increase the narcotic effects.[1]

It is generally believed that, when breathing hyperbaric air, the narcosis is due to the raised partial pressure of nitrogen. Nitrogen is considered an inert (non-reactive) gas as it is thought to participate in no chemical reaction in the human body. Therefore, it must exert its effects by physical means only.

Nitrogen is very soluble in fat, and nerve cells contain a high amount of fat. This enables the nitrogen to enter the nerve cells, where it affects the transmission of impulses.

Many experts now believe that the mechanism of nitrogen narcosis is similar to the action of gaseous general anesthetics, which impair the transmission of impulses between nerve endings in the brain (synaptic transmission).[1]

The reticular center of the brain receives messages (nerve impulses) from throughout the body and re-distributes them through the brain. The nerve cells in the reticular center seem to be very sensitive to the effects of various narcotic agents, including nitrogen. If the reticular center is not functioning properly, brain function becomes disrupted and unconsciousness ensues.

If another narcotic agent such as alcohol, or some other sedative, is also dissolved in the fat of the nerve cells, the effects will combine and the narcosis will become more severe.

Most other inert gases produce a narcosis with similar signs and symptoms to nitrogen narcosis but which varies in potency. The narcotic potency of the inert gases appears to increase with increased solubility in fat and, with the exception of hydrogen, with an increase in molecular weight. Various gases listed in order of increasing narcotic potency are:
Helium (not narcotic at currently attainable pressures), neon, hydrogen, nitrogen, argon, krypton, xenon.

SIGNS AND SYMPTOMS

The manifestations have been compared to the effects of alcohol, the early stages of general anesthesia, hypoxia and hallucinogenic drugs. A list of the signs and symptoms and the depth at which they commonly occur is given in Figure 5.1. It is important to realize that the severity of symptoms and the exact depth of their onset varies greatly between individuals.

At shallower depths brain functions such as memory, concentration, reasoning and judgement are the first affected by narcosis. If a diver is feeling secure in his surroundings a sense of well-being (euphoria) may ensue. However, if the diver is not feeling secure in his surroundings anxiety may result. As the diver goes deeper, movement becomes more difficult and co-ordination becomes poor. A simple task may be difficult to perform. The diver may make serious errors in judgement and may react slowly to directions or stimuli. At extreme depths hallucinations and eventual unconsciousness may occur.

FEATURES OF NITROGEN NARCOSIS

The narcotic effect usually becomes apparent soon after reaching a particular depth and does not worsen as exposure continues at this depth unless the diver's blood carbon dioxide levels become elevated due to anxiety, exertion or some other cause.

At depths of around 130 ft (39 m) the effects can usually be overcome by increased concentration and effort. If you read your gauge and do not understand what it says, concentrate on it until it does make sense. If you still cannot understand the reading, ascend immediately to a depth at which you begin to function adequately.

The effects of narcosis decrease immediately on ascent to shallower depths, although, at times, a diver will not remember events that happened during the dive.

Some divers are more susceptible to narcosis than others. The physical and mental state of the diver will affect his or her predisposition to it, so an individual diver's susceptibility will vary from dive to dive.

FIGURE 5.1

Signs and symptoms of nitrogen narcosis

Depth	Signs and symptoms
33-100 ft (10-30 m)	Mild impairment of performance of unpracticed tasks. Mildly impaired reasoning. Mild euphoria possible.
100-165 ft (30-50 m)	Delayed response to visual and auditory stimuli. Reasoning and immediate memory affected more than motor co-ordination. Calculation errors and wrong choices. Idea fixation. Over-confidence and sense of well-being. Laughter and loquacity (in chambers) which may be overcome by self control. Anxiety (common in cold murky water).
165-230 ft (50-70 m)	Sleepiness, impaired judgement, confusion. Hallucinations. Severe delay in response to signals, instructions and other stimuli. Occasional dizziness. Uncontrolled laughter, hysteria (in chamber). Terror in some.
230-300 ft (70-90 m)	Poor concentration and mental confusion. Stupefaction with some decrease in dexterity and judgement. Loss of memory, increased excitability.
300 ft⁺ (90 m⁺)	Hallucinations. Increased intensity of vision and hearing. Sense of impending blackout, euphoria, dizziness, manic or depressive states, a sense of levitation, disorganization of the sense of time, changes in facial appearance. Unconsiousness. Death.

Note: Death may occur at much shallower depths due to errors caused by impaired judgement or over-confidence.

Certain factors increase the effects of nitrogen narcosis. Some of these are:

* Anxiety, apprehension or inexperience
* Recent intake of alcohol or of certain drugs or medications (e.g. sedatives, hallucinogens, some antihistamines)
* Fatigue, heavy physical work
* Cold water
* Rapid descent
* Poor visibility, reduced sensory input
* Excess carbon dioxide
* Changes in oxygen levels
* Task loading

Factors that reduce the effects of narcosis include:

* Strong motivation to perform a task.
* Concentration on the task at hand.
* Acclimatization - prolonged and frequent exposure gives some degree of adaptation. If a deep dive is planned, it is a good idea to build up to the dive by performing progressively deeper dive during the days prior to the deep dive. These "work-up" dives prior to deep dives help a diver to get more used to the effects of narcosis. However, the risk of bends must be carefully monitored and decompression tables must be followed very conservatively.

Some divers claim that they have never been “narked”, even on dives at times far deeper than 100 ft. It is important to realize that we all suffer from nitrogen narcosis to some degree when we dive on air to 100 ft, or deeper. **When tests are performed on any diver at 100 ft, or deeper, it is possible to demonstrate impairment of concentration and some slowing of thought.** Sometimes, because we are “narked” it is difficult to realize that we are in fact suffering from narcosis. This is similar to the drunk driver who feels perfectly capable of driving safely. Tests would show that his co-ordination is impaired and that his senses are dulled, but the driver might not be aware of this temporary debility.

It does not take much logical thought to swim around at depth and look around us, so we might not notice the effects of narcosis in this situation. However, if we read our gauges it might take a little longer than normal to absorb what they are telling us. If we must perform a task it might become more difficult than it really should be. Although reflexes and thought processes are slowed down, most problems can be sorted out provided that we remain calm, have sufficient time to do it safely, and do not get lost in our determination to solve one problem only. “Task fixation” often occurs when a narcosis-affected diver encounters a problem. In the effort to solve the immediate problem, the diver may forget to check the air supply or bottom time and, in so doing, might create new problems. The “fixated” diver might also, inadvertently, lose buoyancy and, as he sinks, the narcosis will increase, further delay the response time and, therefore, magnify the problem.

If you are suffering from narcosis it is very likely that your buddy is also “narked”. Observe your buddy constantly during any dive, especially a deeper dive, regularly checking his air as well as your own. If your buddy does not appear to be adequately alert, ascend with him to the relative safety of shallower water.

The best way to prevent nitrogen narcosis is to avoid diving to depths known to cause substantial narcotic effects. This is usually somewhere between 100-200 ft (30-60 m). Some professional divers can safely dive to depths approaching 200 ft (60 m) on air, but this is well beyond the scope of recreational divers, who have no need to expose themslves to the great risks involved. When professional divers dive deeper than about 200 ft (60 m) they often substitute the nitrogen in their breathing mix for a less narcotic inert gas such as helium. This eliminates some problems but introduces others.

Safe diving beyond 100 ft (30 m) requires considerable diving experience and an awareness of the ever increasing risk of narcosis and its affect on a diver's judgement and performance. It also requires a diver to be in good physical condition, as well as mentally stable and alert. It is impossible to state an exact depth limit that is acceptable for all sport divers. It depends on the experience and condition of the divers, the task to be done (if any), the prevailing conditions and the diver support available. The combination of narcosis and decompression and air consumption considerations makes deeper diving far more hazardous than diving in shallower water. The greater risk associated with deeper diving cannot normally be justified by recreational divers.

SUMMARY

* Nitrogen narcosis effects all divers breathing air at depths greater than 100 ft (30 m).

* The effects increase progressively with increasing depth, usually appearing on arrival at a depth.

* Narcosis is readily reversible on ascent.

* The exact process that produces narcosis is complex and is not yet fully understood.

* The severity of symptoms and the exact depth of their onset varies between individuals and from dive to dive.

* Initially brain functions such as memory, concentration, reasoning and judgement are affected. Eventually, movement and co-ordination may become affected.

* At depths around 100 ft (30 m) narcosis can usually be overcome by increased concentration and effort.

* Some divers are more susceptible to narcosis than others. The physical and mental state of the diver will affect his predisposition to it.

* Factors which increase the effects of narcosis include: anxiety, apprehension, inexperience, alcohol/drug ingestion, fatigue, hard work, cold water, task loading and high carbon dioxide levels.

* Factors that reduce narcosis include high motivation, concentration and acclimatization.

REFERENCES

1. Bennett, P. (1982), "Inert Gas Narcosis". In: *The Physiology and Medicine of Diving*, 3rd edition, Bennett, P., and Elliott, D. (eds), Best Publishing Co., California.

OTHER SOURCES

Bennett, P. (1981), "Inert Gas Narcosis and the High Pressure Nervous Syndrome". In: *Hyperbaric and Undersea Medicine*, Davis, J. (ed), Medical Seminars, Inc., California.

Dueker, C. (1985), "SCUBA Diving in Safety and Health". Madison Publishing Associates, California.

Edmonds, C. et al (1981), "Diving and Subaquatic Medicine", 2nd edition. Diving Medical Center, Sydney.

Thomas, R. and McKenzie, B. (1981), "The Diver's Medical Companion". Diving Medical Center, Sydney.

RECOMMENDED FURTHER READING

Bennett, P. (1982), "Inert Gas Narcosis". In: *The Physiology and Medicine of Diving*, 3rd edition, Bennett, P., and Elliott, D. (eds), Best Publishing Co., California.

Dueker, C. (1985), "SCUBA Diving in Safety and Health". Madison Publishing Associates, California.

Edmonds, C. et al (1981), "Diving and Subaquatic Medicine", 2nd edition. Diving Medical Center, Sydney.

CHAPTER 7

CARBON DIOXIDE AND DIVING

Carbon dioxide is a waste product of our metabolism. It is carried in our blood in three ways. A small amount is dissolved in the plasma, another small amount is bonded to hemoglobin or plasma proteins, but most of the carbon dioxide in our blood is carried as carbonic acid, which is a weak acid made from a chemical combination of carbon dioxide with water. As the carbon dioxide diffuses from the tissues into the blood, the acidity of the blood increases. This increased acidity is detected by the chemoreceptors in the respiratory center of the brain (medulla), and the rate and depth of breathing is increased until the acidity is reduced to normal levels.

Atmospheric air contains about 0.04% carbon dioxide at a partial pressure of 0.0004 ATA. The partial pressure of carbon dioxide in our lungs is normally 0.05 ATA, the extra being that produced by our body. The carbon dioxide levels in the lungs and arterial blood are identical and are slightly lower than that in the venous blood. The body regulates breathing to maintain these levels at about 0.05 ATA.

When we exercise our circulation increases and more carbon dioxide is produced. The breathing rate increases and flushes out this excess carbon dioxide.

CARBON DIOXIDE BUILD UP DURING DIVING

An excess of carbon dioxide in the blood is called "hypercapnia". Hypercapnia can be caused by any interference with the process of carbon dioxide transport and elimination.

If the same amount of work is done at depth as at the surface, exactly the same amount of carbon dioxide is produced no matter what depth a diver is at. However, diving is often hard work so a lot of carbon dioxide is produced. If this is eliminated adequately, as is usually easily done on land, no problems will arise. At times it can be difficult to eliminate carbon dioxide effectively while diving and this can create some potentially serious problems.

Being immersed means that you have to work harder to breathe, using a regulator means that you have to work harder to breathe. Breathing compressed air means breathing dense gas, which makes more work for the respiratory muscles. All these increase the production of carbon dioxide. The processes are explained in Chapter 2.2.

Deep diving usually means that your regulator is not so easy to breathe from as it is nearer to the surface. The denser gas cannot flow so quickly due to increased resistance in the airways and equipment. This limits the amount of air a diver can get from his regulator, and it requires more work to get it. So, again, there is extra carbon dioxide production and difficulty in getting it out of the body. This problem is magnified by the increased breathing resistance of a poorly adjusted or poorly maintained regulator.

The increased respiratory dead space created by a regulator may allow some expired carbon dioxide to be rebreathed. Although this only happens to a small extent with the masks and regulators normally used by recreational divers, it is a serious consideration for divers using closed or semi-closed rebreathing equipment. It can also occur during helmet diving if the gas flow is insufficient to remove the diver's expired carbon dioxide.

When we dive, the increased pressure causes more oxygen to dissolve in plasma. This **dissolved oxygen supplies a larger part of the tissue's requirements. This means that less hemoglobin-bonded oxygen is required, so less "free" hemoglobin is available to transport carbon dioxide back to the lungs.** Higher venous carbon dioxide levels result.

At depth, the carbon dioxide in the breathing air is breathed at higher partial pressures and this adds to the impaired expiration of carbon dioxide from the lungs. In addition, **if a diver's air supply has been contaminated with extra carbon dioxide the consequences may be disastrous.** For example if a cylinder contains 2% carbon dioxide relatively little effect might be noticed on the surface, but at 130 ft (39 m) the partial pressure of carbon dioxide in the lungs would be about 0.10 ATA. This can cause a diver to go unconscious.

If a diver works hard at depth, so increasing carbon dioxide production even more, he can get into trouble with high blood carbon dioxide levels. High carbon dioxide levels make nitrogen narcosis worse and increase the effects of oxygen toxicity. It also may increase heat loss, alter the heart rhythm and has been accused of predisposing to bends. **If the carbon dioxide level gets too high, and it can on deep SCUBA dives, the diver may go unconscious without warning.** Unconsciousness underwater usually means drowning.

Some individuals tend to retain more carbon dioxide than others and may, consequently, be more at risk of suffering the ill-effects of hypercapnia.

Carbon dioxide retaining has been studied in a few divers over time. Some studies indicated that SCUBA divers may develop a reduced responsiveness to carbon dioxide and, at rest, higher carbon dioxide levels than non-divers.[1] It appears to be a consequence of tolerating the higher carbon dioxide levels due to equipment design during dives. This is more pronounced in certain individuals. Respiratory adaptation to carbon dioxide can affect both state of consciousness and heart rhythm, and a diver would be more subject to loss of consciousness if he were insensitive to carbon dioxide. SCUBA divers who "skip breathe" in an attempt to conserve air put themselves at risk.

Hypercapnia is obviously an important factor that any diver, especially one who tends to dive deeper, should be aware of.

Carbon dioxide acts as a respiratory stimulant and can cause depression of the nervous system. The effect depends on the levels of carbon dioxide in the blood. The rapid breathing caused by hypercapnia can warn a diver of increasing carbon dioxide levels but, if he is exercising, the symptom can be masked by the increased breathing due to the exercise (due, in part, to higher carbon dioxide levels).

CARBON DIOXIDE TOXICITY

If allowed to accumulate in the body, carbon dioxide will exert a toxic effect when a sufficient quantity is present.

SIGNS AND SYMPTOMS

The signs and symptoms of carbon dioxide toxicity depend on the rate of build-up of the carbon dioxide and the amount of carbon dioxide present.

A rapid build-up may cause a diver to become unconscious without any prior warning signs or symptoms except for a desire to breathe deeper and faster.

A gradual build-up, which is more likely to occur with recreational SCUBA diving, will normally cause various other symptoms before loss of consciousness would occur.

As the carbon dioxide level gradually increases the first sign is often an increase in the depth and rate of breathing. *Shortness of breath with rapid, deep breathing occurs*.

As the level continues to increase, the blood vessels dilate and the pulse rate and blood pressure rise. *A throbbing headache*, usually at the front of the head, results from the dilation of blood vessels in the brain. The headache can be severe and can last for many hours after a dive.

The increased breathing rate and throbbing headache are the two symptoms of carbon dioxide excess commonly encountered by sport divers.

If the level continues to rise *dizziness, nausea, confusion, unsteadiness, disorientation and restlessness result. The diver may become flushed and his face may feel warm. Lightheadedness, muscle twitches and jerks, reduced vision, unconsiousness, tremors and convulsions* may occur as the level continues to increase.

A further increase produces depression of the nervous system which reduces the pulse rate, blood pressure and breathing rate. Death can occur and is usually from the stoppage of breathing or the heart.

Although death can occur in rare cases, recovery from carbon dioxide toxicity is the rule.

FIRST AID

In severe cases:

* Remove the diver from the toxic environment
* Monitor the airway, breathing and circulation and resuscitate if necessary.
* Give 100 % oxygen, if available
* Seek medical aid

Milder cases:

If a diver develops symptoms of carbon dioxide toxicity he should immediately **stop moving, take deep, regular breaths and try to relax. The dive should be terminated and the diver should return to the surface with as little effort as possible.** The buoyancy compensator can be carefully adjusted to maintain slight positive buoyancy. This will allow the diver to ascend with the minimum of finning and the consequent exertion.

Once on the surface the diver should be allowed to breathe fresh air, and any tight clothing should be loosened or removed.

100% oxygen can be given, if available. Although it is not clear why it should provide relief from the direct effects of carbon dioxide toxicity, divers have often reported an improvement in symptoms after breathing higher oxygen concentrations.

Ordinary analgesics may provide some relief from the headache.

PREVENTION

A certain amount of hypercapnia is inevitable in divers, especially those who dive deeper. Some of the extra breathing effort is unavoidable as it is inherent to breathing denser gas through a regulator. The degree of hypercapnia can be minimized by:

- Always breathing normally. Never try to conserve air by "skip breathing".
- Using a regulator which provides the minimum resistance to breathing. Some regulators perform far better than others in this respect. These are discussed in Chapter 28.1. Any regulator must be properly adjusted, maintained, and cleaned to minimize deposits of salt, sand and other foreign bodies which will affect its performance. Some unbalanced regulators are not suitable for deep diving as they become harder to breathe from as the cylinder pressure drops.
- Ensuring that the air supply is not contaminated.
- Minimizing exertion during a dive, especially a deep dive.

THE EFFECT OF HYPERCAPNIA ON OTHER DIVING DISORDERS

Hypercapnia has been known, or believed, to predispose various other diving ailments. Its influence on some of these conditions is discussed briefly in the following paragraphs.

Decompression sickness

High levels of carbon dioxide cause the blood vessels to dilate, increasing the blood flow to the body tissues. This vasodilatation will cause more nitrogen to be delivered to various tissues during a dive and, so, increase the potiential for bubble formation, unless overcome by the vasoconstriction of the peripheral vessels due to cold. In addition, extra carbon dioxide present will rapidly diffuse into and enlarge existing bubbles.

Nitrogen narcosis

Hypercapnia does appear to increase the narcotic effects of nitrogen. The depressive effects of both carbon dioxide and nitrogen combine to increase the narcosis.

Oxygen toxicity

Hypercapnia has been shown to increase the effects of oxygen toxicity. One explanation for this is that increased cerebral blood flow caused by hypercapnia increases the amount of oxygen delivered to the brain.

Hypothermia

Carbon dioxide accumulation in the body has severe effects on temperature regulation. When higher concentrations are reached heat production is impaired, while heat loss is increased due to the increased perfusion of the skin and limbs (unless vasodilation due to excess carbon dioxide is overcome by vasoconstriction due to cold).

LOW CARBON DIOXIDE LEVELS - HYPOCAPNIA

"Hypocapnia", which means low carbon dioxide levels usually occurs as a result of overbreathing (hyperventilation). Hyperventilation commonly occurs involuntarily in a anxiety or panic situation, but is at times done voluntarily by breath-hold divers in order to lengthen their breath-hold time.

Hyperventilation, whether voluntary or involuntary, reduces the carbon dioxide levels in the blood without significantly raising the blood oxygen levels. The lower carbon dioxide level delays the breathing stimulus and can allow blood oxygen levels to fall dangerously low before breathing is triggered. The low carbon dioxide level can further complicate the situation by constricting cerebral blood vessels and reducing the oxygen supply to the brain. After hyperventilation during a breath-hold dive, carbon dioxide may not rise quickly enough to stimulate breathing before loss of consciousness results from the low oxygen levels. The swimmer often drowns.

A SCUBA diver who is very anxious might begin to hyperventilate, but is unlikely to suffer significant hypocapnia, especially at depth. The extra carbon dioxide produced by breathing under pressure, and the higher oxygen partial pressures should prevent unconsciousness due to delayed breathing. However, hyperventilation before breath-hold diving has been known to cause a substantial number of cases of near-drowning and drowning. The diver goes unconscious due to hypoxia before, during or after the ascent.

SUMMARY

* High carbon dioxide levels can occur when diving due to:
  - increased breathing effort
  - poor ventilation
  - exertion
  - contamination of air supply
  - decreased carbon dioxide transport.

* The problem increases as the depth of the dive increases.

* Some divers are more susceptible.

* The most common manifestations of carbon dioxide toxicity are rapid, deep breathing and a throbbing headache, but other more severe symptoms can occur if the problem is allowed to continue.

* Hypercapnia is a potientially serious problem for a diver exerting himself at depth. It can cause a diver to lose consciousness underwater.

* First aid in severe cases involves removal from source of toxicity and supporting life. For mild cases, restict movement, breathe deeply and regularly and abort dive. Breathe fresh air or oxygen if available.

* Carbon dioxide toxicity can be minimized by breathing normally, using a good, well-maintained regulator, ensuring clean air, and avoiding exertion at depth.

* High carbon dioxide levels can predispose to bends, nitrogen narcosis, oxygen toxicity and hypothermia.

* Low carbon dioxide levels (hypocapnia) delay the breathing response and may cause hypoxia and consequent loss of consciousness. This is unlikely to occur during a SCUBA dive, especially a deeper dive, but it can result from hyperventilation before a breath-hold dive.

REFERENCES

1. Florio, J. et al (1979), "Breathing Pattern and Ventilatory Response to Carbon Dioxide in Divers". *Journal of Applied Physiology*; 46: 1076-1080.

OTHER SOURCES

Bayne, C. (1981), "Breath-hold Diving". In: *Hyperbaric and Undersea Medicine*, Davis, J. (ed), Medical Seminars Inc., California.

Dueker, C. (1985), "SCUBA Diving in Safety and Health". Madison Publishing Associates, California.

Edmonds, C. et al (1981), "Diving and Subaquatic Medicine", 2nd edition. Diving Medical Center, Sydney.

Lamphier, E. and Camporesi, E. (1982), "Respiration and Exercise". In: *The Physiology and Medicine of Diving*, 3rd edition, Bennett, P. and Elliott, D. (eds), Best Publishing Company, California.

Schaefer, K. (1975), "Carbon Dioxide Effects Under Conditions of Raised Environmental Pressure". In: *Physiology and Medicine of Diving and Compressed Air Work*, Bennett, P., and Elliott, D. (eds), 2nd edition, Balliere Tindall, London.

Thomas R. and McKenzie, B. (1981), "The Diver's Medical Companion". Diving Medical Center, Sydney.

RECOMMENDED FURTHER READING

Dueker, C. (1985), "SCUBA Diving in Safety and Health". Madison Publishing Associates, California.

Lamphier, E. and Camporesi, E. (1982), "Respiration and Exercise". In: *The Physiology and Medicine of Diving*, 3rd edition, Bennett, P. and Elliott, D. (ed), Best Publishing Company, California.

CHAPTER 8

HEAT LOSS

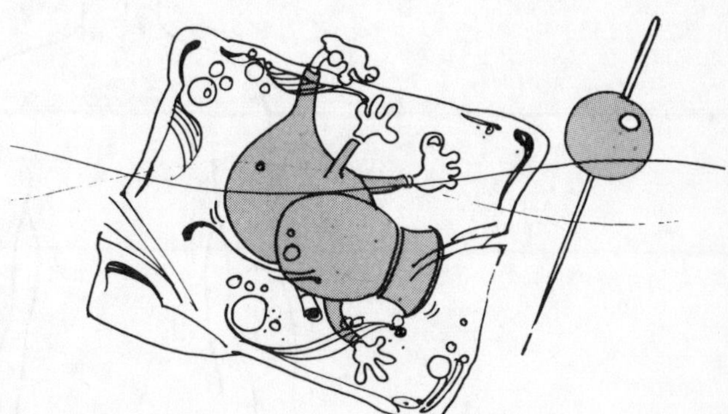

TEMPERATURE REGULATION

All animals have an ideal internal temperature where they function most effectively. Below that temperature their muscles are sluggish, nerve impulses travel slowly and thought processes are slowed down. If it gets cold enough the animal is unable to continue activities, sits down, goes unconscious and dies.

Man is a warm-blooded animal and, as such, attempts to maintain a constant body temperature. Cold-blooded animals, such as reptiles, vary their temperature with the environment. Man evolved in the tropics where, being in the sun, the problem was heat gain with exercise. So we evolved an excellent heat loss system, based on radiation, convection and sweating. Radiation is heat going from a warm body to cooler surroundings. Convection is the process of air movement upwards when it is heated. The warm air rises and sucks cool air in from the side to replace it. This air is then warmed and rises and the process continues. Sweating causes heat loss because turning liquid water into water vapor needs heat. Water on the skin, or on clothes, gets that heat from the body.

The human body copes with cold by vasoconstriction and and increased heat output.

Heat loss is controlled by reducing blood flow to the skin and limbs. The blood vessels to the skin constrict first, followed by those deeper in the arms and legs. This vasoconstriction effectively reduces heat loss from the torso and limbs, but heat can still be lost from other areas. The areas of the body where heat loss is greatest without insulation are the head, the base of the neck over the carotid arteries, the armpits and the groins. The superficial blood vessels in the face and scalp do not vasoconstrict in response to cold and it has been estimated that, in a fully vasconstricted adult, 40% or more of the total heat lost in a cold environment can occur from the scalp, face and neck. In the neck, armpits and groin vasoconstiction is poor and the major arteries are near to the surface, thereby facilitating heat loss.*

* When the skin temperature falls below about 50°F (10°C), blood vessels to the extremities may dilate for a while before constricting again. It has been suggested that this cold vasodilation (which may help to prevent frostbite) increases heat loss from areas where it occurs, but current research suggests that this effect is either minimal or does not occur.

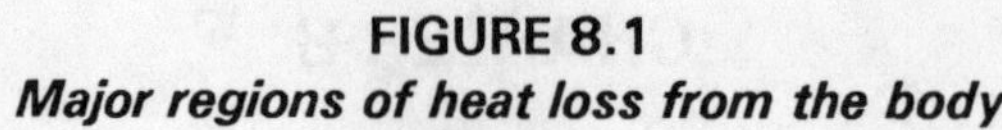

FIGURE 8.1
Major regions of heat loss from the body

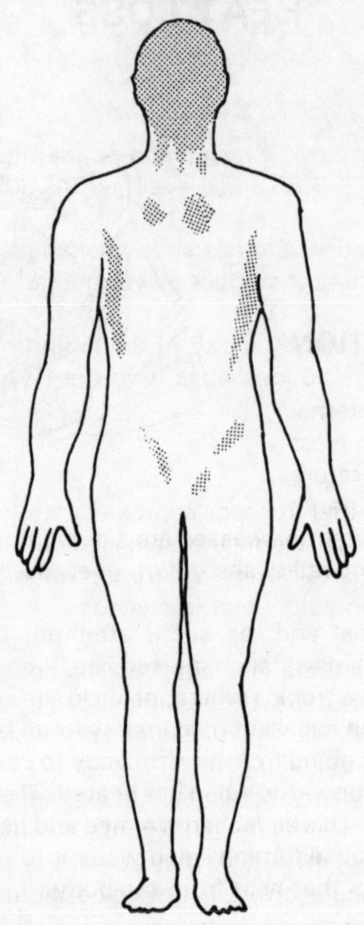

Note: Although it has generally been believed that the armpits and the sides of the chest are areas of high heat loss, there is currently some doubt whether or not this is true.

If heat loss continues the body increases heat production by shivering. Shivering can increase the basal heat output more than fivefold, but shivering stops after a few hours of exposure due to exhaustion and depletion of muscle energy supplies. So this system is not adequate to preserve body temperature for long periods, except in hot areas. To spread across the world man needed insulation (clothes) to retain heat, and fire. In cold, wet, windy conditions once one's insulation is wet, evaporation from the wet insulation draws heat from the body.

HEAT BALANCE

Our internal temperature depends on the balance between heat gain and heat loss. The body has a basal heat output due to the activity of the internal organs such as the heart, liver, respiratory muscles, kidneys and gut in the torso (the core), and from the brain. Heat gain is mostly by muscular contraction.

The normal body "core temperature", which is the temperature of the vital organs, ranges from 96.5°F (35.8°C) to 100°F (37.8°C) and averages 98.6°F (37°C).

Heat loss is influenced by insulation. Clothes act by holding layers of air still over the body, reducing radiation, convection and the effect of sweating.

Human heat regulation is controlled by a part of the brain (the hypothalamus) in response to blood temperature variations and messages from the skin.

HEAT LOSS IN WATER

Heat loss is much increased in water. It needs approximately 1,000 times more heat to warm a given volume of water than to warm the same volume of air. Water conducts heat approximately 23 times faster than air. Heat loss from conduction is increased fivefold in wet clothing and twenty-threefold in cold water immersion.

When we first enter the water there is a high rate of heat loss which decreases when vasoconstriction occurs. **The rate of heat loss is influenced by water temperature, insulation, movement, heat production and, for divers, gas density which depends on depth.**

Adequate insulation allows a balance between heat loss and heat production. Movement, by changing the water that has been warmed by contact with the skin, increases heat loss. So, unless you are well insulated, swimming may actually speed up heat loss in spite of the extra heat generated by the muscular effort. It is often better for a submerged person to avoid moving and huddle into a ball, the Heat Exchange Lessening Posture (HELP), than to try to swim. By tucking the upper arms tightly against the sides of the chest, the forearms over the front, the thighs tucked to protect the groin and keeping the head out of the water, heat is conserved in these areas of greatest heat loss. The buoyancy compensater should be inflated the keep the head out of the water, and the mask left in place to keep spray off the face (Figure 8.2). It has been reported that a person can increase cold water survival time by up to 50% by adopting this position.[1]

FIGURE 8.2
The H.E.L.P. position

A diver's air supply is at sea temperature and has to be warmed to body temperature in the lungs. Each molecule has to be warmed and, as you go deeper, the gas becomes denser and there are more molecules to be warmed. So **a diver loses more heat from his lungs at depth.**

A wetsuit works by trapping a layer of water between the suit and the body. That layer of water warms up to skin temperature. The wetsuit prevents various currents that take heat away from the bare-skinned swimmer. The air in the fabric of the wetsuit, which is a mass of bubbles of nitrogen or air in rubber, acts as an efficient insulator and reduces heat loss. **A diver must wear a hood in cold water.** The head is about ten percent of the body's surface area, and more than half of the head is scalp. **Since the blood vessels in the scalp do not constrict with cold, and because so much blood passes through the head, a lot of heat will be lost if a hood is not worn.** Someone in a well-fitting wetsuit, that does not allow water to move in and out with each movement, can stay quite warm for some time. **The wetsuit is an excellent insulator on the surface but it compresses with depth and becomes a less efficient insulator the deeper a diver goes** (Figure 28.2.1). The use of a wetsuit, by increasing the the insulation around a diver, retains a lot more of the heat generated. However, **a wetsuit does not stop heat loss, it only reduces it.**

A wet wetsuit out of the water can cool the diver by evaporation. The wind-chill effect magnifies this problem. In cold weather it is a good idea to wear a waterproof and windproof jacket to, and from, the dive site.

A drysuit works by trapping a layer of warm air, rather than water, around the diver's body. Air conducts heat away from the body far slower than water does, so as long as the dry suit is functioning properly the diver will stay very warm. A dry-suited diver still needs a hood in cold water. A constant volume dry suit will still insulate well at depth.

As depth increases the water temperature decreases and, at times, if a "thermocline" is present, the temperature drop can be dramatic. Some waters, especially still waters, may have levels of vastly different temperatures. These layers are called "thermoclines". A thermocline is related to seasonal changes, wind conditions, currents, depths and water density. Generally, the water is much colder in the deeper level and this is where the diver's wetsuit is thinner and provides less insulation.

WATER CONTACT REFLEXES

There are a number of reflexes that occur when cold water touches the skin. If the face (the nose and mouth especially) is put into cold water, the body often responds by slowing the heartbeat (bradycardia) and stopping the breathing (apnoea). The bradycardia is known as the diving reflex, and is found to some extent in all mammals and birds. In the *true* diving reflex (not necessarily in we humans), with this bradycardia goes vasoconstiction of everything except the vessels supplying the brain, heart and lungs. This restricts the supply of oxygenated blood to vital organs and increases the survival time without breathing.

Some people suffer from a very dangerous reflex if they fall into very cold water. They develop very rapid and deep breathing which is quite beyond their control. This is sometimes combined with an inability to move. This situation could very likely prove fatal to a diver unless he had a regulator in his mouth and a buddy nearby and/or an inflated buoyancy compensator.

ACCLIMATIZATION TO COLD

Although it appears as though humans do not develop strong adaptive responses to cold, some acclimatization to cold has been observed in a number of groups of individuals exposed to cold environmental conditions for extended periods of time. The adaptation to cold appears to result from combinations of a variety of different physiological responses to cold which may include increased peripheral vasoconstriction, increased shivering, increased metabolic rate and increased subcutaneous (under the skin) insulation.

A 1958 study of Australian aborigines who, until relatively recently slept naked near camp fires, showed that their skin temperatures dropped during the night but their metabolic rates did not increase. However, Caucasians exposed to the same cold stress responded with increased shivering.[2]

Europeans, exposed to cold for six weeks, experienced a 50% increase in their metabolic rates during sleep, and maintained their skin temperature.[3]

Early studies of the Ama divers of Korea, women who for many years wore cotton bathing suits and dived in waters as cold as 50°F (10°C) during winter, showed that they developed a greater body tissue insulation and did not begin to shiver until reaching lower water and skin temperatures than the non-diving control group. It appeared that the divers had learned to restrict their cutaneous circulation better than the non-divers. Although these responses suggested an insulative acclimatization, the Ama also increased their basal metabolic rate by 30% during winter. However, since the Ama began wearing wetsuits, they appear to have lost their adaptation and their responses to cold are now comparable to those of non-diving Korean women. It took five years to lose all the cold adaptation changes they had acquired when diving without wetsuits.[4]

Other studies found that SCUBA divers, exposed to either cold[5] or relatively warm[6] water for extended periods, maintained their core temperatures without increasing their metabolic rates substantially, and did not begin to shiver until reaching lower water and skin temperatures than control subjects. There appeared to be either an increased vasoconstriction or increased efficiency of heat exchange within the body.

It has also been observed that, during the winter months, if a person is regularly exposed to the cold some acclimatization occurs.[7]

HYPOTHERMIA

Hypothermia is when the body's internal temperature drops to a level which causes unwanted changes. Medically it means a drop in body temperature from 98.6°F to about 95°F (37°C to 35°C) or lower.

SIGNS AND SYMPTOMS

The first symptom of heat loss is *feeling cold, especially in the extremities.* Normal skin temperature in cool weather is 90-93°F (32-34°C), which can drop to 70-73°F (21-23°C) before core cooling begins. *Numbness, blueness, pallor or blotching of the skin, especially of the hands, feet and earlobes* occur as the blood vessels to these areas begin to constrict.* *Pain* is sometimes felt in the extremities. The cold affects the transmission of nerve impulses down nerves, and also affects the rate of contraction of muscles. The combination results in malfunction and *difficulty in fine movements* and, as one grows colder, the grosser movements get affected as well. As one's fingers go numb the sensation of touch is impaired, and fine movements are soon impaired. A simple task such as adjusting a mask strap may become more difficult. At this stage the body core temperature may still be normal but, by the time shivering begins, significant body cooling has already occurred. Other responses to cold include shivering, increased heart rate, elevated blood sugar and increased release of adrenal hormones. The initial *shivering* can be suppressed if the diver makes a conscious effort. A diver who is exerting himself might not shiver at this stage because of the muscular activity of exertion. As cooling continues shivering increases. **If the diver does not stop the heat loss *uncontrollable shivering* might occur. A diver should get out of the water before this happens.**

* The cheeks may remain quite red due to the lack of vasoconstriction of blood vessels in the face.

Uncontrollable shivering severely reduces co-ordination and can make it difficult to hold the mouth-piece in place. *A diver who does not shiver in spite of being very cold is already, or is at risk of, suffering severe hypothermia* as the body is not replacing the lost heat. A person under the influence of alcohol often will not shiver as the body has a false sense of warmth. If heat loss continues *weakness* or *fatigue* may set in and make swimming far more difficult. As the brain cools mental changes begin to occur. At this stage the core temperature will have dropped under 95°F (35°C). *Slowness of thought, confusion, slurred speech, inco-ordination, impairment of rational thought and memory, and apathy* may occur. **Cold induced mental changes are probably the danger to the diver because once the brain does not work properly wrong decisions can easily be made. The diver may ignore threats to his safety and finally, realizing the danger, may be unable to rectify the situation because of the loss of power and dexterity in his hands.**

If cooling continues and the core temperature drops below about 90°F (32°C), the symptoms will rapidly become far more severe. *Shivering often stops* and *muscles become increasingly rigid*. The patient's pupils may become dilated. He may lapse into *semi-consciousness* and the *pulse and breathing slow down*. The blood volume is reduced causing the blood to thicken and become sticky, and various chemical changes occur in the blood which, together with the cold, will affect the function of the heart and other major organs. The *heartbeat may become irregular and ventricular fibrillation can occur if the heart is irritated*. The victim is usually *unconscious* by this stage. Further cooling will cause ventricular fibrillation and subsequent *death*.

The above sequence of events describes the development of hypothermia when the heat loss is relatively rapid. However a "silent" or "undetected" hypothermia sometimes results from the long, slow body cooling that may follow several days of diving in water temperatures as high as 81°F (27°C), or higher. It is not uncommon for recreational divers to complain about getting colder towards the end of several days of tropical diving.

This slow cooling may result in reduced performance, fatigue, loss of motivation and impairment of thinking. Some authorities believe that long, slow cooling of the body does not stimulate shivering and the subsequent heat re-generation. As a result the diver might not notice the heat drain from his body until significant hypothermia has developed and shivering finally occurs. Some consider this "silent" hypothermia to be the major hazard to the diver in cold water, as it will make the diver more accident prone without him being aware of it. In commercial diving, investigators have implicated cold as a major cause of diving casualties, particularly the silent, progressive onset of hypothermia of which the diver is not aware.

FIRST AID

First aid for hypothermia must be rapid in order to prevent further heat loss. Mild hypothermia can become far more severe within minutes if heat loss is allowed to continue. The first aid is designed to initially stop the heat loss and then either warm the patient, or allow him to rewarm by himself. Experts disagree about whether or not to actively rewarm a hypothermic patient and, if so, how this can best be done. The debate is primarily about the treatment of a person with severe hypothermia. Some experts feel that it is best to insulate the person and allow them to warm up on their own, while others argue that extra heat should be added, and debate various ways this can best be done. The first aid and treatment must minimize further cooling and some argue that often the only effective way to do this is by adding heat (active rewarming).

It has been observed that, once a drop in core temperature (measured rectally) occurs, it continues to fall for the first 10-20 minutes after rewarming begins. This "afterdrop" has been seen to occur no matter what method of rewarming is used, but appeared to be reduced if the patient was rapidly rewarmed. This provided one of the main arguments for actively rewarming a patient (e.g. placing them in a warm to hot bath).* Afterdrop has been blamed for the sudden collapse and, in some cases, subsequent death of some casualties while being rewarmed. It has been claimed that, when the constricted vessels supplying the skin and limbs dilate as the skin is warmed, the cold blood that has been trapped in these vessels returns to the core, cools the circulating blood, at times further destabilizing the heart and precipitating ventricular fibrillation. It was hoped that warming the blood trapped in the periphery would minimize this effect. However, severely vasoconsticted limbs contain little blood and it appears likely that the after drop is mainly caused by heat being drawn away from the core in order to warm cooler adjacent tissues. In addition, current evidence indicates that afterdrop is largely a rectal temperature phenomenon. When the temperature of the heart is measured, the afterdrop is either much less than measured rectally, or absent. It is likely that early rewarming death results from a different mechansim. When the constricted blood vessels reopen during rewarming, blood pressure is reduced and, since the blood volume is already low from the effects of hypothermia, the heart must work hard to restore blood pressure. The cold heart may not be capable of this increased effort and may fibrillate.

The rapid vasodilation and subsequent drop in blood pressure is one of the arguments used against active rewarming. In addition, there are a number of other problems associated with placing an unconsious, or unstable, patient in a hot bath. Other researchers have suggested that it may be better to rewarm the patient more gently by placing warm objects (such as heat packs or hot water bottles) around the areas of greatest heat loss such as the head, neck and groin. However, there is some evidence that this may in fact hinder the rewarming process by inhibiting the shivering response. Skin temperature receptors are more sensititve to a change in temperature than to the absolute temperature and it is possible to have a dropping core temperature without shivering, or an excessive sensation of feeling cold. So, a slight increase in surface temperature may make a patient feel warmer, so inhibiting shivering but allowing the core temperature to fall further. This has led some experts to recommend that no external heat be added to many hypothermic patients, especially in the field. They argue that all living animals generate heat and, despite a large drop in core temperature, if *adequately* insulated hypothermic patients should rewarm spontaneously.

In light of the above arguments, *probably the safest action for a first-aider to take in the field is to minimize further heat loss by ensuring that the patient is adequately insulated, and allowing slow, passive warming of a hypothermic victim.*[8]

* However, some other evidence indicated that various rewarming methods alter the rate of reversal but do not alter the magnitude of the afterdrop in any case.

Cold

When a diver feels cold and his extremities are beginning to go blue and numb, and/or he is beginning to shiver, he should get out of the water, shelter from the wind and, if possible, replace the wetsuit with warm, dry clothing. A warm, non-alcoholic drink will help rewarm him and a warm shower may provide relief. Alcohol should never be taken as it increases the blood flow to the skin and extremities and may, therefore, increase heat loss. As previously mentioned, alcohol can also suppress shivering.

If no dry clothing is available then leave the diver in his wetsuit, wipe excess water off the surface of his wetsuit and cover him with a windproof layer to prevent evaporation from the wetsuit. A windproof jacket, a large sheet of plastic, or very large plastic bag(s) are suitable. Exercise can also be effective and is not contraindicated if the diver is not exhausted and is walking, well and not significantly hypothermic. However, one must beware of the risk of decompression sickness after diving, and exercise can only be considered for someone who is cold and ***not*** hypothermic.

If correct action is taken at this stage heat loss should be stopped and the diver should not become hypothermic.

Mild Hypothermia

Many of the signs and symptoms of mild hypothermia are similar to those of cold, the difference being the degree. When a cold diver begins to shiver his core temperature has already dropped significantly and, if the shivering becomes uncontrollable and/or the diver becomes unco-ordinated he may be assumed to be suffering from mild hypothermia.

The diver must be removed from the water and protected from the cold, wind and/or rain. If conditions allow and suitable dry clothes or other coverings are available, the wetsuit should be carefully removed and the diver dried and covered warmly. Ensure that the head and neck are protected. The diver can then be placed in an exposure bag, a large plastic bag(s), or wrapped in a space blanket or other plastic sheet if available. Blankets can then be wrapped around to further insulate the diver and another plastic covering can be used to keep the blankets dry if necessary. If no other insulation is available, a number of people dressed in warm, dry clothing, can huddle around the patient.* As the blood vessels to the limbs and skin begin to dilate the blood pressure may drop, so the hypothermic patient should be kept laying down with the legs slighly raised and movement should be minimized to avoid shock.

Warm, sweet, non-alcoholic drinks should be given as long as the patient is not shivering uncontrollably, has a clear and stable level of consciousness and the ability to swallow. Coffee, or other high-caffeine drinks, should not be given as they may stimulate a potentially unstable heart.

* It has often been suggested that bare skin to skin contact is desirable. However, while skin warmth may feel good, it may sometimes reduce shivering and so reduce net heat gain despite temporary improvement in comfort.

If no dry coverings are available or if it is impractical to remove the wetsuit (as may sometimes be the case on a small boat) the wetsuit should be left in place, excess water wiped off its surface and the diver covered and protected from the elements. Plastic bags/sheets and blankets can be used. The wetsuit will provide reasonable insulation as long as it is covered with a windpoof layer to prevent evaporation. It also provides pressure to help counteract the blood pooling effect of vasodilatation when the diver rewarms.

The patient should not be placed near a fire or similar heat source, should not be massaged and should not have a warm shower or bath. He should be placed in a comfortable environment, kept dry, well insulated and laying down, monitored carefully and allowed to rewarm spontaneously. If his condition worsens medical aid should be sought immediately.

Severe Hypothermia

If the diver is very cold and has slow, weak vital signs, altered level of consciousness including slurred speech, staggering gait, decreased mental skills and/or no shivering in spite of being really cold he should be suspected of suffering from severe hypothermia.

Handle the diver very gently and carefully remove him and protect him from the cold environment. ***Send for medical assistance immediately.***

Carefully assess the presence or absence of breathing and pulse for up to two minutes. Both may be hard to detect as they can be very weak and slow. Listen closely to the nose and mouth, feel for the breath and look for chest and/or abdomen movement. Feel for the carotid (neck) and/or femoral pulse (groin). It is unlikely that a radial (wrist) pulse will be detectable due to the reduced blood flow to the limbs. If it is necessary to remove the patient's wetsuit it must be done gently, avoiding unnecessary manipulation of the throat and limbs. The patient's heart will be unstable and rough handling, especially pressure on the neck, armpits or groin, may precipitate ventricular fibrillation. The best way to remove the suit is to carefully cut it off, especially the hood and/or neck section.

There are two schools of thought on whether or not a severely hypothermic patient without vital signs (i.e. "apparently dead") should be resuscitated before being rewarmed. Some believe that although the vital signs may be undetectable adequate respiration and circulation may still be present and, if resuscitation is begun, the patient's heart will probably be sent into ventricular fibrillation. They argue that in the absence of vital signs rescuscitation should be delayed until the patient has been rewarmed. If no vital signs are apparent after rewarming, resuscitation should begin.

The other school of thought, which is probably more relevant to the diving situation, suggests that a rescuer should spend up to about two minutes looking for vital signs before commencing CPR if indicated. There is little controversy about this advice in the case of a witnessed submersion. **However, if resuscitation is commenced it should be continued until the body core temperature has returned to near normal (98.6°F/37°C).** If CPR is applied it should be applied at the normal rates as there seems to be little benefit in further reducing the efficiency of only moderately efficient techniques by reducing the rates of ventilation and/or compression. If the submersion was not witnessed, the victim is apparently dead upon discovery and medical assistance is many hours away, it may sometimes be better not to begin CPR but instead to insulate the patient, maintain a patent airway and get him to medical aid as soon as possible. In this case, possibly the victim's best chance lies in the existance of undetectable life.

If resuscitation is not required, the diver should be dried off and insulated as described previously. Give warm, sweet, non-alcoholic drinks as, and when, described previously. Keep monitoring the patient. ***Ensure medical assistance is given as soon as possible.***

Once the patient is in hospital there are a number of ways that heat can be added. These include warming the gases (air or oxygen) the casualty breathes, putting the trunk in a warm bath and gradually raising the temperature, hot compresses to the chest, giving hot intravenous fluid and passing hot water through the stomach. The heart and blood chemistry are carefully monitored throughout.

When treating a person with hypothermia **do not:**

- exercise or massage them
- give alcohol or coffee (or other high-caffeine drinks)
- put patient in front of a fire or heater or in a shower or bath
- give oxygen, unless it is externally warmed. Oxygen is cool when breathed from a regulator. Breathing cool oxygen will further cool the patient.

Note:

Casualties have at times made dramatic and successful recoveries after resuscitation following long periods (up to 60 minutes) of immersion without breathing in very cold water. The lower oxygen usage resulting from the reduced blood flow to the non-vital organs (diving reflex) and slowed metabolic rate from hypothermia, together with the higher oxygen partial pressures associated with depth, have been used to explain this phenomenon.

In one series of 50 cases of individuals who had been submerged in cold water for periods of between six to sixty minutes, 45 had suffered no detectable neurological impairment after being resuscitated and rewarmed.[8]

It is recommended that resuscitation and rewarming be attempted on any casualty who has been submerged for up to 60 minutes in water of 70°F (21°C) or cooler.

PREVENTION

Hypothermia can be prevented by:

* Wearing an adequate wetsuit. A hood is essential in cold water and gloves and boots are also necessary to maintain dexterity in the hands and prevent cramping in the feet.

* Increasing subcutaneous layers of fat. Fat has a lower thermal conductivity than muscle. Lean people are more prone to hypothermia than those with a more generous subcutaneous fat layer.*

* Reducing exercise in water to reduce heat loss through convection.

* Reducing dive time if getting cold. If possible leave the water when, or before, the hands or feet begin to get numb and/or blue.

* Leave the water if noticing difficulty in performing routine tasks, confusion, or a tendency to repeat tasks or procedures.

* However, this is normally not recommended on general health grounds.

* Leave the water if noticing feelings of being chilled followed by intermittent shivering, even though routine tasks can still be done.

* Adopting the H.E.L.P. position if stranded in the water.

* Refraining from further dives until adequately rewarmed. Divers often disregard the cumulative effects of repetitive diving. After the initial dive a diver might experience superficial skin rewarming and thus feel warmer. However, his core temperature may still be reduced. **Feeling warm is no guarantee that your heat losses have been replaced. The best way to show that your heat losses have been replaced is to start sweating**. This shows that the body needs to lose heat.

* Never drink alcohol before diving. Alcohol may cause an initial sensation of warmth by causing the superficial skin blood vessels to dilate, increasing the blood flow to the skin. Although at times this vasodilation due to alcohol appears to be overridden by vasoconstiction due to cold, this is often not the case and increased circulation to the skin may markedly contribute to heat loss. Alcohol also impairs the shivering response, and reduces the effect of the diving reflex, which would otherwise offer some protection to the hypothermic diver.

It is easy to recognize that hands and feet are cold by the familiar sensations of discomfort, numbness, pain and diminished usefulness. However, a loss of body heat is difficult to recognize and individuals are usually poor judges of their own thermal state. The ability to think clearly and rationally is affected seriously by cold.

The risks of hypothermia to a diver are not normally those of death through heart irregularities brought on by cold. They are much more the risks of cold-induced errors due to clumsiness in muscles, clumsiness in thinking, inappropriate thoughts, and, if the person does go unconscious from cold, drowning through loss of protective reflexes.

SUMMARY

* The human body copes with cold by vasoconstriction and increased heat output.

* The areas of greatest heat loss are the head, neck, and groin.

* The normal core temperature is around 98.6°F (37°C).

* As water conducts heat far better than air does, heat is rapidly lost from a submerged body.

* The rate of heat loss from a diver depends on water temperature, movement, heat production, insulation and depth.

* A well-fitting wetsuit reduces heat loss. A hood is essential in cold water.

* A wetsuit compresses at depth and thus does not insulate as well as in the shallows.

* A wet wetsuit out of the water cools the diver by evaporation.

* Although it appears as though humans do not develop strong adaptive responses to cold, some acclimatization to cold has been observed after extended periods of time.

* Hypothermia is when the body core temperature drops below about 95°F (35°C).

* Signs and symptoms of mild hypothermia include feeling cold, numbness and blueness of extremities and profuse shivering.

* If heat loss is not stopped mild hypothermia can rapidly develop into severe hypothermia.

* Symptoms of a more severe hypothermia include mental changes, muscle rigidity, no shivering despite being very cold, unconsciousness, heart irregularities and death.

* Mental impairment is probably the greatest threat to the diver as it leads to inappropriate decisions and actions.

* First aid for hypothermia is aimed at stopping further heat loss and, in severe cases, preserving life until proper medical assistance is available.

* Hypothermia can usually be prevented by wearing adequate insulation, and leaving the water and drying off before shivering begins.

REFERENCES

1. Department of Transport, Australia (1981), "Safety for Small Craft". Australian Government Printing Service, Canberra.

2. Scholander, P. et al (1958), "Cold adaptation in Australian aborigines". *Journal of Applied Physiology;* 13: 211-218.

3. Scholander, P. et al (1958), "Metabolic accimatization to cold in man". *Journal of Applied Physiology; 12: 1-8.*

4. Hong, S. (1984), "Cold Adaptation in Humans - A Lesson from Korean Women Divers". *SPUMS Journal;* 14 (2): 6-8.

5. Skreslet, S. and Arefjord, F. (1968), "Acclimatization to cold in man induced by frequent SCUBA diving in cold water". *Journal of Applied Physiology;* 24 (2): 177-181.

6. Hanna, J. and Hong, S. (1972), "Critical water temperature and effective insulation in SCUBA divers in Hawaii". *Journal of Applied Physiology*; 33 (6): 770-773.

7. Davies, T. and Johnston, D. (1961), "Seasonal acclimatization to cold in man". *Journal of Applied Physiology*; 16: 231-234.

8. Millar, I. (1990), "Cold and the Diver". *SPUMS Journal*; 20 (1): 33-39.

OTHER SOURCES

Auerbach, P. (1989), "Hypothermia and the Scuba Diver". *The Undersea Journal*; First Quarter, PADI, California.

Edmonds, C. et al (1981), "Diving and Subaquatic Medicine", 2nd edition. Diving Medical Center, Sydney.

Froese, G. and Burton, A. (1957), "Heat loss from the human head". *Journal of Appl Physiol*; 10: 235-241.

Harnett, R. et al (1983), "A Review of the Literature Concerning Resuscitation from Hypothermia: Part 1 - The Problem and General Approaches". *Aviat. Space and Environ. Med.*; 54 (5): 425-434.

Harnett, R. et al (1983), "A Review of the Literature Concerning Resuscitation from Hypothermia: Part 11 - Selected Rewarming Protocols''. *Aviat. Space and Environ. Med.*; 54 (6): 487-495.

Haymes, E. and Wells, C. (1986), "Environment and Human Performance". Human Kinetics, Illinois.

Keatinge, W. (1969), "Survival in Cold Water". Blackwell Scientific Publications, Oxford.

Millar, I., personal communications.

Miller, J. (ed) (1979), "NOAA Diving Manual", 2nd edition. U.S. Dept of Commerce.

Pozos, R. and Wittmers, L. (eds) (1983), "The Nature and Treatment of Hypothermia", Vol. 2. University of Minnesota Press, Minneapolis.

Samuelson, T. et al (1982), "Hypothermia and Cold Water Near Drowning'': Treatment Guidelines". *Alaska Medicine*; 24 (6): 106-111.

Webb, P. (1982), "Thermal Problems". In: *The Physiology and Medicine of Diving*, 3rd edition, Bennett, P. and Elliott, D. (eds), Best Publishing Company, California.

RECOMMENDED FURTHER READING

Edmonds, C. et al (1981), "Diving and Subaquatic Medicine", 2nd edition. Diving Medical Center, Sydney.

Haymes, E. and Wells, C. (1986), "Environment and Human Performance". Human Kinetics, Illinois.

Millar, I. (1990), "Cold and the Diver". *SPUMS Journal*; 20 (1): 33-39.

Samuelson, T. et al (1982), "Hypothermia and Cold Water Near Drowning: Treatment Guidelines". *Alaska Medicine*; 24 (6): 106-111.

CHAPTER 9

DYSBARIC OSTEONECROSIS

Exposure to compressed air at high pressure is known to be associated with the death of portions of the long bones of the arms and legs. The dying-off of bone tissue is known as **bone necrosis.**

Bone necrosis has been associated with conditions unrelated to diving. It has been seen with diseases such as diabetes, where there is a disorder of the fat metabolism. Fatty acids, released from the fat in the bone marrow, can combine with calcium and cause areas of calcification on the bones. This calcification can eventually be detected by X-rays. Bone necrosis has also been noted with alcoholism, steroid treatment, rheumatoid arthritis, syphilis and many other conditions.

The bone death associated with elevated pressures is known as **Dysbaric Osteonecrosis**. The first reports of dysbaric osteonecrosis were published in 1911 when the disease was noted in caisson workers.

CAUSE

The exact cause of dysbaric osteonecrosis is unknown but numerous mechanisms have been suggested.

One common theory suggests that the necrosis is a result of arterial emboli blocking the supply of oxygen and nutrients to the bone. The possible emboli suggested are gas bubbles, the blood platelet clumps that sometimes result from the presence of gas bubbles, "stiff" blood cells (caused by compression) which cannot pass through capillary walls and, so, obstruct circulation, or pieces of fat which have broken off damaged tissue. The fact that lesions (damage) frequently occur in the heads of the bones where end arteries are found supported this theory. However, the large areas of necrosis often found are unlikely to result from the blockage of single arteries.

The long bones of the limbs are rich in the very fatty white bone marrow, and nitrogen is very soluble in this fatty marrow. The large quantities of nitrogen released from this marrow on decompression could cause bubbles, which might swell and press on blood vessels from the outside (extravascular emboli). If the circulation is obstructed bone death might occur.

Oxygen toxicity has also been suggested as another possible cause of dysbaric osteonecrosis. Three possible mechanisms have been proposed:

(i) The high partial pressures of oxygen might cause small blood vessels to constrict sufficiently to cut off adequate blood flow to the bones.

(ii) Bone is made up of live cells which are connected in a matrix by collagen tissue. High pressures of oxygen modifies collagen tissue, which in turn interferes with circulation and nutrition to the bone.

(iii) High oxygen levels cause swelling of the fat cells which raises the pressure inside the bone. This increased pressure may cause some blood vessels to be constricted.

Osmosis, which is the movement of water from one part of the body to another, has also been suggested as a possible cause of aseptic bone necrosis. When the ambient pressure is altered, the body tissues generally behave like a fluid and transmit the pressure evenly and instantaneously. As bone is the only rigid tissue, it is possible that temporary pressure differences might occur within and around it, possibly damaging the living tissue in the bone.

SIGNS AND SYMPTOMS

The earlier stages of dysbaric osteonecrosis are generally asymptomatic and are detected by bone scan or X-ray. It may take three to twelve months before the lesions are detectable by X-ray examination, but technetium bone scans can detect the lesion a week or two after the injury. There is now the development of the magnetic resonance imager, which can probably detect the lesion within hours of it occurring.

The most common areas affected are the long bones of the thigh (femur) and upper arm (humerus), and the tibia (lower leg). There are two main sites for the lesions in the long bones. These are lesions in the head, neck and shaft, and lesions next to joint surfaces (juxta-articular lesions).

If the lesions occur near the joint surfaces of the femur and humerus, the weakened underlying bone that supports the cartilage covering the bone will collapse with weight bearing and activity, causing the joint surface to break down and become irregular. When symptoms eventually occur, their severity depends upon the extent and position of the bone damage. Pain occurs with movement of these joints, and is accompanied by muscle spasms around the joint. Movement becomes restricted and the joint can no longer be used in a normal manner. Once a joint is affected, osteoarthritis develops and, eventually, the joint may collapse, "freeze-up" and cripple the unfortunate sufferer.

The most common sites of these juxta-articular lesions are the hips and shoulders. It has rarely been reported in other joints such as ankles, elbows or wrists. The lesions at times occur symmetrically about the body, such as in both shoulders or both hips.

Lesions in the shafts or in areas away from the joint surface of the femur and humerus do not cause symptoms or disability, and do not seem to weaken the shaft.

FIGURE 9.1
Regions of the femur

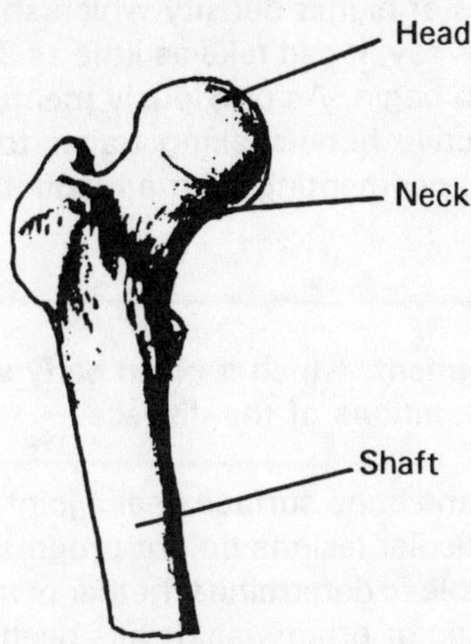

FIGURE 9.2
Sites of dysbaric osteonecrosis
(shaded areas)

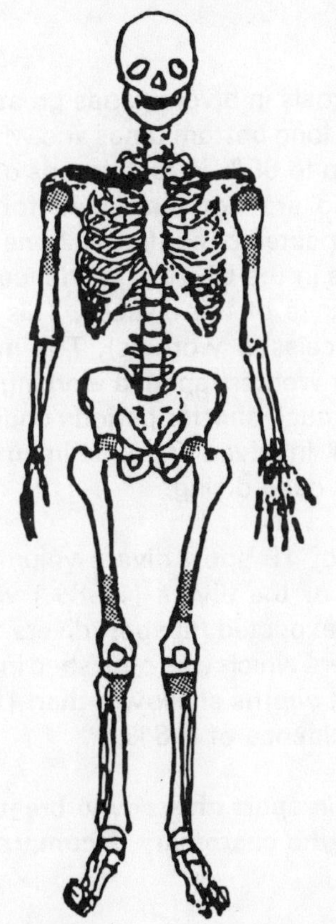

DETECTION

Dead bone cannot be distinguished from live bone, but regenerating new bone on the areas of dead bone produces areas of higher density which show up as an opaqueness on an X-ray. After first detection on X-ray, it can take as little as 3-4 months, or as long as 2-3 years or longer for joint troubles to begin. As previously mentioned, some researchers have also used injections of a radioactive bone-seeking tracer to detect the early stages of bone necrosis, while others are experimenting with a magnetic resonance imager.

TREATMENT

There appears to be no treatment, which if given early when the disease is first detected, will prevent the later manifestations of the disease.

Bone necrosis not involving the bone surface near a joint requires no treatment as it causes no disability. Some juxta-articular lesions do not progress to cause symptoms or disability but, at present, it is not possible to determine whether or not a particular juxta-articular lesion will prove to be asymptomatic or otherwise. It has been suggested that if such a lesion is found early and the joint immobilized for six months or longer, the necrosis might cease. This is usually impractical and it appears that in many such cases the repair process has halted and the circulation has been permanently destroyed. In the worst cases the joint can be replaced by an artificial joint made from plastic or metal.

FEATURES

The incidence of this bone necrosis in divers varies greatly. The fishermen-divers of Japan and Hawaii dive quite deeply for long bottom times and with little or no decompression. Bone lesions have been reported in up to 65% in test groups of these divers.[1] A recent survey of Australian abalone divers (who are not renowned for their respect of decompression schedules!) indicated either suspected or confirmed bone necrosis in 32% of the 108 divers tested.[1] Surveys of naval divers in the UK (4% incidence)[2] and the USA (2.5% incidence)[3] have shown quite a low incidence of the disease. This contrasts with earlier surveys of compressed air workers (e.g. caisson workers). The major difference between the two groups was that compressed air workers spent a working shift (eight hours or longer) under pressure, while the divers had much shorter periods underwater. Many of the naval divers with bone changes had been involved in experimental diving, such as testing new decompression tables and very deep diving.

In Australia in 1976, a group of 19 sport divers volunteered to be X-rayed for signs of dysbaric osteonecrosis. Three of the divers (15.8%) were found to have bone lesions, however, this is far higher than expected for sport divers.[4] A report of the incidence of bone necrosis in 4,980 North Sea divers which was published in 1979, showed no lesions in divers who dived on compressed air at depths shallower than 100 ft (30 m). Dives between 103-165 ft (31-50 m) carried an incidence of 0.8%.[5]

Dysbaric Osteonecrosis is rare in sport divers who breathe air at depths shallower than 165 ft (50 m), and who follow the customary decompression tables.

Although many reports suggest that dysbaric osteonecrosis is a delayed manifestation of decompression sickness, this has yet to be confirmed.

Not all divers with bone lesions have had the bends. The presence of "silent bubbles" has been suggested as an explanation for this.

Many divers who have suffered the bends never develop bone necrosis.

Greatly increased decompression time greatly reduced the bends rate in British compressed air workers, yet did not change the incidence of bone lesions.

Dysbaric osteonecrosis has occurred after only one dive.

The incidence of dysbaric osteonecrosis appears to be greater in divers who:

* spend long times underwater
* have been diving for many years
* dive deeper than 100 ft (30 m)
* undertake experimental diving
* have suffered from bends, especially if inadequately treated
* are fatter or heavier

The most common lesions are shaft lesions which, generally, do not create problems.

PREVENTION

Since the exact cause of these bone lesions is unknown, it is difficult to know what measures need to be taken to prevent dysbaric osteonecrosis.

By avoiding excessively long dives, deep dives, decompression dives and possibly repetitive dives a sport diver will certainly minimize his or her chances of developing this type of bone necrosis.

Avoiding or minimizing bubble formation by diving to conservative No-Decompression Limits, ascending slowly and doing safety stops is a sensible precaution, and may help to prevent bone lesions from forming.

Early recognition of the problem is necessary in order to prevent further damage from continued diving. Cessation of diving should prevent further lesions from developing although, at present, there is no evidence to judge whether or not a diver who already has lesions is any more likely to suffer further lesions if he continues diving.

Routine long bone X-rays are recommended in the following cases:

* 3-4 months after a case of decompression sickness
* all divers exposed to frequent and prolonged repetitive hyperbaric conditions (e.g. professional divers and some instructors).

If bone necrosis is detected diving activity will either have to be modified or ceased, depending on the severity of the lesion.

SUMMARY

- Exposure to compressed air at high pressure is at times associated with the dying-off of bone tissue.
- The exact cause of dysbaric osteonecrosis is not known.
- Various causes have been suggested. These include intravascular and extravascular emboli, oxygen toxicity and osmotic changes.
- The early stages of bone necrosis are usually asymptomatic and detectable only by X-ray.
- The lesions usually occur at the head, neck or shaft of the long bones, or next to the joint surfaces.
- The shaft lesions are usually not serious but lesions near the surface of the joint can be painful and may cause the eventual collapse of the joint.
- There appears to be no treatment which will prevent progression of the process.
- Bone necrosis is rare in sport divers who breathe air at depths shallower than 165 ft (50m), and who follow the customary decompression tables.
- Bone necrosis may be a delayed manifestation of bends, but this has not yet been confirmed.
- If lesions are found, cessation of diving should prevent further lesions developing.

REFERENCES

1. Edmonds, C. (1986), "The Abalone Diver". National Safety Council of Australia, Melbourne.

2. Elliott, D. and Harrison, T. (1971), "Aseptic Bone Necrosis in Royal Navy Divers". *Proceedings of Fourth Symposium of Underwater Physiol., New York*: 251-262, Academic Press

3. Harvey, C. and Sphar, R. (1976), "Dysbaric Osteonecrosis in Divers. A survey of 611 selected Navy divers". *U.S. Navy Submar. Med. Res. Lab.*, NSMRL 832, February: 55.

4. Williams, B. and Unsworth, I. (1976), "Skeletal Changes in Divers". *Aust. Radiol.*; 20:83-94.

5. Knight, J. (1982), "How Common is Dysbaric Osteonecrosis". *SPUMS Journal*; 16: October-December: 12-16.

OTHER SOURCES

Knight, J. (1982), "How Common is Dysbaric Osteonecrosis". *SPUMS Journal*; 16: October-December: 12-16.

Edmonds, C. et al (1981), "Diving and Subaquatic Medicine", 2nd edition. Diving Medical Center, Sydney.

McCallum, I. (1981), "Bone and Joint Problems". In: *Hyperbaric and Undersea Medicine*, Davis, J. (ed), Medical Seminars Inc., California.

McCallum, I and Harrison, J. (1982), "Dysbaric Osteonecrosis". In: *The Physiology and Medicine of Diving*, 3rd edition, Bennett, P. and Elliott, D. (eds), Best Publishing Co, California.

RECOMMENDED FURTHER READING

Edmonds, C. et al (1981), "Diving and Subaquatic Medicine", 2nd edition. Diving Medical Center, Sydney.

Knight, J. (1982), "How Common is Dysbaric Osteonecrosis". *SPUMS Journal*; 16: October-December: 12-16.

McCallum, I and Harrison, J. (1982), "Dysbaric Osteonecrosis". In: *The Physiology and Medicine of Diving*, 3rd edition, Bennett, P. and Elliott, D. (eds), Best Publishing Co, California.

CHAPTER 10

WOMEN AND DIVING

The study of Man underwater has been just that. Dive tables were originally designed for fit, healthy, fit males, and most of the studies of the effects of the underwater environment on humans have been based on male subjects.

The number of women SCUBA divers has grown enormously over the past few years and many questions have been raised about various physiological aspects of women divers.

The two areas of greatest concern are:

(i) the effects of diving during pregnacy on the developing fetus, and

(ii) whether or not women are more susceptible to bends than men are.

These and other aspects of women and diving will be discussed in this chapter.

DIVING DURING PREGNANCY

During the early stages of pregnancy, often before the mother knows she is pregnant, the developing embryo is no more than a clump of cells within the uterus. Damage to these cells during the early stages of pregnancy may have serious consequences, often leading to major birth deformities, or mutations. Drugs that cause a high rate of deformities include thalidomide, although birth deformities will occur at a very low rate in the population naturally.

At this stage it is not adequately known what the effects of increased pressure (including increased partial pressures of nitrogen, oxygen and carbon dioxide) on the developing embryo are. It is known that the embryo is much more sensitive to low partial pressures of oxygen than the mother, a fact which leads to decreased fertility among most mammals when taken to altitude. With diving there are many potential causes of hypoxia in the pregnant mother. Salt water aspiration can at times cause severe hypoxia, which will continue after the dive unless treated. It is thought that severely reduced oxygen levels can increase the possibility of both miscarriage and birth abnormalities. Ill-effects have been observed in the babies of theater nurses, who have inhaled small amounts of anesthetic gases during operations. Some doctors fear that breathing higher partial pressures of nitrogen while diving may have similar effects, although this has not been observed.

Later in pregnancy the developing child depends upon the mother not only for its oxygen and food supply, but also for the removal of waste products and carbon dioxide. The transfer of these materials occurs across the placenta. This is an area of the uterus that specially develops during pregnancy, where the mother's and child's blood supplies come into very close contact with each other. Materials are transferred from one system to the other without the blood of the mother ever mixing with that of the child. If for any reason the mother's blood supply to the placenta is reduced or stopped, the child is deprived of oxygen and, as with a drowned person, brain damage can start to occur within minutes.

Another problem is that if the blood supply is reduced, gradual changes in the developing child, such as reduced size, reduced development and reduced intelligence may result.

The basic question is, does diving cause fetal deformity, premature labour or other pregnancy problems. The answer is not completely clear.

SUGGESTED REASONS WHY DIVING COULD CAUSE FETAL ABNORMALITY

1. Oxygen toxicity

When compressed air is breathed, the partial pressure of oxygen rises progressively with depth and it is feared that sometimes this could have a toxic effect on the fetus.

If a pregnant woman dives deeply or receives hyperbaric oxygen treatment for decompression sickness or arterial gas embolism, oxygen partial pressures may at times be high enough to damage the fetus.

Some doctors suggest that a fetus exposed to very high oxygen pressures late in gestation could develop scarring of the retina of the eye (retrolental fibroplasia), possibly leading to blindness. This problem develops in newborn babies exposed to 100% oxygen. Oxygen partial pressures of 3 ATA or more can also cause some circulatory changes in the fetus. The blood supply is increased to some areas and reduced to others. In the fetus blood is shunted around the lungs and liver by special blood vessels, which only close when the oxygen level in the fetal blood is raised. Premature closing of these vessels, due to the higher oxygen levels from diving or recompression, may cause developmental problems in the fetus, however, to date, this has not been confirmed.

2. Decompression sickness

Most of the concern about diving during pregnancy is over the possibility of decompression sickness in the fetus.

It is known that bubbles can form in, or enter, the blood even when decompression tables are adhered to and it is possible that some of these bubbles could form and/or lodge in vital places within the fetus itself.

Bubbles formed within the mother should be filtered out by the placenta. It has been suggested that bubbles trapped in the placenta might reduce the supply of oxygen and nutrients to the fetus enough to cause damage. This is generally thought to be unlikely as the placenta is like a bloody sponge and, if one channel is closed, another opens. However, **since the lungs of a fetus are not functioning, venous bubbles formed within the fetus will not be filtered out by the lungs, and will pass directly into the arterial system through the foramen ovale. Once in the arterial system the bubbles may cause serious damage since much of the circulation goes directly to the brain and coronary arteries.**

Bubble size is also important. Because the fetal blood vessels are so small they could be obstructed by a bubble so small that, in the mother, it would cause no detectable problem.

Animal Experiments

Many animal studies have been done in an attempt to determine whether or not bubbles form within a fetus after inadequate decompression.

In 1968, a study was conducted in which 28 pregnant dogs were compressed to 6 ATA. Thirteen were exposed for 60 minutes and the rest for 120 minutes. Although marked intravascular bubbling was found in all the mothers and in the amniotic fluid surrounding all the fetuses, none of the fetuses died. Two of the 94 fetuses in the first group and 2 of the 99 fetuses in the second group showed some bubbling.

A similar study was done on rats in 1974. Pregnant rats were compressed to 8.5 ATA for 30 minutes. No bubbles were found in the fetuses despite the mothers dying from massive bubbling.

In 1978, an experiment was conducted in which a monitoring device was implanted within pregnant sheep which were then exposed to various depths for the corresponding No-Decompression Limits. At depths greater than 60 ft (18 m) bubbles were found in the fetuses but not in the mothers. Subsequent experiments indicated that the bubbles in the fetuses may have been precipitated by the surgical insertion of the probe rather than just by the decompression itself. However, a more recent experiment in which bubbles were monitored in sheep and goats by a transcutaneous bubble detector (rather than by one surgically implanted), appears to have confirmed the initial results.

Another experiment was designed to determine if exposure to high pressures of air causes gross fetal malformations, decreased birthweight or death. Pregnant sheep were exposed to pressures of 4.6 ATA during peak development of the embryo. Towards the end of pregnancy the fetuses were examined and no structural deformities were found.

Eleven sheep, about halfway through pregnancy, were taken to 165 ft (50 m) for 20 minutes and then decompressed with stops at 40 ft (12 m) for one minute and 10 ft (3 m) for four minutes. None of the sheep showed signs of bends although bubbles were detected in eight of them. No bubbles were detected in the fetuses and the lambs developed normally after birth. The researchers concluded that if fetal decompression sickness did occur, it was well tolerated by the fetus and did not disturb further growth.

Another study involved bending pregnant sheep late in pregnancy. Mothers who had bends immediately before delivering gave birth to stillborn lambs. However, if the mothers were treated in a recompression chamber the lambs appeared healthy.

Most of the animal experiments seem to indicate that if the pregnant mother does not suffer from bends the fetus will also be unaffected. However, if the mother does suffer from bends the fetus may be damaged.

The problem with these animal experiments is that no animal model can replicate what happens in the human. Rats and dogs have a more efficient way of transferring gas to and from the fetus than do sheep and humans and, consequently, some scientists believe the results of experiments on these animals are not applicable to humans. The sheep is probably the closest model of the human since its placenta more closely resembles the human's.

Human Experience

Ethical problems prevent similar studies to those carried out on animals being done on humans. So, we must rely on surveys to try to determine the effect of diving on the human fetus.

In 1977, 72 women who dived while pregnant were questioned and it was found that more than one third stopped during the first trimester (when they found out they were pregnant), more than one third stopped in the second trimester (mainly due to increased size), and the remainder continued to dive. Most were very experienced divers. The deepest dive was 180 ft (54.5 m) and there were five decompression stop dives performed. All babies were normal, however, there were some complications, e.g. there was one premature birth, one septic abortion, two miscarriages and two cesarian sections.[1] These results did not represent a significant increase over the general pregnant population.

The most comprehensive survey yet undertaken was done in America during 1980, when 208 female divers replied to questionaires placed in diving magazines.[2] 136 of these had dived during pregnancy. It was found that women who had dived during pregnancy had children with more birth defects than those who did not dive. Defects included skeletal deformation, heart deformities and other minor defects. The risk of a birth defect due to diving during pregnancy was put at 5.5% (6/109) from this study. However, it must be said that this is a very small sample group and that, statistically, this figure of 5.5% is not significantly different from the average for the normal population (around 2%), although it is higher.

Eighteen out of the 20 women who dived deeper than 100 ft (30 m) during the first three months of pregnancy reported no fetal or neonatal complications. Two women who dived deeper than 100 ft reported that their babies had been born with deformities. One child's vertibrae had not completely fused, and the other was born with one hand missing. Of the 20 women who made more than 10 dives deeper than 33 ft (10 m) during the first three months of pregnancy, four reported abnormal vaginal bleeding during pregnancy. Two of these four had abortions, one delivered nine weeks prematurely and one (previously mentioned) delivered a baby without a hand. In addition, more than 6% of the babies in the diving group had low birth weights compared to 1.4% in the control group.

Another survey, which included 76 pregnancies reported in 54 women, included 10 women who dived deeper than 100 ft (30 m) during the early stages of pregnancy.[3] Three of the women reported having babies with congenital (from birth) abnormalities. One of the children suffered spina bifida (in which the vertibral arch and the skin failed to cover the spinal cord, leaving it exposed), another suffered from a hole in the heart, and the third baby's penis failed to close properly around the urethra. All three demonstrated a specific sort of abnormality, the "mid-line fusion defect". That is, things down the middle of the body had failed to come together properly.

Women who had dived to shallower depths also reported a higher than expected proportion of birth defects, although most of these could be discounted as defects unrelated to diving. However, one case, a case of spina bifida, was thought to be caused by diving.

The survey concluded that there was no increase in premature labour or fetal abnormality when diving to less than 66 ft (20 m), but an increase in fetal abnormality when diving deeper than 66 ft (20 m).

More recently, a report from a Sydney hospital tells of numerous birth defects in a child born to a mother who undertook about 20 dives during pregnancy to depths up to 110 ft (33 m), and including one emergency ascent from 60 ft (18 m). The mother had not noticed any symptoms of bends and was not recompressed.[4]

3. Hypoxia and hypercapnia from breath-hold diving

Breath-holding is associated with low oxygen levels and high carbon dioxide levels. It has been shown that women who consistently breath-hold dive and exert themselves during pregnancy have a greater chance of having low birth weight babies. The Ama divers of Korea, women who do many deep breath-hold dives for pearls, dive until a few days before giving birth. They have an incidence of 44.6% of prematurity with an infant of less than 2.5 kg, (5.5 pounds) compared to a 15.8% incidence in non-diving women from the same area.[5]

Salt water aspiration from snorkelling (or SCUBA) can cause hypoxia which may affect the fetus if it becomes severe. It has been shown that severe hypoxia in the mother will cause changes in the fetal oxygen content. However, there is no evidence that breath-holding in moderation has any undesirable effect on the fetus. Recreational snorkelling should be fine as long as exertion, thermal stress and substantial water aspiration is avoided.

4. Medications often used during diving activities

Many drugs and medications are potentially harmful to the developing fetus. These include some of the decongestants and anti-seasick medications often used by divers. A pregnant women should consult her doctor before using any medications.

It is impossible to definitely state one way or the other that diving during pregnancy is dangerous to the developing child. However, some signs indicate that at times it might be. This is especially true of deeper diving. In addition, if the mother suffers from bends the fetus may be injured as a direct result of the bends in the mother, or as a result of the mother's subsequent hyperbaric oxygen treatment.

It is also impossible to assess how a child might have developed had the mother behaved differently during pregnancy. It is known, for example, that children born to alcoholic mothers tend to have a high risk of deformity, but what is not known is what effect moderate drinking by the mother may have on the developing embryo. It may result in reduced physical or mental ability but with the variation that normally occurs between different children, it is something which can never be measured or proven. The same applies to diving. Some evidence indicates that deep diving during pregnancy can cause birth defects in the child.

This leads some doctors to fear that all SCUBA diving could be harmful to the developing embryo, although current evidence does not support this conclusion. It must be remembered that many women who dive while pregnant have no problems with their pregnancies or with their babies.

Most authorities recommend that pregnant women should refrain from SCUBA diving. Excessive breath-hold diving should be avoided, but snorkelling on the surface should be fine, as long as the diver stays thermally comfortable, does not exert herself, and minimizes water aspiration and carbon dioxide build-up.

Practically speaking it can be very difficult for a woman to know what to do when trying to get pregnant - which could take some time. Some women are happy to give up diving at this time. Otherwise, it is probably wise not to dive below 20 ft (6 m) (and to avoid multiple ascents), in the second half of the month and, if the period is overdue or the woman thinks that she may be pregnant and has a dive planned for the weekend, a pregnancy test can be done. Urine tests are not as reliable as blood tests as the blood test will be positive before the period is missed. Urine testing kits are readily available and are quite inexpensive.

Many women continue to dive before realizing they are pregnant. If this occurs the expectant mother should not spend the rest of the pregnancy worrying about the possible repercussions. The vast majority of women who reported diving while pregnant gave birth to healthy babies. As with any other concern during pregnancy, a discussion with the obstetrician should help to allay any unreasonable fears.

POTENTIAL PROBLEMS FOR THE MOTHER

Possible problems for the pregnant mother include nausea, vomiting, fatigue and the inability to fit into the wetsuit or to fit a weight-belt in the position where the waist once was. Many expectant mothers have sore breasts, making both a wetsuit and buoyancy compensator uncomfortable to wear, even in the early stages of pregnancy. Practical problems such as getting in and out of a dive boat may create difficulty.

From the fourth month onwards it may become more difficult to equalize the ears and sinuses due to fluid retention and mucosal swelling.

During pregnancy respiratory function becomes progressively impaired. There is a progressive difficulty with the oxygenation of the blood flowing through the lungs, and an increase in the resistance to air flow through the airways. These changes may make it more difficult for the woman to cope with strenuous activity and may increase the possibility of pulmonary barotrauma. The pregnant woman may also be more prone to bends due to the increased blood flow, the increased fluid retention, and the increase in blood clotting mechanisms.

Some women begin to "leak" through the membranes of the fetus into the vagina during the last three months of pregnancy. The discharge often goes unnoticed. If sea water managed to get into the womb it may cause infection and/or premature labour. However, this is only a remote possibility and could happen just as easily in a swimming pool.

Many obsteticians are quite happy for women to go straight back into the water after the birth of their baby, although some recommend a wait of about six weeks. It is important to check with the doctor before recommencing diving activities after childbirth.

Potential problems for the mother during the first few months after pregnancy include:

Enlarged breasts often will not fit into the wetsuit. Nipples can be extremely sensitive to cold water and this can be a problem if the baby wants a feed immediately after the dive. The pelvic ligaments, which gave to let the baby out, can stay lax for up to six months, so it is probably not advisable to be carrying heavy weights for long distances. Lack of fitness may present a problem. In addition, it may be difficult to obtain life-jackets for small babies, which can be a problem if a woman wishes to take the baby with her in a boat. However, most of these problems can be overcome.

EFFECT OF DIVING ON THE SEX OF THE BABY

There is no evidence that recreational diving in either parent makes it more likely that a baby of a particular sex will be born.

Some years ago it was observed that a small group of Royal Navy divers had more female offspring than male offspring. However, subsequent analysis of the data found that the numbers were not statistically significant.

A retrospective survey of the sex of the children of all Royal Australian Navy (RAN) compressed air divers was undertaken to determine whether or not any sex differences were apparent. The survey included 240 children. The results indicated that there was no significant difference in the sex of the children of these RAN divers.[6]

DECOMPRESSION SICKNESS

Women have a greater percentage of fatty tissue than men. Fatty tissue absorbs a lot of nitrogen and releases it slowly. Recent studies in which probes were inserted in muscles and subcutaneous tissue indicate that females do in fact absorb more nitrogen than males do. Hormonal changes during menstruation can result in fluid retention (edema) and fluid shifts. Also, some birth control pills can cause a microsludging or slowing of the circulation. All these factors suggest that women might be more prone to bends than men.

Dr. Bruce Bassett collected and analyzed data on female flight nurses exposed to high altitudes in the U.S. Air Force.[7] Between 1968 and 1977 the incidence of altitude decompression sickness in male students was 0.09%, while in the female nurses it was 0.36%. Bends in the women appeared more rapidly and recurred more frequently. The nurses had four times the bends incidence of the male students, and many have quoted these figures to show that women are more susceptible to bends than men. However, male Air Force Academy cadets exposed to altitude had about the same incidence of bends as the female nurses. So the difference may not be a sex difference but may be due to stress or some other factor.

In 1977, an extensive survey (The MAWD survey) was conducted on women divers, and a portion of it was also sent to some male divers.[1] The data showed that a group of women diving instructors had 3.3 times the incidence of suspected or treated bends than did their male collegues. Other factors such as age and weight/height ratios were not significantly different.

The studies were both retrospective and, therefore, subject to a lot of human factors such as errors of recall, and possible psychological issues such as willingness (or reluctance in men!) to admit to having had bends. Another problem arises in both surveys. Both sets of data involved very small percentages and, when dealing with relatively rare events such as these, it is extremely difficult to determine whether or not the results really are significant. They may be statistically significant but this mathematical result is less reliable for rare events. Both surveys do not really prove that women are more likely than men to get the bends.

A 1986 study by the National Aeronautics and Space Administration (NASA) involved 19 pairs of men and women who were monitored for circulating bubbles with a Doppler probe, and examined for limb bends. The women were found to have fewer circulating bubbles (18% compared to 23%) bubbles but a higher incidence of bends than the men (9% compared to 6%).

Another recent study involved nine pairs of men and women who made decompression dives to between 132 ft (40 m) and 165 ft (50 m). They were then monitored for bubbles using a Doppler probe. Bubbles were detected in three of the women and in seven of the men. The men also showed consistently higher levels of bubbling for a longer time after the dive.

Diving log data from the Naval Diving and salvage Training Centre (NDSTC) demonstrate that there is no increased risk of bends among Navy female divers compared to their male counterparts under similar dive exposures.[8] This data relates to relatively short duration dives and the authors of the report suggest that it may be applied to the sport SCUBA diver as well. They conclude that "if any increased susceptibility to decompression sickness does exist for female sport divers it will be minimal and should not be a deterrent to women diving on the same decompression schedules as men.". However, they add that the women's greater proportion of adipose (fatty) tissue may make them more susceptible to bends after saturation, experimental and multiple repetitive dives, during which the fatty tissues absorb large quantities of gas.

Recompression chamber operators have not reported a proportionally higher number of females being treated for decompression sickness.

DAN's data of the diving accidents in the USA in 1987 and 1988 showed no particlar trend regarding special susceptibility to decompression sickness in women. 22.9% of the injured divers were women, indicating that men were involved in diving accidents (i.e. decompression sickness or arterial gas embolism) four times as often as women. DAN concludes that this probably indicates a larger male diving population but may reflect higher risk diving habits for men.[9]

In light of the current evidence, the consensus is that women are at no greater risk of decompression sickness than men are.[10,11]

EFFECTS OF "THE PILL"

Because of the association between the Pill and the formation of blood clots (thrombosis), and the observed sludging of platelet cells around bubbles in bends, it has been thought that the Pill might aggravate bends. Other side effects of the Pill, such as fluid retention, nausea and cramping theoretically increase the risk of bends. However, blood clotting is an extremely complex mechanism involving many substances. Thrombosis is now seen as a result of a combination of higher dose estrogen pills, age (over 35), smoking and previous ill health. It is more likely that the estrogen in oral contraceptives affects the release of clotting factor proteins from the liver rather than the platelet sludging process of decompression sickness.

The MAWD survey, previously mentioned, included women diving while taking the Pill. It compared 106 women on the Pill with 179 women not on the Pill, doing decompression stop dives. The results showed that 3.7% of the women on the Pill got bent, whereas 3.9% of those not on the Pill got bent. Comparing 301 women on the Pill with 454 not on the Pill and doing no-decompression stop dives, it was found that 1.3% of those on the Pill got bent compared to 2.2% of those who were not on the Pill. There was no significant difference between the bends rate of those who took the Pill and those who did not. However, the numbers were small and, so, not statistically reliable.

DAN statistics show that 25% of the women who suffered from decompression sickness or arterial gas embolism in 1988 were taking the Pill. However, a recent DAN prospective study questionnaire found 26.1% of 188 female divers were also on birth control pills. Although these sub-groups are too small to draw significant results from, the DAN figures provide no evidence that birth control pills are a risk factor in diving accidents.[9]

MAMMARY IMPLANTS IN DIVERS

As a result of questions arising concerning mammary implants and decompression safety, some experiments were conducted to determine the degree of bubbling within these implants after exposure to various pressures.[12] Bubble formation did occur in the implants causing them to increase in volume. It was concluded that bubble formation in an implant should not cause damage to the surrounding tissues, should be absorbed naturally if given sufficient time and can be tolerated safely. Deep, saturation diving should be avoided as inert gas exchange will be very slow and the implant will require a lot of time to get rid of its large gas load. In the worst case, the resulting bubble formation might increase the implant volume enough to cause trauma to the surrounding tissue.

DIVING DURING THE MENSTRUAL PERIOD

Many women wonder whether or not it is safe to dive during menstruation. A common fear is that of shark attack, however, there is no evidence to support this anxiety. Perusal of the statistics of shark attacks indicates that female divers have a much lower incidence of shark attack than males (Is this because sharks are "man eaters"!).

From a purely mechanical point of view there is no need to stop diving during a period. Internally worn protection such as a tampon can be worn effectively.

One complication of the period is fluid retention and although, theoretically, this makes the women more prone to bends as the tissue swelling accompanying the fluid retention may impair blood flow and, hence, nitrogen elimination, has not been verified. DAN figures indicate that 25% of the women who suffered bends or arterial gas embolism in 1988 were menstruating at the time of their injury. However, this is about the same percentage of women from the general population who would be expected to be menstruating and, therefore, does not indicate a higher than expected proportion.[9]

A sensible precaution is to dive more conservatively during the week before and while menstruating.

There are, however, some other problems associated with periods. A number of women suffer from Pre-Menstrual Tension (PMT), or period cramps, which may make them less capable at both a physical and emotional level and may impair their judgement. Those who experience only mild symptoms may find that PMT has little or no effect on their diving. However, those suffering from more severe symptoms such as depression, anxiety or poor concentration are unlikely to be adequately fit to dive and probably will not wish to do so anyway.

Before and during the period there may be an increase of the swelling of the mucosal membrane which may make equalization of the ears and sinuses more difficult.

Whether or not a woman can safely dive during her period really depends on how she feels. If she feels physically and mentally well enough there seems to be no reason not to dive. Apparently some women find that period cramps are relieved by diving.

THERMAL STRESS

Despite the fact that women have a higher percentage of fat and a more even coating of subcutaneous fat than men, it has sometimes been reported that women divers feel cold earlier than their male collegues. Lean women (i.e. those who have less than 27% body fat) have a larger surface area per unit of body mass and, therefore, relatively more surface available for heat loss to the surrounding water. This should cause them to cool at a faster rate. In addition, since heat is created by metabolism and shivering, and since women normally have a smaller muscle mass than men, they should produce less heat. In cold water studies of Japanese male and female Ama divers, men were found to generate more heat in cold water and tolerate the cold better, even though they have less body fat. However, some recent studies indicate that cold tolerance seems to be about equal in men and women.[13]

It has also been reported that the female has fewer functional sweat glands than the male and her body temperature will rise higher than a male's before cooling, through sweating, occurs. This observation has recently been disputed. Early studies indicated that women were significantly less tolerant to heat stress than were men, but the men and women included in the studies were poorly matched. The men were fit and active whereas the women led a more sedentary lifestyle. "Recent studies on responses for men and women to thermal stress indicate that they acclimatize in exactly the same manner and are equally tolerant of thermal stress when allowance is made for previous conditioning. Women typically sweat less than men but enough to control core temperature, and men may have a slight disadvantage in that excessive sweating leads to dehydration".[13]

OTHER FACTORS

Because women are generally smaller than men, they use less oxygen and need to remove less carbon dioxide from their lungs. This means that their respiratory requirements are less, their lungs are smaller and they need to carry less compressed air. This is why a female diver can often use a smaller cylinder than a male. In addition because women have a higher percentage of body fat they have more natural buoyancy, often enabling them to swim and, possibly, survive longer than their male counterparts.

CONCLUSION

The anatomical and physiological differences between men and women may affect various aspects of diving, although the extent of some of these effects is not known. I believe that all divers, both women and men, should dive conservatively and sensibly in order to enjoy the many benefits of diving, while minimizing exposure to the potential hazards.

SUMMARY

* Because women are anatomically and physiologically different to men, there may be differences in how the sexes are affected by diving.

* If a pregnant mother suffers severe hypoxia, the fetus may be endangered.

* At this stage the effects of increased pressure on the developing fetus are not adequately known.

* High partial pressures of oxygen due to very deep SCUBA diving or hyperbaric oxygen treatment may damage the fetus.

* It is feared that the fetus itself may at times develop decompression sickness, although some of the current evidence indicates the fetus may, at times, be less likely to develop bends than the mother.

* Since the lungs of a fetus are not functioning, circulating bubbles will not be filtered out and may enter the arterial system through the foramen ovale. Once in the arterial system these bubbles may cause damage.

* If a pregnant mother suffers from bends, the fetus may be damaged.

* Some surveys indicated that women who dived during pregnancy may have had significanly more birth defects than those who had not dived.

* Surveys have shown that higher rate of birth deformities have occurred after deep dives.

* Women who extensively breath-hold dive and exert themselves during pregnancy appear to have a greater incidence of premature and low birth weight babies.

* Some decongestants and anti-seasick medications may harm the developing embryo.

* Problems for the pregnant diver can include, nausea, vomiting, wetsuit and weight-belt fit, fatigue and getting in and out of boats, as well as possible equalization problems and, possibly, an increased risk of bends.

* There is no evidence that recreational diving affects the sex of the baby.

* Although, theoretically, certain physiological factors would make women more susceptible to bends, it appears that women may have a comparable bends risk to that of men.

* It has not been shown that women taking the Pill are more at risk from bends.

* Women who feel well enough to dive during their period can usually do so safely, although it is wise to dive more conservatively at that time.

* Women appear to tolerate thermal stress similarly to men.

* Women often require less compressed air and have more natural buoyancy.

REFERENCES

1. Bangasser, S. (1978), "Medical Profile of the Woman SCUBA Diver". Proceedings of the 10th International Conference on Underwater Education, NAUI: 31-40.

2. Bolton, M. (1980), "Scuba diving and fetal well-being: a survey of 208 women". *Undersea Biomedical Research*; 7 (3): 183-189.

3. Betts, J. (1985), "Diving and the Unborn Child", *Diver*; 30 (1): 14-15.

4. Turner G. and Unsworth, I. (1982), "Intrauterine Bends?", *SPUMS Journal*; January-March: 24-25.

5. Edmonds, C. (1984), "The Female Diver". *Skindiving*; 14 (4): 119-127.

6. Edmonds, C. (1974), "The Diver". Royal Australian Navy School of Underwater Medicine Report, Project Report 4-74.

7. Bassett, B. (1973), "Decompression Sickness in Female Students Exposed to Altitude During Physiological Training". Ann. Scient. Meet. Aerospace Me. Assoc., 44th Meeting.

8. Zwingelberg, M. et al (1987), "Decompression sickness in women divers". *Undersea Biomedical Research*; 14 (4): 311-317.

9. Divers Alert Network (1989), "Report on 1988 Diving Accidents". Divers Alert Network, North Carolina.

10. Fife , W. ed (1987), "Women in Diving". *Proceedings of The Thirty-fifth Undersea and Hyperbaric Medical Society Workshop*; UHMS Publication No. 71 (WS-WD), Undersea and Hyperbaric Medical Society, Inc.

11. Bennett, P., personal communication.

12. Vann, R. et al (1985), "Mammary Implants in Divers". *SPUMS Journal*; 15 (3): 32-33.

13. Nunneley, S. (1987), "Heat, cold, hard work and the woman diver". In "Women in Diving''. *Proceedings of the Thirty-fifth Undersea and Hyperbaric Medical Society Workshop*; Fife, W. (ed). UHMS Publication No. 71 (WS-WD), Undersea and Hyperbaric Medical Society, Inc.

OTHER SOURCES

Bangasser, S. (1980), "Physiological Concerns of Women Divers". In *Physiology In Depth*, Graver, D. (ed), PADI.

Bangasser, S. (1985), "Current Physiological Aspects of Women Divers". *NAUI News*; February: 15-17.

Bangasser, S., personal communication.

Bassett, B. (1986), "Physiology: The Woman Diver". *Alert Diver*; 2 (4): 4-5.

Bolton-Klug, M et al (1983), "Lack of harmful effects from simulated dives in pregnant sheep". *Am J Obstet Gynecol*; 146: 48-51.

Bove, A. (1988), Diving Medicine. *Skindiver*; 37 (5): 38.

Cush, C. (1987), "Women's susceptibility to decompression sickness questioned". *Underwater USA*; January.

Fife, W. et al (1978), "Susceptibility of fetal sheep to acute decompression sickness". *Undersea Biomedical Research*; 5 (3): 287-292.

Lehner, C. et al (1982), "Fetal health during decompression studies in sheep". *Undersea Biomedical Research*; 9 (1-Suppl): A 71.

Leslie, C. (1990), "SCUBA Diving and Pregnancy". *SPUMS Journal*; 20 (1): 19-26.

Mannerheim, J. (1982), "Sex and SCUBA". *SCUBA Diver*; June: 69-71.

McIver, R. (1968), "Bends resistance in the fetus". In Reprints of Scientific Program. 1968 annual scientific meeting, Aerospace medical Association. Washington. Aerospace Medical Association: 31.

Nemiroff, M. et al (1981), "Multiple hyperbaric exposures during pregnancy in sheep", *Am J Obstet Gynecol*; 140: 651-655.

Powell, M. and Smith, M. (1985), "Fetal and maternal bubbles detected non-invasively in sheep and goats following hyperbaric decompression". *Undersea Biomedical Research*; 12: 59-66.

Sleeper, J. and Bangasser, S. (1979), "Women Underwater". Deepstar Publishing, California.

Stock, M et al (1980), "Response of Fetal Sheep to Simulated No-Decompression Dives". *Journal of Applied Physiology;* 48, January: 776-780.

Viders, H. (1989), "DCS Risk in Female Divers - A 1989 Perspective". *Sources*; 1 (2): 61-64.

RECOMMENDED FURTHER READING

Edmonds, C. (1984), "The Female Diver". *Skindiving*: 14 (4): 119-127.

Fife , W. (ed) (1987), "Women in Diving". *Proceedings of The Thirty-fifth Undersea and Hyperbaric Medical Society Workshop*; UHMS Publication No. 71 (WS-WD), Undersea and Hyperbaric Medical Society, Inc.

Leslie, C. (1990), "SCUBA Diving and Pregnancy". *SPUMS Journal*; 20 (1): 19-26.

Viders, H. (1989), "DCS Risk in Female Divers - A 1989 Perspective". *Sources*; 1 (2): 61-64.

CHAPTER 11

DRUG USE AND THE DIVER

Drugs are chemicals that affect mental and/or physical function. This includes medicines, recreational drugs and drugs of abuse. Most drugs have side-effects, that is they produce changes in the body in addition to the change or effect that is desired. For example, antihistamines, which are often used to combat nasal congestion, often cause drowsiness which can be dangerous for the driver or diver.

The effects of drugs are not always consistent from one environment to another, from one person to another and with an individual from one time to another. The effect of a drug may be altered by pressure, changes in nitrogen, carbon dioxide and oxygen levels, cold, fatigue, mental state, exercise, altered sensory input and various other factors. Thus, even for medications that may reasonably be thought to be useful, both body regulation (autonomic) functions and mood state may change unpredictably. So, for every drug, thought must be given to if, how and when to dive while under its influence.

In determining which drugs are suitable for divers one must eliminate any that would impair exercise capacity, mental acuity or co-ordination. Very few controlled studies have been undertaken to determine the suitability of various drugs for use underwater, and some of the studies done may not be applicable to recreational SCUBA divers diving to the depths normally encountered.

RECREATIONAL DRUGS

Alcohol

Alcohol depresses the brain and so dulls the senses. It interferes with clear thinking and with manual dexterity. Alcohol can combine with nitrogen narcosis to cause a severe state of temporary mental imcompetance. Physical tasks cannot be performed correctly on the surface or underwater and judgement is impaired. Risky or dangerous situations will not be perceived. Even though a diver may not notice any significant decrement in function at the surface, when the effects of cold water, decreased vision and narcosis as well as other dive-related changes are added, the overall effect may be disastrous.

Alcohol has been associated with many drownings. It impairs one's exercise capability making it more difficult to swim as fast or as far as normal. It affects energy production within the body as it reduces the blood sugar level. The brain requires a lot of sugar and low levels of blood sugar reduces concentration and impairs other thought processes. In addition, a low blood sugar level reduces a divers ability to respond to stress and increases susceptibity to cold. Alcohol also increases the risk of vomiting and a diver who vomits underwater is at risk of drowning.

Alcohol is a diuretic (i.e. excretes water) and so dehydrates the body, particularly the brain, and it is this dehydration of the brain which is largely responsible for the hangover headache. However, it has been shown that dehydration of the brain lasts long after the hangover itself. A dehydrated diver is much more prone to bends, particularly neurological bends which affects the brain and spinal cord. In addition, since alcohol can reduce surface tension, which is one of the forces helping to prevent or limit the growth of bubbles, it is theoretically possible that drinking alcohol before or soon after diving may enhance bubble formation. 44.7% (120/268) of the divers who suffered from decompression sickness or arterial gas embolism in the USA in 1988 reported drinking at least one alcoholic drink the night before diving or prior to entering the water on the dive day.[1] Although it appears that alcohol ingestion prior to diving predisposes a diver to bends, this has never been experimentally proven.

Alcohol is metabolized slowly by the body and may affect brain and body metabolism for 24 hours or longer after ingestion. Alcohol dilates blood vessels in the skin and so increases heat loss. The blood vessels in the muscles, the greatest mass of tissues in the body, constrict from alcohol causing a rise in blood pressure.

Long term alcohol abuse is associated with damage to the liver, heart, brain, nerves and various other body organs.

Cigarettes

Diseases produced by long term cigarette smoking include cancers of the lung and mouth, problems with the lung structure and injury to blood vessels, in particular damage to the arteries supplying the heart (coronary arteries).

Smoking is known to cause an increase in blood pressure and heart rate. It causes spasm of the blood vessels of the heart and reduction of the blood flow to it. This results in oxygen starvation and possible damage to the heart itself.

The constriction of blood vessels that occurs immediately on smoking can reduce the blood supply to the heart and may cause it to work less effectively. This would make it difficult to achieve a maximum level of exercise. Constriction of other blood vessels to the muscles may alter the delivery of nitrogen within the body and it has been suggested (but not proven) that this may increase the risk of bends.

Smoking causes immediate irritation of the airways, producing excess mucus secretion and the possibility of airway spasm. Both of these can lead to the obstruction of small airways, air trapping with the possible sequelae of pulmonary barotrauma.

Smoking raises carbon monoxide levels which could compound the problem of an impure air supply. A cigarette before diving may significantly impair neurological function and oxygen carriage and metabolism, thereby putting that diver at an increased risk.

Hallucinogens and Narcotics

The predictable effects of these drugs, which include cardiovascular changes and changes to mental state, would be dangerous to the diver and it is largely unknown what effects pressure might have on these drugs.

Cocaine can produce a variety of responses, from marked changes in mental function to undetected damage of the coronary arteries and heart attack. Mental changes include extremes of happiness, anxiety or depression, restlessness and a reduced awareness of muscle fatigue which may fool a diver into believing he can perform physical tasks that are far beyond him. Cocaine is a very powerful vasoconstictor and at times increases the pulse rate and blood pressure dramatically. These effects may alter nitrogen uptake and its distribution throughout the body and, theoretically, may at times predispose to decompression sickness. Diving while there is still a significant amount of cocaine in the bloodstream may precipitate cardiac problems which could result in sudden death.

Marijuana affects circulation and mental processes. It dilates blood vessels, increases heart rate and causes changes in blood pressure. These may affect nitrogen distribution throughout the body and, theoretically, may predispose to the bends. Marijuana has been reported to cause a variety of undesirable effects underwater. One such report described unpleasant psychic effects such as extreme anxiety and idea fixation, as well as abnormally rapid heat loss.[2] Another unconfirmed report describes a group of divers who experimented with marijuana in warm water. The drug caused the divers to become ultra-relaxed, sleepy, unaware and unable to think or work. Upon reaching a depth of 50-60 ft (15-18 m) each diver became unconscious at some stage.[2]

Marijuana impairs short term memory, affects the sense of timing and may reduce a diver's ability to perform time sharing and/or task loading activites (e.g. buddy breathing). Its effects are potentiated by alcohol and various other drugs and, possibly, by depth. Marijuana can amplify many of the unpleasant diving stimuli a diver is trained to overcome. Small things can become seemingly insurmountable problems for the drugged diver. The feeling of euphoria appears to be rare.

It is important to realize that, like alcohol, these other drugs may still be active in the human body for quite a while after their last use.

Amphetamines

Some studies have been done to determine the effects of certain amphetamines under pressure. They were found to significantly impair judgement, problem-solving ability and muscular co-ordination.[3] Amphetamines also have undesirable cardiovascular effects which increase the chance of developing a disturbance to heart rhythm. Some can cause paranoia and/or hallucinations and may potentiate hypothermia by acting upon the body's temperature regulatory mechanism.

DRUGS USED TO FACILITATE DIVING

Decongestants

Decongestants are used to counter vasodilation and edema of the nasal mucosa. They are commonly used by divers to prevent or treat ear or sinus barotrauma. They act by vasoconstriction, which gives a temporary improvement of the nasal airway. Unfortunately, during the time the nasal airways are cleared the mucosal lining of the nose becomes hypoxic and a rebound nasal congestion, often more severe than the original congestion, may occur.

Decongestants may also cause an increase in the heart rate and force, and central nervous system stimulation, among other effects. The central nervous system stimulation can result in a heightened alertness, trembling and rapid breathing. The stimulation can be initially pleasing but can progress to a frightening awareness of a forceful or rapid heartbeat.

Decongestants are usually administered either topically in the form of nasal sprays or drops, or orally, by tablet.

> *"While the topical administration of phenylephrine (Neo-Synephrine) or of oxymetazoline (Afrin, Drixine) is effective and should produce fewer systemic (circulatory) reactions than oral decongestants, the nasal mucosa is a very good absorptive surface and can produce high blood levels of medications......So, although nasal sprays are generally safe and acceptable, it should be noted that there is a reported case of vertigo and unconsciousness at 136 ft (41 m) in a diver who used excessive amounts of oxymetazoline (Afrin, Drixine) before a dive."* [4]

Oral decongestants are commonly used by divers. Some, such as pseudoephedrine *(Sudafed, Novafed)* are used quite often. Pressure testing with standard doses in rats showed no performance decrement with pseudoephredine, which has been used effectively to depths of 450 ft (136 m) without "unacceptable" side-effects. However, pseudoephredine can have a rebound effect, sometimes immediately and sometimes some hours later. It is also a stimulant and may predispose to palpitations, which may prove dangerous to the diver.

Many divers tend to overuse decongestants. Some doctors argue that a diver who needs decongestants in order to dive should not dive. Decongestants have been known to wear off during a dive, causing an ear or sinus barotrauma. If used, they must be used in the appropriate doses and taken at the appropriate time.

Antihistamines

Rather than causing vasoconstriction, antihistamines act by blocking the release of histamine, which is a catalyst for allergic and physical inflammation. For best effect, antihistamines must be given prior to the occurrence of nasal congestion, however, this is often not feasible.

In the usual doses antihistamines often cause a sedation or depression. Some people become restless and hyperactive. These side-effects often make antihistamines incompatible with diving as the mental changes may affect the diver's judgement and actions. Certain antihistamines have been shown to notably decrease mental alertness, cognitive performance and muscular performance when tested under controlled hyperbaric conditions.

Despite these potential effects, there is a large variation in susceptibility to these side-effects and many divers have reported that they have used certain antihistamines without adverse side-effects.

Anti-Seasickness Drugs

Various types of drugs are used in attempts to prevent motion sickness. All these drugs affect the central nervous system and affect mental alertness and mood. Antihistamines such as dimenhydrinate *(Dramamine)* have been shown to impair function in some divers. Central stimulants (amphetamines) may increase narcosis. Scopolamine has been used to prevent motion sickness. Although quite effective, prolonged use may produce a variety of side-effects which include a dry mouth, drowsiness, disorientation and confusion. Scopolamine is available in a skin patch worn behind the ear - transdermal scopolamine. Tests on transdermal scopolamine in a dry recompression chamber produced no adverse effects, but the results might not be transferable to open water diving conditions.[5,6] However, there have been many anecdotal reports of divers using transdermal scopolamine without apparent problems.

The effectiveness of these drugs varies with individual susceptibility, the intensity and duration of motion, the interval between taking the medication and the onset of motion and the dosage. All of these drugs *may* have some interaction with the threshold of nitrogen narcosis.

It is obvious that there are inherent problems in the use of medications to prevent seasickness, but it is often possible to compromise between the danger of the medication and the danger and discomfort of sea sickness.

> *"The method of achieving this is by giving the drugs and allowing the adverse effects to wear off before the diver subjects himself to either diving or driving. A long-acting antihistamine tablet, such as promethazine (Phenergan), taken 8 hours before the diver dives or drives is sometimes the answer if the dive is in the morning. The diver can take the medication just before he goes to sleep. On awakening in the morning he should have a light breakfast then 1-2 cups of coffee before he commences his diving or driving activities. That way the sedation has usually worn off and the anti-seasick effect is still prominent. The coffee produces enough stimulant to ensure that the sedation has gone, but also works in its own right as an anti-seasick medication.*
>
> *If the diver is doing an afternoon dive or if he has not carried out the above procedure, then a short-acting antihistamine such as cyclizine (Marzine), with one tablet taken about four hours before the boat travel or the driving, with the proviso that he should only dive or drive if there is no sedation evident at the time."* [7]

The depth of the dive should be restricted to less than 100 ft (30 m) to minimize the possibility of any residual drowsiness from the medication compounding the effects nitrogen narcosis.

Steroid-Containing Nasal Sprays

There appears to be no contraindication to the use of intra-nasal, steroid-containing sprays such as dexamethasone *(Turbinaire, Tobispray)* and beclomethasone *(Vancenase, Aldecin, Beconase)*, which are used in the treatment of allergic rhinitis. These medications usually produce no significant mood changes or autonomic changes and act as anti-inflammatory agents.

Those using steroid inhalers for asthma should realize that asthmatics are intrinsically at risk from pulmonary barotrauma and should not SCUBA dive.

Analgesics

Aspirin and acetaminophen *(Tylenol, Datril* etc.*)* have been tested in hyperbaric conditions and found to produce no significant behavioural or psychological problems and, although they reduce fever, they do not lower body temperature and so do not predispose to hypothermia. There is no evidence that these drugs either increase or decrease the risk of bends. Stronger analgesics, however, may alter mental alertness and may prove dangerous to the diver, who should probably not be diving when requiring such medications.

OTHER MEDICATIONS

Sedatives and Tranquilizers

These drugs affect mental function and are used for sedation, tranquilization, sleep and mood elevation. The effects of these medications vary widely between individuals. Pressure appears to affect these medications variably and results from different experiments are not always consistent. The effects of some medications appear unchanged by pressure, others have their properties enhanced while other effects may be counteracted. It is likely that some of these drugs may increase the effects of nitrogen narcosis. People who habitually use these medications should refrain from diving.

Oral Contraceptives

Because of the association between the Pill and the formation of blood clots (thrombosis) and the observed sludging of platelet cells around bubbles in bends, it has been thought that the Pill might aggravate bends. However, thrombosis is now seen as a result of a combination of higher dose estrogen pills (which are not prescribed now), age, smoking and previous ill health. An extensive survey conducted on women divers in the U.S.A. in 1977 found no significant difference between the bends rate of those who took the Pill and those who did not.[8] DAN statistics show that 25% of the women who suffered from decompression sickness or arterial gas embolism in 1988 were taking the Pill. However, a recent DAN prospective study questionnaire found 26.1% of 188 female divers were also on birth control pills. Although these sub-groups are too small to draw significant results from, the DAN figures provide no evidence that birth control pills are a risk factor in diving accidents.[1]

Various other medications are taken by divers from time to time. Often it is the disease itself, rather than the medicine used to treat it, that renders diving unsafe. ***Divers should always consult a diving physician to determine or confirm the appropriateness of diving while taking a particular medication.***

SUMMARY

* Drugs affect mental and/or physical function.

* Most drugs have side-effects in addition to their therapeutic effects.

* The effects of drugs vary widely between individuals and from time to time with an individual.

* The effect of a drug may be altered by pressure, changes in nitrogen, carbon dioxide and oxygen levels, cold, fatigue, mental state and various other factors.

* Alcohol interferes with mental and physical function and can combine with nitrogen narcosis to cause a severe state of temporary mental incompetance. It is associated with many drownings and its diuretic effects may predispose to bends.

* Cigarette smoking is associated with cancer of the lungs and mouth, problems with lung structure and damage to blood vessels, in particular the coronary arteries. It reduces cardiopulmonary fitness.

* The immediate effects of smoking are constriction of blood vessels, which reduces exercise capacity, and irritation of the airways, which produces excess mucus and possible airway spasm and increases the risk of pulmonary barotrauma.

* Narcotics and hallucinogens may have unpredictable effects underwater. The known effects include unpleasant psychic effects, circulatory changes, rapid heat loss, unconsciousness and sudden death.

* Decongestants counter vasodilation and edema of the nasal mucosa. They act by temporary vasoconstriction and can have a rebound effect.

* Certain topical decongestants are usually safe if taken in the correct doses.

* Certain oral decongestants (e.g. Sudafed) are usually safe but have been known to cause problems in some individuals.

* If a decongestant wears off during a dive an ear or sinus barotrauma may occur, possibly on ascent.

* Antihistamines often produce drowsiness and, so, are often incompatible with diving. However, certain antihistamines work effectively against seasickness and may be reasonably safe if taken at the appropriate time and in the appropriate doses.

* Steroid-containing nasal srays appear to be safe for diving.
* Sedatives and tranquilizers affect mental function and are incompatible with diving.
* There has been no evidence to indicate that current oral contraceptives predispose to bends.
* **Divers should always consult a diving physician to determine or confirm the appropriateness of diving while taking a particular medication.**

REFERENCES

1. Divers Alert Network (1989), "Report on 1988 Diving Accidents". Divers Alert Network, North Carolina.
2. Tzimoulis, P. (1988), "The Dangers of Underwater Drug Trips". *Skin Diver*; 37 (4): 8.
3. Thomas, J. (1973), "Amphetamine and Chlordiazepoxide Effects on Behaviour Under Increased Pressures of Nitrogen". *Pharmacologic Biomedical Behaviour*; 1: 421-26.
4. Gillespie, C. (1986), "Drug Use and Diving". *Alert Diver*; 2 (5): 1-4.
5. Davis, M. (1987), "Scopoderm and Diver Performance". *SPUMS Journal*; 17 (1): 23-24.
6. Williams, T. et al (1988), "Effects of Transcutaneous Scopolamine and Depth on Diver Performance". *Undersea Biomedical Research*; 15 (2): 89-98.
7. Edmonds, C. (1982), "Seasickness". *Skindiving*; 12 (2): 39-41.
8. Bangasser, S. (1978), "Medical Profile of the Woman SCUBA Diver". *Proceedings of the 10th International Conference on Underwater Education*, NAUI, California: 31-40.

OTHER SOURCES

Bachrach, A. and Egstrom, G. (1987), "Stress and Performance in Diving". Best Publishing Co., California.

Bove, A. (1987), "Diving Medicine - Alcohol", *Skin Diver;* 36 (9): 32.

Bove, A. (1987), "Diving Medicine - Cigarettes", *Skin Diver*; 36 (10): 22.

Bove, A., "Diving Medicine - Cocaine". *Skin Diver,* 36 (11), 30, November 1987.

Cox, R. (1982), "Offshore Medicine". Springer-Verlag, Berlin, Heidelberg, New York.

Dueker, C. (1985), "SCUBA Diving in Safety and Health". Madison Publishing Associates,

SECTION 2

DECOMPRESSION TABLES

CHAPTER 12

HISTORY OF DECOMPRESSION TABLES

HALDANIAN THEORY

Prior to this century decompression profiles were generally slow, linear decompressions (i.e. continual slow ascent) following slow, linear compressions. Much diving time was wasted in getting to depth and returning from depth and many divers were getting decompression sickness. At the beginning of this century **J.S. Haldane**, a renowned physiologist, was appointed by the British Admiralty to develop safer decompression tables for use by Royal Navy divers, in order to reduce the high incidence of decompression sickness in those divers.

Haldane experimented with goats in a recompression chamber. He kept the goats at a particular pressure for periods of time from 1$^1/_2$ to 2 hours, after which he believed them to be saturated. He then noticed that they could be decompressed to an ambient pressure half that of (what he believed was) saturation before displaying obvious signs of decompression sickness. He believed that they could be decompressed from 2 ATA to 1 ATA, from 4 ATA to 2 ATA, and so on, without becoming bent. He also assumed (incorrectly) that because no signs of decompression sickness were displayed, no bubbles had formed within the goats.

By calculating the nitrogen pressure in the tissues and comparing it to the ambient pressure that the goats could be decompressed to asymptomatically, Haldane observed that, in all cases, the tissue nitrogen tension was 1.58 times the ambient pressure. **He concluded that as long as the ratio of tissue nitrogen tension to ambient pressure did not exceed 1.58 to 1, bubbles would not form and decompression sickness would be avoided.** This became known as the "Critical (Supersatuation) Ratio Hypothesis".

Haldane also proposed that, when a diver first descends to depth, the rate of nitrogen uptake is rapid due to the large difference between the nitrogen tensions in the lungs and in the tissues. As the dive progresses and the pressures become more even, the rate of nitrogen uptake slows down. He suggested that the uptake of nitrogen follows a type of exponential curve. Gas elimination was believed to be the reverse of this process.
Figure 12.1 shows these processes.

FIGURE 12.1
Exponential nitrogen uptake and elimination curves

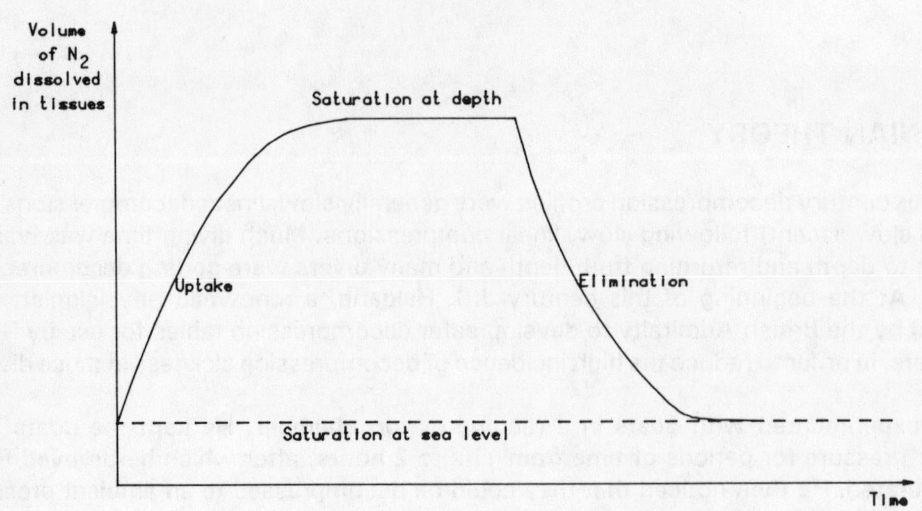

Realizing that different tissues absorb and release nitrogen at different rates, Haldane suggested that the continuous spectrum of tissues within the body could be represented by five tissue groups. He assumed that a specific tissue group absorbed and released nitrogen at the same rate. Haldane then assigned theoretical "half-times" of 5, 10, 20, 40 and 75 minutes to his specific tissue groups. These theoretical tissue types became known as the T_{5}, T_{10}, T_{20}, T_{40} and T_{75} tissues, respectively. *They did not represent specific body tissues.*

Tissue Half Times can be explained as follows:

The "tissue half time" is the time taken before a tissue has absorbed half of the volume of gas that it still needs to absorb in order to become saturated at that ambient pressure.

For example, the T_5 tissue will take five minutes to absorb half of the total volume of gas required for it to become saturated. During the next five minutes it will absorb half of the remaining amount of gas required for it to achieve saturation. This is shown in Table 12.1 and Figure 12.2.

TABLE 12.2

Nitrogen uptake in the T_5 tissue

If V = the total amount of N_2 needed to be absorbed in order to achieve saturation

Interval	Volume of N_2 absorbed during interval	Total volume of N_2 absorbed	% saturation
1st 5 min	1/2 V	1/2 V	50
2nd 5 min	1/4 V	3/4 V	75
3rd 5 min	1/8 V	7/8 V	87.5
4th 5 min	1/16 V	15/16 V	93.8
5th 5 min	1/32 V	31/32 V	96.9
6th 5 min	1/64 V	63/64 V	98.4

This can also be shown diagrammatically as in Figure 12.2 below.

FIGURE 12.2

The loading of the T5 tissue

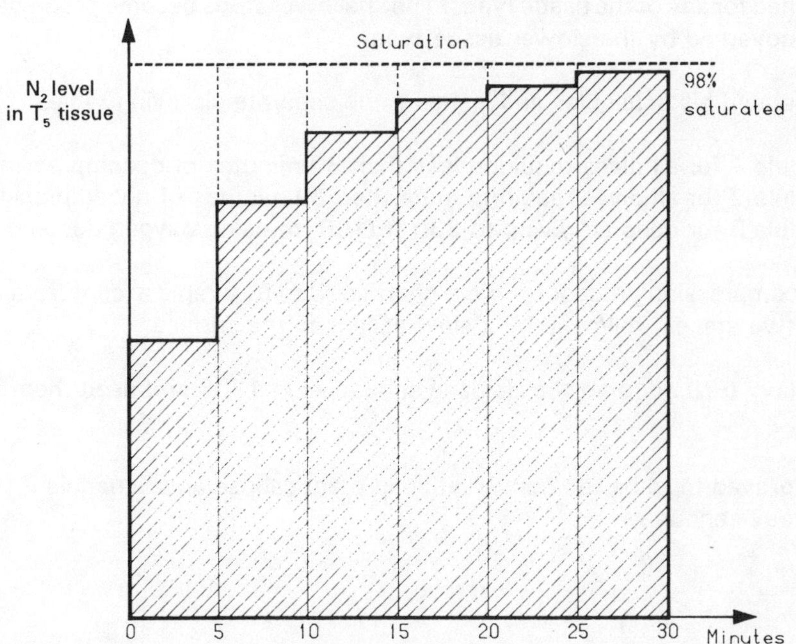

Similarly, the T_{20} tissue takes 20 minutes to absorb half of the nitrogen it requires to become saturated, and so on.

Thus, after 20 minutes, the T_5 tissue will have absorbed 15/16 of the nitrogen that it can hold whereas the T_{20} would only be half-saturated. **A tissue is considered to be completely saturated (98.4%) after six units of half time** so, after 30 minutes (i.e. 6 x 5 min.) the T_5 tissue is considered fully saturated and, after 60 minutes (i.e. 6 x 10 min.) the T_{10} tissue is fully saturated.

Haldane believed desaturation to be the exact opposite to this saturation process. For example, after 5 minutes the T_5 tissue will have released half of the nitrogen required in order for it to return to saturation at sea level.

Using this totally theoretical mathematical model and an empirical observation that animals could tolerate an overpressure (supersaturation) of nitrogen, expressed as a ratio of up to 1.58 to 1 (to ambient pressure), Haldane began to build a decompression schedule. He derived equations which were designed to calculate the amount of nitrogen absorbed after a given time at pressure, and could thus estimate the nitrogen tension in the tissue. Haldane could now calculate the depth that a diver could ascend to before the ratio of tissue nitrogen tension to ambient pressure exceeded the "critical ratio" of 1.58 to 1. He constructed decompression schedules which did not allow this critical ratio to be exceeded in any of the five tissue types.

The deepest stop on Haldane's decompression schedules is very short because it is determined by the tissue with the highest pressure of nitrogen, which is always the fast tissue which releases its gas load quickly. The diver must remain at the stop until the nitrogen pressure in this tissue drops enough to allow a further ascent which ceases when the critical value is reached for any of the tissue types. The shallower stops become progressively longer as they are governed by the slower tissue types.

Haldane tabulated his schedules and issued three separate air diving tables:

- Schedule 1 for all dives requiring less than 30 minutes of decompression time.
- Schedule 2 for all dives requiring more than 30 minutes of decompression time.
- Schedule 3 for deep air diving to 330 ft (100 m) using oxygen decompression.

All of his decompression procedures were characterized by a rapid ascent from depth to the first one or two stages, followed by a slow ascent to the surface.

The Royal Navy (RN) adopted the Haldane schedules in 1908 and used them for the next 50 years.

Schedule 1 proved to to be too conservative in practical use and Schedule 2 proved to be not conservative enough.

FIGURE 12.3

Haldane Decompression Procedure

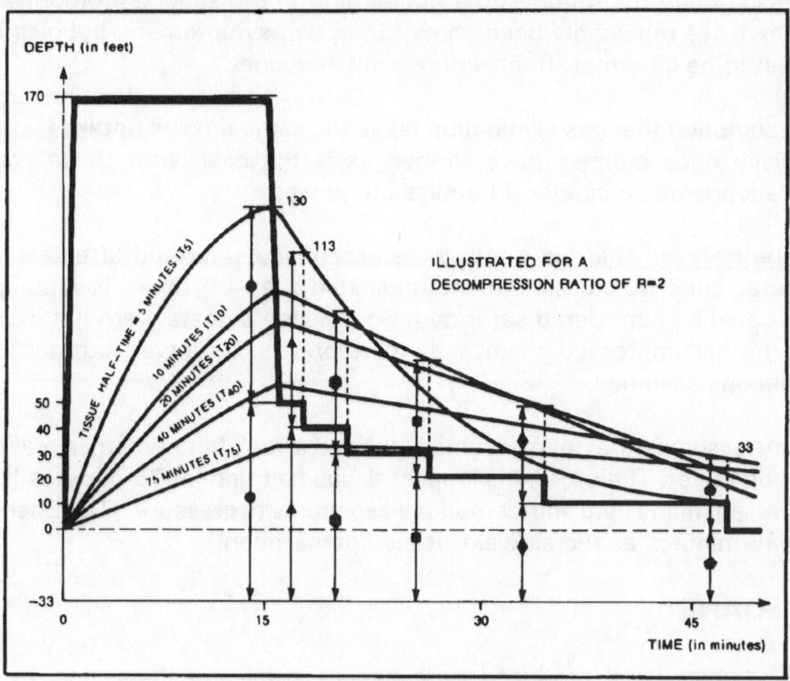

Reprinted from Edmonds, et al (1981), with permission.

Figure 12.3 represents an exposure to 168 ft for 15 minutes and illustrates the procedure Haldane used to calculate a decompression schedule. The procedure involves the following steps:

The tension in each of the five tissue compartments is computed for the exposure of 168 ft for 15 minutes.

The highest tension occurs in the T_5 tissue group and its tension can be calculated to be equivalent to the tissue being saturated at 130 fsw. Since the T_5 compartment contains more gas than the "slower" compartments, it is the "controlling" tissue for the decompression.

The absolute pressure in the T_5 tissue is therefore 130 (from dive) + 33 (from atmosphere) = 163 fsw.

Limiting the diver's ascent by allowing only a 2:1* pressure drop, the diver may ascend to 163/2 = 81.5 "footsworth" of gas, which corresponds to a depth of 81.5 - 33 = 48.5 fsw. Since the decompression stops are in increments of 10 fsw, the first stop occurs at 50 fsw.

The diver must remain at 50 fsw until the tissue tensions fall enough to allow ascent to 40 fsw. Saturation at 40 fsw corresponds to a tension of 40 + 33 = 73 fsw. Since a pressure drop of 2:1 is allowed, the pressure on leaving 50 fsw must not exceed 73 x 2 = 146 fsw. This corresponds to a tissue tension of 146 - 33 = 113 fsw.

Therefore, the diver must remain at 50 fsw until the tension in the T_5 tissue compartment falls to 113 fsw, at which time he may ascend to 40 fsw.

The tensions are computed for all five tissue compartments at each 10 fsw stop. Their tensions must not exceed the 2:1 ratio dictated by the model.

The T_5 tissue compartment limits the ascents from the first three stops. The T_{10} tissue compartment limits the fourth stop, and the T_{20} tissue compartment the fifth. The duration of the fifth stop is controlled by by the T_{40} tissue compartment. When the T_{40} tissue is reduced to 66 "footsworth" of gas, the diver can ascend to the surface (1 ATA or 33 "footsworth" of gas), thereby maintaining a 2:1 ratio and avoiding "bubbling".

* For simplicity, it is assumed that the breathing gas is pure nitrogen. Thus, a ratio of nitrogen tensions of 1.58:1 for air equates to 2:1 with this mix.

Haldane's tables had a number of shortcomings, some of which are the following:

- The assumption that bubbles did not form until the supersaturation ratio exceeded 1.58 to 1 has repeatedly been shown (e.g. by asymptomatic bubbles in ultrasound studies) to be incorrect. Bubbles form much sooner.

- His assumption that gas elimination takes the same time as uptake is often not valid, especially once bubbles have formed as is the case with these schedules. Gas elimination is much slower if bubbles are present.

- Haldane believed that his goats were essentially saturated after 1$^1/_2$-2 hours at a pressure. Subsequent experiments indicated that 4-6 hours is required before the goats could be considered saturated. So Haldane's goats were not in fact saturated when he decompressed them and, therefore, had a lower nitrogen load than his calculations assumed.

  Haldane assumed that man became saturated after 5 hour when, in reality, it takes 24 hours or longer. Therefore, his longest tissue half time of 75 minutes is far too short to represent many long and/or multiple exposures to pressure. (The Buehlmann Tables use 635 minutes as the slowest tissue compartment).

POST HALDANE

In 1912, Sir Leonard **Hill** produced both experimental and theoretical evidence which questioned the use of staged decompression (i.e. decompression requiring stops at particular depths) as suggested by Haldane, over continuous uniform decompression. Hill believed that bubbles form whenever the tissue gas tension exceeds the ambient pressure by a particular amount. In other words bubble formation depends on upon a pressure difference rather than a pressure ratio (Critical Pressure Hypothesis).

In 1954, **Rashbass**, using the observation that a diver seemed able to remain indefinately at 30 ft (9 m) and then ascend directly to the surface, assumed that a diver could tolerate "30 foot's worth" of excess gas in his tissues at any level - that is, that decompression is safe as long as a constant difference of 30 feet of sea water (fsw) is not exceeded.

In 1955, the **U.S. Navy** introduced some schedules based on the Haldanian model but used tissue half-times of 5, 10, 20, 40, 80 and 120 minutes. Instead of using a single critical ratio for all tissues for all depths, the U.S. Navy used ratios (expressed as pressures) that varied from tissue to tissue and from depth to depth. These are the current U.S. Navy schedules, published in 1957.

In 1958, **Hempleman**, a British physiologist, introduced a different decompression concept. He had observed that over a particular depth range the first symptom of decompression sickness to appear was usually pain at or near a joint. He assumed that the tissue involved (e.g. tendon) was, therefore, the tissue with the greatest overpressure of nitrogen for that depth range, and that gas elimination from that tissue must control the decompression. He pictured the body as a single tissue and believed that the quantity of gas absorbed in the body could be calculated by a simple formula which related depth and time. Unlike Haldane, who believed that gas uptake and elimination took identical times, Hempleman assumed that gas elimination was one and a half times slower than uptake. Utilizing the theory that the tissues could tolerate an overpressure of 30 fsw Hempleman constructed a new set of decompression schedules. These schedules, metricated in 1972, are the current Royal Navy schedules.

These schedules have theoretical limitations which have been confirmed in practice. Firstly, the concept that a single tissue (i.e. the slowest tissue) controls decompression only applies over a certain depth range. If deeper dives are performed vestibular symptoms, rather than niggling pain, become the first overt sign of decompression sickness. Secondly, the concept of an allowable overpressure of 30 fsw at all depths is often too conservative.

Hempleman realized these limitations and, in 1968, new schedules were introduced after extensive trialling. These schedules, known as the 1968 Air Diving Tables, still used the concept of a single tissue but used a variable ratio of tissue nitrogen tension to ambient pressure in order to calculate safe decompression. The RN rejected these tables claiming them to be too conservative. They were slightly modified, metricated and re-appeared as the RNPL 1972 tables.

Since the 1960's Professor Albert **Buehlmann** of the University of Zurich has presented various decompression schedules using either nitrogen or helium as the inert gas. The tables assume that gas uptake and elimination occur exponentially and at identical rates. They utilize 12 tissue compartments with half-times for 4-635 minutes, and allow a certain degree of tolerated supersaturation within each compartment.

In 1966, Brian **Hills** introduced his "thermodynamic" approach to decompression. All of the previous theories assumed that the pressure of inert gas in the tissue must exceed the ambient pressure plus the "inherent saturation" by some critical amount before bubbles will form. Hills demonstrated that bubbles (gas phase) are present before these critical levels are reached, and argued that the presence of bubbles reduced the driving force for gas elimination. He proposed that bubbling could be avoided if decompression was performed so that the pressure of inert gas in the tissues remained essentially no higher than the ambient pressure. Hills introduced schedules based on this concept but difficulties were experienced with initial schedule trials. The problems were possibly due to excessively slow diffusion rates being chosen to account for gas uptake.

In 1983, the Defence and Civil Institute of Environmental Medicine (**DCIEM**) of Canada published some schedules based on a decompression model that utilized tissue compartments connected in series, rather than in parallel. The model utilizes the concept of allowable surfacing supersaturation ratios.

During the 1980's some researchers at the University of Hawaii developed a decompression model based on the physical properties of bubble nucleation. Their model, the **Tiny Bubble Group Varying Permeability Model**, assumes the presence of bubble nuclei in our bodies. The nuclei are stabilized by elastic skins and will grow if gas enters them during decompression. If the total volume of gas in the bubbles is less than some critical volume decompression is thought to be safe. Tables based on this model have been produced but are currently untested. They yield NDLs that are more conservative than those of the U.S. Navy for depths shallower than 140 ft (42 m).

The **U.S. Navy** has developed some new decompression models based on the mathematical chance (probability) of bends occurring. The models presume no specific knowledge regarding bubble formation or growth. In 1985, the Navy published two sets of air decompression schedules with an equal chance of bends throughout. One schedule carries a 1% bends risk and the other carries a risk of 5%. The schedules are currently being modified and tested.

In 1988, **PADI** released the Recreational Dive Planner which is based on a Haldanian model similar to that used for the 1957 U.S. Navy Tables. The model assumes that gas uptake and elimination occurs exponentially and at identical rates. The longest tissue half-time used is 60 minutes and it is on this tissue compartment that the repetitive system is based. The table has been designed so that it can be used for multi-level diving and is purely a no-decompression stop table.

SOURCES

Bassett, B. (1985), "The Theoretical Basis of the U.S. Navy Air Decompression Tables". *SPUMS Journal*; July-Sept: 18-23.

Edmonds, C., Lowry, C. and Pennefather, J. (1981), "Diving and Subaquatic Medicine", 2nd edition. Diving Medical Center, Sydney.

Hempleman, H. (1982), "History of Evolution of Decompression Procedures". In: *Physiology and Medicine of Diving*, 3rd edition, Bennett, P. and Elliott, D. (eds), Best Publishing Co., California.

RECOMMENDED FURTHER READING

Hempleman, H. (1982), "History of Evolution of Decompression Procedures". In: *Physiology and Medicine of Diving*, 3rd edition, Bennett, P. and Elliott, D. (eds), Best Publishing Co., California.

CHAPTER 13

THE U.S. NAVY TABLES

13.1 History and design

HISTORICAL BACKGROUND

The first tables developed for the U.S. Navy were the Bureau of Construction and Repair Tables which emerged in 1915. They were based on the Haldanian concept of a decompression ratio, and also used oxygen decompression to achieve depths between 200-300 ft (60-90 m).

In the 1930's, some U.S. Navy researchers undertook a set of decompression experiments using human volunteers. The volunteers were exposed to raised air pressures in a chamber and then decompressed, without stops, back to surface pressure. When the results of these experiments were analyzed it became apparent that Haldane's idea that the ambient pressure could be halved without ill effect was wrong. The researchers (Hawkins et al) concluded that each tissue half-time had its own allowable decompression ratio.

In 1937, it was decided that the T_5 and T_{10} tissue groups could tolerate so much overpressure that they could, in fact, be ignored. Schedules which involved only the T_{20}, T_{40} and T_{75} tissue groups were issued (Yarbrough). The allowable pressure ratios for these tissue types were increased to accommodate exercise at depth. These U.S. Navy Tables gained worldwide acceptance but were eventually found to offer too little protection from bends after long dives. The tables had no real acceptable provision for performing repetitive dives since most dives were done in the surface supply mode with an unlimited air supply. If a repetitive dive was performed the bottom times of the two dives were just added together, no matter how long the surface interval was. No allowance was made for off-gassing during a surface interval.

Later it was decided that the supersaturation ratio must be depth-dependent and deeper stops were introduced (Dwyer, 1956). The T_5 and T_{10} tissues were re-introduced and a new tissue group with a half-time of 120 minutes was added. What had now evolved were various tissue groups or compartments, each with a characteristic supersaturation ratio which varies with the amount of gas dissolved in it. The maximum supersaturation ratios were expressed as maximum permitted excess pressures ("M values"). Tables based on these concepts were introduced by the U.S. Navy by Dwyer in 1955, and tested by des Granges in 1956. The tests involved some 564 man-dives resulting in 26 cases of decompression sickness.[1] The problem of repetitive diving was addressed in 1957. The resulting repetitive dive procedure was tested on 61 repetitive dive combinations. During testing, 122 man-dives were undertaken resulting in 3 cases of bends.[1] The resulting tables were published in the U.S. Navy Manual in 1957 and are the current U.S. Navy Tables.

The tables are based on the Haldanian idea that gas uptake and elimination occur exponentially *and at the same rate*, and they utilize tissue compartments of 5, 10, 20, 40, 80 and 120 minutes. These compartments are not supposed to represent specific body tissues.

There are also separate schedules for exceptional exposures and these utilize additional half-times of 160 and 240 minutes, with allowable supersaturation pressures lower than those for the T_{120} tissue.

FEATURES OF THE U.S. NAVY SYSTEM

The nitrogen tension in each tissue compartment can be calculated and is expressed in feet of sea water (fsw). For example, when saturated at the surface the total gas tension in each tissue type is 33 fsw. Since only 79% of this tension is due to nitrogen, the nitrogen tension is 0.79 x 33 = 26.1 fsw. In general, when a diver is saturated at a depth of **D** fsw, the nitrogen tension in all tissue types is **0.79 (D + 33)** fsw.

After being at depth for a certain time (less than saturation) the different tissue types will each have a particular gas tension. The nitrogen tension can be estimated using the equation: $P_t = P_o + (P_a - P_o)(1 - 2^{-t/T})$ fsw, where P_t is the nitrogen tension in the tissue group after **t** minutes; P_o is the initial nitrogen tension; P_a is the nitrogen pressure in the lungs; **T** is the tissue half-time in minutes; and **t** is the exposure time in minutes.

"M VALUES"

All of the previous systems of calculation used the concept of a maximum permitted supersaturation ratio. It is possible to regard this permitted ratio as a permitted pressure. These permitted pressures became known as **"M values"** (Workman). **An "M value" is the calculated partial pressure of nitrogen in a half-time tissue which is allowed when you reach a given decompression stop.** M values are expressed in feet of sea water absolute. Dividing M values by the barometric pressure at sea level (33 fsw) will give the critical ratio. The limiting M values and supersaturation ratios for surfacing (M_o) are given in Table 13.1.1.

The No-Decompression Limits can be determined by calculating which tissue type will reach its surfacing M value first for a particular depth. For example, when saturated at 60 fsw, the nitrogen tension in all tissue types is 0.79 x 93 = 73.5 fsw. Therefore the T_5 and T_{10} tissues can never reach their surfacing M values which are higher than 73.5 fsw. The first tissue type to reach its maximum is the T_{40} tissue which reaches it after about 60 minutes. Hence, the T_{40} tissue determines the NDL at 60 fsw and is said to "control" the dive at this depth.

Decompression is accomplished by defining maximum values for tissue nitrogen tensions at 10 fsw increments and requiring a diver to stop at a given depth until all tissues have desaturated to these M values. In other words, if the tension in one or more of the tissue types is higher than its allowable value at that depth, the diver must stop and wait until the tension(s) has dropped sufficiently to allow further ascent. The M value for a particular depth (**D**) is found using the formula $\mathbf{M = M_o + a \times D}$ where **a** is a constant which represents the change in M value for every fsw.

TABLE 13.1.1

Limiting surfacing values of U.S. Navy Tables

Half time	M_o value	Ratio
5	104	3.15
10	88	2.67
20	72	2.18
40	58	1.76
80	52	1.58
120	51	1.55

REPETITIVE GROUP DESIGNATORS

The letters A to O, and Z, are Repetitive Group Designators and are, in fact, a measure of the gas tension in the T_{120} tissue. At saturation on the surface the gas tension in the T_{120} tissue is 33 fsw. If, after a dive, the tension in the T_{120} tissue is between 33 and 35 fsw, the diver will be in Repetitive Group A. If the tension is between 35 and 37 fsw, the diver will be in Group B. Each ascending Repetitive Group represents an increase of 2 fsw in the gas tension of the T_{120} tissue.

Surfacing tissue tensions after all dives in the Standard Air Table were computed and the appropriate Repetitive Group assigned.

THE SURFACE INTERVAL CREDIT TABLE

At the beginning of a surface interval a few of the tissue groups may be at, or near, their critical nitrogen level. After a surface interval of just under 10 minutes, the faster tissue compartments have (theoretically) off-gassed enough nitrogen to leave the 120-minute tissue group as the group which is nearest to its critical nitrogen level. Hence, it will control the decompression for a repetitive dive. For this reason the Surface Interval Credit Table cannot be entered unless the surface interval is greater than 10 minutes. Any repetitive dive done within 10 minutes of surfacing is considered to be part of the initial dive.

The Surface Interval Credit Table is table is based on the off-gassing (by exponential decay) of the T_{120} tissue. It gives the amount of time required for the 120-minute tissue to decrease its tissue tension by 2 fsw while at an ambient pressure of 1 ATA.

For example, if you are in Group B when you surface from a dive, the tension in the T_{120} tissue will be between 35 and 37 fsw. The Surface Interval Credit Table indicates that after 2 hours and 11 minutes you will be in Group A. This means that it takes 2:11 hr for the T_{120} tissue to lose the 2 fsw of excess gas to reduce its gas tension to 35 fsw.

RESIDUAL NITROGEN TIME

This is the amount of time it would take the 120-minute tissue to saturate from a tension of 33 fsw to the tension of the various repetitive groups. For example, if you are in Group B you will have a calculated tension of 35-37 fsw in the T_{120} tissue. The time it takes for the tissue tension to rise from 33 to 37 fsw is the **Residual Nitrogen Time (RNT)**. The RNT can be taken to be equivalent to the time already spent at a particular pressure.

THE TABLES

There are five different tables which are used for different purposes. Three of these tables are shown as Tables 13.1.2, 13.1.3 and 13.1.4.

STANDARD AIR TABLE

A portion of this table is shown as Table 13.1.2, the entire table being in Appendix A.

The decompression schedules of the tables are given in 10 ft (3 m) depth increments and, usually, 10-minute bottom time increments. However, depth and bottom time combinations from actual dives rarely exactly match one of the decompression schedules listed in the table being used. As assurance that the selected decompression schedule is always conservative:

(a) always select the schedule depth to be equal to, or the next depth greater than, the actual depth to which the dive was conducted, and

(b) always select the schedule bottom time to be equal to, or the next longer bottom time than the actual bottom time of the dive.

If the Standard Air Decompression Tables, for example, were being used to select the correct schedule for a dive to 96 ft (29 m) for 31 minutes, decompression would be carried out in accordance with the 100 ft (30 m) for 40 minutes schedule.

Never attempt to interpolate between decompression schedules

Ascend at the rate of 60 ft (18 m) per minute when using the tables. Any variations with the rate of ascent must be corrected in accordance with the procedures described in Chapter 13.2.

The diver's chest should be located as close as possible to the stop depth.

The decompression stop times, as specified in each decompression schedule, begin as soon as the diver reaches the stop depth. Upon completion of the specified stop time the diver ascends to the next stop, or to the surface, at the proper ascent rate. **Do not include ascent time as part of stop time.**

If the diver was exceptionally cold during the dive, or if his work load was relatively strenuous, the next longer decompression schedule than the one he would normally follow should be selected. For example, the normal schedule for a dive to 90 ft (27 m) for 34 minutes would be the 90 ft/40 (27 m/40) schedule. If the diver were exceptionally cold or fatigued, he should decompress according to the 90 ft/50 (27 m/50) schedule. *See comment about this on Page 210)*.

TABLE 13.1.2
Portion of U.S. Navy Standard Air Decompression Tables

U.S. Navy Standard Air Decompression Table

Depth (feet)	Bottom time (min)	Time to first stop (min:sec)	Decompression stops (feet) 50	40	30	20	10	Total ascent (min:sec)	Repet-itive group
90 (27 metres)	50	1 20					18	19:30	L
	60	1:20					25	26:30	M
	70	1:10				7	30	38:30	N
	80	1:10				13	40	54:30	N
	90	1:10				18	48	67:30	O
	100	1:10				21	54	76:30	Z
	110	1:10				24	61	86:30	Z
	120	1:10				32	68	101:30	Z
	130	1:00			5	36	74	116:30	Z
100 (30 metres)	25	0.00					0	1:40	★
	30	1.30					3	4:40	I
	40	1:30					15	16:40	K
	50	1:20				2	24	27:40	L
	60	1:20				9	28	38:40	N
	70	1:20				17	39	57:40	O
	80	1:20				23	48	72:40	O
	90	1:10			3	23	57	84:40	Z
	100	1:10			7	23	66	97:40	Z
	110	1.10			10	34	72	117:40	Z
	120	1.10			12	41	78	132:40	Z
	180	1:00		1	29	53	118	202:40	◆
	240	1:00		14	42	84	142	283:40	◆
	360	0:50	2	42	73	111	187	416:40	◆
	480	0:50	21	61	91	142	187	503:40	◆
	720	0:50	55	106	122	142	187	613:40	◆
110 (33 metres)	20	0:00					0	1:50	★
	25	1:40					3	4:50	H
	30	1:40					7	8:50	J
	40	1:30				2	21	24:50	L
	50	1:30				8	26	35:50	M
	60	1:30				18	36	55:50	N
	70	1:20			1	23	48	73:50	O
	80	1:20			7	23	57	88:50	Z
	90	1:20			12	30	64	107:50	Z
	100	1:20			15	37	72	125:50	Z

★ See No Decompression Table for repetitive groups.

◆ Repetitive Dives may not follow exceptional exposure dives.

NO-DECOMPRESSION LIMITS AND REPETITIVE GROUP DESIGNATION TABLE FOR NO-DECOMPRESSION AIR DIVES (Table 13.1.3)

The No-Decompression Table serves two purposes. First it summarizes all the depth and bottom time combinations for which no decompression is required. Secondly, it provides the Repetitive Group Designation for each no-decompression dive. Even though decompression is not required, an amount of nitrogen remains in the diver's tissues after every dive. If he dives again within a 12-hour period, the diver must consider this residual nitrogen when calculating his decompression.

Each depth listed in the No-Decompression Table has a corresponding No-Decompression Limit (NDL) given in minutes. This limit is the maximum bottom time that a diver may spend at that depth without requiring decompression. The columns to the right of the No-Decompression Limits column are used to determine the Repetitive Group Designation which must be assigned to a diver subsequent to every dive. To find the Repetitive Group Designation, enter the table at the depth equal to, or next greater than, the actual depth of the dive. Follow that row to the right to the bottom time equal to, or next greater than, the actual bottom time of the dive. Follow that column to the Repetitive Group Designation.

Depths shallower than 35 ft (10.5 m) do not have a specific No-Decompression Limit. They are, however, restricted in that they only provide Repetitive Group Designations for bottom times up to between five and six hours.* These bottom times are considered the limitations of the No-Decompression Table and no field requirement for diving should extend beyond them.

Any dive below 35 ft (10.5 m) which has a bottom time greater than the No-Decompression Limit given in this table is a decompression dive and should be conducted in accordance with the Standard Air Table.

TABLE 13.1.3

NO-DECOMPRESSION LIMITS AND REPETITIVE GROUP DESIGNATION TABLE FOR NO-DECOMPRESSION AIR DIVES

Depth (feet)	No-decompression limits (min)	Group Designation														
		A	B	C	D	E	F	G	H	I	J	K	L	M	N	O
10		60	120	210	300											
15		35	70	110	160	225	350									
20		25	50	75	100	135	180	240	325							
25		20	35	55	75	100	125	160	195	245	315					
30		15	30	45	60	75	95	120	145	170	205	250	310			
35	310	5	15	25	40	50	60	80	100	120	140	160	190	220	270	310
40	200	5	15	25	30	40	50	70	80	100	110	130	150	170	200	
50	100		10	15	25	30	40	50	60	70	80	90	100			
60	60		10	15	20	25	30	40	50	55	60					
70	50		5	10	15	20	30	35	40	45	50					
80	40		5	10	15	20	25	30	35	40						
90	30		5	10	12	15	20	25	30							
100	25		5	7	10	15	20	22	25							
110	20			5	10	13	15	20								
120	15			5	10	12	15									
130	10			5	8	10										
140	10			5	7	10										
150	5			5												
160	5				5											
170	5				5											
180	5				5											
190	5				5											

* However Repetitive Groups for longer times can be found in Thalmann, E. and Butler, F (1983), "A Procedure for doing Multiple Level Dives on Air using Repetitive Groups". Navy Experimental Diving Unit, Report No. 13-83, Dept. of the Navy.

RESIDUAL NITROGEN TIMETABLE FOR REPETITIVE AIR DIVES (Table 13.1.4)

The quantity of residual nitrogen in a diver's body immediately after a dive is expressed by the Repetitive Group Designation assigned to him by either the Standard Air Table or the No-Decompression Table. The upper portion of the Residual Nitrogen Table is composed of various intervals between 10 minutes and 12 hours, expressed in hours : minutes (2:21 = 2 hours 21 minutes). Each interval has two limits; a minimum time (top limit) and a maximum time (bottom limit).

TABLE 13.1.4

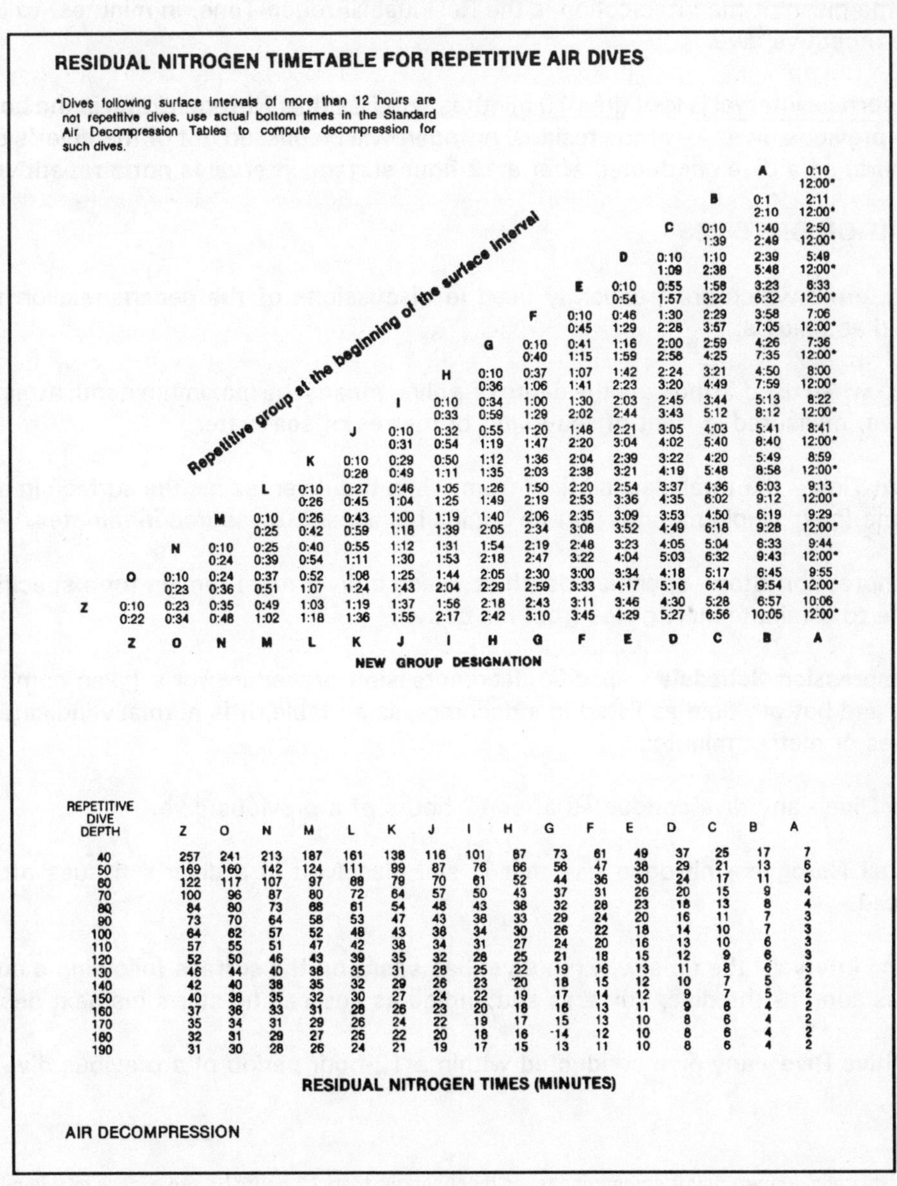

RESIDUAL NITROGEN TIMETABLE FOR REPETITIVE AIR DIVES

*Dives following surface intervals of more than 12 hours are not repetitive dives. use actual bottom times in the Standard Air Decompression Tables to compute decompression for such dives.

Repetitive group at the beginning of the surface interval

A																0:10 12:00*
B															0:1 2:10	2:11 12:00*
C														0:10 1:39	1:40 2:49	2:50 12:00*
D													0:10 1:09	1:10 2:38	2:39 5:48	5:49 12:00*
E												0:10 0:54	0:55 1:57	1:58 3:22	3:23 6:32	6:33 12:00*
F											0:10 0:45	0:46 1:29	1:30 2:28	2:29 3:57	3:58 7:05	7:06 12:00*
G										0:10 0:40	0:41 1:15	1:16 1:59	2:00 2:58	2:59 4:25	4:26 7:35	7:36 12:00*
H									0:10 0:36	0:37 1:06	1:07 1:41	1:42 2:23	2:24 3:20	3:21 4:49	4:50 7:59	8:00 12:00*
I								0:10 0:33	0:34 0:59	1:00 1:29	1:30 2:02	2:03 2:44	2:45 3:43	3:44 5:12	5:13 8:12	8:22 12:00*
J							0:10 0:31	0:32 0:54	0:55 1:19	1:20 1:47	1:48 2:20	2:21 3:04	3:05 4:02	4:03 5:40	5:41 8:40	8:41 12:00*
K						0:10 0:28	0:29 0:49	0:50 1:11	1:12 1:35	1:36 2:03	2:04 2:38	2:39 3:21	3:22 4:19	4:20 5:48	5:49 8:58	8:59 12:00*
L					0:10 0:26	0:27 0:45	0:46 1:04	1:05 1:25	1:26 1:49	1:50 2:19	2:20 2:53	2:54 3:36	3:37 4:35	4:36 6:02	6:03 9:12	9:13 12:00*
M				0:10 0:25	0:26 0:42	0:43 0:59	1:00 1:18	1:19 1:39	1:40 2:05	2:06 2:34	2:35 3:08	3:09 3:52	3:53 4:49	4:50 6:18	6:19 9:28	9:29 12:00*
N			0:10 0:24	0:25 0:39	0:40 0:54	0:55 1:11	1:12 1:30	1:31 1:53	1:54 2:18	2:19 2:47	2:48 3:22	3:23 4:04	4:05 5:03	5:04 6:32	6:33 9:43	9:44 12:00*
O		0:10 0:23	0:24 0:36	0:37 0:51	0:52 1:07	1:08 1:24	1:25 1:43	1:44 2:04	2:05 2:29	2:30 2:59	3:00 3:33	3:34 4:17	4:18 5:16	5:17 6:44	6:45 9:54	9:55 12:00*
Z	0:10 0:22	0:23 0:34	0:35 0:48	0:49 1:02	1:03 1:18	1:19 1:36	1:37 1:55	1:56 2:17	2:18 2:42	2:43 3:10	3:11 3:45	3:46 4:29	4:30 5:27	5:28 6:56	6:57 10:05	10:06 12:00*
	Z	O	N	M	L	K	J	I	H	G	F	E	D	C	B	A

NEW GROUP DESIGNATION

REPETITIVE DIVE DEPTH	Z	O	N	M	L	K	J	I	H	G	F	E	D	C	B	A
40	257	241	213	187	161	138	116	101	87	73	61	49	37	25	17	7
50	169	160	142	124	111	99	87	76	66	56	47	38	29	21	13	6
60	122	117	107	97	88	79	70	61	52	44	36	30	24	17	11	5
70	100	96	87	80	72	64	57	50	43	37	31	26	20	15	9	4
80	84	80	73	68	61	54	48	43	38	32	28	23	18	13	8	4
90	73	70	64	58	53	47	43	38	33	29	24	20	16	11	7	3
100	64	62	57	52	48	43	38	34	30	26	22	18	14	10	7	3
110	57	55	51	47	42	38	34	31	27	24	20	16	13	10	6	3
120	52	50	46	43	39	35	32	28	25	21	18	15	12	9	6	3
130	46	44	40	38	35	31	28	25	22	19	16	13	11	8	6	3
140	42	40	38	35	32	29	26	23	20	18	15	12	10	7	5	2
150	40	38	35	32	30	27	24	22	19	17	14	12	9	7	5	2
160	37	36	33	31	28	26	23	20	18	16	13	11	9	6	4	2
170	35	34	31	29	26	24	22	19	17	15	13	10	8	6	4	2
180	32	31	29	27	25	22	20	18	16	14	12	10	8	6	4	2
190	31	30	28	26	24	21	19	17	15	13	11	10	8	6	4	2

RESIDUAL NITROGEN TIMES (MINUTES)

AIR DECOMPRESSION

Residual Nitrogen Times corresponding to the depth of the repetitive dive are given in the body of the lower portion of the table. To determine the Residual Nitrogen Time for a repetitive dive, locate the diver's Repetitive Group Designation from his previous dive along the diagonal line above the table. Read horizontally to the interval in which the diver's surface interval lies. The time spent of the surface must be between, or equal to, the limits of the selected interval.

Next, read vertically downwards to the new Repetitive Group Designation. This designation corresponds to the present quantity of residual nitrogen in the diver's body. Continue downwards in this same column to the row which represents the depth of the repetitive dive. The time given at the intersection is the Residual Nitrogen Time, in minutes, to be applied to the repetitive dive.

If the surface interval is less than 10 minutes, the Residual Nitrogen Time is the bottom time of the previous dive. All of the residual nitrogen will be passed out of the diver's body after 12 hours, so a dive conducted after a 12 hour surface interval is not a repetitive dive.*

DEFINITION OF TERMS

Those terms which are frequently used in discussions of the decompression tables are defined as follows:

Depth - when used to indicate the depth of a dive, means the maximum depth attained during the dive, measured in feet of sea-water or metres of sea-water.

Bottom Time - the total elapsed time from when the diver leaves the surface in descent to the time (next whole minute) that he begins his ascent, measured in minutes.

Decompression Stop - specified depth at which a diver must remain for a specified length of time to eliminate inert gases from his body.

Decompression Schedule - specific decompression procedure for a given combination of depth and bottom time as listed in a decompression table; it is normally indicated as feet/minutes or metres/minutes.

Single Dive - any dive conducted after 12 hours of a previous dive.

Residual Nitrogen - nitrogen gas that is still dissolved in a diver's tissues after he has surfaced.

Surface Interval - the time which a diver has spent on the surface following a dive; beginning as soon as the diver surfaces and ending as soon as he starts his next descent.

Repetitive Dive - any dive conducted within a 12-hour period of a previous dive.

* It is now known that it sometimes takes much longer than 12 hours before excess nitrogen is eliminated from a diver's body

Repetitive Group Designation - a letter which relates directly to the amount of residual nitrogen in a diver's body for a 12-hour period following a dive.

Residual Nitrogen Time - an amount of time, in minutes, which must be added to the bottom time of a repetitive dive to compensate for the nitrogen still in solution in a diver's tissues from a previous dive.

Single Repetitive Dive - a dive for which the bottom time used to select the decompression schedule is the sum of the Residual Nitrogen Time and the actual bottom time of the dive.

REFERENCES

1. Thalmann, E., and Butler, F. (1983), "A Procedure for doing Multiple Level Dives on Air using Repetitive Groups". Navy Experimental Diving Unit, Report No. 13-83, Dept. of the Navy.

OTHER SOURCES

Bassett, B. (1985), "The Theoretical Basis of the U.S. Navy Air Decompression Tables". *SPUMS Journal*; July-Sept: 18-23.

Bassett, B. (1979), "Theory of Air Decompression for SCUBA Instructors". In: *Decompression In Depth*, PADI, California.

Bell, R. (1979), "The Theoretical Structure and Testing of High Altitude Diving Tables". In: *Decompression In Depth*, PADI, California.

Hempleman, H. (1982), "History of Evolution of Decompression Procedures". In: *The Physiology and Medicine of Diving*, 3rd edition, Bennett, P. and Elliott, D. (eds), Best Publishing Co., California.

Miller, J. ed (1979), "NOAA Diving Manual", 2nd edition. United States Department of Commerce.

U.S. Navy (1985), "U.S. Navy Diving Manual", Vol. 1, Air Diving. U.S. Government Printing Office.

RECOMMENDED FURTHER READING

Bassett, B. (1985), "The Theoretical Basis of the U.S. Navy Air Decompression Tables". *SPUMS Journal*; July-Sept: 18-23.

Hempleman, H. (1982), "History of Evolution of Decompression Procedures". In: *The Physiology and Medicine of Diving*, 3rd edition, Bennett, P. and Elliott, D. eds, Best Publishing Co., California.

13.2 Using the U.S. Navy Tables

There are many different formats of the U.S. Navy Tables available, some of which are shown in Figure 13.2.1.

FIGURE 13.2.1
Various formats of the U.S. Navy Tables

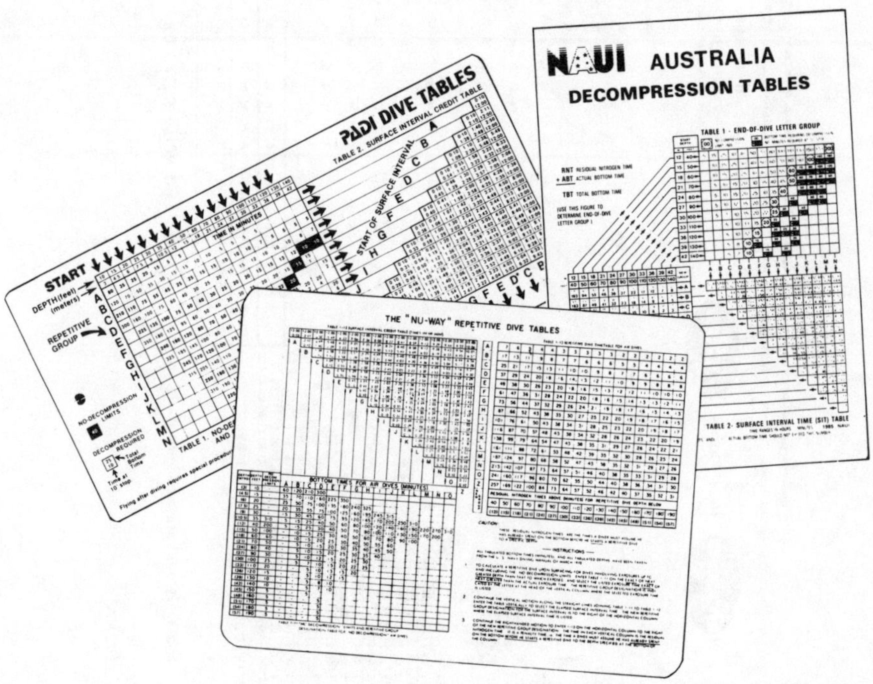

The "No Calculation Dive Tables" will be used for the following examples. These tables are based on the U.S. Navy Tables and, therefore, the same rules and definitions are appropriate. *These tables state that they have been modified for the sport diver. The modifications have only been in the format of the table. The times given are the same as in the U.S. Navy Tables. They have not been shortened in order to make them safer for use by sport divers.* These tables are shown in Figures 13.2.2 and 13.3.3.

FIGURE 13.2.2

Reprinted with permission of S. Harold Reuter, M.D.

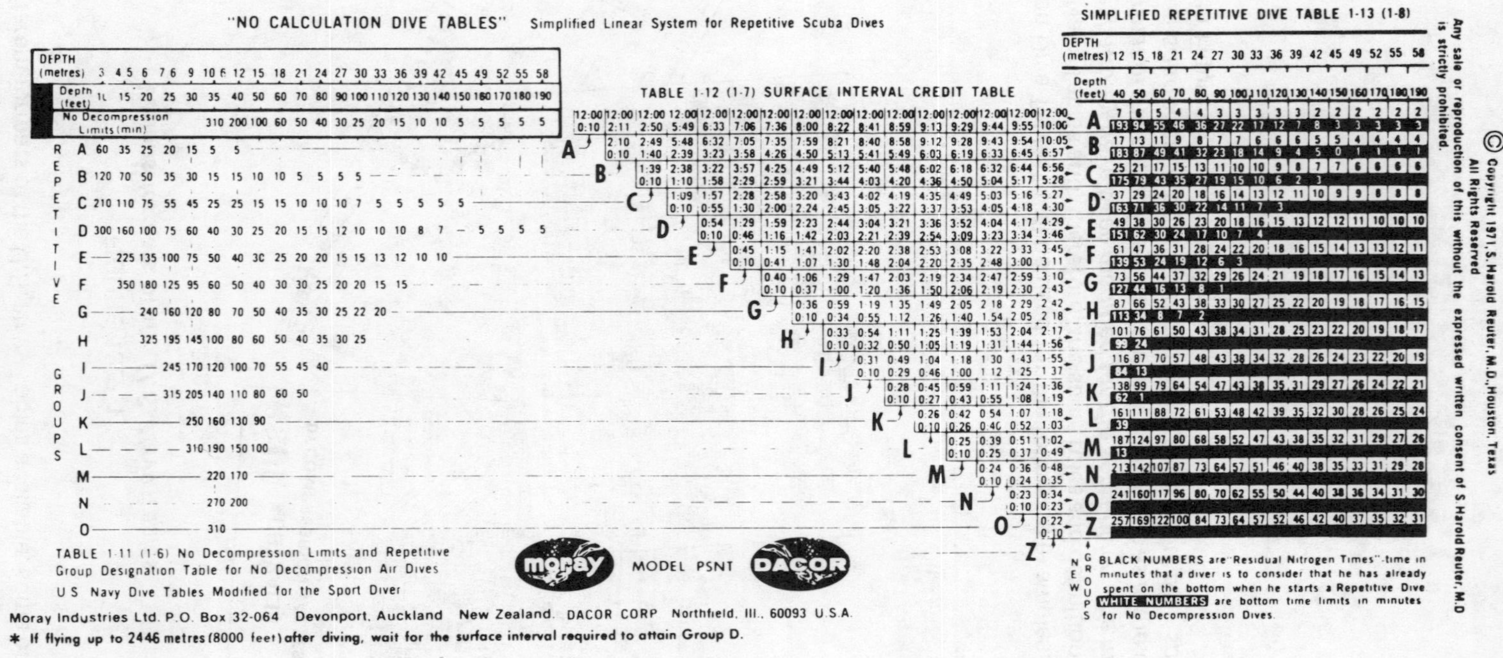

"NO CALCULATION DIVE TABLES" Simplified Linear System for Repetitive Scuba Dives

DEPTH (metres)	3	4.5	6	7.6	9	10.6	12	15	18	21	24	27	30	33	36	39	42	45	49	52	55	58
Depth (feet)	10	15	20	25	30	35	40	50	60	70	80	90	100	110	120	130	140	150	160	170	180	190
No Decompression Limits (min)						310	200	100	60	50	40	30	25	20	15	10	10	5	5	5	5	5
REPETITIVE GROUPS A	60	35	25	20	15	5	5															
B	120	70	50	35	30	15	15	10	10	5	5	5	5									
C	210	110	75	55	45	25	25	15	15	10	10	10	7	5	5	5	5	5				
D	300	160	100	75	60	40	30	25	20	15	15	12	10	10	10	8	7	–	5	5	5	5
E	—	225	135	100	75	50	40	30	25	20	20	15	15	13	12	10	10					
F		350	180	125	95	60	50	40	30	30	25	20	20	15	15							
G			240	160	120	80	70	50	40	35	30	25	22	20								
H			325	195	145	100	80	60	50	40	35	30	25									
I				245	170	120	100	70	55	45	40											
J				315	205	140	110	80	60	50												
K					250	160	130	90														
L					310	190	150	100														
M						220	170															
N						270	200															
O						310																

TABLE 1-11 (1-6) No Decompression Limits and Repetitive Group Designation Table for No Decompression Air Dives

U.S. Navy Dive Tables Modified for the Sport Diver

TABLE 1-12 (1-7) SURFACE INTERVAL CREDIT TABLE

NEW GROUP	A	B	C	D	E	F	G	H	I	J	K	L	M	N	O	Z
A	12:00 0:10	12:00 2:11	12:00 2:50	12:00 5:49	12:00 6:33	12:00 7:06	12:00 7:36	12:00 8:00	12:00 8:22	12:00 8:41	12:00 8:59	12:00 9:13	12:00 9:29	12:00 9:44	12:00 9:55	12:00 10:06
B		2:10 0:10	2:49 1:40	5:48 2:39	6:32 3:23	7:05 3:58	7:35 4:26	7:59 4:50	8:21 5:13	8:40 5:41	8:58 5:49	9:12 6:03	9:28 6:19	9:43 6:33	9:54 6:45	10:05 6:57
C			1:39 0:10	2:38 1:10	3:22 1:58	3:57 2:29	4:25 2:59	4:49 3:21	5:12 3:44	5:40 4:03	5:48 4:20	6:02 4:36	6:18 4:50	6:32 5:04	6:44 5:17	6:56 5:28
D				1:09 0:10	1:57 0:55	2:28 1:30	2:58 2:00	3:20 2:24	3:43 2:45	4:02 3:05	4:19 3:22	4:35 3:37	4:49 3:53	5:03 4:05	5:16 4:18	5:27 4:30
E					0:54 0:10	1:29 0:46	1:59 1:16	2:23 1:42	2:44 2:03	3:04 2:21	3:21 2:39	3:36 2:54	3:52 3:09	4:04 3:23	4:17 3:34	4:29 3:46
F						0:45 0:10	1:15 0:41	1:41 1:07	2:02 1:30	2:20 1:48	2:38 2:04	2:53 2:20	3:08 2:35	3:22 2:48	3:33 3:00	3:45 3:11
G							0:40 0:10	1:06 0:37	1:29 1:00	1:47 1:20	2:03 1:36	2:19 1:50	2:34 2:06	2:47 2:19	2:59 2:30	3:10 2:43
H								0:36 0:10	0:59 0:34	1:19 0:55	1:35 1:12	1:49 1:26	2:05 1:40	2:18 1:54	2:29 2:05	2:42 2:18
I									0:33 0:10	0:54 0:32	1:11 0:50	1:25 1:05	1:39 1:19	1:53 1:31	2:04 1:44	2:17 1:56
J										0:31 0:10	0:49 0:29	1:04 0:46	1:18 1:00	1:30 1:12	1:43 1:25	1:55 1:37
K											0:28 0:10	0:45 0:27	0:59 0:43	1:11 0:55	1:24 1:08	1:36 1:19
L												0:26 0:10	0:42 0:26	0:54 0:40	1:07 0:52	1:18 1:03
M													0:25 0:10	0:39 0:25	0:51 0:37	1:02 0:49
N														0:24 0:10	0:36 0:24	0:48 0:35
O															0:23 0:10	0:34 0:23
Z																0:22 0:10

SIMPLIFIED REPETITIVE DIVE TABLE 1-13 (1-8)

DEPTH (metres)		12	15	18	21	24	27	30	33	36	39	42	45	49	52	55	58
Depth (feet)		40	50	60	70	80	90	100	110	120	130	140	150	160	170	180	190
A	black	7	6	5	4	4	3	3	3	3	3	2	2	2	2	2	2
	white	193	94	55	46	36	27	22	17	12	7	8	3	3	3	3	3
B	black	17	13	11	9	8	7	7	6	6	6	5	5	4	4	4	4
	white	183	87	49	41	32	23	18	14	9	4	5	0	1	1	1	1
C	black	25	21	17	15	13	11	10	10	9	8	7	7	6	6	6	6
	white	175	79	43	35	27	19	15	10	6	2	3					
D	black	37	29	24	20	18	16	14	13	12	11	10	9	9	8	8	8
	white	163	71	36	30	22	14	11	7	3							
E	black	49	38	30	26	23	20	18	16	15	13	12	12	11	10	10	10
	white	151	62	30	24	17	10	7	4								
F	black	61	47	36	31	28	24	22	20	18	16	15	14	13	13	12	11
	white	139	53	24	19	12	6	3									
G	black	73	56	44	37	32	29	26	24	21	19	18	17	16	15	14	13
	white	127	44	16	13	8	1										
H	black	87	66	52	43	38	33	30	27	25	22	20	19	18	17	16	15
	white	113	34	8	7	2											
I	black	101	76	61	50	43	38	34	31	28	25	23	22	20	19	18	17
	white	99	24														
J	black	116	87	70	57	48	43	38	34	32	28	26	24	23	22	20	19
	white	84	13														
K	black	138	99	79	64	54	47	43	38	35	31	29	27	26	24	22	21
	white	62	1														
L	black	161	111	88	72	61	53	48	42	39	35	32	30	28	26	25	24
	white	39															
M	black	187	124	97	80	68	58	52	47	43	38	35	32	31	29	27	26
	white	13															
N	black	213	142	107	87	73	64	57	51	46	40	38	35	33	31	29	28
O	black	241	160	117	96	80	70	62	55	50	44	40	38	36	34	31	30
Z	black	257	169	122	100	84	73	64	57	52	46	42	40	37	35	32	31

NEW GROUPS

BLACK NUMBERS are "Residual Nitrogen Times"-time in minutes that a diver is to consider that he has already spent on the bottom when he starts a Repetitive Dive. WHITE NUMBERS are bottom time limits in minutes for No Decompression Dives.

MODEL PSNT

Moray Industries Ltd. P.O. Box 32-064 Devonport, Auckland New Zealand. DACOR CORP Northfield, Ill., 60093 U.S.A.

* If flying up to 2446 metres (8000 feet) after diving, wait for the surface interval required to attain Group D.

FIGURE 13.2.3

Reprinted with permission of S. Harold Reuter, M.D.

TABLE 1-10 (1-5) U.S. NAVY

Standard Air Decompression Table
(Simplified for the Sport Diver)

DEPTH (metres)	Depth (feet)	Bottom Time (min)	Decompression stops (min) 20 (ft)	Decompression stops (min) 10 (ft)	Repetitive Group
12	40	200		0	(*)
		210		2	N
		230		7	N
15	50	100		0	(*)
		110		3	L
		120		5	M
		140		10	M
		160		21	N
18	60	60		0	(*)
		70		2	K
		80		7	L
		100		14	M
		120		26	N
		140		39	O
21	70	50		0	(*)
		60		8	K
		70		14	L
		80		18	M
		90		23	N
		100		33	N
		110	2	41	O
		120	4	47	O
		130	6	52	O
24	80	40		0	(*)
		50		10	K
		60		17	L
		70		23	M
		80	2	31	N
		90	7	39	N
		100	11	46	O
		110	13	53	O
27	90	30		0	(*)
		40		7	J
		50		18	L
		60		25	M
		70	7	30	N
		80	13	40	N
		90	18	48	O
30	100	25		0	(*)
		30		3	I
		40		15	K
		50	2	24	L
		60	9	28	N
		70	17	39	O
33	110	20		0	(*)
		25		3	H
		30		7	J
		40	2	21	L
		50	8	26	M
		60	18	36	N
36	120	15		0	(*)
		20		2	H
		25		6	I
		30		14	J
		40	5	25	L
		50	15	31	N
39	130	10		0	(*)
		15		1	F
		20		4	H
		25		10	J
		30	3	18	M
		40	10	25	N
42	140	10		0	(*)
		15		2	G
		20		6	I
		25	2	14	J
		30	5	21	K
45	150	5		0	C
		10		1	E
		15		3	G
		20	2	7	H
		25	4	17	K
		30	8	24	L
49	160	5		0	D
		10		1	F
		15	1	4	H
		20	3	11	J
		25	7	20	K
52	170	5		0	D
		10		2	F
		15	2	5	H
		20	4	15	J
55	180	5		0	D
		10		3	F
		15	3	6	I
58	190	5		0	D
		10	1	3	G
		15	4	7	I

*See table 1-11 (1-6) for Repetitive Groups in "No Decompression Dives."

"NO CALCULATION" DIVE TABLES

INSTRUCTIONS FOR USE

For a "no decompression" dive

1. Find the depth you have dived along the top of Table 1-11.
2. Drop down to the figure which denotes your Bottom Time.
3. Go across to the right to Table 1-12.
4. Follow the arrow upward until you find the time spent out of the water since the last dive (Surface Interval).
5. Go across to the right to find the allowable Bottom Time (white numbers) for the next dive. These are listed under the appropriate depths at the top of each column.
   The Black Numbers are "Residual Nitrogen Times" and are only important for figuring "Decompression" Dives.
6. If the "no decompression" limits are exceeded, go to Table 1-10 for Decompression stops and times.
7. If diver's surface interval is less than 10 minutes, add the Bottom Times of the preceeding and following dives, use the maximum depth attained and consider the two dives as one.
8. SHORTENED OR OMITTED DECOMPRESSION: If a diver surfaces after a dive and finds he has not adequately decompressed but has no symptoms of decompression sickness, he has a maximum surface interval of 5 minutes to determine what his decompression for the dive should have been, get back in the water and begin the following decompression procedure:
   a. Make a stop at 40ft. (12m.) for 1/4 the 10ft. (3m.) stop time.
   b. Make a stop at 30ft. (9m.) for 1/3 the 10ft. (3m.) stop time.
   c. Make a stop at 20ft. (6m.) for 1/2 the 10ft. (3m.) stop time.
   d. Make a stop at 10ft. (3m.) for 1 1/2 times the 10ft (3m.) stop time, then surface.

Use of Table 1-10

a) All decompression stops are timed in minutes.
b) Ascent rate is 60 feet per minute.
c) The chest level of the diver should be maintained as close as possible to each decompression depth for the number of minutes listed.
d) The time at each stop is the exact time that is spent at that decompression depth.

DEFINITIONS:

1. Bottom time (in minutes) starts when the diver leaves the surface and ends only when the diver starts a direct ascent back to the surface.
   Always select the exact or next greater bottom time exposure.
2. Depth (in feet) The deepest depth of descent. Always enter the tables on the exact or next greater depth reached.
3. Residual Nitrogen Time—Time in minutes that a diver is to consider he has already spent on the bottom when he starts a repetitive dive.
4. Surface Interval—Time in hours and minutes actually spent on the surface between dives.
5. Repetitive Dive—A dive begun within 12 hours of surfacing from a previous dive.

PLAN YOUR DIVE—DIVE YOUR PLAN

Always carry the Dive Tables on a dive—they may save your life

DIVE	DEPTH	BOTTOM TIME	ARRIVAL TIME AT SURFACE	DEPARTURE TIME NEXT DIVE
1st				
2nd				
3rd				
4th				

Moray Industries Ltd.
P.O. Box 32-064 Devonport,
Auckland New Zealand.

DACOR CORP.
Northfield, Ill., 60093 U.S.A.

MODEL PSNT

A. Planning no-decompression (stop) dives

1. SINGLE, OR FIRST, NO-DECOMPRESSION DIVES

Table 1.11 (in Figure 13.2.2) was designed for planning single dives or the first of a group of dives. Table 1.11 is the left-most table of the "No Calculation Dive Tables"

Example 1.

You are planning to dive to a maximum depth of 80 ft (24 m). What is the No-Decompression Limit (NDL)?

Enter Table 1.11 from the top left corner (in either the *ft* or *m* row) and move right until finding the exact, or next greater tabled, maximum depth of the dive. In this case, move across to the 80 ft (24 m) column and move down the column to the third row which gives the NDLs for the various depths. The NDL for 80 ft (24 m) is, therefore, 40 minutes.

This 40 minutes is the actual allowable bottom time for the dive.

Similarly, the NDL for 100 ft (30 m) is 25 minutes, the NDL for 60 ft (18 m) is 60 minutes and the NDL for 50 ft (15 m) is 100 minutes.

Example 2.

What is the NDL for a single/first dive to a maximum depth of 54 ft (16 m)?

Enter Table 1.11 from the top left corner and move right. There is no column corresponding to 54 ft (16 m) so take the next greater tabled depth, which is 60 ft (18 m). Moving down the 60 ft column the NDL is found to be 60 minutes.

Similarly, the NDL for 66 ft (20 m) is 50 minutes, the NDL for 37ft (11 m) is 200 minutes and for 103 ft (31 m) is 20 minutes.

FINDING THE REPETITIVE GROUP AFTER SINGLE/FIRST NO-DECOMPRESSION DIVES

Example 3.

Find the Repetitive Group (RG) after the previous single dive to 80 ft (24 m) for 40 minutes.

As before, enter Table 1.11 at the top at 80 ft (24 m). Move down the 80 ft column, continue down past row 3 until the 40 (min.) appears again. It is the last figure in the column. Moving across to the right you will find the letter *I*. Thus, the Repetitive Group after a dive to 80 ft (24 m) for 40 minutes is group *I*.

Similarly, the RG after a dive to 100 ft (30 m) for 25 minutes is group *H*.

Example 4.

What is the Repetitive Group (RG) after a dive to 63 ft (19 m) for 30 minutes?

Enter Table 1.11 from the top left and move across to the 70 ft (21 m) column. Move down this column until finding the exact, or next longer tabled, bottom time. In this case you will find the 30-minute bottom time. Move across to the left to find the RG after the dive. It is group *F*.

Example 5.

What is the RG after a dive to 113 ft (34 m) for a bottom time of 11 minutes?

Enter Table 1.11, move across to the 120 ft (36 m) column and then down the column until you find 11 minutes or the next tabled time longer than 11 minutes. Take 12 minutes. Moving across to the right the RG is found to be *E*.

2. REPETITIVE NO-DECOMPRESSION DIVES

During a surface interval nitrogen is off-gassed. After various intervals the Repetitive Groups, which represent the nitrogen levels in the 120-minute tissue, will be reduced. Table 1.12, the "Surface Interval Credit Table", enables us to calculate new Repetitive Groups after surface intervals which are greater than 10 minutes and less than 12 hours.

FINDING THE NEW REPETITIVE GROUP AFTER A SURFACE INTERVAL

Example 6.

If the RG immediately after a dive is H, what is the new group after a surface interval of 2 hours?

Enter Table 1.12 from the left at *H*, and move upwards until you find an interval that includes the 2 hours. You will find it between the interval of 1:42 and 2:23, which is in the fourth row up. Move up to this row and then move right to find the new RG. It is group *E*.

Example 7.

If the RG immediately after a dive is F, find the new group after a surface interval of 2½ hours.

Enter Table 1.12 from the left at *F*, and move up the column until you find an interval including the time of 2½ hours. It is between 2:29 and 3:57, so move along that row to to right to find the new RG; which is *C*.

CALCULATING THE MAXIMUM ALLOWABLE NO-DECOMPRESSION BOTTOM TIME FOR A REPETITIVE DIVE

With these tables a repetitive dive is defined to be any dive within 12 hours of a previous dive(s). When planning a repetitive dive(s) the excess nitrogen still remaining after the surface interval must be taken into account. This is done by adding a "Residual Nitrogen Time" (RNT).

The Residual Nitrogen Time is the amount of time which must be considered already spent at the maximum depth of the repetitive dive before this dive is commenced. It is subtracted from the single dive NDL for that depth, and the result is the no-decompression bottom time still remaining at that depth.

Table 1.13, the right-most table of the "No Calculation Dive Tables", gives the Residual Nitrogen Times and the maximum no-decompression bottom times still available for the various depths of repetitive dives.

Example 8.

If you are in group C immediately before a dive to 80 ft (24 m), find:

(i) the Residual Nitrogen Time (RNT) at 80 ft (24 m)

(ii) the maximum allowable no-decompression bottom time at 80 ft (24 m)

Enter Table 1.13 from the left at group *C*. Move across to the right until intersecting the column corresponding to the exact, or next greater tabled, maximum depth of the repetitive dive. In this case move across to the right to the 80 ft (24 m) column. You will find two numbers in the box. The top number, printed in **black**, is the Residual Nitrogen Time which, in this case, is 13 minutes. This means that before doing the dive you must consider that you have already spent 13 minutes at 80 ft (24 m). This 13 minutes is to account for nitrogen left over from the previous dive(s). To calculate the allowable no-decompression bottom time you must subtract the RNT of 13 minutes from the NDL for 80 ft (24 m) given in Table 1.11.

i.e. Allowable no-deco bottom time = 40 - 13 = 27 minutes.
(NDL) (RNT)

In this particular format of the U.S. Navy Tables this calculation has already been done for you, and is given as the lower of the two numbers in the box. It is the number printed in **white** on black.

Example 9.

At the end of a surface interval after a dive you are in group B. Find:

(i) the Residual Nitrogen Time

(ii) the maximum allowable bottom time for a no-decompression dive to 96 ft (29 m).

Enter Table 1.13 from the left at *B*. Move along this row until intersecting the 100 ft (30 m) column. The RNT is, therefore, 7 minutes and the allowable bottom time is 18 minutes.

PLANNING A PAIR OF NO-DECOMPRESSION DIVES

Example 10.

You are planning two no-decompression dives. The first dive is to 100 ft (30 m) followed 3 hours later by a dive to 73 ft (22 m). Find the maximum allowable bottom time for each dive.

Enter Table 1.11 from the top left and move across to 100 ft (30 m). Moving down to the NDL row, the NDL is found to be *25 minutes*, which is the maximum allowable bottom time for the first dive. Move to the bottom of this 100 ft (30 m) column to the proposed bottom time of 25 minutes, and then across to the right to find the RG after the dive. It is group *H*. Move up the *H* column to find an interval which includes the surface interval of 3 hours. It lies between 2:24 and 3:20. Move across to the right to find the RG after the surface interval. It is *D*.

Enter Table 1.13 from the left at *D* and continue right until intersecting the column corresponding to 80 ft (24 m). The RNT is, therefore, *18 minutes* and the maximum allowable bottom time for the dive is *22 minutes.*

Example 11.

You are planning two no-decompression dives. The first is to 120 ft (36 m), followed 4 hours later by a dive to 110 ft (33 m). Find the maximum allowable bottom time for each dive.

Enter Table 1.11 from the top left and move across to120 ft (36 m). Moving down to the NDL row, the NDL is found to be *15 minutes*, which is the maximum allowable bottom time for the first dive. Move to the bottom of this 120 ft (36 m) column to the proposed bottom time of 15 minutes, and then across to the right to find the RG after the dive. It is group *F*. Move up the *F* column to find an interval which includes the surface interval of 4 hours. It lies between 3:58 and 7:05. Move across to the right to find the RG after the surface interval. It is *B*.

Enter Table 1.13 from the left at *B* and continue right until intersecting the column corresponding to 110 ft (33 m). The RNT is, therefore, *6 minutes* and the maximum allowable bottom time for the dive is *14 minutes.*

FINDING THE REPETITIVE GROUP AFTER A REPETITIVE DIVE

Example 12.

Before a repetitive dive to 100 ft (30 m) you are in group B. If you now dived to 100 ft for a bottom time of 10 minutes, what would be your new Repetitive Group?

From Table 1.13 the RNT at 100 ft (30 m) is *7 minutes* and the maximum no-decompression bottom time is *18 minutes.*

To calculate the RG after this 10-minute dive you must first find the **Equivalent Single Dive Bottom Time** of the dive.

The Equivalent Single Dive Bottom Time is found by adding the Residual Nitrogen Time to the Actual Bottom Time of the dive.

In this case the Equivalent Single Dive Bottom Time is $10_{(BT)} + 7_{(RNT)} = 17$ minutes.

To find the RG after this (repetitive) dive go back to Table 1.11. Enter at the depth of the repetitive dive, 100 ft (30 m), and move down this column until you find the equivalent single dive bottom time of the repetitive dive. In this case take 20 minutes. Move across to the right to find the RG after the dive. It is *F*.

Example 13.

Before a repetitive dive you are in group C. If you now dived to 76 ft (23 m) for a bottom time of 20 minutes, what would be your new Repetitive Group?

From Table 1.13 the RNT at 80 ft (24 m) is *13 minutes.* Adding this 13 minutes to the actual bottom time of 20 minutes gives an Equivalent Single Dive Bottom Time of *33 minutes.*

Enter Table 1.11 at 80 ft (24 m) and move down the column until finding the equivalent bottom time (or next greater tabled) of 33 minutes. In this case take 35 minutes. Move across to the right to get the RG, which is *H*.

PLANNING A GROUP OF THREE NO-DECOMPRESSION DIVES

Example 14.

You are planning to do three no-decompression dives, two of which are repetitive. The first dive, which is to 80 ft (24 m), is followed 2 hours later by a dive to 66 ft (20 m), which is followed 3 hours later by a final dive to 50 ft (15 m). Find the maximum allowable no-decompression bottom times for each of the dives.

Enter Table 1.11 at the top left corner. Move to the right until reaching the 80 ft (24 m) column. Move down to the third row to find the NDL. It is *40 minutes*, which is the maximum allowable bottom time for the first dive.

Continue down the column to the 40 at the end of the column and then move right to get the RG at the end of the first dive. It is *I*.

Move up the *I* column to find the 2-hour surface interval, which lies between 1:30 and 2:02. Move right to find the RG after the surface interval, group *F*.

Continue right until intersecting the 70 ft (21 m) column. The RNT is *31 minutes* and the maximum no-decompression bottom time for the second dive is *19 minutes.* The equivalent bottom time of this second dive is, therefore:

$19_{(BT)} + 31_{(RNT)} =$ *50 minutes*, which is the NDL for a single dive to this depth.

To find the RG after this dive enter Table 1.11 at 70 ft (21 m) and move down this column until finding the equivalent bottom time of 50 minutes. Moving across to the right the RG is *J*.

Move up the *J* column to find the surface interval of 3 hours. It lies between 2:21 and 3:04, so move up to this group and then right to get the RG, which is *E*.

Continue to move right until intersecting the 50 ft (15 m) column. The RNT at 50 ft (15 m) is *38 minutes* and the maximum allowable bottom time is *62 minutes.*

Planning a pair of no-decompression dives:

*** Summary of steps ***

1. Look up the NDL for the first dive (Table 1.11 or 1.10)
2. Find the RG after the first dive (Table 1.11-2)
3. Find the new RG after the surface interval (Table 1.12)
4. Find the RNT at the depth of the repetitive dive (Table 1.13)
5. Find the allowable no-decompression bottom time for the second dive.

Either:
- (i) read it straight off the table if given OR
- (ii) subtract the RNT from the NDL for the depth of the repetitive dive

6. Calculate the RG at the end of the repetitive dive (Table 1.11)
(Equivalent single dive BT = actual BT + RNT)

Example 15.

You are planning two no-decompression dives. The first is to 66 ft (20 m), followed 5 hours later by a dive to 60 ft (18 m). Find the maximum allowable bottom time for each dive.

Following the steps above, the calculations can be recorded as follows:

1. NDL for 66 ft (20 m) = 50
2. RG after first dive = J
3. RG after surface interval of 5 hr = C
4. RNT at 60 ft (18 m) = 17
5. Max. bottom time for 60 ft (18 m) = 60-17 = 43
6. RG after repetitive dive = J

Some divers prefer to draw the profiles and fill in the gaps as they work through the table. This may be done as in Figure 13.2.4.

FIGURE 13.2.4
Drawing a dive profile for Example 15

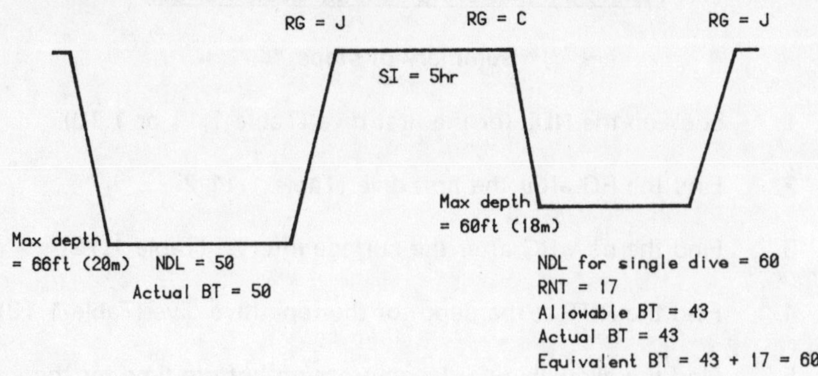

B. Planning decompression (stop) dives

1. SINGLE/FIRST DECOMPRESSION DIVES

If a decompression stop(s) is required for any dive, single or repetitive, it is given in Table 1.10. This particular version of the table has been shortened. It does not include dives which require decompression stops at depths greater than 20 ft (6 m).

Example 16.

Calculate the decompression necessary for a first/single dive to 90 ft (27 m) for 40 minutes.

Enter Table 1.10 from the left at the box corresponding to the exact, or next greater tabled, maximum depth of the dive.

In this case enter the 90 ft (27 m) box. Move right to find the exact, or next longer tabled, bottom time of the dive, which is written in the third column. In this case 40 minutes is tabled so move into the row for 40 minutes (in the 90 ft box), and move right to read off any required decompression stop(s). There is a 7 in the 10 ft (3 m) column so the required decompression is *7 minutes at 10 ft (3 m).*

This means that you must actually spend 7 full minutes at the 10 ft (3 m) stop. The time taken to ascend to the stop is not included in the stop time, it is extra.

Continue to move right along the row to find the RG after the dive. It is *J*.

Example 17.

Calculate the decompression required for a first/single dive to 103 ft (31 m) for 32 minutes.

Enter the 110 ft (33 m) box and look in column 3 for the exact, or next longer, tabled bottom time of 32 minutes. Take 40 minutes. Move across the 40-minute row to the right to find the required decompression. It is *2 minutes at 20 ft (6 m) followed by 21 minutes at 10 ft (3 m).*

You must ascend to 20 ft (6 m) and spend a full 2 minutes at 20 ft before ascending to 10 ft (3 m). You must then spend a full 21 minutes at 10 ft before surfacing.

Moving right, the RG after the dive is *L*.

Notes:

1. The first bottom time in column 3 of each box is the NDL for that depth.
2. A (*) in the final column means that the RG can be found from Table 1.11.

2. REPETITIVE DECOMPRESSION DIVES

Example 18.

You are planning two dives. The first is to a maximum depth of 73 ft (22 m) for a bottom time of 46 minutes. After a surface interval of 3½ hours you wish to dive to 18 m (60 ft) for 50 minutes. Calculate the decompression required.

As 46 minutes is beyond the NDL for 80 ft (24 m), a stop(s) is required and can be found in Table 1.10.

Enter Table 1.10 from the left at the 80 ft (24 m) box. Move right to the bottom time column to find 46 minutes. Take 50 minutes. Move right to find the decompression. It is *10 minutes at 10 ft (3 m).* The RG after the dive is *K*.

Enter Table 1.12 from the left at *K*. Move up the *K* column to find the surface interval of 3½ hour. It lies between 3:22 and 4:19 so move up to this box and then right along the row. You get group *D*.

Continue to move right along the *D* row until intersecting the 60 ft (18 m) column. The RNT is, therefore, 24 minutes. The equivalent single dive bottom time of the second dive is thus $24_{(RNT)} + 50_{(BT)} = 74$ minutes. This dive is equivalent to a single dive of 60 ft (18 m) for 74 minutes, which means that a decompression stop(s) is required and can be found in Table 1.10.

Enter Table 1.10 from the left at the 60 ft (18 m) box and look for 74 minutes in the bottom time column. Take 80 minutes. The required decompression is *7 minutes at 10 ft (3 m)* and the RG after the dive is *L*.

Planning a pair of decompression stop dives

*** Summary of steps ***

1. **Find any decompression stop required for the first dive (Table 1.10)**
2. **Find the RG at the end of the first dive (Table 1.10)**
3. **Find the RG after the surface interval (Table 1.12)**
4. **Find the RNT at the depth of the second dive (Table 1.13)**
5. **Find the equivalent single dive bottom time of the repetitive dive. (actual BT + RNT)**
6. **Find the decompression required for the repetitive dive (Table 1.10).
(Look up max. depth and equivalent single dive bottom time of repetitive dive)**
7. **Find the RG at the end of the repetitive dive (Table 1.10)**

Example 19.

You are planning two dives which will possibly require a decompression stop(s). The first dive is to 90 ft (27 m) for 35 minutes. The second dive, three hours after the first, is to 63 ft (19 m) for 35 minutes. Calculate any decompression stop(s) required.

Following the steps above, the calculations can be recorded as follows:

1. Decompression required first dive of 90 ft (27 m) for 35 minutes = 7 minutes at 10 ft (3 m)
2. RG after first dive = J
3. RG after surface interval of 3 hr = E
4. RNT at 63 ft (19 m) = 26
5. Equivalent single dive bottom time of repetitive dive = 35 + 26 = 61
6. Decompression required for single dive to 63 ft (19 m) for 61 minutes = 14 minutes at 10 ft (3 m)
7. RG after repetitive dive = L

This may be represented in diagramatic form as shown in Figure 13.2.5.

FIGURE 13.2.5
Drawing a profile for Example 19

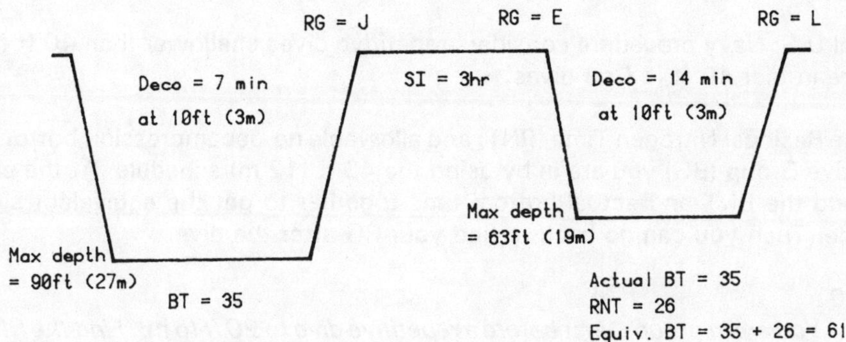

SPECIAL RULES FOR USING THE U.S. NAVY TABLES

1. FINDING THE RESIDUAL NITROGEN TIME BEFORE, AND THE REPETITIVE GROUP AFTER, DIVES TO 35 FT (10.5 M) OR SHALLOWER

Method 1

The original U.S. Navy procedure considers repetitive dives shallower than 40 ft (12 m) as if they were in fact 40 ft (12 m) dives.

You find the Residual Nitrogen Time (RNT) and allowable no-decompression bottom time for the Repetitive Group (RG) you are in by using the 40 ft (12 m) schedule. At the end of the dive you add the RNT and actual bottom time together to get the equivalent single dive bottom time. Then you can go back to find your RG after the dive.

Example 20.

You are in group C just before a repetitive dive to 20 ft (6 m). Find the RNT before the dive. If you then dive for a bottom time of 60 minutes, find the RG at the end of the dive.

Enter Table 1.13 at *C* and move to the 40 ft (12 m) column. The RNT is *25* minutes and the maximum allowable no-decompression bottom time is 175 minutes.

After diving for a bottom time of 60 minutes the equivalent single dive bottom time is $60_{(BT)} + 25_{(RNT)}$ = *85* minutes. To find the RG after the dive, go to Table 1.11, enter the 40 ft (12 m)* column and find the equivalent single dive bottom time of 85 minutes. Taking 100 minutes, the RG is *I*.

Note:

Residual Nitrogen Times and Repetitive Groups for dives shallower than 40 ft (12 m) are now available and are published in Thalmann, E. and Butler, F. (1983).

Method 2

Another method for finding the RNT for a repetitive dive to 35 ft (10.5 m) or shallower was developed relatively recently. It is less conservative than the previous method as it assigns you lower RGs at the end of shallow dives.

Some tables (e.g. the superceded PADI dive tables) already do this by supplying RNTs and RGs after repetitive dives shallower than 40 ft (12 m).

* You do <u>not</u> enter Table 1.11 at 20 ft (6 m) as the RNT you have just added is inappropriate for the times given in this column. The resulting RG would be too low.

This newer method can be explained as follows:

The first concept you must grasp is that if you are in a particular RG it is just a theoretical measure of the nitrogen level within you (i.e. the nitrogen level in the 120-minute tissue compartment). It does not matter what dive profile brought you into the RG. For example, if you are in group D you could have got there by diving to 30 ft (9 m) for 60 minutes, or to 50 ft (15 m) for 25 minutes, or to 80 ft (24 m) for 15 minutes, and so on. All can be viewed as equivalent, theoretically anyway.*

Suppose that you dive to 30 ft (9 m) for 60 minutes. At the end of the dive you will be in group D. Now let's approach the situation from a different angle. What if you were already in group D from a previous dive, say after 70 ft (21 m) for 15 minutes. The two cases can be considered equivalent if you ignore the actual dive profile that got you into group D and just assume that a group D diver is a group D diver, no matter how you got there. If this is done, theoretically, you can use an RNT of 60 minutes (i.e. the time taken to get to group D when doing a single dive to 30 ft/9 m) for the repetitive dive to 30 ft. If you are in group D and are planning to dive to 30 ft, you have already spent the equivalent of 60 minutes there before you start the dive.

Now returning to Example 20, where you are in group C before a dive to 20 ft (6 m) for 60 minutes.

If you enter Table 1.11 at the 20 ft (6 m) column and move down to the *C* row, you will find 75. This 75 minutes can be taken as your RNT for 6 m. After a 60-minute dive the equivalent single dive bottom time will be 75 + 60 = 135 minutes. Looking up 20 ft (6 m) for 135 minutes in Table 1.11, the RG after the dive is *E*. This is lower than the group *I* calculated by the first method.

Example 21.

> *You are in group F just before a repetitive dive to 25 ft (8 m). Find the RNT before the dive. If you then dive for a bottom time of 40 minutes, find the RG at the end of the dive. Use both methods described.*

Method 1

Enter Table 1.13 at F and move to the 40 ft (12 m) column to get the RNT of 61 minutes. Calculate the equivalent single dive bottom time: 61 + 40 = 101 minutes. Enter Table 1.11 at 40 ft (12 m) and look up the RG for 101 minutes (take 110 minutes), which is *J*.

Method 2

Enter Table 1.11 at the 25 ft (8 m) column. Move down to the *F* row to get the RNT at this depth. It is 125. Add on the actual bottom time to get the equivalent bottom time of 165 minutes. Look up 25 ft (8 m) for 165 minutes to get the RG after the dive. It is *H*.

* Although the calculated nitrogen levels in the 120-minute tissue compartment may be identical, the actual nitrogen distribution throughout a diver's body may be very different after the various profiles.

2. COLD OR ARDUOUS DIVES (AND UNDER CONDITIONS THAT PROHIBIT ACCURATE DECOMPRESSION)

The instruction relating to this in the U.S. Navy Manual is given on page 7.4 of the 1985 edition. The following recommendation is taken from the NOAA manual (1979) and seems more appropriate to the non-Navy diver.

For cold or arduous dives and under conditions that prohibit accurate decompression, the next deeper and longer schedule should be used. For example, for a dive to 110 ft (33 m) for 30 minutes in cold water, decompress using the 120 ft (36 m) for 40 minutes schedule.

Example 22.

If, on a dive to 90 ft (27 m) for 27 minutes, you were exceptionally cold, you should consider the dive as a 100 ft (30 m) for 40 minutes dive. Thus, it would require decompression of 15 minutes at 10 ft (3 m).

Example 23.

You are planning a decompression dive to 76 ft (23 m) for 42 minutes. Your depth gauge is not perfectly accurate and your bottom time, ascent rate and decompression stop depth cannot be measured exactly. What schedule should you choose?

These conditions constitute a situation which prohibits accurate decompression. The dive should be avoided if possible! The minimum schedule that should be chosen is that for 90 ft (27 m) for 60 minutes. The required decompression is 25 minutes at 10 ft (3 m).

3. THE EXCEPTION RULE

The following rule has appeared in various editions of the U.S. Navy Diving Manual prior to 1985. However, it does not appear in the 1985 edition of the Manual and it is, therefore, presumably, no longer recommended.

An exception to the tables occurs when a repetitive dive is to the same or greater depth than the previous dive and the surface interval is short enough that the Residual Nitrogen Time is greater than the actual bottom time of the previous dive. In this case, add the actual bottom time of the previous dive to the actual bottom time of the repetitive dive and decompress for the total bottom time and deepest dive.

Example 24.

You have dived to 60 ft (18 m) for a bottom time of 31 minutes and wish to dive to 70 ft (21 m) after a surface interval of 30 minutes. Find the maximum allowable no-decompression bottom time.

After a dive to 60 ft (18 m) for 31 minutes you surface in group *G*. After the surface interval your RG is still *G*. Now if you use the tables in the usual manner your RNT before the 70 ft (21 m) dive is 37 minutes and your maximum allowable no-decompression bottom time is 13 minutes. If, however, you follow the "exception rule", you will take your RNT as 31 minutes (i.e. the actual bottom time of the previous dive since it is shorter than the RNT given). Therefore, your allowable bottom time will be: $50_{\text{(NDL for 21 m)}} - 31 = $ *19 minutes.*

Note: Using the "exception rule" is usually less conservative than using the tables normally.

4. VARIATIONS IN ASCENT RATE

a. Ascent rate greater than 60 ft (18 m) per minute

(i) Rate of ascent greater than 60 ft (18 m) per minute, no decompression required:

Slow the rate of ascent and let the watches catch up/or stop at 10 ft (3 m) for the total ascent time that was required.

A dive was conducted to 100 ft (30 m) with a bottom time of 22 minutes. During ascent, the diver momentarily lost control of his buoyancy and increased his ascent rate to 75 ft (23 m) per minute, reaching 10 ft (3 m) in 1 minute 20 seconds. At a rate of 60 ft (18 m) per minute his ascent time should be 1 minute 40 seconds. He must remain at 10 ft (3 m) for the difference between 1 minute 40 seconds and 1 minute 20 seconds, or a total stop time of 20 seconds.*

(ii) Rate of ascent greater than 60 ft (18 m) per minute, decompression required:

Stop 10 ft (3 m) below the first decompression stop let the watches catch up.

b. Ascent rate less than 60 ft (18 m) per minute

(i) Rate of ascent less than 60 ft (18 m) per minute, delay occurs greater than 50 ft (15m):

Increase <u>bottom time</u> by the difference between the actual ascent time and the time if 60 ft (18 m) per minute were used. Decompress according to the requirements of the new total bottom time.

A dive was conducted to 120 ft (36 m) with a bottom time of 60 minutes. According to the 120 ft/60 (36 m/60) schedule of the Standard Air Decompression Table, the first decompression stop required is 30 ft (9 m). During the ascent the diver was delayed at 100 ft (30 m) and it actually took 5 minutes for him to reach his 30 ft (9 m) decompression stop. If an ascent rate of 60 ft (18 m) per minute were used it would have taken him 1 minute 30 seconds to ascend from 120 ft (36 m) to 30 ft (9 m). The difference between the actual and the 60 ft (18 m) per minute ascent times is 3 minutes 30 seconds.

* Many sport divers exceed this rate of ascent and few make it up by doing the stop that is required.

Increase the bottom time of the dive from 60 minutes to 63 min. 30 sec. and continue decompression according to the schedule which represents the new bottom time ... the 120 ft/70 (36 m/70) schedule.

(ii) Rate of ascent less than 60 ft (18 m) per minute, delay occurs less than 50 ft (15 m):

Increase time of first decompression stop by the difference between the actual ascent time and the time if 60 ft (18 m) per minute were used.

A dive was conducted to 120 ft (36 m) with a bottom time of 60 minutes. From the Standard Air Decompression Table the first decompression stop is at 30 ft (9 m). During the ascent, the diver was delayed at 40 ft (12 m) and it actually took 5 minutes for him to reach his 30ft (9 m) stop. As in the preceding example, the correct ascent time should have been 1 minute 30 seconds, causing a delay of 3 minutes 30 seconds.

Increase the length of the 30 ft (9 m) decompression stop by 3 minutes 30 seconds. Instead of 2 minutes, the diver must spend 5 minutes 30 seconds at 30 ft (9 m).

Author's note: *Many experts now believe that it is in fact preferable to ascend more slowly han the 60 ft (18 m) per minute recommended in the U.S. Navy Manual from where this extract is taken. See Chapter 5.2 for an explanation.*

5. OMITTED DECOMPRESSION

See Chapter 25.

SOURCES

Lewbel, G. (1984), "The Decompression Workbook". Pisces Books, New York.

Miller, J. (ed) (1979), "NOAA Diving Manual", 2nd edition. United States Department of Commerce.

Thalmann, E. and Butler, F. (1983), "A Procedure for doing Multiple Level Dives on Air using Repetitive Groups". Navy Experimental Diving Unit, Report No. 13-83, Dept. of the Navy.

U.S. Navy (1985), "U.S. Navy Diving Manual", Vol. 1, Air Diving. U.S. Government Printing Office.

RECOMMENDED FURTHER READING

Lewbel, G. (1984), "The Decompression Workbook". Pisces Books, New York.

EXERCISES ON THE U.S. NAVY TABLES

1. Find the No-Decompression Limits for single dives to the following depths:

(a)	100 ft (30 m)	(b)	30 ft (9 m)	(c)	76 ft (23 m)
(d)	116 ft (35 m)	(e)	101 ft (30.5 m)		

2. Find the decompression required for the following single or first dives (the times given are bottom times):

   (a) 60 ft (18 m) for 60 min
   (b) 50 ft (15 m) for 75 min
   (c) 63 ft (19 m) for 45 min
   (d) 83 ft (25 m) for 40 min
   (e) 92 ft (28 m) for 30 min
   (f) 120 ft (36 m) for 38 min

3. Find the maximum allowable no-decompression bottom times for the following second dives:

   (a) A dive to 66 ft (20 m), $2^1/_2$ hours after a dive to 92 ft (28 m) for 26 minutes.

   (b) A dive to 50 ft (15 m), 3 hours after a dive to 80 ft (24 m) for 25 minutes.

   (c) A dive to 100 ft (30 m), 5 hours after a dive to 120 ft (36 m) for 12 minutes.

4. Find the decompression required for the following second dives (the times given are bottom times):

   (a) A dive to 110 ft (33 m) for 10 minutes, 1 hour after a dive to 100 ft (30 m) for 20 minutes.

   (b) A dive to 80 ft (24 m) for 30 minutes, $4^1/_2$ hours after a dive to 86 ft (26 m) for 20 minutes.

   (c) A dive to 106 ft (32 m) for 18 minutes, 10 hours after a dive to 140 ft (42 m) for 16 minutes.

   (d) A dive to 26 ft (8 m) for 40 minutes, $1^1/_2$ hours after a dive to 90 ft (27 m) for 20 minutes.

5. Find the maximum allowable no-decompression bottom times for each dive in the following pairs of dives:

   (a) A dive to 92 ft (28 m) followed 2 hours later by a dive to 66 ft (20 m).

(b) A dive to 120 ft (36 m) followed 4½ hours later by a dive to 102 ft (31 m).

(c) A dive to 56 ft (17 m) followed 2½ hours later by another dive to 56 ft (17 m).

(d) A dive to 53 ft (16 m) followed 3 hours later by a dive to 66 ft (20 m).

(e) A dive to 135 ft (41 m) followed 6½ hours later by a dive to 40 ft (12 m).

ANSWERS:

1. (a) 25 (b) no limit (c) 40 (d) 15 (e) 20

2. (a) No deco (b) No deco (c) No deco
   (d) 7 min at 10 ft (3 m) (e) 3 min at 10 ft (3 m)
   (f) 5 min at 20 ft (6 m) and 25 min at 8.5 ft (3 m)

3. (a) 24 (b) 79 (c) 18

4. (a) 7 min at 10 ft (3 m) (b) No deco
   (c) 3 min at 10 ft (3 m) (d) No deco

5. (a) 25, 24 (b) 15, 14 (c) 60,30 (d) 60, 24
   (e) 10, 183

13.3 Adapting the U.S. Navy Tables to sport diving

A. Do the U.S. Navy Tables pertain to the sport diver?

The U.S. Navy Tables were created to prevent bends (not bubbles) in Navy divers. At their acceptance trials in 1956, the schedules produced an overall bends rate of 4.6% (26 cases in 564 dives) for single dives.[1,2] The schedules on which the bends occurred were then re-calculated and tested again (involving very few tests) until no bends occurred. All schedules were then re-calculated in accordance to these modifications. The repetitive schedules were tested on 61 repetitive profiles involving 122 dives. Three cases of bends occurred, an overall incidence of 4.9% (3 cases in 61).[1,3] There is no mention in the report whether or not the repetitive schedules were re-calculated and re-tested to produce no bends; it appears that they were not. Although it is stated that the divers involved in the testing varied in experience, ability and condition, no older divers and women participated.

The U.S. Navy have since done an enormous number of dives and have had a very low overall incidence of decompression sickness. In 1981, thirty five U.S. Navy divers developed bends out of 92,484 dives; an incidence of about 0.04%.[4] In 1987, the Navy recorded 106,965 dives with only 77 cases of bends (0.07%).[5]

The low bends rate of the U.S. Navy may give a distorted view of the actual safety of the tables. The vast majority of U.S. Navy dives are very shallow no-decompression dives, most of which do not even approach the limits of the tables.[6]

The U.S. Navy published a report in 1980 which covered all dives done *to the schedules* between the years 1971-78.[7] They included dives close to the No-Decompression Limits but did not include dives far shorter than the limits. This gave an incidence of 1.4% (13 cases out of 930 dives) for no-decompression dives made by U.S. Navy divers to depths between 40-140 ft (12-42 m).

These figures came from the U.S. Navy dive books. It has often been claimed that the times that are logged in the dive books are rarely the same as the actual dives done.[8] The depths and times recorded may often be in excess of the actual depth and time of the dive. The procedures for recording dives may alter the statistics, and give the effect of a lower incidence of bends for a particular profile than is warranted by the tables.

When some controlled dives were made in laboratory chambers, or in open water, to the No-Decompression Limits, the incidence of bends was four or more times greater than that reported by the Navy. Merrill Spencer and Bruce Bassett independently subjected divers to pressure in recompression chambers.[9,10] They took the divers right to some of the NDLs of the U.S. Navy Tables. e.g. 60 ft (18 m) for 60 minutes, 70 ft (21 m) for 50 minutes and 80 ft (24 m) for 40 minutes. The results suggested that if no-decompression dives are performed to the full limits of the U.S. Navy Tables, the incidence of bends is about 5%. Using Doppler bubble detectors they both detected venous bubbles in about 30% of the divers. Some of the results of these studies are shown in Table 13.3.1.

Table 13.3.1

Comparison of USN, Spencer and Bassett schedules, decompression sickness (DCS) and venous gas emboli (VGE)

Source	Depth/Time (ft/min)	DCS/Dives	DCS	VGE
USN	60/60	2/183	1.1%	No record
USN	60/70	3/62	4.8%	No record
Spencer	60/60	1/13	7.6%	31%
Bassett	60/60 (E)	1/18	5.6%	27.8%
USN	80/40	0/40	0.0%	No record
USN	80/50	2/34	5.9%	No record
Bassett	80/40 (E)	1/16	6.3%	37.5%

(E) Equivalent Flying after Diving Schedule

Note: A dive recorded by the U.S. Navy as 60/70 may in reality be closer to 60/60. Similarly with 80/50. With this in mind, the bends figures of the USN more closely match those of Bassett and Spencer.

A 1986 U.S. Navy report describes some dives conducted to test the algorithm for the U.S. Navy's Air-N_2O_2 decompression computer.[11] The Navy conducted 107 single air dives testing NDLs which ranged from 10-100% longer than the NDLs of the Standard Air Table. The limits tested were: 60 ft (18 m)/66, 100 ft (30 m)/30, 120 ft (36 m)/24, 150 (45 m)/14 and 190 ft (58 m)/10. No cases of bends occurred during this intitial testing and some have argued that this indicates that the standard NDLs are safe. However, when the 100 ft/30 schedule was later re-tested a number of cases of bends did occur. No Doppler bubble monitors were used to determine the level of bubbling in the asymptomatic divers. In addition, these dives involved substantially slower ascent rates at shallow depths. The ascent rates used were: 60 ft (18 m)/minute to 20 ft (6 m), 40 ft (12 m)/minute from 20 ft to 10 ft (3 m) and 30 ft (9 m)/minute from 10 ft to the surface. Short stops, of an unspecified length, were done at 10 ft and it appears that some of the divers may have breathed 100% O_2 during the final part of the ascent. In addition, the NDLs at 40 ft (12 m) and 50 ft (15 m), which are potentially problematic, were not tested.

In summary, it appears that although the U.S. Navy have a low overall bends incidence, if the figures are carefully analyzed significant problems might arise if the tables are dived to, or close to, the limits. Although the U.S. Navy generally uses its tables safely, it does not mean that the tables are safe in themselves. When recreational divers use these tables problems can be expected to occur unless their diving practices and table calculations match U.S. Navy use/practices.

When comparing the U.S. Navy diver to the recreational diver there are a number of differences which may relate to the risk of bends. Most Navy divers are between 17-40 years old, there are very few women divers and none of the divers are obese. In addition, they were all healthy enough to have passed the U.S. Navy physical.

The type of diving that the Navy divers do is usually quite different to what sport divers seem to be doing. It has been reported that the vast majority of U.S. Navy dives are very shallow no-decompression dives, which carry the lowest risk of bends.[6] Repetitive dives are not common in the U.S. Navy practice but are commonly carried out by sport divers. It has also been reported that the U.S. Navy dive supervisors also add safety factors to their decompression table schedules.[8] For instance, if a diver is within 2 minutes or 2 feet of a schedule one goes to the next schedule. At 58 ft you go to the 70 ft schedule and at 58 minutes you go to the 70-minute bottom time (At times 5 ft and 5 minutes are used instead).

To minimize the risk of bends when using the U.S. Navy Tables, the recreational diver must learn to use the tables at least as safely as the U.S. Navy divers do. The sport diver who uses the tables in the same manner as the Navy does may still be at a greater risk of bending than the Navy diver, due to differences in condition and training. It becomes obvious that a sensible sport diver must add significant safety factors ("fudge factors") to the U.S. Navy Tables in order to lower the risk of bends. DAN statistics indicate that about 58% of the recreational divers treated for bends in the U.S.A in 1987 had dived within the U.S. Navy Tables.[12] In 1988, this figure increased to 72%.[13]

B. Adding safety to the U.S. Navy Tables

Many divers have devised methods to add some degree of extra safety to their U.S. Navy Tables calculations. Some methods are obviously better than others. **The methods presented in the following section have never been scientifically tested but are always more conservative than using the tables as written. They should, therefore, provide quite a lot of extra safety, *but still cannot be guaranteed to prevent bends.***

I believe that sport divers are better off using a more appropriate set of tables than the U.S. Navy Tables. At present there are three tables, which are based on the U.S. Navy system, that I believe should be used instead of the Navy tables for sport diving purposes. They are the "Huggins Tables", "The NAUI Tables" (1990) and "The Bassett Tables". These are described in the following chapters. There are also tables based on similar or on other systems which may be more suitable than the U.S. Navy Tables.

A. NO-DECOMPRESSION STOP DIVES

Procedure:

a. *Choose an initial NDL by choosing the NDL for the next greater tabled depth than would normally be used.*

E.g. For a dive to 70 ft (21 m) the NDL is normally 50 minutes. To add safety take the NDL for 80 ft (24 m) as your initial NDL. This is 40 minutes.

For a dive to 103 ft (31 m) you would look up the NDL for 120 ft (36 m), rather than the NDL for 110 ft (33 m) as is usual. So, your initial NDL for this dive is 15 minutes (rather than 20 minutes).

Note: This procedure converts the USN limits into limits which are often very similar to those of Huggins and Bassett.

b. *Reduce this initial NDL further to cater for any predisposing factor(s) to bends present.*

E.g. For a dive to 70 ft (21 m) the initial NDL is 40 minutes. If you expect to get cold reduce this time by at least 4 minutes (10% reduction). If you are 15 pounds (7 kg) overweight take off another 4 minutes (i.e. 10%). Now the actual no-decompression bottom time becomes 40-4-4 = 32 minutes. (This limit is now quite similar to the DCIEM and Buehlmann limits)

c. *Ascend at about 30-33 ft/minute (9-10 m/minute)*

d. *Stop at 15-20 ft (4.5-6 m) for 3-5 minutes before surfacing*

e. *Use the total dive time to find the Repetitive Group after the dive.*

Example 1.

You are planning to do two "no-deco" dives, the first to 66 ft (20 m) followed 3 hours later by a dive to 53 ft (16 m). Using the suggested safety factors, find the allowable "no-deco" bottom time. (Assume that there are no predisposing factors to bends present)

* Look up NDL for 80 ft (24 m) (i.e. next greater depth increment). The limit is *40 minutes* which is the maximum allowable bottom time for this dive.

* Ascend at about 30 ft/min (9 m/minute).

* Safety stop at 15-20 ft (4.5-6 m) for say 3 minutes.

* Total dive time = 40 (bottom) + 3 (stop) + 2 (ascent) = 45 minutes.

* Repetitive Group after dive: Look up 66 ft (20 m) for 45 minutes (i.e. actual dive) which gives group *I*.

* Repetitive Group after surface interval = *D*.

* Residual nitrogen at 53 ft (16 m) = *24* minutes.

* Proposed depth of dive is 53 ft (16 m) so look up NDL for 70 ft (21 m) (i.e. next greater depth increment). NDL = *50* minutes.

* Allowable bottom time = 50 (NDL) - 24 (RNT) = *26* minutes.

* Leave the bottom after 26 minutes.

* Ascend at 30 ft/min (9 m/minute).

* Stop at 15-20 ft (4.5-6 m) for 3-5 minutes.

(Unmodified U.S. Navy times would be 50 minutes and 30 minutes)

Example 2.

You are planning to do two "no-deco" dives, the first to 110 ft (33 m) followed 5 hours later by a dive to 100 ft (30 m). Using the suggested safety factors, find the allowable "no-deco" bottom time. (Assume that there are no predisposing factors to bends present)

* Look up NDL for 120 ft (36 m) (i.e. next greater depth increment). The limit is *15* minutes, which is the maximum allowable bottom time for this dive.

- * Ascend at 30 ft/min (9 m/minute).
- * Safety stop at around 20 ft (6 m) for 3-5 minutes.
- * Total dive time = 15 (bottom) + 5 (stop) + 3.3 (ascent) = 24 min. (approx).
- * Repetitive Group after dive: Look up 110 ft (33 m) for 24 minutes (i.e. actual dive) which gives group *H* (from U.S. Navy decompression table).
- * Repetitive Group after surface interval = *B*.
- * Residual nitrogen at 100 ft (30 m) = 7 minutes.
- * Proposed depth of dive is 100 ft (30 m) so look up NDL for 110 ft (33 m) (i.e. next greater depth increment). NDL = *20* minutes.
- * Allowable bottom time = 20 (NDL) - 7 (RNT) = *13* minutes.
- * Leave the bottom after 13 minutes.
- * Ascend at 30 ft/min (9 m/minute).
- * Stop at 20 ft (6 m) for 3-5 minutes and 10 ft (3 m) for 3 minutes.

  (Unmodified U.S. Navy times would be 20 minutes and 18 minutes)

At times the above method will yield repetitive dive times that may be more conservative than necessary. However, this is not always the case. It is a fairly good method for those divers who do not resent sacrificing a few minutes of dive time, or reducing their depth, to gain a bit of extra safety. For divers who are keen to squeeze out a bit of more dive time, the following method may generally be reasonable, although not quite as safe, especially for repetitive dives to 50 ft (15 m) or shallower, for which the U.S. Navy NDL is often far longer than the equivalent NDLs from other tables:

> Choose the initial NDL for the first dive by looking up the next greater tabled depth increment as described, ascend slowly, do a stop(s) and use the total time underwater to get the RG, as previously described. However, for repetitive dives, choose the initial NDL directly from the table (rather than taking the next greater tabled depth increment) and then reduce it to allow for predisposing factors to bends. For Example 2 this method would give a bottom time of 25 - 7 = 18 minutes for the second dive.

Another method which is often suggested is as follows:

> First reduce the U.S. Navy NDL to cater for any predisposing factor(s) to bends. Then ensure that you leave the bottom with sufficient time left to ascend at 30 ft (9 m) per minute and to reach the surface before your new NDL expires.

This method is often not as conservative as the previous method, especially for shallower dives. For example, for a single dive to 60 ft (18 m) this method allows a maximum (i.e. not allowing for predisposing factors) no-decompression bottom time of 58 minutes. This 58 minutes is substantially longer than the times suggested by the Buehlmann (1986), DCIEM, Huggins and Bassett Tables. However, on the other hand, for some deeper dives this method may prove unnecessarily conservative.

B. DECOMPRESSION STOP DIVES

1. *Choose a decompression schedule by adding one depth increment and one bottom time increment to the schedule that would normally be used.*

   E.g. For a dive to 57 ft (17 m) for a bottom time of 65 minutes use the schedule for 70 ft (21 m) for 80 minutes.

2. *Reduce your ascent rate to about 30 ft (9 m) per minute.*

3. *Select your Repetitive Group (RG) according to the decompression done.*

   E.g. For a dive to 56 ft (17 m) for 65 minutes, if you decompressed as for 70 ft (21 m) for 80 minutes, your RG is *M*.

Note:

If you get cold or work hard during the dive then you can increase your decompression by adding another bottom time increment.

E.g. If you get cold and work hard during the previous dive you can decompress as for a dive to 70 ft (21 m) for 90 minutes. This will often give decompression well in excess of other tables but, if air is available and the conditions are right, it is a cheap insurance!

Example 3.

You are planning a decompression stop dive to 90 ft (27 m) for a bottom time of 38 minutes. What decompression schedule should you use.

* Select the schedule for the next greater tabled depth increment, which will be 100 ft (30 m), and for the next longer time increment, which will be 50 minutes.

  Decompress as for 100 ft (30 m) for 50 minutes. This requires stops of 2 minutes at 20 ft (6 m) and 24 minutes at 10 ft (3 m).

* Ascend at about 30 ft (9 m) per minute.

* The RG after the dive will be *L*

Example 4.

You are planning a dive to 120 ft (36 m) for a bottom time of 20 minutes. The water is cold and you expect to work hard during the dive. What decompression schedule should you select?

* Initially add one depth and one time increment. This gives 130 ft (39 m) for 25 minutes.

* If possible, add another bottom time increment to cater for the cold and exercise. This gives 130 ft (39 m) for 30 minutes. The decompression required is a stop at 20 ft (6 m) for 3 minutes followed by a stop at 10 ft (3 m) for 18 minutes.

* The RG after the dive is *M*.

REFERENCES

1. Thalmann, E. and Butler, F. (1983), "A Procedure for doing Multiple Level Dives on Air Using Repetitive Groups". U.S. Navy Experimental Diving Unit, Report No. 13-83.

2. Des Granges, M. (1956), "Standard Air Decompression Table". U.S. Navy Experimental Diving Unit Report No. 5-57.

3. Des Granges, M. (1957), "Repetitive Diving Decompression Tables". U.S. Navy Experimental Diving Unit Report No. 6-57.

4. Dembert, M. et al (1984), "Health risk factors for the development of decompression sickness among U.S. Navy divers". *Undersea Biomedical Research*; 11 (4): 395-406.

5. Garrahan, R., personal communication.

6. Blood, C. and Hoiberg, A. (1985), "Analyses of variables underlying U.S. Navy diving accidents". *Undersea Biomedical Research*; 12 (3): 351-360.

7. Berhage, T. and Durman, D. (1980), "U.S. Navy Air Decompression Risk Analysis". Naval Medical Research Institute, Report No. NMRI 80-1, Naval Medical Research and Development Command.

8. Bassett, B. (1982), "The Safety of the United States Navy Decompression Tables and Recommendations for Sports Divers". *SPUMS Journal*; Oct-Dec: 16-25.

9. Spencer, M. (1976), "Decompression limits for compressed air determined by ultrasonically detected blood bubbles". *Journal of Applied Physiology*; 40 (2): 229-235.

10. Bassett, B. (1982), "Decompression procedures for flying after diving, and diving at altitudes above sea level". Report No. SAM-TR-82-47, Brooks Air Force Base: United States Air Force School of Aerospace Medicine.

11. Thalmann, E. (1986), "Air-N_2O_2 Decompression Computer Algorithm Development". U.S. Navy Experimental Diving Unit Report No. 8-85.

12. Divers Alert Network (1988), "Preliminary Report on Diving Accidents". Divers Alert Network, North Carolina.

13. Divers Alert Network (1989), "Report on 1988 Diving Accidents". Divers Alert Network, North Carolina.

OTHER SOURCES

Bassett, B., (1984) "Decompression Safety", *IDC Candidate Workshop*, PADI.

Bove, A., Diving Medicine, *Skin Diver*; 36 (6), 18, 1987.

Edmonds, C., "Decompression Sickness", *SCUBA Diver*; June, 1987: 22-25.

Knight, J., "The Safest Table for Sports Divers", *Skin Diver*; 36 (5), 1987.

RECOMMENDED FURTHER READING

Bassett, B., (1982), "The Safety of the United States Navy Decompression Tables and Recommendations for Sports Divers". *SPUMS Journal*; Oct-Dec: 16-25.

EXERCISES ON ADAPTING THE U.S. NAVY TABLES TO SPORT DIVING

1. By adding the suggested safety factors (i.e. taking the NDL for the next greater tabled depth, ascending slowly, doing a safety stop and using total dive time to find the RG after the dive), calculate the maximum allowable no-decompression bottom times for the following dives. Assume no predisposing factors to bends are present.

   (a) A dive to 92 ft (28 m) followed 2 hours later by a dive to 66 ft (20 m).

   (b) A dive to 120 ft (36 m) followed 4½ hours later by a dive to 102 ft (31 m).

   (c) A dive to 56 ft (17 m) followed 2½ hours later by another dive to 56 ft (17 m).

   (d) A dive to 53 ft (16 m) followed 3 hours later by a dive to 66 ft (20 m).

   (e) A dive to 135 ft (41 m) followed 6½ hours later by a dive to 40 ft (12 m).

2. By adding the safety factors suggested (i.e. adding one depth and one time increment to the normal decompression schedule, ascending slowly and using total dive time to determine the RG), find what decompression is required after the following dives, and the RG after the dive.

   (a) A single dive to 63 ft (19 m) for a bottom time of 56 minutes.

   (b) A single dive to 83 ft (25 m) for a bottom time of 50 minutes.

   (c) A single dive to 106 ft (32 m) for a bottom time of 22 minutes.

ANSWERS:

1. * A safety stop(s) of a total of 5 min has been included in each of these calculations.

   (a) Dive 1: Max. bottom time = 20, total dive time = 28
   Dive 2: Max. bottom time = 9

   (b) Dive 1: Max. bottom time = 10, total dive time = 19
   Dive 2: Max. bottom time = 5

   (c) Dive 1: Max. bottom time = 50, total dive time = 55
   Dive 2: Max. bottom time = 20

   (d) Dive 1: Max. bottom time = 50, total dive time = 55
   Dive 2: Max. bottom time = 20

   (e) Dive 1: Max. bottom time = 5, total dive time = 14
   Dive 2: Max. bottom time = 83

2. (a) 23 min at 10 ft (3 m), M
   (b) 9 min at 20 ft (6 m) and 28 min at 10 ft (3 m), N
   (c) 14 min at 10 ft (3 m), J

CHAPTER 14

MORE CONSERVATIVE ALTERNATIVES BASED ON THE U.S. NAVY TABLES

14.1 The Huggins Tables

In 1976, Dr. Merril Spencer published a report in which he stated that he had found that divers who were exposed to some of the U.S. Navy limits developed large counts of "silent bubbles" (venous gas emboli) during and after ascent from depth.[1] He believed that the bubbles resulted from the release of excess nitrogen within the divers' bodies. The bubbles were detected using a Doppler Ultrasonic Bubble Detector. On the basis of this work, Spencer recommended new No-Decompression Limits (NDLs), which were calculated in an attempt to minimize bubble formation after a dive.[1] These limits are shown in Table 14.1.1. Subsequent studies carried out by Dr. Andrew Pilmanis[2] and Dr. Bruce Bassett[3] supported Spencer's findings.

These findings confirmed a growing concern in the sport diving community that the U.S. Navy No-Decompression Limits are not as safe for the recreational diver as they should be. As a result in 1981, Karl Huggins, an Assistant in Research at the University of Michigan, generated a new set of no-decompression tables which are based on Spencer's recommendations. These became known as the "Huggins Tables". They are designed in an attempt to minimize the formation of bubbles, asymptomatic or otherwise.

TABLE 14.1.1

NO-DECOMPRESSION LIMITS (MIN)

Depth ft	Depth m	U.S.Navy	Spencer	Depth ft	Depth m	U.S.Navy	Spencer
30	9	none	225	80	24	40	30
35	10.5	310	165	90	27	30	25
40	12	200	135	100	30	25	20
50	15	100	75	110	33	20	15
60	18	60	50	120	36	15	10
70	21	50	40	130	39	10	5

The Huggins Tables are based on the same concept and format as the U.S. Navy Tables. Using the same six theoretical tissue groups as the Navy tables, with half-times of 5, 10, 20, 40, 80 and 120 minutes, Huggins determined the new, lower, critical nitrogen levels (M values) corresponding to the shortened NDLs recommended by Spencer. These M values are shown in Table 14.1.2. Huggins also determined new Repetitive Group Designators which represent the nitrogen levels in all six tissue groups rather than just in the 120-minute tissue compartment as in the Navy tables. This makes these tables far more suitable for multi-level diving.

These tables have not been officially tested but are more conservative than the U.S. Navy Tables when used to find the limits for single and repetitive no-decompression stop dives.

They consist of a Repetitive Group Table, a Surface Interval Table and a Residual Nitrogen Table. The tables are shown as Tables 14.1.3 and 14.1.4. The only difference in reading the table comes with the arrows "⟶" in the first table. These arrows indicate that the diver must move to the next higher Repetitive Group to the right.

TABLE 14.1.2

COMPARISON OF NEW M VALUES TO U.S. NAVY'S

Tissue Group	Navy	New	% of Navy's
5 min.	104	102.0	98%
10 min.	88	85.0	97%
20 min.	72	67.5	94%
40 min.	58	54.5	94%
80 min.	52	47.5	91%
120 min.	51	43.0	84%

TABLE 14.1.3
No-Decompression Table

DEPTH (FT.)	NO DECOM. LIMITS	BOTTOM TIME AND REPETITIVE GROUP CODE													
		A	B	C	D	E	F	G	H	I	J	K	L	M	N
20	-	10	25	40	60	85	110	135	170	215	275	325			
30	225	5	15	25	40	50	65	75	95	110	130	150	175	205	225
35	165	5	15	20	30	40	50	60	70	85	100	120	135	155	165
40	135	5	10	20	25	35	40	45	55	60	70	85	100	120	135
50	75	-	10	15	20	25	30	35	37	40	50	55	60	70	75
60	50	-	5	10	15	20	23	25	27	30	35	40	45	47	50
70	40	-	5	10	13	15	17	20	23	25	27	30	33	35	40
80	30	-	5	7	→	10	13	15	17	20	→	25	27	→	30
90	25	-	-	5	7	→	10	→	13	15	17	→	20	23	25
100	20	-	-	-	5	7	→	→	10	→	→	13	15	17	20
110	15	-	-	-	-	5	→	7	→	→	10	→	→	13	15
120	10	-	-	-	-	-	5	→	→	7	→	→	10		
130	5	-	-	-	-	-	5								

SURFACE INTERVAL TABLE

A	B	C	D	E	F	G	H	I	J	K	L	M	N	NEW GROUP
12:00 0:10	12:00 2:31	12:00 3:42	12:00 4:43	12:00 5:23	12:00 5:57	12:00 6:21	12:00 6:49	12:00 7:09	12:00 7:30	12:00 7:46	12:00 8:01	12:00 8:18	12:00 8:27	A
	2:30 0:10	3:41 1:20	4:42 2:21	5:22 3:01	5:56 3:35	6:20 3:59	6:48 4:27	7:08 4:47	7:29 5:08	7:45 5:24	8:00 5:39	8:17 5:56	8:26 6:05	B
		1:19 0:10	2:20 1:04	3:00 1:44	3:34 2:18	3:58 2:42	4:26 3:10	4:46 3:30	5:07 3:51	5:23 4:07	5:38 4:22	5:55 4:39	6:04 4:48	C
			1:03 0:10	1:43 0:50	2:17 1:24	2:41 1:48	3:09 2:16	3:29 2:36	3:50 2:57	4:06 3:13	4:21 3:28	4:38 3:45	4:47 3:54	D
				0:49 0:10	1:23 0:43	1:47 1:07	2:15 1:35	2:35 1:55	2:56 2:16	3:12 2:32	3:27 2:47	3:44 3:04	3:53 3:13	E
					0:42 0:10	1:06 0:34	1:34 1:02	1:54 1:22	2:15 1:43	2:31 1:59	2:46 2:14	3:03 2:31	3:12 2:40	F
						0:33 0:10	1:01 0:34	1:21 0:54	1:42 1:15	1:58 1:31	2:13 1:46	2:30 2:03	2:39 2:12	G
							0:33 0:10	0:53 0:30	1:14 0:51	1:30 1:07	1:45 1:22	2:02 1:39	2:11 1:48	H
								0:29 0:10	0:50 0:29	1:06 0:45	1:21 1:01	1:38 1:17	1:47 1:26	I
									0:28 0:10	0:44 0:26	1:00 0:42	1:16 0:58	1:25 1:07	J
										0:25 0:10	0:41 0:24	0:57 0:40	1:06 0:49	K
											0:23 0:10	0:39 0:24	0:48 0:33	L
												0:23 0:10	0:32 0:18	M
													0:17 0:10	N

NEW GROUP	20	30	35	40	50	60	70	80	90	100	110	120	130
A	12	8	7	6	5	4	4	3	3	3	3	2	2
B	28	18	16	14	11	9	8	7	6	6	5	5	4
C	45	29	25	21	17	14	12	9	8	6	6	5	5
D	65	41	34	30	23	19	15	10	8	7	6	5	5
E	86	53	44	37	28	22	17	12	9	8	7	6	5
F	111	66	53	43	32	24	19	14	11	9	7	6	6
G	140	80	62	49	36	27	22	17	12	10	8	7	6
H	175	96	73	57	40	30	24	19	14	11	9	8	7
I	219	113	86	65	45	34	26	21	16	12	10	8	7
J	279	132	103	75	51	38	29	23	18	13	11	9	8
K	369	154	122	88	57	43	32	26	20	15	12	10	8
L	-	178	139	103	64	47	35	28	22	18	13	11	9
M	-	207	158	124	71	52	40	30	25	20	15	12	10
N	-	225	165	135	75	53	41	31	26	21	16	13	11

DEPTH

* NEW *

NO-DECOMPRESSION TABLES

Michigan Sea Grant College Program

The University of Michigan • Michigan State University

Reprinted courtesy of Michigan Sea Grant College Program

REFERENCES

1. Spencer, M. (1976), "Decompression limits for compressed air determined by ultrasonically detected blood bubbles". *Journal of Applied Physiology*; 40 (2): 229-235.

2. Pilmanis, A. (1974), "Intravenous gas emboli in man after selected open ocean air SCUBA dives". *Abstract 5.1.* Undersea Medical Society, Annual Scientific Meeting.

3. Bassett, B. (1982), "Decompression procedures for flying after diving, and diving at altitudes above sea level". Report No. SAM-TR-82-47, Brooks Air Force Base: United States Air Force School of Aerospace Medicine.

OTHER SOURCES

Bove, A. (1987), Diving Medicine. *Skin Diver*; 36 (6): 18.

Huggins, K. (1981), "New No-Decompression Tables Based on No-Decompression Limits Determined by Doppler Ultrasonic Bubble detection". University of Michigan Sea Grant College Program, Report No. MICHU-SG-81-205, Michigan Sea Grant Publications.

Huggins, K. (1985), "Tables, Tables, What's with all these Tables?". In: *I.Q. '85 Proceedings*, Bangasser, S. ed., NAUI, California.

14.2 The Bassett Tables

Dr. Bruce Bassett, a physiologist, was commissioned by the U.S. Air Force to validate some schedules for flying after diving. He had to construct a set of tables which would allow a diver to be flown to an altitude of 10,000 feet (3,000 metres) immediately after surfacing from a dive.

Using the mathematics of the U.S. Navy Tables, Bassett calculated a set of equivalent no-decompression stop dives after which a diver would not reach the critical nitrogen levels (maximum supersaturation ratios) of the U.S. Navy Tables until reaching 10,000 ft. Bassett placed "divers" in a chamber for various periods of time before "surfacing" them and, then, reducing the pressure to its equivalent at 10,000 ft. For example, the divers did not do a 60 ft (18 m) for 60 minutes dive. Instead, they spent 20 minutes at 60 ft and then ascended to 10,000 ft. Bassett believed that the calculated nitrogen pressures in the theoretical half-time tissue compartments on reaching 10,000 ft were identical to that of surfacing after a 60 ft for 60 minutes dive.

If the U.S. Navy Tables are safe, these shorter dives followed by decompression to altitude should have been safe. They were not, as Bassett's divers had a bends incidence of about 6% and silent bubbles were detected in about 30% of the divers.[1] This was unacceptable. Bassett's results were similar to those of Dr. Merril Spencer in Seattle, who had tested the U.S. Navy NDLs in a chamber and found a comparable bends incidence and silent bubble count.[2]

These two sets of dry chamber data and the knowledge that the U.S. Navy divers added depth and time increments before calculating decompression led Dr. Bassett to re-calculate his dive schedule using lesser maximum nitrogen values (M values). That is, he reduced the allowable supersaturation in the various half-time tissue compartments. The two sets of M values are shown in Table 14.2.1.

TABLE 14.2.1

M VALUES OF U.S. NAVY AND BASSETT TABLES

Tissue group	Navy	Bassett	% of Navy's
5 min.	104	95	91%
10 min.	88	83.2	95%
20 min.	72	67	93%
40 min.	58	53.8	93%
80 min.	52	46.5	89%
120 min.	51	44	86%

When Bassett tested his revised decompression procedures in the chamber there were no bends.[1]

Bassett issued a new set of No-Decompression Limits which are more conservative and, he believed, far more appropriate for recreational diving than the U.S. Navy NDLs. These limits are shown in Figure 14.2.2.

TABLE 14.2.2

NO-DECOMPRESSION LIMITS (MIN.)

Depth ft	Depth m	U.S.Navy	Bassett	Depth ft	Depth m	U.S.Navy	Bassett
30	9	none	220	80	24	40	30
35	10.5	310	180	90	27	30	25
40	12	200	120	100	30	25	20
50	15	100	70	110	33	20	15
60	18	60	50	120	36	15	12
70	21	50	40	130	39	10	10
				140	42	10	5

Bassett also recommended that "all dives greater than 30 ft (9 m) end with 3-5 minutes at 10-15 ft (3-4.5 m)". He also suggested that total time underwater be used (rather than just bottom time) to determine the Repetitive Group after a dive.[3]

Dr. Bruce Bassett's Revised Bottom Times "No Decompression" Dive Table

The table, shown as Table 14.2.3, incorporates Bassett's limits, his recommendations and other diving practices designed to reduce the risk of bends.

This table has not been officially tested but is more conservative than the U.S. Navy Tables when used to find the limits for single and repetitive no-decompression dives.

Features of the table are:

1. An ascent rate of 33 ft/minute (10 m/minute) is recommended, as slow ascents seem to produce less bends. Bassett's limits were calculated on an ascent rate of 60 ft/minute (18 m/minute) so this slower ascent is not essential but should provide extra safety.

2. A safety stop of 3-5 minutes at 10-17 ft (3-5 m) is recommended after all dives deeper than 30 ft (9 m) whenever possible.

3. The total time underwater, rather than just the bottom time, is used to calculate the Repetitive Group after a dive.

4. A decompression table is provided as a back-up should the need arise. The decompression table provided is done so to cater for the situation where a diver accidentally overstays his no-decompression time. The times in this table (Table 14.2.4) are those from the U.S. Navy Standard Tables with an extra 5 minutes added to the 10 ft (3 m) stop.

   It is certainly not a recommended decompression table to be used for decompression stop diving but should be more than adequate to cover a diver in the situation described.

5. (a) The Bassett NDLs are given in the third column of Table 1 (in Table 14.2.3). Table 1 is, essentially, the U.S. Navy No-decompression Table with the new NDLs.

   (b) Table 2 is a slightly abbreviated form of the U.S. Navy Surface Interval Table.

   (c) To calculate the allowable bottom times for repetitive dives, Table 3, Dr. John Knight simply subtracted the U.S. Navy Residual Nitrogen Times from the Bassett limits rather than from the U.S. Navy NDLs, as is normally done.

6. The system allows two dives without any calculations. For a third dive deeper than 30 ft (9 m) one does a similar calculation to that with the U.S. Navy Tables. For third, or subsequent, dives to 30 ft (9 m) or less, no further calculation is required; one can dive to the 30 ft (9 m) NDL of 220 minutes.

TABLE 14.2.3
No-Decompression Dive Table

Reprinted with courtesy of Dr. John Knight.

DR BRUCE BASSETT'S REVISED BOTTOM TIMES "NO DECOMPRESSION" DIVE TABLE

ARRANGED FOR REPETITIVE DIVES BY JOHN KNIGHT & JOHN LIPPMANN

BEFORE USING THIS TABLE READ THE OTHER SIDE.

ASCENT RATE 10m A MINUTE

ON ALL DIVES DEEPER THAN 9m (30ft) DO A 3·5 MINUTE SAFETY STOP AT 3·5m. USE THE TOTAL TIME UNDERWATER (BOTTOM TIME + ASCENT TIME + SAFETY STOP TIME) TO FIND THE REPETITIVE GROUP AT THE END OF THE DIVE.

The times in *italics* in the table are OUTSIDE the Bassett Bottom Time limits but are included for ease of calculating the repetitive group using the TOTAL TIME UNDERWATER.

TABLE 1.

Depth M	Depth feet	Bassett Bottom Time Limits	Time Underwater											
9	30	220	15	30	45	60	75	95	120	145	170	205	*250*	*310*
10	35	180	5	15	25	40	50	60	80	100	120	140	160	*190*
12	40	120	5	15	25	30	40	50	70	80	100	110	*130*	*150*
15	50	70		10	15	25	30	40	50	60	70	*80*	*90*	*100*
18	60	50		10	15	20	25	30	40	50	*55*	*60*		
21	70	40		5	10	15	20	30	35	40	*45*	*50*		
24	80	30		5	10	15	20	25	30	*35*	*40*			
27	90	25		5	10	12	15	20	25	*30*		*40*		
30	100	20		5	7	10	15	20	*22*	*25*	*30*			
33	110	15			5	10	13	15	*20*	*25*				
36	120	12			5	10	12	*15*		*20*	*25*			
39	130	10			5	8	10	*15*		*20*				
42	140	5			5	7	*10*		*15*					
Repetitive group at the end of the dive			**A**	**B**	**C**	**D**	**E**	**F**	**G**	**H**	**I**	**J**	**K**	**L**

ABBREVIATED U.S.N. SURFACE INTERVAL TABLE

Enter the table from the top using the appropriate repetitive group. Move across to the left until the appropriate interval is found then move down the column and out of the table into the REPETITIVE DIVE TABLE

(Table 3)

TABLE 2

Group												
A	0:10											
	12:00											
B	2:11	0:10										
	12:00	2:10										
C	2:50	1:40	0:10									
	12:00	2:49	1:39									
D	5:49	2:39	1:10	0:10								
	12:00	5:48	2:38	1:09								
E	6:33	3:23	1:58	0:55	0:10							
	12:00	6:32	3:22	1:57	0:54							
F	7:06	3:58	2:29	1:30	0:46	0:10						
	12:00	7:05	3:57	2:28	1:29	0:45						
G	7:36	4:26	2:59	2:00	1:16	0:41	0:10					
	12:00	7:35	4:25	2:58	1:59	1:15	0:40					
H	8:00	4:50	3:21	2:24	1:42	1:07	0:37	0:10				
	12:00	7:59	4:49	3:20	2:23	1:41	1:06	0:36				
I	8:22	5:13	3:44	2:45	2:03	1:30	1:00	0:34	0:10			
	12:00	8:21	5:12	3:43	2:44	2:02	1:29	0:59	0:33			
J	8:41	5:41	4:03	3:05	2:21	1:48	1:20	0:55	0:32	0:10		
	12:00	8:40	5:40	4:02	3:04	2:20	1:47	1:19	0:54	0:31		
K	8:59	5:49	4:20	3:22	2:39	2:04	1:36	1:12	0:50	0:29	0:10	
	12:00	8:58	5:48	4:19	3:21	2:38	2:03	1:35	1:11	0:49	0:28	
L	9:13	6:03	4:36	3:37	2:54	2:20	1:50	1:26	1:05	0:46	0:27	0:10
	12:00	9:12	6:02	4:35	3:36	2:53	2:19	1:49	1:25	1:04	0:45	0:26
	A	**B**	**C**	**D**	**E**	**F**	**G**	**H**	**I**	**J**	**K**	**L**

TABLE 3

MAXIMUM BOTTOM TIME AVAILABLE FOR A REPETITIVE DIVE

Depth M	Depth feet	A	B	C	D	E	F	G	H	I	J	K	L
9	30	213	203	195	183	171	159	147	133	119	104	82	
12	40	113	103	95	83	71	59	47	33	19	4		
15	50	64	57	49	41	32	23	14	4				
18	60	45	39	33	26	20	14	6					
21	70	36	31	25	20	14	9	3					
24	80	26	22	17	12	7	2						
27	90	22	18	14	9	5	1						
30	100	17	13	10	6	2							
33	110	12	9	5	2								
36	120	9	6	3									
39	130	7	4	2									
42	140	3											

Each of these times takes the diver to the equivalent of the Bassett Bottom Time limits for that depth. If these times are accidentally exceeded, add the excess time to the Bottom Time Limit for that depth in Table 1, then use Table 4 to decompress.

TABLE 14.2.4
Modified Air Decompression Table

TABLE 4
MODIFIED AIR DECOMPRESSION TABLE*

Depth m	Depth feet	Bottom Time minutes	Decompression Stops minutes at 10 feet	Repetitive group
18	60	70	7	K
		80	12	L
21	70	60	13	K
		70	19	L
24	80	50	15	K
		60	22	L
27	90	40	12	J
		50	23	L
30	100	30	8	I
		40	20	K
33	110	25	8	H
		30	12	J
36	120	20	7	H
		25	11	I
39	130	15	6	F
		20	10	H
42	140	15	7	G
		20	11	I
45	150	5	5	C
		10	6	E

* FOR THOSE WHO ACCIDENTALLY EXCEED THE NO-DECOMPRESSION LIMITS

USING THE BASSETT TABLES

Example 1.

What is the maximum allowable bottom time for a single or first no-decompression stop dive to 66 ft (20 m)?

Enter Table 1 from the left at the exact, or next tabled, depth increment. In this case, enter at 70 ft (21 m). Move right to column 3 (Bassett Bottom Time Limits) to find the allowable bottom time. It is *40* minutes. This means that you must leave the bottom after a maximum of 40 minutes, ascend at about 33 ft/min (10 m/minute) and stop at 10-17 ft (3-5 m) for say 3 minutes before surfacing.

To find the RG after the dive you must use the total dive time of $40_{\text{(BT)}} + 2_{\text{(approx. ascent time)}} + 3_{\text{(stop time)}}$ = 45 minutes. Move to the right, across the 70 ft (21 m) row of Table 1, until finding the exact, or next greater tabled, total dive time, then move down the column to get the RG. In this case 45 minutes is tabled and, moving down, the 45-minute column gives an RG of *I*.

Example 2.

You have dived to 60 ft (18 m) for a bottom time of 40 minutes. You ascended slowly and did a safety stop en-route to the surface. After a 2 hour surface interval you wish to dive to 50 ft (15 m). What is the maximum allowable bottom time for the 50 ft (15 m)dive?

For the first dive the NDL was 50 minutes, so you could have had a maximum bottom time of 50 minutes if required. You have spent 40 minutes bottom time, ascended slowly and done a safety stop, so the total time underwater should have been about 45 minutes. To find the RG after the first dive do the following:

* Enter Table 1 at the row for 60 ft (18 m), move right to find 45 minutes, in this case take 50 minutes, and move down to find the RG at the end of the dive. It is group *H*.

To find the new RG after the surface interval:

* Continue downwards to H on Table 2.

* Move across the H row, to the left, until finding the times which include 2 hours, in this case 1:42-2:23.

* Move down this new column to find the group at the end of the surface interval; Group *E*.

To find the maximum allowable no-decompression stop bottom time for the repetitive dive:

* Continue down the E column until intersecting the row corresponding to 50 ft (15 m). You get 32 minutes. This means that you can have a bottom time of *32* minutes at 50 ft (15 m) before ascending slowly, doing a safety stop and surfacing. Your total time underwater would be about 37 minutes.

Note:

The maximum allowable bottom time for the second dive brings you to the Bassett single dive NDL for that depth (found in column 3 of Table 1). i.e. 32 minutes at 50ft (15 m) for this repetitive dive is equivalent to 70 minutes (the Bassett limit for a single 50 ft (15 m) dive taken from Table 1) at 50 ft for a first dive. The difference between the 70 minutes and the 32 minutes is the time already considered spent at 50 ft (15m) before the second dive begins (Residual Nitrogen Time).

Example 3.

Three hours after the second dive in Example 2 you wish to dive to 40 ft (12 m). What is the maximum allowable no-decompression bottom time for the dive?

You must first find the RG after the last dive. This dive was equivalent to a single dive to 50 ft (15 m) for a bottom time of 70 minutes. Adding the ascent and safety stop time of about 5 minutes, the equivalent total time underwater is 70 + 5 = 75 minutes.

Enter Table 1, from the left, at 50 ft (15 m) and move across to the right to find the equivalent time underwater of 75 minutes. Taking 80 minutes and moving down the column, you get an RG of *J*.

Enter Table 2 from the right at J and find the surface interval of 3 hours. It lies between 2:21-3:04. Move down this column to get the RG after the surface interval, which is *E*.

Continue down into Table 3 until intersecting the row corresponding to the depth of the next dive; 40 ft (12 m). The number *71* is the allowable bottom time, in minutes, for this third dive.

Example 4.

During the last dive, after spending only 50 minutes of the allowable bottom time of 71 minutes at 40 ft (12 m), you ascend slowly and stop for 3 minutes at a safety stop. What is your RG after the dive?

Your 50-minute bottom time was 21 minutes shorter than the 70-minute limit for this repetitive dive. This repetitive dive of 50 minutes is equivalent to a single 40 ft (12 m) dive of 120 - 21 = 99 minutes (i.e. 21 min. shorter than the single dive NDL of 120 minutes). Your equivalent time underwater is approximately 99 + 1 + 3 = 103 minutes.

To find your RG after the dive, enter Table 1 at 40 ft (12 m) and move to the right until finding the time underwater of 103 minutes. Taking 110 minutes and moving down, you get an RG of *J*.

Example 5.

Before a repetitive dive your RG is A. You had planned to dive to 100 ft (30 m) for 17 minutes as allowed, but after 15 minutes you notice that you have gone to 110 ft (33m). A glance at Table 3 shows that you were only allowed 12 minutes at this depth so you have overstayed the 100 ft (30 m) limit by 3 minutes. What decompression is necessary?

This repetitive dive of 12 minutes at 110 ft (33 m) is equivalent to a single dive of 15 + 3 = 18 minutes (i.e. 3 minutes longer than the NDL for 110 ft).

Turn to Table 4 and enter from the left at 110 ft (33 m). Moving right, the decompression is found to be *8 minutes at 10 ft (3 m)* and the RG after the dive is *I*.

REFERENCES

1. Bassett, B. (1982), "Decompression procedures for flying after diving, and diving at altitudes above sea level". Report No. SAM-TR-82-47, Brooks Air Force Base: United States Air Force School of Aerospace Medicine.

2. Spencer, M. (1976), "Decompression limits for compressed air determined by ultrasonically detected blood bubbles". *Journal of Applied Physiology*; 40 (2): 229-235.

3. Bassett, B. (1982), "The Safety of the U.S. Navy Decompression Tables and Recommedations for Sports Divers". *SPUMS Journal*; 16, October-December.

OTHER SOURCES

Bassett, B. (1984), "Flying After Diving". In: *I.D.C. Candidate Workshop*, PADI, California.

Bassett, B. (1984), "Decompression Safety". In: *IDC Candidate Workshop*, PADI, California.

Bassett, B., personal communications.

Knight, J. (1987), "The Safest Table for Sports Divers". *Skin Diver*; 36 (5).

Knight, J. (1985), "Towards Safer Diving: Bruce Bassett's Revised No-Decompression Tables". *SPUMS Journal*; 15 (2): 8-15.

RECOMMENDED FURTHER READING

Bassett, B. (1982), "The Safety of the U.S. Navy Decompression Tables and Recommedations for Sports Divers". *SPUMS Journal*; 16, October-December.

Knight, J. (1985), "Towards Safer Diving: Bruce Bassett's Revised No-Decompression Tables". *SPUMS Journal*; 15 (2): 8-15.

14.3 The NAUI Dive Tables

The new NAUI Dive Tables, released in 1990, are modified U.S. Navy Tables. Instead of the U.S. Navy NDLs, the NAUI Tables utilize Maximum Dive Times (MDTs) which are, in fact, the U.S. Navy NDLs reduced by one letter group for dives between 60 ft and 130 ft (18-39 m), by two groups for 50 ft (15 m) dives and three groups for 40 ft (12 m) dives. The maximum ascent rate is 60 ft (18 m)/minute and a precautionary decompression stop of 3 minutes at 15 ft (5 m) is recommended after every dive. The time spent at the safety stop does not have to be counted as "Actual Dive Time" (NAUI's new term for "Actual Bottom Time") which is used to find the Repetitive Group after the dive. Actual Dive Time is therefore taken as the total time underwater and may, or may not, include the time at the safety stop.

The Repetitive Groups are based on the off-gassing of the 120-minute tissue compartment, similarly to those of the U.S. Navy, and the Surface Interval Table is, essentially, the U.S. Navy Surface Interval Table with the previous numerical errors corrected. However, with these tables off-gassing is considered to take 24 hours rather than the 12 hours on which the U.S. Navy Tables are based, and the Group A times have been altered accordingly. This means that a repetitive dive is now considered to be any dive within 24 hours of a previous dive(s). A minimum surface interval of one hour between dives is recommended. Repetitive dives deeper than 100 ft (30 m) are discouraged, as are "bounce" repetitive dives and doing more than three dives in any one day.

Although these tables have not been empirically tested, they are more conservative than the U.S. Navy Tables and should, therefore, be more appropriate for the recreational diver.

SOURCES

Graver, D. (1989), "Proposed Revisions to the NAUI Dive Tables". *Sources*; 1 (3): 27-28.

Graver, D., personal communications.

Graver, D. (1990), "NAUI's New Dive Tables". *Sources*; 2 (2): 17-18.

Telford, H. (1990), "The New NAUI Dive Tables'. *NAUI News - Australia*; 10 (2): 2.

TABLE 14.3.1
The NAUI Dive Tables

Reprinted with permission from NAUI.

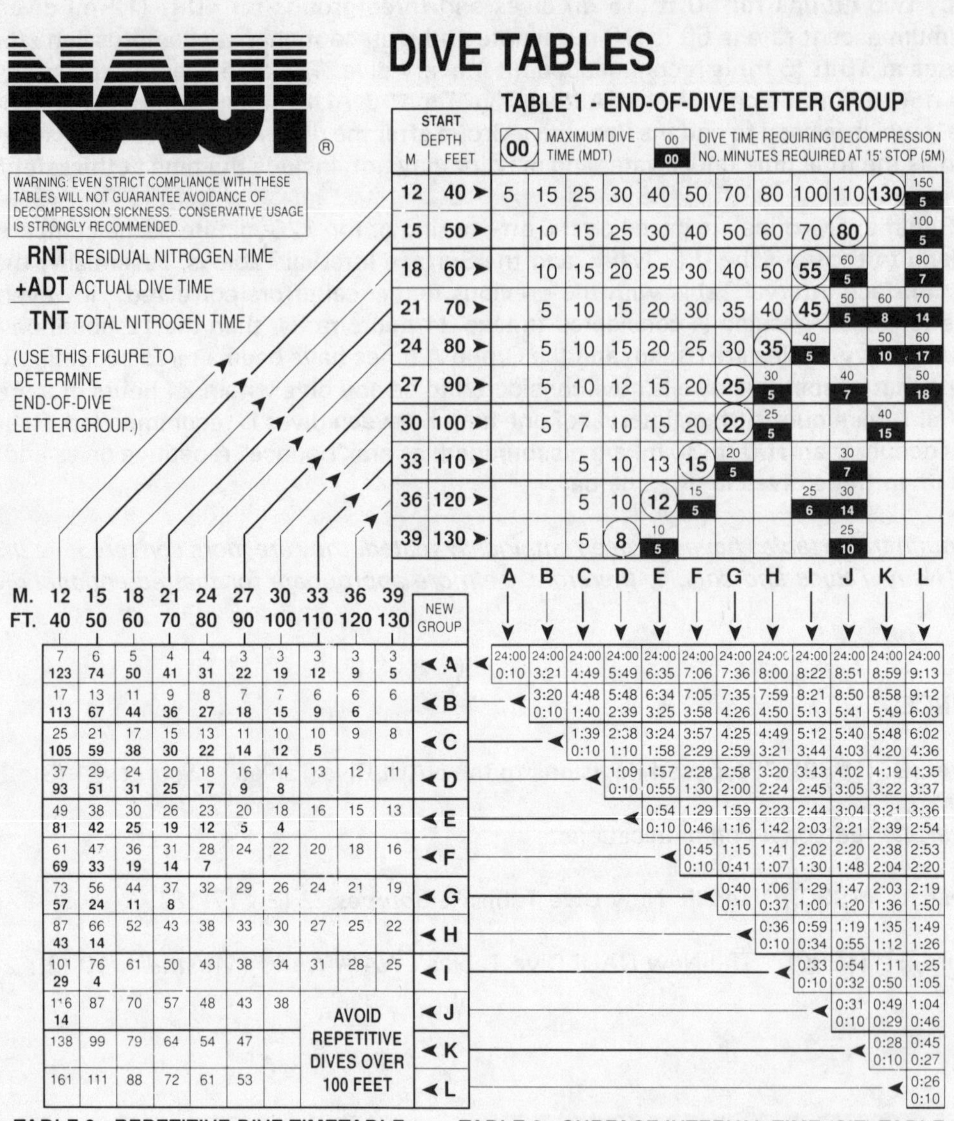

NAUI®

DIVE TABLES

WARNING: EVEN STRICT COMPLIANCE WITH THESE TABLES WILL NOT GUARANTEE AVOIDANCE OF DECOMPRESSION SICKNESS. CONSERVATIVE USAGE IS STRONGLY RECOMMENDED.

RNT RESIDUAL NITROGEN TIME
+ADT ACTUAL DIVE TIME
TNT TOTAL NITROGEN TIME

(USE THIS FIGURE TO DETERMINE END-OF-DIVE LETTER GROUP.)

TABLE 1 - END-OF-DIVE LETTER GROUP

(00) MAXIMUM DIVE TIME (MDT) (circled; shown in bold below)
00 / 00 DIVE TIME REQUIRING DECOMPRESSION / NO. MINUTES REQUIRED AT 15' STOP (5M) (shown as "time / minutes" below)

START DEPTH M	START DEPTH FEET	A	B	C	D	E	F	G	H	I	J	K	L
12	40	5	15	25	30	40	50	70	80	100	110	**130**	150 / 5
15	50		10	15	25	30	40	50	60	70	**80**		100 / 5
18	60		10	15	20	25	30	40	50	**55**	60 / 5		80 / 7
21	70		5	10	15	20	30	35	40	**45**	50 / 5	60 / 8	70 / 14
24	80		5	10	15	20	25	30	**35**	40 / 5		50 / 10	60 / 17
27	90		5	10	12	15	20	**25**	30 / 5		40 / 7		50 / 18
30	100		5	7	10	15	20	**22**	25 / 5			40 / 15	
33	110			5	10	13	**15**	20 / 5			30 / 7		
36	120			5	10	**12**	15 / 5			25 / 6	30 / 14		
39	130			5	**8**	10 / 5					25 / 10		

TABLE 2 - SURFACE INTERVAL TIME (SIT) TABLE

NEW GROUP	A	B	C	D	E	F	G	H	I	J	K	L
A	24:00 0:10	24:00 3:21	24:00 4:49	24:00 5:49	24:00 6:35	24:00 7:06	24:00 7:36	24:00 8:00	24:00 8:22	24:00 8:51	24:00 8:59	24:00 9:13
B		3:20 0:10	4:48 1:40	5:48 2:39	6:34 3:25	7:05 3:58	7:35 4:26	7:59 4:50	8:21 5:13	8:50 5:41	8:58 5:49	9:12 6:03
C			1:39 0:10	2:38 1:10	3:24 1:58	3:57 2:29	4:25 2:59	4:49 3:21	5:12 3:44	5:40 4:03	5:48 4:20	6:02 4:36
D				1:09 0:10	1:57 0:55	2:28 1:30	2:58 2:00	3:20 2:24	3:43 2:45	4:02 3:05	4:19 3:22	4:35 3:37
E					0:54 0:10	1:29 0:46	1:59 1:16	2:23 1:42	2:44 2:03	3:04 2:21	3:21 2:39	3:36 2:54
F						0:45 0:10	1:15 0:41	1:41 1:07	2:02 1:30	2:20 1:48	2:38 2:04	2:53 2:20
G							0:40 0:10	1:06 0:37	1:29 1:00	1:47 1:20	2:03 1:36	2:19 1:50
H								0:36 0:10	0:59 0:34	1:19 0:55	1:35 1:12	1:49 1:26
I									0:33 0:10	0:54 0:32	1:11 0:50	1:25 1:05
J										0:31 0:10	0:49 0:29	1:04 0:46
K											0:28 0:10	0:45 0:27
L												0:26 0:10

TIME RANGES IN HOURS : MINUTES

TABLE 3 - REPETITIVE DIVE TIMETABLE

NEW GROUP	M. 12 / FT. 40	15 / 50	18 / 60	21 / 70	24 / 80	27 / 90	30 / 100	33 / 110	36 / 120	39 / 130
A	7 **123**	6 **74**	5 **50**	4 **41**	4 **31**	3 **22**	3 **19**	3 **12**	3 **9**	3 **5**
B	17 **113**	13 **67**	11 **44**	9 **36**	8 **27**	7 **18**	7 **15**	6 **9**	6 **6**	6
C	25 **105**	21 **59**	17 **38**	15 **30**	13 **22**	11 **14**	10 **12**	10 **5**	9	8
D	37 **93**	29 **51**	24 **31**	20 **25**	18 **17**	16 **9**	14 **8**	13	12	11
E	49 **81**	38 **42**	30 **25**	26 **19**	23 **12**	20 **5**	18 **4**	16	15	13
F	61 **69**	47 **33**	36 **19**	31 **14**	28 **7**	24	22	20	18	16
G	73 **57**	56 **24**	44 **11**	37 **8**	32	29	26	24	21	19
H	87 **43**	66 **14**	52	43	38	33	30	27	25	22
I	101 **29**	76 **4**	61	50	43	38	34	31	28	25
J	116 **14**	87	70	57	48	43	38	AVOID REPETITIVE DIVES OVER 100 FEET		
K	138	99	79	64	54	47				
L	161	111	88	72	61	53				

00 LIGHT FACE NUMBERS ARE RESIDUAL NITROGEN TIMES (RNT)
00 BOLD FACE NUMBERS ARE ADJUSTED MAXIMUM DIVE TIMES (AMDT) • ACTUAL DIVE TIME SHOULD NOT EXCEED THIS NUMBER

CHAPTER 15

NEW U.S. NAVY TABLES

Two groups within the U.S. Navy have been carrying out research into decompression procedures. The groups are the Navy Experimental Diving Unit (NEDU) and the Naval Medical Research Institute (NMRI).

NEDU has developed and tested algorithms for use in the U.S. Navy Underwater Decompression Computer, a wrist-worn diver-carried device. The initial algorithms were designed for breathing mixtures with a constant partial pressure of oxygen (PO_2) of 0.7 ATA in N_2[1,2] but, later, an algorithm which can compute decompression schedules for air or a nitrox (N_2O_2) mix of any PO_2 was developed and tested.[3] During the course of testing, the initial model (which was based on exponential uptake and exponential off-gassing, and utilized 9 tissue compartments with half-times ranging from 5 to 240 minutes) had to be altered as it prescribed inadequate decompression for repetitive dives. The modified model assumes that nitrogen is absorbed by the tissues at an exponential (E) rate and is released at a slower, linear (L) rate while gas phase is present, and exponential thereafter. The algorithm has, thus, been called the E-L Algorithm. Maximum Permissible Tissue Tensions (similar to M values) were calculated for each tissue compartment and ascent is controlled by the tissue which is at, or closest to, its maximum permissible level. Stops are at 10 ft (3 m) intervals and the shallowest stop is at 10 ft. The stop times given are the minimum time that must be spent at the depth before ascent, but these times may be extended if desired.

Testing of the latest algorithm consisted of 837 man-dives on some 38 different profiles. All dives were wet, working dives and a total of 49 cases of bends resulted. *The testing showed that the current U.S. Navy repetitive dive NDLs could probably be extended, but that total decompression times for both bounce and repetitive decompression dives had to be extended considerably compared to the U.S. Navy Standard Air Tables.*[3]

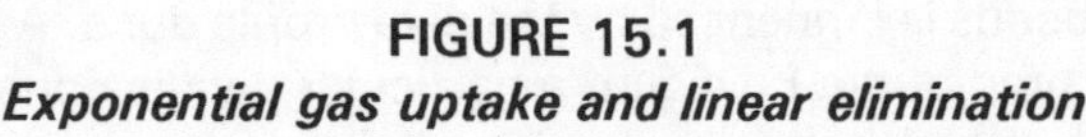

FIGURE 15.1
Exponential gas uptake and linear elimination

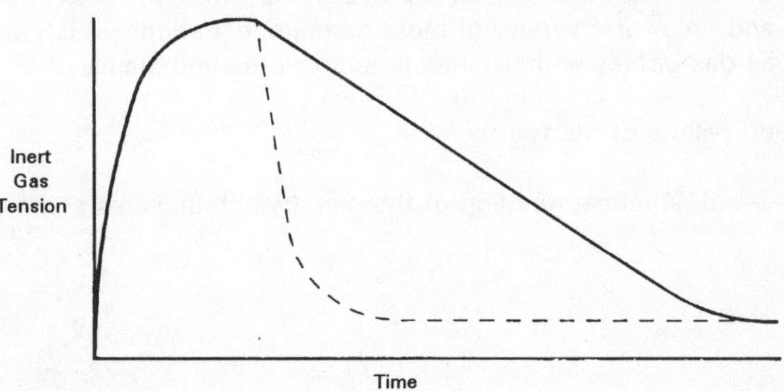

Note: During off-gassing, the linear elimination line initially gives a higher gas content than the exponential elimination curve (dotted line).

The Naval Medical Research Institute (NMRI) has been working on completely different models to those of NEDU. The NMRI models are described in the following paragraphs.

MAXIMUM LIKELIHOOD DECOMPRESSION TABLES

The traditional concept of decompression sickness is that it will occur whenever a certain critical nitrogen level in the tissues is exceeded. However, whether or not a particular dive profile will cause bends varies enormously between individuals, and in a particular individual on different days. None of the traditional decompression models account for this variability in the occurrence of bends.

With the availability of modern biophysical, mathematical and statistical evaluation tools, it has become possible to evaluate the risk of bends in a completely different way.

The U.S. Navy has developed some new decompression models which presume no specific knowledge regarding bubble formation or growth. The models are based purely on the mathematical chance (probability) of bends occurring, and their accuracy has been evaluated statistically. The development of these new models and subsequent tables is described in this chapter.

BACKGROUND

The "probability" of an event occurring is a measure of the chance or likelihood that it will occur. Probability is measured between 0 and 1. If an event has a probability of 0 it cannot occur, and a probability of 1 means that it is certain to occur. The nearer a probability is to 1 the more likely the event will occur, and the nearer the probability is to 0 the less likely the event will occur.

When we stay on the surface our probability of getting decompression sickness, P(DCS), is 0. When we dive our chances of getting bends increases. If we dive very deeply for a very long time our P(DCS) increases even more and, if the decompression procedure is very inadequate, our P(DCS) may get close to 1.

Our chance of getting bends is influenced by the dive profile done. A mathematical equation can be constructed to predict the P(DCS) if a particular dive is done. This equation can be a simple equation which only depends on depth, a slightly more complex equation depending on both depth and time, or a variety of more complex equations which account for other variables such as gas uptake and elimination and/or bubble dynamics.

Such an equation will be of the form:

P(DCS) = some mathematical function of the dive (which includes some constants)

The next step is to use available data from actual dives to find values for any constants (parameters) used in the equation, so that the equation closely matches the data. If a number of exposures to a particular dive profile and whether or not they resulted in bends is known, the P(DCS) for that profile can be estimated. For example, if a particular profile was dived 100 times with 4 resultant bends, the P(DCS) is approximately 4/100 or 0.04.* Inserting the P(DCS) in the left side of the equation will allow any constants to be evaluated. The equations must then be adjusted so that the predicted probabilities match the actual probabilities sufficiently accurately. The resulting equation can then be used to predict the chance of getting bends after doing various dive profiles.

The method adopted by the U.S. Naval researchers is known as the Maximum Likelihood Method. Maximum Likelihood applies a theory, or model, to data, and adjusts the constants within the model (equation) until theoretical predictions and the actual experimental data are in closest possible agreement.

It is then possible to work backwards and calculate what profiles would be necessary to reduce the probability of bends to a pre-defined level. For example, if we wanted to know what time at 60 ft (18 m) would give a bends risk of 5%, we put P(DCS) equal to 0.05 in the equation for 60 ft and find the associated time. In this way entire decompression schedules can be constructed with each entry carrying the same theoretical bends risk. A decompression table with a 1% bends risk for each schedule can be computed or, if preferred, a schedule with 5% bends risk throughout.

THE U.S. NAVY MODELS

The Naval Medical Research Institute is carrying out such an exercise to produce sets of decompression schedules with various associated bends risks. They have constructed a number of decompression models to predict the P(DCS) and have then used vast amounts of data collected from dives carried out over the past years to evaluate the constants in their equations.[4]

The initial data examined came from American, British and Canadian Naval decompression trials, which included more than 1,700 individual exposures to decompression from standard air dives.**

The U.S. Navy used six models to examine their data. Some models had single tissue compartments whereas others had two compartments. Some were also designed to allow a certain amount of nitrogen overpressure in the tissue before symptoms appeared.

* This profile does not have a precise P(DCS) = 0.04. It would be possible to observe four cases of bends out of a sample of 100 dives of a particular profile, even if the true underlying P(DCS) was different to 0.04. A statistical analysis as a result of observing four out of 100 reveals that one can be 95% confident that the true P(DCS) is between 0.011 and 0.099.

** In compiling their data, the U.S. Naval researchers were unable to find any profile that was repeated more than 26 times, and only averaged 5 divers per profile. This meant that there was not enough data to enable precise estimation of the true P(DCS) for an individual profile.[5]

When the various models were applied to the different sets of data it was found that although particular models matched certain sets of data quite well, when the sets of data were combined certain models became less accurate and could not be used successfully. However, some of the other models matched the data quite well.

The various equations were then applied to the current U.S. Navy Tables to estimate the risk associated with various schedules. The level of risk predicted depended on which equation was used and the set of data on which it was used. For standard air exposures (*not* exceptional or extreme exposures), the bends hazard varied greatly between schedules and was from less than 1% to about 23%.[4,5]

These statistical models are independent of variations in diver workload, environmental conditions or acclimatization, so the predicted risks are based on data spanning a large number of divers diving under a broad range of conditions.

THE TABLES

In 1985, the NMRI, encouraged by the success of its bends prediction models, published two new sets of air decompression tables with an equal chance of bends throughout.[6] There are 1% risk schedules and 5% risk schedules. The desired level of risk can be selected from the tables. Normally, a diver would select a low risk schedule but, under some circumstances, the 5% schedule can be used. The 1985 tables are not a final version and are untested as such.

One particular model was chosen to generate the 1985 schedules. It was chosen as it gives a smoother curve for the No-Decompression Limits and because it has a stronger physiological basis. The decompression given by this model is mostly at 10 ft (3 m) which is at odds with some other modern schedules which use deeper stops. The NDLs calculated by this model (Model 5) are shown in Table 15.1. The NDLs calculated by a different model (Model 3) are included simply to provide a comparison.

Table 15.2 compares the NDLs of the 1985 tables with those of the current U.S. Navy Tables and those derived by Dr. Bruce Bassett.

It is apparent from Table 15.2 that the NDLs associated with a 1% risk or less are substantially shorter than the U.S. Navy NDLs, and, in fact, are shorter than those given by virtually all other available tables.

TABLE 15.1

CALCULATED NO-DECOMPRESSION LIMITS *

Depth		Probability of DCS (%) Model 3			Model 5		
ft	m	0.5	1.0	5.0	0.5	1.0	5.0
30	9	160	180	290	120	170	270
35	10.5	130	140	230	85	130	200
40	12	110	120	190	60	100	170
50	15	80	90	140	30	65	120
60	18	7	75	110	15	40	95
70	21	4	60	95	7	25	80
80	24	3	50	80	5	15	65
90	27	2	40	70	5	10	55
100	30	2	15	60	4	8	50
110	33	2	5	55	3	7	45
120	36	-	4	50	3	5	40
130	39	-	4	45	3	5	35
140	42	-	3	40	-	4	30
150	45	-	3	35	-	4	30
160	48	-	3	35	-	3	25
170	51	-	-	32	-	3	25
180	54	-	-	31	-	3	23
190	57	-	-	29	-	3	21
200	60	-	-	27	-	-	20

* Time is in minutes. Descent rate of 75 ft/min (23 m/min).
Ascent rate of 60 ft/min (18 m/min).
Descent time is part of bottom time.

TABLE 15.2

COMPARISON OF NDLS

Depth ft	Depth m	Predicted 5% DCS	Predicted 1% DCS	Current USN	Bassett
30	9	240	170	310	220
40	12	170	100	200	120
50	15	120	70	100	70
60	18	80	40	60	50
70	21	80	25	50	40
80	24	60	15	40	30
90	27	50	10	30	25
100	30	50	8	25	20
110	33	40	7	20	15
120	36	40	5	15	12
130	39	30	5	10	10

Note:

The no-decompression times given in the predicted 5% and 1% columns are taken from the full 5% and 1% risk decompression tables that have been published by the U.S. Navy. In some cases they differ from times predicted by the model, shown in Table 14.1.

These 1985 tables are untested. Most tables have to be modified after testing to reduce the bends rate to an "acceptable" level. Chamber dives often (but not always) produce fewer cases of bends than sea dives, again leading to table modification. What the final, tested tables will be is not as yet clear. However, it is very unlikely that they will be identical to this first proposal.

The idea of decompression tables which allow a diver to pick a likely risk of bends is a good one. However, it is doubtful whether the equations used to predict the risk are actually valid under all circumstances. Some of the data sets had to be excluded because the predictions did not fit the results at all well. A reliable prediction model should fit all the data. The designers of these models drew attention to this and to the unreliability of some of the data used. The data was collected over more than 30 years, and the knowledge of, and emphasis placed upon, various bends symptoms has changed a lot over the years. Some bends symptoms that would have gone unreported in the past would now need to be included in the data. The researchers were also troubled by the short decompression requirements for very deep but short dives.

Relatively recently, the forces behind the NEDU and NMRI tables research have combined and are now co-operating closely. The diving data from NEDU and NMRI, and others from Canada and England are being combined in a **new** decompression data base. All 3,000+ dives were done since 1978 and the Navy has computerized records of the profiles, so any previous worries about data reliabilty have been overcome. The Navy plans to complete an analysis on these new data and then use the most successful model to generate new controlled risk schedules. They intend to produce standard air, repetitive air, and 0.7 ATA oxygen schedules that are consistent with an algorithm for a diver-carried decompression computer. Gaps in the data base will be tested by experimental dives at NEDU. The final product should be in use by the Navy by 1991.[5]

Many thanks to Commander Paul Weathersby (USN) for editing this chapter and for his constructive suggestions and assistance.

REFERENCES

1. Thalmann, E. et al (1980), "Testing of Decompression Algorithms for use in the U.S. Navy Underwater Decompression Computer". U.S. Navy Experimental Diving Unit Report 11-80.

2. Thalmann, E. (1984), "Phase II Testing of Decompression Algorithms for use in the U.S. Navy Underwater Decompression Computer". U.S. Navy Experimental Diving Unit Report 1-84.

3. Thalmann, E. (1986), "Air-N_2O_2 Decompression Computer Algorithm Development". U.S. Navy Experimental Diving Unit Report 8-85.

4. Weathersby, P. et al (1985), "Statistically Based Decompression Tables 1. Analysis of Standard Air Dives: 1950-1970". Naval Medical Research Institute Report NMRI 85-16.

5. Weathersby, P., personal communications.

6. Weathersby, P. et al (1985), "Statistically Based Decompression Tables 2. Equal Risk Air Diving Decompression Schedules". Naval Medical Research Institute Report NMRI 85-17.

OTHER SOURCES

Hoel, P. (1971), "Introduction to Mathematical Statistics". John Wiley and Sons Inc., New York.

Homer, L. and Weathersby, P. (1985), "Statistical aspects of the design and testing of decompression tables". *Undersea Biomedical Research*; 12 (3): 239-49.

Huggins, K. (1985), "Tables, Tables, What's with all these Tables?". In: *I.Q. '85 Proceedings*, Bangasser, S. (ed), NAUI, California.

Knight, J. (1986), "The Ideas Behind the New USN Tables". *SPUMS Journal*; 16 (1):10-16.

Thalmann, E., and Butler, F. (1983), "A Procedure for Doing Multiple Level Dives on Air Using Repetitive Groups". Navy Experimental Diving Unit Report 13-83.

Weathersby, P. et al (1986), "Statistically Based Decompression Tables III: Comparative Risk Using U.S. Navy, British and Canadian Standard Air Schedules". Naval Medical Research Institute Report NRMI 86-50.

Weathersby, P. et al (1986), "Human Decompression Trial in Nitrogen - Oxygen Diving". Naval Medical Research Institute Report NMRI 86-97.

Weathersby, P. et al, "On the Likelihood of Decompression Sickness", *Journal of Applied Physiology*; 57 (3), 815-25, 1984.

CHAPTER 16

SWISS/GERMAN TABLES

16.1 The ZH-L Decompression System

HISTORICAL BACKGROUND

The laboratory of Hyperbaric Physiology of the Medical Clinic of the University of Zurich was established in 1960. The theme of the research, conducted under the guidance of Professor Dr. Albert Buehlmann, was that of assessing the well-being and functional ability of the human being in atmospheres of abnormal pressure and composition. The Swiss, lacking a history of decompression research, were free from the shackles of traditional approaches and could begin to introduce new ideas in this area.

The effects of both nitrogen and helium have been considered throughout their decompression research and the tolerance to nitrogen in decreased ambient pressure has also been investigated due to the local interest in diving in mountain lakes.

FIGURE 16.1.1
Professor Buehlmann (rear) and Hannes Keller prepare for the first simulated dive to 300 m (1000 ft) on 25 April 1961.

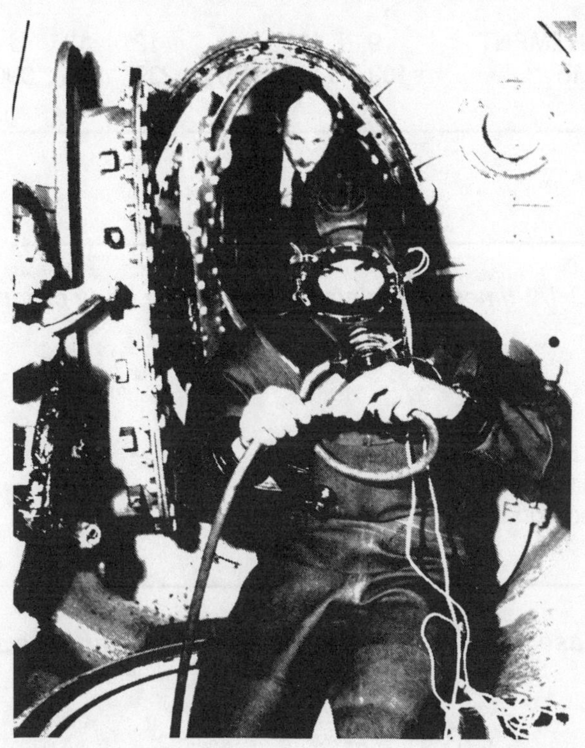

Reprinted courtesy Prof. Dr. A.A. Buehlmann.

The "Swiss Decompression Theory" is only a method of calculating saturation and desaturation in a way which permits safe decompression. All of the empirical factors that are important for this method were determined experimentally in Zurich.

For decades 240 minutes was considered to be the longest half-time for nitrogen in man, but, in the mid 1960's, it was shown that complete saturation with nitrogen takes 3-4 days and, hence, the longest half-time for nitrogen was calculated to be 8-10 hours.[1] Eventually, after various trials and experiments, sixteen tissue compartments with half-times for nitrogen of 2.65 to 635 minutes (and for helium of 1 to 240 minutes) were considered for calculating the equalization of the pressure of the inert gas. Some of these half-times have since been modified to accommodate more recent experimental and practical experience and the half-times currently range from 4 to 635 minutes. The sixteen nitrogen (N_2) half-times currently utilized are shown in Table 16.1.1 The half-times associated with various body organs were identified and some are shown in Table 16.1.2.

TABLE 16.1.1

Sixteen half-time values for N_2 corresponding to various tissue compartments for the ZH-L_{16} system

COMPARTMENT	1	2	3	4	5	6	7	8
N_2 $^1/_2$ TIME	4.0	8.0	12.5	18.5	27.0	38.3	54.3	77.0
COMPARTMENT	**9**	**10**	**11**	**12**	**13**	**14**	**15**	**16**
N_2 $^1/_2$ TIME	109	146	187	239	305	390	498	635

TABLE 16.2

N2 1/2-times associated with various body organs

Organ	N_2 $^1/_2$-time (min.)
Blood, brain, spinal cord	4 - 18.5
Skin and muscles	27 - 239
Joints and bones	239 - 635

Gas uptake and release are considered to be exponential, and are assumed to occur at identical rates.

THE ZH-L_{16} SYSTEM

The Swiss observed that the difference between the pressure of the inert gas in the tissue and the ambient pressure which could be tolerated without producing symptoms of bends, the "overpressure" of nitrogen or helium, increases approximately linearly with increasing ambient pressure. They utilized the commonly accepted notion that tissues with longer half-times (slow tissues) tolerate less excess inert gas than do shorter half-time tissues (fast tissues) at a given ambient pressure.

The ambient pressure that can be tolerated (P amb. tol) when a particular half-time tissue with a calculated inert gas pressure (P i.g.t.) is decompressed is given by:

$$P_{amb.\ tol} = (P_{i.g.t.} - a).b$$

where **a** and **b** are coefficients determined experimentally for various tissue types. Sixteen pairs of coefficients have been determined in order to represent the sixteen tissue half-times. This is known as the ZH-L_{16} system. Various modifications of the ZH-L_{16} system have been used to generate the different sets of the Buehlmann Tables. These modifications, known as ZH-L_{12}, utilize only 12 pairs of coefficients to represent the 16 tissue compartments.

Using the ZH-L_{16} system both staged and continuous decompression can be calculated quite easily and computers can be programmed to carry out the decompression calculations. In fact the "Decobrain 2", "Aladin" (GUIDE), "Aladin Pro" and "Microbrain" dive computers currently utilize modifications of this system.

The following example demonstrates how the system can be used to determine the safe depth of ascent:

> *Consider the tissue compartment with a half-time of 27 minutes. If, at a certain time during a dive, the N_2 tension in this compartment is calculated (by exponential uptake/decay) to be 3.32 bar, and, if this is the controlling tissue (i.e. it has a higher N_2 tension than the other tissue compartments), to which pressure/depth can a diver safely ascend?*
>
> Using $P_{amb.\ tol}$ = $(P\,N_2 - a).b$
> = (3.32 - 0.717) x 0.845
> = 2.2 bar (12.4 msw/40.8 fsw)

FEATURES OF THE ZH-L_{16} SYSTEM

The difference between the maximum depth of the dive and the depth of the first decompression stop increases as dive depth increases, and the rate of ascent to the first stop is governed by both the maximum depth and the controlling half-time tissue. **In practice, for SCUBA divers, the maximum ascent rate recommended for most dives is 10 metres per minute** (33 ft/minute), as Swiss experience shows that this is a safe continuous decompression for saturated tissues in order to prevent bubble formation. This ascent rate enhances gas elimination for dives to depths up to about 30 m (100 ft). However, for deep to very deep dives (i.e. greater than about 30 m) it is recommended to use ascent rates of 15-20 m/minute (50-66 ft/minute) until reaching 30 metres and, thereafter, ascending at 10 m/minute. This is suggested in order to avoid allowing the "slower tissues" to absorb extra gas during the ascent.

Decompression stops are calculated at 0.3 bar (3 msw/10 fsw) intervals.

For short air dives the ZH-L_{12} system gives decompression times which are more conservative than the U.S. Navy and Royal Navy Tables, utilizing a slower ascent rate, slightly longer stays at the deeper stops and giving an overall decompression time in excess of the U.S. Navy and Royal Navy systems. A typical comparison of decompression profiles given by the Buehlmann (1986), U.S. Navy and Royal Navy tables for a decompression dive is shown in Figure 16.1.2.

FIGURE 16.1.2

Comparison of decompression schedules for a dive to 36 m (120 ft) for a bottom time of 30 minutes

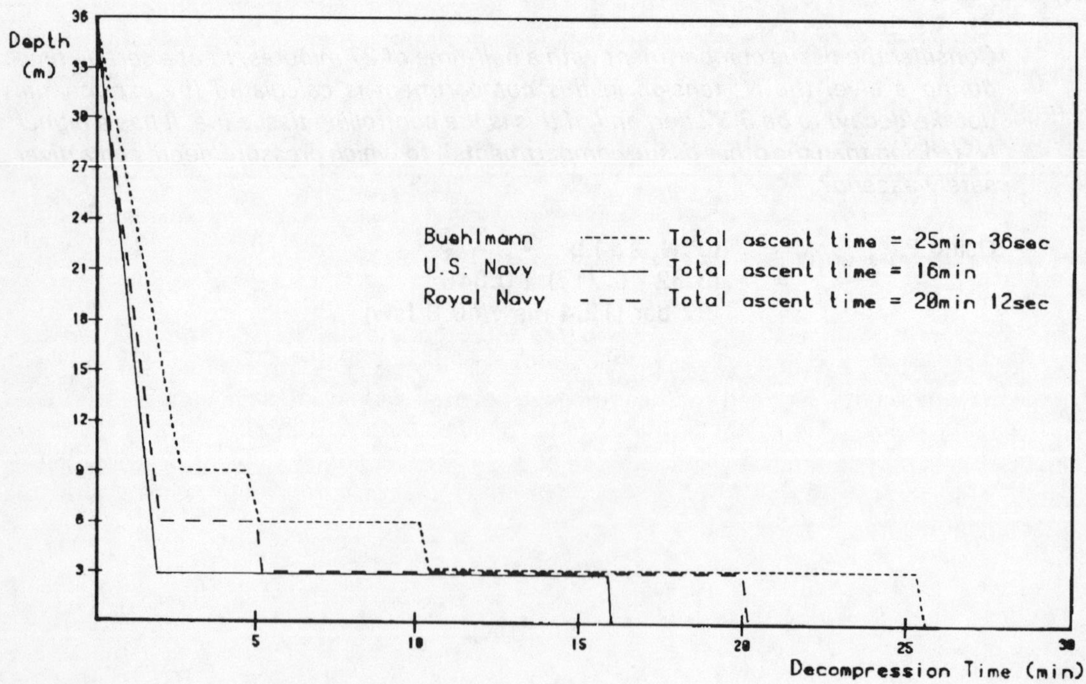

It is apparent from the profile shown that the ascent procedures recommended by the Buehlmann (1986) Tables often lead to a more gentle reduction in pressure, which in turn should minimize bubble formation in the body tissues.

DIVING AT ALTITUDE

As previously mentioned, many Swiss have an avid interest in diving in mountain lakes and consequently, in 1973, decompression tables for diving at sub-atmospheric pressure were developed. They enabled the calculation of decompression after dives of between the altitudes of 0-3200 metres (0-10,500 ft) above sea-level. These tables were then thoroughly tested by Swiss Army divers and published in 1976.[2] Between 1973 and 1983, no cases of decompression sickness were reported although well over 1000 real dives were performed, many of these being repetitive dives.[3]

The current ZH-L_{16} system suggests somewhat different decompressions to those prescribed in the earlier tables but provides a similar nitrogen excess on surfacing. The most recent tables, the Buehlmann (1986) Tables, were tested quite extensively before being released. A total of 544 real dives were carried out at altitude with no cases of decompression sickness resulting. 254 of the dives were carried out in Switzerland at altitudes between 1,000-2,600 metres (3,300-8,500) and 290 dives were done in Lake Titicaca, 3,800 metres (12,500 ft) above sea-level. Most of the dives in Lake Titicaca were no-decompression dives using an ascent rate of 10 m (33 ft)/minute, many of which were repetitive.[4,5,6]

For dives above sea-level it is important to consider whether the divers will reach the mountain lake quickly and then dive immediately, or whether they will be at altitude for some time prior to the dive, thus commencing diving with a sub-normal nitrogen pressure (PN_2) in their tissues. To allow greater safety these tables assume that the diver had travelled to altitude very quickly and, consequently, has not yet adapted to the decreased atmospheric pressure. Adapting to altitude decreases the PN_2 in the tissues and thus provides additional safety. Furthermore, the supersaturation factor on surfacing was chosen to allow for a further reduction in pressure, which may occur as a result of travelling by plane or car to a higher place after the dive.

FLYING AFTER DIVING

Additional experiments have been conducted to determine the surface intervals required before a diver may be subjected to further decreases in atmospheric pressure. On the basis of these experiments, reduced coefficients have been calculated and have been incorporated in the tables to determine the period of time required before flying after diving ("waiting times"). The waiting times were calculated to allow a reduction in ambient pressure to 0.6 bars (i.e. approx 4100 m/13,500 ft), as this is the lowest cabin pressure not regarded as a technical failure.

REPETITIVE DIVING

Joints and bones have the least tolerance to an excess of inert gas and release any excess gas only very slowly. The 120-minute tissue half-time, which is the longest utilized in the U.S. Navy Tables (or the 240 minute tissue in the Exceptional Exposure Tables), may sometimes be inadequate in situations when repetitive dives are undertaken for a number of days in succession, such as on diving holidays. Professor Buehlmann believes that, in these situations, the longer half-times of nitrogen, with the lower tolerance towards nitrogen shown by the slower tissues, must be taken into consideration.*

In the Swiss system, the inert gas pressure in the tissues with nitrogen half times between 305-635 minutes play a leading role during a surface interval and, consequently, with repetitive dives. The Surface Interval Table and Residual Nitrogen Table are both based on all nitrogen half-times up to 635 minutes. This allows a better representation of the body's (theoretical) gas loading during, and after, a surface interval, than can be gained with the single tissue repetitive system such as that used in the U.S. Navy Tables. However, this also means that, despite the longer half-times used, the Buehlmann Tables may give less conservative No-Decompression Limits than the U.S. Navy Tables for some repetitive dive situations.

FIGURE 16.1.3

The hypo/hyperbaric facilities at the University of Zurich.
The water chamber is below the spherical chamber in the front.

Photo courtesy of Prof. Dr. A.A. Buehlmann.

* However, this belief has recently been disputed by one of the dive computer programmers who argues that a 120-minute tissue compartment is adequate for these situations. See comments about this in Chapter 23.

16.2 The Buehlmann (1986) Tables

The Buehlmann Tables, derived using the ZH-L_{12} system, were published in order to provide sports divers with No-Decompression Limits and decompression stops for both single and repetitive dives.

The following definitions and rules apply to the tables:

DEFINITIONS

* **Depths** listed are the maximum depths reached during a dive.
* **Bottom Time** is the time from leaving the surface until commencing the final ascent to the surface or to any decompression stop(s).
* **Decompression Stop Time** is the time actually spent at that stop. It does not include the time taken to ascend to it.
* **Repetitive Group** is a measure of excess nitrogen remaining in the body after a dive.
* **Surface Interval** is the time from surfacing from a dive to commencing the next descent.
* **Residual Nitrogen Time** is a measure of the amount of excess nitrogen still in the body at the end of the surface interval. It is the time that the diver must consider that he has already spent at the planned depth of the repetitive dive when commencing a repetitive dive.

RULES

* The ascent rate must not exceed 10 metres/minute (33 ft/minute)*.
* For interim depths use the next greater depth on the table.
* For interim times use the next longer time on the table.

  E.g. For a dive to 17 m (56 ft) for 73 minutes look up the decompression for 18 m (60 ft) for 80 minutes.
* For "strenous" dives use the decompression prescribed for the next longer time increment.

  E.g. For a strenous dive to 17 m (56 ft) for 73 minutes look up the decompression for 18 m (60 ft) for 90 minutes.
* Repetitive dives require additional time to be added. This time is determined by using the repetitive dive table and is called the Residual Nitrogen Time (RNT). The RNT is a measure of any excess nitrogen already in a diver's body before a repetitive dive.

* This is rounded-off to 30 ft/minute on the imperial version of the tables.

* If the depth of the repetitive dive is in between two increments then take the ***shallower*** figure when calculating the residual nitrogen time (This gives a greater RNT and is thus safer).

* A safety stop of 1 minute at 3 m (10 ft) is required after every no-decompression stop dive at altitudes up to 700 m (2,300 ft), and a stop of 1 minute at 2 m (7 ft) is required after dives at higher altitudes. Professor Buehlmann states that this stop is not necessary for actual decompression purposes but it suggested in order to control the ascent rate and ensure an orderly and safe arrival at the surface.

* The following additional rule precedes Professor Dr. Buehlmann's publication of his full ZH-L_{12} tables. It reads: "Because of the risk of nitrogen narcosis, diving to more than 40 m (132 ft) may not be undertaken without additional security being given from the surface. For diving instructors the limit is increased to 50 m (165 ft). (The Swiss Federal Assurance Court regards that dives deeper than these depths carry "above normal risk" and diving to greater depths may affect a Swiss diver's assurance benefits.)

THE BUEHLMANN (1986) TABLES

TABLE 16.2.1
0 - 700 m table

NO-DECOMPRESSION LIMITS
AIR DIVING DECOMPRESSION TABLE

Depth m	BT min	Stops 6	3	RG
12	**125**		1	G
15	**75**		1	G
	90		7	G
18	**51**		1	F
	70		11	G
21	**35**		1	E
	50		8	F
	60		16	G
24	**25**		1	E
	35		4	F
	40		8	F
	50		17	G
	60	4	24	G
27	**20**		1	E
	30		5	F
	35		10	F
	40	2	13	G
	45	3	18	G
	50	6	22	G
30	**17**		1	D
	25		5	E
	30	2	7	F
	35	3	14	G
	40	5	17	G
	45	9	23	G

m	min	9	6	3	RG
33	**14**			1	D
	20			4	E
	25		2	7	F
	30		4	11	G
	35		6	17	G
	40	2	8	23	G
36	**12**			1	D
	20		2	5	E
	25		4	9	F
	30	2	5	15	G
	35	2	8	23	G
39	**10**			1	D
	15			4	E
	20		3	7	F
	25	2	4	12	G
	30	3	7	18	G
	35	5	9	28	G
42	**9**			1	D
	12			4	D
	15		1	5	E
	18		4	6	F
	21	2	4	10	F
	24	3	6	16	G
	27	4	7	19	G

m	min	12	9	6	3	RG
45	12				5	E
	15			3	5	E
	18		2	4	9	F
	21		3	5	13	G
	24		4	6	18	G
48	9				3	E
	12			2	5	E
	15			4	6	F
	18		3	4	10	F
	21		4	6	16	G
51	9				4	E
	12			3	6	E
	15		2	4	8	F
	18		4	5	13	F
	21	3	4	7	18	G
54	9			1	5	E
	12		1	4	6	E
	15		3	4	10	F
	18	1	3	6	17	G
57	9			2	5	E
	12		2	4	8	E
	15	1	4	5	11	F
	18	3	4	7	18	G

Altitude **0–700 m** above sea level

Ascent rate: 10 m/min → Safety stop: 1 min at 3 m

TABLE 16.2.2
Repetitive dive table (metric)

BUEHLMANN TABLE

REPETITIVE DIVE TIME-TABLE 0–2500 m above sea level

Surface Interval Times

RG at start of surface interval							"0"	✈
A							2	2
B						20	2	2
C					10	25	3	3
D				10	15	30	3	3
E			10	15	25	45	4	3
F		20	30	45	75	90	8	4
G	25	45	60	75	100	130	12	5
G	F	E	D	C	B	A	hrs	hrs

RG at end of surface interval

Example:
Previous dive: 24 m, 35 min = Repetitive Group **(RG) = F**
- after 45 min at surface: **RG = C**
- after 90 min at surface: **RG = A** (intermediate time: use next **shorter** interval time)
- after 4 hrs: flying is permitted
- after 8 hrs: **RG = "0"**, no more Residual Nitrogen Time **(RNT)**

RG for No-Decompression Dives and RNT for Repetitive Dives

Repetitive dive depth m (intermediate depths: use next **shallower** depth)

RG	9	12	15	18	21	24	27	30	33	36	39	42	45	48	51	54	57
A	25	19	16	14	12	11	10	9	8	7	7	6	6	6	5	5	5
B	37	25	20	17	15	13	12	11	10	9	8	7	7	6	5	5	5
C	55	37	29	25	22	20	18	16	14	12	11	10	9	8	7	7	6
D	81	57	41	33	28	24	21	19	17	15	14	13	11	10	9	9	8
E	105	82	59	44	37	30	26	23	21	19	17	16	14	13	12	11	10
F	130	111	88	68	53	42	35	30	27	24	21	19	17	16	15	14	13

Example: RG = C at end of surface interval. Planned depth of repetitive dive = 27 m. **RNT = 18 min,** to be added to Bottom Time (BT) of repetitive dive.

TABLE 16.2.3
0 - 2,300 ft table

NO-DECOMPRESSION LIMITS
AIR DIVING DECOMPRESSION TABLE

Depth ft	BT min	Stops 20	10	RG
40	**125**		1	G
50	**75**		1	G
	90		7	G
60	**51**		1	F
	70		11	G
70	**35**		1	E
	50		8	F
	60		16	G
80	**25**		1	E
	35		4	F
	40		8	F
	50		17	G
	60	4	24	G
90	**20**		1	E
	30		5	F
	35		10	F
	40	2	13	G
	45	3	18	G
	50	6	22	G
100	**17**		1	D
	25		5	E
	30	2	7	F
	35	3	14	G
	40	5	17	G
	45	9	23	G

ft	min	30	20	10	RG
110	**14**			1	D
	20			4	E
	25		2	7	F
	30		4	11	G
	35		6	17	G
	40	2	8	23	G
120	**12**			1	D
	20		2	5	E
	25		4	9	F
	30	2	5	15	G
	35	2	8	23	G
130	**10**			1	D
	15			4	E
	20		3	7	F
	25	2	4	12	G
	30	3	7	18	G
	35	5	9	28	G
140	**9**			1	D
	12			4	D
	15		1	5	E
	18		4	6	F
	21	2	4	10	F
	24	3	6	16	G
	27	4	7	19	G

ft	min	40	30	20	10	RG
150	12				5	E
	15			3	5	E
	18		2	4	9	F
	21		3	5	13	G
	24		4	6	18	G
160	9				3	E
	12			2	5	E
	15			4	6	F
	18		3	4	10	F
	21		4	6	16	G
170	9				4	E
	12			3	6	E
	15		2	4	8	F
	18		4	5	13	F
	21	3	4	7	18	G
180	9			1	5	E
	12		1	4	6	E
	15		3	4	10	F
	18	1	3	6	17	G
190	9			2	5	E
	12		2	4	8	E
	15	1	4	5	11	F
	18	3	4	7	18	G

Ascent rate: 30 ft/min ⟶ Safety stop: 1 min at 10 ft

Altitude **0–2300 ft** above sea level

TABLE 16.2.4
Repetitive dive table (imperial)

BUEHLMANN TABLE

REPETITIVE DIVE TIME-TABLE 0–8200 ft above sea level

Surface Interval Times

RG at start of surface interval

							"0"	✈
						A	2	2
					B	20	2	2
				C	10	25	3	3
			D	10	15	30	3	3
		E	10	15	25	45	4	3
	F	20	30	45	75	90	8	4
G	25	45	60	75	100	130	12	5
G	**F**	**E**	**D**	**C**	**B**	**A**	hrs	hrs

RG at end of surface interval

Example:
Previous dive: 80 ft, 35 min = Repetitive Group **(RG) = F**
- after 45 min at surface: **RG = C**
- after 90 min at surface: **RG = A** (intermediate time: use next **shorter** interval time)
- after 4 hrs: flying is permitted
- after 8 hrs: **RG = "0"**, no more Residual Nitrogen Time **(RNT)**

RG for No-Decompression Dives and RNT for Repetitive Dives

Repetitive dive depth ft (intermediate depths: use next **shallower** depth)

RG	30	40	50	60	70	80	90	100	110	120	130	140	150	160	170	180	190
A	25	19	16	14	12	11	10	9	8	7	7	6	6	6	5	5	5
B	37	25	20	17	15	13	12	11	10	9	8	7	7	6	5	5	5
C	55	37	29	25	22	20	18	16	14	12	11	10	9	8	7	7	6
D	81	57	41	33	28	24	21	19	17	15	14	13	11	10	9	9	8
E	105	82	59	44	37	30	26	23	21	19	17	16	14	13	12	11	10
F	130	111	88	68	53	42	35	30	27	24	21	19	17	16	15	14	13

Example: **RG = C** at end of surface interval. Planned depth of repetitive dive = 90 ft **RNT = 18 min,** to be added to Bottom Time (BT) of repetitive dive.

TABLE 16.2.5
701 - 2,500 m table

NO-DECOMPRESSION LIMITS AIR DECOMPRESSION TABLE

Depth m	BT min	Stops 9	6	4	2	RG
9	**238**				1	**G**
12	**99**				1	**G**
	110				4	**G**
15	**62**				1	**F**
	70				4	**G**
18	**44**				1	**F**
	50				4	**F**
	60				11	**G**
21	**30**				1	**E**
	35				2	**F**
	40				5	**F**
	45				9	**G**
	50			1	13	**G**
	55			3	17	**G**
24	**22**				1	**F**
	30				3	**F**
	35				7	**F**
	40			2	11	**G**
	45			4	16	**G**
27	**18**				1	**D**
	20				2	**E**
	25				4	**F**
	30			2	7	**F**
	35			4	11	**G**
	40		1	6	16	**G**
30	**15**				1	**D**
	20				3	**E**
	25			2	6	**F**
	30		1	4	11	**G**
	35		2	7	15	**G**
	40	1	5	10	20	**G**
33	**12**				1	**D**
	15				2	**E**
	20			2	4	**F**
	25		2	3	9	**G**
	30	1	3	6	14	**G**
	35	2	4	9	20	**G**
36	**10**				1	**D**
	15			1	3	**E**
	20		1	3	6	**F**
	25	1	3	5	12	**G**
	30	3	3	8	19	**G**
39	**9**				1	**D**
	12				3	**E**
	15			2	4	**E**
	18		2	3	7	**F**
	21		3	4	10	**G**
	24	2	3	6	15	**G**
	27	4	4	8	18	**G**
42	**8**				1	**D**
	12			1	4	**E**
	15		1	3	5	**F**
	18		3	4	8	**F**
	21	3	3	5	13	**G**
	24	4	4	7	18	**G**
45	9				3	**D**
	12			3	3	**E**
	15		3	3	6	**F**
	18	2	3	4	11	**F**
	21	4	4	7	16	**G**
48	9			1	4	**E**
	12		1	3	4	**F**
	15	2	2	4	9	**G**
	18	4	5	5	14	**G**
51	6				2	**E**
	9		1	1	3	**F**
	12	1	2	3	5	**F**
	15	3	3	4	11	**G**
54	6				2	**D**
	9		1	3	3	**F**
	12	2	3	3	7	**F**
	15	4	4	6	13	**G**

Altitude **701–2500 m** above sea level

Ascent rate: 10 m/min → Safety stop: 1 min at 2 m

Tables 16.2.1-16.2.5 are protected by copyright and are reprinted courtesy of Prof. Dr. A.A. Buehlmann.

USING THE BUEHLMANN (1986) TABLES

A. PLANNING SINGLE DIVES

Enter Table 16.2.1 (or 16.2.3) at the exact, or next greater, depth box. The top, bold figure in the "Bottom Time" column (column 2) is the No-Decompression Limit (NDL) for that depth. If the planned dive exceeds this time, move down column 2, to the exact, or next longer, time then move right to read off the stops and, if required, the Repetitive Group at the end of the dive.

Example 1.

You are planning a single, no-decompression stop dive to 22 m (73 ft) and wish to know the NDL.

Enter the 24 m (80 ft) box. The NDL is written in bold at the top of the Bottom Time column (column 2). It is *25* minutes. Remember that a safety stop of 1 minute at 3 m (10 ft) is required.

Example 2.

What decompression is required for a dive to 36 m (120 ft) for 18 minutes?

Enter the 36 m (120 ft) box and read down the second column until the exact, or next longer, time is found, in this case 20 minutes. Moving right the decompression is found to be *2 minutes at 6 m (20 ft) followed by 5 minutes at 3 m (10 ft)*. Remember that the maximum ascent rate must be 10 m/minute (33 ft/minute).

The Repetitive Group after the dive, given in the last column, is *E*.

Note:

1. The time taken to ascend from 36 m (120 ft) to the 6 m (20 ft) stop is *not* included in the 6 m (20 ft) stop time of 2 minutes. It should take 3 minutes to ascend to this first stop.

2. The time taken to ascend from 6 m (20 ft) to 3 m (10 ft) (i.e. 20 s) and from 3 m (10 ft) to the surface (20 s) is not included in the 3 m (10 ft) stop time. The diver must spend the entire 5 minutes at 3 m (10 ft).

Example 3.

Calculate the decompression required for a dive to 31 m (102 ft) for 36 minutes.

Enter the 33 m (110 ft) box and move down column 2 until 40 minutes is selected. Moving right, the decompression is found to be *2 minutes at 9 m (30 ft), 8 minutes at 6 m (20 ft) and 23 minutes at 3 m (10 ft)*. The Repetitive Group after the dive is *G*.

B. PLANNING REPETITIVE DIVES

Example 4.

> *Calculate the decompression required for the following pair of dives: 25 m (83 ft) for 20 minutes followed 2½ hours later by a dive to 18 m (60 ft) for 50 minutes.*

Upon entering the 27 m (90 ft) box the NDL for 25 m (83 ft) is found to be 20 minutes. Hence, no decompression stop is required for the first dive. The Repetitive Group immediately after the dive is *E*.

Enter the upper portion of Table 16.2.2 (or 16.2.4), from the left, at *E* (the Repetitive Group), and move right until the 2½ hour surface interval is found. It is between 45 minutes and 4 hours, so, moving down, the Repetitive Group at the end of the interval is found to be *A*.

Enter the lower portion of Table 16.2.2, from the left, at *A*, and move right until intersecting the column corresponding to the depth of the repetitive dive, in this case, 18 m (60 ft). The figure *14* which appears, represents the time to be considered already spent at 18 m (60 ft) before the repetitive dive. This 14 minutes must be added to the proposed bottom time in order to compute the correct decompression. Therefore, this repetitive dive has an equivalent bottom time of 50 + 14 = *64* minutes. From Table 16.2.1 the decompression required is found to be *11 minutes at 3 m (10 ft)*. After the dive the Repetitive Group is *G*.

Example 5.

> *You wish to carry out two no-decompression stop dives, the first to 20 m (66 ft) followed 3 hours later by a dive to 32 m (106 ft). Calculate the maximum allowable bottom time for each dive.*

Enter the 21 m (70 ft) box. The NDL for 21 m (70 ft) is *35* minutes which is the maximum allowable time for the first dive. After this 20 m (66 ft) for 35 minutes dive, the Repetitive Group is *E*. (Remember the safety stop of 1 minute at 3 m (10 ft)).

Entering the upper portion of Table 16.2.2 at *E*, move across to find the surface interval of 3 hours. It lies between 45 minutes and 4 hours, so the Repetitive Group after the surface interval is *A*.

Enter the lower portion of Table 16.2.2, from the left, at *A*, and move right until the 30 m (100 ft) row *(i.e. shallower in this case)* is intersected. The Residual Nitrogen Time is *9* minutes. Thus, your body still has an excess amount of nitrogen as if you had already spent 9 minutes at 32 m (106 ft) before the dive.

Returning to Table 16.2.1 and entering the 33 m (110 ft) box, the NDL is found to be 14 minutes. You have already used 9 minutes of this (i.e. your RNT), so you may still dive for 5 minutes. Hence, the maximum allowable bottom time for the second dive is *5* minutes. Again, do not forget to do the safety stop en route to the surface.

Example 6.

You are planning to do two dives. The first is to 34 m (112 ft) for 18 minutes and the second, five hours later, is to be a no-decompression stop dive to 27 m (90 ft). Calculate the decompression required for the first dive and the maximum allowable no-decompression stop bottom time for the second dive.

Enter the 36 m (120 ft) box, and move down column 2, to 20 minutes. Moving across, the required decompression is *2 minutes at 6 m (20 ft) and 5 minutes at 3 m (10 ft)*. The Repetitive Group is *E*.

Entering the upper part of Table 16.2.2 at *E*, move across to find the surface interval of 5 hours. This row ends at 4.00 hours, which means that, for group *E*, after 4.00 hours, no residual nitrogen needs to be added. In other words, the previous dive can be ignored. This is what RG "0" means. This situation occurs after a surface interval of 2.00 hr for group B, 3.00 hr for group C and up to 12.00 hr for group G. Therefore, to find the allowable bottom time for the second dive, return to Table 16.2.1, enter the 27 m (90 ft) box, and the maximum bottom time is found to be *20* minutes.

Determining the Repetitive Group after dives with Bottom Times less than the No-Decompression Limit

This is done by referring to the lower part of Table 16.2.2, the RG for No-Decompression Dives.

Example 7.

Find the Repetitive Group after a dive to 9 m (30 ft) for 30 minutes.

Enter the lower half of Table 16.2.2 at the 9 m (30 ft) column, and move downwards to find the 30 minutes (or next greater) Bottom Time. In this case we get 37 minutes and, by moving across to the left, the Repetitive Group is found to be Group *B*.

Similarly, after a dive to 30 m (100 ft) for 7 minutes we are in Group *A* (limit is 9 minutes) and, after a dive to 18 m (60 ft) for 38 minutes we are in Group *E* (limit is 44 minutes).

If the Bottom Time is exactly (or more than) the No-Decompression Limit the RG must be taken from Table 16.2.1. (The RG's in Table 16.2.1 do not always coincide with those in Table 16.2.2).

C. FLYING AFTER DIVING

The surface interval required before flying (or otherwise ascending) to normal commercial cabin altitude (2,400 m/8,000 ft) is found in the following manner:

Use the Repetitive Group after the last dive to enter the upper part of Table 16.2.2. Move across until entering the rightmost column, with the picture of the aeroplane. This gives the time required before flying. Theoretically, after this interval it should be safe to fly. (See comments about this in Chapter 20).

Note:

For calculating the waiting times Professor Buehlmann used 0.6 bars (i.e. approx 4100 m/ 13,500 ft) as this is the lowest cabin pressure which is not regarded as a technical failure.

Example 8.

After a dive to 27 m (90 ft) for 20 minutes, you are in Repetitive Group E. Entering Table 16.2.2 at E, and moving across, you will find that after 3 hours it should be safe to fly. If, after the dive, you were in group F, you would have to wait at least 4 hours before flying.

D. DIVING AT ALTITUDE

Table 16.2.1 can be used for diving at altitudes between 0-700 metres. Table 16.2.5 is for use for dives at altitudes 701-2500 metres above sea level. This table is governed by the same rules as the 0-700 metre table and utilizes the same repetitive dive timetable (Table 16.2.2).

The 701-2500 metre table is not currently available in feet.

Buehlmann Tables for altitudes between 2,501 - 4,500 m (8,200-14,800 ft) are reprinted in Appendix E.

Sincere thanks to Professor Dr. Buehlmann for editing the text and examples in this chapter.

REFERENCES

1. Buehlmann, A. et al (1967), "Saturation and desaturation with N_2 and He at 4 ATA". *Journal of Applied Physiology*; 23: 458-462.
2. Boni, M et al (1976), "Diving at diminished atmospheric pressure: air decompression tables for different altitudes". *Undersea Biomedical Research*; 3 (3): 189-204.
3. Buehlmann, A. (1984), "Decompression-Decompression Sickness". Springer-Verlag, Heidelberg.
4. Buehlmann, A. (1987), "Diving at Altitude and Flying After Diving", UHMS Symposium, *The Physiological Basis of Decompression*, Duke University Medical Center.
5. Moody, M. (1988), "Exercise Paddington Diamond". Report on Exercise Paddington Diamond, Lake Titicaca, Bolivia, May 1987. Ordinance Services, Viersen.
6. Moody, M., personal communications.

OTHER SOURCES

Buehlmann, A. (1986), "The Validity of a Multi-Tissue Model in Sport Diving Decompression". *Proceedings of the Diving Officers' Conference*, BS-AC, London.

Buehlmann, A. (1987), "Decompression After Repeated Dives". *Undersea Biomedical Research*; 14 (1): 59-66.

Buehlmann, A., personal communications.

Mueller, B., personal communication.

Aladin Pro Manual, Uwatec, Switzerland.

RECOMMENDED FURTHER READING

Buehlmann, A. (1984), "Decompression-Decompression Sickness". Springer-Verlag, Heidelberg.

EXERCISES ON THE BUEHLMANN (1986) TABLES

1. Determine the No-Decompression Limits (NDLs) and associated Repetitive Groups for dives to the following depths:

   (a) 16 m (53 ft) (b) 22 m (73 ft) (c) 40 m (132 ft)
   (d) 26 m (86 ft)

2. Calculate the decompression required and associated Repetitive Groups after the following single dives:

   (a) 17 m (56 ft) for 67 minutes (b) 24 m (80 ft) for 51 minutes
   (c) 35 m (116 ft) for 15 minutes.

3. Determine the Residual Nitrogen Times after the following dives and Surface Intervals:

   (a) 1st dive: 20 m (66 ft) for 35 minutes
   Surface Interval: 2½ hr
   2nd dive: 16 m.

   (b) 1st dive: 33 m (110 ft) for 20 minutes
   Surface Interval: 30 minutes
   2nd dive: 27 m (90 ft).

4. Calculate the maximum allowable No-Decompression Stop Bottom Time for the following repetitive dives:

   (a) 1st dive: 21 m (70 ft) for 50 minutes
   Surface Interval: 6 hr
   2nd dive: 18 m (60 ft).

   (b) 1st dive: 36 m (120 ft) for 12 minutes
   Surface Interval: 4 hr
   2nd dive: 30 m (100 ft).

5. Calculate the decompression required for the following group of dives:

   1st dive: 17 m (56 ft) for 60 minutes
   Surface Interval: 4 hr
   2nd dive: 47 m (155 ft) for 6 minutes
   Surface Interval: 4½ hr
   3rd dive: 24 m (80 ft) for 25 minutes.

6. Determine the Surface Intervals required before flying after the following dives:

   (a) 15 m (50 ft) for 45 minutes
   (b) 9 m (30 ft) for 70 minutes
   (c) 36 m (120 ft) for 19 minutes.

ANSWERS

1. (a) 51,F (b) 25,E (c) 9,D (d) 20,E

2. (a) 11 min at 3 m (10 ft), G
   (b) 4 min at 6 m (20 ft) and 24 min at 3 m (10 ft), G
   (c) 2 min at 6 m (20 ft) and 5 min at 3 m (10 ft), E

3. (a) 16 (b) 12

4. (a) 37 (b) 17

5. 11 min at 3 m (10 ft), 2 min at 6 m (20 ft) and 5 min at 3 m (10 ft), safety stop of 1 min at 3 m (10 ft).

6. (a) 3 hr (b) 3 hr (c) 3 hr.

16.3 The Buehlmann/Hahn Tables

The Buehlmann/Hahn Tables, derived using a modification of Professor Buehlmann's ZH-L_{16} system, utilize half-times ranging from 2.65 to 635 minutes. These tables were designed by Dr. Max Hahn, a German physical scientist and SCUBA diving instructor. They are the predominent table in Germany. However, these tables represent an earlier state of knowledge than the Buehlmann 1986 Tables which, in the author's opinion, should be used in preference.

In order to take into account inaccuracies of depth gauges, the tabled depths in Tables 16.3.1 and 16.3.2 have been furnished with a safety addition of 2.4%. In Table 16.3.3, 3% + 1 m has been added to the actual depth to give the tabled depth. In addition, a pressure increase of 1 bar for every 10 m of depth was calculated (i.e. a water density of 1.02 kg/l was assumed).

Since the tables are only available in metres the following discussion and example will not include imperial conversions.

DEFINITIONS

The following definitions of terms apply for the interpretation of the decompression tables:

* **Ascent** is an ascent performed according to certain, defined rules.

* **Depth** (Tauchtiefe) is the maximum water depth which has been reached according to a pressure-sensing depth gauge (not a rope!).

  (For decompression, it is actually the pressure rather than the depth which is decisive. In sea water, the actual depth is approx. 1% less, in fresh water approx. 2% more than indicated by a precise depth gauge which has been calibrated to 10 m/1 bar according to DIN 7922.)

* **Bottom time** (Grundzeit) is the time from leaving the surface when descending until commencing the final ascent to the surface or to any decompression stop(s).

* **Dive time** is the total amount of time spent under water.

* **No-Decompression Limit** (NDL) is the maximum bottom time which only just allows you to ascend up to the surface without decompression stops.

* **Decompression times** (Dekopausen) are the periods of time which have to be spent at the decompression stops according to the tables. (They do not include the time taken to ascend to the stops).

* **Total ascent time** is the sum of all decompression times and the time for ascending at 10 m/min.

* **Decompression stops** are the water depths at which decompression times must be spent.

* **Repetitive dives** (Wiederholungstauchgange) are all dives which have to be calculated by adding Residual Nitrogen Time (RNT) to the bottom time.

* **Surface interval** (Oberflachenpause) is the time between two dives which is not spent under water.

* **Repetitive groups** (Wiederholungsgruppe) are letter codes serving for the calculation of the Residual Nitrogen Time (RNT), which is added to the bottom time for repetitive dives.

* **Residual Nitrogen Times (RNT)** (Zeitzuschlag) are added to the actual bottom time of repetitive dives in order to calculate the fictitious bottom time used for reading the tables.

DIRECTIONS FOR USING THE TABLES

Note:

For the purposes of the following exercises, the left-hand side and top right-hand side of Table 16.3.1 will be referred to as Table A. The table at the bottom-right of Table 16.3.1 will be referred to as Table B.

A. If the bottom time is shorter than, or identical to, the No-Decompression Limit, you may ascend without any decompression stop. An ascent rate of 10 m/min is recommended.

E.g. Descent in 1 min to 30 m, time spent there 16 min.
Bottom time: (1 + 16) = 17 min.
Ascent: According to Table A no stop is required. Direct ascent to surface should take 3 min.

B. If the bottom time is longer than the NDL, decompression times must be observed.

E.g. Descent in 2 min to 36 m, time spent there 8 min.
Bottom time: (2 + 8) = 10 min.
Ascent: In 3 min 18 s up to 3 m, stop there for 1 min (from Table A), then take 18 s up to the surface.

C. If the bottom time is an interim time, use the next-longer tabled time.

E.g. Maximum depth of 24 m for a bottom time of 28 min.
Look up 24 m for 30 min bottom time.
Ascent: In 2 min 6 s up to 3 m, stop there for 1 min, then take 18 s up to the surface.

D. If the depth is an interim depth, use the next greater tabled depth.

E.g. Maximum depth of 37 m for a bottom time of 14 min.
Look up 39 m for 15 min.
Ascent: In 3 min 24 s up to 3 m, stop there for 4 min, then take 18 s up to the surface.

E. After any short, intensive exertion or when the water is very cold, read the table for the next-longer time group.

E.g. Maximum depth of 35 m for a bottom time of 5 min with short, intensive exertion while freeing the anchor from rocks.
Look up 35 m for 10 min.

F. After prolonged, intensive exertion you must add 50% to the bottom time.

E.g. Maximum depth of 45 m for a bottom time of 12 min while swimming hard against a strong current.
Look up 45 m for 18 min. The additional air supply needed for the increased decompression must be taken into consideration.

G. **REPETITIVE DIVES:**

In Table B, look up the row of the Repetitive Group (indicated by the letters B, C, D, E, F, G) of the preceding dive, and find the two Surface Interval columns between which your Surface Interval fits. The dividing line between these two columns points down to the appropriate column in the Residual Nitrogen Time table. Look up your RNT in the row of the depth of your planned repetitive dive, given in the left-most column of the table. The RNT must be added to the actual bottom time of the repetitive dive. Using this fictitious increased bottom time, you can look up your decompression schedule in the decompression table according to rules A - F.

E.g. First dive 37 m for 14 min bottom time.
RG = E.
Surface Interval = 1 h.
Second dive to 33 m for 11 min bottom time.
RNT = 8 min
Bottom time = (11 + 8) = 19 min.
Look up 33 m for 20 min in Table A.

H. If the depth of the repetitive dive is an interim depth on the Residual Nitrogen Time table, use the deeper depth figure. This depth should then also be used (according to Rule D) for the ascent calculation on the decompression table.

E.g. First dive 37 m for 14 min bottom time.
RG = E.
Surface Interval = 1 h.
Second dive to 34 m for 11 min bottom time.
RNT = 7 min
Bottom time = (11 + 7) = 18 min.
Look up 36 m for 20 min in Table A.

I. If the Surface Interval is identical to one of the times given in the table for Surface Intervals, use the line and column to the left of this figure.

E.g. First dive 37 m for 14 min bottom time.
RG = E.
Surface Interval = 25 min.
Second dive to 34 m for 11 min bottom time.
RNT = 13 min
Bottom time = (11 + 13) = 24 min.
Look up 36 m for 25 min in Table A.

J. If the Surface Interval is identical to, or shorter than, the smallest time figure given in the appropriate row of Table B, the dives count as one uninterrupted dive (to the max depth reached in either dive) and the bottom times must be added together.

E.g. First dive 37 m for 14 min bottom time.
RG = E.
Surface Interval = 5 min.
Second dive to 35 m for 5 min bottom time and with no exertion.
Sum of bottom times = (14 + 5) = 19 min.
Look up 39 m for 20 min in Table A.

K. After a repetitive dive, the relevent Repetitive Group is the one marked in the table for the last dive.

L. Refrain from doing more than one repetitive decompression stop dive.

After ascent from a repetitive decompression stop dive, a surface interval of at least 12 hours is required before another decompression stop dive is begun.

M. The NDL for a repetitive no-decompression stop dive is found by subtraction of RNT from the NDL given in the table.

E.g. The previous dive had a RG of E. After a Surface Interval of 2 hours, a no-decompression stop dive to 30 m is planned. The NDL is (17 - 9) = 8 min.

N. Flying is permitted only when there is no longer any Residual Nitrogen Time indicated according to the RG of the last dive.

E.g. If RG after last dive is F, you must wait at least 8 hours before flying.

Time groups of Repetitive Group G should be used only in emergencies or as a sum of bottom time and RNT. When these bottom times are taken to their limits, the risk of decompression sickness is increased.

The ascent times given exactly to the second result from a recommmended ascent rate of 10 m/min. However, small deviations are neither avoidable nor dangerous. When ascending from deeper than 25 m, you may ascend at a faster rate until reaching 25 m. This will somewhat reduce nitrogen uptake and air consumption. If you ascend slower than 10 m/min, the ascent time must be added to the bottom time. An ascent at 10 m/min is not added to bottom time.

For safety reasons it is recommended to avoid repetitive dives of increasing depths.

If, in an emergency, the required decompression schedule cannot be carried out, the decompression times should be shortened proportionally in relation to the total decompression time. The first aid measure, until commencement of recompression therapy, should be breathing 100% oxygen.

Statistics have proven that a small percentage of people are more susceptible to decompression sickness. A diver, who has previously suffered from decompression sickness, should always perform the ascent according to Rule E. i.e. read the table at the next-longer time group to the regular one.

End all dives with a few minutes at 2 - 5 metres.

When using the tables and rules cited here, decompression sickness is highly improbable but (as with all tables) not completely impossible. Therefore, the authors and editors of the Buehlmann/Hahn Tables do not accept any liability in connection herewith.

THE BUEHLMANN/HAHN TABLES

TABLE 16.3.1

0 - 250 m table

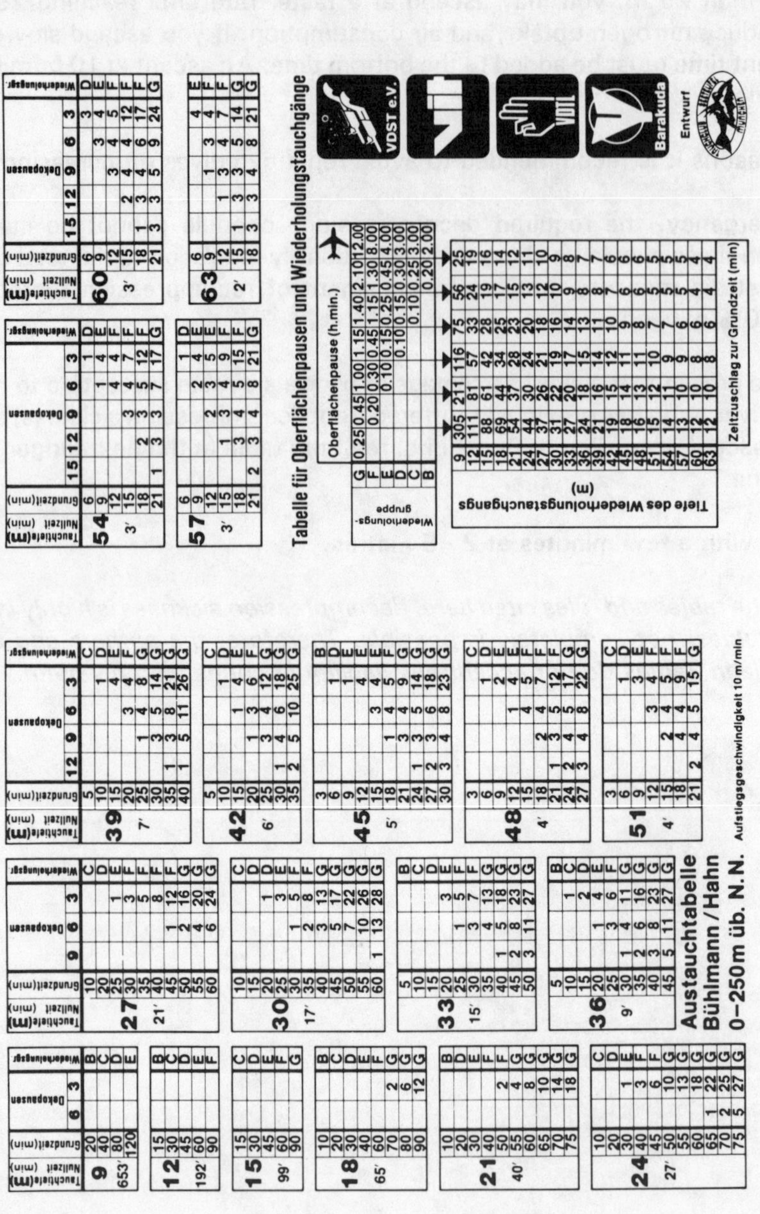

Austauchtabelle Bühlmann/Hahn (0–250 m über N.N.)

Tauchtiefe (m) / Nullzeit (min)	Grundzeit (min)	Dekopausen 15	Dekopausen 12	Dekopausen 9	Dekopausen 6	Dekopausen 3	Wiederholungsgr.
9 / 653′	20						B
	40						C
	80						D
	120						E
12 / 192′	15						B
	30						C
	45						D
	60						E
	90						F
15 / 99′	15						C
	30						D
	45						E
	60						F
	90						G
18 / 65′	10						B
	20						C
	30						D
	40						E
	60						F
	70					2	G
	80					6	G
	90					12	G
21 / 40′	10						B
	20						D
	30						E
	40						F
	50					2	F
	55					4	G
	60					8	G
	65					10	G
	70					14	G
	75					18	G
24 / 27′	10						C
	20						D
	30					1	E
	40					3	F
	45					6	F
	50					10	G
	55					13	G
	60					18	G
	65				1	22	G
	70				2	25	G
	75				5	27	G
27 / 21′	10						C
	20						D
	25					1	E
	30					3	F
	35					5	F
	40					8	F
	45				1	12	F
	50				2	16	G
	55				4	20	G
	60				6	24	G
30 / 17′	10						C
	15						D
	20					1	D
	25					3	E
	30				1	5	F
	35				2	8	F
	40				3	13	G
	45				5	17	G
	50				7	22	G
	55				10	26	G
	60			1	13	28	G
33 / 15′	5						B
	10						C
	15						D
	20					3	E
	25				1	5	F
	30				3	7	F
	35				4	13	G
	40			1	5	18	G
	45			2	8	23	G
	50			3	11	27	G
36 / 9′	5						B
	10					1	C
	15					2	D
	20				1	4	E
	25				3	6	F
	30			1	4	11	G
	35			2	6	16	G
	40			3	8	23	G
	45			5	11	27	G
39 / 7′	5						C
	10					1	D
	15					4	E
	20				3	4	F
	25			1	4	8	G
	30			3	5	14	G
	35		1	3	8	21	G
	40		1	5	11	26	G
42 / 6′	5						C
	10					1	D
	15				1	4	E
	20			1	3	6	F
	25			3	4	12	G
	30		1	4	6	18	G
	35		2	5	10	25	G
45 / 5′	3						B
	6					1	D
	9					1	E
	12					4	E
	15				3	4	E
	18			1	4	5	F
	21			3	4	9	G
	24		1	3	5	14	G
	27		2	3	6	18	G
	30		3	4	8	23	G
48 / 4′	3						C
	6					1	D
	9					2	E
	12				1	4	E
	15				4	5	F
	18			2	4	7	F
	21		1	3	5	12	F
	24		2	4	5	17	G
	27		3	4	8	22	G
51 / 4′	3						C
	6					1	D
	9					3	E
	12				3	4	F
	15			2	4	5	F
	18			4	4	9	F
	21		2	4	5	15	G
54 / 3′	6					1	D
	9				1	4	E
	12				4	4	F
	15			3	4	7	F
	18		2	3	5	12	F
	21	1	3	3	7	17	G
57 / 3′	6					1	D
	9				2	4	E
	12			2	3	5	E
	15		1	3	4	9	F
	18		3	4	5	15	F
	21	2	3	4	8	21	G
60 / 3′	6					3	D
	9				3	4	E
	12			3	4	5	F
	15		2	4	4	12	F
	18	1	3	4	6	17	F
	21	3	3	5	9	24	G
63 / 2′	6					4	E
	9			1	3	4	F
	12		1	3	4	7	F
	15	1	3	3	5	14	G
	18	3	3	4	8	21	G

Austauchtabelle Bühlmann / Hahn 0–250m üb. N.N.

Aufstiegsgeschwindigkeit 10 m/min

Tabelle für Oberflächenpausen und Wiederholungstauchgänge

Wiederholungsgruppe	Oberflächenpause (h.min.)						
G	0.25	0.45	1.00	1.15	1.40	2.10	12.00
F		0.20	0.30	0.45	1.15	1.30	8.00
E			0.10	0.15	0.25	0.45	4.00
D				0.10	0.15	0.30	3.00
C					0.10	0.25	3.00
B						0.20	2.00

Tiefe des Wiederholungstauchgangs (m)	Zeitzuschlag zur Grundzeit (min)					
9	305	211	116	75	56	25
12	111	81	57	33	24	19
15	88	61	42	28	19	16
18	69	44	34	25	17	14
21	54	37	28	23	15	12
24	44	30	24	20	13	11
27	37	26	21	18	12	10
30	31	22	19	16	10	9
33	27	20	17	14	9	8
36	24	18	15	13	8	7
39	21	16	14	11	8	7
42	19	15	12	10	7	6
45	18	14	11	9	6	6
48	16	13	11	8	6	6
51	15	12	10	7	5	5
54	14	11	9	7	5	5
57	13	10	9	6	5	5
60	12	10	8	6	4	4
63	12	10	8	6	4	4

A. PLANNING SINGLE DIVES

The large, bold number in the leftmost column of each box in Table A is the depth in metres. Enter Table A at the exact, or next greater, depth box. The smaller number directly below the depth is the No-Decompression Limit (NDL) for that depth. If the planned bottom time of the dive exceeds this time, move down column 2 to the exact, or next longer, bottom time, then move right to read off the stops and, if required, the Repetitive Group, at the end of the dive. The coloured area in each box* indicates that a decompression stop(s) (other than the safety stop) is required.

Example 1.

You are planning a single, no-decompression stop dive to 22 m and wish to know the NDL.

Enter the 24 m box. The NDL is written below the depth in the first column of the box. It is *27* minutes. Remember that a safety stop is recommended.

Example 2.

What decompression is required for a dive to 36 m for 18 minutes?

Enter the 36 m box and read down the second column until the exact, or next longer time, is found, in this case 20 minutes. Moving right, the decompression is found to be *1 minute at 6 m followed by 4 minutes at 3 m*. Remember that the maximum ascent rate must be 10 m/minute.

The Repetitive Group after the dive, given in the last column, is *E*.

Note:

1. The time taken to ascend from 36 m to the 6 m stop is *not* included in the 6 m stop time of 1 minute. It should take 3 minutes to ascend to this first stop.

2. The time taken to ascend from 6 m to 3 m (i.e. 18 s) and from 3 m to the surface (18 s) is not included in the 3 m stop time. The diver must spend the entire 4 minutes at 3 m.

Example 3.

Calculate the decompression required for a dive to 31 m for 36 minutes.

Enter the 33 m box and move down column 2 until 40 minutes is selected. Moving right, the decompression is found to be *1 minute at 9 m, 5 minutes at 6 m and 18 minutes at 3 m*. The Repetitive Group after the dive is *G*.

* This coloured area is on the actual submersible tables but is not shown here.

B. PLANNING REPETITIVE DIVES

Example 4.

Calculate the decompression required for the following pair of dives: 25 m for 20 minutes followed, $2^1/_2$ hours later, by a dive to 18 m for 50 minutes.

Upon entering the 27 m box the NDL for 25 m is found to be 21 minutes. Hence, no decompression stop is required for the first dive (but the safety stop is still recommended). The Repetitive Group immediately after the dive is *D*.

Enter the upper portion of Table B, from the left, at *D* (the Repetitive Group), and move to the right along the row until the $2^1/_2$ hour surface interval is found. It is between 30 minutes and 3 hours so move down the arrow between 0.30 and 3.00, and enter the lower portion of the table at the corresponding column.

Continue down the column until intersecting the row corresponding to the depth of the repetitive dive (given at the left of the table), in this case 18 m. The figure *14* which appears represents the time to be considered already spent at 18 m before the repetitive dive. This 14 minutes must be added to the proposed bottom time in order to compute the correct decompression. Therefore, this repetitive dive has an equivalent bottom time of 50 + 14 = *64* minutes. From Table A, no decompression stop is required, but a safety stop is advised. After the dive the Repetitive Group is *G*.

Example 5.

You wish to carry out two no-decompression stop dives, the first to 32 m followed, $2^1/_2$ hours, later by a dive to 20 m. Calculate the maximum allowable bottom time for each dive.

Enter the 33 m box in Table A. The NDL for 33 m is *15* minutes, which is the maximum allowable time for the first dive. After this 33 m for 15 minutes dive, the Repetitive Group is *D*.

Entering the upper portion of Table B at *D*, move along the row to the right to find the surface interval of *$2^1/_2$* hours. It lies between 30 minutes and 3.00 hours, so move down the arrow between 0.30 and 3.00 and enter the lower part of the table at the appropriate column. Move down this column until the 21 m row (i.e. the next-deeper tabled depth) is intersected. The Residual Nitrogen Time is *12* minutes. Thus, your body still has an excess amount of nitrogen as if you had already spent 12 minutes at 20 m before the dive.

Returning to Table A and entering the 21 m box, the NDL is found to be 40 minutes. You have already used 12 minutes of this (i.e. your RNT), so you may still dive for 28 minutes. Hence, the maximum allowable bottom time for the second dive is *28* minutes. Again, don't forget to do the safety stop en route to the surface.

Example 6.

You are planning to do two dives. The first is to 34 m for 18 minutes and the second, five hours later, is to be a no-decompression stop dive to 27 m. Calculate the decompression required for the first dive and the maximum allowable no-decompression stop bottom time for the second dive.

Enter the 36 m box and move down column 2 to 20 minutes. Moving across, the required decompression is *1 minute at 6 m and 4 minutes at 3 m*. The Repetitive Group is *E*.

Entering the upper part of Table B at *E*, move across to find the surface interval of 5 hours. This row ends at 4.00 hours which means that, for group *E*, after 4.00 hours, no residual nitrogen needs to be added. In other words, the previous dive can be ignored. This situation occurs after a surface interval of 2.00 hr for group B, 3.00 hr for group C and up to 12.00 hr for group G. Therefore, to find the allowable bottom time for the second dive, return to Table A, enter the 27 m box and the maximum bottom time is found to be *21* minutes.

C. FLYING AFTER DIVING

The surface interval required before flying (or otherwise ascending) to normal commercial cabin altitude (2,400 m) is found in the following manner:

Use the Repetitive Group after the last dive to enter the upper part of Table B. Move across until entering the rightmost column with the picture of the aeroplane. This gives the time required before flying. *Theoretically*, after this interval it should be safe to fly.*

Example 7.

After a dive to 27 m for 20 minutes you are in Repetitive Group D. Entering Table B, at D, and moving across, you will find that after 3 hours it should be safe to fly. If after the dive you were in group F, you would have to wait at least 8 hours before flying.

D. DIVING AT ALTITUDE

Table 16.3.1 can be used for diving at altitudes between 0-250 metres. Table 16.3.2 is for use for dives at altitudes 251-700 metres above sea level and Table 16.3.3 can be used for altitudes between 701-1200 metres. Tables 16.3.2 and 16.3.3 are governed by the same rules as the 0-250 metre table and utilize the same repetitive dive timetable (Table B).

SOURCES

Buehlmann, A., personal communications.

Hahn, M., personal communications.

Lippmann, J. and Bugg, S. (1989), "The Diving Emergency Handbook" (German edition). Springer-Verlag, Heidelberg.

* See comments in Chapter 20.

TABLE 16.3.2
251 -700 m table

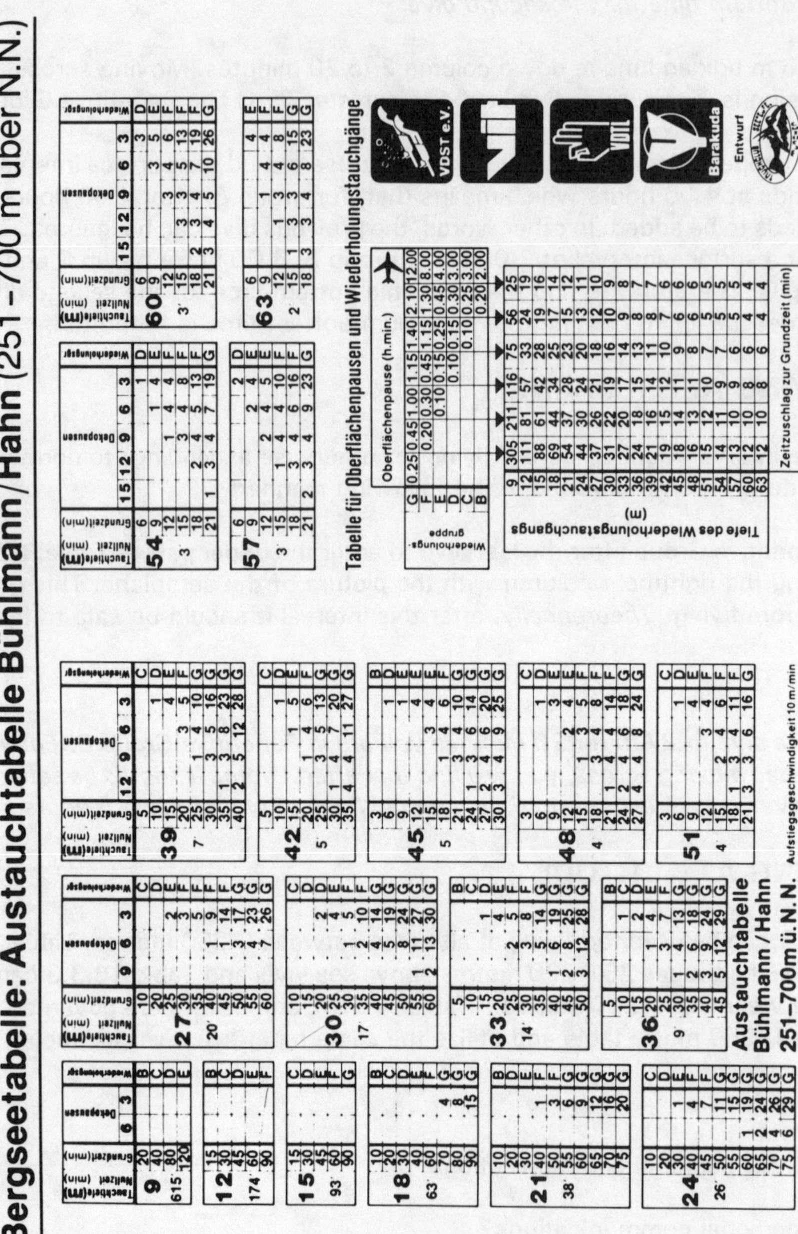

1. Bergseetabelle: Austauchtabelle Bühlmann/Hahn (251 –700 m über N.N.)

Tauchtiefe (m)	Nullzeit (min)	Grundzeit (min)	Dekopausen 15	12	9	6	3	Wiederholungsgr.
9	615′	20						B
		40						C
		80						D
		120						E
12	174′	15						B
		30						C
		45						D
		60						E
		90						F
15	93′	15						C
		30						D
		45						E
		60						F
		90						G
18	63′	10						B
		20						C
		30						D
		40						E
		60						F
		70					4	G
		80					8	G
		90					15	G
21	38′	10						B
		20						D
		30						E
		40					1	F
		50					3	F
		55					6	G
		60					9	G
		65					12	G
		70					16	G
		75					20	G
24	26′	10						C
		20						D
		30					1	E
		40					4	F
		45					7	F
		50					11	G
		55					15	G
		60				1	19	G
		65				2	24	G
		70				4	26	G
		75				6	29	G
27	20′	10						C
		20						D
		25					2	E
		30					3	F
		35					5	F
		40				1	9	F
		45				1	14	F
		50				3	17	G
		55				4	23	G
		60				7	26	G
30	17′	10						C
		15						D
		20					2	D
		25					4	E
		30				1	5	F
		35				2	10	F
		40				4	14	G
		45				5	19	G
		50				8	24	G
		55			1	11	27	G
		60			2	13	30	G
33	14′	5						B
		10						C
		15					1	D
		20					4	E
		25				2	5	F
		30				3	8	F
		35				5	14	G
		40			1	6	19	G
		45			2	8	25	G
		50			3	12	28	G
36	9′	5						B
		10					1	C
		15					2	D
		20				1	4	E
		25				3	7	F
		30			1	4	13	G
		35			2	6	18	G
		40			3	9	24	G
		45			5	12	29	G
39	7′	5						C
		10					1	D
		15					4	E
		20				3	5	F
		25			1	4	10	G
		30			3	5	16	G
		35		1	3	8	23	G
		40		2	5	12	28	G
42	5′	5						C
		10					1	D
		15				1	5	E
		20			1	4	6	F
		25			3	5	13	G
		30		1	4	7	20	G
		35		4	4	11	27	G
45	5	3						B
		6					1	D
		9					1	E
		12					4	E
		15				3	4	E
		18			1	4	6	F
		21			3	4	10	G
		24		1	3	6	14	G
		27		2	4	6	20	G
		30		3	4	9	25	G
48	4	3						C
		6					1	D
		9					3	E
		12				2	4	E
		15			1	3	5	F
		18			3	4	8	F
		21		1	4	4	14	F
		24		2	4	6	18	G
		27		4	4	8	24	G
51	4′	3						C
		6					1	D
		9					4	E
		12				3	4	F
		15			2	4	6	F
		18		1	3	4	11	F
		21		3	3	6	16	G
54	3′	6					1	D
		9				1	4	E
		12			1	4	4	F
		15			3	4	8	F
		18		2	4	5	13	F
		21	1	3	4	7	19	G
57	3′	6					2	D
		9				2	4	E
		12			2	4	5	E
		15		1	4	4	10	F
		18		3	4	6	16	F
		21	2	3	4	9	23	G
60	3′	6					3	D
		9				3	5	E
		12			3	4	6	F
		15		3	3	5	13	F
		18	2	3	4	7	19	F
		21	3	4	5	10	26	G
63	2′	6					4	E
		9			1	4	4	F
		12		1	3	4	8	F
		15	1	3	3	6	15	G
		18	3	3	4	8	23	G

Austauchtabelle Bühlmann / Hahn 251–700m ü. N. N.

Aufstiegsgeschwindigkeit 10 m/min

Tabelle für Oberflächenpausen und Wiederholungstauchgänge

Wiederholungsgruppe	Oberflächenpause (h.min.)						
G	0.25	0.45	1.00	1.15	1.40	2.10	12.00
F		0.20	0.30	0.45	1.15	1.30	8.00
E			0.10	0.15	0.25	0.45	4.00
D				0.10	0.15	0.30	3.00
C					0.10	0.25	3.00
B						0.20	2.00

Tiefe des Wiederholungstauchgangs (m)	Zeitzuschlag zur Grundzeit (min)					
9	305	211	116	75	56	25
12	111	81	57	33	24	19
15	88	61	42	28	19	16
18	69	44	34	25	17	14
21	54	37	28	23	15	12
24	44	30	24	20	13	11
27	37	26	21	18	12	10
30	31	22	19	16	10	9
33	27	20	17	14	9	8
36	24	18	15	13	8	7
39	21	16	14	11	8	7
42	19	15	12	10	7	6
45	18	14	11	9	6	6
48	16	13	11	8	6	6
51	15	12	10	7	5	5
54	14	11	9	7	5	5
57	13	10	9	6	5	5
60	12	10	8	6	4	4
63	12	10	8	6	4	4

TABLE 16.3.3

701 -1,200 m table

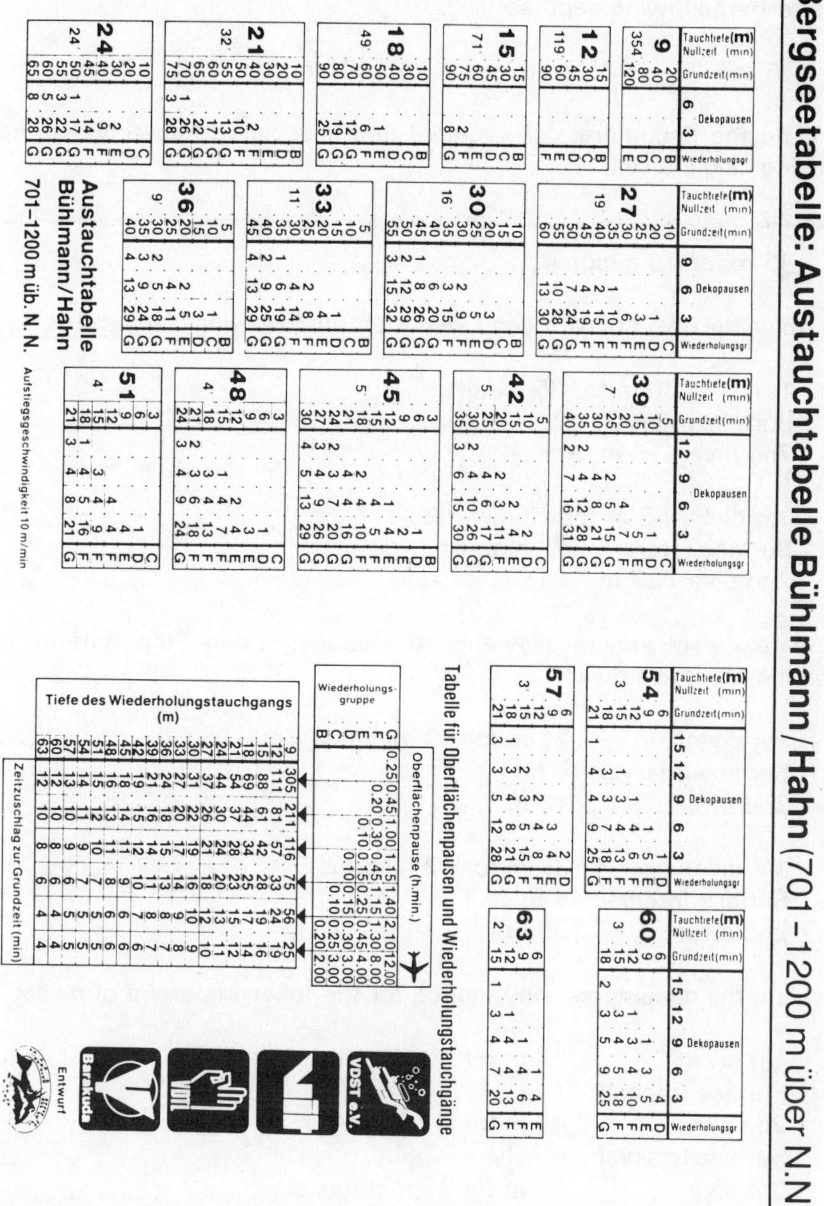

2. Bergseetabelle: Austauchtabelle Bühlmann/Hahn (701-1200 m über N.N.)

Tauchtiefe (m) / Nullzeit (min)	Grundzeit (min)	Dekopausen 15	12	9	6	3	Wiederholungsgr
9 / 354′	20				.	.	B
	40				.	.	C
	80				.	.	D
	120				.	.	E
12 / 119′	15				.	.	B
	30				.	.	C
	45				.	.	D
	60				.	.	E
	90				.	.	F
15 / 71′	15				.	.	B
	30				.	.	C
	45				.	.	D
	60				.	.	E
	75				.	2	F
	90				.	8	G
18 / 49′	10				.	.	B
	30				.	.	C
	40				.	.	D
	50				.	1	E
	60				.	6	F
	70				.	12	G
	80				.	19	G
	90				.	25	G
21 / 32′	10				.	.	B
	20				.	.	D
	30				.	.	E
	40				.	2	F
	50				.	10	F
	55				.	13	G
	60				.	17	G
	65				.	22	G
	70				1	26	G
	75				3	28	G
24 / 24′	10				.	.	C
	20				.	.	D
	30				.	2	E
	40				.	9	F
	45				.	14	F
	50				1	17	G
	55				3	22	G
	60				5	26	G
	65				8	28	G
27 / 19′	10			.	.	.	C
	20			.	.	1	D
	25			.	.	3	E
	30			.	.	6	F
	35			.	1	10	F
	40			.	2	15	F
	45			.	4	19	F
	50			.	7	24	G
	55			.	10	28	G
	60			.	13	30	G
30 / 16′	10			.	.	.	B
	15			.	.	.	C
	20			.	.	3	D
	25			.	.	5	E
	30			.	2	9	F
	35			.	3	15	F
	40			.	6	20	G
	45			1	8	26	G
	50			2	12	29	G
	55			3	15	32	G
33 / 11′	5			.	.	.	B
	10			.	.	.	C
	15			.	.	1	D
	20			.	.	4	E
	25			.	2	8	F
	30			.	4	14	F
	35			1	6	19	G
	40			2	9	25	G
	45			4	13	29	G
36 / 9′	5			.	.	.	B
	10			.	.	1	C
	15			.	.	3	D
	20			.	2	5	E
	25			.	4	11	F
	30			2	5	18	G
	35			3	9	24	G
	40			4	13	29	G
39 / 7′	5		.	.	.	.	C
	10		.	.	.	1	D
	15		.	.	.	5	E
	20		.	.	4	7	F
	25		.	2	5	15	G
	30		.	4	8	21	G
	35		2	4	12	28	G
	40		2	7	16	31	G
42 / 5′	5		.	.	.	.	C
	10		.	.	.	2	D
	15		.	.	2	4	E
	20		.	2	3	11	F
	25		.	4	6	17	G
	30		2	4	10	26	G
	35		3	6	15	30	G
45 / 5′	3		.	.	.	.	B
	6		.	.	.	1	D
	9		.	.	.	2	E
	12		.	.	1	4	E
	15		.	.	4	5	F
	18		.	2	4	10	F
	21		.	4	4	16	G
	24		2	3	7	20	G
	27		3	4	9	26	G
	30		4	5	13	29	G
48 / 4′	3		.	.	.	.	C
	6		.	.	.	1	D
	9		.	.	.	3	E
	12		.	.	2	4	E
	15		.	1	4	7	F
	18		.	3	4	13	F
	21		2	3	6	18	F
	24		3	4	9	24	G
51 / 4′	3		.	.	.	.	C
	6		.	.	.	1	D
	9		.	.	.	4	E
	12		.	.	4	4	F
	15		.	3	4	9	F
	18		1	4	5	16	F
	21		3	4	8	21	G
54 / 3	6	.	.	.	.	1	D
	9	.	.	.	1	5	E
	12	.	.	1	4	6	F
	15	.	1	3	4	13	F
	18	.	3	3	7	18	F
	21	1	4	4	9	25	G
57 / 3′	6	.	.	.	.	2	D
	9	.	.	.	3	4	E
	12	.	.	2	4	8	F
	15	.	2	3	5	15	F
	18	1	3	4	8	21	G
	21	3	3	5	12	28	G
60 / 3′	6	.	.	.	.	4	D
	9	.	.	1	3	5	E
	12	.	1	3	4	10	F
	15	.	3	4	5	18	F
	18	2	3	5	9	25	G
63 / 2′	6	.	.	.	1	4	E
	9	.	.	1	4	6	F
	12	.	1	4	4	13	F
	15	1	3	4	7	20	G

Austauchtabelle Bühlmann/Hahn

701–1200 m üb. N. N.

Aufstiegsgeschwindigkeit 10 m/min

Tabelle für Oberflächenpausen und Wiederholungstauchgänge

Wiederholungsgruppe	Oberflächenpause (h.min.)						
G	0.25	0.45	1.00	1.15	1.40	2.10	12.00
F		0.20	0.30	0.45	1.15	1.30	8.00
E			0.10	0.15	0.25	0.45	4.00
D				0.10	0.15	0.30	3.00
C					0.10	0.25	3.00
B						0.20	2.00

Tiefe des Wiederholungstauchgangs (m)	Zeitzuschlag zur Grundzeit (min)					
9	305	211	116	75	56	25
12	111	81	57	33	24	19
15	88	61	42	28	19	16
18	69	44	34	25	17	14
21	54	37	28	23	15	12
24	44	30	24	20	13	11
27	37	26	21	18	12	10
30	31	22	19	16	10	9
33	27	20	17	14	9	8
36	24	18	15	13	8	7
39	21	16	14	11	8	7
42	19	15	12	10	7	6
45	18	14	11	9	6	6
48	16	13	11	8	6	6
51	15	12	10	7	5	5
54	14	11	9	7	5	5
57	13	10	9	6	5	5
60	12	10	8	6	4	4
63	12	10	8	6	4	4

Sincere thanks to Dr. Max Hahn *for his assistance with the preparation of this section.*

EXERCISES ON THE BUEHLMANN/HAHN TABLES

1. Determine the No-Decompression Limits (NDLs) and associated Repetitive Groups for dives to the following depths:

   (a) 16 m (b) 22 m (c) 40 m (d) 26 m

2. Calculate the decompression required and associated Repetitive Groups after the following single dives:

   (a) 17 m for 67 minutes (b) 24 m for 51 minutes
   (c) 35 m for 15 minutes.

3. Determine the Residual Nitrogen Times after the following dives and Surface Intervals:

   (a) 1st dive: 20 m for 35 minutes
   Surface Interval: $2^1/2$ hr
   2nd dive: 16 m.

   (b) 1st dive: 33 m for 20 minutes
   Surface Interval: 30 minutes
   2nd dive: 27 m.

4. Calculate the maximum allowable No-Decompression Stop Bottom Time for the following repetitive dives:

   (a) 1st dive: 21 m for 50 minutes
   Surface Interval: 6 hr
   2nd dive: 18 m.

   (b) 1st dive: 36 m for 12 minutes
   Surface Interval: 4 hr
   2nd dive: 30 m.

5. Calculate the decompression required for the following group of dives:

   1st dive: 17 m for 60 minutes
   Surface Interval: 4 hr
   2nd dive: 47 m for 6 minutes
   Surface Interval: $4^1/2$ hr
   3rd dive: 24 m for 25 minutes.

   Note: The order of the dives should be re-arranged so that the depths are decreasing.

6. Determine the Surface Intervals required before flying after the following dives:

   (a) 15 m for 45 minutes (b) 9 m for 70 minutes
   (c) 36 m for 19 minutes.

Note:

The answers to these questions can be compared directly to the answers to the questions at the end of Section 16.2.

ANSWERS

1. (a) 65, G (b) 27, E (c) 6, D (d) 21, E

2. (a) 2 min at 3 m, G (b) 13 min at 3 m, G
(c) 2 min at 3 m, D

3. (a) 14 (b) 12

4. (a) 51 (b) 17

5. No deco., 1 min at 6 m and 4 min at 3 m, safety stop of 3 min at 3 m

6. (a) 4 hr (b) 3 hr (c) 4 hr

Note: [illegible] answers to these questions [illegible] at the end of Section 10.2.

Answers

[illegible]

CHAPTER 17

THE DCIEM SPORT DIVING TABLES

HISTORICAL BACKGROUND

Canadian decompression research began in 1962 in what is now named the Defence and Civil Institute of Environmental Medicine (DCIEM). Kidd and Stubbs set out to develop an instrument which would monitor the diver's depth-time profile, and provide instantaneous decompression information when complicated dive profiles were undertaken, or where wide variations of gas mixtures were used. In these situations, the traditional tabular approach to determine decompression was inadequate.

Initially, their decompression computer was based on the traditional Haldane model in order to duplicate the U.S. Navy 1958 Standard Air Tables. However, parameters were changed and the model was modified until a low incidence of decompression sickness was achieved.

A variety of dives were tested, ranging from fixed depth dives, random depth dives and repetitive dives. Within five years they had developed a fairly successful computer based on 5,000 man-dives.

The final configuration of the computer utilized a "serial model", in which tissue compartments are connected in series instead of the parallel arrangement used by Haldane. The model was again modifed in 1970, in order to increase its safety in the 200-300 fsw (60-90 msw) range. The result became known as the KS 1971 Model.

The model was used for some time at DCIEM but a few deficiencies became apparent. One of the problems was that the No-Decompression Limits were much too conservative, in some cases (at shallower depths) being half that of the Royal Navy and U.S. Navy Tables. In other areas the model lacked conservatism, consequently, more research and modifications became necessary.

THE DCIEM MODEL

A very large data-base of decompression information had been accumulated by DCIEM over the years and in order to utilize this information the K.S. Model was chosen as the basis for a new set of air decompression tables. Modifications were made to the K.S. decompression model and the earlier problems and anomalies existing in the K.S. Model were overcome. This modified model became known as the DCIEM 1983 Decompression Model.

The serial model assumes that the tissue compartments are connected in series. Only the first compartment is exposed to ambient pressure and, as gas builds up in this compartment, it bleeds into the next compartment. In Haldane's model each compartment is exposed to ambient pressure and loads up simultaneously. Each of the four tissue compartments in the DCIEM model has the same half-time, which is approximately 21 minutes. The model utilizes the concept of allowable surfacing supersaturation ratios. Critical ratios of 1.92 and 1.73 are used in the initial two compartments, while the pressure levels in the other compartments are not used to calculate the depth from which a diver can safely ascend.

FEATURES OF THE DCIEM 1983 MODEL

The DCIEM Model produces decompression times which are more conservative than the U.S. Navy Tables and the decompression profiles have deeper first stops. **These tables have been rigorously tested during working dives in cold water.** For strenuous dives in cold water, the U.S. Navy procedure is to decompress according to the next longer bottom time. The resulting times are comparable to the DCIEM 1983 times.

The model has been used to generate a complete set of tables, including standard air decompression, repetitive dive procedures, corrections for diving at altitude, in-water oxygen decompression and surface decompression with oxygen.

TESTING

The new tables have been extensively tested using the Doppler ultrasonic bubble detector and bends incidence as safety criteria. About 900 man-dives were performed during the validation dive series over a two year period. Because the model was continuous, and because of the large database of both safe and unsafe dives done on the original K.S. model, it seemed unnecessary to test a larger number of depth and bottom time combinations.

During the tests the divers were monitored for bubbles at the precordial site (right ventricle and/or pulmonary artery) and the subclavian sites (both left and right shoulders). At the precordial site, a reading was first taken when the diver stood at rest, and another reading was taken when he performed a deep knee-bend. At the subclavian site, the diver was initially monitored while at rest and then again after clenching his fist on the side being monitored. The Doppler signals were recorded on audio magnetic tape as well as being assessed aurally by experienced technicians.

The bubble signals were classified according to the Kisman-Masurel (KM) code (shown in Appendix F) which utilizes three criteria, each on a scale from 0 to 4. (Other systems only use 2 criteria to establish bubble grades). The criteria used were the number of bubbles per cardiac cycle, the percentage of cardiac cycles with bubble signals and the amplitude of the bubble signals relative to the background sounds. The resulting 3-digit code is converted to bubble grades from 0 to 4, resulting in a similar bubble grade to that developed by Spencer (and used to assess the PADI Recreational Dive Planner).

The divers were monitored before the dive(s) and at half-hour intervals for at least two hours after diving. When repetitive dives were undertaken, the divers were monitored between the dives as well as after the second dive.

The test dives were conducted in a hyperbaric chamber, with wet-working divers in cold water at 41-50°F (5-10°C), as well as with dry-resting divers. All dives were done using a real-time on-line decompression computer, following the exact decompression profile as specified by the DCIEM 1983 Decompression Model. The Standard Air Table was tested by 267 man-dives. Fifty-five dives had decompression times shorter than 30 minutes, and 90% of these subjects showed no, or few, detectable bubbles. Eighty-four no-decompression stop dives were tested with no detectable bubbles resulting. No cases of bends were observed. The remaining 128 dives (66 single dives and 62 repetitive dive pairs) were near, or at, the normal air diving limit with decompression times between 48 and 88 minutes. Eight cases of bends occurred after single dives, and 4 cases occurred after the second dive of a repetitive dive pair. However, some of these incidents were thought to have other contributing causes and may not have been attributable to the dive profiles alone.

No diving tables can be expected to totally eliminate the occurrence of decompression sickness, but the DCIEM Tables are considered by many experts to be much safer than most other published tables. In the period from October 1987, when the DCIEM Sport Diving Tables were first released, to the time of writing, no cases of decompression sickness were reported in divers who had used the tables. They appear to be sound, well-tested tables (i.e. on "rectangular" dives) which should generally be quite suitable for the recreational diver.* However, a diver's individual susceptibility to bends must still be considered when planning the bottom time for a dive.

In the Instructions for Using The DCIEM Sport Diving Tables c1990, it states:

"The DCIEM air decompression model was tested empirically using a relatively diverse group of human subjects. This takes into consideration certain assumptions about the fitness of the subject. These same considerations apply to divers who use the DCIEM Sport Diving Tables.

It is assumed that:

1. The diver is physically fit, with a good exercise tolerance.
2. The diver is free of any acute or delayed effects of alcohol or drugs of any kind.
3. The diver is not overly fatigued, dehydrated, motion sick, sunburned or otherwise affected in a detrimental way.
4. The diver has no acute illness, especially of a respiratory or musculo-skeletal nature, has had no recent physical trauma and has not recently undergone surgery.
5. The diver has no chronic illnesses such as asthma, high blood pressure, diabetes, epilepsy, inner ear barotrauma or spontaneous pneumothorax.
6. The diver is free of any decompression debt, other than that allowed for or calculated in the DCIEM Sport Diving Tables.

If any of the above apply, or if there is any doubt - do not SCUBA dive. Seek advice from a physician experienced in hyperbaric medicine.

G. Helge Koch M.D., Medical Director, Hyperbaric Department - Toronto General Hospital.

* However, it is important to realize that no testing was conducted to determine their validity for multi-level diving (see Chapter 22).

DCIEM Sport Diving Tables

DEFINITIONS, DESCRIPTION AND RULES

DEFINITION OF TERMS:

Depth - the maximum depth of a dive conducted at sea level.

Bottom Time - the total time from beginning of Descent to beginning of direct Ascent to the surface.

No-D Dive - a dive that does not exceed the No-D Limit for a given depth.

No-D Limit - the maximum Bottom Time that a diver may spend at a given depth without having to conduct a scheduled Decompression Stop before surfacing.

Decompression Stop - a scheduled interruption of the Ascent at a specified depth for a specified time to allow for the elimination of excess nitrogen.

Decompression Dive - a dive that exceeds the No-D Limit and that requires a Decompression Stop.

Repetitive Group (RG) - a dive exposure guide given by letter according to the depth and Bottom Time. *(The RGs are not compatible with Repetitive Groups given in other published tables.)*

Surface interval (SI) - time elapsed between reaching the surface after a dive and beginning the actual Descent on the following dive.

Repetitive Factor (RF) - a residual nitrogen indicator relating to the amount of nitrogen remaining in a diver's body after a Surface Interval.

Repetitive Dive - any dive conducted while the Repetitive Factor is greater than 1.0.

Effective Bottom Time (EBT) - the combined total of actual Bottom Time plus time included to account for residual nitrogen from a previous dive exposure. EBT is applied to Repetitive Dives and to Multi-Level Dives.

Altitude Dive - a dive conducted at an elevation greater than 999 feet (300 metres) above sea-level.

Effective Depth - the equivalent sea level depth for an Altitude Dive.

Descent Rate - the proper Descent Rate is 60 ft (18 m) per minute, or slower.

Ascent rate - the proper rate of ascent is 60 ft (18 m) plus or minus 10 ft (3 m) per minute. However, an ascent rate of 60 ft (18 m) or less is recommended between 20 ft (6 m) and the surface.

Multi-Level Dive - a dive during which bottom time is accumulated at two or more depths. (See Chapter 23 for DCIEM Multi-Level Dive Procedures).

Decompression Time includes ascent time to the decompression stop at the rate of 60 $\pm$ 10 ft/min (18 $\pm$ 3 m/min).

Of interest to the recreational diver are four tables:

Table A. Air Decompression (Table 17.1)
Table B. Surface Interval Table (Table 17.2)
Table C. Repetitive Diving Table (Table 17.2)
Table D. Depth Correction Table for Altitude Diving (Table 17.2)

TABLE 17.1

The Air Decompression Table (Table A)

DCIEM SPORT DIVING TABLES

A: AIR DECOMPRESSION

Depth	No-Decompression Bottom Times (minutes)				Decompression Required Bottom Times			
20' *6m*	30 A 60 B 90 C 120 D	150 E 180 F 240 G 300 H	360 I 420 J 480 K 600 L	720 M ∞				
30' *9m*	30 A 45 B 60 C 90 D	100 E 120 F 150 G 180 H	190 I 210 J 240 K 270 L	300 M	**360**	**400**		
40' *12m*	22 A 30 B 40 C	60 D 70 E 80 F	90 G 120 H 130 I	150 J	160 K 170 L	180 M 190	200	215
50' *15m*	18 A 25 B	30 C 40 D	50 E 60 F	75 G	**85 H 95 I**	**105 J 115 K**	**124 L**	**132 M**
60' *18m*	14 A 20 B	25 C 30 D	40 E	50 F	60 G	70 H 80 I	85 J	92 K
Decompression Stops in minutes			**at 10' *3m***		**5**	**10**	**15**	**20**
70' *21m*	12 A 15 B	20 C	25 D	35 E	40 F	50 G	60 H 63 I	66 J
80' *24m*	10 A 13 B	15 C	20 D	25 E	**29 F**	**35 G**	**48 H**	**52 I**
90' *27m*	9 A	12 B	15 C	20 D	23 E	27 F	35 G	40 H 43 I
100' *30m*	7 A	10 B	12 C	15 D	**18 D**	**21 E**	**25 F 29 G**	**36 H**
110' *33m*		6 A	10 B	12 C	15 D	18 E	22 F	26 G 30 H
120' *36m*		6 A	8 B	10 C	**12 D**	**15 E**	**19 F**	**25 G**
130' *39m*			5 A	8 B	10 C	13 D	16 F	21 G
140' *42m*			5 A	7 B	**9 C**	**11 D**	**14 F**	**18 G**
150' *45m*			4 A	6 B	8 C	10 D	12 E	15 F
Decompression Stops in minutes			**at 20' *6m***		**-**	**-**	**5**	**10**
			at 10' *3m*		**5**	**10**	**10**	**10**

- **ASCENT RATE** is 60' (18m) plus or minus 10' (3m) per minute
  NO-DECOMPRESSION LIMITS are given for first dives
- **DECOMPRESSION STOPS** are taken at mid-chest level for the times indicated at the specified stop depths

→ Table B for **Minimum Surface Intervals** and Repetitive Factors

→ Table C for **Repetitive Dive No-Decompression Limits**

→ Table D for **Depth Corrections** required at Altitudes above 1000' (300m)

TABLE 17.2

Surface Interval, Repetitive Diving and Depth Corrections Tables

B: SURFACE INTERVALS

Rep. Group	0:15 ↘ 0:29	0:30 ↘ 0:59	1:00 ↘ 1:29	1:30 ↘ 1:59	2:00 ↘ 2:59	3:00 ↘ 3:59	4:00 ↘ 5:59	6:00 ↘ 8:59	9:00 ↘ 11:59	12:00 ↘ 14:59	15:00 ↘ 18:00
A	1.4	1.2	1.1	1.1	1.1	1.1	1.1	1.1	1.0	1.0	1.0
B	1.5	1.3	1.2	1.2	1.2	1.1	1.1	1.1	1.1	1.0	1.0
C	1.6	1.4	1.3	1.2	1.2	1.2	1.1	1.1	1.1	1.0	1.0
D	1.8	1.5	1.4	1.3	1.3	1.2	1.2	1.1	1.1	1.0	1.0
E	1.9	1.6	1.5	1.4	1.3	1.3	1.2	1.2	1.1	1.1	1.0
F	2.0	1.7	1.6	1.5	1.4	1.3	1.3	1.2	1.1	1.1	1.0
G	-	1.9	1.7	1.6	1.5	1.4	1.3	1.2	1.1	1.1	1.0
H	-	-	1.9	1.7	1.6	1.5	1.4	1.3	1.1	1.1	1.1
I	-	-	2.0	1.8	1.7	1.5	1.4	1.3	1.1	1.1	1.1
J	-	-	-	1.9	1.8	1.6	1.5	1.3	1.2	1.1	1.1
K	-	-	-	2.0	1.9	1.7	1.5	1.3	1.2	1.1	1.1
L	-	-	-	-	2.0	1.7	1.6	1.4	1.2	1.1	1.1
M	-	-	-	-	-	1.8	1.6	1.4	1.2	1.1	1.1

Repetitive Factors (RF) given for Surface Intervals (hr:min)

C: REPETITIVE DIVING

Depth		1.1	1.2	1.3	1.4	1.5	1.6	1.7	1.8	1.9	2.0
30'	*9m*	272	250	230	214	200	187	176	166	157	150
40'	*12m*	136	125	115	107	100	93	88	83	78	75
50'	*15m*	60	55	50	45	41	38	36	34	32	31
60'	*18m*	40	35	31	29	27	26	24	23	22	21
70'	*21m*	30	25	21	19	18	17	16	15	14	13
80'	*24m*	20	18	16	15	14	13	12	12	11	11
90'	*27m*	16	14	12	11	11	10	9	9	8	8
100'	*30m*	13	11	10	9	9	8	8	7	7	7
110'	*33m*	10	9	8	8	7	7	6	6	6	6
120'	*36m*	8	7	7	6	6	6	5	5	5	5
130'	*39m*	7	6	6	5	5	5	4	4	4	4
140'	*42m*	6	5	5	5	4	4	4	3	3	3
150'	*45m*	5	5	4	4	4	3	3	3	3	3

Repetitive Dive No-D Limits given in minutes according to Depth and RF

D: DEPTH CORRECTIONS

Actual Depth ↓	↓	1000' ↳ 1999'	*300m ↳ 599*	2000' ↳ 2999'	*600m ↳ 899*	3000' ↳ 3999'	*900m ↳ 1199*	4000' ↳ 4999'	*1200m ↳ 1499*	5000' ↳ 5999'	*1500m ↳ 1799*	6000' ↳ 6999'	*1800m ↳ 2099*	7000' ↳ 7999'	*2100m ↳ 2399*	8000' ↳ 10000'	*2400m ↳ 3000*
30'	*9m*	10	*3*	10	*3*	10	*3*	10	*3*	10	*3*	10	*3*	20	*6*	20	*6*
40'	*12m*	10	*3*	10	*3*	10	*3*	10	*3*	10	*3*	20	*6*	20	*6*	20	*6*
50'	*15m*	10	*3*	10	*3*	10	*3*	10	*3*	20	*6*	20	*6*	20	*6*	20	*6*
60'	*18m*	10	*3*	10	*3*	10	*3*	20	*6*	20	*6*	20	*6*	20	*6*	30	*9*
70'	*21m*	10	*3*	10	*3*	10	*3*	20	*6*	20	*6*	20	*6*	30	*9*	30	*9*
80'	*24m*	10	*3*	10	*3*	20	*6*	20	*6*	20	*6*	30	*9*	30	*9*	40	*12*
90'	*27m*	10	*3*	10	*3*	20	*6*	20	*6*	20	*6*	30	*9*	30	*9*	40	*12*
100'	*30m*	10	*3*	10	*3*	20	*6*	20	*6*	30	*9*	30	*9*	30	*9*	40	*12*
110'	*33m*	10	*3*	20	*6*	20	*6*	20	*6*	30	*9*	30	*9*	40	*12*		
120'	*36m*	10	*3*	20	*6*	20	*6*	30	*9*	30	*9*	30	*9*				
130'	*39m*	10	*3*	20	*6*	20	*6*										
140'	*42m*	10	*3*														
Add Depth Correction to Actual Depth of Altitude Dive																	
10'	*3m*	10	*3.0*	10	*3.0*	9	*3.0*	9	*3.0*	9	*3.0*	8	*2.5*	8	*2.5*	8	*2.5*
20'	*6m*	20	*6.0*	19	*6.0*	18	*5.5*	18	*5.5*	17	*5.0*	16	*5.0*	16	*5.0*	15	*4.5*

Actual Decompression Stop Depths (feet/*metres*) at Altitude

Published under government license by Universal Dive Techtronics, Inc.
Ste. 201 2691 Viscount Way, Richmond, B.C., CANADA, V6V 1M9

AIR DECOMPRESSION TABLE: A

Table A provides NO-DECOMPRESSION (STOP) LIMITS FOR FIRST DIVES, Repetitive Group letters and Decompression Stop Times for dives which exceed the No-D Limits.

The NO-DECOMPRESSION LIMITS are the maximum Bottom Times, expressed in minutes, that you may spend at given depths without having to conduct Decompression Stops before surfacing. To determine the **No-D Limit** for a given depth, enter Table A horizontally from the Depth column. Follow the row across to the bold double vertical lines. The largest number to the left of the double lines is the No-D Limit for first dives at that depth.

The letter immediately to the right of each bottom time is the **Repetitive Group (RG)** for that depth/time profile. *(RG letters are not interchangeable with RGs appearing in other tables).* Determine your RG according to the actual or next greater Bottom Time. If no RG letter appears beside your Bottom Time, allow at least **18 hours** to elapse before conducting another dive.

The DECOMPRESSION REQUIRED section is to the right of the bold, double vertical lines. **Decompression Stop** requirements are given at the bottom of each column.

Example: FIRST DIVE: 100 ft (30 m) for 20 minutes
(1st Dive No-D Limit is 15 minutes)

Decompression Stop is 10 minutes at 10 ft (3 m)
(First Dive Repetitive Group = E)

Note:

Deco. Stops for shallow dives - to 60 ft (18 m) are taken at 10 ft (3 m). Deeper dives may require Deco. Stops at both 20 ft (6 m) and 10 ft (3 m). Decompression stops are taken at mid-chest level for the times indicated at the specified depths.

SURFACE INTERVAL TABLE: B

The **Surface Interval (SI)** is the time elapsed between surfacing from a dive and beginning the actual Descent on the following dive. The Surface Interval times across the top of Table B are expressed in hours and minutes. Use the Repetitive Group from your last dive to enter Table B. Match your Repetitive Group row with the column that corresponds with your Surface Interval.

Table B indicates your residual nitrogen level in the form of a **Repetitive Factor (RF)** or Residual Nitrogen Factor. As your Surface Interval increases, your Repetitive Factor decreases until the factor diminishes to 1.0 - the point at which you are considered free of residual nitrogen. *Any SCUBA dive conducted while the Repetitive Factor is greater than 1.0 is a REPETITIVE DIVE.*

If your RF has diminished to 1.0, use the first dive No-D Limits in Table A to plan your dive.

If your RF is greater than 1.0, use the Table C No-D Limits to plan your Repetitive Dive.

If you must dive before a RF appears in Table B, apply the short Surface Interval guidelines that follow:

If your Surface Interval is **less than 15 minutes,** and the dives are to:

a. the SAME DEPTH, add the Bottom Times together and use the total time to determine your decompression requirements and RG from Table A.

b. DIFFERENT DEPTHS, use the RG from the first dive to determine the equivalent time that corresponds to the same RG at the second depth. Add the Bottom Time for the second dive to this time. Use the total time to determine your decompression requirements and RG.

SURFACE INTERVALS REQUIRED BEFORE FLYING AFTER DIVING

After a No-D DIVE, allow enough Surface Interval time to elapse for your RF to diminish to 1.0.

After a DECOMPRESSION STOP DIVE a minimum Surface Interval of **24 hours** is required before flying.

REPETITIVE DIVING TABLE: C

The NO-DECOMPRESSION LIMITS FOR REPETITIVE DIVES are given in Table C. When the actual Bottom Time of a Repetitive Dive exceeds the **No-D Limit** given in Table C, a Decompression Stop is required. Find your No-D Limit by matching the RF with the depth of your Repetitive Dive.

Example: RF of 1.5 at a Depth of 60 ft (18 m)
NO-D LIMIT = 27 minutes

The RG for a Repetitive Dive is found in Table A according to the Depth and **Effective Bottom Time.**

Multiply your actual Bottom Time by the RF to establish the EFFECTIVE BOTTOM TIME or EBT.

Example: RF of 1.5 at a Depth of 60 ft (18 m)
NO-D LIMIT = 27 minutes
Actual Bottom Time = 40 minutes
EBT = 40 minutes x 1.5 = 60 minutes
RG = G (from Table A)
in Table A, a dive to 60 ft (18 m) with an EBT of 60 minutes requires a 5 min. Deco.
Stop at 10 ft (3 m).

Because of the conservatism inherent in the DCIEM air decompression model, the EBT may sometimes result in a lower figure than the first dive No-D Limit given in Table A, although your actual Bottom Time exceeds the Table C Repetitive Dive No-D Limit. This is not a table error. When this situation occurs, conduct a 5 minute Decompression Stop at 10 ft (3 m).

MINIMUM SURFACE INTERVALS FOR NO-D REPETITIVE DIVES

Table C is used in conjunction with Table B to determine the Minimum Surface Interval required to conduct a No-D Repetitive Dive for a given Bottom Time. Match the Repetitive Factor taken from Table C with the Repetitive Group from last dive. The **Minimum Surface Interval** is given at the top of the matching column in Table B.

Example: FIRST DIVE: 80 ft (24 m) for 25 minutes
Repetitive Group = E
PLANNED DIVE: 60 ft (18 m) for 31 minutes

From Table C, a No-Decompression Limit of 31 minutes at a depth of 60 ft (18 m) requires the diver to have a Repetitive Factor of 1.3 at the beginning of the Repetitive Dive.

From Table B, a group E diver acquires a RF of 1.3 after a Minimum Surface Interval of 2 hours.

Note:

For dive exposures exceeding the bottom times in the Sport Diving Tables, refer to the complete Standard Air Tables appearing in the publication "DCIEM Air Decompression Tables and Procedures". (These tables are shown in Appendix B).

USING THE DCIEM SPORT DIVING TABLES

A. SINGLE DIVES

Example 1.

To find the maximum allowable bottom time for a no-decompression stop dive to 60 ft (18 m).

Enter Table A horizontally at 60 ft (18 m) and move across the row. The No-Decompression Limit (NDL) is the number immediately to the left of the bold double vertical lines. The NDL is thus *50* minutes and the Repetitive Group (RG) is *F*.

Example 2.

To find the decompression required after a dive to 95 ft (29 m) for 20 minutes.

Enter Table A horizontally at 100 ft (30 m) (which is the next greater depth for interim depths) and move across the row to 21 minutes (the next longer time for interim times). Moving down, the decompression is found to be *10 minutes at 10 ft (3 m)*. The RG is *E*.

Example 3.

To find the decompression required after a dive to 90 ft (27 m) for 30 minutes.

Enter Table A at 90 ft (27 m) and move across the row to 35 minutes. Moving down, the decompression is found to be *5 minutes at 20 ft (6 m) and 10 minutes at 10 ft (3 m)*. The RG is *G*.

B. REPETITIVE DIVES

Example 4.

Three hours after a dive to 60 ft (18 m) for 50 minutes, you wish to carry out another no-decompression stop dive to 50 ft (15 m). What is the maximum allowable bottom time for the repetitive dive?

After the initial dive the RG is *F*. Enter Table B from the left at F, and move right, until intersecting the column corresponding to the surface interval. In this case 3 hours lies between 3:00-3:59, so the RF is *1.3*.

Enter Table C horizontally at the depth of the repetitive dive, in this case 50 ft (15 m). Move across the row until intersecting the column for an RF of 1.3. The number 50 results. This means that the No-D Limit for the repetitive dive is *50* minutes.

Example 5.

If the repetitive dive in the previous example was undertaken for a bottom time of 50 minutes, find the RG after the dive.

To find the appropriate RG, multiply the actual bottom time of 50 minutes by the RF of 1.3 to get the EBT, in this case *65* minutes. Looking up 50 ft (15 m) for 65 minutes in Table A, the RG after the dive would be *G*.

Example 6.

After a dive to 80 ft (24 m) for 25 minutes you wish to dive again, after an appropriate surface interval. What minimum surface interval is required so that you may dive to 60 ft (18 m) for 30 minutes without the need to make a decompression stop?

Enter Table A at 80 ft (24 m) and move across the row to 25 minutes. The first dive does not require a decompression stop, and the RG is *E*.

Enter Table C at 60 ft (18 m) (i.e. the depth of the proposed repetitive dive), and more across to find an allowable bottom time of 30 minutes. Taking 31 minutes, this occurs within the column for RF = 1.3, which means that after the surface interval you must have an RF of *1.3*.

Before the surface interval your RG was E, so enter Table B at E, and move right to find 1.3. This occurs within the column corresponding to a surface interval of 2:00-2:59, which means that your minimum surface interval must be *2 hours.*

REPETITIVE DIVES REQUIRING DECOMPRESSION STOPS

Example 7.

Four and one half hours after a dive to 95 ft (29 m) for 20 minutes, you wish to dive to 55 ft (17 m) for 50 minutes. What decompression is required?

After the initial dive, the RG is *E*. Enter Table B at E, and move right until intersecting the column including $4^1/_2$ hour (i.e. the column corresponding to 4:00-5:59). The RF is *1.2*. Multiply the proposed bottom time of the second dive, in this case 50 minutes, by 1.2 to get the EBT, in this case *60* minutes. Entering Table A, the appropriate decompression is found to be *5 minutes at 10 ft (3 m).*

Example 8.

After a dive to 60 ft (18 m) for 50 minutes you wish to dive again, after a surface interval of 1 hour 45 minutes, to 60 ft (18 m) for 30 minutes. Calculate the required decompression.

From Table A, the first dive does not require a stop and the RG after the dive is *F*. Entering Table B at F and moving across to the column corresponding to a surface interval of 1 hour 45 minutes gives an RF of *1.5.* The EBT for the second dive is 30 x 1.5 = 45 minutes which is in the No-D range of Table A. However, from Table C, only 27 minutes is allowed for RF = 1.5. Therefore, the decompression required is 5 minutes at 10 ft (3 m).*

Example 9.

Thirteen minutes after a first dive to 60 ft (18 m) for 30 minutes you wish to dive again to 60 ft (18 m) for 25 minutes. Find the required decompression.

From Table A, the first dive requires no stop and the RG is *D. Since the surface interval is shorter than 15 minutes and the dives are to the same maximum depth,* you must add the bottom times of both dives and use the total time, in this case 30 + 25 = 55 minutes, to determine the decompression and RG. The decompression required is *5 minutes at 10 ft (3 m)* and the RG is *G*.

* In this example, if further dives are anticipated, a RG adjustment (as described later in this chapter) may be necessary. However, no RG adjustment is necessary if the second dive is the final dive.

Example 10.

Ten minutes after a first dive to 120 ft (36 m) for 10 minutes you wish to dive again to 70 ft (21 m) for 20 minutes. Find the required decompression.

From Table A, the first dive requires no stop and the RG is *C. Since the surface interval is shorter than 15 minutes and the dives are to different depths,* you must use the RG from the first dive (C) to find the equivalent time for the same RG at the second depth. Entering Table A at 70 ft (21 m), you find that a RG of C corresponds to a bottom time of 20 minutes. Adding this 20 minutes to the proposed bottom time of the second dive gives a total time of 20 + 20 = 40 minutes. Looking up 70 ft (21 m) for 40 minutes in Table A gives a required decompression of *5 minutes at 10 ft (3 m)* and a RG of *F*.

REPETITIVE GROUP ADJUSTMENTS

Certain diving practices - such as deep dives following shallow dives, deep "bounce" dives, and multiple repetitive dives conducted over several consecutive days - are known to increase dramatically the risk of Decompression Sickness. New divers should be cautioned about such practices. No diving table can compensate for lack of common sense.

Dive tables, by their nature of having fixed limits, cannot take into account every possible diving eventuality. In certain instances when a series of similar No-D dives are conducted (similar Depth/Bottom Time/Surface Interval), it is possible to become locked into a "dive table loop" resulting in the same RG and No-D Limit after each dive. Because decompression will eventually be required, it is necessary to break out of a dive table loop. A dive table loop can be broken by altering the dive profile, by extending the Surface Interval, or by adjusting the Repetitive Group.

Unexpected developments, such as a fouled anchor, can sometimes lead to a very short Repetitive Dive. The following dive series illustrates how a short Repetitive Dive can result in a much lower RG than that of the preceding dive:

Example: First Dive: 60 ft (18 m) for 30 minutes
RG = D
Surface Interval = 30 minutes
RF = 1.5

Second Dive: 100 ft (30 m) for 6 minutes
EBT = 6 minutes x 1.5 = 9 minutes
RG = B

When this type of situation occurs, a Repetitive Group adjustment is needed. (Dives should not be conducted in this manner, i.e. deep, repetitive dive following a shallow dive).

Repetitive Group Adjustment Procedures for Repetitive Dives

1. If the RG is the SAME as that of the preceding dive, and the S.I. before the next dive is less than 4 hours, ADD one letter to the RG.

   e.g. 1st Dive RG = C, 2nd Dive RG = C, S.I. after 2nd Dive = 2 hrs, 2nd Dive RG adjusted to D.

   No adjustment necessary if the S.I. is more than 4 hours.

2. If the RG is LOWER than that of the preceding dive, and the S.I. before the next dive is less than 4 hours, ADD one letter to the RG of the PRECEDING DIVE.

   e.g. 1st Dive RG = D, 2nd Dive RG = B, S.I. after 2nd Dive = 1 hr, 2nd Dive RG is adjusted to E.

   If the S.I. is more than 4 hours, ADD one letter to the lower RG.

   e.g. 1st Dive RG = D, 2nd Dive RG = B, S.I. after 2nd Dive = 4 hrs, 2nd Dive RG is adjusted to C.

   These procedures apply to any dive (including a FINAL DIVE) that results in a lower RG.

Special Adjustment for High Exposure RGs:

When the RG of the preceding dive is <u>H or higher</u>, apply a 6 hr guideline to procedures 1 and 2.

3. If FOUR (4) dives are to be conducted in a series, ADD one letter to the 3rd dive RG whenever the S.I. between the 3rd and 4th dives is less then 4 hours.

Example: FOUR (4) DIVE SERIES with 2nd Dive RG = E
S.I. - 1 hour RF = 1.5
3rd Dive: 50 ft (15 m) for 40 minutes
EBT = 40 x 1.5 = 60 minutes
RG = F
S.I. before 4th Dive - 2 hours
3rd Dive RG adjusted to G
RF after 2 hours = 1.5
4th Dive: 40 ft (12 m) for 60 minutes
EBT = 60 x 1.5 = 90 minutes
RG = G

No adjustment is necessary when the S.I. is more than 4 hrs.

Under normal conditions, no more than 3 dives should be conducted in a series. Do not conduct more than 4 dives in a series, or more than one 4 dive series within three days.

Example 11.

Find any decompression stops required in the following sequence of three dives:

Dive 1: 120 ft (36 m) for 12 minutes
S.I. = 3 hr
Dive 2: 120 ft (36 m) for 10 minutes
S.I. = 65 minutes
Dive 3: 80 ft (24 m) for 20 minutes

The decompression required at the end of the first dive is *5 minutes at 10 ft* (3 m) and the RG after the dive is *D*. The RF after the surface interval is 1.2, so the EBT for Dive 2 is 1.2 x 10 = 12 minutes. Dive 2 requires a stop of *5 minutes at 10 ft* (3 m) and the RG after Dive 2 is *D*.

Since this RG is the same as the RG after the first dive and because Dive 3 is within 4 hours of surfacing from Dive 2, you must add one letter to the RG after Dive 2 (Rule 1). Thus, the RG after Dive 2 becomes *E* and the RF before Dive 3 is 1.5. Hence, the EBT for Dive 3 is 1.5 x 20 = 30 minutes and a stop of *10 minutes at 10 ft* (3 m) is required. The RG after Dive 3 is G.

Note:

If the surface interval between the second and third dives in the above example was longer than 4 hours, no adjustment would need to be made to the RG after the second dive; it would remain as D.

Example 12.

Find any decompression stops required after the first two dives and the maximum allowable No-D bottom time for the third dive in the following sequence of three dives:

Dive 1: 90 ft (27 m) for 15 minutes
S.I. = 2½ hours
Dive 2: 70 ft (21 m) for 10 minutes
S.I. = 3 hours
Dive 3: 50 ft (15 m)

No decompression stop is required at the end of the first dive and the RG after the dive is *C*. The RF after the surface interval is 1.2, so the EBT for Dive 2 is 1.2 x 10 = 12 minutes, the RG is *A* and no stop is required. Because the RG after Dive 2 is lower than that of the preceding dive and the surface interval before the next dive is shorter than 4 hours, you must add one letter to the RG of the preceding dive and use this new RG as the RG after Dive 2. So you must use a RG of *D* as the RG after Dive 2 (instead of a RG of A). Therefore, the RF before Dive 3 is 1.2 and the maximum allowable no-decompression stop bottom time is 55 minutes. If this maximum bottom time was used, the RG after the final dive would be *G*.

Example 13.

Dive 1: 90 ft (27 m) for 15 minutes
S.I. = 2½ hours
Dive 2: 70 ft (21 m) for 10 minutes
S.I. = 7 hours
Dive 3: Find the maximum allowable no-decompression stop bottom time at 50 ft (15 m)

RG after Dive 1 is *C*. RF before Dive 2 is 1.2. EBT for Dive 2 is 1.2 x 10 = 12 minutes so the RG after Dive 2 is *A* (from Table A). (If no further dive was planned, this Final Dive RG would be adjusted, according to Rule 3, to *D*). Since a third dive is planned after an interval of longer than 4 hours, increase the RG after Dive 2 by one letter to *B* and use this to enter Table B. Therefore, the RF before Dive 3 is 1.1 and the required bottom time for Dive 3 is *60 minutes*. If this maximum bottom time was used the RG after the final dive would be *G*.

Example 14.

Find any decompression stops required in the following sequence of four dives:

Dive 1: 100 ft (30 m) for 15 minutes
S.I. = 50 minutes
Dive 2: 90 ft (27 m) for 12 minutes
S.I. = 2 hours
Dive 3: 60 ft (18 m) for 25 minutes
S.I. = 3½ hours
Dive 4: 50 ft (15 m) for 30 minutes.

No stop is required after the first dive and the RG after the dive is *D*. The RF before Dive 2 is 1.5, the EBT for the dive is 18 minutes, a stop of *5 minutes at 10 ft (3 m)* is required (since the Actual BT is longer than the No-D bottom time allowed in Table C) and the RG after Dive 2 is adjusted to *E* (from D, by Rule 1). The RF before Dive 3 is 1.3, the EBT for this dive is 33 minutes and no stop is required (as Actual BT does not exceed the No-D time from Table C). The RG after the third dive is first adjusted to *F* (from E, by Rule 3) and then further adjusted to *G* (by Rule 3). The RF before the fourth dive is 1.4, the EBT is 42 minutes and no stop is required. The RG after Dive 4 is adjusted from E to *F* (by Rule 2, since the S.I. before any further dives will be greater than 4 hrs).

Note:

It is recommended that multiple repetitive dives (i.e. more than 2 dives in a series) are avoided when water temperatures are below 40°F (5°C).

OMITTED DECOMPRESSION PROCEDURES

A diver who omits a Decompression Stop may resort to either of the Omitted Decompression Procedures described below. The following procedures are for emergency use only:

a. If no symptoms of DCS are present, the diver may begin the following IN-WATER PROCEDURE:

Within seven (7) minutes of surfacing, secure an adequate air supply and return to the stop 10 ft (3 m) deeper than the first omitted stop. Decompress at this depth for the time of the first omitted stop, then continue the decompression in accordance with the Table A schedule.

Example: 1st Dive: 100 ft (30 m) for 29 minutes
No-D Limit is 15 minutes
Decompression required is 5 min. at 20 ft (6 m) and 10 min. at 10 ft (3 m)

Situation: On ascent, diver omits decompression, but has no symptoms of DCS.

Reaction: Recompress for 5 min. at 30 ft (9 m), 5 min. at 20 ft (6 m) and 10 min. at 10 ft (3 m).

b. When a RECOMPRESSION CHAMBER (RCC) is available within seven (7) minutes of surfacing, the diver may be placed in the RCC and recompressed on Oxygen at a pressure equivalent to a sea level depth of 40 ft (12 m). The diver should remain on Oxygen at this pressure for twice the omitted decompression time. RCC ascent time (on Oxygen) is 2 minutes.

After conducting either of these Omitted Decompression Procedures, the diver must not dive again for at least **24 hours**. During this time, the diver should be closely monitored for symptoms of DCS. If symptoms of DCS occur, transport the diver to the nearest hyperbaric treatment facility.

These procedures are explained in detail in Chapter 25, which contains a number of worked examples.

DEPTH CORRECTION TABLE: D

Table D is used to convert the actual depth at high altitude to an EFFECTIVE DEPTH that corresponds to the Table A and Table C figures intended for sea level use. Table D provides you with the DEPTH CORRECTIONS and ACTUAL STOP DEPTHS needed to conduct dives at altitudes greater than 999 feet (300 metres) above sea level.

Depth Corrections are necessary when diving at altitude because the reduced atmospheric pressure at the surface of the dive site makes the ALTITUDE DIVE equivalent to a much deeper dive at sea level. When you arrive from a lower altitude, your body already has some residual nitrogen as a result of the decrease in atmospheric pressure.

Use the following Depth Correction Procedure if you have acclimatized at the altitude of the dive site for at least 12 hours:

1. **Establish the altitude of the dive site and the actual depth of the Altitude dive;**

2. **Convert the actual depth to EFFECTIVE DEPTH by adding the depth correction given in Table D;**

3. **Apply the EFFECTIVE DEPTH and Bottom Time to Table A to determine the decompression requirements of the Altitude Dive (see Table C for Repetitive Dive No-D Limits);**

4. **If the Altitude Dive is a Decompression Dive, conduct the Decompression Stop at the ACTUAL STOP DEPTH given at the bottom of Table D;**

5. **Decompress at the ACTUAL STOP DEPTH for the Stop Time specified Table A.**

Example: Altitude = 6,000 ft (1,800 m)
Depth = 60 ft (18 m)
Bottom Time = 35 minutes

DEPTH CORRECTION = +20 ft (6 m)
EFFECTIVE DEPTH = 80 ft (24 m)

Deco. Stop = 10 min. at 10 ft (3 m)(from Table A)
Actual Stop Depth = 8 ft (2.5 m) (from Table D)

If you must dive before 12 HOURS have elapsed at the altitude of the dive site, begin the Depth Correction procedure by using the NEXT GREATER DEPTH than the actual depth. Following the example given above, begin the Depth Correction Procedure as if the actual depth were 70 ft (21 m). The EFFECTIVE DEPTH would be 70 ft (21 m) + 20 ft (6 m) = 90 ft (27 m).

The decompression required and Actual Stop Depths would be 5 minutes at 16 ft (5 m), and 10 minutes at 8 ft (2.5 m).*

Chapter 21 includes a number of worked examples using the DCIEM Procedure for Altitude Diving.

MULTI-LEVEL DIVING

The DCIEM Sport Diving Tables can also be used to plan Multi-Level dives. The procedure is described in Chapter 22.

* **The imperial and metric figures given for the Actual Stop Depths are not direct conversions. The metric table for Depth Correction was calculated seperately. Because of the effect of rounding the numbers on the imperial table, the imperial table equivalents may differ slightly from those in the metric table.**

Most of the text of this chapter has been taken directly from the literature and reports accompanying the DCIEM Sport Diving Tables (written by Ron Nishi and Gain Wong). The author wishes to thank DCIEM and UDT Inc. for their co-operation and assistance with the preparation of this chapter, and for permission to reprint the DCIEM Sport Diving Tables and the DCIEM 1984 Standard Air Decompression Tables (Appendix B).

Note:

Since originally released, various changes have been made to the rules for using these tables, and to the tables themselves, in order to make them more user friendly. More changes could still occur so the reader is advised to be vigilant.

SOURCES

Huggins, K. (1987), "Microprocessor Applications to Multi-Level Diving". Michigan Sea Grant College Program, Report No. MICHU-56-87-201.

Lauckner, G. and Nishi, R. (1984), "Decompression Tables and Procedures for Compressed Air Diving Based on the DCIEM 1983 Decompression Model", DCIEM No. 84-R-74, Defence and Civil Institute of Environmental Medicine.

Nishi, R. and Hobson, B. (1986), "The DCIEM/Canadian Forces Air Decompression Tables". DCIEM No. 86-P-23, for publication in the Proceedings of the Canadian Association of Underwater Science: Diving for Science, Assessing the Environment.

Nishi, R. (1986), "New Canadian Air Decompression Tables". DCIEM No. 86-P-06, *Canadian Diving Journal*; Summer: 22-27.

Nishi, R. (1987), "The DCIEM Decompression Tables and Procedures for Air Diving". In: *Decompression in Surface-Based Diving*, Nashimoto, I. and Lanphier, E. (eds), UHMS Publication No. 73 (Dec) 6/15/87.

Nishi, R. and Eatock, B. (1987), "The Role of Ultrasonic Bubble Detection in Table Validation". *Proceedings of the UHMS Workshop on "Validation of Decompression Schedules"*. 13-14 Feb, Bethesda, MD.

Nishi, R., personal communications.

"UDT Guide to the (DCIEM) Sport Diving Tables" (1987). Universal Dive Techtronics, Inc., Toronto.

"UDT Guide to the (DCIEM) Sport Diving Tables (Addendum)" (1988). Universal Dive Techtronics, Inc., Toronto.

"UDT Instructions for using the DCIEM Sport Diving Tables c1989". Universal Dive Techtronics, Inc., Toronto.

"UDT Instructions for using the DCIEM Sport Diving Tables c1990". Universal Dive Techtronics, Inc., Vancouver.

"UDT Recommendations for using the DCIEM Sport Diving Tables (UDT Info. 8)". Universal Dive Techtronics, Inc., Vancouver.

Wong, G., personal communications.

RECOMMENDED FURTHER READING

Two new books about the DCIEM Tables will be released in 1990. One book, titled "DCIEM Air Diving Manual", is written by Ron Nishi, and the other, as yet untitled book, is written by Gain Wong. Both will be available from Atlantis Publications, Toronto.

EXERCISES

1. Find the No-D Limits, (NDL) and corresponding Repetitive Groups (RG) for single dives to the following depths:

   (a) 82 ft (25 m) (b) 145 ft (44 m) (c) 52 ft (16 m)

2. Determine the RG after each of the following dives:

   (a) 50 ft (15 m) for 46 minutes (b) 120 ft (36 m) for 17 minutes

3. Find the Repetitive Factor (RF) after each of the following Surface Intervals (SI):

   (a) Group C after SI of $3^1/_2$ hours
   (b) Group B after SI of 1 hour
   (c) Group H after SI of 5 hours

4. Determine the No-D Limit for each of the following repetitive dives:

   (a) 90 ft (27 m) with RF of 1.4
   (b) 48 ft (15 m) with RF of 1.1
   (c) 115 ft (35 m) with RF of 1.8

5. The following questions relate to a dive to 80 ft (24 m) for 20 minutes, followed 3 hours later by a dive to 61 ft (19 m):

   (a) What is the RG after the first dive?
   (b) What is the RF after the SI?
   (c) What is the No-D Limit for the second dive?
   (d) If the actual bottom time of the second dive was 20 minutes, find the RG after the dive.

6. Repeat question 5 for a dive to 108 ft (33 m) for 10 minutes followed 4 hours later by a dive to 60 ft (18 m).

7. Complete the calculations for the following decompression stop dives:

   The first dive to 115 ft (35 m) for 15 minutes, SI of $1^1/_2$ hours, second dive to 75 ft (23 m) for 30 minutes.

   (a) What decompression stop(s) is (are) required after the first dive?
   (b) What is the RF after the SI?
   (c) What is the decompression requirement and RG after the repetitive dive?

8. Repeat question 7 for the following dives:

   The first dive to 80 ft (24 m) for 28 minutes, followed $2^1/_2$ hours later by 51 ft (16 m) for 40 minutes.

9. Determine the minimum SI necesary to stay within the NDL for the following dives:

(a) First dive to 70 ft (21 m) for 30 minutes.
Second dive to 50 ft (15 m) for 50 minutes.
(b) First dive to 60 ft (18 m) for 50 minutes.
Second dive to 60 ft (18 m) for 30 minutes.

10. Find the decompression requirements and RG after a single dive to 60 ft (18 m) for 35 minutes at an altitude of 8,500 ft (2,575 m) (Assume 12-hour acclimatization).

11. Find the No-D Limits for the following dives to be carried out at an altitude of 4,500 ft (1363 m) (Assume 12-hour acclimatization):

The first dive to 80 ft (24 m) to No-D Limit, SI of 4 hours, second dive to 60 ft (18 m).

12. Find the No-D Limits for the following repetitive dives at sea level:

(a) 70 ft (21 m) for 25 minutes followed 12 minutes later by a dive to 70 ft (21 m).
(b) 80 ft (24 m) for 20 minutes followed 14 minutes later by a dive to 55 ft (17 m).

13. Determine the No-D Limits for the final dive in each of the following dive sequences:

(a) Dive 1: 110 ft (33 m) for 12 minutes
S.I. = 1½ hours
Dive 2: 100 ft (30 m) for 10 minutes
S.I. = 3½ hours
Dive 3: 70 ft (21 m)

(b) Dive 1: 80 ft (24 m) for 24 minutes
S.I. = 3½ hours
Dive 2: 70 ft (21 m) for 20 minutes
S.I. = 4½ hours
Dive 3: 60 ft (18 m)

(c) Dive 1: 80 ft (24 m) for 20 minutes
S.I. = 2 hours
Dive 2: 80 ft (24 m) for 10 minutes
S.I. = 3 hours
Dive 3: 60 ft (18 m) for 20 minutes
S.I. = 3 hours
Dive 4: 60 ft (18 m)

ANSWERS

1.	(a)	20, D	(b)	6, B	(c)	50, F
2.	(a)	E	(b)	F		
3.	(a)	1.2	(b)	1.2	(c)	1.4
4.	(a)	11	(b)	60	(c)	5
5.	(a)	D	(b)	1.2	(c)	25
	(d)	24 min. (EBT), RG = D.				
6.	(a)	B	(b)	1.1	(c)	40
	(d)	22 min. (EBT), RG = C.				
7.	(a)	10 min at 10 ft (3 m)				
	(b)	1.4 (c) 5 min. at 20 ft (6 m) and 10 min. at 10 ft (3 m), H.				
8.	(a)	5 min at 10 ft (3 m)				
	(b)	1.4 (c) 5 min at 10 ft (3 m), G.				
9.	(a)	2.00				
	(b)	3.00				
10.	5 min at 15 ft (4.5 m) and 10 min. at 8 ft (2.5 m), G.					

ANSWERS

[illegible]

CHAPTER 18
THE BS-AC TABLES

18.1 The RNPL/BS-AC Table

Note:

The RNPL/BS-AC Table is only available in metres and, therefore, the following discussion and examples will generally be confined to metric measurement.

In 1958, Hempleman, a British physiologist, introduced a completely different decompression concept to those that were currently in use, and devised some decompression schedules which were based on a completely different model to that of Haldane.

Hempleman had observed that, over a particular depth range, the first symptom of decompression sickness to appear was usually pain at or near a joint. He assumed that the tissue involved (e.g. tendon) was, therefore, the tissue with the greatest overpressure of nitrogen for that depth range, and that gas elimination from that tissue must control the decompression. Hempleman pictured the body as a single tissue (Figure 18.1.1) and believed that the quantity of gas absorbed in the body could be calculated by a simple formula relating depth and time.* Unlike Haldane, who believed that gas uptake and elimination took identical times, Hempleman assumed that gas elimination was one and one half times slower than uptake. He also utilized the theory that decompression is safe if a constant difference, between the gas tension in the tissues and the environment, of 30 feet (9 m) of sea water (fsw) is not exceeded.

The model represents the body as a single "slab" of tissue. One end of the slab is exposed to ambient pressure. As the pressure of inert gas increases it diffuses through the "slab" as shown in Figure 18.1.1. As long as the pressure of the inert gas remains less than a some specified amount (initially 30 fsw) above ambient pressure, bends should be avoided.

These initial schedules, metricated in 1972, are the current Royal Navy Tables. They have theoretical limitations which have been confirmed in practice:

Firstly, the concept that a single tissue (i.e. the slowest tissue) controls decompression only applies over a certain depth range. Secondly, the concept of an allowable overpressure of 30 fsw at all depths is often too conservative.

* Hempleman proposed that :"If this model is near enough correct for most practical purposes and if there is a fixed critical excess quantity of gas which can be tolerated on decompression, then for a dive to a depth P for a time t there will be some critical fixed quantity Q of dissolved gas such that : $Q = P\sqrt{t}$. "

FIGURE 18.1.1
Hempleman's single tissue model

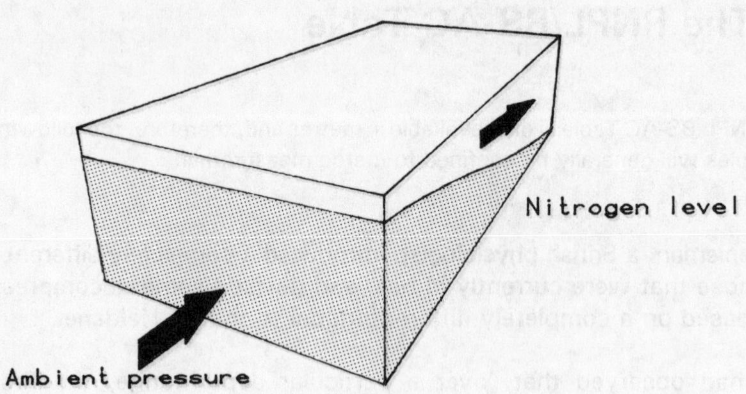

Hempleman realized these limitations and, in 1966, developed a new set of caisson workers' tables for a tunnelling job in Blackpool. This job involved very long exposures of 4-8 hours, and the decompression model was designed to increase the decompression times in this range since existing times were known to be too short. These new tables became known as the Blackpool Tables.

In 1968, Hempleman used the same caisson decompression model to generate a new set of tables for industry. These tables, known as the 1968 Air Diving Tables, still used the concept of a single tissue but used a variable ratio of tissue nitrogen tension to ambient pressure in order to calculate safe decompression.

Both the Royal Navy and industry rejected these tables claiming that the no-stop times were too conservative, and that the no-stop times given by the current RN Tables provided adequate safety. The 1968 Air Diving Tables were slightly modified (which apparently included replacing the no-stop times with the RN no-stop times), metricated and reappeared as the 1972 Metric Air Diving Tables, released by The Royal Naval Physiological Laboratory (RNPL) through the Underwater Engineering Group (UEG) of the Construction Industry Research and Information Association (CIRIA). A portion of these tables is shown as Table 18.1.1. At this time little has been published about these tables.

The metricated version also proved to be commercially unpopular because it was presented in 5 m depth increments, which required substantial extra (and costly) decompression time if the diver slightly exceeded a depth entry.

Initially, with the RN Tables (Appendix C), repetitive dives were handled by adding the bottom times and decompressing for the depth of the deeper dive. Hempleman introduced "concession" rules for use with the 1968 Tables. The halving, quartering and eighthing of times offered much greater flexibility with repetitive diving, and it seemed reasonable to allow this freedom with these more conservative tables. Unfortunately, in 1972, when RNPL was preparing to release the metric version of the 1968 Tables, the RN released its own repeat dive rule - the 6-hour rule, where, if the first dive is shallower than 42 m and above the Limiting Line it can be repeated after 6 hours. This forced Hempleman to alter his repeat dive system and, eventually, gave rise to the confusing set of repeat dive rules governing the RNPL/BS-AC Table.

TABLE 18.1.1
Portion of the RNPL 1972 Tables

Depth not Exceeding (metres)	Bottom Time Not Exceeding (min)	Stoppages at Different Depths (metres) 25 m	20 m	15 m	10 m	5 m	Total Time for Decompression (min)
	45	—	—	—	—	—	$1^1/2$
	50	—	—	—	—	5	5
	55	—	—	—	—	10	10
	60	—	—	—	—	15	15
	65	—	—	—	—	25	25
20	*Limiting* 70	—	—	—	—	30	30
	Line 75	—	—	—	—	40	40
	90	—	—	—	—	60	60
	120	—	—	—	—	90	90
	150	—	—	—	—	110	110
	180	—	—	—	10	110	120
	240	—	—	—	10	120	130
	25	—	—	—	—	—	2
	30	—	—	—	5	5	10
	35	—	—	—	5	10	15
	40	—	—	—	5	15	20
	Limiting 45	—	—	—	5	20	25
	Line 50	—	—	—	10	30	40
25	55	—	—	—	10	40	50
	60	—	—	—	10	60	70
	75	—	—	5	—	80	85
	90	—	—	5	10	100	115
	105	—	—	5	10	120	135
	120	—	—	5	20	120	145
	150	—	—	5	30	120	155
	180	—	5	—	40	125	170

Crown Copyright/MOD Table.

The RNPL 1972 Table is reproduced in full in Appendix D.

You will notice that there is a "Limiting Line" drawn across each depth schedule, and that the depth schedules increase in 5 m increments. The meaning of the "Limiting Line" is as follows:

DIVING BELOW THE LIMITING LINE

(Taken from the Royal Navy Diving Manual - BR 2806)

1. That part of each depth section above the Limiting Line is the ordinary working table where the risk of decompression sickness is negligible. Diving for periods below the Limiting Line carries a greater risk of decompression sickness, and this risk increases with an increase in duration below the line. Intentional diving below the Limiting Line should be undertaken only when a compression chamber is available on the site and, even then, only when circumstances justify the risk. This risk is in no way diminished by the use of oxygen during decompression.

2. A diver who has carried out a dive below the Limiting Line is not to carry out a further dive within 12 hours.

3. He is also to remain in the vicinity of a compression chamber and under surveillance for four hours.

Note:

Below the Limiting Line equates to requiring more than 30 minutes of decompression time.

The British Sub-Aqua Club (BS-AC), searching for a suitable table for its sport-diving members, adapted the RNPL 1972 Table, creating the RNPL/BS-AC Table. In its "short" form the RNPL/BS-AC Table (Table 18.1.2) covers depths to 50 m in 2 m increments (rather than the original 5 m increments), and dive times leading to a total decompression time of 30 minutes (i.e. the tables end at the Limiting Line for each schedule). "No-stop" Times (i.e. No-Decompression Limits) are specified for each depth increment. Where stops are required, all dives to depths not exceeding 20 m require a single stop at 5 m, whilst dives from 20-50 m require a first stop at 10 m, followed by a second at 5 m. The "full" table includes two further depth increments of 5 m (i.e. 55 m and 60 m), again with times leading to a maximum decompression requirement of 30 minutes.

Promoters of the 1972 RNPL Tables have claimed an "incidence factor" of less than 0.05%, but a substantial number of divers have suffered decompression sickness while diving within the RNPL/BS-AC Table (see the discussion later in this chapter). In 1988, the British Sub-Aqua Club released a new, and vastly different, set of tables which, it hopes, will be a improvement on the RNPL/BS-AC Table in ease of use, flexibility and safety.

TABLE 18.1.2
The RNPL/BS-AC Table

Maximum Depth metres	No Stop Time minutes	BOTTOM TIME IN MINUTES					
10	**232**	431	–	–	–	–	
12	**137**	140	159	179	201	229	270
14	**96**	98	106	116	125	134	144
16	**72**	73	81	88	94	99	105
18	**57**	59	66	71	76	80	84
20	**46**	49	55	60	63	67	70
Stops at 5 metres MINUTES		**5**	**10**	**15**	**20**	**25**	**30**

Maximum Depth metres	No Stop Time minutes	BOTTOM TIME IN MINUTES				
22	**38**	42	47	51	55	58
24	**32**	37	41	45	48	51
26	**27**	32	37	40	43	45
28	**23**	29	33	36	39	41
30	**20**	25	30	33	35	37
32	**18**	23	27	30	32	34
34	**16**	21	25	28	30	31
36	**14**	20	23	26	27	29
38	**12**	18	21	24	26	27
40	**11**	17	20	22	24	25
42	**10**	16	19	21	22	24
44	**9**	15	18	20	21	
46	**8**	14	17	18	20	
48	**8**	13	16	17		
50	**7**	12	15	17		
Stops at 10 metres		**5**	**5**	**5**	**5**	**5**
Stops at 5 metres MINUTES		**5**	**10**	**15**	**20**	**25**

The following conditions apply to the RNPL/BS-AC Table:

* Descent rate is 30 m/minute.

* Ascent rate is 15 m/minute.

* Maximum depth is the greatest depth reached, (however briefly) during the dive.

* Bottom time is from the start of descent to the start of ascent.

* "No-Stop Time" is the longest bottom time after which direct ascent to the surface may be made.

  Decompression Time includes time taken to ascend to the stop. (Start timing the stop when you begin the ascent to it, and stop timing it when you leave it).

  The time taken to ascend from the 5 m stop to the surface (20 seconds) is included in the time of the final stop.

* The surface interval is the time from surfacing at the end of one dive, to commencing the descent for the next.

USING THE RNPL/BS-AC TABLE

SECTION A: SINGLE DIVES

Example 1.

You plan to dive to 20 m for 30 minutes. Is any decompression stop(s) required?

Enter Table 18.1.2, from the left, at 20 m and move to the right. The shortest time is *46* minutes, which is the maximum "no-stop" time. Therefore, no stop is required.

Example 2.

You plan to dive to 17 m for 60 minutes. Is any decompression stop(s) required?

Enter the table at 18 m and move to the right to find 60 minutes. Since 60 minutes is not tabled, move on to 66 minutes, which is the next longer tabled time. Move down the column to the stop row. The stop required is *10 minutes at 5 m.*

(This 10 minutes begins when the diver leaves the bottom to ascend to the 5 m stop. The ascent to the stop should take about one minute, so only 9 minutes is actually spent at 5 m.)

Example 3.

You wish to dive to 30 m for 25 minutes. What decompression is required?

Enter the table at 30 m and move to the right to 25 minutes. Move down the column to the stop row. The required stops are *5 minutes at 10 m followed by 5 minutes at 5 m.*

Example 4.

You wish to dive to 26 m for 50 minutes. What decompression is required?

This is "off the table" (i.e. below the Limiting Line) and, hence, carries an increased risk of decompression sickness. The required decompression is found from the RNPL 1972 Tables and is *5 minutes at 15 m followed by 70 minutes at 5 m.* The dive should not be done unless certain specified conditions are met. Recreational divers generally cannot meet these conditions and, therefore, should not do such a dive.

SECTION B: TWO DIVES ONLY, or two dives followed by a dive to 9 m or shallower, in accordance with the third dive table.

TABLE 18.1.3
RNPL/BS-AC Two Dive Concessions

When calculating decompression times for second dives, **the greater depth of the two dives must be used.** The **Surface Interval** is the time from surfacing after the First Dive to descending for the Second Dive.

When **both** dives are shallower than 40 metres, the Time Penalty in Table A should be added to the Second Dive Bottom time.

TABLE A

Surface Interval in hours	Time Penalty to be added to Second Dive bottom time
Less than 2	All of First Dive bottom time
2–4	One half of First Dive bottom time
4–6	One Quarter of First Dive bottom time
More than 6	No Time Penalty need be added

When **either** dive is deeper than 40 metres, the Time Penalty in Table B should be added to the Second Dive bottom time.

TABLE B

Surface Interval in hours	Time Penalty to be added to Second Dive bottom time
Less than 2	All of First Dive bottom time
2– 4	One half of First Dive bottom time
4– 8	One quarter of First Dive bottom time
8–16	One eighth of First Dive bottom time
More than 16	No Time Penalty need be added

Second Dives to 9 metres or less carry no Time Penalty.

The "concessions" (shown as Table 18.1.3) may be applied to the <u>second</u> dive when only two dives are planned or when a third dive to 9 m or shallower is planned in accordance with the third dive table.*

In essence, the concessions give a diver some credit for nitrogen off-gassed during surface intervals of two hours or longer. *They only apply to a the second dive in the circumstances described.* **If a concession has been used to calculate the time allowed or decompression requirement for a second dive, a third dive cannot be carried out within the 24-hour period which began at the start of the first dive in the sequence, unless it is no deeper than 9 m and in accordance with the third dive table (Table 18.1.4).**

Note:

2-4 hr means from 2 hr (which includes 2 hr) up to but not including 4 hr.
4-6 hr means from 4 hr (which includes 4 hr) up to but not including 6 hr.

Example 5.

You plan to dive to 33 m for 12 minutes followed, three hours later, by 25 m for 20 minutes. Calculate the decompression required.

To find the decompression for the first dive, enter the RNPL/BS-AC Table at 34 m. The No-Stop Limit for this depth is 16 minutes, so this 12 minute dive will not require a stop.

To determine the decompression for Dive 2, look up 33 m (i.e. the maximum depth for either dive) for (12/2 + 20) = 26 minutes. The required decompression is thus *5 minutes at 10 m followed by 15 minutes at 5 m.*

Example 6.

You wish to dive to 20 m for 16 minutes followed, 13 hours later, by a dive to 42 m for 10 minutes.

Dive 2 must be treated as a repetitive dive since one of the dives is deeper than 40 m and a 16-hour surface interval is required before no time penalty is applied.

To calculate the required decompression, look up 42 m for (16/8 + 10) = 12 minutes. Stops of *5 minutes at 10 m and 5 minutes at 5 m are required.*

Example 7.

You plan to dive to 36 m for 10 minutes, have a surface interval of one hour, and then dive to 20 m for 10 minutes. What decompression is required?

Dive 1 will not require a stop since the No-Stop Limit is 14 minutes. For Dive 2 you must look up 36 m for (10+10) = 20 minutes, which will require stops of *5 minutes at 10 m and 5 minutes at 5 m.*

* In March 1988 this rule was changed. It is explained in Section D.

Example 8.

> *You plan to dive to 9 m for 32 minutes followed, 5 hours later, by a dive to 24 m for 30 minutes. What decompression will be required?*

Dive 1 will not require a stop as this table provides no limit for a single dive to this depth. For Dive 2 you must look up 24 m for (32/4 + 30) = 38 minutes. Stops of *5 minutes at 10 m and 10 minutes at 5 m* are required.

Example 9.

> *You now plan to perform the two dives in Example 8 in the opposite order. What decompression is now required?*

Dive 1 will not require a stop as the No-Stop Limit for 24 m is 32 minutes. *Dive 2 will also not require a decompression stop* since a second dive to 9 m or less does not require any stop.

Notes:

1. **A second dive to 9 m, or shallower, does not require a decompression stop.**

2. ***If you are calculating the decompression requirement for a dive which is shallower than a previous dive in a repetitive sequence, be very careful to ensure that you use the maximum depth reached on (any of) the previous dive(s) to determine the decompression. Divers commonly forget to do this and, at times, it can cause serious problems.***

SECTION C: MULTIPLE DIVES

A diver may wish, or need, to make more than two dives in a 24-hour period. **The RNPL/BS-AC Table allows a maximum of 8 hours in 24 hours submerged.**

To calculate the decompression required when a sequence of more than two dives is undertaken in a 24-hour period, you must add together the bottom times of each of the dives and decompress for the greatest depth reached during the deepest dive. This is the "Multiple Dive Rule". It applies whenever more than two dives are undertaken in a 24-hour period, except in the special case discussed in Section D and, possibly, in another special situation similar to that described in Example 17.

To determine whether or not the Multiple Dive Rule is to be applied, you start by determining what dives are to be undertaken in the 24-hour period beginning at the start of the initial dive. This can lead to a number of interesting anomalies and can often make it difficult to carry out groups of dives on a number of consecutive days. Some of these problems are dealt with in the discussion later in the chapter.

Example 10.

You wish to dive to 17 m for 25 minutes, followed, five hours later, by a dive to 15 m for 40 minutes, followed, three hours later, by a dive to 10 m for 15 minutes. Calculate the required decompression.

Dive 1 requires no decompression stop. For Dive 2, look up 17 m for 65 minutes, which requires decompression of *10 minutes at 5 m*. For Dive 3, look up 17 m for 80 minutes. The decompression required is *25 minutes at 5 m*.

Example 11.

You are planning to dive to 21 m for 40 minutes, followed, three hours later, by a dive to 8 m for 10 minutes, followed, a further three hours later, by a dive to 12 m for 8 minutes, followed, one hour later, by 9 m for 40 minutes. Calculate the required decompression.

Dive 1 requires decompression of *5 minutes at 10 m and 5 minutes at 5 m.* Dive 2 requires no stops as it is a second dive which is shallower than 9 m. For Dive 3, one must look up 21 m for 58 minutes and must decompress for *5 minutes at 10 m and 25 minutes at 5 m.* For Dive 4 one must look up 21 m for 98 minutes even though the dive is only to 9 m. This is "off the table" so *Dive 4 must not be done.*

Example 12.

You plan to dive to 18 m for 15 minutes, followed, 8 hours later, by a dive to 20 m for 20 minutes, followed, 3 hours later, by a dive to 15 m. Find any stops required for the first two dives and the maximum no-stop bottom time (if any) for the third dive.

For Dive 1, look up 18 m for 15 minutes. No stop is required. For Dive 2 look up 20 m for 35 minutes. Again, no stop is required as a further (46-35) = 11 minutes of bottom time was available. For dive 3, look up a depth of 20 m. The No-Stop Limit at this depth is 46 minutes, of which 35 minutes has already been used up. This leaves *11* minutes of bottom time for the third dive.

Example 13.

You plan to dive to 20 m for 22 minutes, followed, 10 hours later, by a dive to 22 m for 20 minutes, followed, 8 hours later, by a dive to 18 m for 15 minutes. Find the required decompression.

Dive 1 requires no stop. For Dive 2, look up 22 m for 42 minutes, which gives stops of *5 minutes at 10 m and 5 minutes at 5 m*. For Dive 3, look up 22 m for 57 minutes, which gives stops of *5 minutes at 10 m and 25 minutes at 5 m.*

SECTION D: NEW RULES FOR A THIRD DIVE OF 9 M OR SHALLOWER

In March 1988, the BS-AC altered the procedure to be used when calculating the decompression required following a sequence of more than two dives, where the last dive is to a depth of 9 m or shallower.

Previously, for a series of three dives where the third dive was 9 m or shallower, the RNPL/BS-AC "concession" could be used for the second dive and no further calculations were required for the third dive as it was 9 m or shallower. For a series of four dives where the third dive was deeper than 9 m and the fourth dive was 9 m or shallower, the "Multiple Dive Rule" was applied to the first three dives, and the fourth dive, being 9 m or shallower, did not require any decompression stop(s).

However, while researching the BS-AC '88 Tables, it was discovered that these procedures were incorrect. **Third dives of 9 m or shallower must be taken into account**, which means that the "Multiple Dive Rule" should be used.

This will often make a third dive extremely difficult to plan within a day's diving, and can also influence the next day's diving since the first dive of the next day may still be the third dive undertaken within a 24-hour sequence.

The following table, Table 18.1.4, can be used to plan a third dive to a maximum depth of 9 m without the need for decompression stops. It also indicates the surface interval which must follow that third dive in order to re-enter the RNPL/BS-AC table without penalty.

TABLE 18.1.4

Third Dive Table

	Surface interval following 2nd dive minutes 0	30	60	90	hours 4	Surface interval to follow 3rd dive
Third dive no-stop time in minutes for maximum depth of 9 m	-	8	28	115	187	15 hours
	-	-	7	78	147	14 hours
	-	-	-	41	86	13 hours
	-	-	-	-	26	12 hours

Using the new rule for a third dive to 9 m or shallower

1. By referring to the central section of Table 18.1.4, plan the surface interval preceding the third dive. The choices are 0-30 minutes, 30-60 minutes, 60-90 minutes, 90 min-4 hr and more than 4 hours.

2. Read down the column corresponding to the surface interval chosen to determine the maximum no-stop time for the third dive.

3. The final column shows the surface interval required after the third (9 m or shallower) dive so that the RNPL/BS-AC Table can be re-entered without a time penalty.

Example 14.

You are planning the following sequence of dives:

The first is to 20 m for a bottom time of 30 minutes, followed, three hours later, by an 18 m no-stop dive. If you then wish to dive to 8 m two hours later and begin a new day's diving 13 hours after surfacing from the 8 m dive:

(i) What is the maximum allowable bottom time for the second dive?

(ii) What is the maximum allowable no-stop time for the third dive?

Since the third dive is to 9 m or shallower, the "concession" can be used for the second dive and the additional 9 m table can be consulted for the third dive.

Dive 1 requires no stop, and Dive 2 can have a maximum bottom time of (46-15) = *31* minutes.

To find the allowable bottom time for Dive 3, enter Table 18.1.4, from the top, at the column corresponding to a surface interval of 2 hours following the second dive. This is the 90 min-4 hr column. Move down this column to find the time allowed for the 8 m dive. If the dive was to be followed by a 15 hour surface interval, a bottom time of 115 minutes could be chosen. However, since the surface interval following the dive will only be 13 hours, a maximum bottom time of *41* minutes is allowed.

Example 15.

You are planning to do three dives. The first is to 24 m for a bottom time of 28 minutes, the second, after a surface interval of 5 hours, is to be a no-stop dive to 16 m and will begin at 1645. You then wish to do a third dive to 6 m, and then be able to dive again at 0900 the next morning without a time penalty.

(i) What surface interval is required after the second dive?

(ii) What is the maximum allowable no-stop bottom time for the third dive?

Again, as the third dive is 9 m or shallower, the "concession" can be used on the second dive and Table 18.1.4 can be consulted for the third.

No stop is required for the first dive. The maximum no-stop bottom time for the second dive is (32-7) = *25* minutes. You should surface from the second dive at about 1712.

If you plan to dive again after a surface interval of, say, 80 minutes, you would be able to dive for up to 28 minutes but then must wait 15 hours before diving again without penalty. This would mean that you could not dive without penalty until about 1000.

If, instead, you dived to 6 m for a maximum of 7 minutes, you could dive again 14 hours later without penalty, which would allow you to dive at 0900 the next morning. Alternatively, if you allow a surface interval of 91 minutes before doing the third dive, you could dive to 6 m for 41 minutes and then dive without penalty at 0900, as you would end up having a surface interval of between 13 and 14 hours.

SECTION E: PLANNING A PAIR OF NO-DECOMPRESSION STOP DIVES

Example 16.

What are the maximum allowable bottom times so that the following dives would not require decompression stops?

(i) A dive to 21 m followed three hours later by a dive to 16 m.

For Dive 1, look up the No-Stop Lime for 22 m, which is 38 minutes, and which is your maximum bottom time for this dive. Three hours later you must still count 38/2 = 19 minutes of previous bottom time, so Dive 2 must be taken as 21 m (i.e. the maximum depth of either dive). The maximum no-stop time at this depth is 38 minutes but you have already used up 19 minutes of this, leaving you (38-19) = *19* minutes still available for the second dive.

(ii) A dive to 32 m, followed nine hours later, by a 42 m dive.

Remember it would have been safer to do the deeper dive first!

For Dive 1, look up 32 m. Your maximum bottom time is 18 minutes. Nine hours later you must still count 18/8 which is about 3 minutes of this time. For Dive 2, look up the allowable time at 42 m, which is 10 minutes. You have already used 3 minutes of this so you can still dive for a bottom time of (10-3) = 7 minutes.

SUMMARY OF RULES

The RNPL/BS-AC system can be used for more than two dives by using the "Multiple Dive Rule" (i.e. adding the total bottom times and decompressing for the greatest depth). A "concession" to this rule may be used when only two dives are undertaken. **If have have carried out a pair of dives using a "concession" you cannot go over to the "Multiple Dive Rule" to make a third dive of any depth. You must commit yourself to two dives only until the 24-hour period since the start of the first dive has expired, or use the new 9 m table to plan for a third dive to 9 m, or shallower, which is the final dive in a repetitive sequence.**

DISCUSSION

The above section shows a diver how to use the table as designed. Unfortunately, using this table (or any other table) correctly will not guarantee that a diver will not suffer from decompression sickness and, as previously mentioned, quite a number of divers have suffered from the "bends" after diving to times indicated (by this table) as safe. For example, in 1987, 36% (25/69) of the bends cases reported in Britain were divers who had apparently dived within the RNPL/BS-AC Table.[1]

In addition, divers are at times careless, out of condition, some ascend too quickly and some forget to decompress for the greatest depth attained in a dive series when a shallower dive follows a deeper dive. However, there are also some inherent problems within the table itself. A few of these will be outlined below:

1. In many cases the initial No-Stop Limits are too long. They often exceed more modern, safer (Buehlmann (1986), DCIEM, Bassett) NDLs at the shallower depths, and exceed the U.S. Navy limits at the deep end.

2. If you have dived to 40 m or less and wish to dive again to 40 m or less just over 6 hours later, you may do so without considering your previous dive. This often allows a bottom time in excess of many other systems and, although it may often be realistic (e.g. after a short dive), at times it may prove quite unsafe, especially after deep, long initial dives, and/or after a fast ascent.

3. Many experts now believe that the 15 m/minute ascent rate is often too fast.

As mentioned previously, there are a number of anomalies and uncertainties that may arise when this table is used in certain situations.

The RNPL/BS-AC Table was not really designed to cater for multiple dives. As a result many of the "rules" since printed about the table have been the interpretation of the day, sometimes amended with the accumulation of experience and knowledge. Unfortunately, the BS-AC's "Decompression Table Workbook", which is the most comprehensive work on this table, does not express the final stage in this acquisition of knowledge. The BS-AC will not update the workbook as it is delighted to put this table, with all its problems and anomalies, in its final resting place. They hope that introduction of the BS-AC '88 Tables, which have replaced the RNPL/BS-AC Table, will be swift and painless.

Some of these anomalies are discussed here only for the sake of identifying the problems.

* The published rules clearly state that you cannot change over to the Multiple Dive Rule to do a third dive after having used the Concession on a second dive. To many this rule seems illogical and for some time the BS-AC have in fact allowed it to be broken. After using the concession on the second dive it is commonly accepted that the Multiple Dive Rule can be used to plan a third dive. However, this often proves impractical as very little time will be available for the third dive unless all the dives are quite shallow.

* There has been much debate on the length of the surface interval that is required after a second dive, before another dive can be carried out without a penalty being carried over from the first two dives. The only rule that is directly applicable is the Multiple Dive Rule for dives within a 24-hour period. Consider the following example, taken from the 2nd edition of "The Decompression Table Workbook".

Example 17.

Divers wish to make the following series of dives over a two-day period.

DAY 1

First dive at 08.30 - 25 m for 20 minutes
Second dive at 12.00 - 20 m for 15 minutes
Third dive at 19.00 - 18 m for 25 minutes.

DAY 2

Fourth dive at 08.00 - 42 m for 9 minutes
Is this a safe dive series? How should they apply the RNPL/BS-AC Table? Should they use the Multiple Dive Rule or the Two Dive Concession?

Strictly speaking, the Multiple Dive Rule should be applied since there are four dives planned within the 24-hour period from the start of the initial dive. This means that the Multiple Dive Rule should really be used for the second, third and fourth dives. However, the BS-AC has interpreted this quite differently in this particular example. It handles the problem in the following way:

"First, look at the maximum depth to be reached and surface intervals between each dive. The first three dives do not exceed 40 metres: the surface interval between dives two and three exceeds 6 hours - the time needed to eliminate nitrogen after dives not exceeding 40 m depth.

So dives one and two can be treated as one pair: dives three and four as another pair. The Two Dive concession can be applied to both pairs of dives; the series is safe enough.

However, if the third dive took place an hour earlier, at 18.00, the Multiple Dive Rule would have to be applied for dives one, two and three - and decompression requirements after dive three go off the table!

Furthermore, because dive four the next day exceeds 40 metres, and is to be made within 16 hours of dive three, the Multiple Dive Rule extends further to include this dive - which is now an impossibility!

Dive four can only begin at least 16 hours after surfacing from dive three."

ADDING SAFETY TO THE RNPL/BS-AC TABLE

For those divers who dive by the RNPL/BS-AC Table, I recommend the following safety factors for use with the table:

Procedure:

a. *Choose an initial "No-Stop Limit" by choosing the limit for the next greater tabled depth increment than would normally be used.*

E.g. For a dive to 22 m the No-Stop Limit is normally 38 minutes. To add safety take the limit for 24 m as your initial No-Stop Limit. This is 32 minutes.

For a dive to 31 m you would look up the limit for 34 m, rather than the limit for 32 m as is usual. So your initial No-Stop Limit for this dive is 16 minutes (rather than 18).

Note: This procedure converts the RNPL/BS-AC limits into limits which are much closer to those of the Buehlmann (1986) and DCIEM Tables.

b. *Reduce this initial No-Stop Limit to cater for any predisposing factor(s) to bends that are present.*

E.g. For a dive to 21 m the initial limit is 32 minutes. If I expect to get cold I will reduce this time by at least 3 minutes (10% reduction). Now my actual no-decompression stop bottom time becomes 32-3 = 29 minutes.

c. *Ascend at about 10 m/minute.*

d. *Stop at 5-6 m for 3-5 minutes before surfacing.*

e. *Use the total dive time to calculate repetitive dives.*

Example 18.

You are planning to do two "no-stop" dives, the first to 20 m followed, three hours later, by a dive to 16 m. Using the suggested safety factors, find the allowable "no-stop" bottom time. (Assume that there are no predisposing factors of bends present)

* Look up the No-Stop Limit for 22 m (i.e. next greater tabled depth increment). The limit is *38* minutes which is the maximum bottom time for the first dive.
* Ascend at 10 m/minute.
* Stop at 5-6 m for 3-5 minutes, say, 3 minutes.
* Total dive time = 38 + 3 + 2 = 43 minutes.
  (bottom)(stop)(ascent)
* Time of first dive still to be accounted for on second dive = 43/2 = approx. 22 minutes.

* Equivalent depth of second dive: Look up 20 m (i.e. the actual depth of the deeper dive). No-Stop Limit for 20 m = 46 minutes.
* Deduct 22 minutes already used up, leaves *24* minutes allowable bottom time for the second dive. Leave the bottom after 24 minutes.
* Ascend at 10 m/minute.
* Stop at 5-6 m for 3-5 minutes.

Example 19.

You are planning to do two "no-stop" dives, the first to 33 m followed, five hours later, by a dive to 30 m. Using the suggested safety factors find the allowable "no-stop" bottom time. (Assume that there are no predisposing factors to bends present)

* Look up the No-Stop Limit for 36 m (i.e. next greater tabled depth increment). Limit = *14* minutes, which is the maximum bottom time for the first dive.
* Ascend at 10 m/minute.
* Stop at 5-6 m for 3-5 minutes.
* Total dive time = 14 + 5 + 3.3 = 23 min. (approx)
  (bottom) (stop) (ascent)
* Time of first dive still to be accounted for on second dive = 23/4 = approx. 6 minutes
* Equivalent depth of second dive: Look up 33 m (i.e. the actual depth of the deeper dive). No-Stop Limit for 33 m = 16 minutes.
* Deduct 6 minutes already used up, leaves *10* minutes. allowable bottom time for the second dive. Leave the bottom after 10 minutes.
* Ascend at 10 m/minute.
* Stop at 5-6 m for 3-5 minutes.

Example 20.

You are planning to do two "no-stop" dives, the first to 15 m followed, five hours later, by a dive to 24 m. Using the suggested safety factors, find the allowable "no-stop" bottom time. (Assume that there are no predisposing factors to bends present)

* Look up the No-Stop Limit for 18 m. It is *57* minutes, which is the maximum bottom time for the first dive.
* Ascend at 10 m/minute.
* Stop at 5-6 m for 3-5 minutes, say, 3 minutes.
* Total dive time = 57 + 3 + 2 = 62 minutes.
  (bottom) (stop) (ascent)
* Time of first dive still to be accounted for on second dive = 62/4 = approx. 16 minutes.
* Equivalent depth of second dive: Look up 24 m (i.e. the actual depth of the deeper dive). No-Stop Limit for 24 m = 32 minutes.
* Deduct 16 minutes already used up, leaves *16* minutes allowable bottom time for the second dive. Leave the bottom after 16 minutes.
* Ascend at 10 m/minute.
* Stop at 5-6 m for 3-5 minutes.

DIVING AT ALTITUDE

The RNPL/BS-AC Table assumes that dives begin at sea-level and that a diver surfaces to an atmospheric pressure of 1 ATA. If diving at altitudes higher than 100 metres above sea-level, unless the reduced atmospheric pressure is taken into account, the risk of bends will be greatly increased. The simple method to compensate for this is to add a depth penalty to the actual depth of the dive. The penalty varies according to the altitude as follows:

Height above sea level in metres	Depth Penalty to be added to measured depth
Less than 100	No depth penalty need be added
100 - 300	One quarter of measured depth
300 - 2,000	One third of measured depth
2,000 - 3,000	One half of measured depth

This procedure is discussed in detail in Chapter 21.

FLYING AFTER DIVING

Flying, even in a pressurized airliner, exposes the diver to reduced atmospheric pressure, which may lead to bends if undertaken too soon after diving.

The advice given with the tables is the following:

After a **No Stop** dive, do not fly for a period of **2 hours.**
After a dive involving **decompression stops** do not fly for a period of **24 hours.**

The validity of this advice is discussed in Chapter 20.

REFERENCES

1. Shaw, D. (1988), "BS-AC Incidents Report 1987". *SPUMS Journal;* 18 (1): 35-37.

OTHER SOURCES

British Sub-Aqua Club (1977), "Diving Manual". Charles Scribner's Sons, London.

British Sub-Aqua Club (1985). "Sport Diving". Stanley Paul, London.

British Sub-Aqua Club (1988). "The Third Dive Table". *NDC Bulletin*; 12.

British Sub-Aqua Club (1986), "Decompression Talkback". *NDC Bulletin*; 7.

British Sub-Aqua Club (1986). "A Paper Computer for Everyone". *NDC Bulletin*; 6.

Busutilli, M., personal communications.

Ellerby, D., (1988). "Guidelines for the Three-A-Day Diver". *Diver*; 33 (4): 28.

Hazzard, J. (1984). "Decompression Table Workbook", 2nd edition. BS-AC, London.

Hazzard, J., personal communications.

Hennessey, T., personal communication.

Twilley, J. (1984), "Decompression-Part 2-The RNPL/BS-AC Tables". *Subaqua Scene*; 55: 36-37.

RECOMMENDED FURTHER READING

Hazzard, J. (1984), "Decompression Table Workbook", 2nd edition. BS-AC, London.

EXERCISES ON THE RNPL/BS-AC TABLE

1. Find the No-Stop Limits for single dives to the following depths:

   (a) 30 m (b) 9 m (c) 23 m (d) 35 m (e) 30.5 m

2. Find the decompression required for the following single or first dives (the times given are bottom times):

   (a) 18 m for 60 min. (b) 15 m for 75 min.
   (c) 19 m for 45 min. (d) 25 m for 40 min.
   (e) 28 m for 30 min. (f) 36 m for 15 min.

3. Find the maximum allowable no-stop bottom time for the following second dives:

   (a) A dive to 20 m, 2$^1/_2$ hours after a dive to 28 m for 26 minutes.

   (b) A dive to 15 m, 3 hours after a dive to 24 m for 25 minutes.

   (c) A dive to 30 m, 5 hours after a dive to 36 m for 12 minutes.

4. Find the decompression required for the following second dives (the times given are bottom times):

   (a) A dive to 33 m for 10 minutes, 1 hour after a dive to 30 m for 20 minutes.

   (b) A dive to 24 m for 30 minutes, 4$^1/_2$ hours after a dive to 26 m for 20 minutes.

(c) A dive to 32 m for 18 minutes., 10 hours after a dive to 42 m for 16 minutes.

(d) A dive to 8 m for 40 minutes, 1½ hours after a dive to 27 m for 20 minutes.

5. Find any decompression stops required for each of the following dives:

(a) Dive 1: 30 m for 10 minutes
Surface interval = 3 hr
Dive 2: 26 m for 20 minutes
Surface interval = 4 hr
Dive 3: 20 m for 10 minutes

(b) Dive 1: 36 m for 5 minutes
Surface interval = 4 hr
Dive 2: 27 m for 10 minutes
Surface interval = 5 hr
Dive 3: 17 m for 12 minutes

(c) Dive 1: 41 m for 5 minutes
Surface interval = 7 hr
Dive 2: 30 m for 10 minutes
Surface interval = 5 hr
Dive 3: 10 m for 10 minutes

(d) Dive 1: 33 m for 12 minutes
Surface interval = 3 hr
Dive 2: 25 m for 10 minutes
Surface interval = 7 hr
Dive 3: 22 m for 32 minutes
Surface interval = 5 hr
Dive 4: 16 m for 32 minutes

(e) Dive 1: 18 m for 10 minutes
Surface interval = 3 hr
Dive 2: 42 m for 8 minutes
Surface interval = 10 hr
Dive 3: 30 m for 5 minutes

6. Find the maximum allowable no-stop bottom times for each dive in the following pairs of dives:

(a) A dive to 28 m followed 2 hours later by a dive to 20 m.

(b) A dive to 34 m followed 4½ hours later by a dive to 31 m.

(c) A dive to 17 m followed 2½ hours later by another dive to 17 m.

(d) A dive to 16 m followed 3 hours later by a dive to 20 m.

(e) A dive to 41 m followed 6½ hours later by a dive to 12 m.

7. Find any decompression stops required for the second dive and the maximum no-stop bottom time limit for the third dive in the following dive sequences:

   (a) Dive 1: 24 m for 20 minutes
   Surface interval = 5 hr
   Dive 2: 20 m for 10 minutes
   Surface interval = 3 hr
   Dive 3: 18 m

   (b) Dive 1: 20 m for 25 minutes
   Surface interval = 3 hr
   Dive 2: 21 m for 20 minutes
   Surface interval = 3 hr
   Dive 3: 9 m (You wish to dive again after a further surface interval of 13 hours)

8. By adding the suggested safety factors (i.e. taking the NDL for the next greater tabled depth for the initial dive, ascending at 10/minute, doing a safety stop(s) and using total dive time for repetitive dives), calculate the maximum allowable no-stop bottom times for the dives in Question 6. Assume no predisposing factors to bends are present.

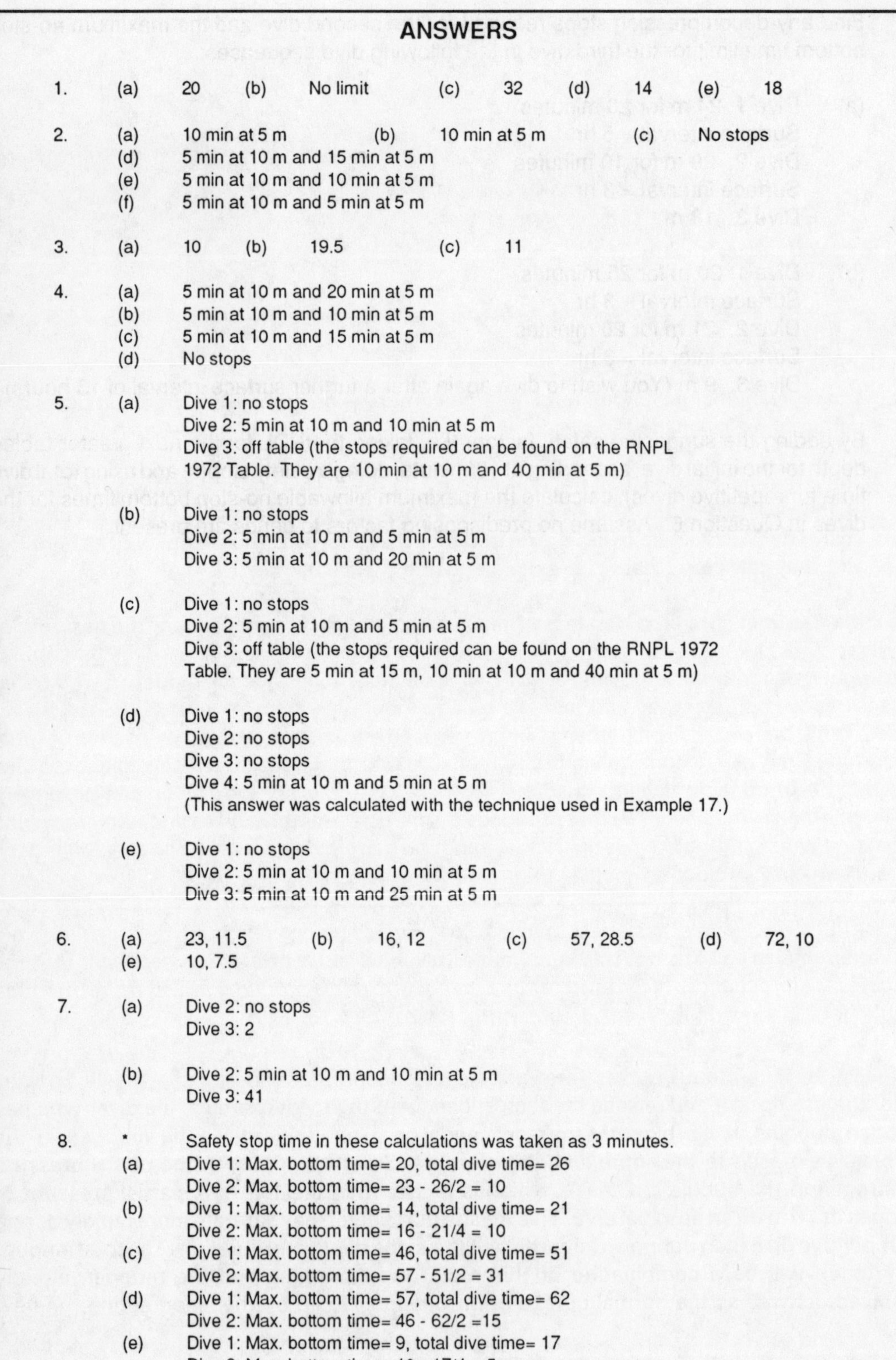

ANSWERS

1. (a) 20 (b) No limit (c) 32 (d) 14 (e) 18

2. (a) 10 min at 5 m (b) 10 min at 5 m (c) No stops
(d) 5 min at 10 m and 15 min at 5 m
(e) 5 min at 10 m and 10 min at 5 m
(f) 5 min at 10 m and 5 min at 5 m

3. (a) 10 (b) 19.5 (c) 11

4. (a) 5 min at 10 m and 20 min at 5 m
(b) 5 min at 10 m and 10 min at 5 m
(c) 5 min at 10 m and 15 min at 5 m
(d) No stops

5. (a) Dive 1: no stops
Dive 2: 5 min at 10 m and 10 min at 5 m
Dive 3: off table (the stops required can be found on the RNPL 1972 Table. They are 10 min at 10 m and 40 min at 5 m)

(b) Dive 1: no stops
Dive 2: 5 min at 10 m and 5 min at 5 m
Dive 3: 5 min at 10 m and 20 min at 5 m

(c) Dive 1: no stops
Dive 2: 5 min at 10 m and 5 min at 5 m
Dive 3: off table (the stops required can be found on the RNPL 1972 Table. They are 5 min at 15 m, 10 min at 10 m and 40 min at 5 m)

(d) Dive 1: no stops
Dive 2: no stops
Dive 3: no stops
Dive 4: 5 min at 10 m and 5 min at 5 m
(This answer was calculated with the technique used in Example 17.)

(e) Dive 1: no stops
Dive 2: 5 min at 10 m and 10 min at 5 m
Dive 3: 5 min at 10 m and 25 min at 5 m

6. (a) 23, 11.5 (b) 16, 12 (c) 57, 28.5 (d) 72, 10
(e) 10, 7.5

7. (a) Dive 2: no stops
Dive 3: 2

(b) Dive 2: 5 min at 10 m and 10 min at 5 m
Dive 3: 41

8. * Safety stop time in these calculations was taken as 3 minutes.
(a) Dive 1: Max. bottom time= 20, total dive time= 26
Dive 2: Max. bottom time= 23 - 26/2 = 10
(b) Dive 1: Max. bottom time= 14, total dive time= 21
Dive 2: Max. bottom time= 16 - 21/4 = 10
(c) Dive 1: Max. bottom time= 46, total dive time= 51
Dive 2: Max. bottom time= 57 - 51/2 = 31
(d) Dive 1: Max. bottom time= 57, total dive time= 62
Dive 2: Max. bottom time= 46 - 62/2 =15
(e) Dive 1: Max. bottom time= 9, total dive time= 17
Dive 2: Max. bottom time= 10 - 17/4 = 5

18.2 The BS-AC '88 Tables

Note:

The BS-AC '88 Tables are only available in a metric version so the following discussion and examples will generally be confined to metric measurement.

BACKGROUND

A number of factors influenced the BS-AC's decision to replace the RNPL/BS-AC Table. Some of these are:

1. The high level of misunderstanding of decompression procedures amongst users and potential users of the table, and

2. The inherent inflexibility of the table itself. The BS-AC recognized that with the advent of the dive computer, the RNPL/BS-AC Table has become more unattractive to the user. The Club wished to have a set of tables that approach the versitility of a computer and that can comfortably co-exist alongside the computer.

The table designer, Dr. Tom Hennessy, has worked alongside Hempleman, the designer of the original RNPL model, for many years. Hennessy initially decided to base the new tables on the same decompression model as the RNPL/BS-AC Table since the model on which that table is based had been tried and tested over a number of years. However, since the RNPL/BS-AC Table has not really had the facility to be used and, hence, tested over series of three or four dives per day, Hennessy had to first ensure that the model could be safely extended to cover these multiple diving situations. He believes that very long dives can produce a similar gas load in the tissues to that produced by multiple repetitive dives and, after receiving some data which indicated that the model might be marginal when used for very long, deep dives, Hennessy decided to modify the model slightly.

The RNPL/BS-AC Table assumes that it is safe to ascend directly to the surface from saturation at 9 m (30 ft), but this is no longer believed to be true. *It now appears that the depth a safe direct ascent from saturation can occur from is around 7 m (23 ft), rather than 9 m.** This ascent criterion is included in the BS-AC '88 Tables.

Hennessy believes that bubbles form after every decompression and that these bubbles affect the gas uptake and release for each subsequent dive. For example, if a diver who has nitrogen bubbles in his blood/tissues descends on a repetitive dive, the nitrogen in the bubbles is exposed to the entire ambient pressure. So at 10 m (33 ft), the partial pressure of nitrogen in the bubble is 2 ATA, which is higher than the 1.6 ATA partial pressure of nitrogen at 10 m on an an initial dive. This means that a diver may saturate more rapidly during the repetitive dive than during an initial dive of the same depth and duration. The total amount of nitrogen will be a combination of this redissolved nitrogen and the nitrogen already dissolved, as well as the normal uptake of nitrogen delivered by the blood during the new

* However, there have been reports of divers suffering from decompression sickness after single dives of 5-6 m.

dive. The gas in the bubbles does not redissolve as soon as it is recompressed. It takes a certain depth and time before the gas will redissolve completely, and, only then will the tissue revert to its normal state where uptake and elimination can be described by the model used for the first dive. Hence, the rates of gas uptake and elimination will alter from dive to dive and it becomes necessary to treat the second and subsequent dives quite differently to the first when trying to predict safe decompression.

Most decompression models assume that gas uptake and elimination occur at the same rate during any dive and the models assume that this rate is the same on a repetitive dive as it is on a single dive. This may be acceptable if significant bubbling has not occurred within the blood and tissues, but, if bubbles are present they will slow down off-gassing and the rates may differ. The original RNPL model assumes that off-gassing is at 2/3 the rate of uptake, and these new tables also assume an assymmetry in the rate of gas uptake and elimination. Hennessy set out to design a set of tables which become progressively more conservative as the number of dives, depth and duration increases.

The U.S. Navy Tables depict the amount of nitrogen in a diver by a single letter code, the Repetitive Group Designator, which is supposed to represent the nitrogen level in the 120-minute theoretical tissue compartment. The system assumes that, after a surface interval of ten minutes, this tissue compartment has the highest nitrogen load and, therefore, controls the decompression. The code is then used to determine the amount of residual nitrogen still remaining in this theoretical tissue (and, therefore, in our entire body) before a repetitive dive, and the original single dive model is used to predict the decompression for the repetitive dive. In reality, it has been shown that on a typical "deepish" dive, seven or eight different absorption rates may play a part in controlling the decompression. The U.S. Navy's approach also assumes that dives which give the same code can be treated identically, whether a short, deep dive or a long, shallow one. It assumes that because the amount of nitrogen that is theoretically dissolved in this one tissue compartment is the same, the dives can be treated equivalently. Unfortunately, our bodies do not work quite so simply. What is not accounted for is that the distribution of the gas load between the various tissues may be quite different in each of the cases, so simply adding some residual nitrogen to the level in one theoretical tissue is often not sufficient.

To avoid using a single dive model to predict repetitive dives, Hennessy has created a number of different tables to be used for different dives. In all, the BS-AC '88 Tables consist of a set of seven separate tables, labelled Table A to Table G.

The first table, Table A, is used for the initial dive. After the dive the diver surfaces with a letter code (the Surfacing Code) which relates to the depth and time of the dive. Following a surface interval, the diver selects a new code (the Current Tissue Code) which relates to the nitrogen load in the tissues after the surface interval, and enters a new table (rather than the original table) which bears the same letter code. The minimum surface interval required to gain credit for off-gassing is 15 minutes, rather than the two hours used in the RNPL/BS-AC Table.

The new tables utilize depth increments of 3 m, rather than 2 m and, instead of giving bottom times, give the time from leaving the surface until arriving at 6 m during the ascent, or at 9 m on dives requiring a 9 m stop. The tables use initial No-Stop Times that are more conservative than those on the RNPL/BS-AC Table.

The BS-AC have not recommended a reduction in the15 m/minute ascent rate and have not included a safety stop after all "no-stop" dives, as is done on various other tables. Instead, the BS-AC '88 Tables require that the ascent to 6 m is at a maximum rate of 15 m/minute (which means that it may be slower than 15 m/minute!), and the ascent from 6 m to the surface must take one minute (which means a rate of 6 m/minute).

Decompression stops are done at 9 m, 6 m *and at the surface*. It is stressed that a surface interval should in essence be treated as a decompression stop and a diver's activities should be modified accordingly. No 3 m stops are given as they are too difficult to do successfully when there is wave action. Decompression times increase in increments of one minute, rather than five minutes as in the RNPL/BS-AC Table. The maximum decompression given is 22 minutes.

The BS-AC '88 Tables are presented in a compact, easy-to-read format *and do not require any calculations at all.* Tables A to G are supplied in a non-submersible but water resistant format, and Tables A, B and C are also printed, in an abreviated form, on a submersible card which should be carried by the diver and used in the event of a memory lapse or a change of dive plan. Presumably Tables D to G are not included on the card due to the very restricted No-Stop Dive Times available to a diver with Current Tissue Codes of D to G.

The tables in their current form are presently untested but appear to be conservative when used for *no-stop dives.*

COMPARING THE BS-AC '88 TABLES TO SOME OTHER TABLES

When the BS-AC '88 Tables are compared to tables such as the U.S. Navy Tables, the Buehlmann (1986) Tables and the DCIEM Tables some trends appear to emerge. These are:

* The tables appear to be conservative for both single and multiple no-stop dives, with the initial No-Stop Limits comparable with those of the Buehlmann (1986) and DCIEM Tables.

* For single/initial dives requiring stops, the decompression given is often, but not always, more conservative than that given by the U.S. Navy Tables, **but is often less conservative than that suggested by the Buehlmann (1986) and DCIEM Tables.**

* For repetitive dives requiring stops, the decompression given by the BS-AC '88 Tables is more conservative than that given by the U.S. Navy Tables, and often comparable to that given by the Buehlmann (1986) and DCIEM Tables.

These trends are demonstrated in Tables 18.2.1, 18.2.2 and 18.2.3 and Figure 18.2.1.

Promoters of the BS-AC '88 Tables argue that even though the Total Decompression Time (TDT) given by these tables is sometimes shorter than that given by some other tables, the risk of decompression sickness is not only dependent on TDT. A longer decompression profile is not necessarily a safer one as other factors (procedural parameters) also affect the risk of bends. Some of these parameters are the ascent rate, the depth and duration of the initial stop, the ease of maintaining the depth of the required stops, the surface interval required before diving again (or flying) and the activities during the surface interval.

If one compares the ascent procedure suggested by the BS-AC '88 Tables to that given by the U.S. Navy Tables, there are a number of differences which include:- a slower ascent rate to 6 m, a longer stay at 6 m, a slower ascent rate from 6 m to the surface (although sometimes a shorter ascent time) and a longer stay at the surface before diving again. Although these comparisons are valid for the U.S. Navy Tables, they do not necessarily apply to other tables. When the BS-AC '88 Tables are compared to the Buehlmann (1986) and DCIEM Tables, especially for first/single dives, the BS-AC Tables often appear less conservative, not only with TDT but also with respect to some of the procedural parameters previously mentioned. Careful examination of Figure 18.2.1 will indicate this trend. Hennessy argues that the Buehlmann and DCIEM Tables are often overly conservative, but this is debatable. Although commercial divers may need to minimize decompression time for the sake of efficiency, a recreational diver who decides to conduct a dive involving mandatory stops and who has planned the dive properly should have no reason not to use a conservative table to gain any extra security that it may provide.

The U.S. Navy Tables, Buehlmann (1986) Tables and DCIEM Tables have been used for comparison with the BS-AC '88 Tables as they have all had a considerable amount of testing and/or usage. Although the basic model on which the BS-AC '88 Tables are based was tested and was used extensively, ***the BS-AC '88 Tables are untested in their current form***.

The BS-AC considered mounting a series of trials using recreational divers but it was decided that, since the bends incidence was expected to be low, unless a very large number of trials were conducted the results would not be statistically conclusive. The practical and financial constraints of a large test series proved prohibitive so, instead, a 4-month period of informal open-sea dives were conducted by a number of BS-AC members before the tables were released. No details of the profiles conducted and the number of dives have been released, but no cases of bends were reported during the period.

Although essentially untested, the BS-AC '88 Tables appear to be quite conservative for no-stop dives and should generally (but obviously not always) be reasonably safe for such dives. *However, divers who plan to use the BS-AC '88 Tables for dives requiring mandatory decompression stops are urged to do so very cautiously and conservatively as the tables are sometimes less conservative in this area than some well-tested tables. Extensive testing needs to be done before the safety of these tables when used for dives involving mandatory stops is determined.*

A 1990 BS-AC report states that, in 1989 after the first full season of usage, there were 41 divers who developed bends after diving according to the BS-AC '88 Tables. Eleven of the divers had misused the tables, 22 had dived within the tables and in the other eight cases there was insufficient information to determine whether the tables had been used correctly. The BS-AC estimate that possibly a million dives could have been conducted using the tables, which would yield an incident rate better than 1 in 10,000.[1] No information is currently available about how many of the bends cases occurred on dives involving mandatory stops and the number that occurred after no-stop dives.[2]

TABLE 18.2.1

Comparison of various schedules

Notes:

- times are in minutes unless otherwise specified
- No-stop bottom time limits for the BS-AC '88 Tables are approximate
- the ascent rate used by the U.S. Navy Tables is 18 m (60 ft)/minute
- the ascent rate used by the Buehlmann Tables is 10 m (33 ft)/minute
- the ascent rate used by the DCIEM Tables is 15 m (50 ft)/minute

Dive 1

Max. depth = 27 m (90 ft) Actual Bottom time = 20

	BS-AC '88	U.S. Navy	Buehlmann	DCIEM
No-Stop Limit (*Bottom* time)	22.5	30	20	20
Stops required	-	-	-	-

Surface Interval = 2 hr

Dive 2

Max. depth = 24 m (80 ft) Actual Bottom time = 15

	BS-AC '88	U.S. Navy	Buehlmann	DCIEM
No-Stop Limit (*Bottom* time)	6.5	22	14	16
Stops required	3 min at 6 m	-	4 min at 3 m	-

Surface Interval = 4 hr

Dive 3

Max. depth = 18 m (60 ft) Actual Bottom time = 40

	BS-AC '88	U.S. Navy	Buehlmann	DCIEM
No-Stop Limit (*Bottom* time)	31	43	37	35
Stops required	1 min at 6 m	-	11 min at 3 m	5 min at 3 m

TABLE 18.2.2

Comparison of various schedules

Dive 1

Max. depth = 36 m (120 ft) Actual Bottom time = 12

	BS-AC '88	U.S. Navy	Buehlmann	DCIEM
No-Stop Limit (*Bottom* time)	12	15	12	10
Stops required	-	-	-	5 min at 3 m

Surface Interval = 1½ hr

Dive 2

Max. depth = 30 m (100 ft) Actual Bottom time = 14

	BS-AC '88	U.S. Navy	Buehlmann	DCIEM
No-Stop Limit (*Bottom* time)	No time available	11	8	10
Stops required	3 min at 6 m	3 min at 3 m	5 min at 3 m	10 min at 3 m

Surface Interval = 8 hr

Dive 3

Max. depth = 27 m (90 ft) Actual Bottom time = 20

	BS-AC '88	U.S. Navy	Buehlmann	DCIEM
No-Stop Limit (*Bottom* time)	13½	23	20	14
Stops required	1 min at 6 m	-	-	10 min at 3 m

TABLE 18.2.3

Comparison of various schedules

Dive 1				
Max. depth =	33 m (110 ft)	Actual Bottom time = 25		
	BS-AC '88	**U.S. Navy**	**Buehlmann**	**DCIEM**
No-Stop Limit (*Bottom* time)	15	20	14	12
Stops required	3 min at 6 m	3 min at 3 m	2 min at 6 m and 7 min at 3 m	10 min at 6 m and 10 min at 3 m
Surface Interval = 2 hr				
Dive 2				
Max. depth =	21 m (70 ft)	Actual Bottom time = 18		
	BS-AC '88	**U.S. Navy**	**Buehlmann**	**DCIEM**
No-Stop Limit (*Bottom* time)	9	24	23	18
Stops required	1 min at 6 m	-	-	-

TABLE 18.2.4

Comparison of No-Stop Limits (Bottom Times)

Depth ft	Depth m	BS-AC '88	RNPL/BS-AC	Buehlmann	DCIEM	U.S. Navy
30	9	242	-	400	300	-
40	12	121	137	125	150	200
50	15	73	72	75	75	100
60	18	50	57	51	50	60
70	21	36	38	35	35	50
80	24	28	30	25	25	40
90	27	22	23	20	20	30
100	30	18	20	17	15	25
110	33	15	16	14	12	20
120	36	12	14	12	10	15
130	39	10	11	10	8	10
140	42	9	10	9	7	10

FIGURE 18.2.1

A comparison of the decompression profiles given by various tables for a dive to 36 m (120 ft) for a bottom time of 30 minutes.

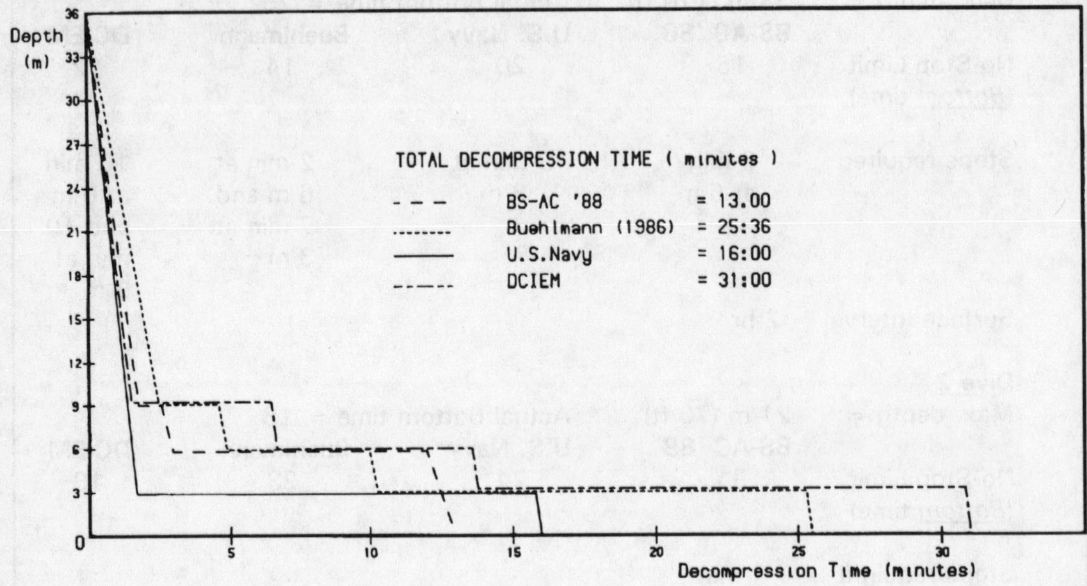

THE TABLES

Tables A, B, C and G are reprinted with permission from the British Sub-Aqua Club and Dr. Tom Hennessy. **The BS-AC '88 Tables are protected by Copyright and the unauthorized copying and reproducing of any part of these tables is expressly forbidden.**

TABLE 18.2.5 (TABLE A)

TABLE A

SURFACE INTERVAL TABLE

LAST DIVE CODE	Minutes 15	30	60	90	Hours 2	3	4	6	10	12	14	15	16
A					A								

DEPTH (metres)	ASCENT (mins)	DIVE TIME (minutes) No-Stop Dives						Decompression Stop Dives							
3	(1)	–	166	∞											
6	(1)	–	36	166	593	∞									
9	1	–	17	67	167	203	243	311	328	336	348	356	363	370	376
12	1	–	10	37	87	104	122	156	169	177	183	188	192	197	201
15	1	–	6	24	54	64	74	98	109	116	121	125	129	133	136
18	1		–	17	37	44	51	68	78	84	88	92	95	98	101
DECOMPRESSION STOP (minutes) at **6 metres**								1	3	6	9	12	15	18	21
SURFACING CODE			**B**	**C**	**D**	**E**	**F**	**G**	**G**	**G**	**G**	**G**	**G**	**G**	**G**

DEPTH (metres)	ASCENT (mins)													
21	1	–	13	28	32	37	51	59	65	68	72	75	77
24	2	–	11	22	26	30	41	49	53	56	59	62	64
27	2	–	8	18	21	24	34	41	45	47	50	52	55
30	2	–	7	15	17	20	29	35	39	41	43	45	47
33	2		–	13	15	17	25	30	34	36	38	40	42
36	2		–	11	12	14	22	27	30	32	34	36	37
39	3		–	10	12	13	20	25	29	30	32	33	35
DECOMPRESSION STOPS (minutes) at **9 metres**									1	1	1	1	2
at **6 metres**							1	3	6	9	12	15	18
SURFACING CODE		*B*	**C**	**D**	**E**	**F**	**G**	**G**	**G**	**G**	**G**	**G**	**G**

DEPTH (metres)	ASCENT (mins)												
42	3		–	9	10	12	21	23	26	28	29	31	32
45	3		–	8	9	10	19	22	24	26	27	28	30
48	3			–	8	9	18	21	23	24	25	26	28
51	3				–	8	17	19	21	22	24	25	26
DECOMPRESSION STOPS (minutes) at **9 metres**								1	1	1	2	2	3
at **6 metres**							2	3	6	9	12	15	18
SURFACING CODE		*B*	*C*	**D**	**E**	**F**	**G**	**G**	**G**	**G**	**G**	**G**	**G**

ASCENT RATE – 15 metres per minute. Take 1 minute from 6m to surface.

DIVE TIME – time from leaving surface to arriving at 6m on return to surface, or arrival at 9m on 2 Stop dives.

TABLE 18.2.6 (TABLE B)

TABLE B

SURFACE INTERVAL TABLE

LAST DIVE CODE	Minutes 15	30	60	90	Hours 2	3	4	6	10	12	14	15	16
B	B (up to 10 hours)									A			

DIVE TIME (minutes)

DEPTH (metres)	ASCENT (mins)	No-Stop Dives					Decompression Stop Dives							
3	(1)	–	∞											
6	(1)	–	80	504	∞									
9	1	–	27	113	148	188	255	282	284	292	300	307	314	321
12	1	–	14	52	67	84	116	129	137	143	148	152	156	160
15	1	–	8	31	40	48	69	78	86	90	94	98	101	105
18	1		–	21	27	32	47	55	61	64	68	71	74	76
DECOMPRESSION STOP (minutes) at **6 metres**							1	3	6	9	12	15	18	21
SURFACING CODE		*B*	**C**	**D**	**E**	**F**	**G**	**G**	**G**	**G**	**G**	**G**	**G**	**G**

DEPTH (metres)	ASCENT (mins)												
21	1		–	15	19	23	35	42	47	50	52	55	57
24	2		–	12	15	19	28	35	39	41	43	45	47
27	2		–	10	12	15	23	29	33	35	36	38	40
30	2		–	8	10	12	20	25	28	30	32	33	35
33	2			–	8	10	17	22	25	26	28	29	31
36	2			–	7	8	15	20	22	24	25	26	28
39	3			–	–	8	14	19	21	23	24	25	26
DECOMPRESSION STOPS (minutes) at **9 metres**									1	1	1	1	2
at **6 metres**							1	3	6	9	12	15	18
SURFACING CODE		*B*	*C*	**D**	**E**	**F**	**G**	**G**	**G**	**G**	**G**	**G**	**G**

DEPTH (metres)	ASCENT (mins)												
42	3					–	15	17	20	21	22	23	24
45	3					–	14	17	18	19	20	21	22
48	3					–	13	16	17	18	19	20	21
51	3					–	12	15	16	17	18	19	
DECOMPRESSION STOPS (minutes) at **9 metres**								1	1	1	2	2	3
at **6 metres**							2	3	6	9	12	15	18
SURFACING CODE		*B*	*C*	*D*	*E*	*F*	**G**	**G**	**G**	**G**	**G**	**G**	**G**

ASCENT RATE – 15 metres per minute. Take 1 minute from 6m to surface.

DIVE TIME – time from leaving surface to arriving at 6m on return to surface, or arrival at 9m on 2 Stop dives.

TABLE 18.2.7 (TABLE C)

TABLE C

SURFACE INTERVAL TABLE

LAST DIVE CODE	Minutes 15	30	60	90	Hours 2	3	4	6	10	12	14	15	16
C	C				B					A			

DEPTH (metres)	ASCENT (mins)	DIVE TIME (minutes) No-Stop Dives					Decompression Stop Dives							
3	(1)	–	∞											
6	(1)		–	359	∞									
9	1		–	49	79	116	182	199	211	220	227	234	241	248
12	1		–	20	31	44	71	83	90	95	100	104	108	112
15	1		–	11	17	24	40	48	54	57	61	64	67	70
18	1		–	7	11	15	27	34	38	40	43	45	47	50
DECOMPRESSION STOP (minutes) at **6 metres**							1	3	6	9	12	15	18	21
SURFACING CODE		*B*	**C**	**D**	**E**	**F**	**G**	**G**	**G**	**G**	**G**	**G**	**G**	**G**

DEPTH (metres)	ASCENT (mins)												
21	1			–	7	10	20	26	29	31	33	35	37
24	2				–	8	16	22	25	26	28	29	31
27	2					–	13	18	21	22	24	25	26
30	2					–	11	16	18	19	20	22	23
33	2					–	10	14	16	17	18	19	20
36	2					–	8	12	14	15	16	17	18
39	3					–	8	12	14	15	16	17	18
DECOMPRESSION STOPS (minutes) at **9 metres**									1	1	1	1	2
at **6 metres**							1	3	6	9	12	15	18
SURFACING CODE		*B*	*C*	*D*	**E**	**F**	**G**	**G**	**G**	**G**	**G**	**G**	**G**

DEPTH (metres)	ASCENT (mins)												
42	3					–	10	●	13	14	15	16	
45	3					–	9	●	12	●	14	●	15
48	3					–	8	●	12	●	13	14	
51	3					–	8	10	11	12	●	13	
DECOMPRESSION STOPS (minutes) at **9 metres**								1	1	1	2	2	3
at **6 metres**							2	3	6	9	12	15	18
SURFACING CODE		*B*	*C*	*D*	*E*	*F*	**G**	**G**	**G**	**G**	**G**	**G**	**G**

ASCENT RATE – 15 metres per minute. Take 1 minute from 6m to surface.
DIVE TIME – time from leaving surface to arriving at 6m on return to surface, or arrival at 9m on 2 Stop dives.

The Symbol ● indicates that the user should move to the next column on the right, i.e. the next decompression time.

TABLE 18.2.8 (TABLE G)

TABLE G

SURFACE INTERVAL TABLE

LAST DIVE CODE	0–15 min	15–30 min	30–60 min	60–90 min	90 min–4 hours	4–16 hours	16 hours
G	G	F	E	D	C	B	A

DIVE TIME (minutes)

DEPTH (metres)	ASCENT (mins)	No-Stop Dives					Decompression Stop Dives							
3	(1)		∞	332	45	19								
6	(1)				∞	484								
9	1							–	9	12	16	19	23	27
12	1									–	6	7	8	10
15	1												–	6
DECOMPRESSION STOP (minutes) at **6 metres**							1	3	6	9	12	15	18	21
SURFACING CODE		*B*	**C**	**D**	**E**	**F**	*G*	**G**	**G**	**G**	**G**	**G**	**G**	**G**

ASCENT RATE – 15 metres per minute. Take 1 minute from 6m to surface.

DIVE TIME – time from leaving surface to arriving at 6m on return to surface, or arrival at 9m on 2 Stop dives.

This combined SURFACE INTERVAL TABLE will assist dive planning. Any benefit to be gained by reducing the DIVE TIME can be seen as a reduced SURFACE INTERVAL before the next dive.

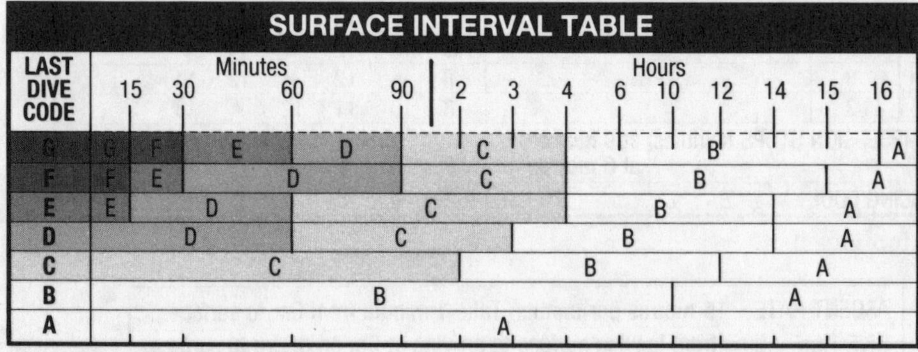

SURFACE INTERVAL TABLE

LAST DIVE CODE	Surface interval (Minutes: 15, 30, 60, 90; Hours: 2, 3, 4, 6, 10, 12, 14, 15, 16)
G	G (to 15 min), F (15–30 min), E (30–60 min), D (60–90 min), C (90 min–4 h), B (4–16 h), A (16 h)
F	F (to 15 min), E (15–30 min), D (30–90 min), C (90 min–4 h), B (4–15 h), A (15 h)
E	E (to 15 min), D (15–60 min), C (60 min–4 h), B (4–14 h), A (14 h)
D	D (to 60 min), C (60 min–3 h), B (3–14 h), A (14 h)
C	C (to 2 h), B (2–12 h), A (12 h)
B	B (to 10 h), A (10 h)
A	A

USING THE BS-AC '88 TABLES

SINGLE/FIRST DIVES

A single or first dive is any dive planned when the Current Tissue Code is A. Code A represents a diver in a saturation state of zero. If a diver has not dived for 16 hours he is considered to have zero saturation and may dive on Table A.

Example 1

What is the maximum No-Stop Dive Time for a single/first dive to 24 m?

Enter Table A, from the left, at 24 m. Move to the right along the row until reaching the last (rightmost) number in the No-Stop Dives column (column 3). The number is 30, which means that the diver has a maximum of *30* minutes from the beginning of his descent until reaching 6 m during his ascent towards the surface. The ascent rate from the bottom to 6 m must not exceed 15 m/minute, and it must take one minute to ascend from 6 m to the surface (an ascent rate of 6 m/minute).

To find the Surfacing Code at the end of the dive, move down the column containing 30 minutes until intersecting the Surfacing Code row. The Surfacing Code after this dive would be *F*.

Example 2

What is the maximum No-Stop Dive Time for a single/first dive to 36 m (120 ft)?

Enter Table A, from the left, at 36 m. Move to the right along the row until reaching the last (rightmost) number in the No-Stop Dives column (column 3). The number is 14 which means that the diver has a maximum of *14* minutes from the beginning of his descent until reaching 6 m during his ascent towards the surface. The ascent rate from the bottom to 6 m must not exceed 15 m/minute so the ascent must commence when no more than 12 minutes of bottom time has elapsed. It must take one minute to ascend from 6 m to the surface.

To find the Surfacing Code at the end of the dive, move down the column containing 14 minutes until intersecting the Surfacing Code row. The Surfacing Code after this dive would be *F*.

Example 3

What decompression is required after a single/first dive to 18 m (60 ft) for a dive time of 60 minutes? (Note that dive time is defined as the time from beginning the descent to arriving at 6 m on return to the surface, or arrival at 9 m on two-stop dives)

Enter Table A, from the left, at 18 m, and move to the right across this row until finding the exact, or next longer, tabled bottom time. In this case 60 minutes is not tabled so select 68 minutes. As this time is beyond the maximum No-Stop Time of 51 minutes, at least one stop is required and can be found by moving down the column containing 68 minutes until intersecting the Decompression Stop row (deep yellow row). The number "1" in the 6 m row means that a stop of *1 minute at 6 m* is required before ascending to the surface at a rate of 6 m/minute.

Notes:

- The dive time of 60 minutes begins when the diver leaves the surface at the start of the dive, and ends when he reaches 6 m to begin the stop.
- The ascent from the bottom to 6 m must be at a rate no faster than 15 m/minute.
- The entire one minute of decompression stop time is spent at 6 m.
- The diver must take one minute to ascend to the surface from the 6 m stop.
- If a decompression stop is required after a dive to 18 m or shallower, it will be a single stop at 6 m. Dives deeper than 18 m may require an additional stop at 9 m.

Example 4

What decompression is required after a single/first dive to 39 m for a dive time of 30 minutes?

Enter Table A at 39 m, and move along the 39 m row until finding the exact, or next longer, tabled dive time. 30 minutes is tabled, so move across to the 30-minute column (which is in the pale yellow section for Decompression Stop Dives), and then move down the column until intersecting the Decompression Stop rows (bright yellow). The required stops are *1 minute at 9 m* followed by *9 minutes at 6 m.* The Surfacing Code at the end of the dive is *G*.

Notes:

- The maximum bottom time of the dive is 30 - 2 = 28 minutes (i.e. ascent to 9 m stop must take at least 2 minutes).
- The 9 m stop begins on reaching 9 m, and ends on leaving 9 m.
- Ascent from 9 m to 6 m must take at least 12 seconds (i.e. at 15 m/minute maximum).
- The 6 m stop begins on reaching 6 m, and ends on leaving 6 m.
- Ascent from 6 m to the surface must take 1 minute (i.e. at a rate of 6 m/minute).
- The diver should rest on the surface and should remain thermally comfortable and well-hydrated (with non-alcoholic fluids).

REPETITIVE OR MULTIPLE DIVES

A repetitive or multiple dive is defined as any dive planned when the Current Tissue Code is higher than A (e.g. B, C etc.). The higher code is designed to account for excess nitrogen still remaining in a diver's tissues as a result of a previous dive(s).

Finding the Current Tissue Code after a surface interval

Example 5

If the Surfacing Code immediately after a dive is C, what is the Current Tissue Code after a surface interval of 2 hours?

This may be done in either of two ways:

Method 1:

Turn to Table C, enter the Surface Interval Table (at the top of Table C) from the left, and move across to the right to 2 hours. After a surface interval of 2 hours the Current Tissue Code becomes *B** so Table B can be used to plan the next dive.

Method 2:

A combined Surface Interval Table is given below Table G. This table can be used in a similar manner to above. Enter the table, from the left, at C, and move to the right along this row until directly under the 2-hour mark, which is at the top of the table. Again after a 2-hour interval, the Current Tissue Code is *B*.

Example 6

If the Surfacing Code immediately after a dive is D, what surface interval is required before the Current Tissue Code is once again A?

Either:

(i) Enter the Surface Interval Table at the top of Table D, from the left, move to the right to the beginning of the section for A. This corresponds to a surface interval of 14 hours.

or

(ii) Enter the extended Surface Interval Table below Table G, from the left at D. Move along the row to the right, until reaching the section for A. Looking directly above the border line between A and B, you will find that the line corresponds to a surface interval of 14 hours.

* B begins at and includes 2 hours and ends at but does not include 12 hours.

Planning Multiple No-Stop dives

Example 7

You are planning two no-stop dives. The first dive is to 30 m, followed, 3 hours later, by a dive to 22 m. Find the maximum allowable dive time for each dive?

Enter Table A, from the left, at the maximum depth of the initial dive, in this case 30 m. Move to the right along the 30 m row until reaching the last (rightmost) time in the section for No-Stop Dives. Hence, the maximum dive time for a no-stop dive is *20* minutes, which means that the diver must begin to ascend after approximately 18 minutes in order to arrive at 6 m on schedule. Move down the column containing the 20 minutes until intersecting the Surfacing Code row. The Surfacing Code is *F*.

To plan the second dive, turn to Table F and enter the Surface Interval Table from the left (or enter the general Surface Interval Table below Table G). Move to the right to find 3 hours, and then look down to find the Current Tissue Code after 3 hours. It is *C*. Enter Table C at the maximum depth of the repetitive dive. In this case 22 m is not tabled, so enter at the 24 m row and move across to the right to determine the No-Stop Dive Time. It is *8* minutes, and the Surfacing Code after the dive would be *F*.

Example 8

You are planning two no-stop dives. The first is to 36 m followed 4 hours later by a dive to 33 m. Find the maximum allowable dive time for each dive.

Enter Table A at 36 m and move along this row to the last figure in the section for No-Stop Dives. Hence, the maximum dive time for a no-stop dive is *14* minutes (i.e. 12 minutes of bottom time and 2 minutes of ascent to 6 m). Move down the column to find the Surfacing Code, which is *F*.

Enter the Surface Interval Table of Table F (or enter the general Surface Interval Table below Table G), and move to the 4-hour line to find the Current Tissue Code after the interval. It is *B*. Enter Table B at 33 m and move right to the last time in the No-Stop Dives section, which is *10* minutes. The Surfacing Code after the dive is *F*.

Example 9

You are planning three no-stop dives. The first dive, which is to 24 m, is followed, 2 hours later, by a dive to 20 m, which is followed, 3 hours later, by a final dive to 15 m. Find the maximum allowable No-Stop Dive Time for each dive.

Enter Table A at 24 m to find the No-Stop Dive Time for the first dive. It is *30* minutes, and the Surfacing Code is *F*.

Turn to Table F and enter the Surface Interval Table (or enter the general Surface Interval Table below Table G) to find the Current Tissue Code after 2 hours. It is *C*. Enter Table C at 21 m (as 20 m is not tabled). The maximum No-Stop Dive Time for the second dive is *10* minutes, and the Surfacing Code after the dive is again *F*.

Enter the Surface Interval Table of Table F to determine the Current Tissue Code after an interval of 3 hours. It is *C*. Turn to Table C and enter at 15 m. The maximum No-Stop Dive Time is, therefore, *24* minutes, and the Surfacing Code at the end of the dive is *F*.

Planning multiple dives involving decompression stops

Example 10

> *You are planning two dives which may require decompression stops. The first dive is to 27 m for a dive time of 35 minutes. The second dive, 3 hours later, is to 19 m for a dive time of 35 minutes. Calculate the required decompression.*

Enter Table A at 27 m and move right along the row to 41 minutes (the next longer tabled dive time since 35 minutes is not tabled). Move down the column to the Decompression Stops row to determine the required stop(s). A stop of *3 minutes at 6 m* is required, and the Surfacing Code is *G*.

Enter the Surface Interval Table of Table G from the left, move across to 3 hours and determine the Current Tissue Code, which is *C*. Enter Table C at 21 m (next deeper tabled depth as 20 m is not tabled) and move to the right to find 35 minutes. It is tabled, so move down the column to find the required stop(s). They are *1 minute at 9 m followed by 15 minutes at 6 m*. The Surfacing Code is *G*.

Example 11

> *You are planning two dives. The first is to a maximum depth of 22 m for a dive time of 50 minutes. After a surface interval of 2½ hours, you wish to dive to 18 m for 50 minutes dive time. Calculate the required decompression.*

Enter Table A at 24 m and look up the dive time of 50 minutes. Selecting 53 minutes, the stops required are*1 minute at 9 m followed by 6 minutes at 6 m.* The Surfacing Code is *G*.

After 2½ *hours* the Current Tissue Code is *C*. Enter Table C at 18 m, move across to 50 minutes and down to find the required stop of *21 minutes at 6 m*. The Surfacing Code is *G*.

FLYING AFTER DIVING

Flying in a pressurized aircraft is not permissible until the SURFACE INTERVAL TABLE indicates that the diver has reached CURRENT TISSUE CODE B. Before flying in an unpressurized aircraft, the diver must reach CURRENT TISSUE CODE A. (See discussion in Chapter 20).

DIVING AT ALTITUDE

Table 1 covers diving in the range from sea level to an altitude of 250 metres. The BS-AC will eventually publish further tables for use at higher altitudes. At present it appears that they may become available in 1990.

MULTI-LEVEL DIVING

The BS-AC has suggested a Multi-level dive procedure based on the BS-AC '88 Tables. This procedure is described in Chapter 22.

REFERENCES

1. Allen, C. and Ellerby, D. (1990), "Decompression Update". *NDC Bulletin*; 16: 1-2.

2. Allen, C., personal communication.

OTHER SOURCES

British Sub-Aqua Club (1986), "Decompression Talkback". *NDC Bulletin*; 7.

British Sub-Aqua Club (1986), "A Paper Computer for Everyone". *NDC Bulletin*; 6.

British Sub-Aqua Club (1988), Diver Training Material - Supplement to Sports Diver and Dive Leader Training Handbook (Lessons ST 6: ST 7: LT 6 using BS-AC '88 Decompression Tables with Theory Questions and Answers). BS-AC, London.

Busuttili, M. (1987), "The BS-AC '88 Sports Diving Decompression Tables". Proceedings from Diving Officers' Conference, BS-AC, London.

Busuttili, M. (1988), "The BSAC '88 Decompression Tables". *NDC Bulletin*; 13.

Busutilli, M., personal communications.

Busuttili, M. (1989), "The BS-AC '88 Decompression Tables - first review". *NDC Bulletin*; 14: 3-5.

Hennessy, T. (1986), "The New BS-AC Tables Project". Proceedings from Diving Officers Conference, BS-AC, London.

Hennessy, T. (1988), "Diving Deeper into the BS-AC '88 Tables". *Diver*; 33 (11): 19.

Hennessy, T., personal communications.

RECOMMENDED FURTHER READING

British Sub-Aqua Club (1988), Diver Training Material - Supplement to Sports Diver and Dive Leader Training Handbook (Lessons ST 6: ST 7: LT 6 using BS-AC '88 Decompression Tables with Theory Questions and Answers). BS-AC, London.

The author wishes to thank Dr. Tom Hennessy for perusing the draft of this chapter and for the material and assistance he provided. Thanks also to the BS-AC for their co-operation and for permission to re-print part of the tables.

EXERCISES ON THE BS-AC '88 TABLES

1. Find the maximum No-Stop Dive Times for single/first dives to the following depths:

   (a) 30 m (b) 9 m (c) 23 m (d) 35 m (e) 30.5 m

2. Find the decompression required for the following single or first dives (the times given are dive times):

   (a) 18 m for 60 min. (b) 15 m for 75 min.
   (c) 19 m for 45 min. (d) 25 m for 40 min.
   (e) 28 m for 30 min. (f) 36 m for 15 min.

3. Find the maximum allowable No-Stop Dive Time for the following second dives:

   (a) A dive to 20 m, $2^1/_2$ hours after a dive to 28 m for 26 minutes.

   (b) A dive to 15 m, 3 hours after a dive to 24 m for 25 minutes.

   (c) A dive to 30 m, 5 hours after a dive to 36 m for 12 minutes.

4. Find the decompression required for the following second dives (the times given are dive times):

   (a) A dive to 33 m for 10 minutes, 1 hour after a dive to 30 m for 20 minutes.

   (b) A dive to 24 m for 30 minutes, $4^1/_2$ hours after a dive to 26 m for 20 minutes.

   (c) A dive to 32 m for 18 minutes, 10 hours after a dive to 42 m for 16 minutes.

   (d) A dive to 8 m for 40 minutes, $1^1/_2$ hours after a dive to 27 m for 20 minutes.

5. Find any decompression stops required for each of the following dives (the times given are dive times):

(a) Dive 1: 30 m for 15 minutes
Surface interval = 3 hr

Dive 2: 26 m for 20 minutes
Surface interval = 4 hr

Dive 3: 20 m for 10 minutes

(b) Dive 1: 36 m for 15 minutes
Surface interval = 4 hr

Dive 2: 27 m for 10 minutes
Surface interval = 5 hr

Dive 3: 17 m for 32 minutes

(c) Dive 1: 41 m for 5 minutes
Surface interval = 7 hr

Dive 2: 30 m for 10 minutes
Surface interval = 5 hr

Dive 3: 10 m for 10 minutes

(d) Dive 1: 33 m for 22 minutes
Surface interval = 3 hr

Dive 2: 25 m for 21 minutes
Surface interval = 7 hr

Dive 3: 22 m for 32 minutes
Surface interval = 5 hr

Dive 4: 16 m for 32 minutes

(e) Dive 1: 18 m for 40 minutes
Surface interval = 3 hr

Dive 2: 42 m for 8 minutes
Surface interval = 10 hr

Dive 3: 30 m for 5 minutes

6. Find the maximum allowable No-Stop Dive times for each dive in the following pairs of dives:

   (a) A dive to 28 m followed 2 hours later by a dive to 20 m.

   (b) A dive to 34 m followed $4^1/_2$ hours later by a dive to 31 m.

   (c) A dive to 17 m followed $2^1/_2$ hours later by another dive to 17 m.

   (d) A dive to 16 m followed 3 hours later by a dive to 20 m.

   (e) A dive to 41 m followed $6^1/_2$ hours later by a dive to 12 m.

7. Find any decompression stops required for the first and second dives and the maximum No-Stop Dive Time for the third dive in the following dive sequences:

   (a) Dive 1: 24 m for 20 minutes
   Surface interval = 5 hr

   Dive 2: 20 m for 10 minutes
   Surface interval = 3 hr

   Dive 3: 18 m

   (b) Dive 1: 20 m for 25 minutes
   Surface interval = 3 hr

   Dive 2: 21 m for 25 minutes
   Surface interval = 3 hr

   Dive 3: 9 m

ANSWERS

1. (a) 20 (b) 243 (c) 30 (d) 14 (e) 17

2. (a) 1 min at 6 m (b) 1 min at 6 m
(c) 1 min at 6 m (d) 3 min at 6 m
(e) 3 min at 6 m (f) 1 min at 6 m

3. (a) 10 (b) 24 (c) 12

4. (a) 18 min at 6 m (b) 3 min at 6 m
(c) 3 min at 6 m (d) No stops

5. (a) Dive 1: No stops
Dive 2: 1 min at 6 m
Dive 3: No stops

(b) Dive 1: 1 min at 6 m
Dive 2: No stops
Dive 3: No stops

(c) Dive 1: No stops
Dive 2: No stops
Dive 3: No stops

(d) Dive 1: 1 min at 6 m
Dive 2: 1 min at 9 m and 6 min at 6 m
Dive 3: 3 min at 6 m
Dive 4: No stops

(e) Dive 1: No stops
Dive 2: 2 min at 6 m
Dive 3: No stops

6. (a) 20, 10 (b) 14, 10 (c) 51, 15 (d) 51, 10
(e) 12, 84

7. (a) Dive 1: No stops
Dive 2: No stops
Dive 3: 32

(b) Dive 1: No stops
Dive 2: 1 min at 6 m
Dive 3: 116

CHAPTER 19

THE PADI RECREATIONAL DIVE PLANNER (RDP)

BACKGROUND

The Standard U.S. Navy Tables were primarily designed as decompression tables suited to military divers with an unlimited air supply, usually working at a single depth on a single task. With the advent of SCUBA the tables were adapted to cater for repetitive diving.

Recreational divers tend to dive differently to military divers. We often spend portions of our dives at different levels rather than a single depth, and we commomly do repetitive dives. Most of us also avoid dives requiring mandatory decompression stops.

Although our diving patterns differ to those of the Navy diver, most recreational divers use navy tables, commonly the U.S. Navy Tables. This introduces a number of problems; some of which are:

1. The NDLs of the U.S. Navy Tables appear to be too long as significant bubble formation has been shown to occur in divers who have dived right to these limits.

2. Although the U.S. Navy divemasters have developed ways to add safety to their table calculations, many recreational divers cannot, or will not, do this effectively.

3. Recreational divers often exceed the ascent rate recommended on the table. In addition, in some situations this ascent rate appears to be too fast.

4. The Navy tables require that a schedule be selected according to the maximum depth and total bottom time of a dive. A diver who has spent very little time at the maximum depth is, therefore, penalized.

5. The long NDLs allowed for an initial dive may allow significant bubble formation and any bubbles formed will delay off-gassing during a subsequent surface interval. This increases the residual nitrogen that must be accounted for on a repetitive dive and, therefore, reduces the no-decompression stop time available for the dive.

For many years various sections of the diving community have debated whether or not the U.S. Navy schedules are appropriate for safe recreational diving. A concern commonly expressed is that some schedules may be too long, posing a higher risk for bends, and that other schedules may unfairly penalize a diver's time, being unnecessarily conservative.

As the demand for an appropriate set of tables for the recreational diver became more and more urgent, PADI, responding to this demand, commissioned a number of individuals to design and test a table which is specifically for recreational diving and which addresses some of the problems described. The introduction of the table by Diving Science and Technology Corporation (DSAT), which is a corporate affiliate of PADI, followed more than three years of research, testing and development.

THE THEORY BEHIND THE TABLES

The RDP is based on the Haldanian system and utilizes tissue compartments with half-times of 5, 10, 20, 30, 40, 60, 80 and 120 minutes.* The maximum allowable nitrogen levels in these tissue compartments (M values) have been reduced below those used by the U.S. Navy. These M values are shown in Table 19.1. The lower M values yield shorter NDLs than are given by the U.S. Navy model (See Table 19.2). The RDP assumes that gas uptake and elimination are symmetrical, that is, they occur at the same rate. This assumption may be acceptable in the absence of bubbles but it can be quite inaccurate when significant bubbling has occurred. This is the reason that PADI/DSAT researched the areas where it was hoped little or no bubbling occurred.

TABLE 19.1

Comparison of M values

Tissue Group	U.S. Navy	PADI RDP	Huggins
5 min.	104	102.9	102.0
10 min.	88	84.1	85.0
20 min.	72	67.2	67.5
30 min.	-	59.8	-
40 min.	58	55.7	54.5
60 min.	-	51.4	-
80 min.	52	49.1	47.5
120 min.	51	46.9	43.0

In theory, optimal dive schedules are found by tracking the gas partial pressures in each individual tissue compartment as it on-gasses during a dive and off-gasses during the surface interval after the dive. Planning of the next dive and its decompression obligation is on the basis of the gas-loading in the "controlling tissue", which is the tissue closest to its maximum safe gas level. This is what is done by most dive computers.

For the sake of simplicity, the U.S. Navy Surface Interval Credit Table is calculated on the basis of a controlling tissue with a 120-minute half-time. This covers all diving situations, including those requiring long decompressions. For the recreational diver, who avoids decompression stop dives and who generally dives shallower than 130 ft (39 m) for relatively short periods, a repetitive system based on the 120-minute tissue compartment may often (but certainly not always) prove to be unnecessarily conservative.# The controlling tissue will often be one with a half-time shorter than 120 minutes.

* The half-times shown above are the only ones mentioned in the actual PADI/DSAT document (Powell et al, 1988). However, in a personal correspondence to the author Drew Richardson, PADI Training Manager, states that the design of the RDP incorporates 14 tissue compartments with half-times from 5 to 480 minutes.

\# However, in reality, if sufficient bubbles have formed after the initial dive to slow down off-gassing and possibly increase on-gassing during repetitive dives, a tissue compartment with a half-time <u>slower</u> than 120-minutes may be required.

Raymond Rogers, the designer of the Recreational Dive Planner (RDP), sought a controlling tissue compartment which he felt was more appropriate to recreational diving than the 120-minute tissue compartment used by the U.S.Navy. Rogers analyzed various typical recreational diving profiles and decided that a tissue compartment with a half-time of 40 minutes was adequate to cover most recreational dives. He discovered, however, that a small percentage of profiles, primarily involving a series of long, shallow dives, required a slower tissue than 40 minutes. Consequently, he chose a tissue compartment with a half-time of 60 minutes on which to base the repetitive system of the RDP. Rogers' computer analyses indicated that a tissue half-time of 60 minutes came closer to the theoretical needs of the recreational diver than any other half-time. However, the question that needed to be answered was whether this theory would hold up in practice - whether or not it would be safe to perform repetitive dives with the 60-minute tissue as the controlling tissue. Various tests have been, and are still being, conducted in an attempt to answer this question. The results, to date, have been positive, but it must be remembered that the tests were conducted under controlled conditions and the results may not always be replicated in the field where conditions may not be as well-controlled.

TESTING THE RDP

The testing of the RDP involved dry hyperbaric-chamber as well as openwater studies. The study used a group of more than 100 volunteer divers who were selected to reflect the recreational diving population in terms of age, gender distribution and percentage of body fat. In the initial phase of the testing, a total of 25 dive schedules were tested; three of them in the open water. The profiles were either repetitive, multi-level or various combinations of these. To maximize nitrogen uptake in the chamber tests, subjects were exercised on rowing machines and the chamber was kept warm to increase blood flow. A Doppler ultrasonic flow meter was used in evaluating the test profiles by monitoring the level of detectable circulating bubbles. Only 17 of the schedules were tested on at least 15 divers, so, only these schedules are considered in the following results.

352 dive schedules were conducted with exercising divers and since many of the schedules consisted of repetitive dives, a total of 743 dives involving exercise were included. After the dives the divers were monitored for bubbles, initially while at rest, and then after doing two deep knee bends. In all, bubbles were detected in 45 of the 352 schedules, which gives an incidence of bubbles of 12.8% per schedule. Many of the schedules included multiple dives and bubbles were detected after a total of 53 of the 743 dives, an incidence of 7.1% per dive.[1]

No case of bends arose in any test and the level of bubbles detected was generally the lowest detectable level (i.e. grade 1 or 2 as shown in Table 19.2). The researchers concluded that it is safe to make repetitive dives controlled by the 40-minute or 60-minute tissue and that minimal bubbling follows such dives.

FIGURE 19.1

Diver being monitored for bubbles - post dive

Photo courtesy Dr. Michael Powell

TABLE 19.2

Grading of Doppler-detected bubbles

0	=	no gas bubbles detected in at least 10 heart cycles
1	=	occasional gas bubbles detected in 10 heart cycles
2	=	few bubbles detectable; some cycles may have 2 to 4 bubbles per cycle
3	=	several gas bubbles detectable per cycle
4	=	gas bubbles present continuously (systole and diastole), gas bubble amplitude louder than flow sounds.

However, some diving scientists have criticized these conclusions.[2,3,4,5] The fear is that although few bubbles were detected, significant bubbling might still be present. Doppler devices only detect moving bubbles and must be aimed correctly to do so effectively.* They do not detect the stationary bubbles trapped in the tissues and it is these bubbles which are thought to produce many of the manifestations of bends.

The repetitive system of the RDP assumes that very few bubbles have formed in the body and, therefore, uses the same mathematics to describe gas uptake and elimination on repetitive dives as on single dives. However, this is also true of almost all of the current decompression tables and computers.# If sufficient bubbling has occurred, off-gassing may be slowed and this mathematics may not be valid. In addition, some researchers also believe that if a repetitive dive is undertaken when bubbles are present, gas uptake will be faster during the repetitive dive than during the initial dive, as the bubbles will provide an extra source of gas for absorption. Hence, allowable times predicted by the model for repetitive dives may not be valid.

Some critics[3,4] argued that many more "wet-chamber" and in-water test dives need to be done to determine the level of bends risk associated with the use of the RDP.** Some fear that the 60-minute half-time, alone, may sometimes be too short to represent the nitrogen load that can build up after many consecutive days of repetitive diving. DAN offered the following statement after the first phase of testing: "The tables have been tested in a reasonable way for up to three repetitive dives in a single day with acceptable results. Using the tables for consecutive days may create risks that do not exist with one day's use: this is also true for the U.S. Navy Tables and all other decompression systems..".

In an attempt to cater for the higher gas loads that may result after multiple repetitive dives and, so that the 60-minute half-time does not, solely, determine repetitive dive times, PADI has introduced special rules to be applied when three or more dives are planned in one day. This avoids pushing the model to it's limits.

PADI is currently well into the second phase of the testing of the RDP. By August 1989, 20 divers had participated in a series of four dives per day for each of six consecutive days. A total of 475 man-dives were conducted in a dry chamber. The test profiles were chosen to test the model as near to the limits as practicable and to provide a wide spectrum of depth-time exposures, including multi-level dives with up to four different levels. However, exercise was limited so that the subjects did not become fatigued and, so, abort a dive. Data on the level of bubbles detected are not yet available, but no cases of bends resulted from these initial tests.[6] Further tests are planned.

As well as being tested under well-controlled conditions, a dive table needs to be proven in the field where conditions may not be as well-controlled as during the tests. PADI reports that the RDP has now been on the market for more than two years without apparent problems.[7] However, in Australia, some divers have been bent while apparently correctly using the RDP.[8]

* See Chapter 4 for an explanation on the use of Doppler flowmeters.

\# With current exceptions being the DCIEM Tables, the RNPL/BSAC Table, the BSAC '88 Tables and an underwater decompression computer used by the U.S. Navy.

** Statistically, for *each schedule* a minimum of 35 dives without bends is needed before a bends rate of less then 2% can be claimed with 95% confidence.

As with any table it will be important to control the rate of ascent. The RDP was tested using an ascent rate of 60 ft (18 m)/minute. If a diver ascends more rapidly much more bubbling could occur. This would delay off-gassing during a subsequent surface interval and make the repetitive times allowed by the tables potentially more hazardous. PADI has launched its S.A.F.E. Diver Campaign to encouage divers to slow down their ascent rates to a maximum of 60 ft (18 m)/minute and to preferably ascend slower. A safety stop at the end of every dive is also highly recommended.

The RDP comes in two versions. There is a table version for those who prefer the conventional tabular layout. It is identical in function and similar in design to the former PADI Dive Tables. *It cannot be used for multi-level diving*. The other version of the RDP is called "The Wheel". By utilizing depth curves, rather than tables, The Wheel minimizes the time restrictions caused by rounding-off conventional tables. No calculations are required when using The Wheel, and it can be used to plan multi-level dives. The Wheel is shown in Figure 19.2.

FIGURE 19.2
The Wheel version of the RDP

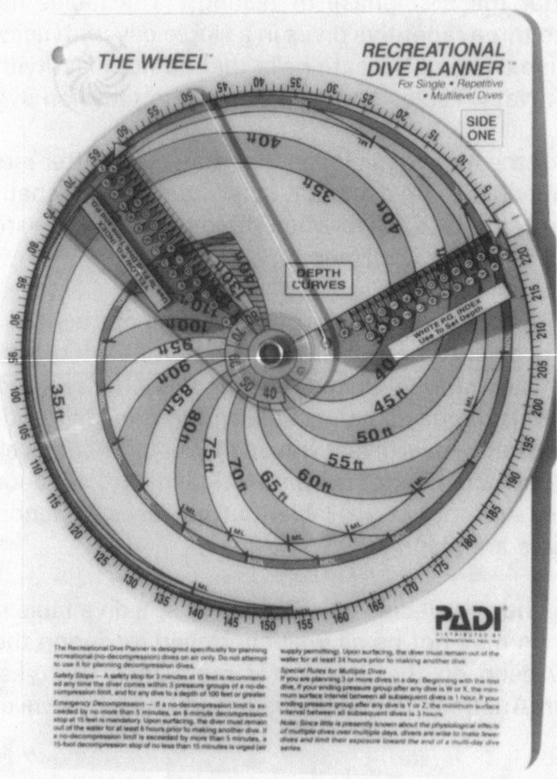

Table 19.3 compares the No-Decompression Limits of the RDP with those of some other tables and a comparision of times allowed by the RDP for a series of repetitive dives is shown in Tables 19.4 and 19.5.

TABLE 19.3

Comparison of No-Decompression Limits

ft	m	U.S.Navy	PADI RDP (imperial)	PADI RDP (metric)	DCIEM	Buehlmann	Huggins
30	9	no limit	360		300	400	225
40	12	200	140	147	150	125	135
50	15	100	80	72 *	75	75	75
60	18	60	55	56	50	51	50
70	21	50	40	37 *	35	35	40
80	24	40	30	29 *	25	25	30
90	27	30	25	20 *	20	20	25
100	30	25	20	20	15	17	20
110	33	20	16	14 *	12	14	15
120	36	15	13	9 *	10	12	10
130	39	10	10	9 *	8	10	5

* These depths were not tabled on the metric RDP, so these times were taken from the next higher tabled depth.

TABLE 19.4

Comparison of allowable times for some repetitive dives

	Bottom time limits (minutes)			
	U.S.Navy	RDP	DCIEM	Buehlmann (1986)
Dive 1				
80 ft (24 m) Actual bottom time (ABT) = 25 minutes.	40	30 *(29)*	25	25
Surface interval = 30 min.				
Dive 2				
60 ft (18 m) ABT = 15 minutes	24	30 *(30)*	26	37
Surface interval = 30 min.				
Dive 3				
60 ft (18 m)	0	26 *(28)*	24	37

Note: Times in *(italics)* are those for the metric RDP.

TABLE 19.5

Comparison of allowable times for some repetitive dives

	Bottom time limits (minutes)			
	U.S.Navy	RDP	DCIEM	Buehlmann (1986)
Dive 1				
120 ft (36 m)				
Actual bottom time (ABT) = 10 minutes.	15	13 *(9)*	10	12
Surface interval = 2 hr.				
Dive 2				
100 ft (30 m)				
ABT = 10 minutes	15	17 *(17)*	11	8 (stop of 5 min at 10ft/3m)
Surface interval = 1 hr.				
Dive 3				
60 ft (18 m)	30	44 *(45)*	29	37

Note: Times in *(italics)* are those for the metric RDP.

Using the PADI RDP (Table Version)

Since the imperial and metric versions of the RDP have a number of different depth increments, they will be dealt with separately.

A. IMPERIAL VERSION

This section relates only to the *imperial version* of the RDP.

GENERAL RULES OF USE

Strictly adhere to the following rules when using The Recreational Dive Planner:

1. Any dive planned to 35 ft or *less* should be calculated as a dive to 35 ft.
2. Use the exact or next-greater depth shown for the depths of all dives.
3. Use the exact or next-greater time shown for the times of all dives.
4. Ascend from all dives no faster than 60 ft/minute.

5. As with any dive tables, be conservative and avoid using the maximum limits provided.

6. When planning a dive in cold water or under conditions that might be strenuous, plan the dive assuming the depth is 10 ft deeper than actual.

7. Plan repetitive dives so each successive dive is to a shallower depth.

8. Limit your maximum depths to your training and experience level (Open Water Divers - 60 ft; divers with greater training and experience - 100 ft, with no dive in excess of 130 ft).

9. Always make a safety stop for 3 minutes at 15 ft after any dive to 100 ft (or greater) and any time you surface within three Pressure Groups of a No-Decompression Limit (NDL)

10. An emergency decompression stop for 8 minutes at 15 ft must be made if a NDL is accidentally exceeded by 5 minutes or less. Upon surfacing, the diver must remain out of the water for at least 6 hours prior to making another dive. If a No-Decompression Limit is exceeded by more than 5 minutes, a 15-foot decompression stop of no less than 15 minutes is urged (air supply permitting). Upon surfacing, the diver must remain out of the water for at least 24 hours prior to making another dive. The RDP is not meant for decompression diving - provisions for an emergency decompression stop are included only as a safety factor if you make a mistake. Proper planning and monitoring of your dives will avoid the need for emergency decompression.

11. Special rules for Multiple dives:

    If you are planning 3 or more dives in a day:
    Beginning with the first dive, if your ending Pressure Group after any dive is W or X, the minimum surface interval between *all* subsequent dives is 1 hour. If your ending Pressure Group after any dive is Y or Z, the minimum surface interval between *all* subsequent dives is 3 hours.

    Note: Since little is presently known about the physiological effects of multiple dives over multiple days, divers are wise to make fewer dives and limit their exposure toward the end of a multi-day dive series.

12. *Flying After Diving Procedures* - For a single no-decompression dive with less than 1 hour of bottom time, *wait 4 hours*; for a single no-decompression dive with more than 1 hour of bottom time or after any repetitive dive, *wait 12 hours*; for any dive requiring emergency decompression, *wait 24 hours.* *

13. *Diving At Altitude* - This planner is not designed for use at altitudes greater than 1000 ft above sea-level. (See Chapter 21 for procedure for diving at altitude).

* In future revisions of the RDP, these guidelines will be replaced by the DAN guidelines given in Chapter 20.

PLANNING NO-DECOMPRESSION STOP DIVES

1. SINGLE OR FIRST NO-DECOMPRESSION STOP DIVES

Table 1 (within Table 19.5) was designed for planning single dives or the first of a group of dives. Table 1 is the left-most table in Table 19.5.

Example 1.

You are planning to dive to a maximum depth of 80 ft. What is the No-Decompression Limit (NDL)?

Enter Table 1 of the RDP, from the top, at 80 ft and move down the column until coming to the *white* number in the *black* box. This is the NDL which, in this case, is *30* minutes. This 30 minutes is the maximum allowable *bottom time* for the dive.

Note:

If you dive to this NDL, you must then make a safety stop of 3 minutes at 15 ft since you have dived to within 3 Pressure Groups (PG) of the NDL. Safety stops need not be added to bottom time with these tables (although the author advises it for the extra safety sometimes gained in any following repetitive dives).

Similarly, the NDL for 100 ft is 20 minutes, the NDL for 60 ft is 55 minutes, and the NDL for 50 ft is 80 minutes.

Example 2.

What is the NDL for a single/first dive to a maximum depth of 54 ft?

Enter Table 1 from the top at 60 ft (i.e. the next greater tabled depth, since 54 ft is not tabled). Move down the column until reaching the *white* number in the *black* box. The NDL is, thus, *55* minutes.

Note:

If this dive is carried out a safety stop would be mandatory (within 3 PGs of the NDL).

Similarly, the NDL for 66 ft is 40 minutes, the NDL for 37 ft is 140 minutes, and for 103 ft is 16 minutes.

Finding the Pressure Group (PG) after single/first no-decompression stop dives

Example 3.

Find the PG after the previous single dive to 80 ft for 30 minutes.

Enter Table 1, from the top, at 80 ft. Move down the column until coming to the exact, or next longer, tabled bottom time. In this case 30 minutes is tabled so move down to 30 minutes, and then right to find the PG after the dive. It is *R*.

TABLE 19.5
Side 1 of the RDP (Imperial version)

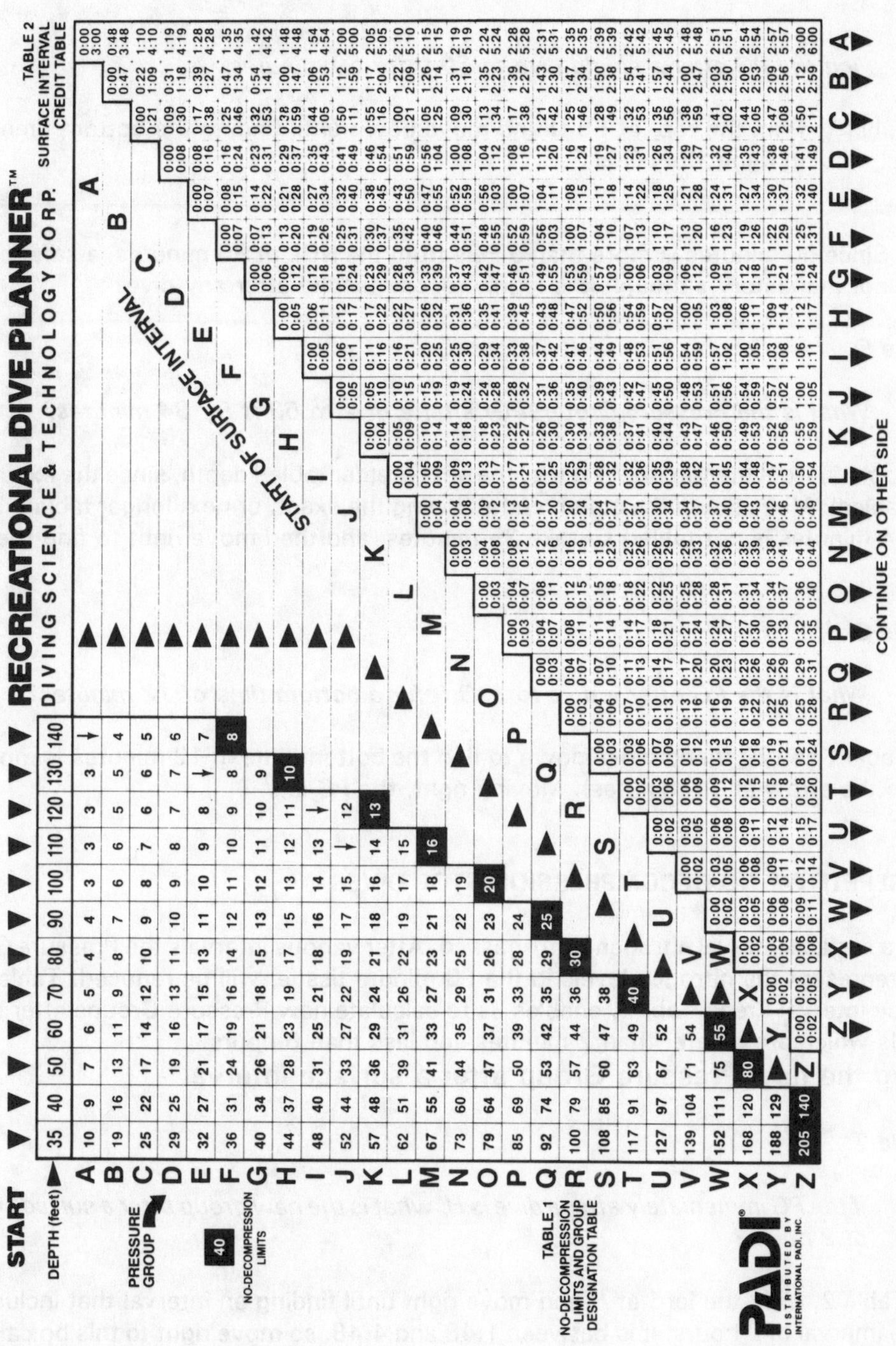

RECREATIONAL DIVE PLANNER™
DIVING SCIENCE & TECHNOLOGY CORP.

START

TABLE 1 NO-DECOMPRESSION LIMITS AND GROUP DESIGNATION TABLE

(Shaded value = NO-DECOMPRESSION LIMITS, e.g. **40**)

PRESSURE GROUP / DEPTH (feet)	35	40	50	60	70	80	90	100	110	120	130	140
A	10	9	7	6	5	4	4	3	3	3	3	↓
B	19	16	13	11	9	8	7	6	6	5	5	4
C	25	22	17	14	12	10	9	8	7	6	6	5
D	29	25	19	16	13	11	10	9	8	7	7	6
E	32	27	21	17	15	13	11	10	9	8	↓	7
F	36	31	24	19	16	14	12	11	10	9	8	**8**
G	40	34	26	21	18	15	13	12	11	10	9	
H	44	37	28	23	19	17	15	13	12	11	**10**	
I	48	40	31	25	21	18	16	14	13	↓		
J	52	44	33	27	22	19	17	15	↓	12		
K	57	48	36	29	24	21	18	16	14	**13**		
L	62	51	39	31	26	22	19	17	15			
M	67	55	41	33	27	23	21	18	**16**			
N	73	60	44	35	29	25	22	19				
O	79	64	47	37	31	26	23	**20**				
P	85	69	50	39	33	28	24					
Q	92	74	53	42	35	29	**25**					
R	100	79	57	44	36	**30**						
S	108	85	60	47	38							
T	117	91	63	49	**40**							
U	127	97	67	52								
V	139	104	71	54								
W	152	111	75	**55**								
X	168	120	**80**									
Y	188	129										
Z	205	**140**										

TABLE 2 SURFACE INTERVAL CREDIT TABLE

START OF SURFACE INTERVAL

	Z	Y	X	W	V	U	T	S	R	Q	P	O	N	M	L	K	J	I	H	G	F	E	D	C	B	A
A																										0:00 3:00
B																									0:00 0:47	0:48 3:48
C																								0:00 0:21	0:22 1:09	1:10 4:10
D																							0:00 0:08	0:09 0:30	0:31 1:18	1:19 4:19
E																						0:00 0:07	0:08 0:16	0:17 0:38	0:39 1:27	1:28 4:28
F																					0:00 0:07	0:08 0:15	0:16 0:24	0:25 0:46	0:47 1:34	1:35 4:35
G																				0:00 0:06	0:07 0:13	0:14 0:22	0:23 0:31	0:32 0:53	0:54 1:41	1:42 4:42
H																			0:00 0:05	0:06 0:12	0:13 0:20	0:21 0:28	0:29 0:37	0:38 0:59	1:00 1:47	1:48 4:48
I																		0:00 0:05	0:06 0:11	0:12 0:18	0:19 0:26	0:27 0:34	0:35 0:43	0:44 1:05	1:06 1:53	1:54 4:54
J																	0:00 0:05	0:06 0:11	0:12 0:17	0:18 0:24	0:25 0:31	0:32 0:40	0:41 0:49	0:50 1:11	1:12 1:59	2:00 5:00
K																0:00 0:04	0:05 0:10	0:11 0:16	0:17 0:22	0:23 0:29	0:30 0:37	0:38 0:45	0:46 0:54	0:55 1:16	1:17 2:04	2:05 5:05
L															0:00 0:04	0:05 0:09	0:10 0:15	0:16 0:21	0:22 0:27	0:28 0:34	0:35 0:42	0:43 0:50	0:51 0:59	1:00 1:21	1:22 2:09	2:10 5:10
M														0:00 0:04	0:05 0:09	0:10 0:14	0:15 0:19	0:20 0:25	0:26 0:32	0:33 0:39	0:40 0:46	0:47 0:55	0:56 1:04	1:05 1:25	1:26 2:14	2:15 5:15
N													0:00 0:03	0:04 0:08	0:09 0:13	0:14 0:18	0:19 0:24	0:25 0:30	0:31 0:36	0:37 0:43	0:44 0:51	0:52 0:59	1:00 1:08	1:09 1:30	1:31 2:18	2:19 5:19
O												0:00 0:03	0:04 0:08	0:09 0:12	0:13 0:17	0:18 0:23	0:24 0:28	0:29 0:34	0:35 0:41	0:42 0:47	0:48 0:55	0:56 1:03	1:04 1:12	1:13 1:34	1:35 2:23	2:24 5:24
P											0:00 0:03	0:04 0:07	0:08 0:12	0:13 0:16	0:17 0:21	0:22 0:27	0:28 0:32	0:33 0:38	0:39 0:45	0:46 0:51	0:52 0:59	1:00 1:07	1:08 1:16	1:17 1:38	1:39 2:27	2:28 5:28
Q										0:00 0:03	0:04 0:07	0:08 0:11	0:12 0:16	0:17 0:20	0:21 0:25	0:26 0:30	0:31 0:36	0:37 0:42	0:43 0:48	0:49 0:55	0:56 1:03	1:04 1:11	1:12 1:20	1:21 1:42	1:43 2:30	2:31 5:31
R									0:00 0:03	0:04 0:07	0:08 0:11	0:12 0:15	0:16 0:19	0:20 0:24	0:25 0:29	0:30 0:34	0:35 0:40	0:41 0:46	0:47 0:52	0:53 0:59	1:00 1:07	1:08 1:15	1:16 1:24	1:25 1:46	1:47 2:34	2:35 5:35
S								0:00 0:03	0:04 0:06	0:07 0:10	0:11 0:14	0:15 0:18	0:19 0:23	0:24 0:27	0:28 0:32	0:33 0:38	0:39 0:43	0:44 0:49	0:50 0:56	0:57 1:03	1:04 1:10	1:11 1:18	1:19 1:27	1:28 1:49	1:50 2:38	2:39 5:39
T							0:00 0:02	0:03 0:06	0:07 0:10	0:11 0:13	0:14 0:17	0:18 0:22	0:23 0:26	0:27 0:31	0:32 0:36	0:37 0:41	0:42 0:47	0:48 0:53	0:54 0:59	1:00 1:06	1:07 1:13	1:14 1:22	1:23 1:31	1:32 1:53	1:54 2:41	2:42 5:42
U						0:00 0:02	0:03 0:06	0:07 0:09	0:10 0:13	0:14 0:17	0:18 0:21	0:22 0:25	0:26 0:29	0:30 0:34	0:35 0:39	0:40 0:44	0:45 0:50	0:51 0:56	0:57 1:02	1:03 1:09	1:10 1:17	1:18 1:25	1:26 1:34	1:35 1:56	1:57 2:44	2:45 5:45
V					0:00 0:02	0:03 0:05	0:06 0:09	0:10 0:12	0:13 0:16	0:17 0:20	0:21 0:24	0:25 0:28	0:29 0:33	0:34 0:37	0:38 0:42	0:43 0:47	0:48 0:53	0:54 0:59	1:00 1:05	1:06 1:12	1:13 1:20	1:21 1:28	1:29 1:37	1:38 1:59	2:00 2:47	2:48 5:48
W				0:00 0:02	0:03 0:05	0:06 0:08	0:09 0:12	0:13 0:15	0:16 0:19	0:20 0:23	0:24 0:27	0:28 0:31	0:32 0:36	0:37 0:40	0:41 0:45	0:46 0:50	0:51 0:56	0:57 1:02	1:03 1:08	1:09 1:15	1:16 1:23	1:24 1:31	1:32 1:40	1:41 2:02	2:03 2:50	2:51 5:51
X			0:00 0:02	0:03 0:05	0:06 0:08	0:09 0:11	0:12 0:15	0:16 0:18	0:19 0:22	0:23 0:26	0:27 0:30	0:31 0:34	0:35 0:39	0:40 0:43	0:44 0:48	0:49 0:53	0:54 0:59	1:00 1:05	1:06 1:11	1:12 1:18	1:19 1:26	1:27 1:34	1:35 1:43	1:44 2:05	2:06 2:53	2:54 5:54
Y		0:00 0:02	0:03 0:05	0:06 0:08	0:09 0:11	0:12 0:14	0:15 0:18	0:19 0:21	0:22 0:25	0:26 0:29	0:30 0:33	0:34 0:37	0:38 0:41	0:42 0:46	0:47 0:51	0:52 0:56	0:57 1:02	1:03 1:08	1:09 1:14	1:15 1:21	1:22 1:29	1:30 1:37	1:38 1:46	1:47 2:08	2:09 2:56	2:57 5:57
Z	0:00 0:02	0:03 0:05	0:06 0:08	0:09 0:11	0:12 0:14	0:15 0:17	0:18 0:20	0:21 0:24	0:25 0:28	0:29 0:31	0:32 0:35	0:36 0:40	0:41 0:44	0:45 0:49	0:50 0:54	0:55 0:59	1:00 1:05	1:06 1:11	1:12 1:17	1:18 1:24	1:25 1:31	1:32 1:40	1:41 1:49	1:50 2:11	2:12 2:59	3:00 6:00

Z Y X W V U T S R Q P O N M L K J I H G F E D C B A

CONTINUE ON OTHER SIDE

PADI® DISTRIBUTED BY INTERNATIONAL PADI, INC

Note:

A safety stop would be required at the end of this dive.

Example 4.

Find the PG after a single dive to 50 ft for 60 minutes.

Enter Table 1, from the top, at 50 ft and move down until finding the bottom time of 60 minutes. Moving right, the PG is *S*.

Note:

Since 60 minutes is more than 3 PGs from the NDL of 80 minutes, a safety stop is not mandatory although it is highly recommended after any dive.

Example 5.

What is the Pressure Group (PG) after a dive to 63 ft for 34 minutes?

Enter Table 1, from the top, at 70 ft (i.e. the next greater tabled depth, since the exact depth is not tabled). Move down the column until finding the exact, or next longer tabled, bottom time. 34 minutes is not tabled so take 35 minutes, and then move right to find the PG. It is *Q*.

Example 6.

What is the PG after a dive to 113 ft for a bottom time of 12 minutes?

Enter Table 1 at 120 ft and move down to find the bottom time of 12 minutes (simply pass through the arrow at 11 minutes). Moving right, the PG is *J*.

2. REPETITIVE NO-DECOMPRESSION STOP DIVES

During a surface interval nitrogen is off-gassed. After various intervals the Pressure Groups, which represent the nitrogen levels in the 60-minute tissue, will be reduced. Table 2, the "Surface Interval Credit Table", enables us to calculate new Pressure Groups after surface intervals which are greater than 2 minutes and less than 6 hours.

Finding the new Pressure Group after a surface interval

Example 7.

If the PG immediately after a dive is H, what is the new group after a surface interval of 2 hours?

Enter Table 2, from the left, at *H* and move right until finding an interval that includes the surface interval of 2 hours. It is between 1:48 and 4:48, so move right to this box and then down the column to the bottom to get the new PG. It is *A*.

Example 8.

If the PG immediately after a dive is F, find the new group after a surface interval of 50 minutes.

Enter Table 2, from the left, at *F* and move right to find a box containing 50 minutes. It is included in 0:47 to 1:34, so move to this box and then down the column to find the PG, which is *B*.

Calculating the maximum allowable no-decompression stop bottom time for a repetitive dive

A repetitive dive is defined to be any dive within 6 hours of a previous dive(s). When planning a repetitive dive, the excess nitrogen still remaining after the surface interval must be taken into account. This is done by adding a "Residual Nitrogen Time" (RNT).

The Residual Nitrogen Time is the amount of time which must be considered already spent at the maximum depth of the repetitive dive before this dive is commenced. It is subtracted from the single dive NDL for that depth and the result is the no-decompression stop bottom time still remaining at that depth.

Table 3 (Table 19.6) gives the Residual Nitrogen Times and the maximum no-decompression stop bottom times still available for the various depths of repetitive dives.

Example 9.

If you are in group C immediately before a dive to 80 ft, find:

(i) *the Residual Nitrogen Time (RNT) at 80 ft*
(ii) *the maximum allowable no-decompression stop bottom time at 80 ft*

Enter Table 3, from the top, at C and move down the column until intersecting the row for 80 ft. You will find two numbers in the box. The top number, printed *on white*, is the Residual Nitrogen Time which, in this case, is *10* minutes. This means that before doing the dive you must consider that you have already spent 10 minutes at 80 ft. This 10 minutes is to account for excess nitrogen left over from the previous dive(s). The remaining allowable no-decompression stop time (i.e. adjusted maximum no-decompression bottom time) is the number printed *on blue.* In this case it is *20* minutes. **The Actual Bottom Time (ABT) of a repetitive dive should never exceed the adjusted maximum no-decompression bottom time.**

Note:

If you planned to do this dive, you must end it with a safety stop of 3 minutes at 15 ft, since you will be within 3 PGs of the NDL.

TABLE 19.6

Side 2 of the RDP (Imperial version)

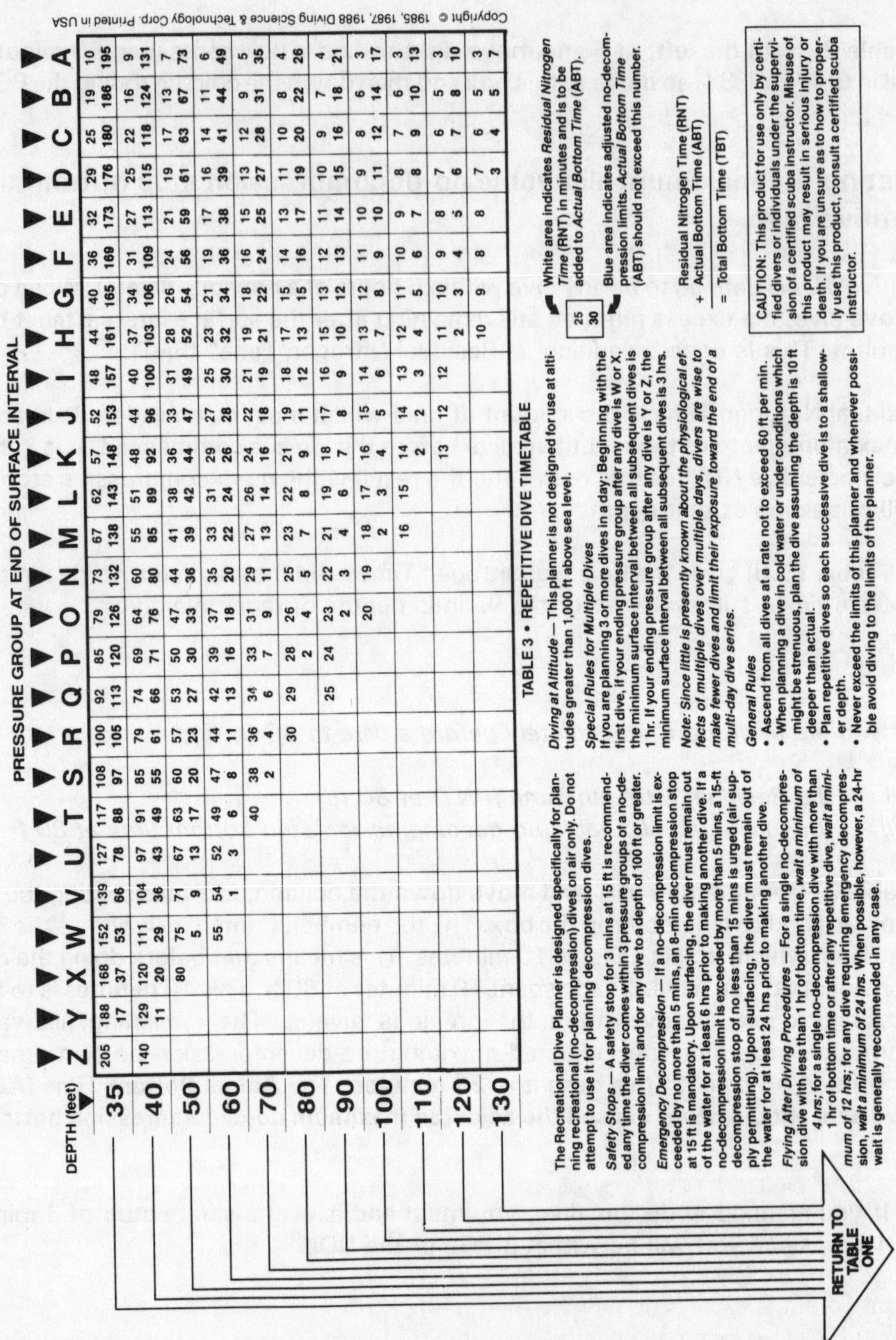

PRESSURE GROUP AT END OF SURFACE INTERVAL

DEPTH (feet)	Z	Y	X	W	V	U	T	S	R	Q	P	O	N	M	L	K	J	I	H	G	F	E	D	C	B	A
35	205	188 / 17	168 / 37	152 / 53	139 / 66	127 / 78	117 / 88	108 / 97	100 / 105	92 / 113	85 / 120	79 / 126	73 / 132	67 / 138	62 / 143	57 / 148	52 / 153	48 / 157	44 / 161	40 / 165	36 / 169	32 / 173	29 / 176	25 / 180	19 / 186	10 / 195
40	140	129 / 11	120 / 20	111 / 29	104 / 36	97 / 43	91 / 49	85 / 55	79 / 61	74 / 66	69 / 71	64 / 76	60 / 80	55 / 85	51 / 89	48 / 92	44 / 96	40 / 100	37 / 103	34 / 106	31 / 109	27 / 113	25 / 115	22 / 118	16 / 124	9 / 131
50			80	75 / 5	71 / 9	67 / 13	63 / 17	60 / 20	57 / 23	53 / 27	50 / 30	47 / 33	44 / 36	41 / 39	38 / 42	36 / 44	33 / 47	31 / 49	28 / 52	26 / 54	24 / 56	21 / 59	19 / 61	17 / 63	13 / 67	7 / 73
60				55	54 / 1	52 / 3	49 / 6	47 / 8	44 / 11	42 / 13	39 / 16	37 / 18	35 / 20	33 / 22	31 / 24	29 / 26	27 / 28	25 / 30	23 / 32	21 / 34	19 / 36	17 / 38	16 / 39	14 / 41	11 / 44	6 / 49
70							40	38 / 2	36 / 4	34 / 6	33 / 7	31 / 9	29 / 11	27 / 13	26 / 14	24 / 16	22 / 18	21 / 19	19 / 21	18 / 22	16 / 24	15 / 25	13 / 27	12 / 28	9 / 31	5 / 35
80									30	29	28 / 2	26 / 4	25 / 5	23 / 7	22 / 8	21 / 9	19 / 11	18 / 12	17 / 13	15 / 15	14 / 16	13 / 17	11 / 19	10 / 20	8 / 22	4 / 26
90										25	24	23 / 2	22 / 3	21 / 4	19 / 6	18 / 7	17 / 8	16 / 9	15 / 10	13 / 12	12 / 13	11 / 14	10 / 15	9 / 16	7 / 18	4 / 21
100												20	19	18 / 2	17 / 3	16 / 4	15 / 5	14 / 6	13 / 7	12 / 8	11 / 9	10 / 10	9 / 11	8 / 12	6 / 14	3 / 17
110														16	15	14 / 2	14 / 2	13 / 3	12 / 4	11 / 5	10 / 6	9 / 7	8 / 8	7 / 9	6 / 10	3 / 13
120																13	12	12	11 / 2	10 / 3	9 / 4	8 / 5	7 / 6	6 / 7	5 / 8	3 / 10
130																			10	9	8	8	7 / 3	6 / 4	5 / 5	3 / 7

TABLE 3 • REPETITIVE DIVE TIMETABLE

RETURN TO TABLE ONE

White area indicates *Residual Nitrogen Time* (RNT) in minutes and is to be added to *Actual Bottom Time* (ABT).

25
30

Blue area indicates adjusted no-decompression limits. *Actual Bottom Time* (ABT) should not exceed this number.

Residual Nitrogen Time (RNT)
\+ Actual Bottom Time (ABT)

= Total Bottom Time (TBT)

The Recreational Dive Planner is designed specifically for planning recreational (no-decompression) dives on air only. Do not attempt to use it for planning decompression dives.

Safety Stops — A safety stop for 3 mins at 15 ft is recommended any time the diver comes within 3 pressure groups of a no-decompression limit, and for any dive to a depth of 100 ft or greater.

Emergency Decompression — If a no-decompression limit is exceeded by no more than 5 mins, an 8-min decompression stop at 15 ft is mandatory. Upon surfacing, the diver must remain out of the water for at least 6 hrs prior to making another dive. If a no-decompression limit is exceeded by more than 5 mins, a 15-ft decompression stop of no less than 15 mins is urged (air supply permitting). Upon surfacing, the diver must remain out of the water for at least 24 hrs prior to making another dive.

Flying After Diving Procedures — For a single no-decompression dive with less than 1 hr of bottom time, *wait a minimum of 4 hrs;* for a single no-decompression dive with more than 1 hr of bottom time or after any repetitive dive, *wait a minimum of 12 hrs;* for any dive requiring emergency decompression, *wait a minimum of 24 hrs.* When possible, however, a 24-hr wait is generally recommended in any case.

Diving at Altitude — This planner is not designed for use at altitudes greater than 1,000 ft above sea level.

Special Rules for Multiple Dives
If you are planning 3 or more dives in a day: Beginning with the first dive, if your ending pressure group after any dive is W or X, the minimum surface interval between all subsequent dives is 1 hr. If your ending pressure group after any dive is Y or Z, the minimum surface interval between all subsequent dives is 3 hrs.

Note: Since little is presently known about the physiological effects of multiple dives over multiple days, divers are wise to make fewer dives and limit their exposure toward the end of a multi-day dive series.

General Rules

- Ascend from all dives at a rate not to exceed 60 ft per min.
- When planning a dive in cold water or under conditions which might be strenuous, plan the dive assuming the depth is 10 ft deeper than actual.
- Plan repetitive dives so each successive dive is to a shallower depth.
- Never exceed the limits of this planner and whenever possible avoid diving to the limits of the planner.

CAUTION: This product for use only by certified divers or individuals under the supervision of a certified scuba instructor. Misuse of this product may result in serious injury or death. If you are unsure as to how to properly use this product, consult a certified scuba instructor.

Example 10.

At the end of a surface interval after a dive you are in group B. Find:

(i) the Residual Nitrogen Time
(ii) the maximum allowable bottom time for a no-decompression stop dive to 96 ft.

Enter Table 3, from the top, at B and move down the column until intersecting the row for 100 ft. The RNT is *6* minutes, and the maximum no-decompression stop bottom time is *14* minutes. A safety stop would be required at the end of the dive.

Planning a pair of no-decompression stop dives

Example 11.

You are planning two no-decompression stop dives. The first dive is to 100 ft, followed, 3 hours later, by a dive to 75 ft. Find the maximum allowable bottom time for each dive.

Enter Table 1 at 100 ft and move down the column to the black box which contains the NDL, which is *20* minutes.

Move right to find the PG, which is *O*. Continue across to the right until finding a box containing the surface interval of 3 hours. It is the 2:24-5:24 box, so move to it and then down the column to get the PG after the surface interval. It is *A*.

Enter Table 3, from the top, at A, and move down the column until intersecting the row for 80 ft. The NDL for the dive is the number printed on blue, and is *26* minutes.

Note:

A safety stop would be mandatory at the end of each dive, but it is not necessary to include the time of the safety stop when determining the PG after the dive. However, by using the total dive time (i.e. bottom time + ascent time + time at safety stop), rather than just the bottom time to determine the PG, extra safety may be achieved.

Example 12.

You are planning two no-decompression stop dives. The first is to 120 ft, followed, 4 hours later, by a dive to 110 ft. Find the maximum allowable bottom time for each dive.

Enter Table 1 at 120 ft and move down to find the NDL in the black box. It is *13* minutes, and is the maximum allowable bottom time for the first dive.

Move right to get the PG after the dive, which is *K*. Continue moving right to find the box which includes the 4-hour surface interval. It is the 2:05-5:05 box. Move across to this box and then down the column to get the new PG, which is *A*.

Enter Table 3 at A and move down to intersect the 110 ft row. The adjusted maximum no-decompression bottom time is *13* minutes.

A safety stop would be mandatory at the end of each dive.

Finding the Pressure Group after a repetitive dive

Example 13.

> *Before a repetitive dive to 100 ft, you are in group B. If you now dived to 100 ft for a bottom time of 10 minutes, what would be your new PG?*

From Table 3, the RNT before the dive is 6 minutes and the maximum no-decompression stop bottom time is 14 minutes.

To find the PG after this 10-minute dive, you must first find the Total Bottom Time (TBT) of the repetitive dive. The TBT is the sum of the Residual Nitrogen Time (RNT) and the Actual Bottom Time (ABT) of the dive. In this case, the TBT = $6_{(RNT)} + 10_{(ABT)}$ = 16 minutes. To find the PG after the dive, return to Table 1. Enter Table 1 at the depth of the repetitive dive, 100 ft, and move down this column to find the TBT of 16 minutes (if the exact time is not tabled select the next greater tabled time). Move right to find the new PG, which is *K*.

Example 14.

> *Before a repetitive dive you are in group C. If you now dived to 75 ft for a bottom time of 15 minutes, what would be your new Pressure Group?*

From Table 3, the RNT at 80 ft before the dive is 10 minutes (and the maximum no-decompression stop bottom time is 20 minutes).

To find the PG after this 15-minute dive, first find the TBT. The TBT = 10 + 15 = 25 minutes.

Turn to Table 1, and look up 80 ft for 25 minutes. You will get a PG of *N*.

Planning a Group of Three No-decompression Stop Dives

Example 15.

> *You are planning to do three no-decompression stop dives, two of which are repetitive. The first dive, which is to 80 ft, is followed, 2 hours later, by a dive to 65 ft, which is followed, 3 hours later, by a final dive to 50 ft. Find the maximum allowable no-decompression stop bottom times for each of the dives.*

Enter Table 1 at 80 ft and move down to find the NDL of *30* minutes, which is the maximum allowable bottom time for the first dive. A safety stop is mandatory.

Move right to find the PG, which is R, and continue across to find the surface interval. It lies in the 1:47-2:34 box, so move across to this box and then down the column to get the new PG, group B.

Enter Table 3 at B and move down to intersect the row for 70 ft. The maximum no-decompression stop bottom time is 31 minutes, and the TBT = 9 + 31 = *40* minutes. A safety stop is mandatory.

Enter Table 1 at 70 ft, move down to find the TBT of 40 minutes and right to find the PG. It is T. Continue right to find the 3-hour surface interval and down to get the new PG, which is A.

Enter Table 3 at A and move down to intersect the 50 ft row. The maximum no-decompression stop bottom time is 73 minutes. A safety stop is mandatory.

Note:

Example 15 can be compared directly to the equivalent problem using U.S. Navy Tables shown on Page 203.

SPECIAL CASES

1. Cold and Strenuous Dives

When planning a dive in cold water, or under conditions that might be strenuous, plan the dive assuming the depth is 10 ft deeper than actual.

For example, if you are planning to dive to 60 ft and you expect to be cold, take the limit for 70 ft as your maximum no-decompression stop bottom time.

If you get cold, or if you work hard during a dive to 85 ft, ensure that you begin your ascent before the NDL for 100 ft expires.

2. Special Rules For Multiple Dives

If you are planning 3 or more dives: Beginning with the first dive, if your ending Pressure Group after any dive is W or X, the minimum surface interval between all subsequent dives is 1 hour. If your ending Pressure Group after any dive is Y or Z, the minimum surface interval between all subsequent dives is 3 hours.

Example 16.

After a dive to 60 ft for 55 minutes your PG will be W. If you are planning a second dive, you must remain at the surface for at least 1 hour. If, after an hour of surface interval you wish to dive to 50 ft, the maximum no-decompression stop bottom time is 49 minutes. If you actually dive to 50 ft for 30 minutes, you will surface with a PG of T. You must still wait at least an hour before diving again, since the previous dive brought you into group W.

Example 17.

After a dive to 60 ft for 54 minutes you are in group V. After a 20-minute surface interval your PG is Q. You then dive to 40 ft for 60 minutes, which puts you into group Z. You must not dive again for at least 3 hours and must have a mininum surface interval of 3 hours between any further dives, until there has been a 6-hour break from diving.

B. METRIC VERSION

This section relates only to the *metric version* of the RDP.

GENERAL RULES OF USE

Strictly adhere to the following rules when using The Recreational Dive Planner:

1. Any dive planned to 10 metres or *less* should be calculated as a dive to 10 metres.

2. Use the exact or next-greater depth shown for the depths of all dives. The 42 metre designation is for emergency purpose only: *do not dive deeper than 40 metres.*

3. Use the exact or next-greater time shown for the times of all dives. **Note: In all cases, if you are ever in doubt about what your pressure group or time reading should be, *always* opt for the more conservative letter or number.**

4. Make a conscious effort to ascend slowly from all dives. In all cases, ascend no faster than 18 metres per minute.

5. As with any dive table, be conservative and avoid using the maximum limits provided.

6. When planning a dive in cold water or under conditions that might be strenuous, plan the dive assuming the depth is 4 metres deeper than actual.

7. Plan repetitive dives so each successive dive is to a shallower depth. Limit repetitive dives to 30 metres or shallower.

8. Limit your maximum depths to your training and experience level (Open Water Divers - 18 metres; divers with greater training and experience - 30 metres, with no dive in excess of 40 metres).

9. If you discover you have accidentally descended below 40 metres, immediately ascend (at a rate not to exceed 18 metres per minute) to 5 metres and make an *emergency decompression stop* for the following time:

   a. 8 minutes - if the No-Decompression Limit for 40 metres is *not* exceeded by more than 5 minutes.

   b. 15 minutes - if the No-Decompression Limit for 40 metres is exceeded by more than 5 minutes.

10. Any dive below 40 metres exceeds the limits of the RDP and must be followed by a surface interval of at least 6 hours.

11. A safety stop is always recommended after every dive. However, always make a safety stop for 3 minutes at 5 metres after any dive to 30 m (or greater) and any time you surface within 3 Pressure Groups of a No-Decompression Limit (NDL). Checking to see whether you are within 3 pressure groups of your NDL should always be your last step when planning a dive.

12. The RDP was not meant for decompression diving - provisions for an emergency decompression stop are included only as a safety factor if you make a mistake. Proper planning and monitoring of your dives will avoid the need for emergency decompression. Emergency decompression - If a No- Decompression Limit is exceeded by no more than 5 minutes, an 8-minute decompression stop at 5 metres is mandatory. Upon surfacing, the diver must remain out of the water for at least 6 hours prior to making another dive. If a No-Decompression Limit is exceeded by more than 5 minutes, a 5-metre decompression stop of no less than 15 minutes is urged (air supply permitting). Upon surfacing, the diver must remain out of the water for at least 24 hours prior to flying or making another dive.

13. Special Rules for Multiple Dives - If you are planning 3 or more dives in a day: Beginning with the first dive, if your ending Pressure Group after any dive is W or X, the minimum surface interval between all subsequent dives is 1 hour. If your ending Pressure Group after any dive is Y or Z, the minimum surface interval between all subsequent dives is 3 hours.

    Note: *Since little is presently known about the physiological effects of multiple dives over multiple days, divers are wise to make fewer dives and limit their exposure toward the end of a multi-day dive series.*

14. *Flying After Diving Procedures* - For a single no- decompression dive with less than 1 hour of bottom time, *wait 4 hours*; for a single no-decompression dive with more than 1 hour of bottom time or after any repetitive dive, *wait 12 hours*; for any dive requiring emergency decompression, *wait 24 hours.* *

15. *Diving At Altitude* - This planner is not designed for use at altitudes greater than 300 m above sea-level (See Chapter 21 for procedure for diving at altitude).

PLANNING NO-DECOMPRESSION STOP DIVES

1. SINGLE OR FIRST NO-DECOMPRESSION STOP DIVES

Table 1 (within Table 19.7) was designed for planning single dives, or the first of a group of dives. Table 1 is the left-most table in Table 19.7.

* In future revisions of the RDP these guidelines will be replaced by the DAN guidelines given in Chapter 20.

TABLE 19.7
Side 1 of the RDP (Metric version)

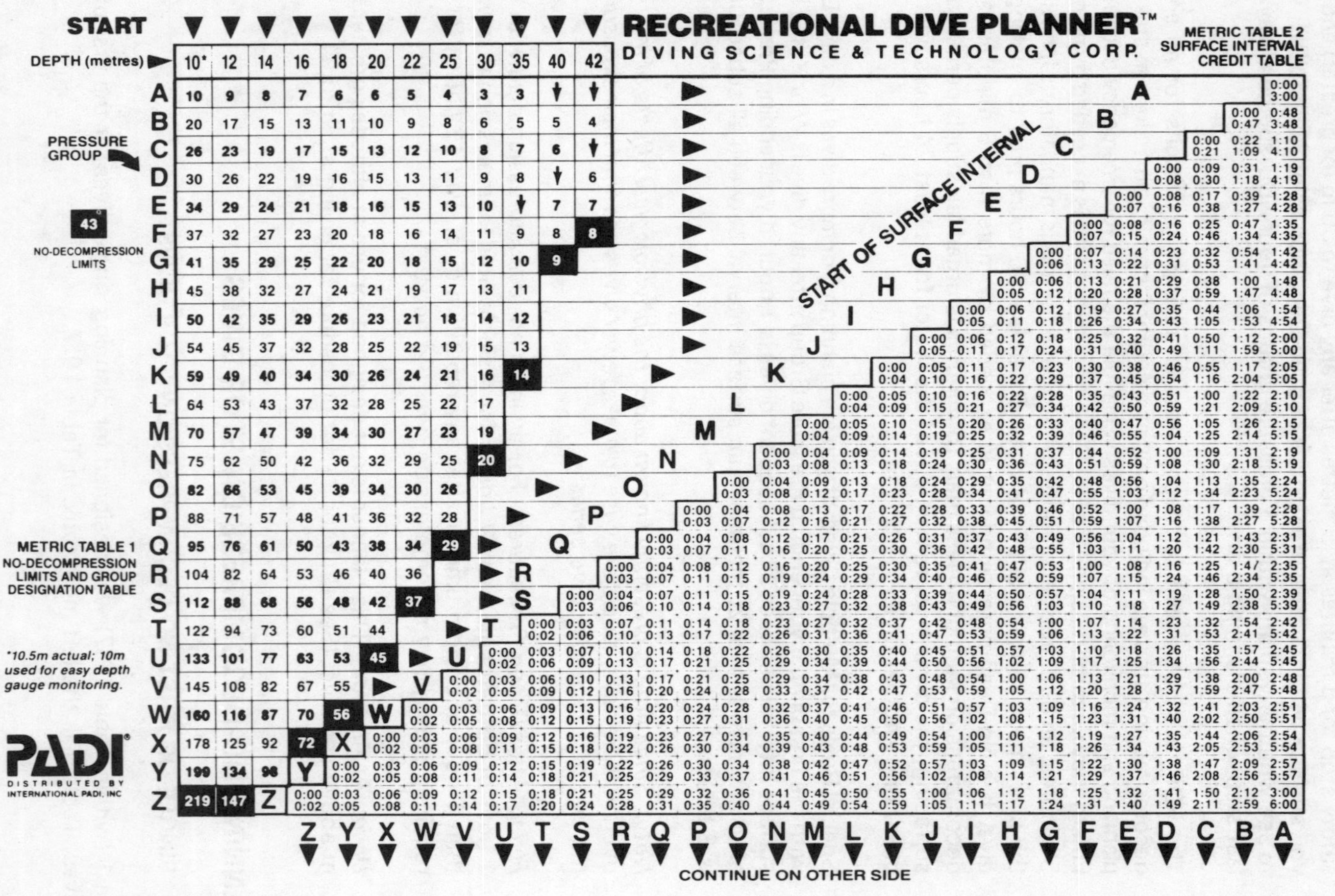

RECREATIONAL DIVE PLANNER™
DIVING SCIENCE & TECHNOLOGY CORP.

START

METRIC TABLE 1 NO-DECOMPRESSION LIMITS AND GROUP DESIGNATION TABLE

PRESSURE GROUP (rows); DEPTH (metres) (columns). Black-box numbers (e.g. 43) = NO-DECOMPRESSION LIMITS.

Pressure Group	10*	12	14	16	18	20	22	25	30	35	40	42
A	10	9	8	7	6	6	5	4	3	3	↓	↓
B	20	17	15	13	11	10	9	8	6	5	5	4
C	26	23	19	17	15	13	12	10	8	7	6	↓
D	30	26	22	19	16	15	13	11	9	8	↓	6
E	34	29	24	21	18	16	15	13	10	↓	7	7
F	37	32	27	23	20	18	16	14	11	9	8	8
G	41	35	29	25	22	20	18	15	12	10	9	
H	45	38	32	27	24	21	19	17	13	11		
I	50	42	35	29	26	23	21	18	14	12		
J	54	45	37	32	28	25	22	19	15	13		
K	59	49	40	34	30	26	24	21	16	14		
L	64	53	43	37	32	28	25	22	17			
M	70	57	47	39	34	30	27	23	19			
N	75	62	50	42	36	32	29	25	20			
O	82	66	53	45	39	34	30	26				
P	88	71	57	48	41	36	32	28				
Q	95	76	61	50	43	38	34	29				
R	104	82	64	53	46	40	36					
S	112	88	68	56	48	42	37					
T	122	94	73	60	51	44						
U	133	101	77	63	53	45						
V	145	108	82	67	55							
W	160	116	87	70	56							
X	178	125	92	72								
Y	199	134	98									
Z	219	147										

*10.5m actual; 10m used for easy depth gauge monitoring.

METRIC TABLE 2 SURFACE INTERVAL CREDIT TABLE

START OF SURFACE INTERVAL

	Z	Y	X	W	V	U	T	S	R	Q	P	O	N	M	L	K	J	I	H	G	F	E	D	C	B	A
A																										0:00 3:00
B																									0:00 0:47	0:48 3:48
C																								0:00 0:21	0:22 1:09	1:10 4:10
D																							0:00 0:08	0:09 0:30	0:31 1:18	1:19 4:19
E																						0:00 0:07	0:08 0:16	0:17 0:38	0:39 1:27	1:28 4:28
F																					0:00 0:07	0:08 0:15	0:16 0:24	0:25 0:46	0:47 1:34	1:35 4:35
G																				0:00 0:06	0:07 0:13	0:14 0:22	0:23 0:31	0:32 0:53	0:54 1:41	1:42 4:42
H																			0:00 0:05	0:06 0:12	0:13 0:20	0:21 0:28	0:29 0:37	0:38 0:59	1:00 1:47	1:48 4:48
I																		0:00 0:05	0:06 0:11	0:12 0:18	0:19 0:26	0:27 0:34	0:35 0:43	0:44 1:05	1:06 1:53	1:54 4:54
J																	0:00 0:05	0:06 0:11	0:12 0:17	0:18 0:24	0:25 0:31	0:32 0:40	0:41 0:49	0:50 1:11	1:12 1:59	2:00 5:00
K																0:00 0:04	0:05 0:10	0:11 0:16	0:17 0:22	0:23 0:29	0:30 0:37	0:38 0:45	0:46 0:54	0:55 1:16	1:17 2:04	2:05 5:05
L															0:00 0:04	0:05 0:09	0:10 0:15	0:16 0:21	0:22 0:27	0:28 0:34	0:35 0:42	0:43 0:50	0:51 0:59	1:00 1:21	1:22 2:09	2:10 5:10
M														0:00 0:04	0:05 0:09	0:10 0:14	0:15 0:19	0:20 0:25	0:26 0:32	0:33 0:39	0:40 0:46	0:47 0:55	0:56 1:04	1:05 1:25	1:26 2:14	2:15 5:15
N													0:00 0:03	0:04 0:08	0:09 0:13	0:14 0:18	0:19 0:24	0:25 0:30	0:31 0:36	0:37 0:43	0:44 0:51	0:52 0:59	1:00 1:08	1:09 1:30	1:31 2:18	2:19 5:19
O												0:00 0:03	0:04 0:08	0:09 0:12	0:13 0:17	0:18 0:23	0:24 0:28	0:29 0:34	0:35 0:41	0:42 0:47	0:48 0:55	0:56 1:03	1:04 1:12	1:13 1:34	1:35 2:23	2:24 5:24
P											0:00 0:03	0:04 0:07	0:08 0:12	0:13 0:16	0:17 0:21	0:22 0:27	0:28 0:32	0:33 0:38	0:39 0:45	0:46 0:51	0:52 0:59	1:00 1:07	1:08 1:16	1:17 1:38	1:39 2:27	2:28 5:28
Q										0:00 0:03	0:04 0:07	0:08 0:11	0:12 0:16	0:17 0:20	0:21 0:25	0:26 0:30	0:31 0:36	0:37 0:42	0:43 0:48	0:49 0:55	0:56 1:03	1:04 1:11	1:12 1:20	1:21 1:42	1:43 2:30	2:31 5:31
R									0:00 0:03	0:04 0:07	0:08 0:11	0:12 0:15	0:16 0:19	0:20 0:24	0:25 0:29	0:30 0:34	0:35 0:40	0:41 0:46	0:47 0:52	0:53 0:59	1:00 1:07	1:08 1:15	1:16 1:24	1:25 1:46	1:47 2:34	2:35 5:35
S								0:00 0:03	0:04 0:06	0:07 0:10	0:11 0:14	0:15 0:18	0:19 0:23	0:24 0:27	0:28 0:32	0:33 0:38	0:39 0:43	0:44 0:49	0:50 0:56	0:57 1:03	1:04 1:10	1:11 1:18	1:19 1:27	1:28 1:49	1:50 2:38	2:39 5:39
T							0:00 0:02	0:03 0:06	0:07 0:10	0:11 0:13	0:14 0:17	0:18 0:22	0:23 0:26	0:27 0:31	0:32 0:36	0:37 0:41	0:42 0:47	0:48 0:53	0:54 0:59	1:00 1:06	1:07 1:13	1:14 1:22	1:23 1:31	1:32 1:53	1:54 2:41	2:42 5:42
U						0:00 0:02	0:03 0:06	0:07 0:09	0:10 0:13	0:14 0:17	0:18 0:21	0:22 0:25	0:26 0:29	0:30 0:34	0:35 0:39	0:40 0:44	0:45 0:50	0:51 0:56	0:57 1:02	1:03 1:09	1:10 1:17	1:18 1:25	1:26 1:34	1:35 1:56	1:57 2:44	2:45 5:45
V					0:00 0:02	0:03 0:05	0:06 0:09	0:10 0:12	0:13 0:16	0:17 0:20	0:21 0:24	0:25 0:28	0:29 0:33	0:34 0:37	0:38 0:42	0:43 0:47	0:48 0:53	0:54 0:59	1:00 1:05	1:06 1:12	1:13 1:20	1:21 1:28	1:29 1:37	1:38 1:59	2:00 2:47	2:48 5:48
W				0:00 0:02	0:03 0:05	0:06 0:08	0:09 0:12	0:13 0:15	0:16 0:19	0:20 0:23	0:24 0:27	0:28 0:31	0:32 0:36	0:37 0:40	0:41 0:45	0:46 0:50	0:51 0:56	0:57 1:02	1:03 1:08	1:09 1:15	1:16 1:23	1:24 1:31	1:32 1:40	1:41 2:02	2:03 2:50	2:51 5:51
X			0:00 0:02	0:03 0:05	0:06 0:08	0:09 0:11	0:12 0:15	0:16 0:18	0:19 0:22	0:23 0:26	0:27 0:30	0:31 0:34	0:35 0:39	0:40 0:43	0:44 0:48	0:49 0:53	0:54 0:59	1:00 1:05	1:06 1:11	1:12 1:18	1:19 1:26	1:27 1:34	1:35 1:43	1:44 2:05	2:06 2:53	2:54 5:54
Y		0:00 0:02	0:03 0:05	0:06 0:08	0:09 0:11	0:12 0:14	0:15 0:18	0:19 0:21	0:22 0:25	0:26 0:29	0:30 0:33	0:34 0:37	0:38 0:41	0:42 0:46	0:47 0:51	0:52 0:56	0:57 1:02	1:03 1:08	1:09 1:14	1:15 1:21	1:22 1:29	1:30 1:37	1:38 1:46	1:47 2:08	2:09 2:56	2:57 5:57
Z	0:00 0:02	0:03 0:05	0:06 0:08	0:09 0:11	0:12 0:14	0:15 0:17	0:18 0:20	0:21 0:24	0:25 0:28	0:29 0:31	0:32 0:35	0:36 0:40	0:41 0:44	0:45 0:49	0:50 0:54	0:55 0:59	1:00 1:05	1:06 1:11	1:12 1:17	1:18 1:24	1:25 1:31	1:32 1:40	1:41 1:49	1:50 2:11	2:12 2:59	3:00 6:00

CONTINUE ON OTHER SIDE

PADI® DISTRIBUTED BY INTERNATIONAL PADI, INC

Example 1.

You are planning to dive to a maximum depth of 25 m. What is the No-Decompression Limit (NDL)?

Enter Table 1 of the RDP, from the top at 25 m, and move down the column until coming to the *white* number in the *black* box. This is the NDL which, in this case, is *29* minutes. This 29 minutes is the maximum allowable *bottom time* for the dive.

Note:

If you dive to this NDL, you must then make a safety stop of 3 minutes at 5 m, since you have dived to within 3 Pressure Groups (PG) of the NDL. Safety stops need not be added to bottom time with these tables (although the author advises it for the extra safety sometimes gained in any following repetitive dives).

Similarly, the NDL for 30 m is 20 minutes, the NDL for 18 m is 56 minutes, and the NDL for 16 m is 72 minutes.

Example 2.

What is the NDL for a single/first dive to a maximum depth of 15 m?

Enter Table 1 from the top at 16 m (i.e. the next greater tabled depth, since 15 m is not tabled). Move down the column until reaching the *white* number in tne *black* box. The NDL is thus *72* minutes.

Note:

If this dive is carried out a safety stop would be mandatory (within 3 PGs of the NDL).

Similarly, the NDL for 19 m is 45 minutes, the NDL for 11 m is 147 minutes and for 31 m is 14 minutes.

Finding the Pressure Group (PG) after single/first no-decompression stop dives

Example 3.

Find the PG after a single dive to 25 m for 29 minutes.

Enter Table 1, from the top, at 25 m. Move down the column until coming to the exact, or next longer, tabled bottom time. In this case 29 minutes is tabled so move down to 29 minutes and then right to find the PG after the dive. It is *Q*.

Note:

A safetv stop would be required at the end of this dive.

Example 4.

Find the PG after a single dive to 15 m for 60 minutes.

Enter Table 1, from the top, at 16 m and move down until finding the bottom time of 60 minutes. Moving right, the PG is *T*.

Note:

Since 60 minutes is more than 3 PGs from the NDL of 72 minutes, a safety stop is not mandatory, although it is highly recommended after any dive.

Example 5.

What is the Pressure Group (PG) after a dive to 19 m for 33 minutes?

Enter Table 1, from the top, at 20 m (i.e. the next greater tabled depth, since the exact depth is not tabled). Move down the column until finding the exact, or next longer tabled, bottom time. 33 minutes is not tabled so take 34 minutes and then move right to find the PG. It is *O*.

Example 6.

What is the PG after a dive to 34 m for a bottom time of 9 minutes?

Enter Table 1 at 35 m and move down to find the bottom time of 9 minutes (simply pass through the arrow below 8 minutes). Moving right, the PG is *F*.

2. REPETITIVE NO-DECOMPRESSION STOP DIVES

During a surface interval nitrogen is off-gassed. After various intervals the Pressure Groups, which represent the nitrogen levels in the 60-minute tissue, will be reduced. Table 2, the "Surface Interval Credit Table", enables us to calculate new Pressure Groups after surface intervals which are greater than 2 minutes and less than 6 hours.

Finding the new Pressure Group after a surface interval

Example 7.

If the PG immediately after a dive is H, what is the new group after a surface interval of 2 hours?

Enter Table 2, from the left, at *H* and move right until finding an interval that includes the surface interval of 2 hours. It is between 1:48 and 4:48, so move right to this box and then down the column to the bottom to get the new PG. It is *A*.

Example 8.

If the PG immediately after a dive is F, find the new group after a surface interval of 50 minutes.

Enter Table 2, from the left, at *F* and move right to find a box containing 50 minutes. It is included in 0:47 to 1:34, so move to this box and then down the column to find the PG, which is *B*.

Calculating the maximum allowable no-decompression stop bottom time for a repetitive dive

A repetitive dive is defined to be any dive within 6 hours of a previous dive(s). When planning a repetitive dive, the excess nitrogen still remaining after the surface interval must be taken into account. This is done by adding a "Residual Nitrogen Time" (RNT).

The Residual Nitrogen Time is the amount of time which must be considered already spent at the maximum depth of the repetitive dive before this dive is commenced. It is subtracted from the single dive NDL for that depth, and the result is the no-decompression stop bottom time still remaining at that depth.

Table 3 (Table 19.6) gives the Residual Nitrogen Times and the maximum no-decompression stop bottom times still available for the various depths of repetitive dives.

Example 9.

If you are in group C immediately before a dive to 24 m, find:

(i) the Residual Nitrogen Time (RNT) at 24 m

(ii) the maximum allowable no-decompression stop bottom time at 24 m

Enter Table 3, from the top, at C and move down the column until intersecting the row for 25 m (i.e. take the next greater tabled depth, since 24 m is not tabled). You will find two numbers in the box. The top number, printed *on white*, is the Residual Nitrogen Time which, in this case, is *10* minutes. This means that before doing the dive you must consider that you have already spent 10 minutes at 24 m. This 10 minutes is to account for excess nitrogen left over from the previous dive(s). The remaining allowable no-decompression stop time (i.e. adjusted maximum no-decompression bottom time) is the number printed *on blue.* In this case it is *19* minutes. **The Actual Bottom Time (ABT) of a repetitive dive should never exceed the adjusted maximum no-decompression bottom time.**

Note:

If you planned to do this dive, you must end it with a safety stop of 3 minutes at 5 m, since you will be within 3 PGs of the NDL.

TABLE 19.8
Side 2 of the RDP (Metric version)

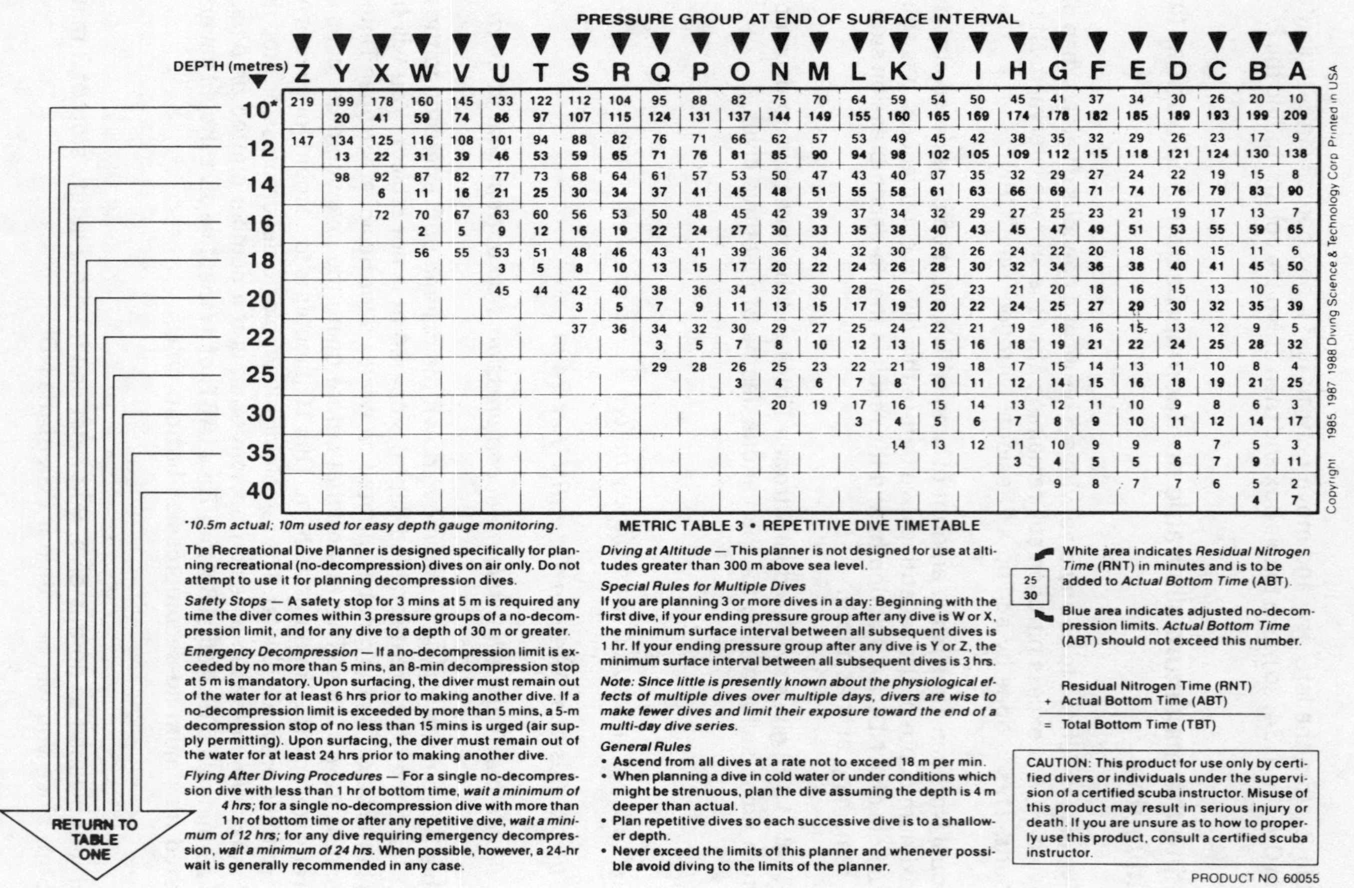

PRESSURE GROUP AT END OF SURFACE INTERVAL

DEPTH (metres)	Z	Y	X	W	V	U	T	S	R	Q	P	O	N	M	L	K	J	I	H	G	F	E	D	C	B	A
10*	219	199 20	178 41	160 59	145 74	133 86	122 97	112 107	104 115	95 124	88 131	82 137	75 144	70 149	64 155	59 160	54 165	50 169	45 174	41 178	37 182	34 185	30 189	26 193	20 199	10 209
12	147	134 13	125 22	116 31	108 39	101 46	94 53	88 59	82 65	76 71	71 76	66 81	62 85	57 90	53 94	49 98	45 102	42 105	38 109	35 112	32 115	29 118	26 121	23 124	17 130	9 138
14		98	92 6	87 11	82 16	77 21	73 25	68 30	64 34	61 37	57 41	53 45	50 48	47 51	43 55	40 58	37 61	35 63	32 66	29 69	27 71	24 74	22 76	19 79	15 83	8 90
16			72	70 2	67 5	63 9	60 12	56 16	53 19	50 22	48 24	45 27	42 30	39 33	37 35	34 38	32 40	29 43	27 45	25 47	23 49	21 51	19 53	17 55	13 59	7 65
18				56	55	53 3	51 5	48 8	46 10	43 13	41 15	39 17	36 20	34 22	32 24	30 26	28 28	26 30	24 32	22 34	20 36	18 38	16 40	15 41	11 45	6 50
20						45	44	42 3	40 5	38 7	36 9	34 11	32 13	30 15	28 17	26 19	25 20	23 22	21 24	20 25	18 27	16 29	15 30	13 32	10 35	6 39
22								37	36	34 3	32 5	30 7	29 8	27 10	25 12	24 13	22 15	21 16	19 18	18 19	16 21	15 22	13 24	12 25	9 28	5 32
25										29	28	26 3	25 4	23 6	22 7	21 8	19 10	18 11	17 12	15 14	14 15	13 16	11 18	10 19	8 21	4 25
30													20	19	17 3	16 4	15 5	14 6	13 7	12 8	11 9	10 10	9 11	8 12	6 14	3 17
35																14	13	12	11 3	10 4	9 5	9 5	8 6	7 7	5 9	3 11
40																				9	8	7	7	6	5 4	2 7

10.5m actual; 10m used for easy depth gauge monitoring.

RETURN TO TABLE ONE

METRIC TABLE 3 • REPETITIVE DIVE TIMETABLE

The Recreational Dive Planner is designed specifically for planning recreational (no-decompression) dives on air only. Do not attempt to use it for planning decompression dives.

Safety Stops — A safety stop for 3 mins at 5 m is required any time the diver comes within 3 pressure groups of a no-decompression limit, and for any dive to a depth of 30 m or greater.

Emergency Decompression — If a no-decompression limit is exceeded by no more than 5 mins, an 8-min decompression stop at 5 m is mandatory. Upon surfacing, the diver must remain out of the water for at least 6 hrs prior to making another dive. If a no-decompression limit is exceeded by more than 5 mins, a 5-m decompression stop of no less than 15 mins is urged (air supply permitting). Upon surfacing, the diver must remain out of the water for at least 24 hrs prior to making another dive.

Flying After Diving Procedures — For a single no-decompression dive with less than 1 hr of bottom time, *wait a minimum of 4 hrs;* for a single no-decompression dive with more than 1 hr of bottom time or after any repetitive dive, *wait a minimum of 12 hrs;* for any dive requiring emergency decompression, *wait a minimum of 24 hrs.* When possible, however, a 24-hr wait is generally recommended in any case.

Diving at Altitude — This planner is not designed for use at altitudes greater than 300 m above sea level.

Special Rules for Multiple Dives

If you are planning 3 or more dives in a day: Beginning with the first dive, if your ending pressure group after any dive is W or X, the minimum surface interval between all subsequent dives is 1 hr. If your ending pressure group after any dive is Y or Z, the minimum surface interval between all subsequent dives is 3 hrs.

Note: Since little is presently known about the physiological effects of multiple dives over multiple days, divers are wise to make fewer dives and limit their exposure toward the end of a multi-day dive series.

General Rules

- Ascend from all dives at a rate not to exceed 18 m per min.
- When planning a dive in cold water or under conditions which might be strenuous, plan the dive assuming the depth is 4 m deeper than actual.
- Plan repetitive dives so each successive dive is to a shallower depth.
- Never exceed the limits of this planner and whenever possible avoid diving to the limits of the planner.

25
30

White area indicates *Residual Nitrogen Time* (RNT) in minutes and is to be added to *Actual Bottom Time* (ABT).

Blue area indicates adjusted no-decompression limits. *Actual Bottom Time* (ABT) should not exceed this number.

Residual Nitrogen Time (RNT)
\+ Actual Bottom Time (ABT)
= Total Bottom Time (TBT)

CAUTION: This product for use only by certified divers or individuals under the supervision of a certified scuba instructor. Misuse of this product may result in serious injury or death. If you are unsure as to how to properly use this product, consult a certified scuba instructor.

PRODUCT NO 60055

Example 10.

At the end of a surface interval after a dive you are in group B. Find:

(i) the Residual Nitrogen Time

(ii) the maximum allowable bottom time for a no-decompression stop dive to 29 m.

Enter Table 3, from the top, at B and move down the column until intersecting the row for 30 m. The RNT is *6* minutes and the maximum no-decompression stop bottom time is *14* minutes. A safety stop would be required at the end of the dive.

Planning a pair of no-decompression stop dives

Example 11.

You are planning two no-decompression stop dives. The first dive is to 30 m, followed, 3 hours later, by a dive to 23 m. Find the maximum allowable bottom time for each dive.

Enter Table 1 at 30 m and move down the column to the black box which contains the NDL, which is *20* minutes.

Move right to find the PG, which is *N*. Continue across to the right until finding a box containing the surface interval of 3 hours. It is the 2:19-5:19 box, so move to it and then down the column to get the PG after the surface interval. It is *A*.

Enter Table 3, from the top, at A and move down the column until intersecting the row for 25 m. The NDL for the dive is the number printed on blue, and is *25* minutes.

Note:

A safety stop would be mandatory at the end of each dive, but it is not necessary to include the time of the safety stop when determining the PG after the dive. However, by using the total dive time (i.e. bottom time + ascent time + time at safety stop), rather than just the bottom time to determine the PG, extra safety may be achieved.

Example 12.

You are planning two no-decompression stop dives. The first is to 36 m, followed, 4 hours later, by a dive to 33 m. Find the maximum allowable bottom time for each dive.

Enter Table 1 at 40 m and move down to find the NDL in the black box. It is *9* minutes and is the maximum allowable bottom time for the first dive.

Move right to get the PG after the dive, which is *G*. Continue moving right to find the box which includes the 4-hour surface interval. It is the 1:42-4:42 box. Move across to this box and then down the column to get the new PG, which is *A*.

Enter Table 3 at A and move down to intersect the 35 m row. The adjusted maximum no-decompression bottom time is *11* minutes.

A safety stop would be mandatory at the end of each dive.

Finding the Pressure Group after a repetitive dive

Example 13.

Before a repetitive dive to 30 m, you are in group B. If you now dived to 30 m for a bottom time of 10 minutes, what would be your new PG?

From Table 3, the RNT before the dive is 6 minutes, and the maximum no-decompression stop bottom time is 14 minutes.

To find the PG after this 10-minute dive you must first find the Total Bottom Time (TBT) of the repetitive dive. The TBT is the sum of the Residual Nitrogen Time (RNT) and the Actual Bottom Time (ABT) of the dive. In this case, the TBT = $6_{(RNT)} + 10_{(ABT)} = 16$ minutes. To find the PG after the dive, return to Table 1. Enter Table 1 at the depth of the repetitive dive, 30 m, and move down this column to find the TBT of 16 minutes (if the exact time is not tabled select the next greater tabled time). Move right to find the new PG, which is *K*.

Example 14.

Before a repetitive dive you are in group C. If you now dived to 23 m for a bottom time of 15 minutes, what would be your new Pressure Group?

From Table 3, the RNT at 25 m before the dive is 10 minutes (and the maximum no-decompression stop bottom time is 20 minutes).

To find the PG after this 15-minute dive, first find the TBT. The TBT = 10 + 15 = 25 minutes.

Turn to Table 1 and look up 25 m for 25 minutes. You will get a PG of *N*.

Planning a group of three no-decompression stop dives

Example 15.

You are planning to do three no-decompression stop dives, two of which are repetitive. The first dive, which is to 24 m, is followed, 2 hours later, by a dive to 20 m, which is followed, 3 hours later, by a final dive to 15 m. Find the maximum allowable no-decompression stop bottom times for each of the dives.

Enter Table 1 at 25 m and move down to find the NDL of *29* minutes, which is the maximum allowable bottom time for the first dive. A safety stop is mandatory.

Move right to find the PG, which is Q, and continue across to find the surface interval. It lies in the 1:43-2:30 box, so move across to this box and then down the column to get the new PG, group B.

Enter Table 3 at B and move down to intersect the row for 20 m. The maximum no-decompression stop bottom time is 35 minutes, and the TBT = 10 + 35 = *45* minutes. A safety stop is mandatory.

Enter Table 1 at 20 m, move down to find the TBT of 45 minutes and right to find the PG. It is U. Continue right to find the 3-hour surface interval, and down to get the new PG, which is A.

Enter Table 3 at A and move down to intersect the 16 m row. The maximum no-decompression stop bottom time is 65 minutes. A safety stop is mandatory.

Note:

Example 15 can be compared directly to the equivalent problem using U.S. Navy Tables shown on Page 203.

SPECIAL CASES

1. Cold and Strenuous Dives

When planning a dive in cold water, or under conditions that might be strenuous, plan the dive assuming the depth is 4 m deeper than actual.

For example, if you are planning to dive to 18 m and you expect to be cold, take the limit for 22 m as your maximum no-decompression stop bottom time.

If you get cold, or if you work hard during a dive to 27 m, ensure that you begin your ascent before the NDL for 35 m expires (i.e. it is treated as a dive to 31 m).

2. Special Rules For Multiple Dives

If you are planning 3 or more dives: Beginning with the first dive, if your ending Pressure Group after any dive is W or X, the minimum surface interval between all subsequent dives is 1 hour. If your ending Pressure Group after any dive is Y or Z, the minimum surface interval between all subsequent dives is 3 hours.

Example 16.

After a dive to 18 m for 56 minutes your PG will be W. If you are planning a second dive, you must remain at the surface for at least 1 hour. If, after an hour of surface interval, you wish to dive to 15 m, the maximum no-decompression stop bottom time is 43 minutes. If you actually dive to 15 m for 30 minutes, you will surface with a PG of T. You must still wait at least an hour before diving again, since the previous dive brought you into group W.

Example 17.

After a dive to 18 m for 54 minutes you are in group V. After a 20-minute surface interval, your PG is Q. You then dive to 12 m for 60 minutes, which puts you into group Z. You must not dive again for at least 3 hours, and must have a mininum surface interval of 3 hours between any further dives, until there has been a 6-hour break from diving.

Some of the above text has been taken directly from some PADI promotional and educational material and I wish to thank PADI International Inc. for permission to use it and for permission to re-print their tables. *Special thanks to Drew Richardson (Director of Training and Education, PADI International) for his constructive comments, support and encouragement. Thanks also to Terry Cummins (Director, PADI Australia) for his support.*

Note:

Since originally released, various changes have been made to the rules for using these tables. More changes could still occur so the reader is advised to be vigilant.

REFERENCES

1. Powell, M. et al (1988), "Doppler Ultrasound Monitoring of Gas Phase Formation Following Decompression in Repetitive Dives". Diving Science and Technology.

2. Bennett, P., personal communication.

3. Gorman, D. and Parsons, D., personal communication and correspondence to Drew Richardson, PADI USA.

4. Hills, B., personal communication and correspondence to Dr. David Davies, Secretary, SPUMS.

5. Nishi, R., personal communication.

6. Rogers, R. and Powell, M. (1989), "Controlled Hyperbaric Chamber Tests of Multi-Day, Repetitive Dives". (Presented at UHMS Meeting, June 9, 1989).

7. Richardson, D., personal communication.

8. Statistics of Division of Accident Prevention, Brisbane (in prep).

OTHER SOURCES

Diving Science and Technology Corp. (1987), "Recreational Dive Planning ... The Next Generation". PADI.

Powell, M. et al (1988), "Doppler Ultrasound Monitoring of Gas Phase Formation Following Decompression in Repetitive Dives". Diving Science and Technology.

Richardson, D. (1988), "The Evolution of the Recreational Dive Planner". *The Undersea Journal*; First Quarter.

Richardson, D. (1988), "Editorial- A Word About Decompression DSAT Research and Doppler" *The Undersea Journal*; Third Quarter.

Richardson, D. (1988), "Slower Ascent Rates: The PADI S.A.F.E. Diver Campaign. *The Undersea Journal*; Third Quarter.

Richardson, D. (1988), "Multiple Dives over Multiple Days: An Area of Growing Interest and Concern". *The Undersea Journal*; Third Quarter.

Richardson, D. (1988), "Questions and Answers: On the Recreational Dive Planner, DSAT and the Table Research". *Undersea Journal*; Third Quarter.

Rogers, R. (1988), "Renovating Haldane". *The Undersea Journal;* Third Quarter.

Shreeves, K. (1988), "New PADI Dive Tables". *Skin Diver*; 37 (2).

RECOMMENDED FURTHER READING

Powell, M. et al (1988), "Doppler Ultrasound Monitoring of Gas Phase Formation Following Decompression in Repetitive Dives". Diving Science and Technology.

Richardson, D. (1988), "Editorial- A Word About Decompression DSAT Research and Doppler". *The Undersea Journal*; Third Quarter.

Richardson, D. (1988), "Multiple Dives over Multiple Days: An Area of Growing Interest and Concern". *The Undersea Journal*; Third Quarter.

Richardson, D. (1988), "Questions and Answers: On the Recreational Dive Planner, DSAT and the Table Research". *Undersea Journal*; Third Quarter.

Rogers, R. (1988), "Renovating Haldane". *The Undersea Journal;* Third Quarter.

EXERCISES ON THE RDP (Imperial version)

1. Find the No-Decompression Limits for single dives to the following depths:

   (a) 100 ft (b) 30 ft (c) 75 ft (d) 115 ft

   (e) 102 ft

2. Find the maximum allowable no-decompression stop bottom time for the following second dives:

   (a) A dive to 65 ft, 2½ hours after a dive to 96 ft for 20 minutes.

   (b) A dive to 50 ft, 2 hours after a dive to 80 ft for 25 minutes.

   (c) A dive to 100 ft, 4 hours after a dive to 120 ft for 12 minutes.

3. Find the maximum allowable no-decompression stop bottom times for each dive in the following pairs of dives:

   (a) A dive to 95 ft, followed, 2 hours later, by a dive to 66 ft.

   (b) A dive to 120 ft, followed, 2½ hours later, by a dive to 105 ft.

   (c) A dive to 56 ft, followed, 2½ hours later, by another dive to 56 ft.

   (d) A dive to 52 ft, followed, 3 hours later, by a dive to 65 ft.

   (e) A dive to 130 ft, followed, 6½ hours later, by a dive to 40 ft.

ANSWERS

(Times in minutes)

1. (a) 20 (b) 205 (c) 30 (d) 13 (e) 16

2. (a) 35 (b) 67 (c) 17

3. (a) 20, 31 (b) 13, 13 (c) 55, 44
   (d) 55, 35 (e) 10, 140.

EXERCISES ON THE RDP (Metric version)

1. Find the No-Decompression Limits for single dives to the following depths:

   (a) 30 m (b) 9 m (c) 22 m (d) 34 m

   (e) 33 m

2. Find the maximum allowable no-decompression stop bottom time for the following second dives:

   (a) A dive to 19 m, 2$^1/_2$ hours after a dive to 29 m for 20 minutes.

   (b) A dive to 15 m, 2 hours after a dive to 24 m for 25 minutes.

   (c) A dive to 30 m, 4 hours after a dive to 35 m for 12 minutes.

3. Find the maximum allowable no-decompression stop bottom times for each dive in the following pairs of dives:

   (a) A dive to 28 m, followed, 2 hours later, by a dive to 20 m.

   (b) A dive to 35 m, followed, 2$^1/_2$ hours later, by a dive to 32 m.

   (c) A dive to 17 m, followed, 2$^1/_2$ hours later, by another dive to 17 m.

   (d) A dive to 16 m, followed, 3 hours later, by a dive to 20 m.

   (e) A dive to 40 m, followed, 6$^1/_2$ hours later, by a dive to 12 m.

ANSWERS

(Times in minutes)

1. (a) 20 (b) 219 (c) 37 (d) 14 (e) 14.

2. (a) 39 (b) 59 (c) 17.

3. (a) 20, 35 (b) 14, 11 (c) 56, 45

   (d) 72, 39 (e) 9, 138.

SECTION 3

ALTITUDE CONSIDERATIONS AND DIVING

CHAPTER 20
FLYING AFTER DIVING

After diving, we ascend with excess nitrogen in our body tissues, and the amount of this excess nitrogen remaining after a dive depends on a number of factors, which include:

- the depth of the dive
- the amount of time spent underwater
- the amount of physical exertion during the dive
- the effectiveness of our circulation
- the effectiveness of off-gassing during the ascent and after the dive (which depends on the amount of bubble formation, among other factors).

During a short dive, little gas is absorbed by the "slower" body tissues and the body will rid itself of the excess gas fairly quickly. However, during longer dives, the "slower" body tissues will absorb far more nitrogen and it will take a lot longer for the body to unload this extra gas. In addition, if bubbles (symptomatic or asymptomatic) have formed in our blood or body tissues, they will hinder the release of the excess nitrogen, which will be retained for longer.

If we ascend to a higher altitude (by either flying or by driving up a mountain) before enough of this extra gas is released, the reduced atmospheric pressure could allow new bubbles to begin to form, and will also allow any existing bubbles to increase in size.

Doppler monitoring has confirmed the presence of venous bubbles in humans who were taken to altitudes of 3,300 to 10,000 feet (1,000 to 3,000 metres) three hours after a single no-decompression stop dive to 50 ft (15 m) for 100 minutes, and also after a single no-decompression stop dive to 130 ft (39 m) for 10 minutes. Bubbles appeared within minutes of flight. In an earlier study, bubbles were also detected when flying at a cabin altiude of 25,000 feet (7,600 metres) 24 hours after diving.[1]

If sufficient bubble formation occurs **we can get decompression sickness by flying, driving (or otherwise ascending to altitude) too soon after having dived.** It is, therefore, necessary to spend sufficient time at the surface before ascending to higher altitudes in order to allow some of this extra gas to diffuse out of the body. The difficult part is determining how much surface interval is required.

A number of guidelines for this have emerged over the years and the suggested surface intervals vary greatly. Most of the rules give suggested surface intervals before flying to maximum commercial cabin altitudes of 0.74 ATA, which equates to an altitude of 8,000 feet (2,400 metres). However, at times, even modern airliners may have a cabin pressure as low as 0.58 ATA, which equates to an altitude of 13,000 feet (4,000 metres).

Some of these guidelines will be discussed briefly.

Cross Corrections to the U.S. Navy Tables

By dividing the barometric pressure at sea level by the barometric pressure at altitude, a number greater than one is obtained.

For example, at 10,000 feet (3,000 metres), the factor would be 1.00 ATA/0.69 ATA (14.7 psi/10.11 psi) = 1.45. This number is then multiplied by the actual depth of the dive to obtain an "equivalent" depth with which to enter the U.S. Navy Tables. To make a dive of 100 ft (30 m), at an altitude of 10,000 feet (3,000 metres), you would enter the table at 100 x 1.45 = 145 ft (30 x 1.45 = 43.5 m) to obtain your No-Decompression Limit of 5 minutes. For flying immediately after diving at sea-level, you can perform the same calculation to obtain the dive time limit.

At an altitude of 8,500 feet (2,600 metres), the limits obtained would be: 40 ft (12 m)/60 min., 60 ft (18 m)/30 min., 80 ft (24 m)/20 min., 100 ft (30 m)/10 min. and 130 ft (39 m)/ 5 min.

Dr. Bruce Bassett tested similar schedules in a U.S. Air Force study, and his results indicated that this procedure could be expected to yield a significant number of decompression casualties.[2]

The D-Group Rule

This rule suggests that it should be safe to fly to 8,000 feet (2,400 meters), as stated in the NOAA Diving Manual, or to 10,000 feet (3,000 metres), as stated by C.L. Smith in *Altitude Procedures for the Ocean Diver*, as long as one is in Repetitive Group D (or lower, i.e. A,B,C) of the U.S. Navy Tables.

This rule has been applied in two ways. The first implies that one can fly directly to 8,000 feet (2,400 metres)* immediately after dives to 40 ft (12 m)/30 min., 60 ft (18 m)/20 min., 80 ft (24 m)/15 min., 100 ft (30 m)/10 min., and so on. The other application is using the Surface Interval Credit Table to find the proposed safe interval before flying to 8,000 feet (or 10,000 feet), following dives which result in a Repetitive Group greater than D. For example, after diving to 80 ft (24 m) for 25 minutes you are in Group F, but, after a surface interval of 1$^1/_2$hours, you will be in Group D and, theoretically, should be safe to fly to 8,000 feet (2,400 metres).

* or to 10,000 ft according to Smith.

Although the NOAA suggestion is correct, in theory, according to the mathematics of the U.S. Navy Tables, the mathematics has its limitations and this rule is often not conservative enough.[3,4,5] Smith's assertion often violates the supersaturation levels allowed by the U.S. Navy Tables and is, thus, felt to be even less safe than that of NOAA.

One U.S. researcher has gathered 47 cases where the diver had been in Group D, or lower, for between 7 to 40 hours before flying, did not show symptoms before flying, but had symptoms in the aircraft or shortly after landing.[5]

Edel's recommendations

Edel and co-workers, contracted to NASA to establish guidelines for flying after diving, proposed the following procedure for flying to altitudes of 5,000-8,000 feet (1,500-2,400 metres). Their recommendation was that a two hour surface interval be observed prior to flying in commercial aircraft, following dives made only within the No-Decompression Limits of the U.S. Navy Standard Air Decompression Tables, during the preceding 12 hours.[6] Mild symptoms of decompression sickness were ignored in these experiments, and the recommendation did not apply to repetitive or decompression stop dives. It was suggested that, if decompression stop dives were made (or should have been made), then the diver should allow 24 hours between surfacing and flying.

The British adopted this system for use with their tables, and extended it to altitudes between 5,000-9,000 feet (1,500-2,700 metres).

This system is in accordance with the theory and mathematics of the U.S. Navy Tables, however, its main failing is that it does not really take into account the length of the dive. It might be OK to fly two hours after some short no-decompression stop dives, since, after a short dive we unload excess gas fairly quickly. However, the two hour interval is often insufficient after longer dives, or after repetitive dives. In addition, even though obvious symptoms of bends may not result, there may still be a substantial amount of bubble formation which just may cause less obvious but, possibly, serious problems. For example, these guidelines will let you fly two hours after a dive to 130 ft (39 m) for 10 minutes, or a dive to 50 ft (15 m) for 100 minutes and the study previously mentioned[1] detected substantial intravascular bubbling three hours after such dives.

Swiss Recommendations

The Swiss specify a number of different surface intervals ("waiting times"), which depend on the length and depth of the previous dive. After a short dive you can fly sooner than after a longer dive. These suggested intervals, varying from 2 to 5 hours in duration on the Buehlmann (1986) Tables (and between 2-12 hours on the Buehlmann/Hahn Tables), only apply to dives done in accordance with the Buehlmann Tables, which utilize conservative single dive No-Decompression Limits and an ascent rate generally not exceeding 33 ft (10 m)/minute. These "waiting times" were tested for altitudes up to 0.6 ATA (13,500 ft/ 4,100 m).[7] Details of this procedure are shown in Chapter 16.

Example 1.

Find the surface interval required before flying, in a commercial airliner, after a single dive to 60 ft (18 m) for 50 minutes.

The Repetitive Group after the dive is F. Enter the Surface Interval Table at F, and move to the right until intersecting the column with the airplane. The required surface interval is *4 hours*.

Example 2.

Find the surface interval required before flying, in a commercial airliner, after the following pair of dives:
A dive to 100 ft (30 m) for 15 minutes bottom time, followed, 3 hours later, by a dive to 50 ft (15 m) for 40 minutes bottom time.

The Repetitive Group after the first dive is C, and, after the second dive, is D. Enter the Surface Interval Table at D, and move to the right until intersecting the column with the airplane. The required surface interval is *3 hours*.

The BS-AC '88 Tables recommendations

The following recommendations accompany the BS-AC '88 Tables:

A diver who wishes to fly in a pressurized aircraft must wait until he has a Current Tissue Code of *B*. A diver who wishes to fly in an unpressurized aircraft must wait until he has a Current Tissue Code of *A*.

In the case of a pressurized aircraft, the interval required before flying is between 0 to 4 hours, depending on the Surfacing Code after the last dive. Intervals of 10 to 16 hours are required before flying in an unpressurized aircraft.

Example 3.

Find the surface interval required before flying, in a commercial airliner, after a single dive to 60 ft (18 m) for a bottom time of 50 minutes.

From Table A, the Surfacing Code after the dive is F. Enter the Surface Interval Table at F, and move to the left until reaching B. This corresponds to a surface interval of *4 hours*.

Example 4.

Find the surface interval required before flying, in a commercial airliner, after the following pair of dives:
A dive to 100 ft (30 m) for a bottom time of 15 minutes, followed, 3 hours later, by a dive to 50 ft (15 m) for 40 minutes bottom time.

The Surfacing Code after the first dive is E, and, after 3 hours it is C. Enter Table C and look up 15 m for the second dive. The Surfacing Code after the dive is G.
Enter the Surface Interval Table at G, and move to the left until reaching B. This corresponds to a surface interval of *4 hours.*

The DCIEM Sport Diving Tables Recommendations

After a single No-D DIVE, allow enough Surface Interval time to elapse for your Repetitive Factor to diminish to **1.0**. (This will take 9-18 hours, depending on the Repetitive Group after the final dive.)

After a REPETITIVE DIVE or a DECOMPRESSION STOP DIVE a minimum Surface Interval of **24 hours** is required before flying.

Example 5.

> *Find the surface interval required before flying, in a commercial airliner, after a single dive to 60 ft (18 m) for a bottom time of 50 minutes.*

The Repetitive Group after the dive is F. From Table B, a minimum surface interval of *15 hours* is required for the Repetitive Factor to reduce to 1.0.

Example 6.

> *Find the surface interval required before flying, in a commercial airliner, after a single dive to 90 ft (27 m) for a bottom time of 25 minutes.*

Since the dive requires a decompression stop, a minimum surface interval of *24 hours* is required.

Example 7.

> *Find the surface interval required before flying, in a commercial airliner, after the following pair of dives:*
> *A dive to 100 ft (30 m) for a bottom time of 15 minutes, followed, 3 hours later, by a dive to 50 ft (15 m) for 40 minutes bottom time.*

Since Dive 2 is repetitive, a minimum surface interval of 24 hours is required before flying.

DMAC guidelines

The British Admiralty, hoping to solve some of the confusion surrounding the problem of flying after diving, convened a meeting of The Diving Medical Advisory Committee (DMAC) in 1982. Present at this meeting were experts from aviation and Diving Medicine from throughout the world. They considered the current evidence, and suggested the following DMAC Guidelines which address the time interval between diving and flying to either 2,000 feet (600 metres) (helicopter) and 8,000 feet (2,400 metres) (commercial aircraft)[8]:

		Time before flying at cabin altitude	
		2000 ft (600 m)	**8000 ft (2400 m)**
1.	No-decompression dives. *(Total time under pressure less than 60 minutes within previous 12 hours)*	2 hours	4 hours
2.	All other air diving. *(Less than 4 hours under pressure)*	12 hours	12 hours
3.	Air or Nitrox saturation. *(More than 4 hours under pressure)*	24 hours	48 hours

While designed for commercial divers in the North Sea, these recommendations may ***generally*** be relevant to sport divers. However for no-decompression stop dives made *to the limits* at 60 ft (18 m) or deeper (i.e. which do have bottom times less than 60 minutes), Rule 1 may not always be sufficiently conservative. Additionally, if substantial bubble formation has occurred after *any* dive, bends may still result.

Notes:

1. These guidelines were drawn up to address single dives, and no clear guidelines were given about the periods required before flying after repetitive dives. In light of this, it is suggested that a minimum period of 12 hours is spent at the surface before flying after a repetitive dive.[9]

2. These DMAC guidelines did not apply to any particular set of decompression tables.[9]

DAN's Recommendations

In the past, the Divers Alert Network (DAN) advised vacationing divers to wait a full 24 hours after diving before flying.

Guidelines developed during a Undersea and Hyperbaric Medical Society Workshop on Flying and Diving in Bethesda in February 1989, officially supported DAN's 24-hour rule. However, recommendations arising from the workshop provide divers with the option of reducing that waiting time to 12 hours, after certain diving schedules. There is scientific evidence to support a range of options for sport divers who plan to fly after diving. The following are the recommendations arising from the workshop[10]:

SCUBA Diving Schedule	Time before Flying (cabin pressure altitude 8,000 ft/2,400 m)
Less than 2 hours No-D diving (within the past 48 hours)	12 hours
Multiday - Unlimited diving	24 hours
Decompression stop diving	24-48 hours*
	* (if possible wait 48 hr)

DAN cautioned that these guidelines cannot be guaranteed to prevent bends in all cases and that they may need to be amended in the future as further data and knowledge are developed.

Since the workshop, controversy arose as a result of business loss these guidelines may have caused dive operators and possible inconvenience to vacationing divers. After re-examining the limited data, workshop participants offered the following compromise:

DAN's Current Position on Recreational Flying After Diving (July 1991)

"Until such time as there is futher **objective** data available, DAN proposes that for the Recreational Diving Industry in the USA the original conclusions of the UHMS committee be used with some small modifications:

1. **A minimum surface interval of 12 hours** is required in order to be reasonably assured a diver will remain symptom free upon ascent to altitude in a commercial jet airliner (altitude up to 8,000 feet). *(Note: The Workshop participants did not discuss the risk of flying or driving to lower elevations, or the effect of dives at altitude. These guidelines therefore may be too conservative for these applications.)*

2. Divers who plan to make **daily, multiple dives for several days** or make dives that require decompression stops should take special precautions and wait for an extended surface interval beyond 12 hours before flight. The greater the duration before flight the less likely is DCS to occur.

3. There can never be a flying after diving rule that is guaranteed to prevent DCS completely. Rather there can be a **guideline** that represents the best estimate for a conservative, safe, surface interval for the majority of divers. There will always be an occasional diver whose physiological makeup or special diving circumstances will result in bends.

4. Further research is recommended to provide significant data upon which to provide more specific guidelines for the future."

Dive Computers

Many dive computers give an indication on when, according to the model programmed into the computer, it should be safe to fly. These suggested intervals vary from computer to computer but most will allow flying relatively soon after a short dive, however, longer periods on the surface are required before flying after longer periods of diving. *It is interesting to note that, currently, some of the computers will allow a diver to fly one hour or less after a single dive to 130 ft (39 m) for 10 minutes,[11] when substantial bubbling has been found in divers who flew three hours after such a dive.[1]* Most of the current computers fail to account for substantial bubble formation and, if this has occurred, the suggested intervals may be far too short.

We can never be exactly sure when it becomes "safe to fly" after a dive as it will depend on the degree of bubble formation and for how long it persists. There is a gradual reduction of risk with time. It must now be apparent to you that, just as with decompression tables, where no table is completely safe for all divers all of the time, no guidelines for flying after diving can be guaranteed completely safe at all times. Flying shortly after a single, short dive might prove to be quite different to flying after a series of repetitive dives and some of the guidelines do not consider this. In addition, if we have formed "silent bubbles" during a dive, we may be "teetering on the edge of being bent" for many hours, or days, after the dive, and ascending to altitude will allow these bubbles to expand, possibly causing bends. It appears that, at times, bubbles can take days, or even weeks, to resolve.

In the light of the sparse and conflicting evidence about flying after diving, many authorities suggest that ***flying be avoided for at least 24 hours after diving.*** This is a very sensible rule to follow, especially if repetitive dives have been done over a number of consecutive days, as is often done on diving holidays. Some people believe this rule to be too conservative, but a substantial and growing number of unfortunate divers have been bent after flying some days after their last dive.

If a diver has had symptoms of decompression sickness and has not received full recompression treatment, flying can be risky, even more than a week after the dive.

Flying after recompression treatment

In the USA, it is currently recommended that a diver who has received treatment for decompression sickness should not fly for at least 3-7 days after the treatment, depending on residual symptoms, and, then, only with approval from the treating hyperbaric physician.[12] In Australia, some experienced hyperbaric physicians currently recommend avoiding flying for at least 4 weeks after treatment since they believe excess inert gas may still be present for some weeks after treatment.[13]

In summary, the following procedure is recommended:

To minimize the risk of contracting decompression sickness by flying after having dived, a diver should avoid flying for at least 12 hours after any dive. However, extending the surface interval beyond 12 hours will reduce the risk of DCS, especially after multi-day, repetitive diving or decompression stop dives.

Note:

At times a diver may find himself in a situation where he may need to dive at sea level and then, shortly afterwards, drive over a mountain pass. *This situation should be treated in the same manner as flying after diving*. However, some people treat the dive at sea-level as a dive at the altitude that they must later ascend to, and use altitude tables, or altitude conversions, to determine the allowable dive time(s). Although this procedure may prove sound mathematically, and, apparently, has often been used successfully, it is not recommended. Despite the fact that the shorter dive time should reduce the likelihood, or amount, of bubble formation, if significant bubble formation does occur, unless sufficient time is spent at sea level to allow the bubbles to resolve, these bubbles will be expanded during the ascent to altitude, and may become problematic.

FLYING BEFORE DIVING

Tissues off-gas while flying and, depending on the duration of the flight, some tissues may take hours, or days, to return to their normal sea-level nitrogen levels.

Some divers believe that, if they fly to a sea-level dive site and then dive before their tissue nitrogen levels have returned to normal, they will have less chance of getting the bends. Since they began the dive with lower nitrogen levels, the belief is that they should surface with lower nitrogen levels than a diver who had done the same dive, but who had not previously flown.

Unfortunately, the situation is not as straightforward as it might seem. The diver's tissues might not respond as expected, and many other factors can affect the outcome. Flying has numerous physiological and psychological effects on us. We might arrive at our destination fatigued, dehydrated, disorientated, irritated and nervous. Certain biological reactions to the aircraft environment may also take their toll. Some of these factors can increase the likelihood of bends.

A diver should not dive until he feels physically and mentally well enough to do so safely.

SUMMARY

* Bends can be precipitated by ascending to altitude too soon after diving.

* A substantial number of divers have suffered decompression sickness after flying many days after last diving.

* We can never be exactly sure when it becomes "safe to fly" after a dive as it will depend on the degree of bubble formation and for how long it persists. There is a gradual reduction of risk with time.

* Many of the available guidelines for flying after diving are not conservative enough. Some do not consider the length of the dive, or whether or not a repetitive dive(s) were done.

* A good policy is to wait at least 24 fours before flying after any dive.

* Do not fly if you are "jet-lagged". Wait until you feel well enough to dive safely.

SOURCES

1. Balldin, V. (1980), "Venous gas bubbles while flying with cabin altitudes of airliners or general aviation aircraft 3 hours after diving". *Aviat Space Environ Med*; 51 (7): 649-652.

2. Bassett, B. (1984), "Flying After Diving". *I.D.C. Candidate Workshop*, PADI.

3. Divers Alert Network (1987), "Flying after diving results in bends". *Alert Diver*; 3 (1).

4. Divers Alert Network (1989), "Flying after diving 1987 accidents". *Alert Diver*; 5 (1).

5. Lang, M. and Hamilton, B. (eds) (1989), "Proceedings of Dive Computer Workshop". University of Southern California Sea Grant Publication No. USCSG-TR-01-89. University of Southern California, Santa Catalina Island.

6. Edel, P. et al (1969), "Interval at sea level pressure required to prevent decompression sickness in humans who fly in commercial aircraft after diving". *Aerospace Med.*; 40: 1105-1110.

7. Buehlmann, A., personal communication.

8. Diving Medical Advisory Committee (1982), "Recommendations for Flying After Diving". DMAC 07, Diving Medical Advisory Committee, London.

9. Hollobone, T., personal communication.

10. Divers Alert Network (1990), "Flying After Diving Workshop Supports DAN's 24-Hour Rule". DAN Bulletin, Divers Alert Network, North Carolina.

11. Lippmann, J. (1990), "Dive computers and flying after a dive to 39 m for 10 minutes". *SPUMS Journal*; 20 (1): 6-7.

12. Wachholz, C., personal communication.

13. Acott, C. and Gorman, D., personal communications.

OTHER SOURCES

Bassett, B. (1982), "Decompression procedures for flying after diving, and diving at altitudes above sea level". Report No. SAM-TR-82-47, Brooks Air Force Base: United States Air Force School of Aerospace Medicine.

Bassett, B. (1979), "And Yet Another approach to the Problems of Altitude Diving and Flying After Diving". In: *Decompression in Depth*; PADI, California.

Buehlmann, A. (1984), "Decompression-Decompression Sickness". Springer-Verlag, Heidelberg.

Buehlmann, A. (1987), "Diving At Altitude and Flying After Diving", UHMS Symposium, *The Physiological Basis of Decompression*, Duke University Medical Centre.

Diving Medical Advisory Committee (1982), "Recommendations for Flying After Diving". *SPUMS Journal*; April-June: 38-39.

Dueker, C. (1979), "SCUBA Diving in Safety and Health", Diving Safety Digest, Madison Publishing Associates, California.

Emmerman, M. (1987), "Flying and Diving, A New Look". Lifeguard Systems Inc., New York.

McLeod, M. (1985), "Altitude Diving and Flying After Diving". *Alert Diver*; 1 (3): 4-5.

Miller J. (ed), "NOAA Diving Manual", 2nd edit. United States Department of Commerce.

Smith, C. (1976), "Altitude Procedures for the Ocean Diver". NAUI, California.

"UDT Instructions for using the DCIEM Sport Diving Tables c1990". Universal Dive Techtronics, Inc., Vancouver.

RECOMMENDED FURTHER READING

Bassett, B. (1984), "Flying After Diving". *I.D.C. Candidate Workshop*, PADI, California.

Bassett, B. (1979), "And Yet Another approach to the Problems of Altitude Diving and Flying After Diving". In: *Decompression in Depth*; PADI, California.

Emmerman, M. (1987), "Flying and Diving, A New Look". Lifeguard Systems Inc., New York.

CHAPTER 21

DIVING AT ALTITUDE

More than 70 percent of the earth's surface is covered by water, most of this being our oceans and seas. Consequently, most diving is carried out at sea level in salt water. As you know there are many other bodies of water such as lakes, quarries, dams and rivers. Divers, strange, inquisitive creatures that we are, often wish to explore these places.

Many of these bodies of water are at altitudes higher than sea level where the atmospheric pressure is reduced, and where the water is fresh, rather than salty. The lesser density of the fresh water causes loss of buoyancy and affects depth gauge readings. The lower atmospheric pressure also affects depth gauge readings and, in addition, will greatly increase a diver's risk of bends if not compensated for in decompression calculations. These changes, as well as possible differences in water temperature and visibility, will affect the manner in which we carry out such dives. Significant changes in diving practice and equipment usage are necessary in order to compensate for these differences.

These changes will be discussed in detail in the following chapter.

A. Buoyancy Changes

As mentioned previously, fresh water (density = 62.366 lb/ft^2 or 1 kg/l) is less dense than salt water (density = 64.043 lb/ft^2 or 1.025 kg/l) and, therefore, gives us less support. Because we lose buoyancy in fresh water, we must remove some of the weight from our weight-belt in order to re-establish neutral buoyancy in our diving gear. The actual amount of weight to be removed depends on the volume of the diver in his gear, and is usually about 2$^1/_2$ percent of his gross weight. In practice, most divers seem to remove about 3 to 10 pounds (1.5 to 4.5 kg) from their weight-belts.

An interesting phenomenon occurs at high altitudes. Wetsuits, which are impregnated with small air bubbles, begin to swell as the bubbles expand with the reduced atmospheric pressure. This expansion makes the suit bulkier and more buoyant. This phenomenon is relatively minor and only needs to be considered if a shallow dive is planned at a high altitude. As soon as moderate depth is reached, the water pressure will again compress the wetsuit and the added buoyancy will be lost.

B. Changes to Depth Gauge Readings

All depth gauges used by divers determine depth by measuring pressure. These gauges will not function accurately in fresh water, unless calibrated for fresh water use. Many diving instruments are, in fact, calibrated for fresh water and, therefore, indicate a depth that is slighltly deeper than the actual depth when used in sea water. The accuracy depends on the salinity. In a gauge that is calibrated for sea water, the error due to fresh water alone is only about 3 percent, so, if we dive in fresh water at sea level we are actually about 3 percent deeper than is indicated by our depth gauge.

Although this may at first appear to be a potentially serious problem, it usually does not present a problem. For most recreational diving the main purpose of the depth gauge is not to provide the actual depth, but to *provide a measure of the pressure that our body is under* so that the correct decompression schedule can be applied. If our depth gauge is calibrated for sea water and reads 33 ft (10 m) while we are diving in the ocean, then we are at an ambient pressure of about 2 ATA, and our depth should actually be 33 ft (10 m). If the gauge reads 33 ft (10 m) while underwater in a mountain lake, our body is still under a pressure of approximately 2 ATA, even though we are slightly deeper than 33 ft (10 m). To find a decompression schedule, we need to know the maximum pressure that we have been to, rather than the actual maximum depth. A well-calibrated, zero-adjust depth gauge should provide this information.

Many depth gauges will not function accurately at reduced atmospheric pressure. Some types of depth gauge give completely erroneous readings at any appreciable altitude above sea level. Most of the gauges are designed to read zero at 1 ATA and will become inaccurate when atmospheric pressures fall significantly below this. The higher the altitude, the greater the error in the depth gauge reading. Exceptions to this are gauges with a zero-adjustment mechanism, gauges which read the atmospheric pressure and compensate automatically, and capillary gauges.

Effects on Different Types of Depth Gauges

The non-zero-adjust diaphragm, open bourdon tube and closed bourdon tube gauges all indicate depths that are shallower than the actual depth, and the amount of inaccuracy will probably depend on the depth. They are designed to read zero at an ambient pressure of 1 ATA. If the gauge has a pin preventing the needle moving past (i.e. shallower than) the zero mark, then, on the surface at altitude the needle will be pushed hard against the pin and will not leave the zero mark until the pressure has increased sufficiently on descent. Consequently, in the water the gauge will give a reading that is shallower than the actual depth. If the gauge has no pin at zero it will read less than zero on the surface at altitude, again reading too shallow underwater. The depth readings can be corrected by adding a depth corresponding to the difference between the atmospheric pressure at the altitude site, and 1 ATA. An additional correction may be required to compensate for fresh water.

Some of the newer diaphragm gauges include an adjustment screw, so that the gauge can be set to zero, hence, adjusted to the reduced atmospheric pressure before entering the water. These are the zero-adjust gauges. Bourdon tube gauges cannot be zero-adjusted. Adjusting the gauge to zero improves the accuracy of the reading but still may not provide true depth if the difference between fresh and salt water has not been accounted for. The gauge will show a depth which is about 3 percent shallower than the actual depth if it was calibrated for sea water. Some of the newer dive computers will read the atmospheric pressure and automatically adjust for it. With some, it is essential to ensure that they are activated on the surface before submerging. Many of them are calibrated for fresh water and, therefore, will read actual depth.

A simple procedure to determine actual depth from non-zero-adjust gauges is to first add 1 foot per 1,000 feet (30 cm per 300 metres) of altitude, then add 3 percent of the gauge reading in order to account for the fresh water, if required. For zero-adjust gauges only the latter calculation may be necessary. It is claimed that the average error of this procedure is less than 1/2 ft (15 cm) over a wide range of altitudes.

Due to the reduced density in the air entrapped within a capillary gauge, less water pressure is required at altitude, than at sea level, to compress the air to a given volume. As a result, the capillary gauge will always indicate a depth greater than the actual depth. In fact, a capillary gauge gives an equivalent sea-level depth (i.e. the Theoretical Ocean Depth, discussed later in this chapter) which can be used for planning decompression. Unfortunately, it becomes difficult to read a capillary gauge accurately at depths greater than about 50 ft (15 m). If the true depth of the water is required, the simple procedure to determine the true depth from a capillary gauge (calibrated for sea water) is to subtract 3 percent of its reading per 1000 feet (300 metres) of elevation. Evidently this works well at altitudes above 3,000 feet (900 metres). At less than 1000 feet (300 metres) no correction is required. If a decompression stop(s) is required after a dive at altitude, it is wise to use a capillary gauge to determine the depth of the stop(s). The stop(s) will be slightly deeper than suggested, but this is safer than being shallower, as is likely with other gauges.

A depth gauge which is used for altitude diving must have the facility to be adjusted for the atmospheric pressure of the dive site.

If the actual depth of a dive in fresh water and/or at altitude is required, it can be determined by using a marked downline (i.e. straight, weighted line marked in 10 ft (3 m), or other, increments).

C. Changes to Decompresssion Procedures

When we ascend to altitude from sea-level our tissues contain higher relative nitrogen pressures (tensions) than are present in normal atmospheric conditions. Nitrogen is off-gassed from the tissues until, eventually, the body nitrogen levels are in equilibrium with the new ambient nitrogen level. A period of 12-24 hours is required to eliminate this excess nitrogen. Divers who reach a dive site at altitude quickly (by plane) and dive immediately will have more excess nitrogen than those who have partly adapted during a slow drive to altitude.

Most decompression tables are based on the concept that there is a critical ratio, of nitrogen pressure in the body tissues to ambient pressure, which can be tolerated without bubbles being formed.

i.e. If $\frac{\text{Tissue } N_2 \text{ Pressure}}{\text{Ambient Pressure}}$ exceeds a particular value bubbles will form.

If the nitrogen pressure in the tissues increases too much, this ratio will increase beyond the critical level. Similarly, if the ambient pressure is reduced, the ratio will again increase and may exceed the critical level.

The tables are designed so that a diver surfaces without this critical ratio being exceeded. Most tables apply to a diver who surfaces to the normal atmospheric pressure of 1 ATA, but, when we ascend from a dive at altitude we ascend to an atmospheric pressure which is less than 1 ATA. If, while at altitude, we have dived near to the limits of the standard sea level table, the reduced ambient pressure may cause this critical ratio to be exceeded, bubbles may form, and decompression sickness may ensue. Therefore, standard tables cannot be safely used for diving at altitude.

A number of special tables, or adjustments to standard tables, have emerged over the years, and some of these will be discussed in the following section.

CROSS CORRECTIONS FOR DIVING AT ALTITUDE

This method, originally published in 1967, has been widely used in the USA in conjunction with the U.S. Navy Tables. The method involves determining a Theoretical Ocean Depth (TOD) for a dive at altitude by multiplying the actual diving depth at altitude* by the ratio of atmospheric pressure at sea level to that at altitude. The TOD and the actual bottom time are then used to enter the U.S. Navy Tables to determine the diving schedule at altitude.

The equation for determining the TOD is:

$$\text{Theoretical Ocean Depth} = \frac{\text{Actual depth} \times \text{Atmos. press. at sea level}}{\text{Atmos press. at altitude}}$$

For example, at an altitude of 7,000 feet (2,100 metres)**, where the atmospheric pressure is about 0.77 ATA (586.4 mmHg), a dive to an actual (gauge) depth 30 fsw (9 msw) would have a TOD of:

$$\text{TOD} = \frac{30 \times 760}{586.4} = 38.9 \text{ fsw } (11.8 \text{ msw})$$

This theoretical depth is 8.9 fsw deeper than the same depth at sea level. Thus, the correction says that for a 30 fsw dive at 7,000 feet above sea level we would select a 40 fsw (12 msw) schedule from the U.S. Navy Standard Tables.

If the diver has been at altitude for over 12-24 hours and all of his tissues are, therefore, equilibrated at the new, reduced nitrogen pressure at the start of the dive, it can be shown mathematically that the calculated nitrogen tensions within the diver all lie within the "critical tissue pressures" of the U.S. Navy Tables. If the diver were to ascend instantaneously to altitude and then dive immediately, his nitrogen tension(s) may just exceed the critical value.[1] Since, in practice, this would be difficult to achieve, the Cross Conversions can be assumed to lie within the levels deemed acceptable by the U.S. Navy Tables and should provide the same degree of safety that the U.S. Navy Standard Tables provide at sea level. **Although the corrections have apparently been quite widely used with good results, they have never been experimentally validated.**

* The actual depth is taken as the depth shown on the gauge in feet of sea water (fsw) or metres of sea water (msw). As previously mentioned, this depth reading will not be accurate but is acceptable for these purposes.

** The imperial-metric conversions given throughout this chapter have generally be rounded of.

TABLE 21.1

Theoretical Ocean Depth (TOD) at Altitude for a Given Actual Diving Depth in Fresh Water

Theoretical Ocean Depth (TOD) at Altitude for a Given Actual Diving Depth in Fresh Water

Actual Depth, fsw	Altitude, ft 0	1000	2000	3000	4000	5000	6000	7000	8000	9000	10000
0	0	0	0	0	0	0	0	0	0	0	0
10	10	10	10	11	11	12	12	13	13	14	14
20	20	20	21	22	23	23	24	25	26	27	28
30	29	30	31	33	34	35	36	38	39	41	43
40	39	40	42	44	45	47	49	51	52	55	57
50	49	51	52	54	56	59	61	63	66	68	71
60	59	61	63	65	68	70	73	76	79	82	85
70	68	71	73	76	79	82	85	88	92	95	99
80	78	81	84	87	90	94	97	101	105	109	113
90	88	91	94	98	102	105	109	114	118	123	128
100	98	101	105	109	113	117	122	126	131	136	142
110	107	111	115	120	124	129	134	139	144	150	156
120	117	121	126	131	135	141	146	152	157	164	170
130	127	131	136	141	147	152	158	164	171	177	184
140	137	142	147	152	158	164	170	177	184	191	199
150	146	152	157	163	169	176	182	190	197	205	213
160	156	162	168	174	181	187	195	202	210	218	227
170	166	172	178	185	192	199	207	215	223	232	241
180	176	182	189	196	203	211	219	227	236	245	255
190	185	192	199	207	214	223	231	240	249	259	270
200	195	202	210	218	226	234	243	253	262	273	284
210	205	212	220	228	237	246	255	265	276	286	298
220	215	222	231	239	248	258	268	278	289	300	312
230	224	233	241	250	260	270	280	291	302	314	326
240	234	243	252	261	271	281	292	303	315	327	340
250	244	253	262	272	282	293	304	316	328	341	355
Stops											
0	0	0	0	0	0	0	0	0	0	0	0
10	10	10	10	9	9	9	8	8	8	7	7
20	21	20	19	18	18	17	16	16	15	15	14
30	31	30	29	28	27	26	25	24	23	22	21
40	41	40	38	37	35	34	33	32	30	29	28
50	51	49	48	46	44	43	41	40	38	37	35
Ascent Rate											
60	62	59	57	55	53	51	49	47	46	44	42

Reprinted with permission from E.R. Cross

USING THE CROSS CORRECTIONS

Luckily, if a diver wishes to use the Cross Corrections in order to dive at altitude he does not have to sit down and do the mathematical calculations. These calculations have already been done and the results are provided in Table 21.1. Table 21.1 has also been corrected for fresh water and rate of ascent.

We will now use this table to re-do the previous example of a dive to 30 fsw (9 msw) at an altitude of 7,000 feet (2,100 metres).

Enter the top section of Table 21.1, from the left, at the planned dive depth of 30 fsw and move right until intersecting the column corresponding to an altitude of 7,000 feet. You get the number 38, which corresponds to a Theoretical Ocean Depth of 38 fsw (as before). The No-Decompression Limit (NDL) for this 30 fsw dive at altitude would be 200 minutes, which is the NDL for a 40 fsw (12 msw) dive at sea level.

If a decompression stop is required it is done at slightly shallower depths than at sea level. The modified stop depths are found in the following manner:

Enter the middle section of Table 21.1, from the left, at the stop depth given by the U.S. Navy Standard Table. Move towards the right until intersecting the row corresponding to the required altitude. The resulting number gives the new (equivalent) stop depth.

The ascent rate must be reduced for dives at altitude, and the new ascent rate is found as follows:

Enter the lower part of Table 21.1, from the left, and move across to the right until intersecting the row corresponding to the required altitude. The resulting number is the required ascent rate. In this case the ascent rate is 47 fsw/minute (14 msw/minute).

Example 1.

Find the NDL for a dive to 60 fsw (18 msw) at an altitude of 10,000 feet (3,000 metres) above sea level.

Enter the top section of Table 21.1, from the left, at 60 fsw and move right until intersecting the 10,000 ft column. You get 85 fsw, which is the depth that you use to enter the U.S. Navy Tables. The NDL to be used will thus be *30* minutes, which is the NDL for 90 fsw (27 msw).

To find the ascent rate, enter the lower part of the table, from the left, and move across to the 10,000 ft column. The ascent rate is thus reduced to 42 fsw/minute (13 msw/minute).

Example 2.

Calculate the decompression required for a dive to 100 fsw (30 msw) for 20 minutes at an altitude of 5,000 feet (1,500 metres).

Enter the top section of Table 21.1, from the left, at 100 fsw and move right until reaching the 5000 ft column. The TOD is, therefore, 117 fsw (35.5 msw).

Look up 120 fsw (36 msw) for a bottom time of 20 minutes in the U.S. Navy Tables. The decompression given is *2 minutes at 10 fsw (3 msw).*

Enter the middle part of Table 21.1, from the left, at 10 fsw and move to the right until reaching the 5,000 ft column. The modified stop depth is thus 9 fsw (2.7 msw).

Enter the lower part of Table 21.1, from the left, and move across until again reaching the 5,000 ft column. The required ascent rate is thus 51 fsw/minute (15 msw/minute).

Repetitive Dives

The system can be extended to repetitive dives by using the TOD of the repetitive dive to find the Residual Nitrogen Time before the dive, and subtracting this time from the NDL for the TOD of the repetitve dive.

Example 3.

Four hours after the dive in Example 2, the diver wishes to dive to a depth of 60 fsw (18 msw). Calculate the maximum allowable no-decompression stop bottom time for the second dive.

After the first dive the RG is *H*. Enter the U.S. Navy Surface Interval Credit Table at H and find the new RG after four hours surface interval. It is *C*. Use Table 21.1 to find the TOD of the repetitive dive; it is 70 fsw (21 msw). Use the U.S. Navy Repetitve Dive Table to find the Residual Nitrogen Time (RNT) at the TOD of the repetitive dive. The RNT is *15* minutes. Subtract this RNT from the NDL for the TOD of the repetitve dive, which is 50 minutes. Therefore, the maximum bottom time is *35* minutes.

Non-Acclimatized Divers

The above system applies to a diver who has acclimatized to the altitude of the dive site by spending 12-24 hours at that level. As previously mentioned, if a diver were to ascend quickly to altitude and dive immediately, his (theoretical) nitrogen levels may exceed those allowed by the U.S. Navy Tables. To overcome this problem a diver who is not acclimatized can select a Repetitive Group (RG) from Table 21.2 The RGs in Table 21.2 are identical to the RGs of the U.S. Navy Standard Air Table and can be used as such.

For example, a diver who has just arrived at 10,000 feet (3,000 metres) and wishes to dive immediately can assume that he is in group G before the dive. If he wishes to dive to a gauge depth 50 fsw (15 msw), he must first look up the TOD from Table 21.1, which gives 71 fsw. He must now use the U.S. Navy Repetitive Dive Table to find the Residual Nitrogen Time for an RG of G at 80 fsw (24 msw), which is 32 minutes. His NDL for the dive is, therefore, 40 - 32 = 8 minutes. If he waits until he is acclimatized, his NDL would be 40 minutes.

TABLE 21.2

Repetitive dive groups for non-acclimatized divers

Elevation feet	metres*	RG before acclimatization
1000	300	B
2000	600	B
3000	900	C
4000	1200	D
5000	1500	D
6000	1800	E
7000	2100	E
8000	2400	F
9000	2700	F
10000	3000	G

* Approximate conversions

Repetitive Dives at Different Altitudes

Example 4.

After doing the dive in Example 1 for a bottom time of 30 minutes, the diver drives back to sea-level and wishes to dive again. If the surface interval after the first dive has been five hours, find the maximum allowable no-decompression stop bottom time for a dive in the sea to 50 fsw (15 msw).

The RG after the first dive, of 30 minutes at a TOD of 90 fsw (27 msw), is *H*. After the surface interval the new RG is *B*. The RNT for the repetitive dive is thus 13 minutes and the required bottom time is *87* minutes.

Example 5.

After doing a sea-level dive of 70 fsw (21 msw) for 20 minutes, a diver drives to a mountain lake at an altitude of 6,000 feet (1,800 metres). Here, she wishes to dive to a depth of 60 fsw (18 msw). The surface interval since the first dive has been three hours. What is the maximum allowable no-decompression stop bottom time for this dive at altitude?

In this situation, the initial sea-level dive must be treated as if it had been done at an altitude of 6,000 ft (1,800 metres). To find the RG after the first dive, first find the TOD; which is 85 fsw. Use the U.S. Navy Tables to find the RG after a dive to 90 fsw (27 m) for 20 minutes. It is *F*. The new RG after the surface interval will be *C*.

The TOD of the repetitive dive is 73 fsw (22 msw). The RNT for the repetitive dive is, therefore, 13 minutes. Hence, the required bottom time is 40 - 13 = *27* minutes.

PROCEDURES FOR USING THE PADI RDP AT ALTITUDE

There are special rules and procedures that must be applied when using the Repetitive Dive Planner (Wheel or Table) at altitudes from 1,000 feet (300 metres) to 10,000 feet (3,000 metres). Two tables (shown together as Tables 21.3), derived from the Cross Corrections, are used to find the Theoretical Ocean Depth and the depth of the safety/decompression stop. For extra safety, the depths were not converted to fresh water equivalents but the calculations were deliberately kept as for salt water, giving slightly deeper TODs. Also, for the sake of conservatism, repetitive dive restrictions were added, although they were not required by the model.

These rules were published in PADI's *The Undersea Journal - Second Quarter 1989* and are re-printed here with permission of PADI International Inc. **These procedures have not as yet been validated by any extensive testing.**

TABLE 21.3

THEORETICAL DEPTH AT ALTITUDE

Actual Depth	Theoretical Depth at Various Altitudes (in feet)									
	1000	2000	3000	4000	5000	6000	7000	8000	9000	10,000
0	0	0	0	0	0	0	0	0	0	0
10	10	11	11	12	12	12	13	13	14	15
20	21	21	22	23	24	25	26	27	28	29
30	31	32	33	35	36	37	39	40	42	44
40	41	43	45	46	48	50	52	54	56	58
50	52	54	56	58	60	62	65	67	70	73
60	62	64	67	69	72	75	78	81	84	87
70	72	75	78	81	84	87	91	94	98	102
80	83	86	89	92	96	100	103	108	112	116
90	93	97	100	104	108	112	116	121	126	131
100	103	107	111	116	120	124	129	134	140	
110	114	118	122	127	132	137				
120	124	129	134	139						
130	135	140								

SAFETY/EMERGENCY DECOMPRESSION STOP DEPTH

Altitude										
Stop	1000	2000	3000	4000	5000	6000	7000	8000	9000	10,000
Depth	14	14	13	13	12	12	12	11	11	10

THE RULES

1. Arriving at Altitude

When you arrive at a high altitude destination, you must take into account that you have "surfaced" to a lower ambient pressure. You may wait 6 hours to adjust to the altitude, or if you want to dive sooner, make an adjustment using the following guidelines. Before you begin diving, you need to determine your Pressure Group from the change in pressure. Upon arrival at altitude between 1,000 feet and 8,000 feet, count down two (2) Pressure Groups for each 1,000 feet (round up fractions of 1,000 feet) for your starting Pressure Group. You may dive immediately or allow a "surface interval" to move you into a lower Pressure Group. Above 8,000 feet, wait 6 hours before diving.

For example, if you are diving in a lake at 4,264 feet (rounded up to 5,000), on arrival count ten Pressure Groups to find you are in Pressure Group J *before* you get in the water. If you elect to not dive immediately, after one hour, Side Two of the Wheel, or Table Two of The Table, shows that you have moved into Group C.

2. Rate of Ascent

The rate of ascent on a high-altitude dive *may not exceed* 30 feet per minute.

3. Repetitive Diving

Make no more than two dives per day when diving at altitude.

4. Depths

To use the Recreational Dive Planner at high altitudes, you must convert your actual depth - the distance you actually are from the surface - to a theoretical depth - a depth that accounts for the lower pressure at altitude when using dive tables. Use the accompanying Theoretical Depth at Altitude table to convert your actual depth into a theoretical depth for use on the RDP. All table calculations, No-Decompression Limits and Pressure Groups must be based on the *theoretical* depth. The absolute maximum depth for a dive at altitude is a *theoretical* 130 feet. *Always use theoretical depth when calculating with The Wheel or The Table.*

For example, to dive to 60 feet in a lake at 4,265 feet, find 60 feet in the left-hand column (of Table 21.3) under Actual Depth. Follow across to the right until you are under the 5,000 feet column, and read 72. You must treat the dive as if it were a dive to 72 feet. (Note: The Wheel's 5-foot depth increments help minimize much of the rounding that is necessary when using the Theoretical Depth at Altitude table. On The Wheel, this dive is calculated as 75 feet, on The Table, as 80 feet.)

5. Safety and Emergency Decompression Stops

Make safety or emergency decompression stops at the depth listed on the Safety/Emergency Decompression Stop Depth table. Three-minute safety stops should be made on all dives. In the event that an emergency decompression stop is required, follow the RDP's guidelines for emergency decompression, but use the appropriate depth from the Safety/Emergency Decompression Stop Depth table. For example, at 4,265 feet (rounded up to 5,000 feet), you make a stop at 12 feet instead of the usual 15 feet. The amount of time does not change.

6. Flying After Diving at Altitude

The rules for flying after diving do not change for flying after diving at altitude: For a single no-decompression dive with less than 1 hour bottom time, wait a minimum of 4 hours; for a single no-decompression dive with more than 1 hour bottom time, or after any repetitive dive, wait a minimum of 12 hours. When possible, a 24-hour wait is generally recommended.

If driving through mountains immediately after diving, do not ascend to an altitude significantly greater than the altitude of the dive. If (after diving) you intend to drive to a higher altitude than that of your dive, to be conservative plan your dive conversions for the highest altitude you will reach.

Example 6. (using imperial RDP)

> *A diver arrives at a lake at an altitude of 5,412 ft. He plans to dive after 30 minutes to an actual depth of 38 ft. What is his NDL?*

Firstly 5,412 ft must be rounded up to 6,000 ft. Since the diver is not waiting for 6 hours before diving, he must add two Pressure Groups for every 1,000 ft of altitude, which gives 12 Pressure Groups and puts him in Group L when arriving at altitude. After a surface interval of 30 minutes he is in Group G (according to Table 2 on The Table or Side 2 on the Wheel).

To find the Theoretical Depth at Altitude, enter Table 21.3, from the left, at 40 ft and move along the row until intersecting the 6,000 feet column. The Theoretical Depth is, therefore, 50 ft.

Turn to the RDP (Table or Wheel) to find the NDL for a diver in Group G diving to 50 ft. It is *54 minutes*.

Example 7. (using imperial RDP)

> *A diver wishes to make a 20-minute dive to 60 ft at an altitude of 6,873 ft. What is the minimum time he must wait before making this dive?*

6,873 ft rounds up to 7,000 ft, so he must count up 14 Pressure Groups and is in Group N on arrival at altitude.

An actual depth of 60 ft converts to a theoretical depth of 78 ft (rounded to 80 ft) when at an altitude of 6,873 ft.

Using either Table 3 of The Table or Side 1 of The Wheel, it can been seen that the diver must be in Group C or above to make a 20-minute dive to 80 ft. To move from Group N to Group C the diver must wait 1 hour 9 minutes.

Note:

> It should take the diver 5 minutes to ascend from 60 ft to the surface. This is made up of 2 minutes of ascent time (at 30 ft/minute) plus the 3-minute safety stop.

The table below provides depth conversion information for use with metric RDP's. The rules given above also apply to the metric RDP.

TABLE 21.4

THEORETICAL DEPTH AT ALTITUDE

ACTUAL DEPTH (M)	THEORETICAL DEPTH AT VARIOUS ALTITUDES (Metres)												
	300	600	900	1200	1500	1800	2100	2400	2700	3000	3300	3600	3900
10	10	11	11	12	12	12	13	13	14	14	15	16	16
12	12	13	13	14	14	15	15	16	17	17	18	19	19
14	15	15	16	16	17	17	18	19	19	20	21	22	23
16	17	17	18	18	19	20	21	21	22	23	24	25	26
18	19	19	20	21	22	22	23	24	25	26	27	28	29
20	21	21	22	23	24	25	26	27	28	29	30	31	32
22	23	24	25	25	26	27	28	29	31	32	33	34	36
24	25	26	27	28	29	30	31	32	33	35	36	37	39
26	27	28	29	30	31	32	34	35	36	38	39	41	42
28	29	30	31	32	34	35	36	38	39	40	42		
30	31	32	33	35	36	37	39	40	42				
32	33	34	36	37	38	40	41						
34	35	37	38	39	41	42							
36	37	39	40	42									
38	39	41	42										
40	41												

IMPORTANT: When using the Metric RDP at altitude, the maximum ascent rate is 9 metres/minute.

Example 8. (using metric RDP)

> *A diver arrives at a lake at an altitude of 1,600 m. He plans to dive after 30 minutes to an actual depth of 11 m. What is his NDL?*

Firstly 1,600 m must be rounded up to 1,800 m. Since the diver is not waiting for 6 hours before diving, he must add two Pressure Groups for every 300 m of altitude, which gives 12 Pressure Groups and puts him in Group L when arriving at altitude. After a surface interval of 30 minutes he is in Group G (according to Table 2 on The Table or Side 2 on the Wheel).

To find the Theoretical Depth at Altitude, enter Table 21.4, from the left, at 12 m and move along the row until intersecting the 1,800 m column. The Theoretical Depth is, therefore, 15 m.

Turn to the RDP (Table or Wheel) to find the NDL for a diver in Group G diving to 15 m. It is *47 minutes.*

Example 9. (using metric RDP)

> *A diver wishes to make a 20-minute dive to 18 m at an altitude of 2,000 m. What is the minimum time he must wait before making this dive?*

2,000 m rounds up to 2,100 m, so he must count up 14 Pressure Groups and is in Group N on arrival at altitude.

An actual depth of 18 m converts to a theoretical depth of 23 m (rounded to 25 m) when at an altitude of 2,000 m.

Using either Table 3 of The Table or Side 1 of The Wheel, it can been seen that the diver must be in Group B or above to make a 20-minute dive to 23 m. To move from Group N to Group B the diver must wait at 1 hour 31 minutes.

Note:

> It should take the diver 5 minutes to ascend from 18 m to the surface. This is made up of 2 minutes of ascent time (at 9 m/minute) plus the 3-minute safety stop.

THE ROYAL NAVY SYSTEM

Note:

> Metres are the primary unit used, so this discussion is presented in metres, although, at times, imperial equivalents are given.

The Royal Navy use a similar, but much simplified, system in order to determine the Theoretical Ocean Depth (TOD) of a dive at altitude.

Rather than present a lengthy table as was done by Cross, the British presented four simple rules for determining the TOD. These rules are as follows:

Height above sea level in metres	Depth Penalty to be added to measured depth
Less than 100	No depth penalty need be added
100 - 300	One quarter of measured depth
300 - 2,000	One third of measured depth
2,000 - 3,000	One half of measured depth

Using the Cross Corrections for a dive at 300 metres (1,000 feet) one must only add about 4% of the actual depth in order to determine the TOD. The British system, requiring 25% of the depth to be added, is far more conservative at these altitudes. At altitudes between 300-2,000 metres (1,000-6,600 feet) the Cross Corrections require the addition of about 30%, which is comparible to the British recommendations. For altitudes between 2,000-3,000 metres (6,600-10,000 feet), Cross requires the addition of 46% of the actual depth, which is again comparable to the 50% addition suggested by the British system. For dives at altitudes low within these altitude ranges, the British system is more conservative than for dives at altitudes high within the range. For example, within the range of 2,000-3,000 metres, the system provides more safety at altitudes nearer to 2,000 metres, than it does at altitudes approaching 3,000 metres.

Hence, it becomes obvious that the British rules generally provide far greater Theoretical Ocean Depths and, therefore, usually give more conservative dive profiles for dives done at altitude. However, like the Cross Corrections, **these corrections have never been validated experimentally.**

For example, for our previous dive of 9 m (30 ft) at an altitude of 2,100 metres (7,000 feet), this system requires us to add one half of the actual depth in order to find the TOD. In this case, the TOD would be 13.5 m (44.6 ft). As you can see this is more conservative than the 11.8 m (38.9 ft) given by the Cross Corrections for the same dive. The no-stop bottom time given by this British system (using the RNPL/BS-AC Table) would be 96 minutes, compared to the 200 minutes (using the U.S. Navy Tables) suggested by Cross.

No alteration to the ascent rate or decompression stop depth was suggested with this procedure.

Although this system was developed for use with the Royal Navy Tables, it has been used with the RNPL/BS-AC Table for a number of years. Some divers have applied the British conversions to the U.S. Navy Tables and this does not seem unreasonable since it yields more conservative times than those allowed when the Cross Conversions are applied. However, once again, the technique has never been validated.

USING THE BRITISH RECOMMENDATIONS

Example 10.

Using the RNPL/BS-AC Table, find the NDL for a dive to 18 m (60 ft) at an altitude of 2,900 metres (9,500 feet).

As 2,900 metres lies within the range of 2,000 -3,000 metres we must add one half of the actual dive depth. This gives a Theoretical Ocean Depth of 27 m (90 ft), for which the RNPL/BS-AC Table gives a no-stop time of *23* minutes.

Example 11.

Using the RNPL/BS-AC Table, calculate the decompression required for a dive to 30 m (100 ft) for 20 minutes at an altitude of 1,500 metres (5,000 feet).

As 1,500 metres lies within the 300-2,000 metre range we must add one third to the actual depth of the dive. This gives a TOD of 40 m (132 ft) with which to enter the RNPL/BS-AC Table. This (equivalent) dive of 40 m for 20 minutes requires decompression stops of *5 minutes at 10 m and 10 minutes at 5 m*. (The Cross system with the U.S. Navy Tables gives 2-minute stop at 3 m (10 ft)).

TABLE 21.5

No-Decompression Limits (NDL), based on the RNPL/BS-AC Table, for dives at various altitudes.

100-300 metres

$Depth_{(m)}$	9	10	12	14	16	18	20	22	24	26	28	30	32	34	36	38	40	42	44	46	48	50
$NDL_{(min)}$	137	96	72	57	46	32	27	23	20	16	14	12	11	9	8	8	7	beyond table				

300-2,000 metres

$Depth_{(m)}$	9	10	12	14	16	18	20	22	24	26	28	30	32	34	36	38	40	42	44	46	48	50
$NDL_{(min)}$	137	96	72	46	38	32	23	20	18	14	12	11	9	8	8	beyond table						

2,000-3,000 metres

$Depth_{(m)}$	9	10	12	14	16	18	20	22	24	26	28	30	32	34	36	38	40	42	44	46	48	50
$NDL_{(min)}$	96	72	57	38	32	23	20	16	14	11	10	8	8	beyond table								

THE SWISS ALTITUDE PROCEDURE*

The Swiss, with their avid interest in diving in mountain lakes, have continuously researched the problems of altitude diving since at least the early 1970's. Their initial altitude tables, which were published in 1973, have undergone numerous revisions, all with quite intensive testing - currently far more testing than with any other altitude procedure. The resulting incidence of bends has, apparently[2], been very low. In order to allow greater safety, these tables assume that the diver has travelled to altitude very quickly and, consequently, has not yet adapted to the decreased atmospheric pressure. Adapting to altitude reduces the nitrogen tension in the tissues and, thus, provides additional safety.

The latest version of these tables, the Buehlmann (1986) Tables, includes three tables. The first is for dives between sea level and an altitude of 700 metres (2,300 feet). The second is for use at altitudes between 701-2,500 metres. The third is for repetitive dives at all altitudes. These tables are shown in Chapter 16.2.

* Metres are the primary unit used, so this discussion is presented in metres, although, at times, imperial equivalents are given.

The Buehlmann (1986) Tables were tested extensively before being released. A total of 544 real dives were carried out at altitude, with no cases of decompression sickness resulting. 254 of the dives were carried out in Switzerland at altitudes between 1,000-2,600 metres.[3] 290 dives were done in Lake Titicaca, 3,800 metres above sea level. Most of the dives in Lake Titicaca were no-decompression stop dives, many of which were repetitive.[4] A special set of schedules was generated for these altitudes, and it is shown as Appendix E.

The times given by these tables for no-decompression stop dives at altitude are often in excess of those dictated by the Cross Corrections to the U.S. Navy Tables, and this has deterred some divers from using them. However, ***if the diver adheres to the recommended maximum ascent rate of 10 m (33 ft)/minute*** sufficient safety should be provided by these tables for *most divers most of the time.*

USING THE BUEHLMANN (1986) TABLES

Example 12.

Find the NDL for a dive to 18 m (60 ft) at an altitude of 2,400 metres (8,000 feet).

Entering Table 16.2.5 (Page 256), from the left, at 18 m the NDL is the bold figure at the top portion of the second column relating to the 18 m depth increment. Hence, the NDL is *44* minutes.

Example 13.

Calculate the decompression required for a dive to 30 m (100 ft) for 20 minutes at an altitude of 1,500 metres (5,000 feet).

Enter Table 16.2.5 at the 30 m section and find the exact, or next greater, bottom time in the second column. In this case, we can find the exact bottom time of 20 minutes. Moving right, the required decompression is seen to be *3 minutes at 2* m.* (This is slightly greater than suggested by the Cross system and, in addition, utilizes the slower ascent rate.)

The Buehlmann (1986) Table is explained in detail in Chapter 16.

THE DCIEM RECOMMENDATIONS

The DCIEM Sport Diving Tables are designed for divers who work hard in cold water. The tables have been tested extensively using the Doppler ultrasonic bubble detector and have emerged from the testing with a very low bubbles and bends incidence. These tables are shown and explained in detail in Chapter 17.

* For dives at altitudes greater than 700 metres, the depths of the decompression stops have been reduced in order to accommodate changes in atmospheric pressure.

The DCIEM Sport Diving Tables include a table of depth corrections for diving at altitude. They apply directly to divers who have spent at least 12 hours at that altitude and must be modified for non-acclimatized divers. This system works in a similar manner to the Cross Corrections to the U.S. Navy Tables, in that it provides a Theoretical Ocean Depth, called the Effective Depth, for the dive, and modified decompression stop depths. At altitudes above 4999 feet (1499 metres), the ascent rate is reduced to 50 ft (15 m)/minute.

Despite the similarities, this system is not compatible with the Cross system.

These depth corrections have not been experimentally validated by DCIEM but are more conservative than most other altitude procedures.

The DCIEM Sport Diving Tables are shown in full in Chapter 17. They will need to be referred to to complete the following exercises.

THE DEPTH CORRECTION TABLE FOR ALTITUDE DIVING (TABLE D)

TABLE 21.6

Depth Corrections for Altitude Diving (Table D)

D: DEPTH CORRECTIONS

Actual Depth ↓	↓	1000' ↳ 1999	*300m ↳ 599*	2000' ↳ 2999	*600m ↳ 899*	3000' ↳ 3999	*900m ↳ 1199*	4000' ↳ 4999	*1200m ↳ 1499*	5000' ↳ 5999	*1500m ↳ 1799*	6000' ↳ 6999	*1800m ↳ 2099*	7000' ↳ 7999	*2100m ↳ 2399*	8000' ↳ 10000	*2400m ↳ 3000*
30'	*9m*	10	*3*	10	*3*	10	*3*	10	*3*	10	*3*	10	*3*	20	*6*	20	*6*
40'	*12m*	10	*3*	10	*3*	10	*3*	10	*3*	10	*3*	20	*6*	20	*6*	20	*6*
50'	*15m*	10	*3*	10	*3*	10	*3*	10	*3*	20	*6*	20	*6*	20	*6*	20	*6*
60'	*18m*	10	*3*	10	*3*	10	*3*	20	*6*	20	*6*	20	*6*	20	*6*	30	*9*
70'	*21m*	10	*3*	10	*3*	10	*3*	20	*6*	20	*6*	20	*6*	30	*9*	30	*9*
80'	*24m*	10	*3*	10	*3*	20	*6*	20	*6*	20	*6*	30	*9*	30	*9*	40	*12*
90'	*27m*	10	*3*	10	*3*	20	*6*	20	*6*	20	*6*	30	*9*	30	*9*	40	*12*
100'	*30m*	10	*3*	10	*3*	20	*6*	20	*6*	30	*9*	30	*9*	30	*9*	40	*12*
110'	*33m*	10	*3*	20	*6*	20	*6*	20	*6*	30	*9*	30	*9*	40	*12*		
120'	*36m*	10	*3*	20	*6*	20	*6*	30	*9*	30	*9*	30	*9*				
130'	*39m*	10	*3*	20	*6*	20	*6*										
140'	*42m*	10	*3*														
Add Depth Correction to Actual Depth of Altitude Dive																	
10'	*3m*	10	*3.0*	10	*3.0*	9	*3.0*	9	*3.0*	9	*3.0*	8	*2.5*	8	*2.5*	8	*2.5*
20'	*6m*	20	*6.0*	19	*6.0*	18	*5.5*	18	*5.5*	17	*5.0*	16	*5.0*	16	*5.0*	15	*4.5*
Actual Decompression Stop Depths (feet/*metres*) at Altitude																	

Table D is used to convert the actual depth at high altitude to an EFFECTIVE DEPTH that corresponds to the Table A and Table C figures intended for sea level use. Table D provides you with the DEPTH CORRECTIONS and ACTUAL STOP DEPTHS needed to conduct dives at altitudes greater than 999 feet (300 metres) above sea level.

Depth Corrections are necessary when diving at altitude because the reduced atmospheric pressure at the surface of the dive site makes the ALTITUDE DIVE equivalent to a much deeper dive at sea level. When you arrive from a lower altitude, your body already has some residual nitrogen as a result of the decrease in atmospheric pressure.

Use the following Depth Correction Procedure if you have acclimatized at the altitude of the dive site for at least 12 hours:

1. Establish the altitude of the dive site and the actual depth of the Altitude dive;
2. Convert the actual depth to EFFECTIVE DEPTH by adding the depth correction given in Table D;
3. Apply the EFFECTIVE DEPTH and Bottom Time to Table A to determine the decompression requirements of the Altitude Dive (see Table C for Repetitive Dive No-D Limits);
4. If the Altitude Dive is a Decompression Dive, conduct the Decompression Stop at the ACTUAL STOP DEPTH given at the bottom of Table D;
5. Decompress at the ACTUAL STOP DEPTH for the Stop Time specified Table A.

Example: Altitude = 6,000 ft (1,800 m)
Depth = 60 ft (18 m)
Bottom Time = 35 minutes

DEPTH CORRECTION = +20 ft (6 m)
EFFECTIVE DEPTH = 80 ft (24 m)

Deco. Stop = 10 min. at 10 ft (3 m) (from Table A)
Actual Stop Depth = 8 ft (2.5 m) (from Table D)

If you must dive before 12 HOURS have elapsed at the altitude of the dive site, begin the Depth Correction procedure by using the NEXT GREATER DEPTH than the actual depth. Following the example given above, begin the Depth Correction Procedure as if the actual depth were 70 ft (21 m). The EFFECTIVE DEPTH would be 70 ft (21 m) + 20 ft (6 m) = 90 ft (27 m).

The decompression required and Actual Stop Depths would be 5 minutes at 16 ft (5 m), and 10 minutes at 8 ft (2.5 m).*

* The metric and imperial figures given for the Actual Stop Depths are not direct conversions. The metric table for Depth Correction was calculated separately. Because of the effect of "rounding" the numbers on the imperial table, the metric table equivalents may be slightly different from the imperial table.

Example 14.

What decompression stop(s), if any, would be required after a dive to 60 ft (18 m) for 30 minutes at an altitude of 5,000 feet (1500 m)?

Enter Table D at the proposed depth of the dive, 60 ft (18 m). Move across the depth row until intersecting the column including 5,000 ft (1500 m); the 5000-5999 ft (1500-1799 m) column. The resulting 20 (6) means that 20 ft (6 m) must be added to the actual depth of the dive before entering Table A (Table 17.1) to determine any decompression stops. Looking up 80 ft (24 m) for 30 minutes in Table A, the resultant decompression is 10 minutes at 10 ft (3 m). However, the decompression is actually carried out at a slightly different depth. To determine this depth, re-enter Table D, towards the bottom, at 10 ft (3 m) and move across to the appropriate altitude column. The 10 ft (3 m) stop is done at 9 ft (3 m).

Example 15.

What is the No-D Limit for a dive to 80 ft (24 m) at an altitude of 6000 ft (1800 m)?

Enter Table D at the 80 ft (24 m) row and move across the row to intersect the 6000-6999 (1800-2099) column. 30 (9) means that 30 ft (9 m) must be added to the depth of the dive. Look up the NDL for 110 ft (33 m) in Table A. The No-D Limit is, thus, *12* minutes.

Example 16.

Find the No-D Limit for a dive to 60 ft (18 m) at an altitude of 9,500 feet (2,900 metres).

Enter Table D at the 60 ft (18 m) row and move across the row until intersecting the column corresponding to the required altitude, which is the 8,000-10,000 ft (2,400-3,000 m) column. The 30 (9) means that we must add 30 ft (9 m) to the actual depth in order to find the Effective Depth. In this case the Effective Depth is 90 ft (27 m). Enter Table A at 90 ft (27 m) in order to determine the NDL of *20* minutes. (This is more conservative than the NDL given by the other systems for a similar dive.)

D. Other Changes

TEMPERATURE

Most mountain lakes are substantially colder than the ocean, sometimes with temperatures as low as 37°F (4°C). So, when planning to dive at altitude, it is necessary to ensure that your wetsuit will be adequate. It is often preferable to wear a drysuit instead of a wetsuit. If you are cold, you will not enjoy the dive as much and you will also be predisposed to decompression sickness. In addition, some decompression schedules require that certain safety factors be added to the schedules when the diver is cold. It is important to ensure that this is done.

Mountain lakes are usually still, and, often, in still waters one can find levels of vastly different temperatures. These layers of varying temperature are called "thermoclines". A thermocline is related to seasonal changes, wind conditions, currents, depths and water density. Generally, the water is colder in the deeper layer, but this is not always the case. For example, during an expedition to Lake Titicaca (at an altitude of 12,580 ft (3,812 m)), divers recorded the following temperatures during a dive:[4]

Air	64°F (18°C)
16.5 ft (5 m)	46°F (8°C)
33 ft (10 m)	54°F (12°C)
83 ft (25 m)	57°F (14°C)

The temperature change due to a thermocline can be quite dramatic.

FIGURE 21.1
Divers preparing to dive in Lake Titicaca, 12,580 feet (3,812 metres) above sea-level

FIGURE 21.2
Diving on ancient ruins in Lake Titicaca

Photos courtesy Major Marc Moody

Visibility

Still waters often contain a lot of silt. The silt settles if the water is undisturbed and, often, under these conditions visibility can be exceptional. If, however, the silt is disturbed, visibility may deteriorate dramatically. This presents an enormous problem to cave divers who must use guidelines in case silting occurs. When diving in fresh water it is necessary to be aware of this potential problem and to take appropriate precautions, where necessary.

If a thermocline is present the visibility may change from one layer to the next. The surface layers are often less clear than the deeper and, generally, colder layers.

Hypoxia After Ascent From A Dive At Altitude

A diver surfacing from a dive at altitude is moving from a breathing gas which contains a high oxygen partial pressure, to an atmosphere in which the oxygen levels are lower than normal. As a result, the diver may experience symptoms of hypoxia and breathing difficulties for a period after the dive. This will be accentuated if the diver has been exerting himself. In this situation, blackout after ascent could occur. A diver must anticipate this problem and mimimize exertion after ascent.

CHOOSING A DECOMPRESSION SCHEDULE FOR DIVING AT ALTITUDE

Choosing which procedure to use for altitude diving can be a daunting task. The choice will depend on a number of factors, which include the familiarity with a particular table and the purpose of the dive at altitude. It is essential that you thoroughly familiarize yourself with the altitude procedure of your choice in order to minimize the chance of making a mistake when calculating the schedule.

If the dive you are planning is simply for recreation, then it is wise to choose a conservative set of tables, such as the DCIEM Tables. Recreational diving is supposed to be enjoyable and getting the bends is far from being enjoyable. If you have a task to be carried out at altitude and, hence, need to maximize the time underwater, then a less conservative set of tables, such as the Buehlmann (1986) Tables, might be chosen. If the water is cold and/or the task requires exertion appropriate precautions must be taken. The DCIEM procedure takes this into account but the other tables require appropriate adjustments.

The Buehlmann (1986) Tables are the simplest to use because no calculations or conversions need to be carried out. You simply enter the appropriate table at the actual dive depth in order to find your schedule. The Cross, Royal Navy and Canadian systems require that you calculate the Theoretical Ocean Depth before entering the standard table. At times, this can lead to errors in the calculations. The Buehlmann Tables have undergone much more testing than any other altitude diving procedure and, apparently, have resulted in a very low incidence of decompression sickness. At times, these schedules are less conservative than the other schedules but the ascent rate is always much slower and this seems to make quite a lot of difference. It is essential never to exceed the maximum ascent rate of 10 m/minute (33 ft/minute) when using these tables. This will be very difficult to achieve unless a shotline, or other simliar ascent line, is followed during the ascent, or unless an appropriate ascent rate indicator is used. In the absence of these securities, I believe that these tables should not be dived as written. In this case one can select the No-Decompression Limit for the next greater depth increment when planning a no-decompression stop dive, or decompressing for the next greater depth and time increment for a decompression stop dive.

SUMMARY

* As fresh water is less dense than salt water we are less buoyant and, so, require less weight.

* Many depth gauges will not measure the depth accurately in fresh water as they are calibrated to measure the pressure change associated with depths of sea water.

* Many depth gauges will not account for the reduced atmospheric pressure at altitude. Altitude diving requires a well-calibrated, zero-adjustable depth gauge.

* Most mountain lakes are substantially colder than the ocean. Thermoclines often exist in these lakes.

* Still waters often contain a lot of silt. Visibility will diminish greatly if the silt is disturbed.

* When we ascend to altitude, nitrogen is off-gassed from our tissues until the nitrogen tension in the tissues is in equilibrium with the reduced nitrogen tension in the atmospheric air.

* It takes 12-24 hours before equilibrium is reached and we are acclimatized to the particular altitude.

* Most decompression tables are based on the diver surfacing to a pressure of 1 ATA. At altitude, a diver surfaces to less than 1 ATA, and this must be accounted for if bends is to be avoided.

* Most tables require an additional depth correction to be added to the measured depth of the dive to account for the reduced atmospheric pressure.

* The Swiss decompression tables are, currently, the only tables that have been substantially tested for diving at altitude.

REFERENCES

1. Bassett, B. (1979), "And Yet Another approach to the Problems of Altitude Diving and Flying After Diving". In: *Decompression in Depth*; PADI, California.

2. Buehlmann, A., personal communication.

3. Buehlmann, A. (1987), "Diving At Altitude and Flying After Diving". UHMS Symposium, *The Physiological Basis of Decompression*, Duke University Medical Centre, Durham.

4. Moody, M. (1988), "Exercise Paddington Diamond". Ordinance Services, Viersen.

OTHER SOURCES

Bassett, B. (1982), "Decompression procedures for flying after diving, and diving at altitudes above sea level". Report No. SAM-TR-82-47, Brooks Air Force Base: United States Air Force School of Aerospace Medicine.

Bell, R. et al (1979), "The Theoretical Structure and Testing of High Altitde Diving Tables". In: *Decompression in Depth*; PADI, California.

Boni, M. (1976), et al "Diving at Diminished Atmospheric Pressure: Air Decompression Tables for Different Altitudes", *Undersea Biomedical Research*; 3 (3): 189-204.

British Sub-Aqua Club (1977), "Diving Manual". Charles Scribner's Sons, London.

British Sub-Aqua Club (1985), "Sport Diving". Stanley Paul, London.

Buehlmann, A. (1984), "Decompression-Decompression Sickness". Springer-Verlag, Heidelberg.

Buehlmann, A. (1986), "The Validity of a Multi-Tissue Model in Sport Diving Decompression". Proceedings of the Diving Officers' Conference, BS-AC, London.

Buehlmann, A., personal communications.

Dueker, C. (1979), "SCUBA Diving in Safety and Health". Diving Safety Digest, Madison Publishing Associates, California.

Hazzard, J. (1984), "Decompression Table Workbook", 2nd edition. BS-AC, London.

McLeod, M. (1985), "Altitude Diving and Flying After Diving". *Alert Diver*; 1 (3): 4-5.

Miller J. (ed) (1979), "NOAA Diving Manual", 2nd edit. United States Department of Commerce.

Moody, M., personal communications.

Richardson, D. (ed) (1989), "Procedures for Using the Recreational Dive Planner at Altitude". *The Undersea Journal*; First Quarter 1989.

Smith, C. (1976), "Altitude Procedures for the Ocean Diver". NAUI, California.

RECOMMENDED FURTHER READING

Bassett, B. (1979), "And Yet Another approach to the Problems of Altitude Diving and Flying After Diving". In: *Decompression in Depth*; PADI, California.

Miller J. (ed) (1979), "NOAA Diving Manual", 2nd edit. United States Department of Commerce.

TABLE 21.7

Comparison of No-Decompression Limits for various altitude procedures at different altitudes.

Sea level	**Depth**	*(ft)*	**40**	**50**	**60**	**70**	**80**	**90**	**100**	**110**	**120**	**130**
		(m)	**12**	**15**	**18**	**21**	**24**	**27**	**30**	**33**	**36**	**39**
	Table											
	U.S. Navy		200	100	60	50	40	30	25	20	15	10
	RNPL/BSAC		137	72	57	38	32	23	20	16	14	11
	Buehlmann		125	75	51	35	25	20	17	14	12	10
	DCIEM		150	75	50	35	25	20	15	12	10	8
	PADI RDP		140	80	55	40	30	25	20	16	13	10
2000 ft *(600 m)*	**Depth**	*(ft)*	**40**	**50**	**60**	**70**	**80**	**90**	**100**	**110**	**120**	**130**
		(m)	**12**	**15**	**18**	**21**	**24**	**27**	**30**	**33**	**36**	**39**
	Table											
	U.S. Navy		100	60	50	40	30	25	20	15	10	10
	RNPL/BSAC		72	46	32	23	18	14	11	9	8	-
	Buehlmann		125	75	51	35	25	20	17	14	12	10
	DCIEM		75	50	35	25	20	15	12	8	7	6
	PADI RDP		80	55	40	30	25	20	16	13	10	8
4000 ft *(1200 m)*	**Depth**	*(ft)*	**40**	**50**	**60**	**70**	**80**	**90**	**100**	**110**	**120**	**130**
		(m)	**12**	**15**	**18**	**21**	**24**	**27**	**30**	**33**	**36**	**39**
	Table											
	U.S. Navy		100	60	50	40	30	20	15	10	10	5
	RNPL/BSAC		72	46	32	23	18	14	11	9	8	-
	Buehlmann		99	62	44	30	22	18	15	12	10	9
	DCIEM		75	50	25	20	15	12	10	8	6	-
	PADI RDP		80	55	40	25	20	16	13	10	8	-
6000 ft *(1800 m)*	**Depth**	*(ft)*	**40**	**50**	**60**	**70**	**80**	**90**	**100**	**110**	**120**	**130**
		(m)	**12**	**15**	**18**	**21**	**24**	**27**	**30**	**33**	**36**	**39**
	Table											
	U.S. Navy		100	50	40	30	25	20	10	10	5	5
	RNPL/BSAC		72	46	32	23	18	14	11	9	8	-
	Buehlmann		99	62	44	30	22	18	15	12	10	9
	DCIEM		50	35	25	20	12	10	8	7	6	-
	PADI RDP		80	40	30	25	20	13	10	8	-	-
8000 ft *(2400 m)*	**Depth**	*(ft)*	**40**	**50**	**60**	**70**	**80**	**90**	**100**	**110**	**120**	**130**
		(m)	**12**	**15**	**18**	**21**	**24**	**27**	**30**	**33**	**36**	**39**
	Table											
	U.S. Navy		60	50	40	25	20	15	10	5	5	5
	RNPL/BSAC		57	32	23	18	14	10	8	7	-	-
	Buehlmann		99	62	44	30	22	18	15	12	10	9
	DCIEM		50	35	20	15	10	8	7	-	-	-
	PADI RDP		55	40	25	20	16	10	8	-	-	-

TABLE 21.8

Barometric pressure at various altitudes

Altitude		Barometric Pressure	
feet	metres*	mmHg	ATA
Sea-level		760.0	1.00
1,000	300	732.9	0.96
2,000	600	706.6	0.93
3,000	900	681.1	0.90
4,000	1,200	656.3	0.86
5,000	1,500	632.3	0.83
6,000	1,800	609.0	0.80
7,000	2,100	586.4	0.77
8,000	2,400	564.4	0.74
9,000	2,700	543.2	0.71
10,000	3,000	522.6	0.69

* Approximate conversions

REVIEW EXERCISES

Use the Cross Corrections to the U.S. Navy Tables to solve Questions 1 and 2.

1. Find the TOD for the the following dives at altitude:
   (i) Actual depth = 80 ft (24 m)
   Altitude = 9,500 ft (2,900 m)
   (ii) Actual depth = 50 ft (15 m)
   Altitude = 6,600 ft (2,000 m)
   (iii) Actual depth = 70 ft (21 m)
   Altitude = 5,000 ft (1,500 m)

2. Find the NDLs for each of the (single) dives in Question 1.

3. Repeat Question 1 using the Royal Navy Corrections to adjust the depths given by the RNPL/BS-AC Table.

4. Repeat Question 2 using the Royal Navy Corrections to adjust the times given by the RNPL/BSAC Table.

5. Use the Buehlmann (1986) Tables to find the NDLs for the dives in Question 1.

6. Use the DCIEM Tables to find the NDLs for the dives in Question 1.

7. Use the PADI RDP to find the NDLs for the dives in Question 1.

ANSWERS

1.	(i)	113 ft (34 m)	(ii)	63 ft (19 m)		
	(iii)	82 ft (25 m)				
2.	(i)	15 min	(ii)	50 min	(iii)	30 min
3.	(i)	36 m	(ii)	22.5 m	(iii)	28 m
4.	(i)	14 min	(ii)	32 min	(iii)	23 min
5.	(i)	16 min (Appendix E)	(ii)	62 min	(iii)	30 min
6.	(i)	10 min	(ii)	35 min	(iii)	20 min
7.	(i)	13 min	(ii)	40 min	(iii)	25 min *

* Answers given are for imperial version

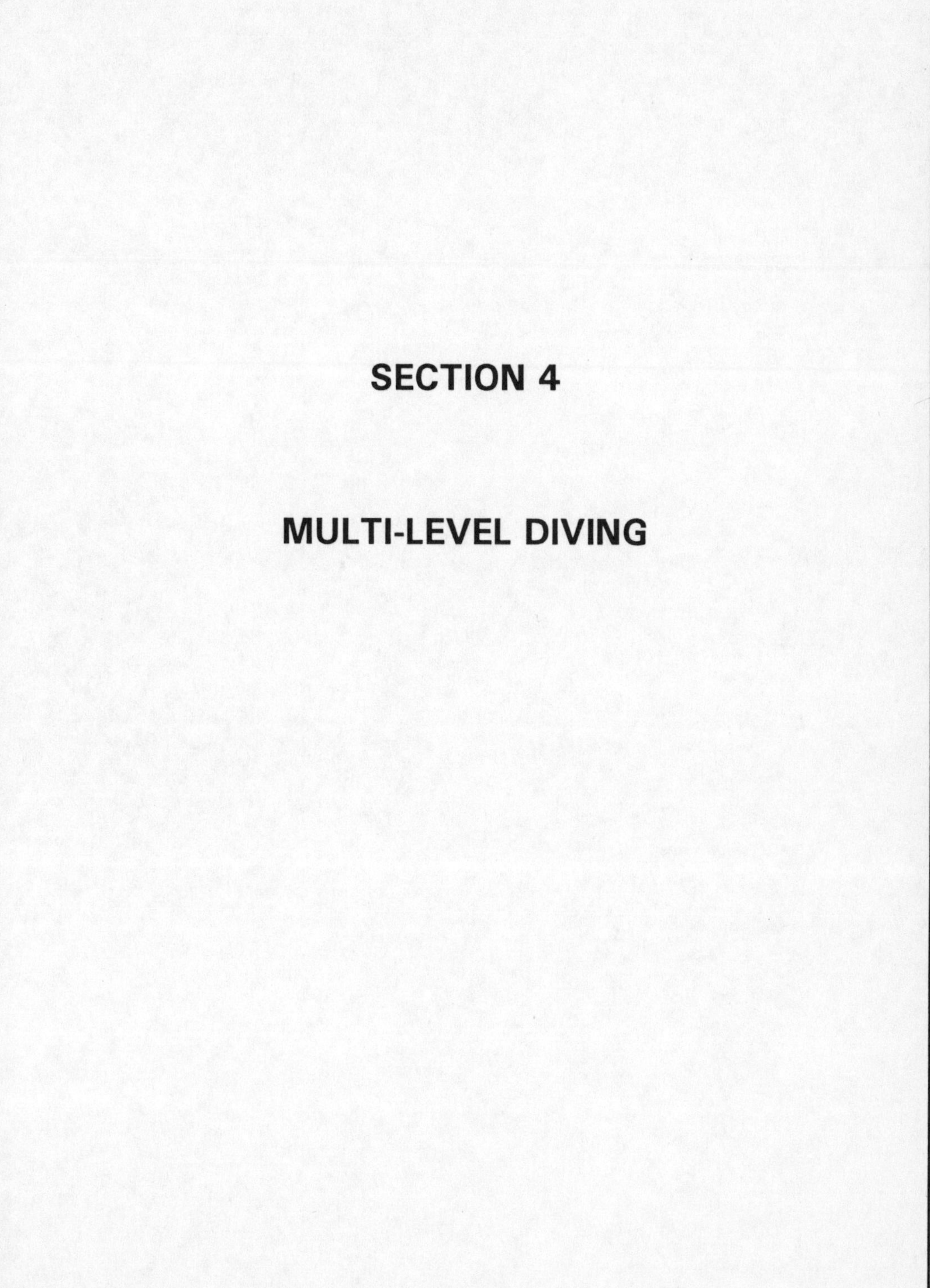

SECTION 4

MULTI-LEVEL DIVING

CHAPTER 22

MULTI-LEVEL DIVING USING TABLES

The U.S. Navy Tables were designed for use by Navy divers, whose diving is task-orientated, frequently requiring the divers to stay in one place and, consequently, at one depth for most of the dive. The diver generally goes to the maximum depth, spends the dive there and returns to the surface after completing any required decompression stops.

Sport divers often dive quite differently to this. Sometimes our depth varies considerably during a dive and, at times, very little of the bottom time is spent at the actual maximum depth of the dive. Consequently, some sport divers feel that, in these circumstances, the practice of looking up the maximum depth for the total bottom time is overly conservative.

For example, consider a dive where you go to 80 ft (24 m) for 5 minutes and then wish to spend the rest of the dive at 40 ft (12 m). The U.S. Navy Tables give a NDL of 40 minutes at 80 ft (24 m), so, using the tables by the rules, you must consider that the entire dive has been spent at 80 ft (24 m) and begin to ascend to the surface after 40 minutes. No consideration is given to the fact that you have spent most of the dive far shallower than 80 ft (24 m).

In 1976, Dennis Graver first published a way of extrapolating the U.S. Navy Tables in order to account for the shallower sections of a *"Multi-Level"* dive.[1]

A "Multi-Level" dive is defined here as a dive where the diver spends significant bottom time shallower than the maximum depth and, so, extends the bottom time beyond the limits for a rectangular profile dive to the maximum depth.

THE REPETITIVE GROUP METHOD (GRAVER METHOD)

Many different dives will put you into the same Repetitive Group (RG). Using the U.S. Navy Tables you will be in group B after a dive to 80 ft (24 m) for 5 minutes, or to 60 ft (18 m) for 10 minutes, or 40 ft (12 m) for 15 minutes, and so on. Graver proposed that within a RG all dives are more or less equivalent with respect to the nitrogen content of the tissues. In other words, whether you dived to 80 ft (24 m) for 5 minutes to get into group B, or whether you dived to 40 ft (12 m) for 15 minutes, your nitrogen load will be about the same.*

If you surfaced after diving to 80 ft (24 m) for 5 minutes, you would surface in group B. If, instead of surfacing, you ascended to 40 ft (12 m), you would still be in group B and your previous 5 minutes at 80 ft (24 m) could be seen as equivalent to having already spent 15 minutes at the 40 ft (12 m) depth. In other words, the 15 minutes required to get into group B at 40 ft (12 m) can be taken as Residual Nitrogen Time at that depth. Since the NDL for 40 ft (12 m) is 200 minutes, theoretically, you could still spend a further 185 minutes at 40 ft (12 m) without needing to make a stop.

* In reality this is not true as the distribution of the gas load between the various tissues may be very different.

Similarly, if after the 5 minutes at 80 ft (24 m), you had ascended to 60 ft (18 m), instead of 40 ft (12 m), the 5 minutes at 80 ft (24 m) could be seen as equivalent to 10 minutes at 60 ft (18 m), i.e. the time at 60 ft (18 m) to go into group B. Since the NDL at 60 ft (18 m) is 60 minutes, you can, in theory, spend a further 60-10 = 50 minutes at this depth before requiring a decompression stop.

This procedure assumes that the actual NDLs of the shallower sections are still applicable to this multi-level situation. In other words, after spending 5 minutes at 80 ft (24 m) and ascending to 60 ft (18 m), does the 60 minute NDL for 60 ft (18 m) still apply?

To answer this, one has to go back to the mathematical model for the U.S. Navy Tables, and calculate the theoretical nitrogen pressure in the various half-time tissue compartments after each section of a multi-level dive. If, at any stage during a multi-level dive, the nitrogen pressure exceeds the critical value for that compartment, a decompression stop will be required. It can be shown that when the above multi-level method is used right to the NDLs, in some cases the critical pressure in a particular tissue, or tissues, may be exceeded. This creates a much greater potential for bends. An example of this is shown in Table 22.1.

TABLE 22.1

Tissue Nitrogen Pressures (fsw) during a Multi-level dive

Depth/Time (fsw/min.)	Tissue Groups (Half-Time (Mo Value))					
	5(104)	**10(88)**	**20(72)**	**40(58)**	**80(52)**	**120(51)**
120/15	109.02	87.35	64.50	47.77	37.62	33.94
90/5	103.10	90.23	69.70	51.87	40.15	35.74
70/10	85.69	87.53	78.81	62.62	47.91	41.55
% of Max. Allowable Press. at surfacing	**83%**	**100%**	**110%**	**108%**	**93%**	**82%**

Reprinted from Huggins and Somers (1981)

When 101 allowable (i.e. in theory, by this method) multi-level dives were analyzed using the U.S. Navy model and formulae, it was found that many of the dive profiles built up potentially dangerous nitrogen levels in the five faster tissue groups.[2] The reason for the violation is that the Repetitive Groups and Residual Nitrogen Times are based solely upon the gas pressure in the 120-minute tissue compartment, assuming that it has the highest nitrogen load during a surface interval. However, a surface interval of just under 10 minutes is necessary before this compartment's nitrogen level controls the decompression.

Before a 10-minute surface interval has elapsed, one, or more, of the other tissues will have a higher gas load and must be taken into consideration. A multi-level dive has no 10-minute surface interval between sections, and the Repetitive Group method does not take this problem into consideration. Therefore, the Repetitive Groups given are not always valid.

Graver realized this potential problem and made some recommendations in order to make the method a bit safer. These were:

1. Limit the procedure to no-decompression stop dives to 130 ft (39 m) or less.
2. The depths must become progressively shallower during the dive.
3. Shorten the NDLs to:

40 ft (12 m)/170	90 ft (27 m)/25
50 ft (15 m)/70	100 ft (30 m)/20
60 ft (18 m)/55	110 ft (33 m)/15
70 ft (21 m)/45	120 ft (36 m)/15
80 ft (24 m)/30	

Despite Graver's recommendations, some experts argue that this method is not sound as it still pushes the diver too close to the limits. Huggins recommended further modifications to this Repetitive Group method.[2]
These were:

1. Use the following NDLs: 120 ft (36 m)/12, 70 ft (21 m)/40 and 60 ft (18 m)/50 instead of those previously suggested.
2. Take a 10 ft (3 m) stop for 5-15 minutes.
3. Keep at least one RG back from the limits on the table, especially females, older divers and less fit divers; and
4. Include ascent times to each higher level in the bottom time for the previous level.

Despite these recommendations, Huggins did not favor the method as he felt that these "safety factors" would not, or could not, be used consistently.

REPETITIVE GROUP - RESIDUAL NITROGEN METHOD

This method also utilizes the U.S. Navy Tables and treats the various levels of a multi-level dive as repetitive dives without any surface interval. It was first published by Bove in 1983.[3]

For example, consider a diver who spends 5 minutes at 80 ft (24 m) and then ascends to 40 ft (12 m). How long can he spend at 40 ft (12 m) before a stop is required?

Using the tables as designed, the diver has around 35 minutes of bottom time still available. However, using the Repetitive Group-Residual Nitrogen method it can be extended, as follows:

If he had surfaced after 5 minutes at 80 ft (24 m), he would have had an RG of B. If, after a surface interval between 10 minutes and 2 hrs 10 mins (i.e. RG is still B), he were to descend to 40 ft (12 m), he would have an RNT of 17 minutes and 183 minutes of bottom time available before a decompression stop was required.

The Repetitive Group-Residual Nitrogen method treats a multi-level dive as if the diver had surfaced between levels and then redescended with the same RG. Various safety precautions were suggested for use with the method. These included restricting the dive to two levels only, staying shallower than 39 m (130 ft), reducing the NDLs and doing a safety stop, among others.

However, since there is no 10-minute surface interval between the different depth levels, this method suffers the same shortcomings as the Repetitive Group method. At times, the nitrogen pressures in the theoretical tissue compartments can become too high, exceeding the critical levels on which the U.S. Navy Tables are based and increasing the potential for bends.

Other methods, based on the U.S. Navy Tables, to compute times for multi-level dives have emerged over the years. Many of these methods suffer from the same problem as those described above.

USING THE HUGGINS TABLES FOR MULTI-LEVEL DIVING

Rather than using U.S. Navy Tables as the basis of multi-level dive calculations, many divers have adopted the more conservative "Huggins" tables, published in 1981.[4] These tables, described in detail in Chapter 14.1 and shown as Table 14.1.3, were built on the same model as the U.S. Navy Tables, with the same theoretical tissue compartments. However, Huggins reduced the maximum allowable tissue nitrogen levels to levels indicated by Doppler ultrasonic detection work to be less likely to produce bubbles and, hence, bends. Also, by basing the RGs on all six tissue groups, rather than the single tissue used by the U.S. Navy, Huggins avoided the need for a 10-minute surface interval in order to allow the nitrogen levels in the faster compartments to fall below that of the 120-minute compartment. The shorter NDLs that resulted seem to be much more suitable for multi-level diving, and, in fact, for general sport diving, whether multi-level or not.

If a diver uses the Repetitive Group (Graver) method based on the Huggins tables, rather than on the U.S. Navy Tables, it appears that the new, lower critical nitrogen levels are not exceeded in any of the theoretical tissue types.[4] Multi-level divers who use the Huggins tables will, therefore, greatly increase their bottom times (compared to standard single-level procedures), but build up lower (theoretical) body nitrogen levels than they would if they based their multi-level technique on U.S. Navy Tables.

The "Huggins" Tables are used in exactly the same way as the U.S. Navy Tables. They include a No-Decompression Table which gives RGs for various bottom times, a Surface Interval Credit Table and a Residual Nitrogen Table. **The tables have not been tested, but they are more conservative than the U.S. Navy Tables and should, therefore, be safer than those tables. *However, no testing has been done to assess the safety of using the Huggins Tables for multi-level diving.***

Example 1.

> *You are planning to dive to 100 ft (30 m) for 5 minutes, before ascending to 66 ft (20 m) for 10 minutes. You will then ascend to 50 ft (15 m). If you used the Repetitive Group method with Huggins Tables, for how long could you remain at 50 ft (15 m) before a decompression stop is required?*

FIGURE 22.1

The multi-level profile described in Example 1

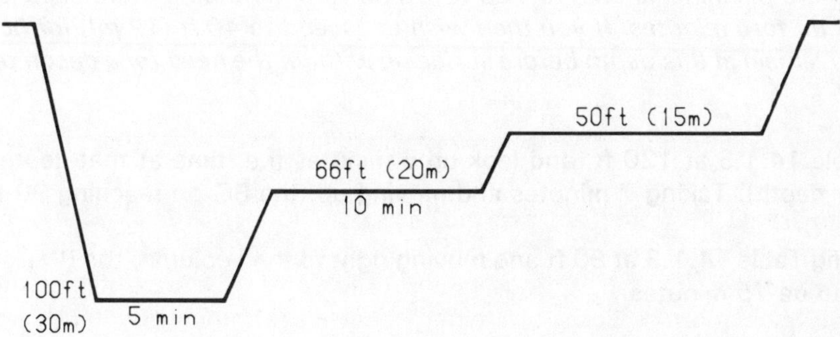

Enter the bottom left-hand portion of Table 14.1.3 at 100 ft, and look up a bottom time of 6 minutes (i.e. include the one minute of ascent time to the next level as a safety factor). Taking 7 minutes, and moving up the column, the RG is *E*. You must now determine how long would have been required at the 66 ft (20 m) depth to get into group E. To do this, re-enter the bottom left-hand portion of Table 14.1.3 at 70 ft (21 m) and move right until intersecting the E column. You get a bottom time of 15 minutes. This 15 minutes is your RNT for the 66 ft (20 m) depth. To find the RG after the 66 ft (20 m) segment, re-enter Table 14.1.3 at 70 ft, and look up a bottom time of $15_{\text{(RNT)}} + 10_{\text{(BT)}} + 0.5_{\text{(ascent to next level)}} = 25.5$ min. Taking 27 minutes and moving up the column, the RG after the 66 ft (20 m) segment is *J*.

To find the RNT at 50 ft (15 m), re-enter Table 14.1.3 at 50 ft, and move right until intersecting the J column. You get 50 minutes, which is the time that must be considered already spent at this level. Since the NDL for 50 ft is 75 minutes, you have 75 - 50 = 25 minutes left to spend at 50 ft (15 m). After 25 minutes at this level and a direct ascent to the surface, your RG would be *N*.

I suggest that you leave 50 ft (15 m) a few minutes earlier and spend these minutes doing a safety stop at 10-20 ft (3-6 m) before surfacing. Your RG after the dive will be *N*.

Note:

If you spend the entire 25 minutes at 50 ft (15 m) before doing a safety stop and surfacing, your RG will still be N. The reason for this is that group N represents the maximum nitrogen load in any of the tissues and, theoretically anyway, off-gassing from all theoretical tissues will occur at any depth shallower than 21.4 ft (6.5 m). This means that you should off-gas at the safety stop and surface with a lower nitrogen load than you had when you left 50 ft (15 m). This would only be true with an RG of N. With a lower RG, on-gassing may still occur in some of the tissues.

Example 2.

> *You are planning to dive to 120 ft (36 m) for5 minutes, before ascending to 90 ft (27 m) for6 minutes. If you then wish to ascend to 40 ft (12 m), for how long could you remain at this depth before surfacing without the need for a decompression stop?*

Enter Table 14.1.3 at 120 ft, and look up 6 minutes (i.e. time at that depth + ascent to shallower depth). Taking 7 minutes and moving up, the RG on reaching 90 ft (27 m) is *I*.

Re-entering Table 14.1.3 at 90 ft and moving right to the I column, the RNT at 90 ft (27 m) is found to be *15* minutes.

To find the RG on reaching 40 ft (12 m), look up 90 ft for 15 + 6 + 1 = 22 minutes, which gives group *M*. A previous stay of 120 minutes at 40 ft (12 m) would have put you in group M, so the RNT at 40 ft (12 m) is 120 minutes. Since the NDL for 40 ft is 135 minutes, you can spend 135 - 120 = *15* minutes at this depth before ascending.

Leave the bottom a few minutes earlier and stop at 15-20 ft (4.5-6 m) for a few minutes before surfacing. Your RG after the dive will be N.

USING THE DCIEM SPORT DIVING TABLES FOR MULTI-LEVEL DIVING

A Multi-Level Dive is a dive during which bottom time is spent at two or more depths.

The DCIEM multi-level diving procedures are based on the repetitive dive procedures used for surface intervals of less than 15 minutes. These procedures are known as the Step System. During a multi-level dive, the normal decompression process built into the ascent rate is interrupted. Additional precautions are included in the multi-level diving procedures to compensate for the interrupted decompression resulting from partial ascents.

Guidelines for Multi-level Dives

1. Conduct the **deepest part of the dive first** and ascend to **progressively shallower depths**, keeping under the **No-D Limit** at each and every Step.

If any bottom time - or EBT - should touch or exceed the No-D Limit, conduct a decompression stop for the greater of 5 min. at 10 ft (3 m) or the decompresion requirement specified in Table A;

2. Limit the number of Steps to four (4) or less. If a 4th Step is included, conduct it at a depth of 30 ft (9 m) or less;

3. Before surfacing from a No-D multi-level dive, conduct a "safety stop" at a depth of 15 ft (4.5 m) for at least 3 minutes. The actual time spent at a safety stop is more critical than the precise depth (within a range of about 10-20 ft (3-6 m)).

4. Allow for a minimum Surface Interval of one hour after a multi-level dive.

<u>**First Dive - Multi-Level Procedure**</u>

Find the Repetitive Group (RG) for Step 1 according to the depth and actual bottom time (Table A).

Use the RG from Step 1 to determine an equivalent time for the same (or next higher) RG at Step 2. Add the planned actual bottom time at Step 2 to the equivalent time that corresponds to the RG. The total of the two times is the Effective Bottom Time (EBT). Find the RG for Step 2 according to the depth and EBT.

Use the RG from Step 2 to determine an equivalent time for the same RG at Step 3. Add the actual bottom time at Step 3 to the equivalent time. The total of the two times is the EBT. Find the RG for Step 3 according to the depth and EBT. Repeat this process for Step 4, if necessary.

Example: NO-D FIRST DIVE (3 STEP)

Step 1: 90 ft (27 m) for 15 minutes
Step 2: 60 ft (18 m) for 20 minutes
Step 3: 30 ft (9 m) for 30 minutes

Step 1: 90 ft (27 m) - *No-D Limit is 20 minutes*
actual bottom time = 15 minutes, RG = C

Step 2: 60 ft (18 m) - *No-D Limit is 50 minute*
equivalent time for RG "C" = 25 minutes
ADD actual bottom time = 20 minutes
EBT = 25 + 20 = 45 minutes, RG = F

Step 3: 30 ft (9 m) - *No-D Limit is 300 minutes*
equivalent time for RG "F" = 120 minutes
ADD actual bottom time = 30 minutes
EBT = 120 + 30 = 150 minutes, RG = G

Example: DECOMPRESSION STOP REQUIRED FIRST DIVE (3 STEP)

Step 1: 90 ft (27 m) for 15 minutes
Step 2: 70 ft (21 m) for 15 minutes
Step 3: 50 ft (15 m) for 15 minutes

Step 1: 90 ft (27 m) - *No-D Limit is 20 minutes*
actual bottom time = 15 minutes,
RG = C

Step 2: 70 ft (21 m) - *No-D Limit is 35 minutes*
equivalent time for RG "C" = 20 minutes
actual bottom time = 15 minutes
EBT = 20 + 15 = 35 minutes

EBT at Step 2 touches No-D Limit so a decompression stop of 5 minutes at 10 ft (3 m) will be required at end of dive. RG = E

Step 3: 50 ft (15 m) - *No-D Limit is 75 minutes*
equivalent time for RG "E" = 50 minutes
actual bottom time = 15 minutes
EBT Time = 50 + 15 = 65 minutes, RG = G

Decompress at 10 ft (3 m) for 5 minutes before surfacing.

Repetitive Dive - Multi-Level Procedure

On repetitive Multi-level dives the *RG at Step 1 must be equal to or greater than the RG of the previous dive.* For example, if the RG for Step 1 is C and the RG of the preceding dive is D, the RG for Step 1 is adjusted to D. Beyond Step 1, the procedures followed for repetitive dives are identical to those used for first dives.

Use Table C to determine the No-D Limit for Step 1 according to the depth and Repetitive Factor (RF). (The actual bottom time for Step 1 should not exceed this No-D Limit). Multiply the actual bottom time by the RF to determine the EBT for Step 1. Find the RG for Step 1 according to the depth and EBT.

Use the RG from Step 1 to establish an equivalent time for the same RG at Step 2. Add the actual bottom time at Step 2 to the equivalent time. The total of the two times is the EBT for Step 2. Find the RG for Step 2 according to the depth and EBT.

Use the RG from Step 2 to establish an equivalent time for the same RG at Step 3. Add the actual bottom time at Step 3 to the equivalent time. The total of the two times is the EBT for Step 3. Find the RG for Step 3 according to the depth and EBT. Repeat this process for Step 4, if necessary.

Example: NO-D REPETITIVE DIVE with RF of 1.7 (3 Step)

Step 1: 80 ft (24 m) for 10 minutes
Step 2: 50 ft (15 m) for 25 minutes
Step 3: 30 ft (9 m) for 30 minutes

Step 1: 80 ft (24 m) - *No-D Limit for RF 1.7 is 12 minutes* (Table C - actual bottom time not to exceed 12 minutes)
ADD actual bottom time = 10 minutes
EBT = 10 x 1.7 = 17 minutes, RG = D

Step 2: 50 ft (15 m) - *No-D Limit is 75 minutes* equivalent time for RG "D" = 40 minutes
ADD actual bottom time = 25 minutes
EBT = 40 + 25 = 65 minutes, RG = G

Step 3: 30 ft (9 m) - *No-D Limit is 300 minutes*
equivalent time for RG "G" = 150 minutes
ADD actual bottom time = 30 minutes
EBT = 150 + 30 = 180 minutes, RG = H

Note:

The DCIEM multi-level procedure has not been extensively tested, but is more conservative and, therefore, safer than <u>some</u> of the other methods commonly practiced by recreational divers.

Example 3.

You are planning to dive to 100 ft (30 m) for 5 minutes before ascending to 66 ft (20 m) for 10 minutes. You will then ascend to 50 ft (15 m). If you used the DCIEM Multi-level Procedure, for how long could you remain at 50 ft (15 m) before a decompression stop is required?

Enter Table A (Table 17.1) at the 100 ft (30 m) row, and move along the row to find 5 minutes. The associated RG is A.

At 66 ft (20 m) an RG of A corresponds to a bottom time of 12 minutes, which is considered the time already spent at 66 ft (20 m). The EBT at 66 ft (20 m) is taken as
12 + 10 = 22 minutes, which gives a RG of D.

At 50 ft (15 m), an RG of D corresponds to 40 minutes, which is taken as the time already spent at 50 ft (15 m). Since the NDL for 50 ft (15 m) is 75 minutes, there is still 75 - 40 = 35 minutes of bottom time remaining. However, if you touch this No-D Limit, a 5 minute stop at 10 ft (3 m) will be required. *(The Huggins Table gives 25 minutes at this depth, the PADI Wheel gives 42 minutes* and the Suunto SME-ML dive computer gives 46 minutes.)*

* or 35 minutes on metric Wheel

Example 4.

You are planning to dive to 120 ft (36 m) for 5 minutes before ascending to 90 ft (27 m) for 6 minutes. If you then wish to ascend to 40 ft (12 m), what is the No-D Limit at the 40 ft (12 m) level?

Enter Table A at 120 ft (36 m), and move along the row to find 5 minutes. The associated RG is A.

At 90 ft (27 m), a RG of A corresponds to a bottom time of 9 minutes, which is considered the time already spent at 90 ft (27 m). The EBT at 90 ft (27 m) is taken as 9 + 6 = 15 minutes, which gives a RG of C.

At 40 ft (12 m), a RG of C corresponds to 40 minutes, which is taken as the time already spent at 40 ft (12 m). Since the NDL for 40 ft (12 m) is 150 minutes, there is still 150 - 40 = 110 minutes of bottom time remaining. *(The Huggins Tables give 15 minutes at this depth.)*

Example 5.

A diver dives to 70 ft (21 m) for 40 minutes before ascending to 50 ft (15 m) for a further 15 minutes. What decompression is required?

The diver has exceeded to No-D Limit at Step 1 by 5 minutes and should have ascended to 10 ft (3 m) a do a 5 minute stop before surfacing. However, since he continued to dive, his 40 minutes at 70 ft (21 m) was equivalent to 60 minutes at 50 ft (15 m) and his EBT = 60 + 15 = 75 minutes, which is the No-D Limit at 50 ft (15 m). Since he has touched the No-D Limit he must do an additional 5 minutes of safety stop, giving total decompression of 10 minutes at 10 ft (3 m).

THE BS-AC '88 TABLES MULTI-LEVEL PROCEDURE

The BS-AC has suggested a multi-level dive procedure based on the BS-AC '88 Tables.[5] It is essentially a Repetitive Group procedure and involves swapping from one table to another. The procedure is as follows:

The first portion of the dive time is timed from leaving the surface to arriving at the second level. The second portion begins on arrival at the second level and ends on arrival at the third level, and so on. The final level used in a dive time calculation must be below 6 m; you cannot include a 6 m or 3 m re-entry in a Multi-level dive.

Ascent between the various levels is at a maximum rate of 15 m/minute, and the ascent from 6 m to the surface is at a rate of 6 m/minute.

On final surfacing, the usual Surfacing Code (SC) applies and is used for subsequent dive planning.

Divers are advised to go to the maximum depth at the start of the dive, to work progressively shallower throughout the dive and to avoid re-descent during the dive. However, if a diver does descend to a deeper level during the dive, and this level is more than 6 m deeper than the previous maximum level, the diver is advised to move to the next higher table.* For example, if you are diving on Table A and have reached a maximum depth of 30 m before ascending to 24 m, and then you re-descend to 30 m, you must assume that you began the dive on Table B and do the entire Multi-level calculation accordingly.

It is recommended that, if a Multi-level dive is contemplated, it is planned in advance on the surface, rather than underwater.

To date, there has been no testing to determine the safety of applying the Multi-level dive procedure to the BS-AC '88 Tables, which themselves are untested in their current format.

Example 6.

You wish to conduct a single Multi-level dive. The first portion of the dive will be spent at 30 m, and you will then ascend to 15 m, arriving after 7 minutes of dive time has elapsed. After a further 10 minutes you intend to be at 9 m. For how long can you remain at 9 m before a decompression stop is required?

Enter Table A at the 30 m row and look up 30 m for 7 minutes. Moving down the column, the SC is *C*. Enter Table C at 15 m and look up the 10 minutes of dive time for the second portion of the dive. Taking 11 minutes and moving down the column, the SC is *D*. Entering Table D at 9 m, the available dive time is *29 minutes.* This means that you must arrive at 6 m by the time the 29 minutes has expired and then take one minute to ascend from 6 m to the surface.

Example 7.

You wish to conduct a single Multi-level dive using the BS-AC '88 Tables. You intend to dive to 21 m before ascending to 15 m, and arriving there after 13 minutes. You then plan to remain at 15 m for 16 minutes before ascending directly to 9 m. How long can you spend at 9 m before requiring a stop?

Enter Table A at 21 m and look up 13 minutes. Moving down the column, the SC is *C*. Enter Table C at 15 m and look up the 16 minutes of dive time plus the extra time taken to ascend to the 9 m level. Taking 17 minutes and moving down the column, the SC is *E*. Entering Table E at 9 m, the available dive time is *9 minutes*, at the end of which you must be at 6 m to begin the final, slow ascent.

Example 8.

You have begun a single dive to 11 m. After 13 minutes at 11 m you are forced to descend to 18 m to retrieve a lost torch. You descend directly to 18 m (arriving after 14 minutes of elapsed dive time) and by the time you find the torch and return to 11 m, a further 6 minutes of dive time has elapsed. For how long can you remain at 11 m before a stop is necessary?

* This is to attempt to cater for the faster gas loading that may occur when bubbles, if present, are compressed during a re-descent.

Since this dive involves a re-descent, you must begin the entire calculation on Table B, rather than Table A.

Looking up 12 m for 14 minutes on Table B gives a SC of *C*. From Table C, 6 minutes at 18 m yields a SC of *D*. From Table D, 8 minutes of dive time is still available, which includes the time taken to ascend from 11 m to 6 m.

THE PADI WHEEL

The Wheel has been designed specifically to cater for multi-level diving. The instruction booklet, accompanying the Wheel, contains a number of detailed examples on its use in multi-level dive situations, so further examples will not be presented here. Users of the Wheel are advised to read the instructions very carefully, and to ensure that they have mastered the Wheel before using it to calculate a multi-level dive.

The multi-level procedure using the Wheel is currently the only table-based multi-level procedure that has undergone any significant testing to determine its safety.*

COMBAT SWIMMER MULTI-LEVEL DIVE (CSMD) PROCEDURE

In 1983, the U.S. Navy published a report titled "A Procedure for diving multiple-level dives on air using repetitive groups".[6] It was reported that the Navy's current combat swimmer mission scenarios involve long transits at 30 ft (9 m), or shallower, with deeper excursions interspersed throughout the profile. In the absence of a surface interval, the standard U.S. Navy rules would require the diver to decompress for the deepest depth, and total bottom time, of the entire mission. This approach was felt to be overly restrictive. In addition, the absence of RNTs for depths shallower than 40 ft (12 m), and the absence of RGs for 30 ft (9 m) dives longer than 310 minutes prompted the Navy to develop the new procedure.

The technique divides each dive into segments: those deeper than 30 ft (9 m) and those 30 ft (9 m) or shallower. Deep and shallow segments must alternate, and each dive can last up to 12 hours. The maximum depth of the excursions beyond 30 ft (9 m) is restricted to 120 ft (36 m), so that decompression will never be required at a depth greater than 30 ft (9 m).

In this procedure, Repetitive Groups are transferred between depths in a similar way to the Repetitive Group (Graver) method previously described. For segments deeper than 30 ft (9 m), the RG is determined in the normal (single-level dive) manner, and any required decompression is taken during the subsequent shallow segment of the dive. Decompression is done at 30 ft (9 m), 20 ft (6 m) and 10 ft (3 m). The 10 ft (3 m) stop is allowed to be taken at any depth between 10-20 ft (3-6 m) in order to avoid wave action. It is believed that taking the stop deeper may actually enhance the off-gassing. The diver must spend a minimum of 30 minutes at 20 ft (6 m), or shallower, to allow the faster tissues to unload, and, therefore, ensure that decompression will be controlled by the slowest tissue. This interval serves the same purpose as the normal 10-minute interval on the surface in the standard U.S. Navy procedure. After each segment, the diver has a new RG and a new RNT, which is then carried over to the next segment.

* Details of the testing are provided in Chapter 19.

This method was designed for use with the Navy's closed-circuit mixed gas system, in order to allow the Navy diver to spend up to 12 hours underwater without surfacing. The procedure has been tested and is considered to be safe but, as yet, no test reports have been released to the public. The system is complex and is not designed to be worked out underwater. It appears to be quite inappropriate for use by the sport diver.

OFF-GASSING IN THE SHALLOWS?

Most multi-level dive procedures encourage a diver to spend some time in shallow water towards the end of the dive, rather than to ascend directly to the surface from depth. The aim of this is to allow some of the excess nitrogen to diffuse out of the diver's body while still under pressure.

It may be beneficial for a diver to spend some time doing a "safety stop" at the end of any dive, whether a multi-level dive or not. Although certain experimental evidence[7] indicates that we may, at times, surface with less excess gas after doing a safety stop than we would have if no stop was done, wherever possible, the time spent at the stop should be included when calculating the RG at the end of the dive. In this way, if any extra gas is taken aboard during the safety stop, it will be accounted for if a repetitive dive is planned.

IS MULTI-LEVEL DIVING SAFE?

The safety of most multi-level diving techniques has not, as yet, been determined. It is difficult enough to test the large array of possible single-depth dive profiles, so it is impossible to validate the endless number of possible combinations of depth and time during various multi-level dives.

The few tests that were done to test the validity of the multi-level program used by the "Edge" diving computer[8], and the growing number of tests being conducted to test the application of the PADI Wheel to multi-level diving[9,10], indicate that certain profiles may be safe. However, although there have been many anecdotal reports of divers multi-levelling without incident, **currently there is insufficient evidence to determine the safety of most multi-level techniques**.

It is not known whether multi-level diving magnifies potential decompression problems, or whether some types of profile actually reduce these problems. It seems likely that working shallower throughout a dive is a sensible practice, whereas working progressively deeper during a dive appears to be risky as it may lead to greater inert gas loads in the tissues and, possibly, a longer direct ascent, both of which are conducive to bubble formation. Consequently, if multi-level dives are planned, they should be done so very conservatively and the depths of the levels should become progressively shallower.

Unfortunately, calculation errors are often made when tables are used for multi-level dive calculations. To minimize these errors, ***the dive profile should be planned before entering the water***. By using a dive computer, a diver avoids the possiblity of making these errors.

However, the ***dive computer must be reliable and conservative*** in order to maximize the safety of the multi-level dive. Unfortunately, dive computers sometimes fail, and most of the current models appear to lack the appropriate conservatism when used for certain dive profiles, especially those during which a diver increases, rather than decreases, depth levels.

The following rules are suggested to minimize the risks involved with multi-level diving.

RULES FOR MULTI-LEVEL DIVING

1. Use the Huggins, DCIEM Tables, BS-AC '88 Tables, or the PADI Wheel, rather than a multi-level technique based on the U.S. Navy Tables. The Huggins and BS-AC '88 Tables appear to be more conservative than the others. The times allowed by the Wheel and the DCIEM Tables vary with respect to each other, depending on the dive.

   OR

   Use a reliable and ***conservative*** dive computer.

2. If using tables, plan the dive profile before diving and then stick to the plan or dive more conservatively than the plan.

3. Reduce the NDLs **substantially** to cater for any predisposing factors to decompression sickness that are relevant to you.

4. ***Do the deepest level first, and work progressively shallower throughout the dive.*** Re-descending during the dive may increase the rate of gas uptake and so make the dive far more hazardous.

5. Ascend no faster than 60 ft (18 m)/minute between levels and to the surface. An ascent rate of about 30 ft (9 m)/minute seems reasonable, especially for depths shallower than about 80-100 ft (24-30 m).*

6. If using tables, include the time taken to ascend to a level in the "bottom" time of the previous level.

7. Spend at least 3 minutes between 15-20 ft (4.5-6 m) before surfacing, and include this time when calculating the RG after surfacing, where appropriate.

* However, a faster ascent rate may significantly reduce the amount of inert gas absorbed during the ascent at greater depths.

TABLE 22.3

Comparision of allowable times for a Multi-level dive

	Bottom time limits		
	Huggins	**PADI Wheel**	**DCIEM**
Step 1:			
110 ft (33 m)	15	16 (15)	12
Actual bottom time = 10 minutes			
Step 2:			
70 ft (21 m)	13	19 (16)	20
Actual bottom time = 10 minutes			
Step 3:			
40 ft (12 m)	0	72 (72)	90

The times in brackets are from the metric Wheel.

TABLE 22.4

Comparision of allowable times for a pair of Multi-level dives

	Bottom time limits		
	Huggins	**PADI Wheel**	**DCIEM**
DIVE 1			
Step 1:			
120 ft (36 m)	10	13 (13)	10
Actual bottom time = 5 minutes			
Step 2:			
80 ft (24 m)	17	20 (20)	15
Actual bottom time = 10 minutes			
Step 3:			
40 ft (12 m)	50	87 (91)	90
Actual bottom time = 50 minutes			
Surface Interval = 1 1/2 hours			

	Bottom time limits		
	Huggins	**PADI Wheel**	**DCIEM**
DIVE 2			
Step 1:			
70 ft (21 m)	14	24 (22)	16
Actual bottom time = 10 minutes			
Step 2:			
50 ft (15 m)	0	37 (31)	*

* A decompression stop would be required here. However, if Step 2 was at 40 ft (12 m) or shallower, plenty of No-D bottom time would be available.

The times in brackets are from the metric Wheel.

SUMMARY

* A "Multi-Level" dive is defined here as a dive where the diver spends significant bottom time shallower than the maximum depth and, so, extends the bottom time beyond the the limits for a rectangular profile dive to the maximum depth.

* Various techniques have been introduced for planning multi-level dives. Some techniques, based on the U.S. Navy Tables, create a higher gas load in the tissues than is allowed by the tables and may be more likely to cause bends.

* Most multi-level techniques involve transferring a Repetitive Group between depths. However, this may not always be appropriate.

* The safety of most multi-level diving techniques has not been determined, although it appears that some types of profile may be safer than others (i.e. starting at the deepest level and working shallower).

* A reliable, conservative dive computer or a table which has been designed, or appropriately adapted, to cater for multi-level diving should be used. e.g. Huggins Tables, DCIEM Tables, PADI Wheel or BS-AC '88 Tables.

* Predisposing factors to bends must be accounted for, ascent should be slow, and a safety stop should be done.

* Do the deepest level first, and work progressively shallower throughout the dive.

* Total dive time should be used to determine the time allowed for any subsequent repetitive dive(s).

REFERENCES

1. Graver, D. (1976), "A Decompression Table Procedure for Multi-Level Diving". In: Fead, L. (ed). *Proceedings of The Eighth International Conference on Underwater Education.* NAUI, California.

2. Huggins, K., and Somers, L. (1981), "Mathematical Evaluation of Multi-Level Diving". Report No. MICHU-SG-81-207, Michigan Sea Grant Publications.

3. Bove, A. (1983), RX for Divers. *Skin Diver;* 33 (3), March: 10.

4. Huggins, K. (1981), "New No-Decompression Tables Based on No-Decompression Limits Determined by Ultrasonic Bubble Detection". Report No. MICHU-SG-81-205, Michigan Sea Grant Publications, University of Michigan.

5. Busuttili, M. (1989), "The BS-AC '88 Decompression Tables - first review". *NDC Bulletin*; 14: 3-5.

6. Thalmann, E., and Butler, F. (1983), "A Procedure for Doing Multiple Level Dives on Air Using Repetitive Groups", Navy Experimental Diving Unit, Report No. 13-83, Department of the Navy.

7. Kindwall, E. et al (1975), "Nitrogen Elimination in Man During During Decompresion". *Undersea Biomedical Research*; 2 (4): 285-297.

8. Huggins, K. (1983), "Doppler Evaluation of Multi-Level Diving Profiles". Report No. MICHU-SG-84-300, Michigan Sea Grant Publications, University of Michigan.

9. Powell, M., Spencer, M. and Rogers, R. (1988), "Doppler Ultrasound Monitoring of Gas Phase Formation in Divers Performing Multilevel and Repetitive Dives". Diving Science and Technology, PADI, California.

10. Rogers, R. and Powell, M. (1989), "Controlled Hyperbaric Chamber Tests of Multi-Day, Repetitive Dives". (Presented at UHMS Meeting, June 9, 1989).

OTHER SOURCES

Bove, A. (1983), RX for Divers. *Skin Diver;* 33 (4), May: 12.

Graver, D. (1979), "Using the U.S. Navy Dive Tables for Sport Diving". In: *Decompression In Depth*, PADI, California.

Huggins, K. (1987), "Microprocessor Applications to Multi-Level Air Decompression Problems", Report No. MICHU-SG-77-201, Michigan Sea Grant Publications, University of Michigan.

Huggins, K. (1985), "Multi-Level Diving, How Safe Is It?", *Proceedings of International Conference on Underwater Education, I.Q. `85*, NAUI, California.

Huggins, K. (1985), "Tables, Tables, What's with all these Tables?", *I.Q. '85 Proceedings*, Bangasser, S. (ed), NAUI, California.

Huggins, K., personal communication.

Lewbel, G. (1986), "Trends in Multi-Level Diving in the USA", *Skindiving*; 16 (1): 100-102.

PADI (1987), "Recreational Dive Planning...The Next Generation". PADI, California.

"UDT Instructions for using the DCIEM Sport Diving Tables c1990". Universal Dive Techtronics, Inc., Vancouver.

"UDT Recommendations for using the DCIEM Sport Diving Tables (UDT Info. 8) c1990". Universal Dive Techtronics, Inc., Vancouver.

Wong, G., personal communications.

RECOMMENDED FURTHER READING

Huggins, K. (1985), "Multi-Level Diving, How Safe Is It?". *Proceedings of International Conference on Underwater Education, I.Q. `85*, NAUI, California.

Powell, M., Spencer, M. and Rogers, R. (1988), "Doppler Ultrasound Monitoring of Gas Phase Formation in Divers Performing Multilevel and Repetitive Dives". Diving Science and Technology, PADI, California.

CHAPTER 23

DIVE COMPUTERS

Since decompression sickness in humans first reared its ugly head, back in the mid-1800's, scientists, and others, have sought ways to improve and simplify decompression calculations and procedures.

Haldane introduced his model and schedules at the beginning of this century and, since then, many decompression tables have been published. Although some of the very latest tables include methods for compensating for parts of a dive spent shallower than the maximum depth, most tables require a diver to choose a no-decompression stop, or decompression stop schedule according to the maximum depth and bottom time of a dive. The calculation assumes that the entire bottom time was spent at the maximum depth, and that the diver's body has absorbed the associated amount of nitrogen. However, many dives do not follow that pattern. A diver's depth normally varies throughout a dive and, often, very little of the bottom time is actually spent at the maximum depth. In this case, a diver's body should, theoretically, contain far less dissolved nitrogen than is assumed to be present when using the tables in the conventional manner. Some divers feel penalized for the time of the dive not spent at the maximum depth.

FIGURE 23.1

A typical dive profile

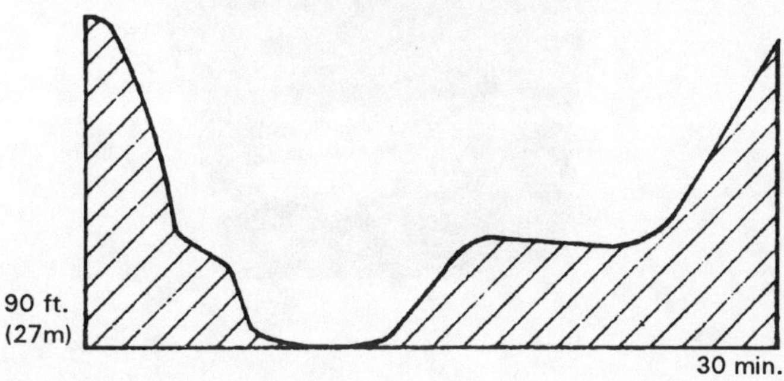

In Figure 23.1, the bold line represents the actual dive profile, whereas the broken line represents the profile that must be looked up when using a decompression table in the conventional manner. The shaded area represents the time when less nitrogen should be absorbed than the tables assume has been absorbed.

The ideal situation is to have a device that tracks the exact dive profile and then calculates the decompression requirement according to the actual dive done. Such devices have emerged since the mid-1950's, some gaining some notoriety.

Probably the best known of the early decompression meters is the *SOS decompression meter* (Figure 23.2) which was designed in 1959 and emerged in the early 1960's. The meter, which is still currently available, appears to represent a diver's body as one tissue. It contains a ceramic resistor through which gas is absorbed, before passing into a constant volume chamber. Within the chamber is a bourdon tube which bends as the pressure changes, and the pressure level, which represents the amount of absorbed gas, is displayed on an attached gauge. On ascent, gas escapes back through the resistor and, eventually, when enough gas has escaped the gauge will indicate that a safe (supposedly) ascent is possible.

FIGURE 23.2
The S.O.S. decompression meter

A number of problems arise with the use of the SOS meter. Individual meters often vary greatly, and the no-decompression stop times for initial/single dives deeper than 60 ft (18 m) exceed the U.S. Navy NDLs. The meters give inadequate decompression for repetitive dives when compared to the U.S. Navy, and most other, tables. In 1971, the first six divers requiring treatment at the Royal Australian Navy School of Underwater Medicine chamber were divers who had ascended according to SOS decompression meters.[1]

FIGURE 23.3
Schematic diagram of the S.O.S. decompression meter

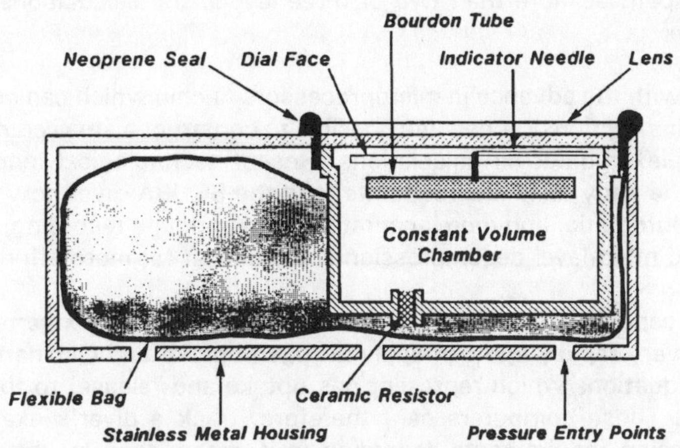

Reprinted from Huggins (1987)

The Defence and Civil Institute of Environmental Medicine (DCIEM) of Canada developed a decompression meter in 1962. It utilized four resistor-compartments to simulate nitrogen uptake and elimination in a diver. Initially, the compartments were set up in parallel so that each compartment was exposed to ambient pressure and, thus, absorbed gas simultaneously. When tested, this configuration produced an unacceptable bends incidence. The four units were then re-arranged in a series arrangement so that only the first was exposed to ambient pressure and gas passed from one compartment into the next. This configuration was tested on almost 4,000 test dives and produced a very low incidence of bends.[1] The meter gave effective half-times from 5 to more than 300 minutes and it indicated current depth and safe ascent depth. The DCIEM unit never became available to recreational divers as it would have proved to be very expensive and would have required extensive, and costly, maintenance.

In 1975, Farallon released its *Multi-Tissue Decomputer*, which was designed to be a no-decompression stop meter. It consisted of four permeable membranes, two of which absorbed gas and two which released it. In 1976, the Royal Australian Navy tested two meters and found them to give very divergent results. One became more conservative while the other became more radical.[2] In addition, various mechanical problems eventuated. Tests done in the USA confirmed that the NDLs given by the meter often greatly exceeded those of the U.S. Navy Tables.[3]

Over the past ten years or so, various methods of extrapolating the U.S. Navy (and some other) Tables to credit a diver for the shallower portions of a multi-level dive have emerged. Most of these methods, described in Chapter 22, require manipulations that are too complex for many divers, and require the dive plan to be known in advance and rigidly followed. Most techniques are unvalidated and their safety in certain situations is a subject of dispute. In addition, if time is spent at more than two or three levels, the calculations may become prohibitively complex.

By the mid-1970's, with the advance in microprocessors (a chip which can contain a series of pre-programmed instructions), it became possible to construct a small computer capable of doing very complex multi-level calculations. Recent technological innovations have overcome some of the early technical restraints, and the SCUBA diver now has access to the convenience of automatic, and more accurate, depth and time recording, together with accurately computed multi-level decompression schedules at far more affordable prices.

A microprocessor is capable of reading a pressure transducer (which converts pressure into electrical impulses) very rapidly and can apply nitrogen uptake and elimination algorithms (the mathematical equations which represent gas uptake and release) to this information every few seconds. These computers can, therefore, track a diver's exact profile and calculate decompression requirements according to it, rather than by the "rounded-off" profile which is used with decompression tables.

FIGURE 23.4

The internal components of an Aladin Pro dive computer

Some of the computers (e.g. Suunto SME-USN, Decobrain 1) have actual decompression tables programmed into their memory, and read the table to give the diver the appropriate decompression information. The tables programmed into these devices list decompression information in discrete increments of depth (usually 10 ft/3 m) and time (often 5-10 minutes), so they still do not give the exact (theoretical) decompression requirement for the actual dive done. The Decobrain 1 allowed table-like multi-level dive calculations but got confused easily.

To overcome this situation, most current dive computers are programmed with the actual decompression model on which the table is based, rather than on the table itself. For example, if a computer is programmed with the model of the U.S. Navy Tables, it can simulate the loading and unloading of all six tissue compartments used in the U.S. Navy model and portray their theoretical nitrogen content at any particular depth and time during a dive or surface interval. In this manner, the exact decompression requirement given by the model can be calculated almost instantly.

The current generation of computers are based on either the U.S. Navy model, models based on Spencer's NDLs or reduced U.S. Navy NDLs, or on the Swiss (ZH-L) system. They generally appear to follow their models accurately.

These modern dive computers offer the diver a number of advantages over the tables. They eliminate the problem of divers making errors in their decompression calculations since the computers do the calculations automatically and accurately, in accordance to their model. By following the actual profile, rather than just the maximum depth, and by accounting for a variety of tissues, rather than a single tissue, during a surface interval, the computers allow the diver much more bottom time on most dives, especially repetitive dives. They normally also measure depth and time very accurately, and many give the diver an indication of ascent rate which, in itself, is a very valuable function.

Despite, and in some cases, because of some of these features, some reputable diving scientists, doctors and educators remain very critical of these devices. Some argue that a diver will become too machine-dependent and would be at a loss, and in a potentially dangerous situation, if his computer failed while in use. However, other reputable diving scientists and educators feel that modern decompression computers are less likely to fail than divers are while reading the tables, and that there are some reasonable bail-out procedures in case of meter failure. *Probably the major fear of the computer critics is that some computers bring a diver far too close to, or beyond, the limits of safe diving, especially during deep and/or repetitive dives.*

The decompression models programmed into the model-based computers are designed to simulate nitrogen uptake and release in a diver's body. However, they are just models and cannot completely predict the gas flow in and out of our actual tissues. Our physiology is not always so predictable as many factors influence the rate of gas uptake and elimination and the possibility of consequent decompression sickness. So, even though the computers follow their models exactly and the theoretical tissues programmed into the computer load and unload as expected, our bodies might not be behaving quite so predictably. There is no safety margin built into most computers which substantially compensates for this difference.

Tables, on the other hand, usually contain an inherent safety margin and, in addition, since we must "round-up" any intermediate depth and/or time to the nearest higher or longer tabled depth and/or time, we partly, but not always fully, compensate for our own body's deviation from the model.

A table-based, non-multi-level computer retains any inherent and/or "round-up" safety margin of the table. A table-based, multi-level computer retains a small amount of the margin and a model-based computer retains no margin at all unless it is built into the model itself.

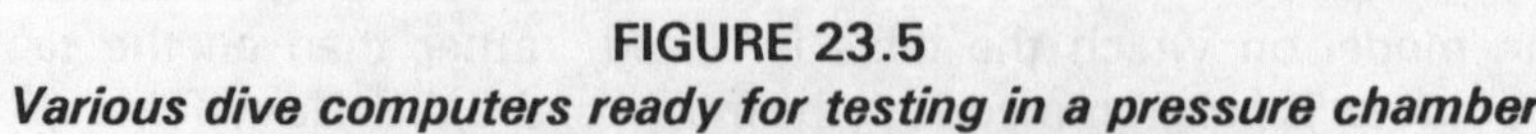

FIGURE 23.5
Various dive computers ready for testing in a pressure chamber

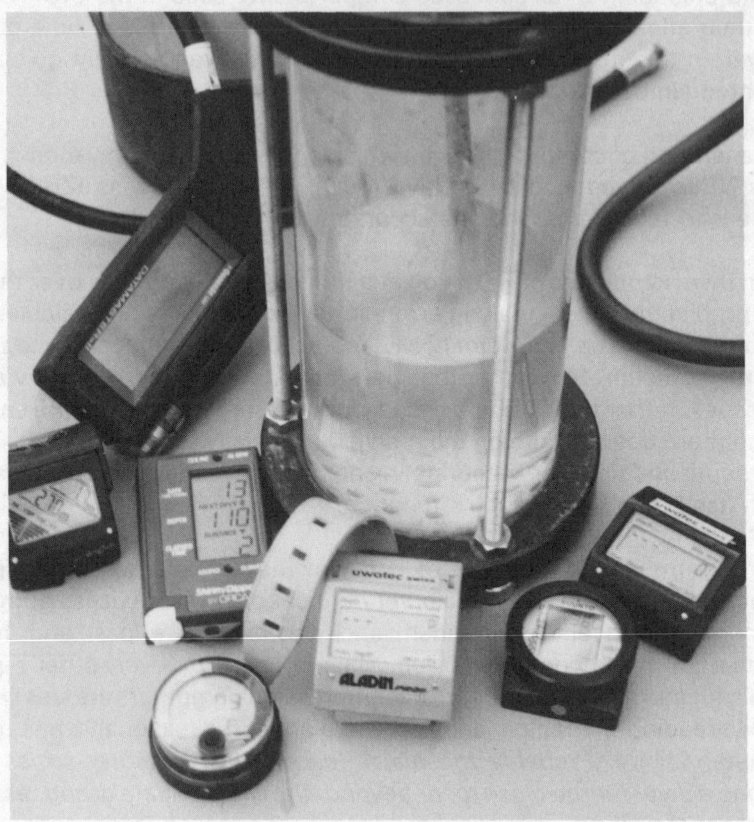

COMPARING COMPUTERS TO TABLES FOR NO-DECOMPRESSION STOP DIVES

When no-decompression stop times allowed by various computers are compared to those allowed by various tables (even those based on the same model) for the same dive, vast differences often appear. These differences become greater for repetitive dives. Tables 23.1, 23.2 and 23.3 compare the times allowed by various computers and tables for three series of repetitive dives that were carried out in a water-filled pressure chamber. A variety of other simulated, and real, dives were conducted, with similar results. Some of the reasons for these differences will be discussed in this section.

TABLE 23.1

Dive times allowed by various computers and tables

The times given are in minutes unless otherwise specified

Dive 1. **Depth** = 120 ft (36 m)

Allowable no-deco. time:

Edge = 11
Skinnydipper = 10
SME-ML = 10
Aladin (Guide) = 9
Aladin Pro = 12
Micro Brain = 8
Micro Brain Pro Plus = 8
Datamax Sport = 13

U.S. Navy Tables = 15
Buehlmann (1986) Tables = 12

Bottom time = 10
Ascent time = 1.3*
Deco. required:
Micro Brain Pro Plus = 1 minute at 10 ft (3 m)

Surface interval = 60

Dive 2. **Depth** = 100 ft (30 m)

Allowable no-deco. time:

Edge = 19
Skinnydipper = 19
SME-ML = 19
Aladin (Guide) = 15
Aladin Pro = 15
Microbrain = 13
Micro Brain Pro Plus = 12
Datamax Sport = 15

U.S. Navy Tables = 11
Buehlmann (1986) Tables = 8

Bottom time = 18
Deco. required:
Edge = none
Skinnydipper = none
SME-ML = none
Aladin = none
Aladin Pro = 2 min at 10 ft (3 m)
Microbrain = 2 min at 10 ft (3 m)
Micro Brain Pro Plus = 3 min at 10 ft (3 m)
Datamax Sport = 1 min at 10 ft (3 m)
U.S. Navy Tables = 15 min at 10 ft (3 m)
Buehlmann Tables = 2 min at 20 ft (6 m) + 7 min at 10 ft (3 m)
Ascent time = 2.3

* Note that the ascent was about three times as fast as it should have been. None of these computers reduced the allowable times for the following repetitive dive in order to try to compensate for any extra bubble formation occurring as result of a faster than recommended ascent.

TABLE 23.2

Dive times allowed by various computers and tables

The times given are in minutes unless otherwise specified

<u>**Dive 1.**</u> **Depth** = 90 ft (27 m)

Allowable no-deco. time:

SME-ML(R1) = 22
Skinnydipper = 23*
Aladin = 19
Aladin Pro = 20
Micro Brain = 18
Micro Brain Pro Plus = 15
Datamax Sport = 25

U.S. Navy Tables = 30
Buehlmann (1986) Tables = 20

Bottom time = 18 **Deco. required** = none (Micro Brain Pro Plus initially indicated 2 min at 10 ft (3 m) but cleared during the ascent)

Ascent time = 3.5 min

Surface interval = 32

<u>**Dive 2.**</u> **Depth** = 100 ft (30 m)

Allowable no-deco. time:

SME-ML(R1) = 16
Skinnydipper = 16
Aladin = 14
Aladin Pro = 12
Micro Brain = 13
Micro Brain Pro Plus = 12
Datamax Sport = 12

U.S. Navy Tables = 3
Buehlmann (1986) Tables = 6

Bottom time = 16

Deco. required:

SME-ML(R1) = none
Skinnydipper = none
Aladin = 4 min at 10 ft (3 m)
Aladin Pro = 7 min at 10 ft (3 m)
Micro Brain = 4 min at 10 ft (3 m)
Micro Brain Pro Plus = 4 min at 10 ft (3 m)
Datamax Sport = 4 min at 10 ft (3 m)
U.S. Navy Tables = 15 min at 10 ft (3 m)
Buehlmann Tables = 2 min at 20 ft (6 m) + 7 min at 10 ft (3 m)

Ascent time = 2.5 min to 10 ft (3 m)
Deco. done = 7 min at 10 ft (3 m)
Surface interval = 32

* This time given by the Edge should be identical

TABLE 23.2 (Continued)

<u>**Dive 3.**</u> **Depth** = 120 ft (36 m)

Allowable no-deco. time:

SME-ML(R1) = 10	U.S. Navy Tables = 0
Skinnydipper = 10*	Buehlmann (1986) Tables = 0
Aladin = 9	
Aladin Pro = 6	
Micro Brain = 8	
Micro Brain Pro Plus = 8	
Datamax Sport = 0	

Bottom time = 10

Ascent time to 10 ft (3 m) = 2
Deco. required:

SME-ML(R1) = none
Skinnydipper = none
Aladin = deco. was indicated but cleared during ascent
Aladin Pro = 3 min at 10 ft (3 m)
Micro Brain = 5 min at 10 ft (3 m)
Micro Brain Pro Plus = 3 min at 10 ft (3 m)
Datamax Sport = out of range

U.S. Navy Tables = 15 min at 20 ft (6 m) + 31 min at 10 ft (3 m)
Buehlmann Tables = 4 min at 20 ft (6 m) + 9 min at 10 ft (3 m)

* The time given by the Edge should be identical.

TABLE 23.3

Dive times allowed by various computers and tables

The times given are in minutes unless otherwise specified

Dive 1. **Depth** = 100 ft (30 m)

Allowable no-deco. time:

SME-ML(R1) = 18
Skinnydipper = 19
Aladin Pro = 16
Micro Brain Pro Plus = 12
Datamax Sport = 20
U.S. Navy Tables = 25
Buehlmann (1986) Tables = 17

Bottom time = 10
Deco. required = none
Ascent time = 3

Surface interval = 60

Dive 2. **Depth** = 100 ft (30 m)

Allowable no-deco. time:

SME-ML(R1) = 18
Skinnydipper = 19
Aladin Pro = 15
Micro Brain Pro Plus = 12
Datamax Sport = 17
U.S. Navy Tables = 11
Buehlmann (1986) Tables = 8

Bottom time = 10

Deco. required:

SME-ML(R1) = none
Skinnydipper = none
Aladin Pro = none
Datamax Sport = none
U.S. Navy Tables = none
Buehlmann Tables = 5 minutes at 10 ft (3 m)

Ascent time = 3

Surface interval = 60

TABLE 23.3 (Continued)

Dive 3. **Depth** = 100 ft (30 m)

Allowable no-deco. time:

SME-ML(R1) = 18 U.S. Navy Tables = 0
Skinnydipper = 19 Buehlmann (1986) Tables = 8
Aladin Pro = 15
Micro Brain Pro Plus = 12
Datamax Sport = 15

Bottom time = 10

Deco. required:

SME-ML(R1) = none
Skinnydipper = none
Aladin Pro = none
Micro Brain Pro Plus = none
Datamax Sport = 12 minutes at 10 ft* (3 m)
U.S. Navy Tables = 15 minutes at 10 ft (3 m)
Buehlmann Tables = 5 minutes at 10 ft (3 m)

Ascent time = 3

* Pre-dive scrolled NDLs indicated that 15 minutes of no-decompression stop time was available, but after 7 minutes at 100 ft a decompression stop was required

SINGLE DIVES

Table 23.4, below, compares the single dive NDLs of various computers to those of the U.S. Navy and Buehlmann (1986) Tables.

TABLE 23.4

Comparison of NDLs of various computers and tables

Depth (ft)	(m)	USN	Buehlmann (1986)	Spencer	Aladin	Aladin Pro	Datamaster Sport	Datamax Sport	Edge	S/Dipper	Micro Brain	MicroBrain Pro Plus	SME-ML (R1)
30	9	-	400	225	-	354	260	260	225	225	199	220	215
40	12	200	125	135	124	121	136	136	133	133	113	106	132
50	15	100	75	75	72	70	78	78	75	75	65	64	74
60	18	60	51	50	49	49	55	55	52	52	46	44	53
70	21	50	35	40	35	35	40	40	39	39	30	31	38
80	24	40	25	30	25	25	31	31	31	31	22	20	29
90	27	30	20	25	19	20	25	25	24	24	17	15	23
100	30	25	17	20	16	16	20	20	19	19	13	12	18
110	33	20	14	15	13	14	16	16	13	13	10	10	13
120	36	15	12	10	9	12	13	13	10	10	8	8	11
130	39	10	10	5	7	10	11	11	9	9	7	7	9
140	42	10	9	0	6	8	9	9	7	7	7	7	7
150	45	5	0	0	5	7	6	8	7	7	6	6	6
160	48	5	0	0	4	6	3	7	6	6	5	5	5
170	51	5	0	0	4	5	0	6	5	5	4	4	4
180	54	5	0	0	4	4	0	5	5	5	4	4	4
190	57	5	0	0	4	4	0	5	4	4	3	3	4
200	60	0	0	0	4	3	0	5	4	4	3	3	3

Notes:

1. Times given for Orca computers are for the imperial models and also apply to the Delphi. The NDLs for the metric Orca models vary slightly.
2. Times given for the Oceanic computers apply to the European version. The times for the standard version differ for depths between 150-200 ft (45-60 m).
3. Times given for the Micro Brain computers are for the metric version and, in some cases, differ slightly to the imperial version.

Various computer NDLs may change periodically as manufacturers alter the models.

Single rectangular dives

It can be seen from Table 23.4 that the single dive No-Decompression Limits of the computers are more conservative than the U.S. Navy limits, and are generally similar to the limits of the Buehlmann (1986) Tables. Therefore, *for a single rectangular dive these computers will usually give a more conservative no-decompression stop time than the U.S. Navy Tables.*

It has been shown experimentally that divers who dive right to some of the U.S. Navy NDLs will be quite likely to bubble during, or after, the ascent.[4,5] By reducing the maximum allowable supersaturation ratios and, thereby, shortening the initial NDLs and, in some cases, slowing down the ascent, these computers (and many modern tables) attempt to minimize bubble formation during or after a dive.

Single multi-level dives

On a multi-level dive the computers will normally extend the allowable no-decompression stop dive time far beyond that allowed by the tables, especially if the levels become progressively shallower.

This occurs because the computer constantly calculates the (theoretical) gas uptake or release at all levels of the dive, rather than just at the maximum depth as tables do. This function is demonstrated in Figure 23.6 which shows a dive profile allowed by a Suunto SME-ML. At each level of the dive there was 1 minute of no-decompression stop time left when ascent was commenced to the next level.

FIGURE 23.6
Single multi-level no-decompression stop dive on a Suunto SME-ML

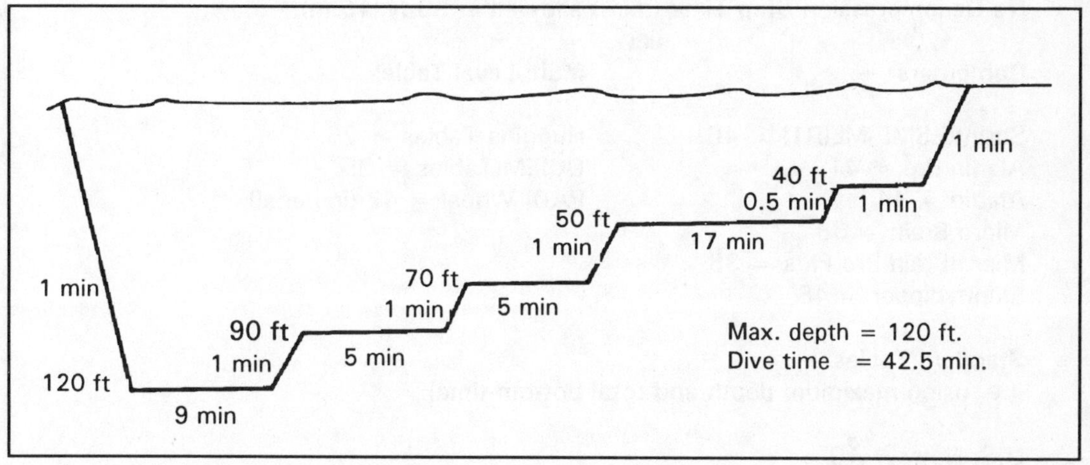

The (single) dive shown in Figure 23.6 required no decompression stop according to the computer, but required decompression of 15 minutes at 20 ft (6 m) and 31 minutes at 10 ft (3 m) according to the U.S. Navy Tables.

Figure 23.7 compares the times allowed by some dive computers to the times allowed by various table-based, multi-level methods for a single, multi-level dive of 100 ft (30 m) for 5 minutes, followed by 66 ft (20 m) for 10 minutes, followed by ascent to 50 ft (15 m).

FIGURE 23.7

Comparison of dive time allowed at 50 ft (15 m) by various computers and tables for a single, multi-level dive of 100 ft (30 m) for 5 minutes, followed by 66 ft (20 m) for 10 minutes, followed by ascent to 50 ft.

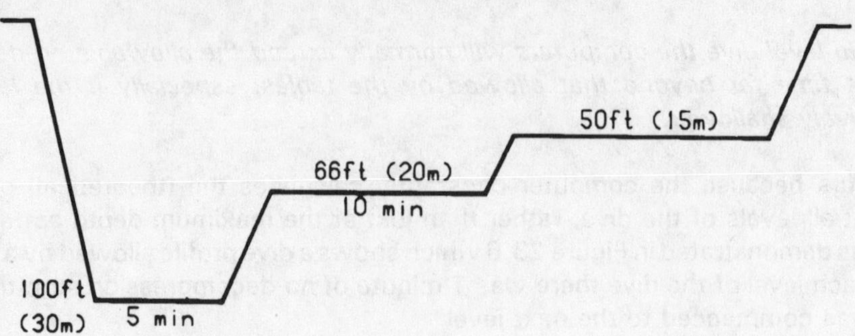

Time spent at 100 ft (30 m) = 5 minutes
Time spent at 66 ft (20 m) = 10 minutes

No-Decompression Stop Time (min.) allowed at 50 ft (15 m):

Computers

Suunto SME-ML(R1) = 46
Aladin Pro = 41
Aladin = 44
Micro Brain = 38
Micro Brain Pro Plus = 38
Skinnydipper = 48*

Multi-Level Tables

Huggins Tables = 25
DCIEM Tables = 35
PADI Wheel = 42 (imperial)

Standard Tables
(i.e. using maximum depth and total bottom time)

U.S. Navy = 10
Buehlmann (1986) = 2
DCIEM = 0
PADI RDP = 5

* This time should be identical to that given by the Edge

FIGURE 23.8

Comparison of some dive computers on a single, multi-level dive of increasing depths

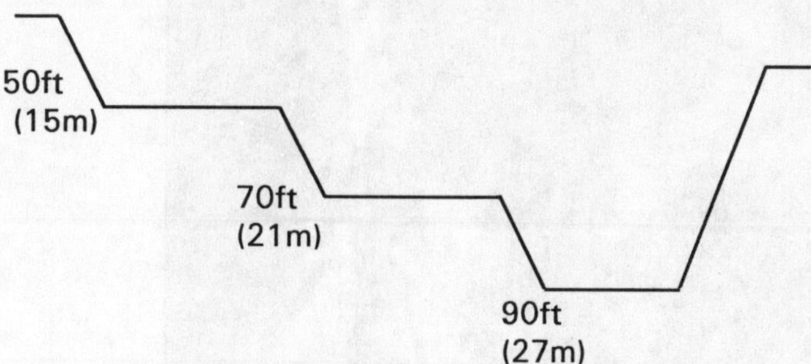

Level 1: 50 ft (21 m)

No-Deco. stop times:

Aladin Pro = 70
Datamax Sport = 78
Micro Brain Pro Plus = 64
Skinnydipper = 75
SME-ML(R1) = 74
Aladin = 71

Time at level 1 = 15

Level 2: 70 ft (21 m) for 10 minutes

No-Deco. stop times:

Aladin Pro = 24
Datamax Sport = 28
Micro Brain Pro Plus = 21
Skinnydipper = 28
SME-ML(R1) = 26
Aladin = 25

Time at level 2 = 15

Level 3: 90 ft (27 m)

No-Deco. stop times:

Aladin Pro = 5
Datamax Sport = 10
Micro Brain Pro Plus = 5
Skinnydipper = 11
SME-ML(R1) = 9
Aladin = 6

* Times are in minutes

FIGURE 23.9
The author comparing some computers after diving

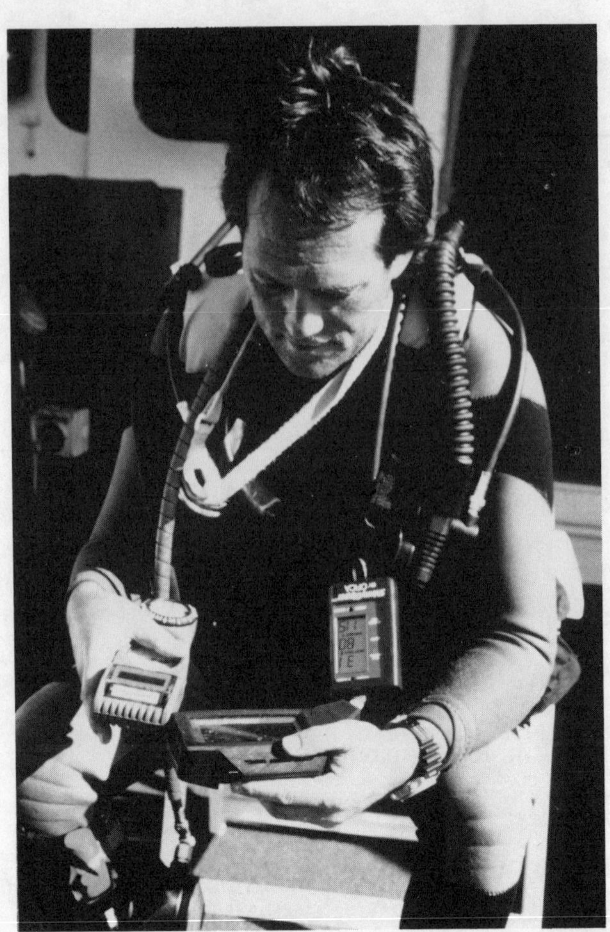

REPETITIVE DIVES

The dives shown in Tables 23.1, 23.2 and 23.3 were rectangular dives so that the multi-level capability of the computers was minimized and the times allowed by the computers could be compared to the times allowed by the tables.

It is obvious that the computers allowed substantially more time for these repetitive dives than the tables would give. We know that it is unwise, and at times hazardous, to dive the U.S. Navy Tables to their limits, especially on repetitive rectangular dives. How then can the generous times given by these computers be justified?

As previously mentioned, divers who dive right to some of the U.S. Navy limits will be quite likely to bubble during, or after, the ascent. Some of these divers will develop manifestations of bends, but most will be asymptomatic. In either case, these bubbles will slow down the off-gassing process and give rise to more residual nitrogen for repetitive dives than there would be if no bubbling had occurred.

By shortening the initial NDLs and slowing down the ascent rate, these computers attempt to minimize the bubble formation after the initial dive. This should enhance off-gassing, reduce residual nitrogen and thus enable longer no-decompression stop bottom times for repetitive dives. The Buehlmann Tables work on this premise. They utilize shorter initial NDLs than the U.S. Navy Tables, followed by a slow ascent, and this is why they sometimes allow longer no-decompression stop bottom times than are given by the U.S. Navy Tables for repetitive dives. However, as you can see from the examples, using the Buehlmann Tables for repetitive dives is still more conservative than using most computers.

Because most tables are based on the off-gassing of a single, slow, tissue during the surface interval, they often have a safety margin built into them, whereas the computers carry no such margin. Repetitive Groups and Residual Nitrogen Times given in tables are designed to account for the highest gas loading that is theoretically possible, and are often based on a single tissue compartment only.* Since this tissue is a slow tissue, it off-gasses slowly on the surface. These tables (e.g. U.S. Navy Tables) assume that all of the tissue compartments are unloading at this rate and, so, may over-estimate the theoretical gas loads of the faster tissue compartments. This results in shorter repetitive dive times than would be allowed if the actual (theoretical) gas load in the faster compartments was considered. So, this crudeness of the table's calculations may lead to longer surface intervals than are required by the model, but introduces a margin of safety by assuming the diver has more residual nitrogen than the model dictates. However, many depth and time combinations may lead to the same Repetitive Group although, in reality, the nitrogen contents in the various body tissues are quite different.

Computers calculate repetitive dive times according to the exact (rather than the maximum possible) gas loading given by the model, taking into account all the tissues used in the model. This usually allows more dive time on repetitive dives than is allowed by tables. However, in some situations the times can be similar. The deeper NDLs are determined by fast tissues which absorb gas rapidly and which off-gas rapidly at the surface. Repetitive Groups are usually based on slower tissues. If repetitive dives are compared for NDLs in the depth range where the Repetitive Group tissue controls the NDL (i.e. shallow to moderate depths), then the limits given by the tables and the computer should be close.

On some long dive sequences or in situations where repetitive dives are done over many consecutive days, the computers are sometimes slower to unload as they are programmed with slower tissues than are used to determine the Repetitive Groups in most tables. This may occassionally lead to the situation where certain tables will allow you to begin a new day's diving without considering residual nitrogen from the previous day's (or night's) diving, whereas a computer may still carry over a penalty for certain shallower dives. However, if this occurs it will normally only apply to the first dive of the day and the computer will then allow longer bottom times than most tables would allow for the following dives that day.

* This is not the case with the Buehlmann (1986) Tables which take into account the gas loading in all the theoretical tissue compartments.

An interesting report[6] describes a program that was written to simulate a dive computer with 1,530 tissue compartments with half-times ranging from six seconds to 24 hours, and maximum acceptable nitrogen levels based on Dr. Merrill Spencer's calculations. The single dive NDLs predicted by the model were similar to those utilized in the PADI RDP for dives deeper than 40 ft (12 m). The researcher was curious to investigate whether a computer programmed with such a broad range of tissue compartments (and, therefore, capable of "remembering" a dive for up to six days) would predict substantially different dive times for multi-day repetitive dives than other models which utilized only a few theoretical tissues. He programmed his computer so that each of the theoretical tissues was filled to its maximum acceptable nitrogen limit, and compared the NDLs given 12 hours after this theoretical dive with the NDLs allowed if no dive had been done for the previous week. There was no difference at all in the NDLs for dives deeper than 40 ft (12 m). This is because the NDLs for these depths are determined by tissue compartments with relatively short half-times, which release their nitrogen load reasonably quickly and will have off-gassed completely within 12 hours. **(However, this assumes that bubble formation is minimal and that a Haldanian model can be applied; and this is not always the case.)** The substantial differences that did occur were at shallow depths, where the NDLs are determined by the slower tissue compartments, but where bottom times are beyond the limits of recreational diving. This experiment demonstrates that no dive computer, based on a Haldanian model, can predict decompression problems that may be associated with multi-day diving, no matter how many tissue compartments are used and how slow the half-times are.

ARE THE COMPUTERS SAFE?

The safety of these devices is still the subject of many a heated debate. The main criticisms focus on the following arguments:

1. The models on which the computers are based are not completely accurate. Decompression computers will retain inaccuracies until the devices can directly measure an individual's actual tissue nitrogen levels.

2. Any inherent safety margin of the tables, as well as the extra security gained by "rounding-off" the tables is lost in the computers. This will give a diver more time, but will at times put him more at risk.

3. Although some of the models on which the tables are based have been well-tested for fixed-depth dives, there have only been relatively few well-controlled, documented tests of the validity of the multi-level applications. The number of these tests has been insufficient to determine the validity of the multi-level applications with any statistical significance. (However, the growing number of tests conducted to validate the PADI RDP may help to determine the safety of some of the computer algorithms.)

Before releasing the "Edge" in 1983, Orca Industries conducted a study to evaluate the safety of the algorithm programmed into the "Edge". Twelve divers did a series of 10 "chamber dives". Nine of the profiles were multi-level, no-decompression stop profiles and the tenth required a decompression stop. The divers were monitored with Doppler bubble detectors. In the 119 profiles completed, bubbles were detected in one diver, and were the lowest grade of bubbles.[7] None of the divers showed definite signs of bends. Two divers were slightly fatigued, one had some skin itchiness (which often occurs in chamber dives) and another had slight tingling in one leg. Tingling was a condition this subject often had after diving but it was reported as it was stronger than usual. No conclusions could be drawn as to whether the manifestations of fatigue and tingling were due to decompression stress or other factors. However, significantly more dives are needed to establish the risk of decompression sickness for the various schedules. For example, *for each schedule* a minimum of 35 dives without bends is needed before a bends rate of less than 2% can be claimed with 95% confidence.[8]

By late 1987, Orca Industries reported that more than 500,000* dives had been done by divers using the "Edge", and that 14 cases of bends in divers "properly" using the "Edge" had been reported to Orca and the Divers Alert Network (DAN).[9]

Uwatec, the manufacturers of the "Aladin" ("GUIDE"), reported that between 50,000 and 100,000* incident-free dives had been done using the "Aladin" by the end of October, 1987.[10] These dives included 290 documented dives done by a British scientific expedition in Lake Titicaca, 12,580 feet (3,812 m) above sea-level.[11]

Since then, the number of divers using dive computers has increased greatly and by now some millions of dives would have been carried out by computer-users, the vast majority of the dives being incident free. With so many apparently safe dives carried out by computer-users, it might appear that the computers are, indeed, safe devices. However, as with tables, it is difficult to determine whether it is the computers themselves that are safe, or if the apparent safety lies in how divers are using them and the type of dives that they are normally using them on. Since most of the computer-assisted dives are undocumented, it is not known whether or not the divers dived to the limits given by their computers. If the units are not dived to their limits then we still do not know how safe the actual limits are. This is especially relevant to multi-level and repetitive dives.

More than 200 divers were treated for bends in Australasia in 1987. The vast majority of cases displayed neurological effects. Many of these cases arose after dives, often repetitive dives, that were conducted in accordance with, and, at times, well within conventional tables. Some had done a multi-level dive but had surfaced within the NDL specified by the table for the maximum depth.[12]

With such a high incidence of bends when diving within conventional limits, some fear that more cases might be expected to occur when the limits are extended, especially for repetitive dives. As computers become more and more common a better understanding should emerge.

By the end of 1988, 121 cases of bends in divers using computers had been reported to DAN, 77 of these occurring during 1988 alone.[13] In the USA, computer related decompression sickness increased from 14% (31/220) of the total bends cases in 1987, to 36.6% in 1988.[14]

In the United Kingdom in 1987, 16% (11/69) of the divers treated for bends had been using a dive computer[15], and, in 1988, this figure had risen to about 34% (30/89). Six of these 30 divers had misused their computers, but 20 of them had been diving within the limits of

* To my knowledge at the time of writing, the vast majority of these dives have not been documented or validated.

their dive computer.[16] Analysis of the 1988 British data shows that the vast majority (20/30) of the computer-users who got bends had dived deeper than 100 ft (30 m). Overall, the British estimated that the bends rate in computer-users was comparable to that of table-users.

The 1989 British statistics show that nearly 33% (45/137) of the divers who reported bends had been using a dive computer. Fifteen of these divers reported diving within the limits of their dive computers and others got bends after misusing their computers.[17,18] Interestingly, six of the 15 divers who got bent within the limits of their computer were later examined by echocardiography, and five of these six divers had a patent foramen ovale which would have predisposed them to bends. The BS-AC estimate that, in 1989, there were 7,500-8,000 dive computers being used in Britain and, by assuming that each dive computer owner dives 50 times a year, calculated that, possibly, half a million dives were done using computers in 1989. This "guestimate" yields and incident rate better than 1 in 10,000.[19]

DAN, in a detailed analysis of the bends cases reported in the USA in 1987, attempted to estimate the bends rate in both computer-users and table-users. Although they found no significant difference in their *estimates* of the bends rate, they did notice that the type of dive profile causing the bends seemed to differ between computer-users and table-users. Computer-users got more bends after multi-level dives and decompression stop dives, but seemed to have a lower bends incidence on dives shallower than 100 ft (30 m). 77% of the divers who suffered from bends after using a dive computer had done repetitive dives. Although this is 17% higher than the bends rate for divers who used tables for repetitive dives, the difference is not statistically significant.[20]

DAN's analysis of their 1988 statistics showed similar trends to the previous year. Computer-users appear to have engaged in different diving patterns to table-users. A comparison of the profiles undertaken by the bends sufferers is shown in Table 23.5. The predominent risk factors for both tables and computers were diving beyond 80 ft (24 m) and repetitive diving.[14] Computers appear to yield a very high bends rate for these types of dives.

TABLE 23.5

Table vs. Computer Profiles

	U.S. NAVY TABLES		COMPUTERS	
	no.	%	no.	%
Deeper than 80 ft (24 m)	97	67	62	81
Square profile	89	61	32	42
Multi-day	69	48	42	55
Repetitive	83	57	62	81
Single day	76	52	35	45

I believe that, to a large extent, the bends rate in dive computer users will depend on how divers dive when they use their computers - on the type of dive profile and on their rate of ascent.

It appears that a diver who ascends slowly will have less chance of getting bends, especially neurological bends, than one who ascends more rapidly. I believe that a diver should ascend no faster than about 30 ft/minute (9 m/minute when shallower than about 80 ft (24 m). Many computers include a warning mechanism to tell a diver when he is exceeding the recommended ascent rate. The rate varies between computers but I believe it should roughly equate with the above recommendation. **This function is an essential function of any dive computer.**

If you exceed the recommended ascent rate at any stage during a dive, especially at, or near, the end of a dive, reduce your dive time substantially from that given by the computer for the rest of that dive, and for repetitive dives. If bubbles form as a result of the faster ascent, they will slow down off-gassing and make the times allowed by the computer far less realistic.

I also highly recommend that a diver goes to the maximum depth early in the dive and then gradually works shallower. If a diver begins a dive in the shallows and then progressively gets deeper and deeper before ascending to the surface, the nitrogen load in the "slower" tissues is likely to contribute more than usual to bubbles which are subsequently formed in the "fast" or "medium" tissues during, or following, the ascent.

If you are using a dive computer I recommend that you should:

* **Ascend slowly.** Never exceed the recommended ascent rate, and generally ascend at about 30 ft (9 m)/minute or slower.

* **Go to the maximum depth early in the dive and progressively and slowly work shallower.** End the dive with at least 5 minutes at 15-20 ft (4.5-6 m). *Avoid rectangular dive profiles.*

* **Do not dive right to the limits given by the computers.** They do not cater for individual susceptibility to bends.

* **Avoid using the computer for deep, repetitive dives, especially those with rectangular profiles and/or those requiring a mandatory decompression stop(s)** (in fact avoid doing deep repetitive and/or decompression stop dives altogether, if possible).

* In the event of a computer failure during a dive, ascent slowly to 15-20 ft/4.5-6 m (nearer to 20 ft if possible), and spend at least five minutes there before surfacing. If a mandatory stop(s) was indicated before the computer failure and you cannot remember it, spend as much time at 20 ft (6 m) as possible, leaving enough air to return to the boat safely. Do not re-enter the water for at least 18 hours, or for the time needed for the dive computer to totally off-gas (had it not malfunctioned), **whichever is longer.**

* If using a dive computer for multi-day, repetitive diving, take a break around the third or fourth day to allow your body to rid itself of some of the extra nitrogen load it has accumulated.

* Do not begin to use a dive computer if you have had a pressure exposure in the previous 24 hours.

THE FUTURE?

Dive computers are here to stay and they will develop enormously as knowledge and technology advance further. The current models are based only on depth and time, but future computers might be programmed to include other variables such as degrees of individual susceptibility to bends, exertion, water temperature and delayed off-gassing due to a rapid ascent. The ultimate computer would measure the nitrogen level within an individual diver's tissues.

Some scientists believe that many of the current dive computer algorithms need to be modified to give more conservative times for "high risk" dive profiles. These "high risk" dive profiles include deep dives, especially deep repetitive dives, multi-day repetitive dives and multi-level dives during which a diver descends deeper, rather than working shallower, during the dive. Some of the computer manufacturers are already in the process of changing their algorithms to cater for these situations.

For example, with the current programs one can take an Edge, Skinnydipper or Suunto SME-ML(R1) and dive to 100 ft (30 m) for 10 minutes without a stop, have a one hour surface interval, dive again to 100 ft for 10 minutes, again without a stop, have another hour on the surface and do it again, and again. This is demonstrated in Table 23.3. Many experts have grave reservations about the computers allowing such dives. The algorithms of certain computers have been, or are currently being, modified to prohibit such a situation.

I believe that it is also important for dive computers to be programmed to reduce repetitive dive times if the diver exceeds the recommended ascent rate. This may partly compensate for the slower off-gassing that may occur if significant bubble formation results from the rapid ascent.

Whatever decompression algorithm is used, it must be thoroughly tested over a broad range of diving profiles which should include the high risk profiles previously described. Extensive chamber testing should be followed by numerous, well-controlled open-water trials. In this way, a more accurate assessment of the risk associated with the use of a dive computer may be ascertained.

Dive computers are a wonderful invention and, in the years to come, they may replace tables altogether. However, there are still a number of problems that need to be sorted out with the algorithms in order to maximize their safety. Divers must also be thoroughly educated in their use so that they are totally familiar with the particular computer they are using, aware of the short-comings of that computer (and they all do have them!) and with the safe diving practices that should be adopted when using a computer.

SUMMARY

* Dive computers are designed to calculate the decompression requirement for the actual dive profile, rather than for the "rounded-off" profile which is used with tables.

* Almost all current computers are programmed with an actual decompression model, rather than with tables.

* Computers eliminate errors in table calculations and, usually, provide much more bottom time than is given by the tables.

* Tables include inherent, or added, margins which provide a degree of safety if our body absorbs more nitrogen than predicted by the model. Computers do not include such margins as they follow the model exactly.

* For single rectangular dives, the computers usually give more conservative NDLs than the tables.
* On a multi-level dive, the computers will normally extend the allowable no-decompression stop bottom time far beyond that allowed by the tables, especially if the diver works shallower throughout the dive.

* **The computers usually allow far more time for repetitive dives than is allowed by tables. This is an area of risk for both tables and computers, as is multi-day diving.**

* **The safety of dive computers has not been determined as too few validated tests have been done to determine the bends risk associated with their use.** However, this is also true for most decompression tables!

* **The computers generally rely on a slow ascent rate, and the times given are less valid if a diver has ascended faster than recommended.**

* Computers can, and do, fail, and the diver must have an appropriate back-up procedure.

* If using a computer it is important to:
  - Ascend at the appropriate rate
  - Go to depth early and then work shallower throughout the dive.
  - Do not dive right to the limits. Allow for predisposing factors to bends.
  - End all dives with a few minutes at 15-20 ft (4.5-6 m).

* For multi-day diving, rest every third or fourth day.

* Avoid rectangular dives, deep dives, especially deep, repetitive dives, and dives (especially repetitive dives) requiring a mandatory decompression stop(s).

REFERENCES

1. Edmonds, C (1987), "Bendomatic Decompression Meters". *SCUBA Diver*; October: 22-27.

2. West, D. and Edmonds, C. (1976), "Evaluation of the Farallon Decompression Meter". *RAN SUM Report;* 1.

3. Flynn, E. and Bayne, C. (1978), "Inert Gas Exchange: Experiments and Concepts." In: *Diving Medical Officer Student Guide*. Naval School of Diving and Salvage.

4. Bassett, B. (1982), "The Safety of the U.S. Navy Decompression Tables and Recommendations for Sport Divers". *SPUMS Journal*; Oct-Dec: 16-25.

5. Spencer, M. (1976), "Decompression limits for compressed air determined by ultrasonically detected blood bubbles". *Journal of Applied Physiology*; 40 (2): 229-235.

6. Lewis, J. (1989), "How Much Memory Does Your Dive Computer Need?". *The Undersea Journal*; 4th Quarter.

7. Huggins (1987), "Microprocessor Applications to Multi-Level Air Decompression Problems". Michigan Sea Grant College Program Report No. MICHU-SG-87-201, Michigan Sea Grant Publications, University of Michigan.

8. Shields, T. (1982), "Re-trial at sea of 70 and 80 metre 15 minute Trimix decompression schedules. AMTE(E) R82-409.

9. Barshinger, C. (1988), "Decompression Computers". *Skin Diver*; 37 (2): 32.

10. Voellm, E. (1987), personal communication.

11. Moody, M. (1988), "Exercise Paddington Diamond". Ordinance Services, Viersen.

12. Gorman, D. and Parsons, D. (1987), "Decompression Meters - Philosophical and Other Objections". *SPUMS Journal*; 17 (3): 119.

13. Bennett, P., personal communication.

14. Divers Alert Network (1989), "Report on 1988 Diving Accidents". Divers Alert Network, North Carolina.

15. Shaw, D. (1987), "NDC Diving Incidents Report". *Proceedings of Diving Officers' Conference*, BS-AC, London.

16. Allen, C. (1988), "NDC Diving Incidents Report". *Proceedings of Diving Officers' Conference*, BS-AC, London.

17. Allen, C. (1989), "NDC Diving Incidents Report". *Proceedings of Diving Officers' Conference*, BS-AC, London.

18. Allen, C., personal communication.

19. Allen, C. and Ellerby, D. (1990), "Decompression Update". *NDC Bulletin*; 16: 1-2.

20. Divers Alert Network (1988), "Preliminary Report on Diving Accidents", Divers Alert Network, North Carolina.

OTHER SOURCES

Buehlmann, A., personal communications.

Chadwell, C. (ed) (1988), "Multi-level Diving - Instructor Guide". Sea Quest, California.

Douglas, D. (1987), "Time to reflect on diving in the computer age". *Diver*; 32 (7): 5.

Edmonds, C. and Anderson, T. (1987), "Assessment of the Orca EDGE Dive Computer". *SPUMS Journal*; 17 (3): 119-127.

Ellerby, D. (1987), "Decompression Computers - Their Use". *Proceedings of Diving Officer's Conference*, BS-AC, London.

Ellerby, D. (1987), "Decompression - BC and AC". *NDC Bulletin*; 11: 1-3.

Ellerby, D. (1987), "Budget Brain". *Diver*; 32 (7); 24-25.

Ellerby, D. and Todd, M. (1988). "Which Dive Computer?". *Diver*; 33 (3): 15-17.

Fulton, J. (1987), "Orca Industries stands by its EDGE". *SCUBA Diver*; October: 22-27.

Graver, D. (1988), "Electronic Dive Monitors". *NAUI News*; May: 33-37.

Hahn, M., personal communications.

Hermann, J., personal communications.

Huggins, K. (1981), and Somers, L., "Mathematical Evaluation of Multi-Level Diving". Report No. MICHU-SG-81-207, Michigan Sea Grant Publications, University of Michigan.

Huggins, K. (1983), "Doppler Evaluation of Multi-Level Diving Profiles". Report No. MICHU-SG-84-300, Michigan Sea Grant Publications, University of Michigan.

Huggins, K. (1985), "Multi-Level Diving, How Safe Is It?". *Proceedings of International Conference on Underwater Education, I.Q.'85*, NAUI, California.

Huggins, K., personal communications.

Huggins, K (1988), "History of Decompression Devices". *NAUI News*; May: 22-30

Huggins, K. (1988), "History of Decompression Devices - Part 2". *NAUI News*; July: 49-51.

Lang, M. and Hamilton, R. (eds) (1989), "Proceedings of Dive Computer Workshop". University of Southern California Sea Grant Publication No. USCSG-TR-01-89, University of Southern California, Santa Catalina Island.

Murphey, M. (1988), "Subaquatic Computers Compared" *NAUI News*; May: 31-32.

Nikkola, A., personal comminication.

Thalmann, E. (1984), "Phase II testing of decompression algorithms for use in the U.S. Navy underwater decompression computer." U.S. Navy Experimental Diving Unit Report 1-84.

Thalmann, E. (1986), "Air N_2O_2 decompression computer algorithm development." U.S. Navy Experimental Diving Unit Report 8-85.

Vann, R. (1988), "Decompression Sickness and Diver-Carried Computers". *Alert Diver*; 4 (3).

RECOMMENDED FURTHER READING

Chadwell, C. (1988), "Multi-level Diving - Instructor Guide". Sea Quest, California.

Divers Alert Network (1988), "Preliminary Report on Diving Accidents", Divers Alert Network, North Carolina.

Edmonds, C (1987), "Bendomatic Decompression Meters". *SCUBA Diver*; October: 22-27.

Edmonds, C. and Anderson, T. (1987), "Assessment of the Orca EDGE Dive Computer". *SPUMS Journal*; 17 (3): 119-127.

Huggins (1987), ":Microprocessor Applications to Multi-Level Air Decompression Problems". Michigan Sea Grant College Program Report No. MICHU-SG-87-201, Michigan Sea Grant Publications, University of Michigan.

Huggins, K (1988), "History of Decompression Devices". *NAUI News*; May: 22-30

Huggins, K. (1988), "History of Decompression Devices - Part 2". *NAUI News*; July: 49-51.

Lang, M. and Hamilton, R. (eds) (1989), "Proceedings of Dive Computer Workshop". University of Southern California Sea Grant Publication No. USCSG-TR-01-89, University of Southern California, Santa Catalina Island.

Vann, R. (1988), "Decompression Sickness and Diver-Carried Computers". *Alert Diver*; 4 (3).

Following is a list of some current models of dive computers along with various characteristics of these computers. The list is not exhaustive. The information has mainly been taken from the literature accompanying the devices. To my knowledge, at the time of writing, much of this information has not been independently validated. Some of the features described may change as the units are modified.

ALADIN (GUIDE)

Model: Swiss ZH-L_6
Number of theoretical tissues: 6
Half times: 4, 12, 27, 54, 109, 305
Critical limits: Lower tolerance limits than Buehlmann
Tables in order to compensate for fewer tissues than the 16 accounted for in the original model.
Repetitive dive control: All theoretical tissues
Decompression functions: Remaining no-decompression stop time, need and depth for decompression stop.
Depth gauge accuracy: ±1.7 ft (0.5 m)
Depth range: 0-330 ft (0-99.9 m)
Altitude range: 0-13,200 ft (0-4,000 m)
Temperature range: 15-120°F (-10-50°C)
Recommended ascent rate: 33 ft/minute (10 m/minute)
Ascent rate indicator: None

ALADIN PRO (MONITOR 2)

Model: Swiss ZH-L_6 2.1
Number of theoretical tissues: 6
Half times: 6, 14, 34, 64, 124, 320
Critical limits: Lower tolerance limits than Buehlmann
Tables in order to compensate for fewer tissues than the 16 accounted for in the original model. (same as for Aladin)
Repetitive dive control: All theoretical tissues with retarded desaturation for repetitive dives
Decompression functions: Remaining no-decompression stop time, decompression stop time, decompression stop depth, total ascent time, desaturation time, time to fly, adaptation time for altitude diving, scrolled NDLs for repetitive dives.
Depth gauge accuracy: ± 1.7 ft (0.5 m)
Depth range: 0-330 ft (0-99.9 m)
Altitude range: 0-13,200 ft (0-4,000 m)
Temperature range: 15-120°F (-10-50°C)
Recommended ascent rate: 33 ft/minute (10 m/minute)
Ascent rate indicator: Arrow flashes if ascent rate is between 40-53 ft/min (12-16 m/min). *Alarm sounds* if ascent rate exceeds 53 ft/min (16 m/min)

EDGE

Model: Haldanian
Number of theoretical tissues: 12
Half times: 5-480 minutes.
Critical limits: Lower critical limits (M values) than U.S. Navy. Derived from Doppler studies.
Repetitive dive control: All theoretical tissues
Decompression functions: Tissue nitrogen levels, ceiling depth, remaining no-decompression stop times, remaining decompression stop time, repetitive no-decompression stop time, total ascent time, time to fly.
Depth gauge accuracy: ±1 fsw (0.3 msw)
Depth range: 0-160 fsw (0-49 msw)
Altitude range: 0-1,150 ft (0-350 m)
Temperature range: 16.8-123°F (-15-50°C)
Recommended ascent rate: 20 ft (6 m)/minute from 0-60 ft (0-18 m), 40 ft (12 m)/minute from 61-120 ft (18.5-36 m), 60 ft (18 m)/minute from 121-200 ft (36.5-60 m)
Ascent rate indicator: Visual warning when recommended ascent rate is exceeded.

DATAMASTER 2

Model: Modified U.S. Navy (Haldanian)
Number of theoretical tissues: 6
Half times: 5, 10, 20, 40, 80, 120
Critical limits: Spencer M-Values
Repetitive dive control: 120-minute tissue on surface (no subsurface elimination)
Decompression functions: Remaining dive time controlled by NDLs or available air, no-decompression stop warning area, emergency decompression stop time, repetitive group, repetitive no-decompression stop time.
Depth gauge accuracy: +1%
Depth range: 0-249 ft (0-75.5 m)
Altitude range: 0-2,000 ft (0-606 m)
Temperature range: 32-150°F (0-65.5°C)
Recommended ascent rate: 40 ft/minute (12 m/minute)
Ascent rate indicator: No

DATAMASTER SPORT

Model: Modified Haldanian
Number of theoretical tissues: 6
Half times: 5, 10, 20, 40, 80, 120
Critical limits: Spencer M-Values
Repetitive dive control: 60-minute control for compartments faster than 80 minutes. 80-minute and 120-minute control maintained (reciprocal subsurface elimination)
Decompression functions: Remaining dive time controlled by NDLs or available air, no-decompression stop warning area, decompression stop time, repetitive no-decompression stop time, stops for repetitive decompression stop dives.
Depth gauge accuracy: +1%
Depth range: 0-249 ft (0-75.5 m)
Altitude range: 0-2,000 ft (0-606 m)
Temperature range: 32-150°F (0-65.5°C)
Recommended ascent rate: Under 20 ft (6 m) = 30 ft (9 m)/min, 20-60 ft (6-18 m) = 40 ft (12 m)/min, over 60 ft (18 m) = 60 ft (18 m)/min
Ascent rate indicator: "Depth" and "FT" enunciators flash.

DATAMAX SPORT

Model: Modified Haldanian
Number of theoretical tissues: 12
Half times: 5-480 minutes
Critical limits: Spencer M-Values
Repetitive dive control: 60-minute control for compartments faster than 60 minutes. Tissue compartments with half-times of 60 minutes or slower are controlled by whichever has the highest load (reciprocal subsurface elimination).
Decompression functions: Available no-decompression stop time, caution zone, time and depth of decompression stops required for stops of 10, 20 and 30 ft (3, 6 and 9 m), Scrolled NDLs for repetitive dives.
Depth gauge accuracy: +1%
Depth range: 0-249 ft (0-75.5 m)
Altitude range: 0-3,000 ft (0-912 m) - full functions. 3,000-10,000 ft (912-3020 m) - does not compute decompression but acts as depth gauge, bottom timer and ascent rate indicator
Temperature range: not specified
Recommended ascent rate: Under 20 ft (6 m) = 30 ft (9 m)/min, 20-59 ft (6-18 m) = 45 ft (14 m)/min, 60 ft (18 m) and beyond = 60 ft (18 m)/min
Ascent rate indicator: Depth display flashes.

DELPHI

Model: Haldanian
Number of theoretical tissues: 12
Half times: 5-480 minutes
Critical limits: Lower critical limits (M values) than U.S. Navy. Derived from Doppler studies. Modified from Edge/Skinnydipper values for continuous altitude compensation.
Repetitive dive control: All theoretical tissues
Decompression functions: Tissue nitrogen levels, remaining no-decompression stop time, total ascent time in decompression, repetitive no-decompression stop time, ceiling depth, time to fly.
Depth gauge accuracy: ±1.5 fsw (0.45 msw)
Depth range: 0-199 fsw (English model), 0-100 msw (Metric model), 0-300 fsw (English professional model)
Altitude range: 0-10,000 ft (0-3,000 m), continuous compensation
Temperature range: 0-122°F (-9-50°C)
Recommended ascent rate: 20 ft (6m)/minute from 0-60 ft (0-18 m), 40 ft (12 m)/minute from 61-120 ft (18.5-36 m), 60 ft (18 m)/minute from 121-200 ft (36.5-60 m)
Ascent rate indicator: Lighted bar at proper rate, down arrow and LED when rate exceeded

MICRO BRAIN

Model: Modified ZH-L_{16} (Buehlmann/Hahn P3)
Number of theoretical tissues: 6
Half times: 4-397 min
Critical limits: Lower tolerance limits than BuehlmannTable in order to compensate for fewer tissues than the 16 accounted for in the original model.
Repetitive dive control: All theoretical tissues
Decompression functions: Remaining no-decompression stop time (bar graph), ceiling and/or decompression stops, scrolled NDLs for repetitive dives.
Depth gauge accuracy: ±1 ft (0.3 m)
Depth range: 0-330 fsw (0-100 msw)
Altitude range: 0-6,600 ft (0-2,000 m)
Temperature range: 14-122°F (-10-50°C)
Recommended ascent rate: 33 ft/minute (10 m/minute)
Ascent rate indicator: Visual warning if ascent rate exceeds 40-50 ft/minute (12-15 m/minute).

MICRO BRAIN PRO PLUS

Model: Modified ZH-L_{16} (Buehlmann/Hahn P4)
Number of theoretical tissues: 6
Half times: 6-600 min
Critical limits: Lower tolerance limits than Buehlmann Table in order to compensate for fewer tissues than the 16 accounted for in the original model.
Repetitive dive control: All theoretical tissues
Decompression functions: Remaining no-decompression stop time (bar graph), decompressiontime, decompression stop depth, total ascent time, desaturation time, time to fly, scrolled NDLs for repetitive dives, dive simulation and planning function.
Depth gauge accuracy: $\pm$1 ft (0.3 m)
Depth range: 0-270 fsw (0-82 msw)
Altitude range: Acts as decompression computer to altitude of 6,560 ft (2,000 m) but only after appropriate acclimatization. Acts as depth gauge to 14,764 ft (4,500 m).
Temperature range: 14-122°F (-10-50°C)
Recommended ascent rate: 33 ft/minute (10 m/minute)
Ascent rate indicator: Visual warning if ascent rate exceeds 33-40 ft/minute (10-12 m/minute).

SUUNTO SME - ML (R1)

Model: Haldanian
Number of theoretical tissues: 9
Half times: 2.5, 5, 10, 20, 40, 80, 120, 240, 480 minutes
Critical limits: Lower critical limits (M values) than U.S. Navy. Derived from Doppler studies by Spencer.
Repetitive dive control: All theoretical tissues
Decompression functions: Remaining no-decompression stop time, remaining decompression stop time and ceiling depth, wrong decompression stop depth, repetitive no-decompression stop times.
Depth gauge accuracy: $\pm$2 ft (0.6 m)
Depth range: 0-230 ft (0-70 m)
Altitude range: 0-1500 ft (0-454 m)
Temperature range: 32-104°F (0-40°C)
Recommended ascent rate: 33 ft/minute (10 m/minute)
Ascent rate indicator: Visual warning when ascent rate exceeded.

SKINNYDIPPER

Model: Haldanian
Number of theoretical tissues: 12
Half times: 5-480 minutes
Critical limits: Lower critical limits (M values) than U.S. Navy. Derived from Doppler studies.
Repetitive dive control: All theoretical tissues
Decompression functions: Remaining no-decompression times, decompression indicator and ceiling, repetitive no-decompression time, time to fly.
Depth gauge accuracy: ±1.5 fsw (0.45 msw)
Depth range: 0-199 fsw (0-66 msw)
Altitude range: 0-2,000 ft (0-606 m)
Temperature range: 24.8-122°F (-4-50°C)
Recommended ascent rate: 20 ft (6m)/minute from 0-60 ft (0-18 m), 40 ft (12 m)/minute from 61-120 ft (18.5-36 m),60 ft (18 m)/minute from 121-200 ft (36.5-60 m)
Ascent rate indicator: Visual warning when recommended ascent rate is exceeded

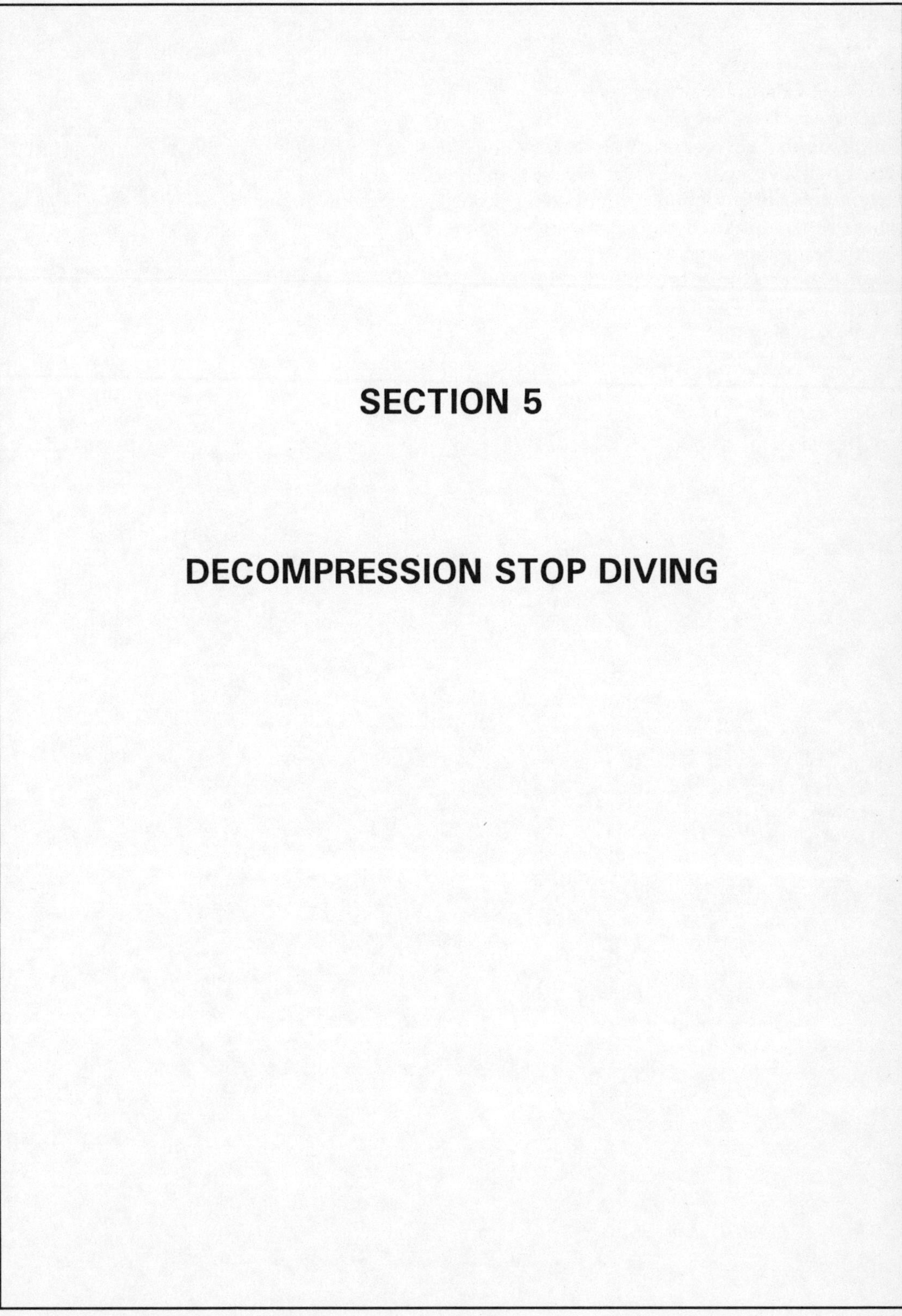

SECTION 5

DECOMPRESSION STOP DIVING

CHAPTER 24

DECOMPRESSION STOP DIVING

At times it is necessary for some divers to plan and conduct dives involving mandatory decompression stops. Although these decompression stop dives can, and should, normally be avoided by divers diving for recreational purposes, they are often an unavoidable part of a commercial, scientific or military diver's job.

The main danger of decompression stop diving is the greatly increased risk of bends if any of the decompression stops are missed, or carried out incorrectly. Once the No-Decompression Limit has expired, a diver can no longer ascend directly to the surface without increasing his chance of bends substantially. Equipment failure, exhaustion of the air supply, panic, disorientation and harassment by a shark are among the many factors which may cause a diver to surface without completing the required stops. For these reasons **decompression stop dives require a very high level of experience, planning, preparation and support and should only be attempted, when necessary, by very experienced divers who are adequately fit and prepared, and who have enough support to conduct the dive as safely as is possible.**

Decompression stop dives can be conducted similarly to deep dives and some of the descent and ascent systems used for deep dives can often be adopted.* It is essential that the divers are able to find their way to the decompression stage, bars or line at the end of the dive, so appropriate steps should be taken to ensure that this is achieved. It is highly desirable that an adequately equipped and staffed recompression chamber is available at the site of diving operations. The chamber can be used in the event of omitted decompression, or if signs/ symptoms of bends arise after the dive.

It has often been stated that decompression stop diving carries an inherently greater risk of bends than dives which require no stops. Although this is certainly true for particular profiles it appears that it is not necessarily a general truth, as many variable factors come into play. Dr. Bruce Bassett conducted an analysis of the dives logged by the U.S. Navy between 1971 and 1978.[1] He concluded that, "the risk of decompression sickness in U.S. Navy diving is no different in no-decompression or decompression diving".

So, although it appears that the U.S. Navy divers may not get more bends as a result of decompression stop diving, it must be realized that they are throughly trained, prepared and equipped for such dives, and have a high level of surface support and control. In addition, it has been reported that U.S. Navy divers may do more decompression than specified by the U.S. Navy Tables.[1] Recreational divers normally do not have the same level of preparedness and support and, consequently, have far less chance of doing decompression stop dives properly. If the decompression is not done correctly bends is a likely result. This is too often the case with recreational divers.

DAN figures indicate that approximately 30% of the divers treated for bends in the USA in both 1987 and 1988 had conducted decompression stop dives.[2,3] Since it is unlikely that 30% of U.S. recreational divers conduct decompression stop dives, this figure appears to indicate a substantial risk.

* ***A number of these systems are presented and discussed in "The Essentials of Deeper Diving" by John Lippmann. The book also provides practical guidelines for conducting deeper and/or decompression stop dives.***

A report on DCS resulting from commercial off-shore air-diving operations in the UK sector of the North Sea from 1982-88 provides some interesting data. Most of this diving was done using U.S. Navy Tables. About 31% of the dives were "no-stop" dives, which resulted in a DCS incidence of one bend for every 4102 dives. About 12% of the dives required "in-water" stops, resulting in a DCS rate of 1 bend for every 619 dives, (the rest of the dives involved surface decompression). Thus, the bends rate was more than six times higher for dives requiring decompression stops than for no-decompression stop dives. In addition, for the dives requiring stops, the bends rate increased with the length of required decompression time. Thus, for a dive requiring more than 30 minutes of decompression, the risk of a bend was 1 in 250 dives.[4]

If decompression stop dives are planned it is essential to attempt to choose a schedule that accounts for the condition of the divers, and of the sea. If the divers work hard during the dive, more decompression is required. If the divers become cold, more decompression is required. In addition, other predisposing factors to bends must also be accounted for. **A conservative, well-tested decompression table should be used.** It may be more appropriate to use the DCIEM or the Buehlmann (1986) Tables, rather than the U.S. Navy Tables, as these tables are *generally* far more conservative than the U.S. Navy Tables when used for decompression stop dives. A comparison of the decompression requirements after a dive to 120 ft (36 m) for a bottom time of 30 minutes is shown in Figure 24.1.

FIGURE 24.1

Comparison of decompression requirements after a dive to 120 ft (36 m) for a bottom time of 30 minutes

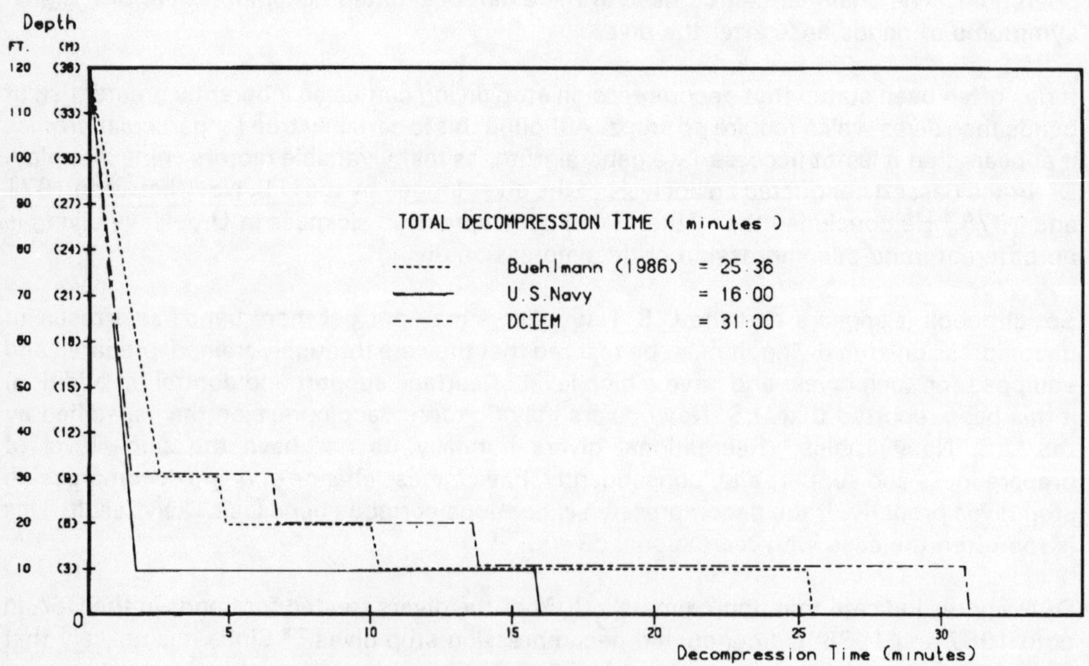

Figures 24.2 and 24.3 show the percentage risk of decompression sickness for 10 minute, 30 minute, 60 minute and 90 minute dives at different depths using either U.S. Navy Tables or DCIEM Tables. The broken line indicates a 5% risk of bends. These risk analyses are based on data from the U.S. Navy Medical Research Institute.[5]

The analyses examined three sets of decompression tables: the U.S. Navy Air Decompression Tables, The British Navy Tables (RN Table 11) and the Canadian Forces Tables (DCIEM). All three tables shared some general trends. The bends risk increased dramatically with longer bottom times. The risk also increased with increased depth but not with such a marked effect as with time. For example, for dives of three hours or longer the risk was between 10-50%. Short duration dives (30 minutes or less) carried a risk of less than 2%, whereas intermediate length and depth dives had incidences between 2 and 15%. Overall, the U.S. Navy Tables were predicted to carry the highest risk and the DCIEM Tables the lowest, due to the substantially longer decompression times suggested by the Canadian Tables.

FIGURE 24.2

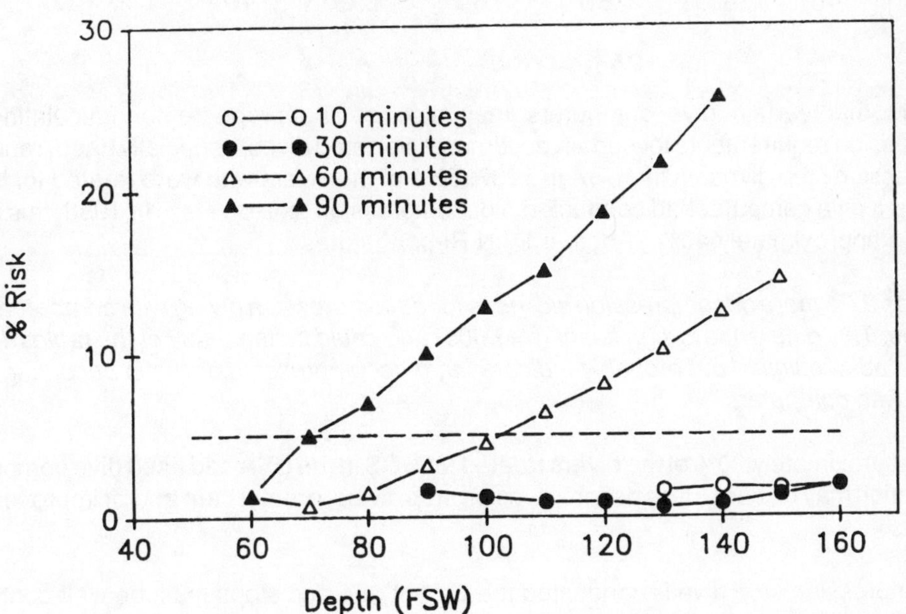

FIGURE 24.3

DCIEM Decompression Tables Risk Analysis

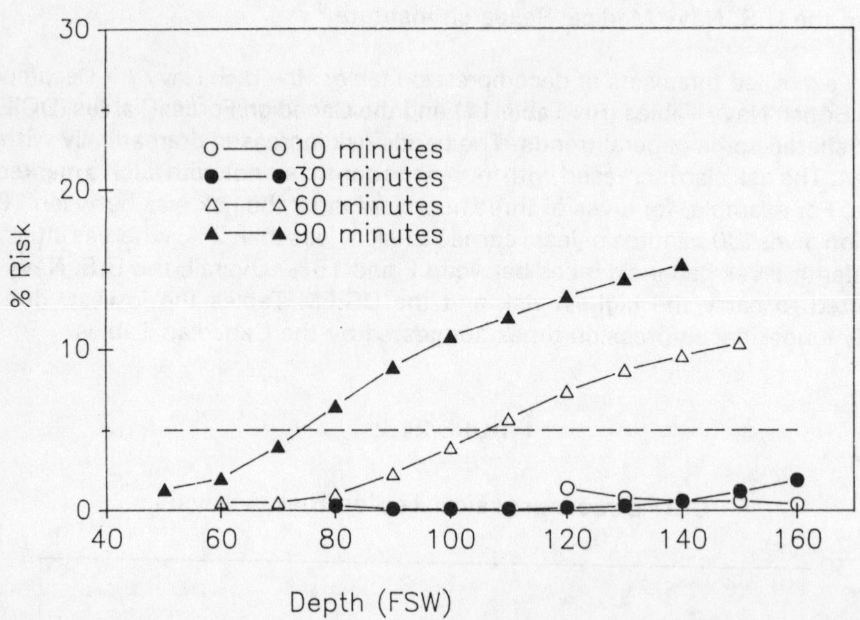

It appears that certain dive computers may also be inappropriate for calculating the decompression requirements for certain decompression stop dives, especially deep, repetitive decompression stop dives. In the USA in 1987, 52% of the divers who were treated for bends after using a dive computer had conducted a decompression stop dive(s)[2]. In 1988, this figure reduced to approximately 40%.[3] Another DAN Report[6] states:

"There was 27% more decompression sickness for decompression diving with computers than with tables. This difference is significant (p=0.005) and could be the result of the tables' longer no-stop exposure limits, but probably indicates that decompression diving is becoming more common with computers".

In 1989, approximately 20% of the divers treated for DCS in the USA had used dive computers. The reduction may be due to less decompression stop diving, greater care and/or improved dive computers.

If a decompression stop dive is conducted the ascent rate and stops must be well-controlled and performed accurately. Suitable support lines and equipment are absolutely essential so that there will be virtually no room for error.

Some factors to consider are:

Positioning during decompression

Ideally, the divers should be positioned on a stable platform with their chests at the level of the stop. They should not be hanging onto a movable line and moving up and down with wave motion and/or buoyancy changes.

Some experiments have indicated that off-gassing may be enhanced when a diver is positioned horizontally, but at this stage a seated or standing position is still generally recommended.

Exercise during decompression

Increased circulation, resulting from exercise, increases the gas supply to the tissues and speeds up their saturation with nitrogen. In addition, the build-up of carbon dioxide associated with exercise may also aggravate bubble formation, and the contraction of muscles causes low pressure areas which can act as nuclei for bubbles.

An early controlled study showed that exercised divers developed bends more often than rested divers. However, some more recent work at Duke University showed that divers who mildly exercised during stops could have their stop times reduced by as much as 30%.[4] It also showed that heavy exercise on the bottom can increase decompression time threefold. It was assumed that, if bubble formation was slight enough, exercise could accelerate gas elimination, but, when bubbles were large, gas elimination was hampered and exercise did not assist the off-gassing. However, there were not enough results to provide statistical validity.

Although it appears that mild exercise may at times assist off-gassing during decompression stops it is very difficult to define what level of exercise, if any, is desirable for a particular decompression situation. At this stage, it appears wise to refrain from exercise during decompression stops. However, gently moving and stretching will prevent divers adopting a fixed posture which could restrict circulation to and, hence, off-gassing from, one particular area.

Exercise after decompression has been shown to increase the risk of bends, so divers should avoid any exertion for at least 12 hours after a decompression stop dive.

Temperature control

It appears that raising a diver's temperature during decompression increases gas elimination and reduces the chance of bends after the diver surfaces. Conversely, if a diver becomes cold while decompressing, off-gassing may be inadequate and one would expect that the chance of bends may increase. However, one series of experiments demonstrated that divers who were cold at the onset and throughout a dive had fewer doppler detectable bubbles than warm divers.[8] These cold divers may have absorbed less nitrogen during the dive due to their reduced circulation. This would explain the low bubble count. However divers should be adequately insulated to avoid becoming cold during any part of the dive.

Decompression Using Oxygen

As oxygen breathing increases the rate of nitrogen elimination, it is possible to reduce decompression time by up to 40% by switching from air to 100% oxygen during relatively shallow decompression stops. However, **when oxygen is breathed at partial pressures greater than 1.6 ATA, acute oxygen toxicity can occur, often causing epileptic-like convulsions.** This generally restricts oxygen decompression to depths of about 30 ft (9 m) or shallower.

There are a number of special tables available which outline the appropriate decompression. Most of the oxygen decompression tables are for surface decompression in a decompression chamber breathing oxygen. If a diver begins to convulse or shows other signs of toxicity, the oxygen concentration can be reduced and the patient can be carefully monitored and appropriately treated. However, the Royal Navy (RN), RNPL, Canadian Forces (DCIEM) and a few other organizations have published tables which utilize in-water decompression stops on oxygen. In all cases there are stringent conditions that must be met and specific equipment used, usually including that the divers wear full-face masks. If a diver who is not wearing a full-face mask were to convulse, it is likely that the regulator would fall from his mouth, probably causing him to drown. In addition, if a diver were to ascend while convulsing, he may end up with a ruptured lung, caused by the expansion of the gas trapped in his lungs.

The Royal Navy utilize in-water oxygen decompression for dives deeper than 178 ft (54 m). The first oxygen stop is a short stop at 60 ft (18 m) and it is followed by progressively shallower stops.[9] The RNPL 1972 Tables introduce oxygen decompression stops where decompression time on air alone would exceed 31 minutes. The stops are at 33 ft (10 m) and/or 16.5 ft (5 m).[10] The DCIEM in-water oxygen decompression tables utilize a single 30 ft (9 m) stop.[11]

The main purpose of these tables is to reduce decompression time compared to that required with air decompression. However, relatively little testing has been done to assess the risk of DCS with these tables. Some of the testing that has been done indicates that there is still a significant risk of bends.[12, 13]

Some abalone divers, pearl divers, deep wreck divers, cave divers and others have begun using oxygen for in-water decompression to try to reduce their risk of DCS. Most of these divers do not decompress by a specific oxygen decompression table, but instead use an air decompression table and breathe oxygen, rather than air for some of the shallow stops, using the time given for air decompression stops. This should add safety to the decompression but, since most of these divers do not wear full-face masks they would be in serious danger if they convulsed. **It is important to realize that at depths approaching 30 ft (9 m) the possibility of oxygen toxicity problems still exist, and that the risk increases dramatically at depths beyond 30 ft (9 m).** Accordingly, such divers are advised to restrict oxygen breathing to depths of **20 ft (6 m)** or shallower, and to ensure that they do not inadvertently descend deeper.

Because of the potential for acute oxygen toxicity, most hyperbaric experts strongly recommend that recreational divers totally refrain from breathing oxygen underwater.

Due to the high level of dive-fitness, experience, equipment and support required to conduct decompression stop dives safely, it is strongly recommended that recreational divers refrain from doing dives requiring mandatory decompression stops.

REFERENCES

1. Bassett, B. (1982), "The Safety of the United States Navy Decompression Tables and Recommendations for Sports Divers". *SPUMS Journal*; Oct/Dec: 16-25.

2. Divers Alert Network, "Preliminary Report on Diving Accidents 1988". Divers Alert Network, North Carolina.

3. Divers Alert Network, "Report on 1988 Diving Accidents". Divers Alert Network, North Carolina.

4. Wilmshurst, P. (1990), "Learning from the Professionals". *Diver*; 35(7): 33-34.

5. Weathersby, P. et al (1986), "Statistically Based Decompression Tables III: Comparitive Risk Using U.S. Navy, British and Canadian Standard Air Schedules". Naval Medical Research Institute Report No. NRMI 86-50, Department of the Navy.

6. Vann, R. et al (1988), "Decompression Sickness and Diver-Carried Computers". *Alert Diver*; 4 (3).

7. Hamilton, B. (1985), "Decompression Tables Underlying Assumptions". *Triage*; 9, January.

8. Dunford, R. and Hayward, J. (1981), "Venous gas bubble production following cold stress during a no-decompression dive". *Undersea Biomedical Research*; 8 (1): 41-49.

9. B.R. 2806, "Diving Manual". Ministry of Defence, Weapons Department (Naval), March 1972.

10. RNPL Metric Air Diving Tables. Report UR7 CIRIA Underwater Engineering Group.

11. Canadian Forces Air Diving Tables and Procedures. Department of National Defence Canada and Defence and Civil Institute of Environmental Medicine, April 1986.

12. Lauckner, G. et al (1984), "Evaluation of DCIEM 1982 Decompression Model for Compressed Air Dives (Series G-K). DCIEM Report No. 84-R-73.

13. Lauckner, G. et al (1985), "Evaluation of DCIEM 1983 Decompression Model for Comporessed Air Dives (Series L-Q). DCIEM Report No. 85-R-18.

OTHER SOURCES

Vann, R. (1982), "Decompression Theory and Application". In: *The Physiology and Medicine of Diving*, Bennett, P. and Elliott, D. (eds), Best Publishing Co., California: 352-382.

Vann, R. et al (1985), "Exercise and Decompression". *Alert Diver*; 2 (1): 3.

RECOMMENDED FURTHER READING

Vann, R. (1982), "Decompression Theory and Application". In: *The Physiology and Medicine of Diving*, Bennett, P. and Elliott, D. eds., Best Publishing Co., California: 352-382.

Vann, R. et al (1988), "Decompression Sickness and Diver-Carried Computers". *Alert Diver*; 4 (3).

CHAPTER 25

OMITTED OR INTERRUPTED DECOMPRESSION

It is important to realize that an omitted decompression procedure is not only relevant to divers who plan to do a decompression stop dive. Sometimes, what was planned to be a no-decompression stop dive can inadvertantely become a dive requiring decompression stops. A diver might unknowingly exceed the maximum depth and, after discovering this might lack adequate air to complete necessary stops. A depth gauge might be faulty, thereby causing the diver to exceed the planned depth. A previous dive may not have been considered. These situations should not occur since the buddy should provide the necessary "double check" in order to avoid them. Unfortunately, they still manage to happen.

If a diver surfaces from a dive without having completed the required decompression, it is likely that bubbles have begun to form within his blood and body tissues. At the surface, excess gas within the diver's body will diffuse into these bubbles, causing them to grow. Eventually, symptoms of decompression sickness might develop.

Most decompression tables have associated omitted decompression procedures which can be used in the event of inadequate decompression. These procedures generally require an ***asymptomatic*** diver to return to a specified depth, within a very short time of having surfaced and to decompress in accordance with a revised schedule. ***If symptoms are present, the diver must remain on the surface and be treated for decompression sickness.*** Some of these omitted decompression procedures are shown later in this chapter.

The rationale behind these procedures is as follows:

When the diver returns to depth, bubbles within his body are compressed. This compression increases the pressure of the gas within the bubbles which, in turn, causes gas to diffuse from them. Thus, the size of the bubbles is reduced and, hopefully, the diver will return to the surface with smaller, and possibly fewer, bubbles.

The success of these procedures has been varied. At times bends seems to have been prevented, while, on other occasions, divers have suffered from bends despite the recommended procedure having been followed. At times these procedures can in fact create, or worsen, potential problems for the diver. One problem is that compression on descent may cause some of the bubbles trapped in the lung capillaries to become small enough to pass through the lungs and into the arterial circulation. If an arterial gas embolism were to result, the consequences could be disastrous, especially if the diver became unconscious while underwater. Secondly, although compression will cause an immediate decrease in the size of any bubbles, the higher partial pressures of nitrogen at depth might eventually drive more nitrogen into some tissues and, so, promote bubble growth. In addition, problems such as potential hypothermia and the inability to carry out the omitted decompression procedure completely and correctly, often make the procedure of dubious value.

In the light of the abovementioned problems and of the significant incidence of decompression sickness even after the complete and correct use of an in-water omitted decompression procedure, it is recommended that the following procedure be adopted:

If decompression has been omitted or interrupted and the diver is symptom-free, he should:

* **Remain on the surface**
* **Keep still and quiet**
* **Breathe 100% oxygen**
* **Drink non-alcoholic fluids**
* **Contact a diving physician for advice**
* **Do not dive again for at least 24 hours and then only if no signs/symptoms of bends had occurred**

If symptoms are present, the full first aid regimen for decompression sickness should be implemented.

If there is no oxygen available and appropriate medical advice is not readily accessible, a diver might decide to adopt an in-water omitted decompression procedure. If this is contemplated, it is essential that the following conditions are satisfied:

1. *The diver must be completely asymptomatic.*
2. He must be back underwater at the first stop within the specified time of having surfaced from the original dive.
3. There is enough air to complete *all* required stops.
4. A suitable buddy is available.
5. The sea conditions are suitable.
6. The diver is adequately insulated.

Warning:

The following are not treatment tables and should not be used if the diver is displaying signs/symptoms of decompression sickness.

A. UNITED STATES NAVY OMITTED OR INTERRUPTED DECOMPRESSION

This procedure is only available to a diver who has omitted, or interrupted, decompression given by the U.S. Navy Tables. It is based on the Standard Air Decompression Table. Special care must be taken to detect signs/symptoms of decompression sickness. **If signs/symptoms of decompression sickness are present, full recompression treatment in a recompression chamber is required.**

Procedure:

Ascent from 20 ft (6 m) or shallower

If a diver fails to complete a stop(s) of 20 ft (6 m) or shallower, indicates that he is well and can be returned to his stop depth within 1 minute, he may complete his normal decompression stops. The decompression stop from which ascent occurred is lengthened by 1 minute. If the 1 minute surface interval is exceeded and the diver remains asymptomatic, return the diver to the stop from which he ascended, and multiply the 20 ft (6 m) and/or 10 ft (3 m) stop times by $1^1/_2$. An alternative procedure is available if a recompression chamber is available. The diver must be observed for 1 hour after surfacing.

Ascent from deeper than 20 ft (6 m)

When no recompression chamber is available, use the following in-water procedure to make up omitted decompression in asymptomatic divers after they have ascended prematurely from stops deeper than 20 ft (6 m).

Recompress the diver in the water as soon as possible (preferably less than a 5-minute surface interval). Keep the diver at rest, provide a standby diver and maintain a good communication and depth control.

1. Repeat all stops below 40 ft (12 m) then:
2. Stop at 40 ft (12 m) for $^1/4$ of the time of the omitted 10 ft (3 m) stop.
3. Stop at 30 ft (9 m) for $^1/3$ of the omitted 10 ft (3 m) stop time.
4. Stop at 20 ft (6 m) for $^1/2$ of the omitted 10 ft (3 m) stop time.
5. Stop at 10 ft (3 m) for $1^1/2$ times the omitted 10 ft (3 m) stop time.

Assume an ascent rate of one minute between stops
(i.e. one foot every 6 seconds). The diver must be observed for 1 hour after surfacing.

USING THE U.S. NAVY PROCEDURE

Example 1.

A diver, using the U.S. Navy Tables, has dived to 120 ft (36 m) for a bottom time of 25 minutes, and surfaces without having completed the required decompression of 6 minutes at 10 ft (3 m). What should he do?

Ideally, the diver should remain at rest on the surface, breathe 100% oxygen, drink appropriate fluids (condition permitting) and contact a diving physician. If this is not possible and *if the required pre-conditions are satisfied* the diver may adopt the following U.S. Navy procedure:

If he can be at the 10 ft (3 m) stop within 1 minute of surfacing, he should go to 10 ft (3 m) and remain there for 7 minutes before ascending.

However, if he is on the surface for longer than 1 minute, he should go to 10 ft (3 m) and remain there for 9 minutes before surfacing.

Note: He must be asymptomatic.

Example 2.

A diver has just surfaced from a dive to 100 ft (30 m) for a bottom time of 23 minutes. Immediately on surfacing she realizes that she had not taken a previous dive into account, and that she was in Repetitive Group E prior to this last dive. If she decided to follow the U.S. Navy Omitted Decompression Schedule (having satisfied the pre-conditions), what stop(s) would be required?

Since she was in Group E before the dive, the Residual Nitrogen Time that she had forgotten to add was 18 minutes. Therefore the schedule she should have followed was that for 100 ft (30 m) for a bottom time of 41 minutes. The decompression omitted was 2 minutes at 20 ft (6 m) followed by 24 minutes at 10 ft (3 m).

According to U.S. Navy procedure she should:

(i) Surface interval within 1 minute:
Go to 20 ft (6 m) and remain there for 3 minutes, then ascend to 10 ft (3 m) for 24 minutes before surfacing.

(ii) Surface interval longer than 1 minute:
Go to 20 ft (6 m) for 3 minutes, followed by 3 m (10 ft) for 36 minutes before surfacing.

Example 3.

A professional diver, using the U.S. Navy Tables, has dived to 130 ft (39 m) for a bottom time of 60 minutes, and surfaces without having completed the required decompression of 9 minutes at 30 ft (9 m), 23 minutes at 20 ft (6 m) and 52 minutes at 10 ft (3 m). What should he do?

Accordingly to U.S. Navy procedure, as soon as possible (preferably within 5 minutes) he should:

1. Go to 40 ft (12 m) for for 13 minutes.
Take 1 minute to ascend to 30 ft (9 m).

2. Stay at 30 ft (9 m) for 18 minutes.
   Take 1 minute to ascend to 20 ft (6 m).
3. Stay at 20 ft (6 m) for 26 minutes.
   Take 1 minute to ascend to 10 ft (3 m).
4. Stay at 10 ft (3 m) for 78 minutes.
   Take 1 minute to ascend to the surface.

B. THE BRITISH PROCEDURE

On Page 349 of the superceded BS-AC Diving Manual it states:

"If a diver has made a free or buoyant ascent which prevented him carrying out necessary decompression stops, he should get another aqualung immediately and return with the standby diver to a depth 10 m deeper than his first planned stop. He should remain there for five minutes and then continue decompressing for a dive ten minutes longer than his original one".

This recommendation was based on a surface decompression procedure designed to decompress divers in a chamber, rather than in the sea. Sometimes, when the water was cold, or the surface conditions were rough, decompression in a dry chamber on the surface was preferred to doing it in the water. When tested, the surface decompression procedure yielded an incidence of bends of 4.3% which, at the time, was felt to be acceptable. However, there is currently some concern that this technique may have caused long-term neurological damage to some of the divers involved.

It must be noted that this incidence of more than 4% bends resulted when done by professionals, under ideal conditions, in a dry chamber. One would expect a far higher bends rate when a similar procedure is attempted, in the water, by amateur divers.

The BS-AC have not included this procedure in their new "Sport Diving" manual and no longer recommend it.

C. THE OMITTED DECOMPRESSION PROCEDURE FOR THE BUEHLMANN (1986) TABLES

If a diver has omitted or interrupted the required decompression given by the Buehlmann (1986) Table, he must return, within two minutes, to the last stop level, and perform the decompression required for the next longer bottom time than the actual bottom time of the dive.

The diver must be asymptomatic and must be accompanied by a suitable diver.

Example 4.

A diver has dived to 27 m (90 ft) for 28 minutes. The required decompression is 5 minutes at 3 m (10 ft). If he only completes 2 minutes of the decompression at 3 m (10 ft) before accidentally surfacing, he could:

Return to 3 m (10 ft) and complete decompression for a bottom time of 35 minutes. The required decompression would be 10 minutes at 3 m (10 ft).

Example 5.

A diver has dived to 39 m (130 ft) for 20 minutes. The required decompression is 3 minutes at 6 m (20 ft) and 7 minutes at 3 m (10 ft). She completes the 3 minutes at 6 m (20 ft) but has only spent 1 minute at 3 m (10 ft) before running out of air. What is the omitted decompression procedure required?

If she has ready access to another tank, is asymptomatic and can be accompanied by a suitable buddy, she could:

Return, within 2 minutes, to the 3 m (10 ft) stop and remain there for 12 minutes before surfacing.

D. OMITTED DECOMPRESSION PROCEDURE FOR THE BUEHLMANN/ HAHN TABLES

Pre-requisites:

(a) Adequate air to complete all required stops.
(b) No signs or symptoms of decompression sickness have developed.
(c) He has to be back underwater within 5 minutes of surfacing (after the end of the dive) at half of his dived depth.

Warning:

1. The procedure of the Omitted/Delayed Decompression is meant to be used in clear emergency cases, as the procedure carries a greater risk of decompression sickness than if regular decompression was followed.

2. The Delayed Decompression is not to be used if any of the above pre-requisites ((a) to (c)) is not fulfilled.

3. This procedure is not meant as treatment and cannot be used if the diver is displaying signs/symptoms of decompression sickness.

Procedure for Omitted/Delayed Decompression:

1. Dive again within 3 minutes of surfacing.

2. Dive to a depth that is half of the maximum depth of the dive from which you have inadequately decompressed, within 5 minutes of surfacing.

3. Stay at that depth for 5 minutes.

4. Ascend and decompress for a dive with the same maximum depth of the original dive, but with a bottom time 10 minutes longer.

Example 6.

A diver has dived to 27 m for 28 minutes. The required decompression is 3 minutes at 3 m. If he accidentally surfaces, he could:

Dive again, within 3 minutes of surfacing, and descend to 13.5 m within 5 minutes of surfacing. Remain at 13.5 m for 5 minutes, before decompressing for a dive of 27 m for 38 minutes. The required stop is 8 minutes at 3 m.

Example 7.

A diver has dived to 39 m for 20 minutes. The required decompression is 3 minutes at 6 m and 4 minutes at 3 m. She completes the 3 minutes at 6 m, but has not completed the stop at 3 m before running out of air. What is the omitted decompression procedure required?

The diver could dive again, within 3 minutes of surfacing, and descend to 19.5 m within 5 minutes of surfacing. Remain at 19.5 m for 5 minutes, before decompressing for a dive of 39 m for 30 minutes. The diver must now ascend to 9 m for 3 minutes, 6 m for 5 minutes and 3 m for 14 minutes.

E. THE DCIEM OMITTED DECOMPRESSION PROCEDURE

A diver who omits a Decompression Stop may resort to either of the Omitted Decompression Procedures described below. The following procedures are for emergency use only:

a. If no symptoms of DCS are present, the diver may begin the following IN-WATER PROCEDURE:

Within seven (7) minutes of surfacing, secure an adequate air supply and return to the stop 10 ft (3 m) deeper than the first omitted stop. Decompress at this depth for the time of the first omitted stop, then continue the decompression in accordance with the Table A schedule.

Example: 1st Dive: 100 ft (30 m) for 29 minutes
No-D Limit is 15 minutes
Decompression required is 5 min. at 20 ft (6 m) and 10 min. at 10 ft (3 m)

Situation: On ascent, diver omits decompression, but has no symptoms of DCS.

Reaction: Recompress for 5 min. at 30 ft (9 m), 5 min. at 20 ft (6 m) and 10 min. at 10 ft (3 m).

b. When a RECOMPRESSION CHAMBER (RCC) is available within seven (7) minutes of surfacing, the diver may be placed in the RCC and recompressed on Oxygen at a pressure equivalent to a sea level depth of 40 ft (12 m). The diver should remain on Oxygen at this pressure for twice the total omitted decompression time. RCC ascent time (on Oxygen) is 2 minutes.

After conducting either of these Omitted Decompression Procedures, the diver must not dive again for at least **24 hours**. During this time, the diver should be closely monitored for symptoms of DCS. If symptoms of DCS occur, transport the diver to the nearest hyperbaric treatment facility.

Example 8.

After diving to 140 ft (42 m) for a bottom time of 14 minutes, a diver is required to decompress for 5 minutes at 20 ft (6 m) and then 10 minutes at 10 ft (3 m). When ascending to the 20 ft (6 m) stop, the diver loses control of his buoyancy and surfaces. What decompression is now required?

In this situation, since the diver missed the first stop he must descend (within 7 minutes) to 30 ft (9 m) for 5 minutes, before ascending to 20 ft (6 m) and completing the original schedule. His decompression is therefore: 5 minutes at 30 ft (9 m), 5 minutes at 20 ft (6 m) and 10 minutes at 10 ft (3 m). The diver must be asymptomatic.

Example 9.

After diving to 140 ft (42 m) for a bottom time of 14 minutes a diver is required to decompress for 5 minutes at 20 ft (6 m) and then 10 minutes at 10 ft (3 m). After completing the 20 ft (6 m) stop, the diver loses control of his buoyancy and fails to complete the stop at 10 ft (3 m). What decompression is now required?

In this case the diver must return to 20 ft (6 m) for a total of 10 + 5 = 15 minutes before ascending to 10 ft (3 m) for 10 minutes. The diver must be asymptomatic.

F. THE PROCEDURE FOR USE WITH THE PADI RDP

The PADI Recreational Dive Planner is not meant to be used for decompression diving. Provisions for an emergency decompression stop are included only as a back-up if you make a mistake.

An emergency decompression stop of 8 minutes at 15 ft (5 m on metric) must be made if a No-Decompression Limit is exceeded by 5 minutes, or less. Upon surfacing, the diver must remain out of the water for at least 6 hours prior to making another dive. If a No-Decompression Limit is exceeded by more than 5 minutes, a 15-foot (5 m on metric) decompression stop of no less than 15 minutes is urged (air supply permitting). Upon surfacing, the diver must remain out of the water for at least 24 hours prior to making another dive.

SUMMARY

* Omitted decompression procedures generally require an asymptomatic diver to return to a specified depth within a short time of having surfaced, and to decompress in accordance to a revised schedule.

* The following are some of the many pre-conditions that must be met before attempting such a procedure:

  - divers must be asymptomatic, have enough air, be adequately insulated, accompanied by an unaffected attendant
  - weather and sea conditions must be suitable

* Potential problems include:

  - Arterial gas embolism caused by compressed bubbles passing through the lungs and into the arterial circulation
  - increased bubble size after ascent, due to more gas entering existing bubbles

* **Surface procedure is strongly advised.** It is:

  - Remain on surface, rest, breathe 100% oxygen, drink appropriate fluids, contact a diving physician for advice and do not dive again for at least 24 hours and then only if no signs/symptoms of bends had occurred

SOURCES

British Sub-Aqua Club (1977), "Diving Manual". Charles Scribner's Sons, New York.

British Sub-Aqua Club (1985), "Sport Diving". Stanley Paul, London.

Buehlmann, A., personal communications.

Instructions for using the DCIEM Sport Diving Tables. Universal Dive Techtronics, Richmond, B.C., 1990.

Lippmann, J. and Bugg, S. (1989), "The Diving Emergency Handbook" - German Edition. Springer-Verlag, Heidelberg.

Miles, S. and Mackay, D. (1976), "Underwater Medicine", 4th edition. Granada Publishing Ltd, London.

Nishi, R. (1986), "New Canadian Air Decompression Tables". DCIEM No. 86-P-06, *Canadian Diving Journal*; 22-27, Summer.

"The Wheel-Instructions for Use". PADI, California, 1989.

U.S. Navy (1985), "U.S. Navy Diving Manual, Vol. 1, Air Diving". U.S. Government Printing Office: 8.22-8.24.

Weathersby, P., personal communication.

Wilmshurst, P. (1988), "Re-Entry Decompression". *NDC Bulletin*; 12: 2.

EXERCISES

U.S. Navy Tables

Determine the in-water decompression stops needed to attempt to compensate for omitted decompression after the following dives:

1. 56 ft (17 m) for 68 minutes (can be back at first stop within 1 minute).

2. 90 ft (27 m) for 45 minutes (cannot be back at stop within 1 minute).

3. 130 ft (39 m) for 28 minutes (cannot be back at stop within 1 minute).

   (i) Ascent occurred from the 20 ft (6 m) stop.
   (ii) Ascent occurred from the 10 ft (3 m) stop.

4. 100 ft (30 m) for 42 minutes (can be back at first stop within 1 minute).

   (i) Ascent occurred from the 20 ft (6 m) stop.
   (ii) Ascent occurred from the 10 ft (3 m) stop.

5. 90 ft (27 m) for 90 minutes.

6. 140 ft (42 m) for 40 minutes.

Buehlmann (1986) Tables

1. Determine the in-water decompression stops needed to attempt to compensate for omitted decompression after the following dives:

   a. 20 m (66 ft) for 45 minutes (no stops completed).
   b. 27 m (90 ft) for 40 minutes (no stops completed).
   c. 33 m (110 ft) for 22 minutes (first stop completed).
   d. 39 m (130 ft) for 12 minutes (no stop completed)

Buehlmann/Hahn Tables

1. Determine the in-water decompression stops needed to attempt to compensate for omitted decompression after the following dives:

   a. 20 m for 45 minutes.
   b. 27 m for 40 minutes.
   c. 33 m for 22 minutes.
   d. 39 m for 12 minutes.

DCIEM Tables

1. Determine the in-water recompression times needed to compensate for omitted decompression after the following dives:

   a. 70 ft (21 m) for 50 minutes.
   b. 85 ft (26 m) for 33 minutes.
   c. 115 ft (35 m) for 16 minutes.
   d. 60 ft (18 m) for 51 minutes.

ANSWERS

U.S. Navy Tables

1. 3 minutes at 10 ft (3 m)
2. 27 minutes at 10 ft (3 m)
3. (i) $4^1/2$ minutes at 20 ft (6 m) and 27 minutes at 10 ft (3 m)
   (ii) 27 minutes at 10 ft (3 m)
4. (i) 3 minutes at 20 ft (6 m) and 24 minutes at 10 ft (3 m)
   (ii) 25 minutes at 10 ft (3 m)
5. 40 ft (12 m) for 12 minutes
   30 ft (9 m) for 16 minutes
   20 ft (6 m) for 24 minutes
   10 ft (3 m) for 72 minutes
6. 40 ft (12 m) for $6^1/2$ minutes
   30 ft (9 m) for $8^2/3$ minutes
   20 ft (6 m) for 13 minutes
   10 ft (3 m) for 39 minutes

Buehlmann (1986) Tables

1. a. 10 ft (3 m) for 16 minutes
   b. 20 ft (6 m) for 3 minutes and 10 ft (3 m) for 18 minutes
   c. 10 ft (3 m) for 11 minutes
   d. 10 ft (3 m) for 7 minutes

Buehlmann/Hahn Tables

1. a. 10 m for 5 minutes and 3 m for 4 minutes
   b. 13.5 m for 5 minutes, 6 m for 2 minutes and 3 m for 16 minutes
   c. 16.5 m for 5 minutes, 6 m for 4 minutes and 3 m for 13 minutes
   d. 19.5 m for 5 minutes, 9 m for 1 minutes, 6 m for 4 minutes and 3 m for 8 minutes

DCIEM Tables

1. a. 20 ft (6 m) for 10 minutes and 10 ft (3 m) for 10 minutes
   b. 30 ft (9 m) for 5 minutes, 20 ft (6 m) for 5 minutes and 10 ft (3 m) for 10 minutes
   c. 30 ft (9 m) for 5 minutes, 20 ft (6 m) for 5 minutes and 10 ft (3 m) for 10 minutes
   d. 20 ft (6 m) for 5 minutes and 10 ft (3 m) for 5 minutes

SECTION 6

ADMINISTRATION OF OXYGEN TO DIVERS

CHAPTER 26

OXYGEN

Oxygen is a colorless, odorless and tasteless gas that constitutes about 21% of the air we breathe. We need oxygen to effectively metabolize food and provide energy for cell function. The body consumes oxygen and produces heat and other forms of energy, as well as carbon dioxide.

The blood carries oxygen in two forms: dissolved in plasma and chemically combined with hemoglobin.

Oxygen is not very soluble in plasma at normal temperatures and pressures, so very little is normally dissolved in plasma. The vast majority of oxygen is chemically combined with hemoglobin, in fact, it is about sixty times the amount dissolved in plasma.

When breathing air at normal atmospheric pressures, the hemoglobin is 97.5% saturated with oxygen. The partial pressure of oxygen in the lungs must be raised to about 2.5 times its normal level before the hemoglobin is fully saturated. As the oxygen rich blood reaches the tissues the hemoglobin releases some oxygen to the tissues, but still remains about 75% saturated.

Oxygen is important in the management of shock and resuscitation and it is the drug of choice in the first aid and treatment of a number of diving-related injuries. It is a "drug", in that it must be used correctly, too little, and too much, can have serious effects.

EFFECTS OF TOO LITTLE OXYGEN - HYPOXIA, ANOXIA

When our body tissues receive too little oxygen they become hypoxic, and, if no oxygen is received, anoxia results. **Hypoxia** is a state of low oxygen levels, and **anoxia** is a complete lack of oxygen.

Hypoxia causes cells to change to non-oxygen (anaerobic) metabolism, which may create a shortage of cell energy and always causes an increase in blood acidity. The increase in blood acidity impairs cellular function, in particular, the ability of the brain and the heart to function properly. Body cells cannot survive for long without oxygen. Brain cells are particularly sensitive to oxygen starvation and will die off in minutes as they cannot change to non-oxygen metabolism.

There are many ways that tissue hypoxia can occur. Too little oxygen in the gas we breathe will affect the whole body. This will occur when the partial pressure of oxygen falls below 0.16 ATA. Lung damage will cause similar effects. Poisoning with carbon monoxide prevents hemoglobin taking up oxygen because it preferentially takes up the carbon monoxide. Cyanide prevents the cells taking up oxygen by poisoning enzyme systems. Blockage of an artery, cutting off the blood supply, causes hypoxia beyond the blockage by preventing the arrival of oxygen-carrying blood. The same happens when blood flow through a part of the body is reduced by constriction of arteries, perhaps due to the effects of cold (blue fingers and ears), or a fall in blood pressure.

EFFECTS OF TOO MUCH OXYGEN - OXYGEN TOXICITY

Oxygen breathed at partial pressures greater than about 0.6 ATA damages the body. The level of toxicity depends on the partial pressure of oxygen and the time of exposure.

Put simply, at low pressures oxygen damages the lungs, while at pressures greater than 2 ATA the most noticeable effect is on the brain, causing convulsions.

Pulmonary Oxygen Toxicity

When oxygen is breathed at partial pressures greater than 0.6 ATA but below 2 ATA, the damage arises slowly and mainly affects the lungs. Prolonged oxygen poisoning will permanently damage lungs, and kills.

Oxygen damages the lungs by causing swelling of the alveolar walls, so increasing the distance oxygen has to diffuse to enter the blood. This swelling stiffens the lungs and makes breathing more difficult. This damage will reverse when the oxygen concentration goes back to normal. However, if the oxygen breathing continues, the cells in the alveolar walls will be damaged and may then die. Death from hypoxia will occur in spite of high oxygen partial pressures.

Continual breathing of 100% oxygen at the surface will cause irritation of the respiratory tract and lungs within 24 hours. Symptoms such as *coughing, wheezing, shortness of breath and pain behind the breastbone* may occur. Lower partial pressures can be breathed for longer before causing ill-effects.

Although this Pulmonary Oxygen Toxicity is a major consideration in diving habitats it does not generally threaten the recreational diver unless he requires recompression for bends or arterial gas embolism. In these circumstances the periods of oxygen breathing are carefully monitored and "air breaks" (periods of breathing air) are given, if required.

Central Nervous System Oxygen Toxicity

When oxygen is breathed at partial pressures greater than 1.6 ATA it produces toxicity far more rapidly and affects the brain. This is known as Central Nervous System (CNS) or Acute Oxygen Toxicity. The exact cause is unknown but a common theory suggests that the high oxygen levels might inhibit certain enzymes that are required for biochemical reactions in the brain.

The partial pressure at which this acute oxygen toxicity occurs varies. Some factors seem to affect the pressure at which the toxicity occurs. High levels of carbon dioxide and high temperatures increase susceptibility, as well as doing heavy work and being underwater, rather than in a dry chamber. Susceptibility varies between individuals and with the same individual from day to day.

The most dramatic direct result of acute oxygen toxicity is an epileptic-like convulsion which may occur with, or without, warning. Commonly, minor symptoms such as *nausea, muscle twitching (particularly lips), vertigo, lightheadedness, visual abnormalities, irritibility and numbness precede the convulsion.* The convulsions usually last for about two minutes. Initially, the body becomes rigid and the casualty loses consciousness. Breathing stops and the airway can become obstructed. If decompression (e.g. ascent) occurs at this stage a lung injury could result. After about 30 seconds the convulsion begins and breathing resumes. If a convulsion occurred in a diver using a normal SCUBA regulator, the regulator would probably be dislodged and the diver may drown.

A recreational diver should never normally be exposed to oxygen partial pressures of 1.6 ATA or more. A diver breathing air would have to go to 218 fsw (66 msw) in order to reach such an oxygen level. In addition, the narcotic effects of nitrogen seem to delay the onset of acute oxygen toxicity. However, elevated carbon dioxide levels increase the likelihood of oxygen toxicity.

Some Australian abalone divers, scientific divers and deep wreck divers have begun to breathe oxygen during decompression stops. If they were to breathe pure oxygen deeper than 20 fsw (6 msw) they would be breathing an oxygen partial pressure of 1.6 ATA and would be risking acute oxygen toxicity.

Normally, the only time that a recreational diver might be susceptible is if he is being treated for bends or arterial gas embolism. Routine treatment involves 100% oxygen breathing at a partial pressure of 2.8 ATA which is equivalent to a depth of 60 fsw (18 msw). During recompression, the diver is carefully monitored for signs of toxicity and the oxygen level is reduced if necessary. Also, as mentioned before, convulsions are less likely to occur at rest in a dry chamber.

OXYGEN THERAPY

When air is breathed at higher pressures, as with SCUBA diving, or when a higher concentration of oxygen is breathed, since the hemoglobin is almost fully saturated it cannot hold much more oxygen. However, the higher partial pressure of oxygen causes more of it to dissolve into the plasma.

The amount of oxygen delivered to a tissue depends on the quantity of oxygen in the blood and the rate of blood flow (perfusion). By maximizing the oxygen concentration we can maximize the hemoglobin saturation and increase the amount of oxygen dissolved in plasma. This increases the chances of survival of poorly perfused tissues.

When breathing air at 1 ATA there is 0.3 ml of oxygen dissolved in each 100 ml of blood plasma. Breathing 100% oxygen at 1 ATA enables 2.3 ml of oxygen to be dissolved in each 100 ml of blood. This has many benefits for the injured diver, some of which are outlined below:

Decompression sickness and arterial gas embolism

* By breathing 100% oxygen (that is, no nitrogen) the diver is avoiding adding more nitrogen to the body. This has the advantage of speeding elimination of nitrogen and reducing the size of the bubbles.

A gas diffuses from an area of high concentration to areas of lower concentration and, the greater the difference in concentrations of the gas, the faster the diffusion occurs When breathing 100% oxygen the injured diver is not inhaling the large amounts of nitrogen present in air. Excluding nitrogen from the lungs encourages the nitrogen in the blood to diffuse into the lungs, and lowers the partial pressure of nitrogen in the arterial blood. This arterial blood then passes through the tissues and, since it now contains less nitrogen than the tissues, nitrogen diffuses from the tissues, and from the bubbles, into the blood and is taken to the lungs and eliminated. This cycle continues until all the excess nitrogen is removed.

This effect is reduced greatly as the oxygen level falls below 100%.

* Any reduction in blood flow due to bubble formation may cause hypoxia in affected tissues. The higher oxygen partial pressures will help to oxygenate any hypoxic tissues. The distance that oxygen diffuses into the tissues from the capillaries partly depends on its partial pressure in the blood. Raising the partial pressure increases the distance that oxygen can diffuse before it is all used up.

* Higher oxygen concentrations can help alleviate any respiratory distress that may be present.

* Higher oxygen concentrations reduce the shock associated with decompression sickness and arterial gas embolism (see below).

Pulmonary barotrauma (burst lung)

Administering 100% oxygen can reduce the respiratory difficulties associated with pulmonary barotrauma as it increases the transfer of oxygen across damaged or poorly perfused lung surface, thereby offsetting the impairment due to the damage. It also hastens the elimination of nitrogen from the pockets of air associated with a pneumothorax (collapsed lung) or mediastinal emphysema.

Carbon monoxide toxicity

Carbon monoxide, which may be a contaminant in a diver's breathing air, combines far more readily with hemoglobin than oxygen does. This reduces the major means of oxygen transport through the body. Increasing the concentration of inspired oxygen enables more oxygen to dissolve into the blood plasma, thereby improving the oxygen supply to the tissues. Hyperbaric oxygen increases this effect and helps break the bond between the hemoglobin and carbon monoxide.

Shock

Shock, which is a reduction in the body's effective circulation, accompanies many injuries. It reduces the circulation's ability to carry oxygen around the body. The effect of the reduced circulation can be partly offset by increasing the concentration of the inhaled oxygen, as more oxygen will be carried by the blood.

Near drowning and salt water aspiration

Conditions such as near drowning and salt water aspiration reduce the effectiveness of ventilation and cause various degrees of respiratory distress. Higher inspired oxygen levels help to offset these problems.

Resuscitation

By raising the blood oxygen levels, oxygen-assisted rescuscitation will help offset the reduced ventilation and perfusion that occur prior to, and during, resuscitation.

> In summary, 100% oxygen provides the following benefits to the diver:
>
> * Washes out dissolved nitrogen
> * Washes out the nitrogen in bubbles thus reducing bubble size
> * Improves tissue oxygenation
> * Reduces respiratory distress
> * Reduces shock

Oxygen breathing should not be considered a final treatment for diving emergencies. It is a supplement to normal diving first aid procedures and should increase the effect of those procedures and give the casualty the greatest chance of a full, and speedy, recovery. Even though a casualty may appear to have improved greatly, or even completely since breathing oxygen, he must still receive immediate specialist attention.

The breathing of oxygen is a first aid measure and must never be substituted for the recompression required for decompression sickness and arterial gas embolism, regardless of the response.

WHEN SHOULD OXYGEN BE ADMINISTERED?

The ultimate goal is to deliver 100% oxygen to the victim from the time the accident is recognized until medical authorities order it discontinued (or the supply is exhausted).

Oxygen breathing should be commenced as soon as possible to gain the maximum benefit.

A paper, published in the USA, describes a study of ten matched pairs of divers who suffered from the bends. Only one of each pair had been given oxygen while en route to a treatment facility. Nine out of the ten divers treated with oxygen made an apparently complete recovery after recompression, compared to five of the group who received no oxygen as first aid. The one diver who received oxygen and did not recover had only received oxygen after an initial delay of one hour.[1]

If only a limited supply of oxygen is available it should be given in heavy concentrations from the time the accident is recognized, until the supply of oxygen is exhausted.

Ideally, all divers should have access to oxygen should it be needed after a dive. The sooner an injured diver receives oxygen, the better. *All dive charter boats should carry suitable oxygen equipment, and ensure that their staff are adequately trained to use it.*

LIMITATIONS ON OXYGEN USE

Air breaks

The periods of oxygen breathing should be recorded (i.e. time(s) put on and time(s) taken off oxygen), *and the patient's response to oxygen should also be recorded.*

The doctor who will recompress the diver will then know how long the higher partial pressure of oxygen has been breathed for, and will use this information to minimize the effects of pulmonary oxygen toxicity during the subsequent hyperbaric oxygen treatment. If a patient has had long periods of oxygen breathing without breaks, by the time he arrives at the chamber for recompression, treatment options may have been substantially diminished. For this reason some treatment facilities prefer that the casualty breathes air for 5 minutes after each 25 minutes on oxygen, while en route to the chamber. The air breaks minimize the toxic effects of the oxygen on the lungs. However, since the "air breaks" are generally unnecessary if the transport time is shorter than about four hours, other facilities prefer that oxygen breathing continues, without breaks, until arrival at the chamber. If air breaks are given and the patient's condition deteriorates when taken off oxygen, he should recommence oxygen breathing immediately.

If a bad response to oxygen occurs, ensure that the diver breathes air for 15 minutes before oxygen is tried again.

There are certain people to whom administration of oxygen could be very dangerous. Luckily, they are normally so short of breath that they could never go diving. These ill people, suffering from chronic bronchitis, might stop breathing and die if given high concentrations of oxygen. Carbon dioxide provides the major stimulus for breathing for humans. However, some sufferers from chronic bronchitis have accustomed their bodies to such high carbon dioxide levels that they receive their main breathing trigger from reduced oxygen levels. If such a sufferer is given a high oxygen concentation, his breathing may cease. Fortunately for the diving first aider, a sufferer of chronic bronchitis should not pass a diving medical examination and, therefore, should never need to be given oxygen as first aid for a diving injury. To avoid the above possibility, divers should normally restrict themselves to giving oxygen to divers thought to be suffering from a diving-related problem.

EQUIPMENT

There are many different types of oxygen equipment on the market and these differ from Country to Country. Much of it requires advanced knowledge and skills which can be gained only through the appropriate training.

A diver must be thoroughly familiar with any oxygen equipment that he may use. A first-aider is normally safe from litigation as long as he delivers first aid within his level of training. A first-aider who goes beyond his level of training may create a potentially dangerous situation for the casualty and may expose himself to the threat of litigation. In addition, various Countries/States have regulations regarding oxygen usage, and a rescuer should be aware of pertinent regulations.

Oxygen therapy has two main components: a source of oxygen and the delivery system.

Oxygen source

Oxygen cylinders come in a number of different sizes. Like SCUBA cylinders, they are manufactured from either steel or aluminium alloy and, since they hold gas under high pressure, they must be carefully handled, maintained and tested at regular intervals. The cylinders should be rated by the appropriate authority for oxygen use. Cylinders should be stored indoors, protected from the weather and not subjected to extremes of hot or cold. The cylinders and valves must also be kept free from oil, grease and other flammable substances. They should be kept full so that the maximum amount of oxygen will be available, if required.

Oxygen cylinders are color-coded, but the color varies between Countries. In Australia and the United Kingdom the cylinders are black with a white top, whereas, in the USA and Canada the entire cylinder is green and, in Germany, it is blue. The cylinders should also be clearly labelled.

Although oxygen itself is not flammable, it readily supports combustion. The presence of even minute amounts of hydrocarbon oil or grease in a high-pressure oxygen atmosphere may cause an explosion. Leakage from a cylinder, or exhaust oxygen from a patient undergoing treatment, can very quickly produce a high oxygen content in enclosed spaces. This creates a greatly increased risk of fire or explosion due to the far greater ignitibility of substances in this environment. Therefore, oxygen cylinders must never be stored or used in an inadequately ventilated area, or near ignitable, or burning, substances.

For divers, enough oxygen must be provided for any anticipated transport time between the dive site and the nearest hospital. As well as having an adequate capacity, the cylinder must be compact enough to fit on the dive boat. Larger boats or permanent sites may have the potential for a large oxygen store, but consideration should be given for the possible need for the equipment to accompany a casualty while being transported to a hospital or recompression chamber. For this reason, it may sometimes be preferable to have a number of smaller cylinders rather than just a large one. Cylinder size varies from Country to Country but the minimum capacity should be around 400 liters (14.3 cu. ft). One such cylinder should provide approximately 30-90 minutes of oxygen when delivered by demand valve, about 40 minutes if used with a constant flow delivery system set at 10 liters per minute, and around 25-30 minutes at 15 liters per minute. Larger cylinders will last proportionately longer and, since divers often dive in areas remote from medical facilities, are often desirable. In Australia, the Divers Emergency Service (DES) recommends a minimum cylinder capacity of 1500 liters (53.6 cu. ft) for use by divers. If used with a demand delivery system, this should last 2-5 hours.

The smaller cylinders should be fitted with a pin-indexed medical oxygen valve which will mate with the appropriate oxygen regulator.

Delivery systems

There is an array of delivery devices designed for giving oxygen to conscious and/or unconscious patients. However, very little oxygen equipment has been designed specifically for diving accidents. *To maximize the benefits of oxygen first aid in diving accidents, 100% oxygen must be delivered.* ***To achieve this a demand delivery system must be used.***

FIGURE 26.1
Oxygen equipment designed for divers

Photo courtesy DAN.

Demand systems

The equipment necessary to deliver oxygen in this manner is very similar in principle to SCUBA equipment. The high pressure oxygen is delivered from the cylinder through a pressure regulator (first stage) to a demand valve (second stage), which supplies oxygen when the victim breathes spontaneously.

A demand valve with a tight-sealing, double-seal, oro-nasal mask (covers mouth and nose) is capable of delivering 100% oxygen to both the conscious and unconscious (breathing) victim. However, it is often difficult to get an adequate seal, especially if the first aider is unfamiliar or out of practice with the equipment, and, if the seal is inadequate, the oxygen concentration can fall well below the desired 100%.

Because tight-fitting masks are often uncomfortable, and because of the difficulty in achieving an adequate seal with certain masks, some demand valves can be adapted to suit a *conscious* diver by replacing the mask with a regulator mouth-piece, and sealing the casualty's nose with a nose clip, fingers or a diver's facemask. If the nose is not sealed, the oxygen concentration will drop well below 100%.

A demand system can also be used to provide an oxygen concentration in excess of 90% to an unconscious non-breathing diver. The rescuer breathes the oxygen from the demand valve (with his nose sealed) and then exhales his expired breath into the casualty.

FIGURE 26.2

A demand valve oxygen delivery system with tight-sealing mask

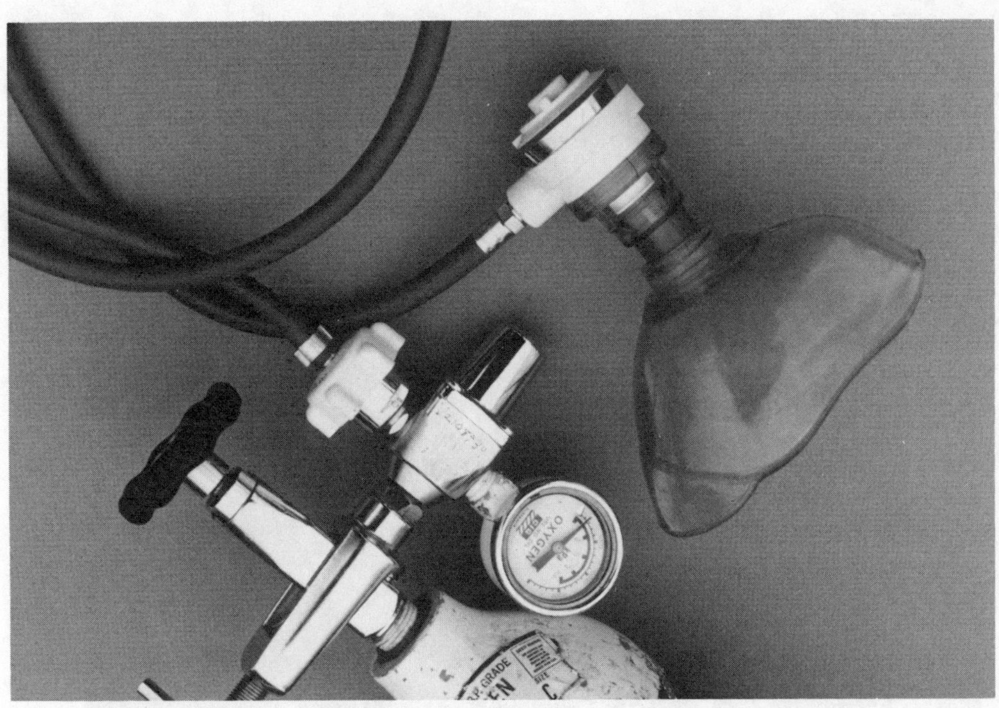

FIGURE 26.3
A demand valve oxygen delivery system with SCUBA mouth-piece

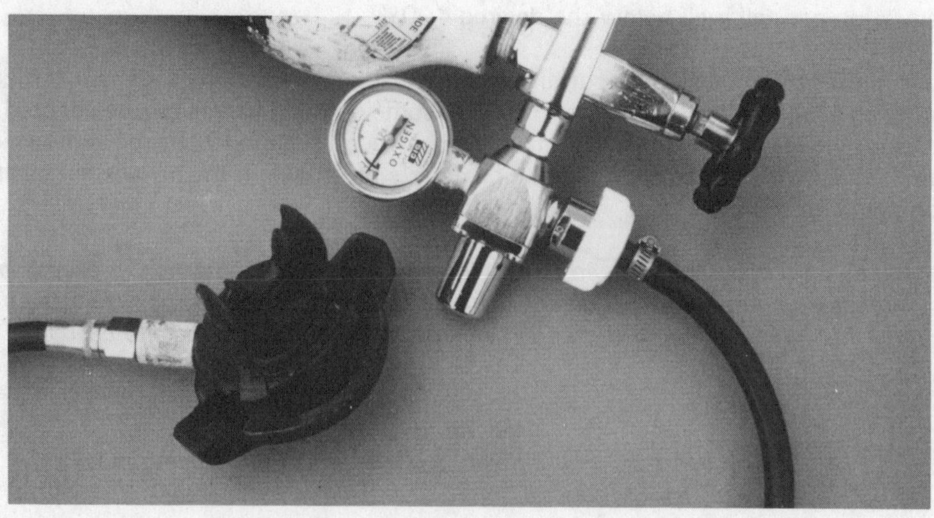

FIGURE 26.4
A conscious diver breathing 100% oxygen through a demand valve

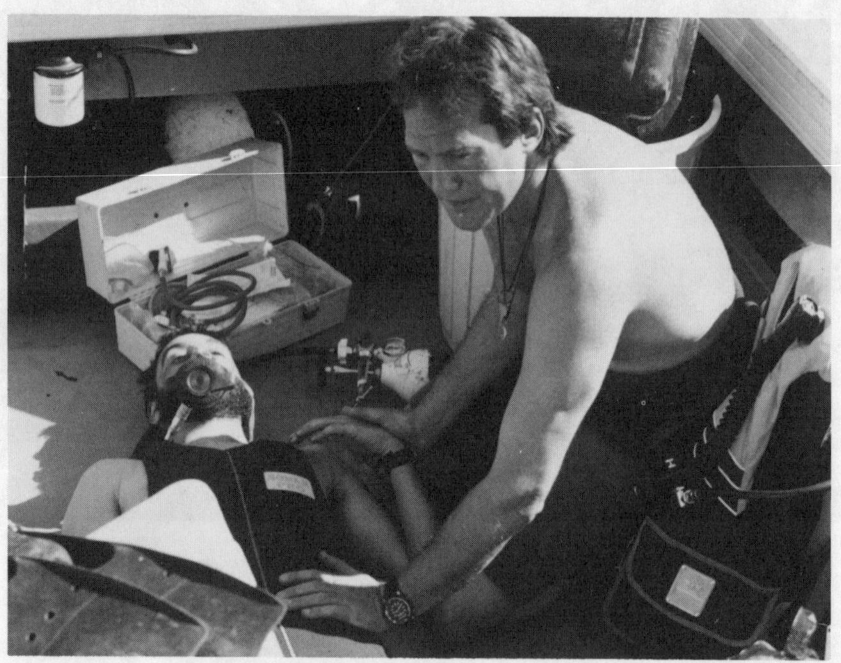

Note: The diver is wearing a nose clip.

Constant flow systems

The most commonly available oxygen delivery systems are those that deliver a constant flow of oxygen at either a fixed, or variable, flow rate. The oxygen concentration delivered by a constant flow system depends on the effectiveness of the seal, the flow rate, the type of delivery system (e.g. mask or nasal cannulae) and the rate and depth of the patient's breathing. In almost all cases the oxygen concentration will be well below 100%. It varies from about 25-35% with a loose-fitting mask or nasal cannulae, to up to 98% with a tight-sealing mask-valve-bag system with an additional oxygen reservoir bag attached, and a flow rate of 12-15 liters per minute (Laerdal, Ambu, Air-Viva).[2,3] (Concentrations up to 100% have been reported in an anesthetic mask and bag system with a high flow rate, but this requires specialized skill). Although most of these systems do not normally provide the maximum benefit, especially for a victim of bends or arterial gas embolism, they are still valuable in the first aid for these, and other, diving injuries, as well as for shock and for supplementing the oxygen supply during resuscitation.

Nasal cannulae, correctly positioned and with an oxygen flow rate of 4 liters/minute, will provide up to about 36% percent oxygen in a spontaneously breathing patient. Higher flow rates are uncomfortable for the patient and will not raise the oxygen concentration. However, the cannulae can be used to greatly increase the oxygen level in resuscitation by inserting them in the nose of either the patient or rescuer while performing Expired Air Resuscitation (Rescue Breathing). A flow rate of 3 liters/minute has been shown to be sufficient to increase blood oxygen levels by up to 85%. Higher flow rates did not increase oxygen levels and used up the oxygen supply more quickly.[4]

There are a number of different masks available. The concentration of oxygen delivered by these masks depends on how well the mask seals, the flow rate, the breathing rate of the patient and whether or not a resevoir bag is used in conjunction with the mask. A tight-sealing mask will minimize air dilution. If the flow rate is too low, carbon dioxide can build up in the mask, causing the patient to hyperventilate and greatly reducing the potential oxygen concentration. High flow rates will minimize carbon dioxide retention but will also use up the oxygen supply more rapidly. The oxygen concentration will fall if the patient's breathing rate increases.

Some masks are fitted with a venturi system to decrease the oxygen concentration. These are designed for use by chronic bronchitics and ensure that a fixed, low oxygen percentage is delivered. Such masks are generally not suitable for diving emergencies.

FIGURE 26.5
A loose-fitting oxygen therapy mask and binasal cannulae

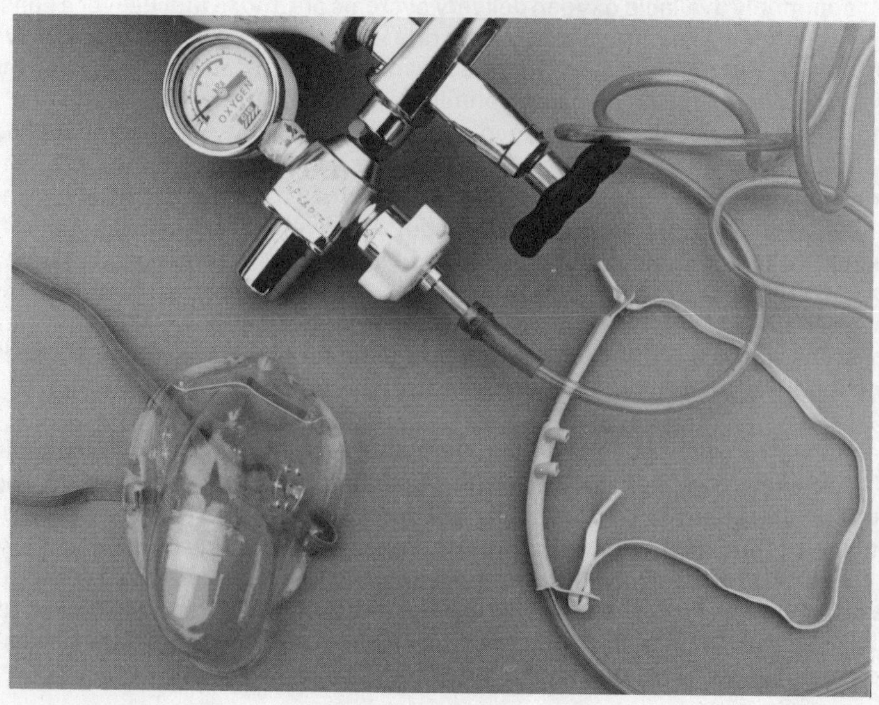

FIGURE 26.6
A Laerdal mask-valve-bag system with oxygen reservoir bag

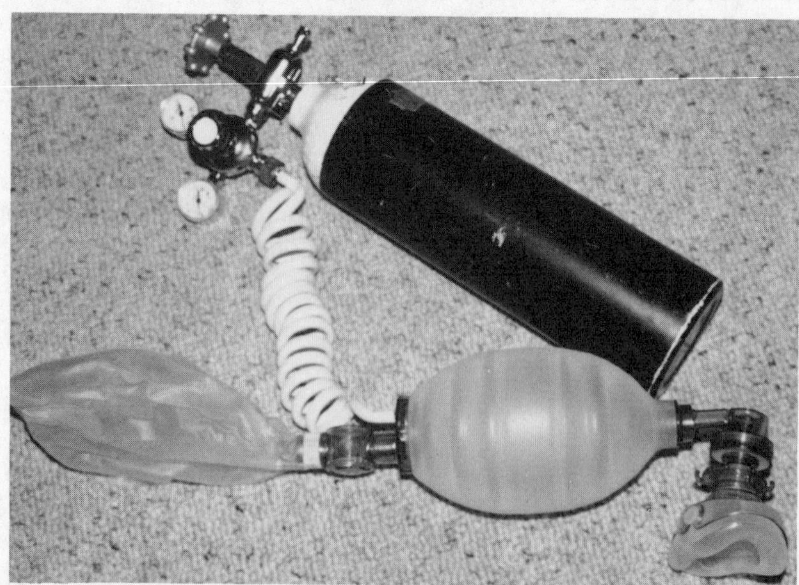

A commonly available mask is the Laerdal "Pocket Mask". These masks can give a good seal and, if provided with an oxygen inlet valve, these may give oxygen concentrations up to 80%, with a flow rate of 15 liters/minute, to a breathing patient.[5] They can also be used for Expired Air Resuscitation (Rescue Breathing) either with, or without, oxygen supplementation in situations when mouth-mouth or mouth-nose contact may not be acceptable due to facial injuries, poisons or infectious disease. It has been claimed that in oxygen assisted expired air resuscitation with a flow rate of 10 liters/minute, oxygen concentrations of up to 50% can be achieved.[5]

It must be emphasized that the oxygen concentrations quoted above are the maximum possible. It is likely that the oxygen concentrations actually achieved when some of this equipment is used by someone who is unfamiliar with it may be substantially lower.

FIGURE 26.7

Laerdal Pocket Mask with oxygen inlet and non-return valve

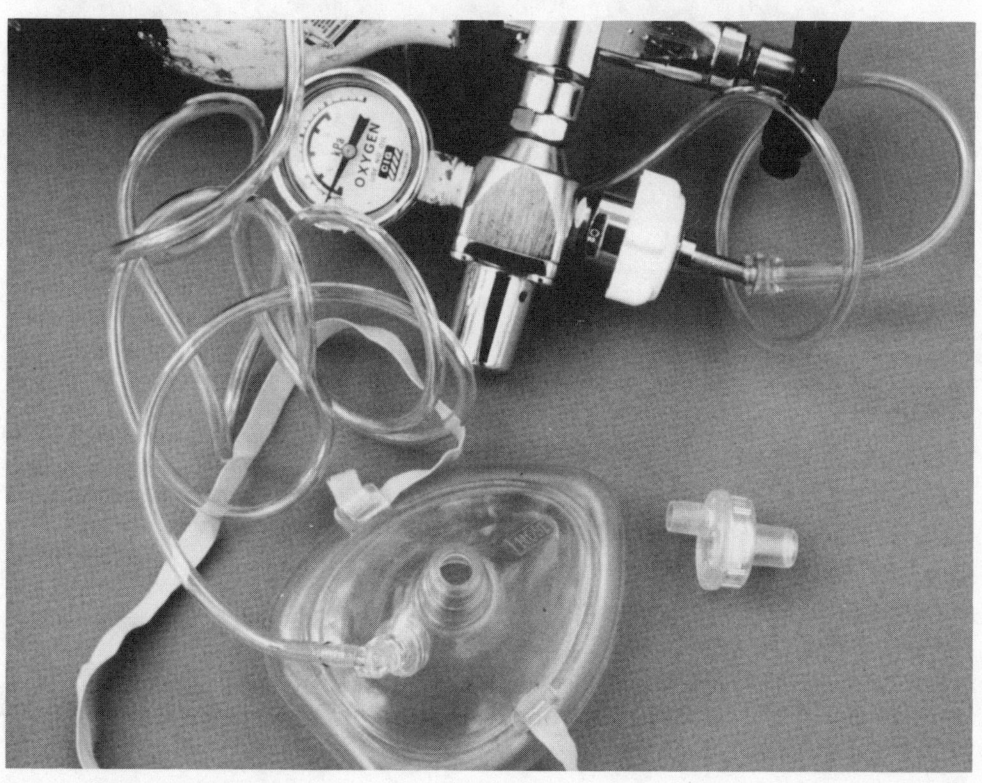

FIGURE 26.8
Oxygen-assisted Expired Air Resuscitation using a pocket mask

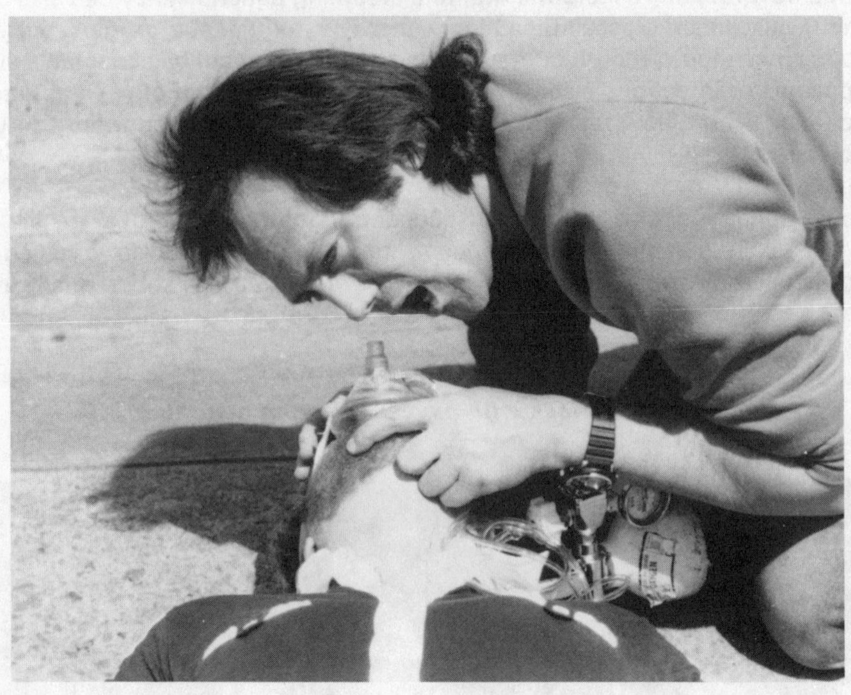

Warning:

Some oxygen equipment, especially the equipment used for oxygen resuscitation, is capable of delivering high pressure oxygen and, although it can be extremely effective in trained, skilled hands, it may be ineffectual, and potentially hazardous, if used incorrectly. It should never be used by those untrained in its use.

PLACES TO OBTAIN OXYGEN EQUIPMENT IN AN EMERGENCY

If oxygen equipment is not available at the dive site it can often be found nearby. If suitable oxygen equipment can be obtained without delaying the subsequent treatment, it might prove to be beneficial.

The following places might have a supply of *medical* oxygen:

Hospitals, doctor's surgeries, dentists, veterinarians, ambulance stations, fire stations, public swimming pools, schools, life-saving clubs, dive shops, airports.

SUMMARY

* Body cells cannot survive long without oxygen. Brain cells will die off in minutes if starved of oxygen.

* Oxygen is toxic when breathed at partial pressures greater than 0.6 ATA. The degree of toxicity depend on the partial pressure and the length of exposure.

* Pulmonary oxygen toxicity occurs when oxygen is breathed at pressures greater than 0.6 ATA for prolonged periods. Coughing, wheezing and shortness of breath may occur.

* Acute oxygen toxicity can occur when oxygen partial pressures of more than 1.6 ATA are breathed, even for short periods. This affects the brain and often results in convulsions.

* A recreational diver who adheres to safe sport diving procedures should not, normally, be at risk of oxygen toxicity.

* When oxygen is breathed at higher than normal partial pressures, more will dissolve in the plasma. This has many benefits for the first aid and treatment of a number of diving accidents.

* Breathing 100% oxygen:
  - contains no inert gas (e.g. nitrogen)
  - washes out dissolved nitrogen and nitrogen in bubbles
  - improves tissue oxygenation
  - reduces respiratory distress
  - reduces shock

* Oxygen should be given as soon as possible to gain the maximum benefit.

* A diver must be thoroughly familiar with any oxygen equipment that he may use.

* Near 100% oxygen can only be given with a demand valve and appropriate tight-sealing oro-nasal mask, or via a regulator mouth-piece, and sealing the patient's nose.

* Constant flow systems are not nearly as effective as demand systems for most diving injuries, but are useful in treating shock and for giving oxygen-enriched expired air resuscitation.

Equipment care and maintenance

* Keep oxygen equipment clean, dry and in a safe location. Never allow oil, grease or other flammable substances to come into contact with the equipment.

* Store in a well-ventilated area, well away from sources of heat and combustible materials.

* Always ensure that the cylinder is full, and turned off, before storing. Always depressurize the regulator before storing.

* Check the contents and functioning of the equipment regularly.

* Thoroughly wash, disinfect and dry the mask and tubing after use. Wash in warm water with mild detergent, then soak in a mild disinfectant solution before rinsing and thoroughly drying.

Rules for using oxygen

When administering oxygen it is important to:

* Ensure that the area is well ventilated and that there is nothing highly combustible, or burning, in the immediate vicinity (This includes cigarettes, boat fuel and a running boat engine or compressor).

* Carefully record the periods of oxygen breathing.

* Carefully record the patient's response to oxygen. If a bad response to oxygen occurs, ensure that the diver breathes air for 15 minutes before oxygen is tried again.

* If the appropriate recompression facility requires it, ensure that the patient breathes air for 5 minutes after each 25 minutes on oxygen *(unless his condition deteriorates when taken off oxygen).*

* Divers should generally restrict oxygen administration to a diver suffering from a diving-related problem unless appropriately trained.

Remember:

The breathing of oxygen is a first aid measure and must never be substituted for the recompression required for decompression sickness and arterial gas embolism, regardless of the response.

REFERENCES

1. Betts, J. (1985), "Oxygen Onus". *Diver*; 30 (10): 11.

2. Acott, C. (1985), "Oxygen Therapy". *Skindiving*; 16 (1): 22-26.

3. Acott, C., personal communication.

4. Komesaroff, D. (1980), "The Use of Bi-Nasal Oxygen Cannulae in Expired Air Resuscitation". Technical Committee Research Project, The Royal Life Saving Society of Australia.

5. Laerdal Medical, "Pocket Mask - Directions for Use".

OTHER SOURCES

Airdive Equipment P/L. (1986), "Regulators used with pure oxygen". Engineering Bulletin No. 137, Melbourne.

British Sub-Aqua Club, "Safety and Rescue for Divers". Stanley Paul, London.

Clark, J. (1981), "Oxygen Poisoning". In: *Hyperbaric and Undersea Medicine*, Medical Seminars Inc., California.

Clark, J. (1982), "Oxygen Toxicity". In: *The Physiology and Medicine of Diving, 3rd edition*, Bennett, P. and Elliott. D. (eds), Best Publishing Co., California: 200-238.

Corry, J. (1985), "Oxygen's Role in Dive Accident Management". *NDA News*; Nov/Dec: 31.

Corry, J. (1986), "Diver Rescue Management". *Proceedings of the Diving Officers' Conference*, BS-AC, London.

Davies, T. (1986), "Oxygen to the Rescue". *Diver*; 31 (5): 16-17.

Davis, J. and Youngblood, D. (1981), "Definitive Treatment of Decompression Sickness and Arterial Gas Embolism". In: *Hyperbaric and Undersea Medicine*, Medical Seminars Inc., California.

Davis, J. (1981), "Hyperbaric Oxygen Therapy: Applications in Clinical Practice". In: *Hyperbaric and Undersea Medicine*, Medical Seminars Inc., California.

Davis, J. and Elliott. D. (1983), "Treatment of the Decompression Disorders". In: *The Physiology and Medicine of Diving, 3rd edition*, Bennett, P. and Elliott. D. (eds), Best Publishing Co., California: 473-487.

Dick, A. (1985), "Oxygen and Diving Accidents". *Alert Diver*; 2 (1).

Dovenbarger, J. (1988), "Oxygen Use in Dive Accidents". *Alert Diver*; 4 (2).

Edmonds, C., Lowry, C. and Pennefather, J. (1981), "Diving and Subaquatic Medicine", 2nd edition. Diving Medical Center, Sydney.

Knight, J., personal communications.

Taylor, L. (1986), "Rx: Oxygen - The Legal Issues". *Alert Diver*; 2 (5).

Taylor, L. (1989), "A Diver's Guide to Oxygen Therapy - Part 1". *Sources*; 1 (2): 30-35.

Taylor, L. (1989), "A Diver's Guide to Oxygen Therapy - Part 2". *Sources*; 1 (3): 72-74.

Towse, J. (1985), "Oxygen First Aid in Suspected Bends Incidents". *Subaqua Scene*; 67: 10.

RECOMMENDED FURTHER READING

Acott, C. (1985), "Oxygen Therapy". *Skindiving*; 16 (1): 22-26.

Betts, J. (1985), "Oxygen Onus". *Diver*; 30 (10): 11.

Corry, J. (1986), "Diver Rescue Management". *Proceedings of the Diving Officers' Conference*, BS-AC, London.

Dovenbarger, J. (1988), "Oxygen Use in Dive Accidents". *Alert Diver*; 4 (2).

Taylor, L. (1986), "Rx: Oxygen - The Legal Issues". *Alert Diver*; 2 (5).

Taylor, L. (1989), "A Diver's Guide to Oxygen Therapy - Part 1". *Sources*; 1 (2): 30-35.

Taylor, L. (1989), "A Diver's Guide to Oxygen Therapy - Part 2". *Sources*; 1 (3): 72-74.

CHAPTER 27

EMERGENCY IN WATER RECOMPRESSION USING OXYGEN

Over the years various procedures were developed to treat divers who had contracted decompression sickness in areas remote from recompression facilities. Some of these procedures involved returning the diver to the water, breathing air. The injured diver would descend to depth and, then, very gradually, return to the surface. The idea of the treatment was to use the pressure of the water (in the absence of a pressure chamber) to compress the bubbles within the diver's body. It was hoped that, eventually, sufficient gas would diffuse from the bubbles to allow the diver to re-surface without symptoms. Even relatively recently there have been reports of divers with symptoms of bends redescending to complete omitted or extra decompression in an effort to eliminate the symptoms.[1,2,3]

Occasionally some of these treatments appeared to be successful, however, on other occasions there were disastrous consequences with divers and, at times, their attendants surfacing with serious decompression sickness.

Some treatments involved the patient and their attendant descending to depths up to 165 ft (50 m) and remaining submerged for periods of five hours or longer. These types of profiles were, obviously, riddled with potential problems.

The depth required posed problems for both the patient and the attendant. Nitrogen narcosis could be a hindrance and consequent danger, and the compression of the wetsuit promoted hypothermia. Since the treatment took many hours, weather conditions could easily deteriorate, the seas could rise and the advent of night could further jeopardize the safety of the divers and surface attendants. Enormous quantities of air were required and, if the air supply ran out, the divers would be forced to surface prematurely. If the treatment was aborted prematurely, both the patient and attendant faced the possibility of serious decompression sickness.

Due to the many hazards associated with recompressing a sick diver in the water, breathing air, and because of the persistent need for some form of emergency recompression treatment for divers who contracted bends in remote areas, Dr. Carl Edmonds, then at the Royal Australian Navy School of Underwater Medicine, developed an alternative to this treatment.[4]

The Edmonds Procedure

This procedure is described only to provide an insight into the physical and physiological concepts involved, and not to encourage the reader to attempt to carry out such a procedure. ***It is an emergency procedure available only to appropriately trained and equipped personnel and, even then, only under exceptional circumstances.***

By substituting oxygen for air as the breathing gas, the depth and time involved in recompressing a diver in the water could be dramatically reduced. It is necessary to return the diver to only 30 ft (9 m) ***(any deeper would introduce the possibility of acute oxygen toxicity),*** and the overall treatment is reduced to approximately three hours.

The benefits of using oxygen, rather than air, are manifold. No more nitrogen is introduced to the diver's body, and the excess nitrogen already present is drawn out far more rapidly due to the increased nitrogen pressure gradient. The possible problems of narcosis and decompression sickness in the attentants are eliminated, and the potential for hypothermia is reduced, although still not eliminated. If the treatment is aborted prematurely, the divers can ascend directly to the surface without the need for extra decompression. The shallower depth often enables the treatment to be executed in much more sheltered areas, thereby reducing the chance of the sea conditions becoming such a danger.

The advantages of breathing oxygen at 30 ft (9 m), rather than at the surface, include the compression of the offending bubbles and increased oxygenation. The bubbles are approximately halved in volume, whatever shape or size they are. The diameter of round bubbles is reduced by about 20 percent. The diameter of a long bubble in a blood vessel will not be reduced at all, but the length will be reduced, so reducing the frictional resistance and increasing the chances of the bubble moving on.[5] There is a large nitrogen pressure gradient out of the bubble. The higher partial pressure of oxygen also provides far greater oxygenation to hypoxic tissues within the diver's body.

The procedure has been used successfully on many occasions by trained diving medical personnel,[6] but still remains controversial. *Some doctors fear that the patient might still suffer from oxygen convulsions at 30 ft (9 m) depth* * *and, unless appropriate precautions are taken, a drowning or pulmonary barotrauma could result. If the diver were to accidentally descend deeper than 30 ft (9 m) while breathing 100% oxygen, the risk of oxygen convulsions would increase dramatically. (To avoid this possibility, the diver is attached to a measured line, attached to a stable platform on the surface). Some doctors are loathe to recompress a sick diver in the water in case some bubbles, trapped in his lungs, become small enough to pass through the lungs and into the arterial circulation, possibly causing an arterial gas embolism. Another fear is that hypothermia could present a problem unless adequate precautions are taken.*

* There was one report of a diver having oxygen convulsions while being treated underwater at 26 ft (8 m) on oxygen.[7] However, since the diver had aspirated water during the treatment, it has been argued that the tremors may have been due to salt water aspiration rather than oxygen toxicity.[8]

FIGURE 27.1
Diver rigged for in-water recompression using oxygen (Edmonds procedure)

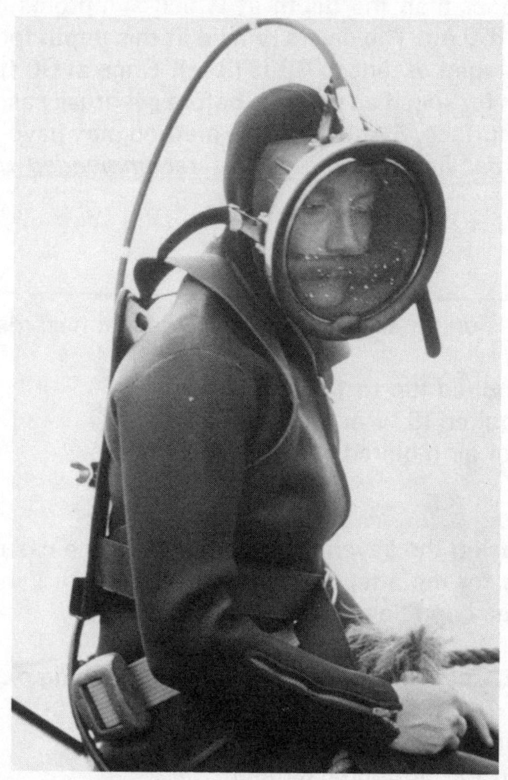

Photo courtesy Drs. J. Knight and J. Mannerheim

B. The U.S. Navy Procedure

The U.S. Navy have published an In-Water Oxygen Recompression procedure.[9] The Navy recommend that recompression in the water should be considered an option of last resort, to be used only when no recompression facility is on site and there is no prospect of reaching a recompression facility within 12 hours. *It is stated that, in divers with severe decompression sickness symptoms, or symptoms of arterial gas embolism, the risk of increased harm to the diver from in-water recompression probably outweighs any anticipated benefit. They suggest that, generally, these individuals should not be recompressed in the water, but should be kept at the surface on 100% oxygen, if available, and evacuated to a recompression facility, no matter what the delay.*

Although the U.S. Navy procedure utilizes a 100% oxygen re-breather, the technique is similar (but not identical) to the Edmonds procedure. The decompression seems to be roughly equivalent in both techniques.

Note:

Some Hawaiian diving fishermen have adopted an in-water recompression procedure which utilizes both air and oxygen breathing. The stricken diver and an attendant descend to a depth which is 30 ft (9 m) deeper than the depth at which symptoms disappear. The maximum allowable depth is 165 ft (50 m). The divers remain at this depth for a specified period before commencing a gradual, staged ascent to 30 ft (9 m). Once at 30 ft (9 m), the stricken diver switches to 100% oxygen for specified periods, before eventually ascending to the surface and breathing oxygen on the surface.[10] Although this method may have at times been successful, ***it is fraught with potential hazards and is not recommended under any circumstances whatsoever.***

SUMMARY

* In-water recompression on air carries many potential hazards which include:

- the depth required (up to 165 ft/50 m)
- the times required (5 hr or longer)
- the amount of air required
- hypothermia
- narcosis
- risk of increasing the severity of the bends in the casualty
- risk of bends for the attendant
- dangerous sea conditions

* Some of the benefits of in-water recompression breathing oxygen, rather than air, are:

- no nitrogen is added during the treatment
- large gradient for nitrogen excretion
- maximum depth reduced to 30 ft (9 m)
- time reduced to about 3 hours
- less air required for attendant
- risk of hypothermia reduced
- narcosis eliminated
- less chance of increasing the severity of the bend than if air is used
- minimal risks for attendant
- can abort treatment and surface at any stage
- easier to find sheltered areas of 30 ft (9 m) depth

* The major potential hazards of in water recompression using oxygen are:

- oxygen convulsions at depths approaching/beyond 33 ft (10 m)
- hypothermia
- possibility of bubbles, compressed by redescent, entering the arterial system

> ***WARNING:***
>
> ***Both of the in-water oxygen techniques described were not designed to be carried out by divers in the absence of supervision by appropriately trained and equipped diving medical personnel.*** **Obviously, if an emergency in-water oxygen treatment is being considered in the absence of an adequately accessible recompression chamber, its benefits must be carefully weighed against potential problems, and the procedure should be commenced only if all of the recommended equipment and appropriate diving and diving medical expertise and supervision are available, and conditions are suitable.**
>
> ***The Divers Alert Network (DAN), of the USA, strongly recommends that in-water recompression using either air or oxygen never be attempted.***

REFERENCES

1. Barker, A. (1982), "Charlie's $3 Million Dollar Dive". *Skindiving in Australia and the South Pacific*; 12 (2).

2. Allen, C. (1988), "Diving Incidents Report". Proceedings of Diving Officers' Conference, BS-AC, London.

3. Allen, C. (1989), "Diving Incidents Report". Proceedings of Diving Officers' Conference, BS-AC, London.

4. Edmonds, C., Lowry, C., and Pennefather, J. (1981), "Diving and Subaquatic Medicine", 2nd edition. Diving Medical Centre, Sydney.

5. Knight, J. (1987), "Diver Rescue, Decompression Sickness and its Treatment Underwater". *SPUMS Journal*; 17 (4): 147-154.

6. Edmonds, C., personal communication.

7. Anon, (1981), "Oxygen convulsion during in-water prophylactic treatment at 8 m". *SPUMS Journal*; 11 (Oct-Dec): 23.

8. Edmonds, C. (1982), "Salt water aspiration syndrome misdiagnosed as oxygen convulsions". *SPUMS Journal*; 12 (July-Sept): 14.

9. U.S. Navy (1985), U.S. Navy Diving Manual, Vol. 1, Air Diving. U.S. Government Printing Office.

10. Krassof, D. (1985), "Hawaiian Emergency Air/Oxygen Treatment for Decompression Sickness". *NAUI Australian News*; 5 (5).

OTHER SOURCES

Knight, J. (1984), "In-Water Oxygen Recompression Therapy for Decompression Sickness". *SPUMS Journal*; 14 (3):32-34.

Wilmshurst, P. (1988), "Re-Entry Decompression". *NDC Bulletin*; 12: 2.

SECTION 7

OTHER CONSIDERATIONS

CHAPTER 28

SOME EQUIPMENT CONSIDERATIONS

28.1 Regulator Performance at Depth

A good quality regulator is important for any diving, but it is especially important for deep diving. There are a number of exceptionally good regulators now available.

Three variables affect how, or whether, a regulator will deliver air - the depth, the cylinder pressure and the demand.

1. As depth increases it becomes more difficult for a regulator to deliver the denser air, and the resistance to exhalation also increases.

2. As the cylinder pressure drops it becomes more difficult for a regulator to deliver air. Some regulators can draw air from an almost empty tanks, whereas others will deliver no air from a cylinder at the same pressure.

3. The harder a diver works (i.e. the more rapid and deep the breathing), the greater the exhalation resistance.

A regulator to be used for deeper diving should, theoretically, have a balanced first stage (piston or diaphragm) and a good second stage, preferably servo or venturi (aspirate) assisted. One of the benefits of a balanced regulator is that its breathing characteristics should not alter as the air supply depletes. Most regulators with an unbalanced piston first stage will require more breathing effort as the tank pressure decreases. This is because the high pressure air provides one of the opening forces for the first stage valve. As the breathing effort increases, there will be an increase in fatigue and carbon dioxide levels in the diver, and a reduction in effective ventilation.

A high performance regulator should require little respiratory effort to smoothly provide for the diver's respiratory needs during any combination of work-load and depth. Combinations of deeper diving and strenuous activity can cause respiratory demands which exceed the capabilities of a regulator. Without a high performance regulator, a diver, working hard at depth, may be starved for air just when it is needed the most. In addition, a regulator used for deeper diving must have minimal resistance to exhalation to minimize the retention of exhaled carbon dioxide.

Regulator manufacturers all boast various characteristics of their products. Ultimately, it does not really matter whether or not a regulator is balanced or unbalanced, has a piston or a diaphragm first stage, or whether it is servo-assisted or otherwise. What really matters is how well the regulator actually performs under test and/or diving conditions.

In August 1987, the U.S. Navy published a report which detailed the results of tests that it had conducted on various regulators to determine which regulators would perform to their satisfaction at depths down to 198 fsw (60 msw).[1] The tests included evaluation of breathing resistance, work of breathing, first stage performance, performance in cold water and a "human factors openwater study". The Navy selected 51 regulators/systems that were readily available, and found only eight which met, or exceeded, their new performance criteria at 198 fsw. These, listed in alphabetical order, were:

1. AGA Divator Mk 11 FFM with U.S. Divers Royal first stage.
2. AGA Divator Mk 11 breathing valve with AGA mouthpiece and U.S. Divers Royal SL first stage.
3. POSEIDON Cyklon 5000
4. POSEIDON Odin
5. POSEIDON Thor
6. SCUBAPRO Mk X/G-250
7. U.S. Divers Conshelf SE-2
8. U.S. Divers Pro Diver

There were a number of other regulators that did not meet the Navy's new standards, but, that the Navy still considered to be quite safe. There were some regulators that could not be tested properly since they could not be adapted to the test criteria.

Any regulator, especially one used for deeper diving, should be fitted with a good "octopus" rig which works every time (not just any old spare second stage regulator). The only exception to this is if a "pony bottle" of some sort is used. There are various means of securing an octopus rig to oneself, but, the bottom line to them all is that the system must be readily accessible by the diver who is wearing it. An octopus regulator which is stored away in the pocket of the BC is often not readily accessible.

One octopus-breathing procedure dictates that the (primary) second stage regulator being used by the donor is the one handed to the out-of-air diver. If this is the preferred system, the primary second stage should have a longer hose to enable it to be passed more easily to the diver who is out of air. After giving his primary second stage to his buddy, the donor can then quickly locate his "octopus" and use it himself. This "octopus" regulator must be readily accessible to its wearer, who must be able to lift it to his mouth by a single movement of a single hand. It is best positioned somewhere between the wearer's mouth and nipples. It can be secured by means of an easily removable neck strap, or can be attached to a short line attached to an appropriate quick-release clip on the BC. The advantage of this system is that the out-of-air diver receives air very quickly, but, the disadvantage is that the donor will temporarily lose his air supply. Many divers prefer to retain the second stage they are breathing from, handing the "octopus" to their out-of-air buddy. In this case, the "octopus" should have a long hose and must be readily accessible to both its wearer and his buddy. It should be positioned somewhere between the mouth and the nipples of its wearer and attached by an easily (but not unwantedly) removed clip, rubber tie or equivalent. Some recent experiments in which novice divers conducted a variety of out-of-air drills, concluded that, where an "octopus" was used to assist the ascent, the divers much preferred to use the system in which the donor kept his primary second stage and handed his "octopus" to the out-of-air diver. However, the most popular system was the using of a Spare Air[R] cylinder.[2]

It has been shown that with low tank pressures and heavy breathing, such as might be encountered in a stressful situation, the work effort needed to obtain air can triple when an octopus regulator is being used.[3] This, in itself, may lead to dangerously high carbon dioxide levels which, at times, may cause unconsciousness. In addition, when two distressed divers breathe from the same regulator (i.e. one is on octopus), serious problems could develop if the regulator (including the octopus) is not properly maintained, or if it is inadequate. It is conceivable that, although there might be air in the cylinder, it might be not possible to withdraw it. These problems are magnified at depth.

28.2 Buoyancy Considerations

A wetsuit is made from neoprene, impregnated with tiny air bubbles. As the density of the soft rubber in neoprene is 1.1, almost all of the buoyancy provided by a wetsuit is provided by the air trapped in the neoprene. When a diver descends, these air bubbles are compressed, according to Boyle's Law, and buoyancy is lost. A wetsuit that provides 10 pounds (4.5 kg) of buoyancy at the surface will only provide about 5 pounds (2.3 kg) of buoyancy at 33 ft (10 m) where the ambient pressure is 2 ATA. At an ambient pressure of 5 ATA, which occurs at 132 ft (40 m), its buoyancy will be reduced to about 2 pounds (0.9 kg).

FIGURE 28.2.1
Compression of a wetsuit at depth

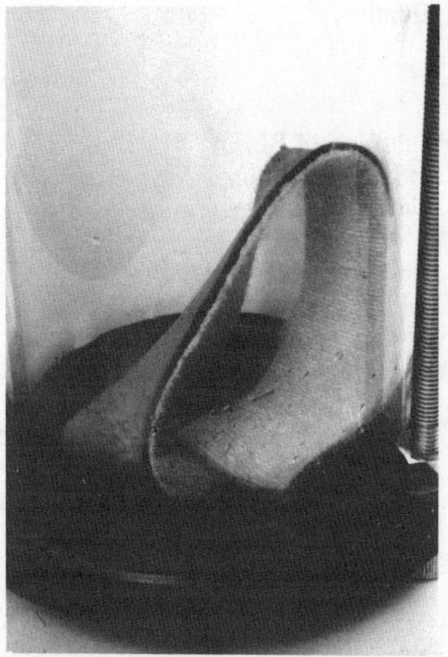

The above photos show a piece of 1/4 inch (7 mm) neoprene, initially at 1 ATA and then at 100 ft/30 m (4 ATA). Note how much the neoprene has compressed.

In addition to wetsuit compression, the gas spaces within a diver's body compress at depth, further reducing his buoyancy.

If a diver, wearing a 1/4 inch (7 mm) full wetsuit (and correctly-weighted on the surface), has not compensated for wetsuit compression by inflating his BC, he can be up to 15 pounds (7 kg) overweight on reaching 132 ft (40 m). The diver must, therefore, add quite a large amount of air to his BC to get the 15 pounds of lift needed to regain neutral buoyancy. It is desirable to add air to the BC during the descent, and *essential to be neutrally buoyant at the target depth*. At times, divers do forget to add air to their BC's at depth and, occasionally, the consequences are serious.

A series of experiments was conducted to determine the time required to inflate a BC at various depths.[4] The BC had an internal volume of approximately 18.2 liters (i.e 40 pounds lift) and the "reserve" pressure in the cylinder was 515 psi (35 Atm). The tests showed that it required about 57 seconds to inflate the BC at 100 ft (30 m) using the power inflator. It was not possible to completely inflate the BC at 100 ft if the diver continued to breathe from the regulator during the inflation, as the air supply ran out before the BC was fully inflated. The results are presented in Table 28.2.1.

TABLE 28.2.1

Time required for inflation of BC at depth with a power inflator attached to a tank at reserve pressure.

Depth:						
	fsw	0	33	66	99	132
	msw	0	10	20	30	40
Duration of BC inflation without simultaneous respiration		12	25	39	57	78
Duration of BC inflation with respiration at 15 breaths a minute		18	40	(50)*	**	**

(Times in seconds)

* Unable to fully inflate BC before tank emptied
** Tank emptied before adequate inflation of BC.

The results indicate that *if a diver has not attained neutral buoyancy at depth by adding air to his BC when there was plenty of air in the tank, he may not have sufficient air left to enable him to regain neutral buoyancy for the ascent.* This means that he may have to work hard and, therefore, use up a lot of air in order to ascend. **At times, especially if the diver is overweighted, he might have great difficulty ascending without ditching his weight-belt.**

This situation was tragically demonstrated in Australia in 1988. An inexperienced diver dived to 140 ft (42 m) on a wreck. After he failed to surface, searchers went in and located his body on the sea-bed. Despite there being almost 500 psi (34.5 atm) of air still in the victim's cylinder, the divers were unable to raise his body by inflating his BC, but, when his weight-belt was released, his body rapidly ascended to the surface. Later examination revealed that the victim was substantially overweighted on the surface and, with the loss of buoyancy from wet-suit compression, was probably more than 15 pounds (7 kg) overweighted at 140 ft. It would have been extremely difficult for the diver to ascend from the bottom without adding a lot of air to his BC (which he may not have been able to do) or without dropping his weight-belt. When his BC was later tested, it took 45 seconds to fully inflate at 140 ft, with 500 psi in the cylinder.

The lift provided by currently available BC's varies between about 11-55 pounds (5-25 kg). It is essential that a diver wears a BC with sufficient lift to enable him to maintain neutral buoyancy at the depths to which he dives. The ability to maintain neutral buoyancy at any stage during a dive enables a diver to consume less air and conserve energy, which becomes even more important during a deeper dive. A diver who must exert himself to maintain his position will increase his risk of bends. *Remember that a BC should also provide sufficient buoyancy to support the diver comfortably on the surface, should float an unconscious diver face upwards and should be highly visible on the surface.* How many of the current BC's fulfill all of these criteria?

A diver, especially one who is planning to do a deeper dive, should have just enough weight to be neutrally buoyant at 10 ft (3 m) with about 500 psi (34 Atm) of air in his cylinder, as at the end of the dive.* A diver carrying extra weight must work harder to move around.

A diver who is overweighted at depth, low on air, cannot inflate his BC and is having difficulty ascending, should ditch his weight-belt and make an emergency buoyant ascent, unless his buddy can quickly rectify, or overcome, the problem. The ascent rate can be slowed by venting air from the BC, if necessary, and extending the arms and legs and arching the back in a "spread-eagle" posture, as well as angling the fins to create the maximum drag. Exhalation should be increased substantially to avoid pulmonary barotrauma.

A diver who finds himself in a situation where he fears he may become unconscious during ascent, should remove his weight-belt and hold it in his hand and away from his body. If he becomes unconscious the belt will fall away and the diver should rise to the surface.

* Empty tanks have a positive buoyancy of 3 to 10 pounds (1.3-4.5 kg) depending on their composition and size. This extra buoyancy, if not accounted for, can affect a diver's ability to maintain the correct depth at a safety/ mandatory decompression stop.

REFERENCES

1. Morson, P. (1987), "Evaluation of Commercially Available Open Circuit SCUBA Regulators". Navy Experimental Diving Unit Report No. 8-87, Navy Experimental Diving Unit, Dept. of the Navy.

2. Griffiths, T. and Marchese-Ragona, S. (1988), "A Comparison of Five Selected Out-of-Air Response Techniques". *NAUI News*; Nov/Dec: 49-52.

3. "Technical Limitations of the Octopus". *Undercurrent*; 10 (7): 5-7, 1985.

4. Min, W. (1989), "Buoyancy and unnecessary death". *SPUMS Journal*; 19 (1): 12-17.

OTHER SOURCES

"U.S. Navy 1987 Tests of 51 Regulators". *Undercurrent*; 12 (11/12), 1-20, 1987.

RECOMMENDED FURTHER READING

Min, W. (1989), "Buoyancy and unnecessary death". *SPUMS Journal*; 19 (1): 12-17.

"U.S. Navy 1987 Tests of 51 Regulators". *Undercurrent*; 12 (11/12), 1-20, 1987.

"Technical Limitations of the Octopus". *Undercurrent*; 10 (7): 5-7, 1985.

CHAPTER 29

AIR SUPPLY CALCULATIONS

Calculation of Air Consumption

WHY CALCULATE AIR CONSUMPTION?

For most types of recreational diving it is unnecessary to calculate the amount of air expected to be consumed during the dive. Usually, divers simply monitor their contents gauge and leave the bottom with sufficient air to make a safe ascent to the surface. For dives within the No-Decompression Limits and with direct access to the surface, this is a completely satisfactory process.

Problems may arise, however, when direct access to the surface is not possible due to decompression requirements, because a diver has penetrated a wreck or a cavern, or because a task must be completed before surfacing.

Many cave divers overcome this problem by using the "One Third Rule". i.e. They swim into the cave until they have used one third of their air supply, at which stage they begin to come back. Their return to the entrance should also use one third of their supply, which leaves the final third of the tank as a reserve in the event of an emergency. This has proven to be a fairly safe and effective practice for this type of diving.

When planning to carry out a particular underwater task such as a salvage operation, it is sensible practice to estimate the air requirements in advance so that the task does not have to be aborted due to exhaustion of the air supply.

If decompression stop diving is planned, it is <u>essential</u> to ensure that there will be enough air available to complete the necessary decompression stops. On too many occasions divers have failed to complete their stops because their air supply has run out, and a significant number have suffered from decompression sickness as a result.

These situations can generally be avoided by calculating the anticipated air requirements before the dive and ensuring that enough air is available to meet these requirements.

There are a number of useful products available designed to avoid, or simplify, the calculations necessary to determine a diver's likely air consumption. However, it is sometimes an advantage to know how to calculate air consumption and supply considerations from first principles. A number of these techniques are presented in this chapter.

> ***Warning:***
>
> ***Before relying on calculations such as these to determine air demand and/or supply for any dive during which the diver cannot ascend directly to the surface at any stage, a diver must first master the calculations and then test their accuracy and suitablity during dives which allow direct access to the surface throughout.***

RESPIRATORY MINUTE VOLUME (RMV)

In order to calculate the air consumption we must first understand the following term:

The "Respiratory Minute Volume" (RMV) is the amount of air consumed in one minute on the surface.

RMV's vary from diver to diver and a diver's own RMV changes due to variations in his breathing rate. If we are unfit, cold and/or anxious we breathe more than when fit, comfortable and/or relaxed. When swimming against a current we breathe more than when we drift with it. Many other factors affect our breathing rate and, consequently, RMV, and must be considered when calculating the anticipated air consumption for a dive.

At rest, a tidal volume of 500 ml and a breathing rate of 12 breaths/minute provides an RMV of 6 liters/minute. Slow walking requires an RMV of about 15 l/minute, and to swim at a comfortable speed of 0.8 to 1 knot requires approximately 28 l/minute (1 cu. ft/minute).

TABLE 29.1

Activity level and Respiratory Minute Volume

Activity	RMV l.	RMV cu. ft.
bed rest	6	0.21
sitting quietly	7	0.25
walking (2 mph)	16	0.57
running (8 mph)	50	1.80
slow SCUBA swim (0.5 knot)	18	0.64
average SCUBA swim (0.85 knot)	28	1.0
fast SCUBA swim (1 knot)	40	1.4
peak swimming (1.2-1.4 knots)	60-75	2.1-2.7

The above figures are averages and vary from diver to diver and from time to time for a particular diver. Factors such as cold and anxiety may increase these rates considerably.

Under normal comfortable diving conditions, an experienced diver's RMV would generally lie between 14-28 l/minute (0.5 to 1 cu.ft/minute), but can increase to more than three times the normal rate if the diver is under stress or is exerting himself.

Since, in the USA, many contents gauges are calibrated in pounds per square inch (psi), divers RMV's are often expressed in psi/minute, rather than liters/minute or cubic feet/ minute. However, *it is important to realize that, with SCUBA divers, an RMV measured in psi/minute (or other pressure/time units) will vary with a change in cylinder size. The only true measures of breathing rate are volume/time units such as liters/minute or cu. ft/minute.*

CALCULATING THE EXPECTED AIR CONSUMPTION DURING A DIVE FROM FIRST PRINCIPLES

Think about the following question: If a particular diver takes one hour to empty his tank on the surface, approximately how long would it take him to empty it at a depth of 33 ft (10 m) underwater?

It depends on a couple of factors. Firstly, we'll assume that his breathing rate is the same in both situations.

The tank would last about one half of the time (1/2 hour) at 33 ft (10 m). The diver will use up twice as much air with each breath at that depth, because the air must be twice as dense (twice the pressure) in order to expand the diver's lungs to their normal volume. If the diver was at 66 ft (20 m), where the ambient pressure is 3 ATA, he would need three times the amount of surface air in each breath, and the tank would last about 20 minutes.

It becomes obvious that the amount of air consumed depends on the ambient pressure. If the diver is exerting himself his breathing rate would increase and more air would be used. The longer the diver is submerged, the more the air consumed.

It can now be seen that the amount of air consumed during a dive is dependent on the combination of three factors:

The ambient pressure (the depth of the dive), the amount of air breathed in each minute (RMV) and the number of minutes spent submerged. This can be expressed as follows:

Air Consumed = Pressure x Time x Respiratory Minute Volume

* If the ambient pressure is in ATA, the time in minutes and the RMV in psi per minute (psi/min), the air consumed will be calculated in psi.

* If the ambient pressure is in ATA, the time in minutes and the RMV in cubic feet per minute (cu.ft/min), the air consumed will be calculated in cubic feet.

* If the ambient pressure is in ATA, the time in minutes and the RMV in liters per minute (l/min), the air consumed will be calculated in liters.

* If the ambient pressure is in ATA, the time in minutes and the RMV in atmospheres per minute (atm/min), the air consumed will be calculated in atmospheres.

* If the ambient pressure is in ATA, the time in minutes and the RMV in bars per minute (bar/min), the air consumed will be calculated in bars.

METHOD 1

The simplest and most conservative method for calculating the anticipated air consumption during a dive is achieved by assuming that the entire dive time (i.e. descent, time on bottom, ascent and decompression stop time if applicable) is spent at the maximum depth. This method generally over-estimates the air requirement as long as the diver's RMV does not increase greatly.

The following examples illustrate this method:

Example 1.

Calculate the amount of air expected to be consumed (in psi/min) by a diver, whose RMV is 30 psi/min, if she is planning a no-decompression stop dive to 66 ft (20 m) for a bottom time of 25 minutes.

The total dive time, $T = 25_{\text{(bottom time)}} + 2_{\text{(ascent time at about 30 ft/min)}} = 27$ minutes.

$$AC_{(psi)} = P_{(ATA)}{}^{*} \times T_{(min)} \times RMV_{(psi/min)}$$

$$= 3 \times 27 \times 30 = 2430 \text{ psi}$$

Example 2.

A diver plans to dive to 100 ft (30 m) for a bottom time of 20 minutes. Calculate the anticipated air consumption (in psi) if his RMV is 25 psi/min and if he plans a safety stop of 3 minutes at 10 ft (3 m).

$$T = 20_{\text{(bottom time)}} + 3_{\text{(ascent)}} + 3_{\text{(safety stop)}}$$

$$= 26 \text{ minutes.}$$

$$AC = P \times T \times RMV = 4 \times 26 \times 25 = 2600 \text{ psi}$$

* The following formula can be used to convert the depth, in feet or metres, to ambient pressure, in atmospheres absolute:

$$P_{ATA} = \frac{D' + 33}{33} \quad \text{or} \quad P_{ATA} = \frac{Dm + 10}{10}$$

Example 3.

Calculate the amount of air expected to be consumed (in cu. ft) by a diver, whose RMV is 0.5 cu. ft/min, if he is planning a no-decompression stop dive to 120 ft (36 m) for a bottom time of 10 minutes.

The total dive time, $T = 10_{(\text{bottom time})} + 4_{(\text{ascent time})} = 14$ minutes.

$$AC_{(\text{cu.ft})} = P_{(\text{ATA})} \times T_{(\text{min})} \times RMV_{(\text{cu.ft/min})}$$

$$= 4.6 \times 14 \times 0.5 = 32.2 \text{ cu. ft}$$

Example 4.

Calculate the amount of air expected to be consumed (in liters) by a diver, whose RMV is 20 l/min, if he is planning a no-decompression stop dive to 50 ft (15 m) for a bottom time of 40 minutes.

The total dive time, $T = 40_{(\text{bottom time})} + 2_{(\text{ascent time})} = 42$ minutes.

$$AC_{(\text{l})} = P_{(\text{ATA})} \times T_{(\text{min})} \times RMV_{(\text{l/min})}$$

$$= 2.5 \times 42 \times 20 = 2100 \text{ l}$$

Example 5.

Calculate the amount of air expected to be consumed (in atm) by a diver, whose RMV is 3 atm/min, if he is planning a no-decompression stop dive to 60 ft (18 m) for a bottom time of 20 minutes.

The total dive time, $T = 20_{(\text{bottom time})} + 2_{(\text{ascent time})} = 22$ minutes.

$$AC_{(\text{atm})} = P_{(\text{ATA})} \times T_{(\text{min})} \times RMV_{(\text{atm/min})}$$

$$= 2.8 \times 22 \times 3 = 185 \text{ atm}$$

Example 6.

Calculate the amount of air expected to be consumed (in bars) by a diver, whose RMV is 3 bar/min, if he is planning a no-decompression stop dive to 60 ft (18 m) for a bottom time of 20 minutes.

The total dive time, $T = 20_{(\text{bottom time})} + 2_{(\text{ascent time})} = 22$ minutes.

$$AC_{(bar)} = P_{(ATA)} \times T_{(min)} \times RMV_{(bar/min)}$$

$$= 2.8 \times 22 \times 3 = 185 \text{ bar}$$

METHOD 2

This method allows for the fact that most of the dive is not actually spent at the maximum pressure. During the descent and ascent the pressure varies between a minimum at the surface and a maximum at the greatest depth. During a decompression stop the pressure is less than at the maximum depth. The previous method calculates the air consumed during these portions of the dive at the maximum pressure, thereby overestimating the air required. However, by calculating the air consumed at the average pressure during the ascent* and at the actual pressure at any decompression stop, the accuracy of the computations can be improved.

Averaging the pressure for the ascent

Consider a diver diving to 66 ft (20 m). During the ascent the pressure changes between maximum of 3 ATA at the 66 ft (20 m) depth, to a minimum of 1 ATA at the surface. Therefore, the average pressure during the ascent (and descent) is found to be:

$$P_{ave} = \frac{1 + 3}{2} = 2 \text{ ATA}$$

and, in general, $P_{ave} = \dfrac{P_{minimum} + P_{maximum}}{2}$

By following the steps below we can now estimate more accurately the amount of air used by the diver in Example 2.

Step 1 **Calculate the air consumed during bottom time (AC_{bottom})**

$$AC_{bottom} = P_{maximum} \times t_{bottom} \times RMV$$

$$= 4 \times 20 \times 25 = 2000 \text{ psi}$$

Step 2 **Calculate the air consumed during ascent, (AC_{ascent})**

Here, we calculate the air needed to ascend directly to the surface at a rate of about 30 ft (9 m)/min.

Ascent time, t_{ascent} = maximum depth/30
= *100/30 = 3.3, say 4 min.*

* Some texts suggest that this averaging of pressure should be done both on descent and on ascent and it is true that this, at least theoretically, provides a slightly more accurate computation. However, the calculation is far simpler (and a bit safer) if the averaging is restricted to the ascent only. For rectangular dives the difference is only a few breaths of air. Example 8 indicates how the descent may be treated seperately.

Average pressure on ascent $= P_{ave} = \frac{1 + 4}{2} = 2.5$ ATA

$$\mathbf{AC_{ascent} = P_{ave} \times t_{ascent} \times RMV}$$

$$= 2.5 \times 4 \times 25 = 250 \text{ psi}$$

Step 3 **Calculate air consumed during any decompression stops (AC_{deco})**

Check the decompression requirements with the appropriate tables.

$$\mathbf{AC_{deco} = P_{deco} \times t_{deco} \times RMV}$$

When two stops are required the above calculation will have two parts.

In this case, using U.S. Navy Tables, no decompression stops are required, but, because the diver wishes to do a safety stop the air consumed while at the stop can be computed.

Pressure at 10 ft (3 m) stop, P_{10} = 1.3 ATA
Time at 10 ft stop, t_{10} = 3 min.
Air consumed at 10 ft stop, AC_{10} = *1.3 x 3 x 25 = 97.5 psi, say 98 psi*
Since this is the only stop, AC_{deco} = 98 psi

Step 4 **Calculate the total air consumption, AC_T**

$$\mathbf{AC_T = AC_{bottom} + AC_{ascent} + AC_{deco}}$$

$$= 2000 + 250 + 98 = 2348 \text{ psi}$$

Example 7.

A diver is planning a decompression stop dive (using DCIEM Tables) to 120 ft (36 m) for a bottom time of 20 minutes. If his RMV is 20 psi/minute, calculate his anticipated air consumption.

Step 1 $AC_{bottom} = P_{maximum} \times t_{bottom} \times RMV$

$$= 4.6 \times 20 \times 20 = 1840 \text{ psi}$$

Step 2 $AC_{ascent} = P_{ave} \times t_{ascent} \times RMV$

$P_{ave} = \frac{1 + 4.6}{2} = 2.8$ ATA, $t_{ascent} = 4$ min.

$AC_{ascent} = 2.8 \times 4 \times 20 = 224$ psi

Step 3 $AC_{deco} = P_{deco} \times t_{deco} \times RMV$

Using DCIEM Tables, a dive of 120 ft (36 m) for 20 minutes requires stops of 10 minutes at 20 ft (6 m) and 10 minutes at 10 ft (3 m).

AC_{20} = *1.6 x 10 x 20 = 320 psi*
AC_{10} = *1.3 x 10 x 20 = 260 psi*
Hence AC_{deco} = *320 + 260 = 580 psi*

Step 4 AC_T = $AC_{bottom} + AC_{ascent} + AC_{deco}$

= *1840 + 224 + 580 = 2644 psi*

Example 8.

A pair of divers have been commissioned to inspect the wall of the dam shown in Figure 29.1. Their plan is to enter the water at A, decend to B, at the maximum depth of 90 ft (27 m), swim across to C and, finally, ascend at D. They will swim at a rate of 50 ft (15 m)/minute and, while doing so, expect their RMV's to be 25 psi/min. If the divers follow the DCIEM Tables, how much air would each diver be expected to consume?

FIGURE 29.1
Dive profile for Example 8

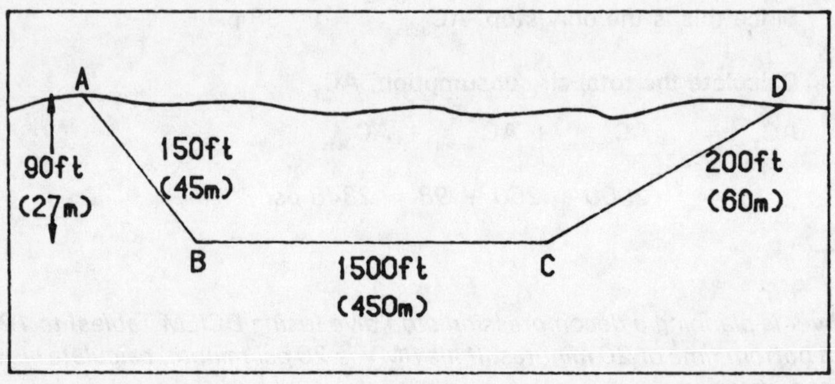

This calculation is done in four parts: The descent, the time at depth, the ascent and any decompression stop(s).

1. **The descent**

P_{ave} = $\frac{1 + 3.7}{2} = 2.4$ ATA

$t_{descent}$ = 3 min. (i.e. 150 ft at 50 ft/min)

$AC_{descent}$ = $P_{ave} \times t_{descent} \times RMV$

= 2.4 x 3 x 25 = 180 psi

2. At depth

P_{max} = 3.7 ATA

t_{depth} = 1500/50 = 30 min.

AC_{depth} = $P_{max} \times t_{depth} \times RMV$

= 3.7 x 30 x 25 = 2775 psi

3. The ascent

AC_{ascent} = $P_{ave} \times t_{ascent} \times RMV$

= 2.4 x 4 x 25 = 240 psi

4. The decompression

Look up 90 ft (27 m) for 3 + 30 + 4 = 37 minutes.* The decompression required is 10 minutes at 20 ft (6 m) and 10 minutes at 10 ft (3 m).

AC_{20} = *1.6 x 10 x 25 = 400 psi*

AC_{10} = *1.3 x 10 x 25 = 325 psi*

Hence AC_{deco} = *400 + 325 = 725 psi*

$\mathbf{AC_T}$ = $\mathbf{AC_{descent} + AC_{depth} + AC_{ascent} + AC_{deco}}$

= 180 + 2775 + 240 + 725 = 3920 psi

ADD A SAFETY MARGIN

Because of possible increases in the RMV, it is always advisable to add a safety margin to the expected air consumption. It is recommended that a margin of *at least* 20% extra should be added for general diving, and of at least 33% for penetration and/or decompression stop diving. Unfortunately, if a diver's RMV dramatically increases, this margin could be clearly inadequate. Remember, if your RMV triples for a part of the dive you will consume three times the amount of air expected to be consumed during that part of the dive. The only real solution to this potential problem is to ensure that there is adequate air to cover all eventualities. This is easily done when a surface supply system is used, but not so with SCUBA. The problem can be partially overcome by *always planning to surface with* ***plenty*** *of reserve air remaining in the tank.* This reserve air can be drawn upon if the calculated safety margin proves to be inadequate.

* Since the ascent rate (which is approx. 23 ft (7 m)/min) is slower than that utilized by the DCIEM Tables, it is wise to add the ascent time to the bottom time when calculating the decompression schedule.

Calculating the capacity of a cylinder

Most of us are aware that a 50 cubic foot cylinder is so named because it will hold around 50 cu. ft (i.e. 50 x 28 = 1400 l) of air when filled to its rated pressure. Similarly, an 80 cu. ft tank will hold around 80 cu. ft (2240 l) of air at its rated pressure, and so on.

Sometimes it is necessary to calculate approximately how much air is in a partially filled cylinder, and this can be achieved quite easily by using the following formula:

$$V = \frac{P\,Vr}{Pr} \quad \text{where}$$

V = current cylinder volume
P = current cylinder pressure
Vr = rated volume of full cylinder
Pr = rated pressure of full cylinder

Example 9.

Calculate the volume of air in a 90 cu. ft cylinder, rated at 3,000 psi, when the cylinder pressure is 500 psi.

$$V = \frac{P\,Vr}{Pr}$$

$$= 500 \times {}^{90}/_{3000} = 15 \text{ cu. ft } (15 \times 28 = 420 \text{ l})$$

Example 10.

Calculate the volume of air in a 50 cu. ft cylinder, rated at 2,475 psi, when the cylinder pressure is 2,000 psi.

$$V = \frac{P\,Vr}{Pr}$$

$$= 2000 \times {}^{50}/_{2475} = 40.4 \text{ cu. ft } (1131 \text{ l})$$

Example 11.

Calculate the volume of air in a 90 cu. ft cylinder, rated at 3,000 psi, when the contents gauge indicates 150 bar.

First convert bar to psi by multiplying by 14.5, so 150 bar is equal to 150 x 14.5 = 2175 psi.

$$V = \frac{P\,Vr}{Pr}$$

$$= 2175 \times {}^{50}/_{3000} = 36.3 \text{ cu. ft } (1016 \text{ l})$$

In some Countries (e.g. Australia and Britain), the water capacity of a cylinder is stamped on the neck of the cylinder, adjacent to the letters WC. The water capacity is a measure of the internal volume of the empty cylinder. It is measured by filling the empty cylinder with fresh water and measuring the weight of the water. Since one liter of fresh water weighs 2.2 pounds (1 kg), if the water contained in the cylinder weighs 22 pounds (10 kg) its volume is 10 liters and the cylinder will contain 10 liters of air at atmospheric pressure. The WC is either given in pounds and ounces, kilograms or liters.

If the water capacity of a cylinder is known, its contents can be calculated by using the following formula:

Cylinder capacity (liters) = **water capacity x gauge pressure** (l or kg) (atm or bar)

Example 12.

Calculate the volume of air in a cylinder, with a WC 10 liters, when the contents gauge indicates 150 bar.

Using CC = WC x GP
= 10 x 150 = 1500 liters

Since we are able to calculate the expected air consumption during a dive and the amount of air within a cylinder, it is now possible to estimate whether or not enough air is available with which to carry out a particular dive. Consider the following example:

Example 13.

A diver, whose RMV is 20 psi/min, is planning to dive to 100 ft (30 m) for 20 minutes bottom time, and do a safety stop of 3 minutes at 20 ft (6 m) before surfacing. Her tank (rated capacity = 79.87 cu. ft, rated pressure = 3000 psi) is filled to 2900 psi. Will she have enough air to safely complete the dive?

Step 1 **Calculate the expected air consumption**

AC_{bottom} = 4 x 20 x 20 = 1600 psi
AC_{ascent} = 2.5 x 3 x 20 = 150 psi
AC_{deco} = 1.6 x 3 x 20 = 96 psi
AC_T = 1600 + 150 + 96 = 1846 psi

Step 2 **Add a safety margin**

In this case I will add 20% extra. 20% of 1846 = 369 psi

Air required = 1846 + 369 + 500 = 2715 psi

(calculated)(safety margin)(reserve)

So, it appears that she has enough air to do the dive safely.

Calculating your own RMV

The best way to estimate your average RMV under diving conditions is to measure your air consumption during a dive. This can be done in the following way:

1. Descend to a known depth and record the reading on your contents gauge on arrival at that depth.

2. Remain at that depth for five minutes or longer and swim around as you would normally do during a dive.

3. Before you leave that depth record the time spent at that depth and the air contents on leaving the depth.

You now have all the information required to calculate your RMV. The following formula can now be used to determine your RMV, which can be calculated in liters/minute, cu. ft/minute, psi/minute or various other units, as required:

$$RMV = \frac{\text{Air consumed}}{\text{Pressure x Time}} = \frac{AC}{P \times T}$$

Calculating your RMV in psi/minute

To calculate the RMV in psi/minute the following units should be used in the formula:

AC must be in psi, *P* in ATA and *T* in minutes.

Example 14.

If you stayed at 33 ft (10 m) for 10 minutes and your contents gauge read 2800 psi on arrival and 2300 psi on leaving 33 ft:

AC = 2800 - 2300 = 500 psi
P = 2 ATA
T = 10 minutes

$$RMV = \frac{500}{2 \times 10} = 25 \text{ psi/minute}$$

Note: An RMV calculated in psi/min will alter if the size of cylinder is changed. The conversion formula described further on can be used to estimate the change in RMV.

Calculating your RMV in cu. ft/minute

To calculate the RMV in cu. ft/minute the following units should be used in the formula:

AC must be in cu. ft, *P* in ATA and *T* in minutes.

Example 14.

You stayed at 33 ft (10 m) for 10 minutes and your contents gauge read 2800 psi on arrival and 2200 psi on leaving 33 ft. Your tank is rated at 50 cu. ft at 3000 psi. Calculate your RMV in cu. ft/min.

Contents of tank *at* 2800 psi = $2800 \times \frac{50}{3000}$ = *46.7 cu. ft*

Contents of tank *at* 2200 psi = $2200 \times \frac{50}{3000}$ = *36.7 cu. ft*

AC = 46.7 - 36.7 = 10 cu. ft
P = 2 ATA
T = 10 minutes

RMV = $\frac{10}{2 \times 10}$ = 0.5 cu. ft/minute

Note: An RMV calculated in cu. ft/min will alter if the size of cylinder is changed. The conversion formula described further on can be used to estimate the change in RMV.

Calculating your RMV in liters/minute

To calculate the RMV in l/minute the following units should be used in the formula:

AC must be in liters, *P* in ATA and *T* in minutes.

Example 16.

You stayed at 40 ft (12 m) for 15 minutes and your contents gauge read 190 bar on arrival and 140 bar on leaving 40 ft. Your tank is rated at 72.4 cu. ft at 3000 psi (3000/14.5 = 207 bar). Calculate your RMV in l/min.

Contents of tank at rated pressure = 72.4 x 28 = 2027 *l*

Contents of tank *at* 190 bars = $2027 \times \frac{190}{207}$ = *1861 l*

Contents of tank *at* 140 bars = $2027 \times \frac{140}{207}$ = *1371 l*

AC = 1861 - 1371 = 490 *l*
P = 2.2 ATA
T = 15 minutes

RMV = $\frac{490}{2.2 \times 15}$ = 14.8 l/minute

Calculating your RMV in atm/minute

To calculate the RMV in atm/minute the following units should be used in the formula:

AC must be in atm, *P* in ATA and *T* in minutes.

Example 17.

You stayed at 40 ft (12 m) for 15 minutes and your contents gauge read 190 atm on arrival and 140 atm on leaving 40 ft. Calculate your RMV in atm/min.

AC = 190 - 140 = 50 atm
P = 2.2 ATA
T = 15 minutes

$$\text{RMV} = \frac{50}{2.2 \times 15} = 1.5 \text{ atm/minute}$$

Note: An RMV calculated in atm/min will alter if the size of cylinder is changed. The conversion formula described further on can be used to estimate the change in RMV.

Calculating your RMV in bar/minute

To calculate the RMV in bar/minute the following units should be used in the formula:

AC must be in bar, *P* in ATA and *T* in minutes.

Example 18.

You stayed at 40 ft (12 m) for 15 minutes and your contents gauge read 190 bar on arrival and 140 bar on leaving 40 ft. Calculate your RMV in bar/min.

AC = 190 - 140 = 50 bar
P = 2.2 ATA
T = 15 minutes

$$\text{RMV} = \frac{50}{2.2 \times 15} = 1.5 \text{ bar/minute}$$

Note: An RMV calculated in bar/min will alter if the size of cylinder is changed. The conversion formula described below can be used to estimate the change in RMV.

CONVERTING RMV FROM ONE CYLINDER TO ANOTHER

It is important to realize that an RMV calculated in psi/min (or another pressure/time unit) is dependent on the size of the cylinder being used. If a diver measures his RMV at 25 psi/min while using a 72 cu. ft cylinder, his RMV will be less than 25 psi/minute if using an 80 cu. ft cylinder and greater if using a 50 cu. ft cylinder. If a diver knows his RMV for a particular cylinder and wishes to estimate it for a different size cylinder, he may do so by multiplying his known RMV by a conversion factor. This conversion factor can be found in the following way:

To convert from tank A to tank B:

$$\text{Conversion factor} = \frac{\text{Rated capacity of A}}{\text{Rated capacity of B}} \times \frac{\text{rated press. of B}}{\text{rated press. of A}}$$

For example to convert from an 80 cu.ft tank (rated at 80.70) with a rated (i.e. fill or service pressure) pressure of 3000 psi to a 50 cu.ft tank (rated at 50.43) with a rated pressure of 3000 psi, the conversion factor is:

$$CF = \frac{80.70}{50.43} \times \frac{3000}{3000} = 1.6$$

If your RMV with the 80 cu.ft tank was measured at 30 psi/min it could be expected to change to 30 x 1.6 = 48 psi/min when using the 50 cu.ft tank.

CONVERTING RMV FROM ONE UNIT TO ANOTHER

If you know your RMV in a particular unit and wish to convert it to another unit, you may do so by using another conversion formula.

Converting RMV from psi/minute to cu. ft/minute

$$RMV_{cu.ft/min} = RMV_{psi/min} \times \frac{\text{tank capacity (cu. ft)}}{\text{tank pressure (psi)}}$$

Example 19.

Convert an RMV of 25 psi/minute to cu. ft/minute using an 80 cu. ft, 3000 psi cylinder.

$$RMV_{cu.ft/min} = 25 \times \frac{80}{3000} = 0.67$$

Converting RMV from atm/minute to l/minute

$$RMV_{l/min} = RMV_{atm/min} \times \frac{\text{tank capacity (l)}}{\text{tank pressure (atm)}}$$

Example 20.

Convert an RMV of 2 atm/minute to l/minute using a 2016 l, 204 atm cylinder.

$$RMV_{l/min} = 2 \times \frac{2016}{204} = 19.8$$

TABLE 29.2

Pressure conversion factors

1 atmosphere	=	14.7 pounds per square inch (psi)
	=	1.013 bar
	=	101 kilopascals (kPa)
	=	0.1 megapascals (MPa)
	=	760 millimetre mercury (mmHg)
	=	33.05 feet of sea water (fsw)
	=	33.95 feet of fresh water (ffw)
	=	10.07 metres of sea water (msw)
	=	10.34 metres of fresh water (mfw)

SUMMARY

* It is necessary to calculate air consumption requirements for dives requiring mandatory decompression stops, penetration dives and for dives involving a time-consuming task.

* Respiratory Minute Volume (RMV) is the amount of air consumed in one minute on the surface.

* Air consumed = Pressure (ATA) x Time (min) x RMV

* A safety margin of *at least* 20% extra should be added to the expected air consumption for general diving and a margin of of at least 33% for penetration and/or decompression stop diving.

* In addition to the safety margin, a diver must always plan to surface with plenty of reserve air in his tank.

SOURCES

British Sub-Aqua Club (1985), "Sport Diving". Stanley Paul, London.

Dueker, C. (1985), "SCUBA Diving in Safety and Health". Madison Publishing Associates, California.

Graver, D. (ed), "Advanced Diving - Technology and Techniques". NAUI, California.

Miller J. (ed) (1979), "NOAA Diving Manual", 2nd edit. United States Department of Commerce.

Tucker, W. (1980), "Diver's Handbook of Underwater Calculations". Cornell Maritime Press, Maryland.

U.S. Navy (1985), "U.S. Navy Diving Manual", Vol. 1., Air Diving, U.S. Government Printing Office, Washington.

RECOMMENDED FURTHER READING

Tucker, W. (1980), "Diver's Handbook of Underwater Calculations". Cornell Maritime Press, Maryland.

INDEX TO APPENDICES

A. U.S. Navy Standard Air Decompression Table.

B. Decompression Tables for Compressed Air Diving based on the DCIEM 1983 Decompression Model.

C. Royal Navy Decompression Tables - RN Table 11.

D. RNPL (1972) Decompression Tables.

E. Buehlmann High Altitude Table.

F. Kisman-Masurel (KM) Code for Bubble Grading.

G. U.S. Navy Recompression Therapy Tables 6 and 6A.

H. Royal Navy Recompression Therapy Table 62.

APPENDIX A

U.S. NAVY STANDARD AIR DECOMPRESSION TABLE

U.S. Navy Standard Air Decompression Table

Depth (feet)	Bottom time (min)	Time to first stop (min:sec)	Decompression stops (feet) 50	40	30	20	10	Total ascent (min:sec)	Repetitive group
40	200	0:00					0	0:40	★
(12 metres)	210	0:30					2	2:40	N
	230	0:30					7	7:40	N
	250	0:30					11	11:40	O
	270	0:30					15	15:40	O
	300	0:30					19	19:40	Z
	360	0:30					23	23:40	♦
	480	0:30					41	41:40	♦
	720	0:30					69	69:40	♦
50	100	0:00					0	0:50	★
(15 metres)	110	0:40					3	3:50	L
	120	0:40					5	5:50	M
	140	0:40					10	10:50	M
	160	0:40					21	21:50	N
	180	0:40					29	29:50	O
	200	0:40					35	35:50	O
	220	0:40					40	40:50	Z
	240	0:40					47	47:50	Z
60	60	0:00					0	1:00	★
(18 metres)	70	0:50					2	3:00	K
	80	0:50					7	8:00	L
	100	0:50					14	15:00	M
	120	0:50					26	27:00	N
	140	0:50					39	40:00	O
	160	0:50					48	49:00	Z
	180	0:50					56	57:00	Z
	200	0:40				1	69	71:00	Z

★ See No Decompression Table for repetitive groups.

♦ Repetitive Dives may not follow exceptional exposure dives.

NOTE: The figure in brackets is the depth in feet converted to metres.

U.S. Navy Standard Air Decompression Table

Depth (feet)	Bottom time (min)	Time to first stop (min:sec)	Decompression stops (feet) 50	40	30	20	10	Total ascent (min:sec)	Repet-itive group
60	240	0:40				2	79	82:00	♦
	360	0:40				20	119	140:00	♦
	480	0:40				44	148	193:00	♦
	720	0:40				78	187	266:00	♦
70	50	0:00					0	1:10	★
(21 metres)	60	1:00					8	9:10	K
	70	1:00					14	15:10	L
	80	1:00					18	19:10	M
	90	1:00					23	24:10	N
	100	1:00					33	34:10	N
	110	0:50				2	41	44:10	O
	120	0:50				4	47	52:10	O
	130	0:50				6	52	59:10	O
	140	0:50				8	56	65:10	Z
	150	0:50				9	61	71:10	Z
	160	0:50				13	72	86:10	Z
	170	0:50				19	79	99:10	Z
80	40	0:00					0	1:20	★
(24 metres)	50	1:10					10	11:20	K
	60	1:10					17	18:20	L
	70	1:10					23	24:20	M
	80	1:00				2	31	34:20	N
	90	1:00				7	39	47:20	N
	100	1:00				11	46	58:20	O
	110	1:00				13	53	67:20	O
	120	1:00				17	56	74:20	Z
	130	1:00				19	63	83:20	Z
	140	1:00				26	69	96:20	Z
	150	1:00				32	77	110:20	Z
	180	1:00				35	85	121:20	♦
	240	0:50			6	52	120	179:20	♦
	360	0:50			29	90	160	280:20	♦
	480	0:50			59	107	187	354:20	♦
	720	0:40		17	108	142	187	455:20	♦
90	30	0:00					0	1:30	★
(27 metres)	40	1:20					7	8:30	J

★ See No Decompression Table for repetitive groups.

♦ Repetitive Dives may not follow exceptional exposure dives.

U.S. Navy Standard Air Decompression Table

Depth (feet)	Bottom time (min)	Time to first stop (min:sec)	Decompression stops (feet) 50	40	30	20	10	Total ascent (min:sec)	Repetitive group
90 (27 metres)	50	1:20					18	19:30	L
	60	1:20					25	26:30	M
	70	1:10				7	30	38:30	N
	80	1:10				13	40	54:30	N
	90	1:10				18	48	67:30	O
	100	1:10				21	54	76:30	Z
	110	1:10				24	61	86:30	Z
	120	1:10				32	68	101:30	Z
	130	1:00			5	36	74	116:30	Z
100 (30 metres)	25	0:00					0	1:40	★
	30	1:30					3	4:40	I
	40	1:30					15	16:40	K
	50	1:20				2	24	27:40	L
	60	1:20				9	28	38:40	N
	70	1:20				17	39	57:40	O
	80	1:20				23	48	72:40	O
	90	1:10			3	23	57	84:40	Z
	100	1:10			7	23	66	97:40	Z
	110	1:10			10	34	72	117:40	Z
	120	1:10			12	41	78	132:40	Z
	180	1:00		1	29	53	118	202:40	◆
	240	1:00		14	42	84	142	283:40	◆
	360	0:50	2	42	73	111	187	416:40	◆
	480	0:50	21	61	91	142	187	503:40	◆
	720	0:50	55	106	122	142	187	613:40	◆
110 (33 metres)	20	0:00					0	1:50	★
	25	1:40					3	4:50	H
	30	1:40					7	8:50	J
	40	1:30				2	21	24:50	L
	50	1:30				8	26	35:50	M
	60	1:30				18	36	55:50	N
	70	1:20			1	23	48	73:50	O
	80	1:20			7	23	57	88:50	Z
	90	1:20			12	30	64	107:50	Z
	100	1:20			15	37	72	125:50	Z

★ See No Decompression Table for repetitive groups.

◆ Repetitive Dives may not follow exceptional exposure dives.

U.S. Navy Standard Air Decompression Table

Depth (feet)	Bottom time (min)	Time to first stop (min:sec)	Decompression stops (feet) 70	60	50	40	30	20	10	Total ascent (min:sec)	Repetitive group
120 (36 metres)	15	0:00							0	2:00	★
	20	1:50							2	4:00	H
	25	1:50							6	8:00	I
	30	1:50							14	16:00	J
	40	1:40						5	25	32:00	L
	50	1:40						15	31	48:00	N
	60	1:30					2	22	45	71:00	O
	70	1:30					9	23	55	89:00	O
	80	1:30					15	27	63	107:00	Z
	90	1:30						19	37	132:00	Z
	100	1:30					23	45	80	150:00	Z
	120	1:20				10	19	47	98	176:00	♦
	180	1:10			5	27	37	76	137	284:00	♦
	240	1:10			23	35	60	97	179	396:40	♦
	360	1:00		18	45	64	93	142	187	551:00	♦
	480	0:50	3	41	64	93	122	142	187	654:00	♦
	720	0:50	32	74	100	114	122	142	187	773:00	♦
130 (39 metres)	10	0:00							0	2:10	★
	15	2:00							1	3:10	F
	20	2:00							4	6:10	H
	25	2:00							10	12:10	J
	30	1:50						3	18	23:10	M
	40	1:50						10	25	37:10	N
	50	1:40					3	21	37	63:10	O
	60	1:40					9	23	52	86:10	Z
	70	1:40					16	24	61	103:10	Z
	80	1:30				3	19	35	72	131:10	Z
	90	1:30				8	19	45	80	154:10	Z
140 (42 metres)	10	0:00							0	2:20	★
	15	2:10							2	4:20	G
	20	2:10							6	8:20	I
	25	2:00						2	14	18:20	J
	30	2:00						5	21	28:20	K
	40	2:00					2	16	26	46:20	N
	50	1:50					6	24	44	76:20	O
	60	1:50					16	23	56	97:20	Z

★ See No Decompression Table for repetitive groups.

♦ Repetitive Dives may not follow exceptional exposure dives.

U.S. Navy Standard Air Decompression Table

Depth (feet)	Bottom time (min)	Time to first stop (min:sec)	Decompression stops (feet) 90	80	70	60	50	40	30	20	10	Total ascent (min:sec)	Repetitive group
140	70	1:40						4	19	32	68	125:20	Z
	80	1:40						10	23	41	79	155:20	Z
	90	1:30					2	14	18	42	88	166:20	◆
	120	1:30					12	14	36	56	120	240:20	◆
	180	1:20				10	26	32	54	94	168	386:20	◆
	240	1:10			8	28	34	50	78	124	187	511:20	◆
	360	1:00		9	32	42	64	84	122	142	187	684:20	◆
	480	1:00		31	44	59	100	114	122	142	187	801:20	◆
	720	0:50	16	56	88	97	100	114	122	142	187	924:20	◆
150	5	0:00									0	2:30	C
(45 metres)	10	2:20									1	3:30	E
	15	2:20									3	5:30	G
	20	2:10								2	7	11:30	H
	25	2:10								4	17	23:30	K
	30	2:10								8	24	34:30	L
	40	2:00							5	19	33	59:30	N
	50	2:00							12	23	51	88:30	O
	60	1:50						3	19	26	62	112:30	Z
	70	1:50						11	19	39	75	146:30	Z
	80	1:40					1	17	19	50	84	173:30	Z
160	5	0:00									0	2:40	D
(48 metres)	10	2:30									1	3:40	F
	15	2:20								1	4	7:40	H
	20	2:20								3	11	16:40	J
	25	2:20								7	20	29:40	K
	30	2:10							2	11	25	40:40	M
	40	2:10							7	23	39	71:40	N
	50	2:00						2	16	23	55	88:40	Z
	60	2:00						9	19	33	69	132:40	Z
	70	1:50					1	17	22	44	80	166:40	◆
170	5	0:00									0	2:50	D
(51 metres)	10	2:40									2	4:50	F
	15	2:30								2	5	9:50	H
	20	2:30								4	15	21:50	J
	25	2:20							2	7	23	34:50	L
	30	2:20							4	13	26	45:50	M
	40	2:10						1	10	23	45	81:50	O

★ See No Decompression Table for repetitive groups.

◆ Repetitive dives may not follow exceptional exposure dives.

U.S. Navy Standard Air Decompression Table

Depth (feet)	Bottom time (min)	Time to first stop (min:sec)	Decompression stops (feet) 110	100	90	80	70	60	50	40	30	20	10	Total ascent (min:sec)	Repetitive group
170	50	2:10								5	18	23	61	109:50	Z
(51 metres)	60	2:00							2	15	22	37	74	152:50	Z
	70	2:00							8	17	19	51	86	183:50	◆
	90	1:50						12	12	14	34	52	120	246:50	◆
	120	1:30				2	10	12	18	32	42	82	156	356:50	◆
	180	1:20			4	10	22	28	34	50	78	120	187	535:50	◆
	240	1:20			18	24	30	42	50	70	116	142	187	681:50	◆
	360	1:10		22	34	40	52	60	98	114	122	142	187	873:50	◆
	480	1:00	14	40	42	56	91	97	100	114	122	142	187	1007:50	◆
180	5	0:00											0	3:00	D
(54 metres)	10	2:50											3	6:00	F
	15	2:40										3	6	12:00	I
	20	2:30									1	5	17	26:00	K
	25	2:30									3	10	24	40:00	L
	30	2:30									6	17	27	53:00	N
	40	2:20								3	14	23	50	93:00	O
	50	2:10							2	9	19	30	65	128:00	Z
	60	2:10							5	16	19	44	81	168:00	Z
190	5	0:00											0	3:10	D
(57 metres)	10	2:50									1		3	7:10	G
	15	2:50									4		7	14:10	I
	20	2:40							2		6		20	31:10	K
	25	2:40							5		11		25	44:10	M
	30	2:30					1		8		19		32	63:10	N
	40	2:30					8		14		23		55	103:10	O
	50	2:20			4		13		22		33		72	147:10	◆
	60	2:20			10		17		19		50		84	183:10	◆

Depth (feet)	Bottom time (min)	Time to first stop (min:sec)	Decompression stops (feet) 130	120	110	100	90	80	70	60	50	40	30	20	10	Total ascent (min:sec)
200	5	3:10													1	4:20
(60 metres)	10	3:00												1	4	8:20
	15	2:50											1	4	10	18:20
	20	2:50											3	7	27	40:20

All dives below 200 ft (61 m) are exceptional exposure dives.

◆ Repetitive Dives may not follow exceptional exposure dives.

U.S. Navy Standard Air Decompression Table

Depth (feet)	Bottom time (min)	Time to first stop (min:sec)	Decompression stops (feet) 130	120	110	100	90	80	70	60	50	40	30	20	10	Total ascent (min:sec)
200	25	2:50											7	14	25	49:20
(61 metres)	30	2:40										2	9	22	37	73:20
	40	2:30									2	8	17	23	59	112:20
	50	2:30									6	16	22	39	75	161:20
	60	2:20								2	13	17	24	51	89	199:20
	90	1:50					1	10	10	12	12	30	38	74	134	324:20
	120	1:40				6	10	10	10	24	28	40	64	92	180	473:20
	180	1:20		1	10	10	18	24	24	42	48	70	106	142	187	685:20
	240	1:20		6	20	24	24	36	42	54	68	114	122	142	187	842:20
	360	1:10	12	22	36	40	44	56	82	98	100	114	122	142	187	1058:20
210	5	3:20													1	4:30
(64 metres)	10	3:10												2	4	9:30
	15	3:00											1	5	13	22:30
	20	3:00											4	10	23	40:30
	25	2:50										2	7	17	27	56:30
	30	2:50										4	9	24	41	81:30
	40	2:40									4	9	19	26	63	124:30
	50	2:30								1	9	17	19	45	80	174:30
220	5	3:30													2	5:40
(67 metres)	10	3:20												2	5	10:40
	15	3:10											2	5	16	26:40
	20	3:00										1	3	11	24	42:40
	25	3:00										3	8	19	33	66:40
	30	2:50									1	7	10	23	47	91:40
	40	2:50									6	12	22	29	68	140:40
	50	2:40								3	12	17	18	51	86	190:40
230	5	3:40													2	5:50
(70 metres)	10	3:20											1	2	6	12:50
	15	3:20											3	6	18	30:50
	20	3:10										2	5	12	26	48:50
	25	3:10										4	8	22	37	74:50
	30	3:00									2	8	12	23	51	99:50
	40	2:50								1	7	15	22	34	74	156:50
	50	2:50								5	14	16	24	51	89	202:50

All dives below 200 ft (61 m) are exceptional exposure dives.

Repetitive Dives may not follow exceptional exposure dives.

U.S. Navy Standard Air Decompression Table

Depth (feet)	Bottom time (min)	Time to first stop (min:sec)	Decompression stops (feet) 120	110	100	90	80	70	60	50	40	30	20	10	Total ascent (min:sec)
240	5	3:50												2	6:00
(73 metres)	10	3:30										1	3	6	14:00
	15	3:30										4	6	21	35:00
	20	3:20									3	6	15	25	53:00
	25	3:10								1	4	9	24	40	82:00
	30	3:10								4	8	15	22	56	109:00
	40	3:00							3	7	17	22	39	75	167:00
	50	2:50						1	8	15	16	29	51	94	218:00
250	5	3:50											1	2	7:10
(76 metres)	10	3:40										1	4	7	16:10
	15	3:30									1	4	7	22	38:10
	20	3:30									4	7	17	27	59:10
	25	3:20								2	7	10	24	45	92:10
	30	3:20								6	7	17	23	59	116:10
	40	3:10							5	9	17	19	45	79	178:10
	60	2:40				4	10	10	10	12	22	36	64	126	298:10
	90	2:10	8	10	10	10	10	10	28	28	44	68	98	186	514:10
260	5	4:00											1	2	7:20
(79 metres)	10	3:50										2	4	9	19:20
	15	3:40									2	4	10	22	42:40
	20	3:30								1	4	7	20	31	67:20
	25	3:30								3	8	11	23	50	99:20
	30	3:20							2	6	8	19	26	61	126:20
	40	3:10						1	6	11	16	19	49	84	190:20
270	5	4:10											1	3	8:30
(82 metres)	10	4:00										2	5	11	22:30
	15	3:50									3	4	11	24	46:30
	20	3:40								2	3	9	21	35	74:30
	25	3:30							2	3	8	13	23	53	106:30
	30	3:30							3	6	12	22	27	64	138:30
	40	3:20						5	6	11	17	22	51	83	204:30

All dives below 200 ft (61 m) are exceptional exposure dives.
Repetitive Dives may not follow exceptional exposure dives.

U.S. Navy Standard Air Decompression Table

Depth (feet)	Bottom time (min)	Time to first stop (min:sec)	Decompression stops (feet) 80	70	60	50	40	30	20	10	Total ascent (min:sec)
280	5	4:20							2	2	8:40
(85 metres)	10	4:00					1	2	5	13	25:40
	15	3:50				1	3	4	11	26	49:40
	20	3:50				3	4	8	23	39	81:40
	25	3:40			2	5	7	16	23	56	113:40
	30	3:30			3	7	13	22	30	70	150:40
	40	3:20	1	6	6	13	17	27	51	93	218:40
290	5	4:30							2	3	9:50
(88 metres)	10	4:10					1	3	5	16	29:50
	15	4:00				1	3	6	12	26	52:50
	20	4:00				3	7	9	23	43	89:50
	25	3:50			3	5	8	17	23	60	120:50
	30	3:40			5	6	16	22	36	72	162:50
	40	3:30	3	5	7	15	16	32	51	95	228:50

Depth (feet)	Bottom time (min)	Time to first stop (min:sec)													Total ascent (min:sec)
300	5	4:40											3	3	11:00
(91 metres)	10	4:20									1	3	6	17	32:00
	15	4:10								2	3	6	15	26	57:00
	20	4:00							2	3	7	10	23	47	97:00
	25	3:50						1	3	6	8	19	26	61	129:00
	30	3:50						2	5	7	17	27	39	75	172:00
	40	3:40					4	6	9	15	17	34	51	90	231:00
	60	3:00	4	10	10	10	10	10	14	28	32	50	90	187	460:00

All dives below 200 ft (61 m) are exceptional exposure dives.

Repetitive Dives may not follow exceptional exposure dives.

APPENDIX B

DECOMPRESSION TABLES FOR COMPRESSED AIR DIVING BASED ON THE DCIEM 1983 DECOMPRESSION MODEL

The Department of National Defence, Defence and Civil Institute of Environmental Medicine (DCIEM), and Universal Dive Techtronics, Inc. disclaim any and all responsibilities for the use of these tables and procedures.

Warning:

These tables have recently undergone a number of changes, some of which have been included as footnotes. More alterations may still occur before the tables are re-released in 1991. The tables are included here only for the purpose of comparison. Divers intending to use these tables must ensure that they obtain a current and complete set of tables and procedures.

CANADIAN FORCES AIR DIVING TABLE 1 (FEET)
STANDARD AIR

Depth (fsw)	Bottom Time (min)	Stop Times (min) at Different Depths (fsw)							Decom. Time (min)	Repet. Group
		70	60	50	40	30	20	10		
30	30	-	-	-	-	-	-	-	-	A
	60	-	-	-	-	-	-	-	-	C
	90	-	-	-	-	-	-	-	-	D
*	120	-	-	-	-	-	-	-	-	F
	150	-	-	-	-	-	-	-	-	G
	180	-	-	-	-	-	-	-	-	H
	380	-	-	-	-	-	-	-	-	
	390	-	-	-	-	-	-	7	7	
	400	-	-	-	-	-	-	10	10	
	420	-	-	-	-	-	-	14	14	
	450	-	-	-	-	-	-	19	19	
	480	-	-	-	-	-	-	23	23	
40	30	-	-	-	-	-	-	-	-	B
	60	-	-	-	-	-	-	-	-	D
	90	-	-	-	-	-	-	-	-	G
**	120	-	-	-	-	-	-	-	-	H
	150	-	-	-	-	-	-	-	-	J
	175	-	-	-	-	-	-	-	-	L
	190	-	-	-	-	-	-	10	10	
	200	-	-	-	-	-	-	14	14	
	210	-	-	-	-	-	-	18	18	
	220	-	-	-	-	-	-	22	22	
	240	-	-	-	-	-	-	28	28	
	270	-	-	-	-	-	-	38	38	
	300	-	-	-	-	-	-	48	48	
	330	-	-	-	-	-	-	57	57	
	360	-	-	-	-	-	-	66	66	

* NDL for 30 fsw changed to 300, RG = M
For BT = 330, stop at 10 fsw/3, RG = N
For BT = 360, stop at 10 fsw/5, RG = 0

** NDL for 40 fsw changed to 150, RG = J
For BT = 160, stop at 10 fsw/3, RG = K
For BT = 170, stop at 10 fsw/5, RG = L
For BT = 180, stop at 10 fsw/8, RG = M

CANADIAN FORCES AIR DIVING TABLE 1 (FEET)
STANDARD AIR

Depth (fsw)	Bottom Time (min)	Stop Times (min) at Different Depths (fsw)							Decom. Time (min)	Repet. Group
		70	60	50	40	30	20	10		
50	20	-	-	-	-	-	-	-	-	A
	30	-	-	-	-	-	-	-	-	C
	40	-	-	-	-	-	-	-	-	D
	50	-	-	-	-	-	-	-	-	E
	60	-	-	-	-	-	-	-	-	F
	75	-	-	-	-	-	-	-	-	G
*	100	-	-	-	-	-	-	6	6	I
	120	-	-	-	-	-	-	12	12	K
	130	-	-	-	-	-	-	18	18	L
	140	-	-	-	-	-	-	24	24	M
	150	-	-	-	-	-	-	29	29	
	160	-	-	-	-	-	-	33	33	
	170	-	-	-	-	-	-	38	38	
	180	-	-	-	-	-	-	43	43	
	200	-	-	-	-	-	-	53	53	
	220	-	-	-	-	-	-	63	63	
	240	-	-	-	-	-	-	74	74	
	260	-	-	-	-	-	-	86	86	
	280	-	-	-	-	-	-	97	97	
60	10	-	-	-	-	-	-	-	-	A
	20	-	-	-	-	-	-	-	-	B
	30	-	-	-	-	-	-	-	-	D
	40	-	-	-	-	-	-	-	-	E
	50	-	-	-	-	-	-	-	-	F
	60	-	-	-	-	-	-	5	5	G
	80	-	-	-	-	-	-	10	10	I
	90	-	-	-	-	-	-	19	19	J
	100	-	-	-	-	-	-	26	26	K
	110	-	-	-	-	-	-	32	32	L
	120	-	-	-	-	-	2	37	39	M
	130	-	-	-	-	-	2	43	45	
	140	-	-	-	-	-	3	49	52	
	150	-	-	-	-	-	3	55	58	
	160	-	-	-	-	-	4	62	66	
	170	-	-	-	-	-	4	70	74	
	180	-	-	-	-	-	5	77	82	
	190	-	-	-	-	-	5	85	90	
	200	-	-	-	-	-	11	90	101	
	210	-	-	-	-	-	15	96	111	
	220	-	-	-	-	-	19	102	121	
	230	-	-	-	-	-	23	108	131	
	240	-	-	-	-	-	27	114	141	

* After 50 fsw/20, RG = B (not A)

CANADIAN FORCES AIR DIVING TABLE 1 (FEET)
STANDARD AIR

Depth (fsw)	Bottom Time (min)	Stop Times (min) at Different Depths (fsw)							Decom. Time (min)	Repet. Group
		70	60	50	40	30	20	10		
70	10	-	-	-	-	-	-	-	-	A
	20	-	-	-	-	-	-	-	-	C
	25	-	-	-	-	-	-	-	-	D
	35	-	-	-	-	-	-	-	-	E
	40	-	-	-	-	-	-	5	5	F
	50	-	-	-	-	-	-	10	10	G
	60	-	-	-	-	-	2	11	13	H
	70	-	-	-	-	-	3	19	22	J
	80	-	-	-	-	-	4	27	31	K
	90	-	-	-	-	-	5	34	39	M
	100	-	-	-	-	-	6	41	47	N
	110	-	-	-	-	-	7	48	55	
	120	-	-	-	-	-	8	56	64	
	130	-	-	-	-	-	9	65	74	
	140	-	-	-	-	-	11	74	85	
	150	-	-	-	-	-	17	81	98	
	160	-	-	-	-	-	22	89	111	
	170	-	-	-	-	-	27	98	125	
	180	-	-	-	-	-	31	107	138	
	190	-	-	-	-	-	36	115	151	
	200	-	-	-	-	2	39	123	164	
80	10	-	-	-	-	-	-	-	-	A
	15	-	-	-	-	-	-	-	-	C
	20	-	-	-	-	-	-	-	-	D
	25	-	-	-	-	-	-	-	-	E
	30	-	-	-	-	-	-	6	6	F
	40	-	-	-	-	-	2	10	12	G
	50	-	-	-	-	-	4	12	16	H
	55	-	-	-	-	-	5	17	22	I
	60	-	-	-	-	-	6	22	28	J
	65	-	-	-	-	-	7	27	34	J
	70	-	-	-	-	-	8	31	39	K
	75	-	-	-	-	-	9	35	44	L
	80	-	-	-	-	-	9	40	49	M
	85	-	-	-	-	-	10	44	54	
	90	-	-	-	-	-	11	48	59	
	95	-	-	-	-	-	11	53	64	
	100	-	-	-	-	2	10	58	70	
	110	-	-	-	-	3	14	66	83	
	120	-	-	-	-	3	20	76	99	
	130	-	-	-	-	4	24	87	115	
	140	-	-	-	-	5	29	98	132	
	150	-	-	-	-	5	35	109	149	
	160	-	-	-	-	6	40	120	166	

CANADIAN FORCES AIR DIVING TABLE 1 (FEET)
STANDARD AIR

Depth (fsw)	Bottom Time (min)	Stop Times (min) at Different Depths (fsw)							Decom. Time (min)	Repet. Group
		70	60	50	40	30	20	10		
90	10	-	-	-	-	-	-	-	-	A
	15	-	-	-	-	-	-	-	-	C
	20	-	-	-	-	-	-	-	-	D
	25	-	-	-	-	-	-	8	8	E
	30	-	-	-	-	-	3	9	12	F
*	40	-	-	-	-	-	6	11	17	H
	45	-	-	-	-	-	7	16	23	I
	50	-	-	-	-	-	9	21	30	J
	55	-	-	-	-	-	10	27	37	K
	60	-	-	-	-	2	9	32	43	L
	65	-	-	-	-	3	9	37	49	
	70	-	-	-	-	4	9	42	55	
	75	-	-	-	-	4	10	47	61	
	80	-	-	-	-	5	10	53	68	
	85	-	-	-	-	5	11	59	75	
	90	-	-	-	-	6	15	62	83	
	95	-	-	-	-	6	18	68	92	
	100	-	-	-	-	7	21	73	101	
	110	-	-	-	-	8	26	87	121	
	120	-	-	-	-	8	33	101	142	
100	5	-	-	-	-	-	-	-	-	A
	10	-	-	-	-	-	-	-	-	B
	15	-	-	-	-	-	-	-	-	D
	20	-	-	-	-	-	-	8	8	E
	25	-	-	-	-	-	3	10	13	F
	30	-	-	-	-	-	6	10	16	G
	35	-	-	-	-	-	8	11	19	H
	40	-	-	-	-	-	9	18	27	I
	45	-	-	-	-	3	8	25	36	J
	50	-	-	-	-	4	9	30	43	K
	55	-	-	-	-	5	9	37	51	L
	60	-	-	-	-	6	9	43	58	
	65	-	-	-	-	7	10	48	65	
	70	-	-	-	-	8	10	55	73	
	75	-	-	-	-	8	15	59	82	
	80	-	-	-	-	9	18	65	92	
	85	-	-	-	2	8	22	71	103	
	90	-	-	-	2	8	25	79	114	
	95	-	-	-	3	8	29	87	127	
	100	-	-	-	3	9	32	95	139	
	105	-	-	-	4	8	36	104	152	
	110	-	-	-	4	9	39	112	164	

* After 90 fsw/10, RG = B (not A)

CANADIAN FORCES AIR DIVING TABLE 1 (FEET)
STANDARD AIR

Depth (fsw)	Bottom Time (min)	Stop Times (min) at Different Depths (fsw)							Decom. Time (min)	Repet. Group
		70	60	50	40	30	20	10		
110	5	-	-	-	-	-	-	-	-	A
	10	-	-	-	-	-	-	-	-	B
	12	-	-	-	-	-	-	-	-	C
	15	-	-	-	-	-	-	5	5	D
	20	-	-	-	-	-	3	9	12	F
	25	-	-	-	-	-	6	10	16	G
	30	-	-	-	-	-	9	11	20	H
	35	-	-	-	-	4	7	19	30	I
	40	-	-	-	-	5	8	26	39	J
	45	-	-	-	-	6	9	33	48	K
	50	-	-	-	-	8	9	39	56	M
	55	-	-	-	-	9	9	46	64	N
	60	-	-	-	3	7	11	53	74	
	65	-	-	-	3	8	16	58	85	
	70	-	-	-	4	8	20	64	96	
	75	-	-	-	5	8	23	73	109	
	80	-	-	-	5	8	28	81	122	
	85	-	-	-	6	8	32	91	137	
	90	-	-	-	6	9	35	101	151	
	95	-	-	-	7	9	40	111	167	
	100	-	-	-	7	10	44	120	181	
	105	-	-	-	8	13	46	129	196	
	110	-	-	-	8	16	50	136	210	
120	5	-	-	-	-	-	-	-	-	A
	10	-	-	-	-	-	-	-	-	C
	15	-	-	-	-	-	-	10	10	D
	20	-	-	-	-	-	6	9	15	F
*	25	-	-	-	-	-	9	11	20	G
	30	-	-	-	-	5	7	17	29	I
	35	-	-	-	-	6	9	25	40	J
	40	-	-	-	-	8	9	33	50	K
	45	-	-	-	3	7	9	41	60	M
	50	-	-	-	4	7	10	49	70	N
	55	-	-	-	5	7	15	54	81	
	60	-	-	-	6	8	19	61	94	
	65	-	-	-	7	8	23	70	108	
	70	-	-	-	7	9	27	80	123	
	75	-	-	2	6	9	32	91	140	
	80	-	-	3	6	9	37	103	158	
	85	-	-	3	7	10	41	114	175	
	90	-	-	3	7	14	44	124	192	
	95	-	-	4	7	16	49	134	210	
	100	-	-	4	7	20	53	142	226	

* After 120 fsw/20, stop at 20 fsw/5 and 10 fsw/10

CANADIAN FORCES AIR DIVING TABLE 1 (FEET)
STANDARD AIR

Depth (fsw)	Bottom Time (min)	Stop Times (min) at Different Depths (fsw)							Decom. Time (min)	Repet. Group
		70	60	50	40	30	20	10		
130	5	-	-	-	-	-	-	-	-	A
	8	-	-	-	-	-	-	-	-	B
	10	-	-	-	-	-	-	5	5	C
	15	-	-	-	-	-	4	9	13	E
	20	-	-	-	-	-	8	10	18	G
	25	-	-	-	-	5	7	12	24	H
	30	-	-	-	-	7	8	23	38	J
	35	-	-	-	3	6	9	32	50	K
	40	-	-	-	5	6	10	40	61	M
	45	-	-	-	6	7	10	50	73	N
	50	-	-	-	7	8	16	55	86	
	55	-	-	2	6	8	21	64	101	
	60	-	-	3	6	8	26	75	118	
	65	-	-	4	6	9	31	86	136	
	70	-	-	5	6	9	36	100	156	
	75	-	-	5	7	11	40	113	176	
	80	-	-	6	7	15	44	125	197	
	85	-	-	6	7	18	49	135	215	
	90	-	-	7	7	22	54	144	234	
140	7	-	-	-	-	-	-	-	-	B
	10	-	-	-	-	-	-	7	7	D
	15	-	-	-	-	-	6	9	15	F
	20	-	-	-	-	4	7	11	22	G
	25	-	-	-	-	7	8	19	34	I
	30	-	-	-	4	6	9	29	48	K
	35	-	-	-	6	6	10	39	61	L
	40	-	-	-	7	7	10	49	73	N
	45	-	-	3	6	7	17	56	89	O
	50	-	-	4	6	8	22	65	105	
	55	-	-	5	6	9	27	78	125	
	60	-	-	6	6	9	33	91	145	
	65	-	-	7	6	11	38	106	168	
	70	-	2	5	7	15	42	120	191	
	75	-	3	5	8	18	47	133	214	
	80	-	3	6	8	21	54	143	235	
	85	-	4	6	8	25	61	151	255	
	90	-	4	6	8	30	68	157	273	

CANADIAN FORCES AIR DIVING TABLE 1 (FEET)
STANDARD AIR

Depth (fsw)	Bottom Time (min)	Stop Times (min) at Different Depths (fsw)							Decom. Time (min)	Repet. Group
		70	60	50	40	30	20	10		
150	7	-	-	-	-	-	-	-	-	B
	10	-	-	-	-	-	-	9	9	D
	15	-	-	-	-	-	8	10	18	F
	20	-	-	-	-	6	8	11	25	H
*	25	-	-	-	4	6	8	25	43	J
	30	-	-	-	6	7	9	35	57	K
	35	-	-	3	5	7	10	46	71	M
	40	-	-	4	6	8	16	54	88	O
	45	-	-	6	6	8	22	65	107	
	50	-	-	7	6	9	28	78	128	
	55	-	3	5	6	10	34	94	152	
	60	-	4	5	7	13	39	110	178	
	65	-	4	6	7	17	44	125	203	
	70	-	5	6	7	21	50	139	228	
	75	-	6	5	8	25	58	148	250	
	80	-	6	6	8	29	67	155	271	
160	6	-	-	-	-	-	-	-	-	B
	10	-	-	-	-	-	3	9	12	D
	15	-	-	-	-	4	7	10	21	G
	20	-	-	-	3	5	8	16	32	H
	25	-	-	-	6	6	9	30	51	K
	30	-	-	4	5	6	10	42	67	M
	35	-	-	5	6	7	14	52	84	N
	40	-	-	7	6	8	21	62	104	
	45	-	3	5	6	9	28	76	127	
	50	-	4	5	7	9	35	93	153	
	55	-	5	6	7	14	39	112	183	
	60	-	6	6	7	18	45	129	211	
	65	3	4	6	8	22	53	142	238	
	70	3	5	6	8	27	62	152	263	
170	5	-	-	-	-	-	-	-	-	B
	10	-	-	-	-	-	5	9	14	D
	15	-	-	-	-	6	7	10	23	G
	20	-	-	-	5	6	8	22	41	I
	25	-	-	3	5	6	10	35	59	K
	30	-	-	6	5	7	11	48	77	M
	35	-	3	4	6	8	19	58	98	O
	40	-	4	5	6	9	26	72	122	
	45	-	6	5	6	10	34	91	152	
	50	3	4	5	7	14	39	111	183	
	55	3	5	5	8	19	45	129	214	
	60	4	5	6	8	23	54	144	244	
	65	5	5	6	8	29	64	154	271	
	70	5	5	7	12	31	76	160	296	

* NDL for 150 fsw changed to 6 min.

CANADIAN FORCES AIR DIVING TABLE 1 (FEET)
STANDARD AIR

Depth (fsw)	Bottom Time (min)	Stop Times (min) at Different Depths (fsw)								Decom. Time (min)	Repet. Group
		80	70	60	50	40	30	20	10		
180	5	-	-	-	-	-	-	-	-	-	B
	10	-	-	-	-	-	-	7	9	16	E
	15	-	-	-	-	-	8	7	11	26	H
	20	-	-	-	-	7	6	8	27	48	J
	25	-	-	-	5	5	7	10	40	67	M
	30	-	-	3	5	5	8	15	53	89	O
	35	-	-	5	5	6	8	24	66	114	
	40	-	3	4	5	6	9	32	85	144	
	45	-	4	4	5	7	14	38	107	179	
	50	-	5	4	6	7	19	45	127	213	
	55	-	5	5	6	8	24	53	144	245	
	60	3	3	5	7	9	29	65	155	276	
190	5	-	-	-	-	-	-	-	-	-	
	10	-	-	-	-	-	-	8	10	18	
	15	-	-	-	-	4	5	8	13	30	
	20	-	-	-	4	5	6	9	31	55	
	25	-	-	3	4	5	7	11	46	76	
	30	-	-	5	5	5	8	20	58	101	
	35	-	3	4	5	6	9	29	76	132	
	40	-	5	4	5	7	12	36	100	169	
	45	-	6	4	6	7	18	43	123	207	
	50	3	4	4	6	8	24	52	141	242	
	55	4	4	5	6	10	28	65	154	276	
200	5	-	-	-	-	-	-	-	4	4	
	10	-	-	-	-	-	4	6	10	20	
	15	-	-	-	-	6	5	8	18	37	
	20	-	-	-	6	4	7	9	36	62	
	25	-	-	5	4	5	8	14	51	87	
	30	-	3	4	5	6	8	24	67	117	
	35	-	5	4	5	7	9	34	89	153	
	40	3	3	5	5	8	16	40	115	195	
	45	4	4	4	6	8	22	49	137	234	
	50	5	4	5	6	10	27	62	153	272	

CANADIAN FORCES AIR DIVING TABLE 1 (FEET)
STANDARD AIR

Depth (fsw)	Bottom Time (min)	Stop Times (min) at Different Depths (fsw)										Decom. Time (min)
		100	90	80	70	60	50	40	30	20	10	
210	5	-	-	-	-	-	-	-	-	-	6	6
	10	-	-	-	-	-	-	-	5	7	10	22
	15	-	-	-	-	-	-	7	6	8	22	43
	20	-	-	-	-	4	3	5	7	10	40	69
	25	-	-	-	-	6	5	5	8	18	55	97
	30	-	-	-	5	4	5	6	9	29	76	134
	35	-	-	3	4	4	5	7	14	36	103	176
	40	-	-	5	3	5	6	8	19	46	130	222
	45	-	-	6	4	4	7	8	27	57	149	262
	50	-	3	4	4	5	7	13	31	74	160	301
220	5	-	-	-	-	-	-	-	-	-	7	7
	10	-	-	-	-	-	-	-	7	7	10	24
	15	-	-	-	-	-	5	4	6	8	27	50
	20	-	-	-	-	5	4	5	7	10	46	77
	25	-	-	-	4	4	4	6	9	22	61	110
	30	-	-	3	4	4	5	7	9	33	87	152
	35	-	-	5	3	5	5	8	17	40	117	200
	40	-	3	3	4	5	6	8	24	52	142	247
230	5	-	-	-	-	-	-	-	-	-	8	8
	10	-	-	-	-	-	-	-	8	7	11	26
	15	-	-	-	-	-	6	4	7	9	30	56
	20	-	-	-	-	6	4	6	7	14	48	85
	25	-	-	-	6	4	4	7	8	26	69	124
	30	-	-	5	3	4	6	7	12	36	100	173
	35	-	4	3	3	5	6	8	20	46	131	226
	40	-	5	3	4	5	6	10	27	61	151	272
240	5	-	-	-	-	-	-	-	-	-	9	9
	10	-	-	-	-	-	-	5	5	7	11	28
	15	-	-	-	-	-	7	5	6	9	34	61
	20	-	-	-	5	3	4	6	8	17	53	96
	25	-	-	4	3	4	5	7	9	29	78	139
	30	-	4	2	4	4	6	7	16	39	113	195
	35	-	5	3	4	5	6	8	24	52	142	249
	40	4	2	4	4	5	7	13	30	71	159	299

CANADIAN FORCES AIR DIVING TABLE 1 (METRES)
STANDARD AIR

Depth (msw)	Bottom Time (min)	Stop Times (min) at Different Depths (msw)							Decom. Time (min)	Repet. Group
		21	18	15	12	9	6	3		
9	30	-	-	-	-	-	-	-	-	A
	60	-	-	-	-	-	-	-	-	C
	90	-	-	-	-	-	-	-	-	D
	120	-	-	-	-	-	-	-	-	F
	150	-	-	-	-	-	-	-	-	G
	180	-	-	-	-	-	-	-	-	H
	400	-	-	-	-	-	-	-	-	
	405	-	-	-	-	-	-	5	5	
	420	-	-	-	-	-	-	10	10	
	450	-	-	-	-	-	-	15	15	
	480	-	-	-	-	-	-	20	20	
12	30	-	-	-	-	-	-	-	-	B
	60	-	-	-	-	-	-	-	-	D
	90	-	-	-	-	-	-	-	-	G
	120	-	-	-	-	-	-	-	-	H
	150	-	-	-	-	-	-	-	-	J
	175	-	-	-	-	-	-	-	-	L
	190	-	-	-	-	-	-	5	5	
	200	-	-	-	-	-	-	10	10	
	210	-	-	-	-	-	-	15	15	
	220	-	-	-	-	-	-	19	19	
	240	-	-	-	-	-	-	26	26	
	270	-	-	-	-	-	-	35	35	
	300	-	-	-	-	-	-	44	44	
	330	-	-	-	-	-	-	53	53	
	360	-	-	-	-	-	-	62	62	

NOTE: Similar changes to those shown on the imperial tables have been made to the metric tables.

CANADIAN FORCES AIR DIVING TABLE 1 (METRES)
STANDARD AIR

Depth (msw)	Bottom Time (min)	Stop Times (min) at Different Depths (msw)							Decom. Time (min)	Repet. Group
		21	18	15	12	9	6	3		
15	20	-	-	-	-	-	-	-	-	A
	30	-	-	-	-	-	-	-	-	C
	40	-	-	-	-	-	-	-	-	D
	50	-	-	-	-	-	-	-	-	E
	60	-	-	-	-	-	-	-	-	F
	75	-	-	-	-	-	-	-	-	G
	100	-	-	-	-	-	-	5	5	I
	120	-	-	-	-	-	-	10	10	K
	125	-	-	-	-	-	-	13	13	K
	130	-	-	-	-	-	-	16	16	L
	140	-	-	-	-	-	-	21	21	M
	150	-	-	-	-	-	-	26	26	
	160	-	-	-	-	-	-	31	31	
	170	-	-	-	-	-	-	35	35	
	180	-	-	-	-	-	-	40	40	
	200	-	-	-	-	-	-	50	50	
	220	-	-	-	-	-	-	59	59	
	240	-	-	-	-	-	-	70	70	
	260	-	-	-	-	-	-	81	81	
	280	-	-	-	-	-	-	91	91	
18	10	-	-	-	-	-	-	-	-	A
	20	-	-	-	-	-	-	-	-	B
	30	-	-	-	-	-	-	-	-	D
	40	-	-	-	-	-	-	-	-	E
	50	-	-	-	-	-	-	-	-	F
	60	-	-	-	-	-	-	5	5	G
	80	-	-	-	-	-	-	10	10	I
	90	-	-	-	-	-	-	16	16	J
	100	-	-	-	-	-	-	24	24	K
	110	-	-	-	-	-	-	30	30	L
	120	-	-	-	-	-	-	36	36	M
	130	-	-	-	-	-	2	40	42	
	140	-	-	-	-	-	2	46	48	
	150	-	-	-	-	-	3	52	55	
	160	-	-	-	-	-	3	59	62	
	170	-	-	-	-	-	4	65	69	
	180	-	-	-	-	-	4	73	77	
	190	-	-	-	-	-	5	80	85	
	200	-	-	-	-	-	7	87	94	
	210	-	-	-	-	-	13	91	104	
	220	-	-	-	-	-	17	97	114	
	230	-	-	-	-	-	21	103	124	
	240	-	-	-	-	-	24	109	133	

CANADIAN FORCES AIR DIVING TABLE 1 (METRES)
STANDARD AIR

Depth (msw)	Bottom Time (min)	Stop Times (min) at Different Depths (msw)							Decom. Time (min)	Repet. Group
		21	18	15	12	9	6	3		
21	10	-	-	-	-	-	-	-	-	A
	20	-	-	-	-	-	-	-	-	C
	25	-	-	-	-	-	-	-	-	D
	30	-	-	-	-	-	-	-	-	D
	35	-	-	-	-	-	-	-	-	E
	40	-	-	-	-	-	-	5	5	F
	50	-	-	-	-	-	-	10	10	G
	60	-	-	-	-	-	-	12	12	H
	70	-	-	-	-	-	3	17	20	J
	80	-	-	-	-	-	4	25	29	K
	90	-	-	-	-	-	5	32	37	M
	100	-	-	-	-	-	6	39	45	N
	110	-	-	-	-	-	7	46	53	
	120	-	-	-	-	-	7	54	61	
	130	-	-	-	-	-	8	62	70	
	140	-	-	-	-	-	9	71	80	
	150	-	-	-	-	-	15	77	92	
	160	-	-	-	-	-	20	85	105	
	170	-	-	-	-	-	25	93	118	
	180	-	-	-	-	-	29	101	130	
	190	-	-	-	-	-	34	109	143	
	200	-	-	-	-	-	38	117	155	
24	10	-	-	-	-	-	-	-	-	A
	15	-	-	-	-	-	-	-	-	C
	20	-	-	-	-	-	-	-	-	D
	25	-	-	-	-	-	-	-	-	E
	30	-	-	-	-	-	-	5	5	F
	40	-	-	-	-	-	-	11	11	G
	50	-	-	-	-	-	4	11	15	H
	55	-	-	-	-	-	5	15	20	I
	60	-	-	-	-	-	6	21	27	J
	65	-	-	-	-	-	7	25	32	J
	70	-	-	-	-	-	7	30	37	K
	75	-	-	-	-	-	8	34	42	L
	80	-	-	-	-	-	9	37	46	M
	85	-	-	-	-	-	9	42	51	
	90	-	-	-	-	-	10	46	56	
	95	-	-	-	-	-	11	50	61	
	100	-	-	-	-	-	11	55	66	
	110	-	-	-	-	2	12	64	78	
	120	-	-	-	-	3	18	72	93	
	130	-	-	-	-	4	23	82	109	
	140	-	-	-	-	4	28	93	125	
	150	-	-	-	-	5	33	104	142	
	160	-	-	-	-	5	39	114	158	

CANADIAN FORCES AIR DIVING TABLE 1 (METRES)
STANDARD AIR

Depth (msw)	Bottom Time (min)	Stop Times (min) at Different Depths (msw)							Decom. Time (min)	Repet. Group
		21	18	15	12	9	6	3		
27	10	-	-	-	-	-	-	-	-	A
	15	-	-	-	-	-	-	-	-	C
	20	-	-	-	-	-	-	-	-	D
	25	-	-	-	-	-	-	7	7	E
	30	-	-	-	-	-	2	9	11	F
	40	-	-	-	-	-	6	10	16	H
	45	-	-	-	-	-	7	14	21	I
	50	-	-	-	-	-	8	20	28	J
	55	-	-	-	-	-	9	26	35	K
	60	-	-	-	-	2	8	31	41	L
	65	-	-	-	-	3	8	36	47	
	70	-	-	-	-	3	9	40	52	
	75	-	-	-	-	4	9	46	59	
	80	-	-	-	-	4	10	51	65	
	85	-	-	-	-	5	10	56	71	
	90	-	-	-	-	5	14	60	79	
	95	-	-	-	-	6	17	64	87	
	100	-	-	-	-	6	20	70	96	
	110	-	-	-	-	7	26	82	115	
	120	-	-	-	-	8	31	95	134	
30	5	-	-	-	-	-	-	-	-	A
	10	-	-	-	-	-	-	-	-	B
	15	-	-	-	-	-	-	-	-	D
	20	-	-	-	-	-	-	8	8	E
	25	-	-	-	-	-	3	9	12	F
	30	-	-	-	-	-	5	10	15	G
	35	-	-	-	-	-	7	11	18	H
	40	-	-	-	-	-	9	16	25	I
	45	-	-	-	-	3	8	23	34	J
	50	-	-	-	-	4	8	29	41	K
	55	-	-	-	-	5	9	34	48	L
	60	-	-	-	-	6	9	40	55	
	65	-	-	-	-	6	10	46	62	
	70	-	-	-	-	7	10	52	69	
	75	-	-	-	-	8	14	56	78	
	80	-	-	-	-	8	18	61	87	
	85	-	-	-	-	9	21	67	97	
	90	-	-	-	2	8	24	75	109	
	95	-	-	-	3	8	27	82	120	
	100	-	-	-	3	8	31	90	132	
	105	-	-	-	3	9	34	98	144	
	110	-	-	-	4	8	38	106	156	

CANADIAN FORCES AIR DIVING TABLE 1 (METRES)
STANDARD AIR

Depth (msw)	Bottom Time (min)	Stop Times (min) at Different Depths (msw)							Decom. Time (min)	Repet. Group
		21	18	15	12	9	6	3		
33	5	-	-	-	-	-	-	-	-	A
	10	-	-	-	-	-	-	-	-	B
	12	-	-	-	-	-	-	-	-	C
	15	-	-	-	-	-	-	5	5	D
	20	-	-	-	-	-	3	9	12	F
	25	-	-	-	-	-	6	10	16	G
	30	-	-	-	-	-	9	10	19	H
	35	-	-	-	-	3	8	16	27	I
	40	-	-	-	-	5	8	24	37	J
	45	-	-	-	-	6	9	31	46	K
	50	-	-	-	-	7	9	38	54	M
	55	-	-	-	-	8	10	44	62	N
	60	-	-	-	2	7	10	51	70	
	65	-	-	-	3	7	15	55	80	
	70	-	-	-	4	7	19	62	92	
	75	-	-	-	4	8	23	68	103	
	80	-	-	-	5	8	26	77	116	
	85	-	-	-	5	9	30	86	130	
	90	-	-	-	6	9	34	95	144	
	95	-	-	-	6	9	38	105	158	
	100	-	-	-	7	9	42	114	172	
	105	-	-	-	7	12	45	123	187	
	110	-	-	-	8	15	48	130	201	
36	5	-	-	-	-	-	-	-	-	A
	10	-	-	-	-	-	-	-	-	C
	15	-	-	-	-	-	-	10	10	D
	20	-	-	-	-	-	6	9	15	F
	25	-	-	-	-	-	9	10	19	G
	30	-	-	-	-	4	8	14	26	I
	35	-	-	-	-	6	8	24	38	J
	40	-	-	-	-	8	8	32	48	K
	45	-	-	-	3	6	10	38	57	M
	50	-	-	-	4	7	10	46	67	N
	55	-	-	-	5	7	13	53	78	
	60	-	-	-	6	7	18	59	90	
	65	-	-	-	6	8	22	66	102	
	70	-	-	-	7	8	27	75	117	
	75	-	-	-	8	8	31	86	133	
	80	-	-	2	6	9	35	97	149	
	85	-	-	3	6	10	40	107	166	
	90	-	-	3	7	13	42	118	183	
	95	-	-	4	6	16	46	128	200	
	100	-	-	4	7	19	50	136	216	

CANADIAN FORCES AIR DIVING TABLE 1 (METRES)
STANDARD AIR

Depth (msw)	Bottom Time (min)	Stop Times (min) at Different Depths (msw)							Decom. Time (min)	Repet. Group
		21	18	15	12	9	6	3		
39	5	-	-	-	-	-	-	-	-	A
	8	-	-	-	-	-	-	-	-	B
	10	-	-	-	-	-	-	5	5	C
	15	-	-	-	-	-	4	8	12	E
	20	-	-	-	-	-	8	10	18	G
	25	-	-	-	-	5	7	11	23	H
	30	-	-	-	-	7	8	22	37	J
	35	-	-	-	3	6	9	30	48	K
	40	-	-	-	4	7	9	39	59	M
	45	-	-	-	6	7	10	47	70	N
	50	-	-	-	7	7	15	53	82	
	55	-	-	2	6	8	20	61	97	
	60	-	-	3	6	8	25	70	112	
	65	-	-	4	6	8	30	82	130	
	70	-	-	4	7	9	34	94	148	
	75	-	-	5	6	11	39	106	167	
	80	-	-	5	7	14	42	118	186	
	85	-	-	6	7	17	47	129	206	
	90	-	-	6	8	20	52	138	224	
42	7	-	-	-	-	-	-	-	-	B
	10	-	-	-	-	-	-	7	7	D
	15	-	-	-	-	-	6	9	15	F
	20	-	-	-	-	4	7	10	21	G
	25	-	-	-	-	7	8	17	32	I
	30	-	-	-	4	6	8	28	46	K
	35	-	-	-	5	7	9	37	58	L
	40	-	-	-	7	7	10	46	70	N
	45	-	-	3	5	8	16	53	85	O
	50	-	-	4	6	8	21	62	101	
	55	-	-	5	6	8	27	73	119	
	60	-	-	6	6	9	32	86	139	
	65	-	-	6	7	10	37	99	159	
	70	-	-	7	7	14	40	114	182	
	75	-	3	5	7	18	45	126	204	
	80	-	3	6	7	21	51	137	225	
	85	-	4	5	8	25	57	146	245	
	90	-	4	6	8	28	65	152	263	

CANADIAN FORCES AIR DIVING TABLE 1 (METRES)
STANDARD AIR

Depth (msw)	Bottom Time (min)	Stop Times (min) at Different Depths (msw)							Decom. Time (min)	Repet. Group
		21	18	15	12	9	6	3		
45	7	-	-	-	-	-	-	-	-	B
	10	-	-	-	-	-	-	9	9	D
	15	-	-	-	-	-	8	9	17	F
	20	-	-	-	-	6	7	11	24	H
	25	-	-	-	4	5	8	23	40	J
	30	-	-	-	6	6	9	34	55	K
	35	-	-	3	5	7	10	44	69	M
	40	-	-	4	6	7	15	52	84	O
	45	-	-	5	6	8	21	61	101	
	50	-	-	6	7	8	27	73	121	
	55	-	3	5	6	9	33	88	144	
	60	-	3	5	7	12	38	103	168	
	65	-	4	5	8	16	42	119	194	
	70	-	5	5	8	20	48	132	218	
	75	-	5	6	8	24	55	142	240	
	80	-	6	6	8	28	63	150	261	
48	6	-	-	-	-	-	-	-	-	B
	10	-	-	-	-	-	-	11	11	D
	15	-	-	-	-	4	6	10	20	G
	20	-	-	-	-	8	8	14	30	H
	25	-	-	-	6	6	8	29	49	K
	30	-	-	3	5	7	9	40	64	M
	35	-	-	5	5	8	13	49	80	N
	40	-	-	6	6	8	20	59	99	
	45	-	3	5	6	9	26	72	121	
	50	-	4	5	7	9	33	88	146	
	55	-	5	5	7	13	38	105	173	
	60	-	6	5	8	17	43	122	201	
	65	-	7	5	8	22	50	135	227	
	70	3	4	6	8	26	58	146	251	
51	6	-	-	-	-		-	-	-	B
	10	-	-	-	-		5	8	13	D
	15	-	-	-	-	5	7	10	22	G
	20	-	-	-	5	5	8	20	38	I
	25	-	-	3	5	6	9	33	56	K
	30	-	-	5	5	7	10	46	73	M
	35	-	3	4	6	8	18	55	94	O
	40	-	4	5	6	8	26	68	117	
	45	-	5	5	7	9	32	85	143	
	50	-	6	6	7	13	37	105	174	
	55	3	4	6	7	18	44	122	204	
	60	4	4	6	8	23	51	137	233	
	65	5	4	6	9	27	61	148	260	
	70	5	5	6	12	30	72	155	285	

CANADIAN FORCES AIR DIVING TABLE 1 (METRES)
STANDARD AIR

Depth (msw)	Bottom Time (min)	Stop Times (min) at Different Depths (msw)								Decom. Time (min)	Repet. Group
		24	21	18	15	12	9	6	3		
54	5	-	-	-	-	-	-	-	-	-	B
	10	-	-	-	-	-	-	6	9	15	E
	15	-	-	-	-	-	7	7	11	25	H
	20	-	-	-	-	6	6	8	25	45	J
	25	-	-	-	5	5	7	9	39	65	M
	30	-	-	3	4	6	7	15	50	85	O
	35	-	-	5	4	6	8	23	62	108	
	40	-	-	6	5	7	9	30	80	137	
	45	-	4	4	5	7	13	36	101	170	
	50	-	4	5	5	8	18	42	121	203	
	55	-	5	5	6	8	23	51	137	235	
	60	-	6	5	6	9	28	61	149	264	
57	5	-	-	-	-	-	-	-	-	-	
	10	-	-	-	-	-	-	8	9	17	
	15	-	-	-	-	4	5	7	11	27	
	20	-	-	-	4	4	6	9	29	52	
	25	-	-	-	7	5	7	10	44	73	
	30	-	-	5	4	6	8	19	55	97	
	35	-	3	4	5	6	9	27	72	126	
	40	-	4	4	5	7	11	35	93	159	
	45	-	5	5	5	8	17	41	116	197	
	50	3	3	5	6	8	22	50	135	232	
	55	4	3	5	7	9	27	61	149	265	
60	5	-	-	-	-	-	-	-	-	-	
	10	-	-	-	-	-	-	10	9	19	
	15	-	-	-	-	5	6	8	16	35	
	20	-	-	-	5	5	6	10	33	59	
	25	-	-	5	4	5	7	14	48	83	
	30	-	3	4	4	6	9	23	62	111	
	35	-	5	4	5	6	10	32	84	146	
	40	-	6	4	6	7	15	38	109	185	
	45	4	3	5	6	8	21	47	131	225	
	50	5	4	4	7	9	27	58	147	261	

CANADIAN FORCES AIR DIVING TABLE 1 (METRES)
STANDARD AIR

Depth (msw)	Bottom Time (min)	Stop Times (min) at Different Depths (msw)										Decom. Time (min)
		30	27	24	21	18	15	12	9	6	3	
63	5	-	-	-	-	-	-	-	-	-	5	5
	10	-	-	-	-	-	-	-	5	6	10	21
	15	-	-	-	-	-	-	7	6	8	20	41
	20	-	-	-	-	-	7	5	7	9	39	67
	25	-	-	-	-	6	4	6	8	17	52	93
	30	-	-	-	5	4	4	7	8	28	71	127
	35	-	-	3	3	4	6	7	12	35	97	167
	40	-	-	4	4	4	6	8	19	43	123	211
	45	-	-	5	4	5	6	9	25	54	142	250
	50	-	3	3	4	6	6	13	29	70	154	288
66	5	-	-	-	-	-	-	-	-	-	7	7
	10	-	-	-	-	-	-	-	7	6	10	23
	15	-	-	-	-	-	4	5	5	9	24	47
	20	-	-	-	-	5	4	5	7	10	43	74
	25	-	-	-	4	4	4	6	8	21	58	105
	30	-	-	3	3	4	5	7	9	32	81	144
	35	-	-	5	3	4	6	7	16	39	110	190
	40	-	3	3	4	4	7	8	23	49	135	236
	45	-	4	3	4	5	7	11	28	65	151	278
69	5	-	-	-	-	-	-	-	-	-	8	8
	10	-	-	-	-	-	-	-	8	7	10	25
	15	-	-	-	-	-	6	4	6	9	28	53
	20	-	-	-	-	6	4	6	7	12	47	82
	25	-	-	-	6	3	5	6	9	24	65	118
	30	-	-	5	3	4	5	7	12	35	93	164
	35	-	3	3	4	4	6	8	19	44	123	214
	40	-	5	3	4	5	6	9	27	57	146	262
72	5	-	-	-	-	-	-	-	-	-	9	9
	10	-	-	-	-	-	-	4	5	7	11	27
	15	-	-	-	-	-	7	5	6	9	32	59
	20	-	-	-	4	4	4	5	8	16	50	91
	25	-	-	4	3	4	5	6	9	28	73	132
	30	-	-	6	3	5	5	8	15	37	106	185
	35	-	5	3	4	4	6	9	23	49	135	238
	40	3	3	3	4	6	6	13	28	67	153	286

APPENDIX C

ROYAL NAVY DECOMPRESSION TABLES
RN TABLE 11

Section 1—General

5101. DECOMPRESSION—INTRODUCTION

1. The physiological problems associated with increased environmental pressure and the requirement for subsequent decompression in stages are discussed in Chapter 1.

2. This and other sections in this chapter deal with the decompression requirement in greater detail and amplify the regulations laid down in Chapter 2, Section 3.

5102. METHODS AVAILABLE

1. Decompression may be carried out in one of three ways:

a. In the water while the diver is ascending on a shot rope or lazy shot

b. In a compression chamber on the surface

c. In a submersible compression chamber.

2. In each case the method used may be varied by the type of gas the diver is breathing.

3. The simplest of these methods and the one most commonly used with dives of relatively short duration is decompression in the water.

4. Compression chambers are used with the surface-decompression technique and during advanced operations involving the use of submersible compression chambers.

5. Whichever method is used a common factor is the decompression schedule. Different schedules are available depending on the circumstances, most of them relying on 'stage' decompression, i.e. ascending to a calculated depth or stage for a given time and then ascending to a further stage. These stages are all set out in Section 6, which contains all the decompression tables in current use.

5103. HARD WORK—INCREASED DECOMPRESSION

1. When a diver exerts himself under pressure, his body absorbs more gas than usual and he will require a longer period of decompression to eliminate this gas.

2. On all occasions, therefore, when hard physical work is carried out by a diver, the decompression routine for the dive is to be taken as that for the next longer time increment for the dive, as given in the decompression tables.

5104. PROCEDURE AFTER DIVING IN EXCESS OF 35 METRES

1. A diver who has carried out a dive deeper than 35 m for a period above the limiting line in Table 11 is to remain within four hours' travelling time of a compression chamber for 12 hours after completing the dive.

2. A diver who has carried out a dive of 35 m or more for a period below the limiting line in Table 11 must remain in the immediate vicinity of a compression chamber (i.e. on board) for a period of four hours after completing the dive, and within four hours' travelling time of a chamber for a further 12 hours.

3. If no compression chamber is available, the diver should be kept under observation on board for the first four hours quoted in para. 2 above.

5105–5110. Spare.

5111. REPETITIVE DIVES

1. Dives to depths of less than 10 metres, or equivalent air depths of 10 metres, have no time restriction or requirement for further decompression when preceded by deeper dives and do not count as 'dives' in the terms of this article.

2. Dives carried out breathing pure oxygen may be followed by deeper dives without modification of the appropriate decompression schedule.

3. A diver who has carried out a dive to depths greater than 42 metres or dived below the limiting line is not to carry out a further dive within 12 hours of surfacing.

4. If the time interval between dives above the limiting line exceeds six hours, then no modification of decompression is required, *provided the second dive does not exceed 42 metres.*

5. If the time interval between dives above the limiting line is less than six hours, the procedure for combined dives must be followed as in Article 5112.

5112. STOPS FOR A COMBINED DIVE

1. The stops for a combined dive are obtained by adding together the duration of the first and each subsequent dive to obtain a total time for the combined dives. This total time and the depth of the deepest dive made are used to obtain the stops in the relevant table as for a single dive.

2. The total time of the combined dives (i.e. the sum of successive durations) is not to be allowed to exceed a total time for decompression (Column 4 or 6 in the appropriate table) of 75 minutes or the next lower figure in this column if 75 is not quoted.

3. Dives carried out using pure oxygen are not to be included in this calculation.

EXAMPLE (TABLE 11)

4. For example, if a diver descends to 26 m on air for a duration of 32 minutes, he should carry out stoppages for 10 minutes. If he then dives within eight hours to the same depth for 36 minutes, this is added to the previous duration to give a total time of 68 minutes, which calls for further stoppages of 45 minutes.

5. This is apparently a dive below the limiting line. It is, however, acceptable because the durations are being aggregated. In this example the limitation is imposed by the maximum acceptable total time for ascent of 70 minutes given in column 4, there being no figure of 75.

6. If it is necessary for the diver to go down again, the duration of his last dive must not exceed 22 minutes. If, for instance, he dived for 24 minutes, his total duration would be 92 minutes (32 + 36 + 24), calling for a total time for ascent of 80 minutes, which is in excess of that allowed by para. 2 above. The last dive of 22 minutes would mean a stoppage time of 70 minutes.

5113. DIVING BELOW THE LIMITING LINE

1. That part of each depth section above the limiting line is the ordinary working table where the risk of decompression sickness is negligible; diving for periods below the line carries a greater risk of decompression sickness, and this risk increases with an increase of duration below the line. Intentional diving below the limiting line should be undertaken only when a compression chamber is available on the site and even then only when circumstances justify the risk. This risk is in no way diminished by the use of oxygen during decompression.

2. A diver who has carried out a dive below the limiting line is not to carry out a further dive within 12 hours.

3. He is also to remain within the vicinity of a compression chamber and under surveillance for four hours (Article 5104, para. 2).

5114–5120. Spare.

5121. DIVING AT ALTITUDE

1. Most diving takes place at sea level where the pressure on the surface is one bar absolute.

2. If a dive is carried out at altitude (e.g. in a mountain lake), the surface pressure is less than one bar absolute. Because of this, decompression schedules must be adjusted to prevent the onset of decompression sickness in the rarefied atmosphere.

3. Water will invariably be fresh, but stoppages should be used as though it were salt, so increasing the safety margin of the schedule.

4. Adjustments should be made to the schedules as follows:

a. Dives between altitudes of 100 *m and* 300 *m*: Add 0·25 of the depth to give the depth of the dive.

b. Dives between altitudes of 300 *m and* 2000 *m*: Add 0·3 of the depth to give the depth of the dive.

c. Dives between altitudes of 2000 *and* 3000 *m*: Add 0·5 of the depth to give the depth of the dive.

5. For example, a dive to a depth of 24 m from an altitude of 1000 m should be treated in the decompression tables as a dive to a depth of 32 m.

6. No adjustments are required for altitudes of less than 100 m.

5122. DECOMPRESSION SICKNESS—FLYING RESTRICTIONS

1. To avoid the risk of contracting decompression sickness by flying after having dived, the following rules, applicable to commercial cabin altitude, normally between the equivalents of 5000 and 9000 feet, are to be applied:

Type of dive	*Period before flying*
No-stop dive	2 hours
Dive involving stoppages	24 hours

Section 6—Decompression Tables

5601. USE OF TABLES

1. The decompression table to be used will depend on the type and duration of dive conducted.

2. This section contains all the schedules that can be employed both for preventing and curing decompression sickness and air embolisms.

3. Those used for prevention are carried out as part of the dive and are referred to as diving tables. The serial numbers of these tables are included in the series commencing with Tables 11 and 12. The remainder of the tables, that is those whose serial numbers commence with 51, 61, 71 and 81, are employed for curing cases of decompression sickness, whether they occur during or after the dive, and are referred to as therapeutic tables.

4. The procedure for applying these schedules is contained in Articles 5602, 5603 and in the preamble to each table.

5602. APPLICATION OF DIVING TABLES

1. Different diving tables are provided for different sets of circumstances, but their format and application are nonetheless similar.

2. Their limitations are also similar. Therefore, in cases where either the depth or duration of the dive is in doubt, stoppages for the next greater figure in the appropriate column are to be employed.

3. The tables are applied as follows:

a. *Depth* (*Column 1*). This column has increments in depth of three metres, and the figure to be used is the one immediately exceeding the deepest depth to which the diver descended in his dive. Thus stoppages for 30 m would be used for a dive to 28 m. If there was any doubt about the accuracy of the depth of 28 m, stoppages for 33 m would be used.

b. *Duration* (*Column 2*). The duration of the dive is the interval of time in minutes between the diver leaving the surface at the start of the dive and leaving the bottom to commence the ascent. The figure to be used is the one immediately exceeding the actual duration. Thus a dive to 30 m for 23 minutes would employ stoppages against a duration of 25 minutes. If there was any doubt about the accuracy of this time interval, stoppages against a duration of 30 minutes would be used.

c. *Stoppages* (*Column 3*). Stoppages are given opposite each depth increment for different durations. The time for the first stop commences when the diver leaves the bottom and the time for each subsequent stop commences when the diver leaves the preceding stop. In other words the ascent time is to be included in the stoppage time throughout.

d. *Oxygen stoppages.* Oxygen is breathed while carrying out stoppages in a compression chamber, and in the water after deep dives. As an exception to sub-para. *c* above, the ascent time is not to be included in the stoppage time when changing from air to oxygen breathing. The time for oxygen stops is taken as starting when the report 'Diver breathing oxygen' is received. The preceding ascent time is ignored and counted as dead time. Subsequent ascent times are, however, to be included in the stoppage times.

e. *Changing to air stoppages.* If for any reason a diver ceases to breathe oxygen during his decompression and reverts to air, the oxygen stops are to be increased 2½ times to determine the time to be spent on air.

f. *Limiting line.* See Article 5113.

g. *Rate of ascent.* See Article 5202.

5603. APPLICATION OF THERAPEUTIC TABLES

1. Different therapeutic tables are provided for different sets of circumstances and are applied as described in the preamble to each series.

2. Additionally there are some common factors, which are outlined below.

a. *Descent time.* Descent time, which varies between tables, is not included in the elapsed time.

b. *Elapsed time.* The timing of each table starts when maximum pressure is reached, and is given in hours and minutes opposite each step of the table.

c. *Stoppages.* The duration of stoppages is given, oxygen being breathed as indicated.

d. *Ascent.* The rate of ascent varies between tables, but with all tables the ascent becomes critical near the surface, where the rate of change of pressure is greatest. If, as the compression chamber nears the surface, air begins to escape round the door seal, compensation by admitting more compressed air may be needed. In addition, the gauges may indicate that the surface has been reached when there is still some pressure in the chamber. If this occurs the chamber must continue to be vented at the established rate until pressure is equalised.

e. *Surfacing.* On arrival at the surface both patient and attendant must remain in the chamber for one minute in case of return of symptoms.

5604–5610. Spare.

5611. TABLE 11: AIR TABLE

1. Table 11 is employed for dives down to depths of 55 m.

2. The table is applied as described in Article 5602.

CHAPTER 5
TABLE 11
AIR TABLE

(1) DEPTH NOT EXCEEDING (*metres*)	(2) DURATION TIME LEAVING SURFACE TO BEGINNING OF ASCENT NOT EXCEEDING (*min.*)	(3) STOPPAGES AT DIFFERENT DEPTHS (*min.*)					(4) TOTAL TIME FOR DECOMPRESSION (*min.*)
		15 m	12 m	9 m	6 m	3 m	
9	No limit	—	—	—	—	—	—
12	135	—	—	—	—	—	—
	165	—	—	—	—	5	5
	195	—	—	—	—	10	10
	225	—	—	—	—	15	15
	255	—	—	—	—	20	20
	330	—	—	—	—	25	25
	390	—	—	—	—	30	30
	660	—	—	—	—	35	35
	Limiting Line						
	over 660	—	—	—	—	40	40
15	85	—	—	—	—	—	—
	105	—	—	—	—	5	5
	120	—	—	—	—	10	10
	135	—	—	—	—	15	15
	145	—	—	—	—	20	20
	160	—	—	—	—	25	25
	170	—	—	—	5	25	30
	190	—	—	—	5	30	35
	Limiting Line						
	240	—	—	—	10	40	50
	360	—	—	—	30	40	70
	450	—	—	—	35	40	75
	over 450	—	—	—	35	45	80
18	60	—	—	—	—	—	—
	70	—	—	—	—	5	5
	80	—	—	—	5	5	10
	90	—	—	—	5	10	15
	100	—	—	—	5	15	20
	110	—	—	—	5	20	25
	120	—	—	—	5	25	30
	130	—	—	—	5	30	35
	Limiting Line						
	140	—	—	—	10	30	40
	150	—	—	—	10	40	50
	160	—	—	—	15	40	55
	180	—	—	—	20	40	60
	200	—	—	5	30	40	75
	255	—	—	10	35	45	90
	325	—	—	20	40	45	105
	495	—	—	35	40	45	120
	over 495	—	—	35	40	50	125
21	40	—	—	—	—	—	—
	55	—	—	—	—	5	5
	60	—	—	—	5	5	10
	70	—	—	—	5	10	15
	75	—	—	—	5	15	20
	85	—	—	—	5	20	25
	90	—	—	—	5	25	30
	95	—	—	5	5	25	35
	Limiting Line						
	105	—	—	5	5	35	45
	120	—	—	5	10	40	55
	135	—	—	5	20	45	70
	150	—	—	5	30	45	80
	165	—	—	10	30	50	90
	180	—	—	15	35	50	100
	210	—	—	25	40	50	115
	240	—	5	30	40	50	125

SECTION 6

TABLE 11 (*contd.*)

Air Table

(1) DEPTH NOT EXCEEDING (*metres*)	(2) DURATION TIME LEAVING SURFACE TO BEGINNING OF ASCENT NOT EXCEEDING (*min.*)	(3) STOPPAGES AT DIFFERENT DEPTHS (*min.*)					(4) TOTAL TIME FOR DECOMPRESSION (*min.*)
		15 m	12 m	9 m	6 m	3 m	
	30	—	—	—	—	—	—
	40	—	—	—	—	5	5
	50	—	—	—	5	5	10
	55	—	—	—	5	10	15
	60	—	—	—	5	15	20
	70	—	—	—	5	20	25
	75	—	—	—	5	25	30
24	**Limiting Line**						
	80	—	—	5	5	30	40
	90	—	—	5	10	35	50
	105	—	—	5	20	40	65
	120	—	5	5	30	45	85
	140	—	5	10	35	50	100
	160	—	10	30	40	50	130
	25	—	—	—	—	—	—
	30	—	—	—	—	5	5
	40	—	—	—	5	5	10
	45	—	—	—	5	10	15
	50	—	—	—	5	15	20
	55	—	—	—	5	20	25
	60	—	—	5	5	20	30
	65	—	—	5	5	25	35
27	**Limiting Line**						
	70	—	—	5	10	30	45
	75	—	—	5	15	30	50
	80	—	—	5	20	35	60
	90	—	—	5	25	40	70
	100	—	—	5	30	45	80
	110	—	5	15	35	45	100
	120	—	5	20	35	50	110
	135	5	5	25	40	50	125
	150	5	10	35	40	50	140
	20	—	—	—	—	—	—
	25	—	—	—	—	5	5
	30	—	—	—	5	5	10
	35	—	—	—	5	10	15
	40	—	—	—	5	15	20
	45	—	—	—	5	20	25
	50	—	—	5	5	20	30
	55	—	—	5	5	25	35
30	**Limiting Line**						
	60	—	—	5	10	30	45
	70	—	—	5	20	35	60
	75	—	5	5	20	40	70
	80	—	5	5	30	40	80
	90	—	5	15	30	45	95
	105	—	5	25	35	50	115
	120	5	10	30	40	50	135

CHAPTER 5

TABLE 11 (*contd.*)

AIR TABLE

(1) DEPTH NOT EXCEEDING (*metres*)	(2) DURATION TIME LEAVING SURFACE TO BEGINNING OF ASCENT NOT EXCEEDING (*min.*)	(3) STOPPAGES AT DIFFERENT DEPTHS (*min.*) 18 m	15 m	12 m	9 m	6 m	3 m	(4) TOTAL TIME FOR DECOMPRESSION (*min.*)
	17	—	—	—	—	—	—	—
	20	—	—	—	—	—	5	5
	25	—	—	—	—	5	5	10
	30	—	—	—	—	5	10	15
	35	—	—	—	—	5	15	20
	40	—	—	—	—	5	20	25
	45	—	—	—	5	5	20	30
	Limiting Line							
	50	—	—	—	5	10	25	40
33	55	—	—	—	5	15	30	50
	60	—	—	—	5	20	35	60
	65	—	—	5	5	20	40	70
	70	—	—	5	10	20	45	80
	75	—	—	5	15	25	45	90
	80	—	—	5	20	30	45	100
	90	—	5	5	20	40	45	115
	100	—	5	10	25	40	50	130
	110	—	5	20	30	45	50	150
	120	5	5	25	40	45	50	170
	14	—	—	—	—	—	—	—
	20	—	—	—	—	—	5	5
	25	—	—	—	—	5	5	10
	30	—	—	—	—	5	15	20
	35	—	—	—	—	5	20	25
	40	—	—	—	5	5	25	35
	Limiting Line							
	45	—	—	—	5	10	25	40
36	50	—	—	—	5	15	30	50
	55	—	—	5	5	20	35	65
	60	—	—	5	10	25	40	80
	70	—	—	5	20	30	45	100
	75	—	5	5	20	35	45	110
	80	—	5	10	25	35	45	120
	90	—	5	15	30	40	50	140
	100	5	5	20	35	45	50	160
	110	5	15	25	40	45	50	180
	120	5	20	30	40	45	50	195

SECTION 6

TABLE 11 (*contd.*)

AIR TABLE

(1) DEPTH NOT EXCEEDING (*metres*)	(2) DURATION TIME LEAVING SURFACE TO BEGINNING OF ASCENT NOT EXCEEDING (*min.*)	(3) STOPPAGES AT DIFFERENT DEPTHS (*min.*)							(4) TOTAL TIME FOR DECOMPRESSION (*min.*)
		21 m	18 m	15 m	12 m	9 m	6 m	3 m	
	11	—	—	—	—	—	—	—	—
	15	—	—	—	—	—	—	5	5
	20	—	—	—	—	—	5	5	10
	25	—	—	—	—	—	5	10	15
	30	—	—	—	—	—	5	20	25
	35	—	—	—	—	5	5	20	30
	Limiting Line								
	40	—	—	—	—	5	10	25	40
	45	—	—	—	5	5	15	30	55
39	50	—	—	—	5	5	20	35	65
	55	—	—	—	5	10	25	40	80
	60	—	—	—	5	15	30	45	95
	70	—	—	5	10	20	30	50	115
	75	—	—	5	15	25	40	50	135
	80	—	—	5	20	30	45	50	150
	90	—	5	5	25	40	45	50	170
	100	5	5	15	30	40	45	50	190
	110	5	10	25	30	45	45	50	210
	120	5	15	30	40	45	45	50	230
	9	—	—	—	—	—	—	—	—
	10	—	—	—	—	—	—	5	5
	15	—	—	—	—	—	5	5	10
	20	—	—	—	—	—	5	10	15
	25	—	—	—	—	—	5	15	20
	30	—	—	—	—	5	5	20	30
	Limiting Line								
	35	—	—	—	—	5	10	25	40
	40	—	—	—	5	5	15	30	55
42	45	—	—	—	5	10	15	35	65
	50	—	—	—	5	15	20	40	80
	55	—	—	5	5	15	25	45	95
	60	—	—	5	5	20	35	45	110
	65	—	—	5	10	25	40	45	125
	70	—	—	5	15	30	40	50	140
	75	—	5	5	20	30	45	50	155
	80	—	5	10	20	35	45	50	165
	85	—	5	15	25	40	45	50	180
	95	5	5	20	35	40	45	50	200
	105	5	15	25	35	45	45	50	220
	115	5	20	35	40	45	45	50	240

CHAPTER 5

TABLE 11 (*contd.*)

AIR TABLE

(1) DEPTH NOT EXCEEDING (*metres*)	(2) DURATION TIME LEAVING SURFACE TO BEGINNING OF ASCENT NOT EXCEEDING (*min.*)	(3) STOPPAGES AT DIFFERENT DEPTHS (*min.*)							(4) TOTAL TIME FOR DECOMPRESSION (*min.*)
		21 m	18 m	15 m	12 m	9 m	6 m	3 m	
	8	—	—	—	—	—	—	—	—
	10	—	—	—	—	—	—	5	5
	15	—	—	—	—	—	5	5	10
	20	—	—	—	—	—	5	15	20
	25	—	—	—	—	5	5	20	30
	Limiting Line								
	30	—	—	—	—	5	10	25	40
	35	—	—	—	5	5	10	30	50
	40	—	—	—	5	10	15	35	65
45	45	—	—	—	5	15	20	40	80
	50	—	—	5	5	15	25	45	95
	55	—	—	5	10	20	30	50	115
	60	—	—	5	15	25	35	50	130
	65	—	5	5	15	30	40	50	145
	70	—	5	10	20	30	45	50	160
	75	—	5	15	25	35	45	50	175
	80	5	5	20	30	40	45	50	195
	85	5	10	25	35	40	45	50	210
	90	5	15	30	40	45	45	50	230
	10	—	—	—	—	—	5	5	10
	15	—	—	—	—	—	5	10	15
	20	—	—	—	—	5	5	15	25
	25	—	—	—	—	5	10	20	35
	Limiting Line								
	30	—	—	—	5	5	10	25	45
	35	—	—	—	5	10	15	30	60
	40	—	—	—	5	10	20	40	75
48	45	—	—	5	5	15	25	45	95
	50	—	—	5	10	20	30	45	110
	55	—	—	5	15	25	40	45	130
	60	—	5	5	20	25	40	50	145
	65	—	5	10	20	35	45	50	165
	70	—	5	15	25	40	45	50	180
	75	5	5	20	30	40	45	50	195
	80	5	10	25	35	40	45	50	210
	85	5	15	30	40	45	45	50	230

SECTION 6

TABLE 11 (*contd.*)

AIR TABLE

(1) DEPTH NOT EXCEEDING (*metres*)	(2) DURATION TIME LEAVING SURFACE TO BEGINNING OF ASCENT NOT EXCEEDING (*min.*)	(3) STOPPAGES AT DIFFERENT DEPTHS (*min.*)								(4) TOTAL TIME FOR DECOMPRESSION (*min.*)
		24 m	21 m	18 m	15 m	12 m	9 m	6 m	3 m	
	10	—	—	—	—	—	—	5	5	10
	15	—	—	—	—	—	—	5	10	15
	20	—	—	—	—	—	5	5	15	25
	Limiting Line									
	25	—	—	—	—	—	5	10	25	40
	30	—	—	—	—	5	5	15	30	55
	35	—	—	—	—	5	10	20	35	70
51	40	—	—	—	5	5	15	25	35	85
	45	—	—	—	5	10	20	30	40	105
	50	—	—	5	5	10	25	35	45	125
	55	—	—	5	5	15	30	40	50	145
	60	—	—	5	10	20	35	45	50	165
	65	—	5	5	15	25	35	45	50	180
	70	—	5	10	15	30	40	45	50	195
	75	—	5	15	20	35	45	45	50	215
	80	5	5	20	25	40	45	45	50	235
	10	—	—	—	—	—	—	5	5	10
	15	—	—	—	—	—	5	5	10	20
	20	—	—	—	—	—	5	10	15	30
	Limiting Line									
	25	—	—	—	—	5	5	10	25	45
	30	—	—	—	—	5	10	15	35	65
	35	—	—	—	5	5	15	20	40	85
54	40	—	—	—	5	10	20	25	45	105
	45	—	—	5	5	10	25	35	45	125
	50	—	—	5	5	15	30	40	50	145
	55	—	—	5	10	20	35	45	50	165
	60	—	5	5	15	25	40	45	50	185
	65	—	5	10	20	30	40	45	50	200
	70	—	5	15	25	35	45	45	50	220
	75	5	5	20	30	40	45	45	50	240
	10	—	—	—	—	—	—	5	5	10
	15	—	—	—	—	—	5	5	15	25
	20	—	—	—	—	—	5	10	20	35
	Limiting Line									
	25	—	—	—	—	5	5	15	25	50
	30	—	—	—	5	5	10	20	35	75
57	35	—	—	—	5	5	15	30	45	100
	40	—	—	5	5	10	20	35	45	120
	45	—	—	5	5	15	25	40	50	140
	50	—	—	5	10	20	30	45	50	160
	55	—	5	5	15	25	35	45	50	180
	60	—	5	10	20	30	40	45	50	200
	65	5	5	10	25	35	45	45	50	220
	70	5	10	15	30	40	45	45	50	240
	10	—	—	—	—	—	—	5	10	15
	15	—	—	—	—	—	5	5	15	25
	Limiting Line									
	20	—	—	—	—	5	5	10	20	40
	25	—	—	—	—	5	10	15	30	60
60	30	—	—	—	5	5	15	20	40	85
	35	—	—	—	5	10	20	30	45	110
	40	—	—	5	5	15	25	40	45	135
	45	—	—	5	10	20	30	45	50	160
	50	—	5	5	15	25	35	45	50	180
	55	—	5	10	20	30	40	45	50	200
	60	5	5	10	25	35	45	45	50	220
	65	5	10	15	30	40	45	45	50	240

APPENDIX D

RNPL (1972) DECOMPRESSION TABLES

Background

As a result of testing Royal Navy and other air decompression tables at depths in excess of 30m (100 ft) and for bottom times in excess of 15 minutes, it was realised that these schedules yielded a higher number of bends than was desirable (in some instances over 20% in a group of healthy young divers). Selection of men resistant to bends can reduce this value, but the only known method of selection is by diving and discovering. Such a testing procedure will bring back the higher bends rates. Further, there is considerable evidence that whereas some men are resistant to bends for long dives at shallow depths this may not be true when the diving schedule changes to short periods at deep depths. The desirable solution to the problem in the light of these unresolved complexities was to evolve decompression schedules which markedly reduced the overall bends incidence.

Caisson and tunnel work in compressed air has encountered similar difficulties, and minor modifications of their schedules have failed to influence the situation. Accordingly, entirely new decompression procedures were requested from the Royal Navy Physiological Laboratory (RNPL). These tables have been called 'The Blackpool Tables' because they were first tested on compressed air work at Blackpool in 1966. A certificate of exemption to enable contractors legally to employ these new Tables has been granted by HM Factory Inspectorate, and all major compressed air work in this country, since their introduction, has been carried out using them. Over 50 000 entries into compressed air in caissons and tunnels have been made at pressures in excess of 10m (30 ft) of sea water, including some working times in excess of 8 hours at pressures of nearly 30m (100 ft) of sea water. To date there have been no fatalities, only a few cases of serious acute decompression sickness, and a low incidence of bends. Thus, by adopting a more conservative decompression schedule, there is a good basis for believing that diving may be conducted more safely, and for longer periods, than previously.

These new Air Diving Tables have been calculated on exactly the same principles as those of the Blackpool Tables. However, experience has shown that some of the modifications in the Air Diving Tables 1968 were slightly over-cautious and, accordingly, a return has been made to the old established no-stop dive times.

The limits of depth and time given in the Tables represent what is considered to be normal usage plus a further allowance for any emergencies or unusual commitments which may occur. These Tables have now been tested over a range of pressures, times, water conditions and numbers of different men necessary to establish their reliability. They should prove safe in use but there is always a small number of seemingly unavoidable incidents which occur following the use of even extremely well-established procedures and no relaxation of recognised safe practices is therefore permissible.

Using the Tables

Note: For all practical purposes related to the use of these Tables, the unit of the bar may be taken to be the equivalent of 10m standard seawater.

STANDARD DIVES

1. The bottom time is taken as the time between leaving the surface and leaving the bottom.
2. All descents to depth are to be not faster than 30m/min (100 ft/min).
3. All ascents are to be at 15m/min (50 ft/min).
4. All time spent ascending from one stop to another (including from depth to the first stop) is included in the next stop time.
5. Air and pure oxygen decompression should be used for any dive where decompression time on air alone would exceed 31 min.
6. If pure oxygen is not available, or in case of emergency, multiply the oxygen stop time by 2 and add to the air stop time (if any) to give the equivalent air decompression stop time.
7. Ascent to the first stop must always be on air.

COMBINED DIVES

1. For regular air diving, no more than 8 h in any period of 24 h must be spent under pressure (bottom times plus decompression times).
2. **If the surface interval between two dives is 2 h or less:** Add the bottom times of the two dives together, and decompress for this bottom time at the deeper of the two dive depths.
3. **If the surface interval between two dives is greater than 2 h but less than 4 h:** Add one half of the bottom time of the first dive to the bottom time of the second dive, and decompress for this bottom time at the deeper of the two dive depths.
4. **If the surface interval is greater than 4 h but less than 8 h:** Add one quarter of the bottom time of the first dive to the bottom time of the second dive, and decompress for this bottom time at the deeper of the two dive depths.
5. **If the surface interval is greater than 8 h but less than 16 h:** Add one eighth of the bottom time of the first dive to the bottom time of the second dive, and decompress for this bottom time at the deeper of the two dive depths.
6. **After a 16-h surface interval:** The diver need take no account of the previous dive.
7. If both dives are to depths less than 40m and the bottom times are above the double black lines in the decompression Tables, the above rules can be amended to state that if the surface interval is greater than 4 h but less than 6 h then add one quarter of the bottom time of the first dive to the bottom time of the second dive and decompress for this bottom time at the deeper of the two dive depths. After a 6-h surface interval, the diver need not take any account of the previous dive.
8. If the second dive does not exceed a depth of 9m then it is safe to surface from this second dive without stoppages.

SURFACE DECOMPRESSION

1. **Surface decompression:** By this technique, the diver is brought directly from depth to the surface and quickly installed in a compression chamber where he is repressurised for subsequent normal decompression according to the Tables.

2. **Rate of ascent in the water:** 15m/min (50 ft/min).

3. **Repressurisation in chamber:** The diver must be repressurised in the chamber within 5min of leaving the seabed. Immediately the diver is closed up in the chamber, it is to be pressurised to the air pressure equivalent to the depth which would have been the diver's first stop under normal decompression in the water PLUS 10m. The diver is then to spend 5min at this pressure before commencing the ascent.

4. **Decompression:** Thereafter, normal decompression procedures are to be followed, but the stops during the ascent are to be taken for the incremented duration (i.e. the actual dive time plus the time of the water ascent and entry into the chamber plus the 5min period described in 3 above). The incremented duration should not exceed the maximum permissible bottom time shown in the Tables.

DIVING AT ALTITUDE

1. Most diving takes place at sea level where the pressure on the surface is 1 atm. absolute.

2. If a dive is carried out at altitude (e.g. in a mountain lake), then the surface pressure is less than 1 atm. absolute. Because of this, decompression schedules must be adjusted to prevent the onset of decompression sickness in the rarified atmosphere.

3. Water will invariably be fresh, but stoppages should be calculated assuming it to be salt. This will increase the safety margin of the schedule.

4. Adjustments should be made to the Tables as follows:

   (a) **Dives between altitudes of 100m and 300m:** Add one quarter of the actual depth to give the calculated depth of the dive.

   (b) **Dives between altitudes of 300m and 2000m:** Add one third of the actual depth to give the calculated depth of the dive.

   (c) **Dives between altitudes of 2000m and 3000m:** Add one half of the actual depth to give the calculated depth of the dive.

   For example, a dive to a depth of 24m from an altitude of 1000m should be treated in the decompression Tables as a dive to a depth of 32m.

5. There are no adjustments to the Tables required at altitudes of less than 100m.

RNPL Air Diving Tables

Read pages 5 and 6

DEPTH NOT EXCEEDING: 9 m (approx. 30 ft)
No limit

Read pages 5 and 6

DEPTH NOT EXCEEDING: 10 m (approx. 33 ft)

Bottom time not exceeding (min)	Stoppages at different depths (min)							Total time for decompression (min)
	Air			Oxygen or air				
				O_2	Air	O_2	Air	
	25 m	20 m	15 m	10 m		5 m		
230								1
420							5	5
480							10	10

Read pages 5 and 6

DEPTH NOT EXCEEDING: 15 m (approx. 49 ft)

Bottom time not exceeding (min)	Stoppages at different depths (min)							Total time for decompression (min)
	Air			Oxygen or air				
				O_2	Air	O_2	Air	
	25 m	20 m	15 m	10 m		5 m		
80								1
85							5	5
90							10	10
100							15	15
110							25	25
120							30	30
150						25	–	25
180						30	–	30
240						40	–	40

RNPL AIR DIVING TABLES

Read pages 5 and 6

DEPTH NOT EXCEEDING: 20 m (approx.66 ft)								
Bottom time not exceeding (min)	Stoppages at different depths (min)							Total time for decompression (min)
	Air			Oxygen or air				
				O_2	Air	O_2	Air	
	25 m	20m	15m	10m		5m		
45								1½
50							5	5
55							10	10
60							15	15
65							25	25
70							30	30
75						20	–	20
90						30	–	30
120						45	–	45
150						55		55
180				5	–	55		60
240				5	–	60		65

Read pages 5 and 6

DEPTH NOT EXCEEDING: 25 m (approx.82 ft)								
Bottom time not exceeding (min)	Stoppages at different depths (min)							Total time for decompression (min)
	Air			Oxygen or air				
				O_2	Air	O_2	Air	
	25m	20m	15m	10m		5m		
25								2
30					5	–	5	10
35					5	–	10	15
40					5	–	15	20
45					5	–	20	25
50				5	–	15	–	20
55				5	–	20	–	25
60				5	–	30	–	35
75			5	–	–	40	–	45
90			5	5	–	50	–	60
105			5	5	–	60	–	70
120			5	10	–	60	–	75
150			5	15	–	60	–	80
180		5	–	20	–	60	5	90

RNPL AIR DIVING TABLES

Read pages 5 and 6

DEPTH NOT EXCEEDING: 30 m (approx.98 ft)								
Bottom time not exceeding (min)	Stoppages at different depths (min)							Total time for decompression (min)
	Air			Oxygen or air				
				O_2	Air	O_2	Air	
	25 m	20 m	15 m	10 m		5 m		
20								2
25					5	–	5	10
30					5	–	10	15
35					5	–	20	25
40				5	–	20	–	25
45				5	–	25	–	30
50			5	–	–	35	–	40
55			5	5	–	40	–	50
60			5	5	–	45	–	55
75			5	5	–	55	-	65
90			5	10	–	60	–	75
120		5	–	20	10	60	5	100

Read pages 5 and 6

DEPTH NOT EXCEEDING: 35 m (approx.115 ft)								
Bottom time not exceeding (min)	Stoppages at different depths (min)							Total time for decompression (min)
	Air			Oxygen or air				
				O_2	Air	O_2	Air	
	25 m	20 m	15 m	10 m		5 m		
15								2½
20					5	–	5	10
25					5	–	15	20
30					5	–	25	30
35				5	–	20	–	25
40			5	5	–	30	–	40
45			5	5	–	40	–	50
50			5	5	–	45	–	55
55			5	5	–	50	–	60
60			5	5	–	55	–	65
75		5	–	15	–	60	--	80

RNPL AIR DIVING TABLES

Read pages 5 and 6

DEPTH NOT EXCEEDING 40 m (approx.131 ft)								
Bottom time not exceeding (min)	Stoppages at different depths (min)							Total time for decompression (min)
	Air			Oxygen or air				
				O_2	Air	O_2	Air	
	25 m	20 m	15 m	10 m		5 m		
11								3
15					5	–	5	10
20					5	–	10	15
25					5	–	25	30
30			5	–	–	25		30
35			5	5	–	35	–	45
40			5	5	–	45	–	55
45			5	5	–	50	–	60
50		5	–	10	–	55	–	70
55		5	–	10	–	60	–	75
60		5	–	15	–	60	–	80

Read pages 5 and 6

DEPTH NOT EXCEEDING 45 m (approx.148 ft)								
Bottom time not exceeding (min)	Stoppages at different depths (min)							Total time for decompression (min)
	Air			Oxygen or air				
				O_2	Air	O_2	Air	
	25 m	20 m	15 m	10 m		5 m		
9								3
15					5	–	10	15
20					5	–	20	25
25			5	5	–	20		30
30			5	5	–	35	–	45
35			5	5	–	45	–	55
40		5	–	5	–	50	–	60
45		5	–	10	–	55	–	70
50		5	5	15	–	60	–	85
55		5	5	20	–	60	5	95

RNPL AIR DIVING TABLES

Read pages 5 and 6

DEPTH NOT EXCEEDING: 50 m (approx.164 ft)								
Bottom time not exceeding (min)	Stoppages at different depths (min)							Total time for decompression (min)
	Air			Oxygen or air				
				O_2	Air	O_2	Air	
	25 m	20 m	15 m	10 m		5 m		
7								3½
10					5	–	5	10
15					5	–	10	15
20			5	5	–	15	–	25
25			5	5	–	30	–	40
30			5	5	–	40	–	50
35		5	–	5	–	50	–	60
40		5	5	10	–	60	–	80
45		5	5	15	–	60	–	85
50	5	–	5	20	–	60	5	95

Read pages 5 and 6

DEPTH NOT EXCEEDING: 55 m (approx.180 ft)								
Bottom time not exceeding (min)	Stoppages at different depths (min)							Total time for decompression (min)
	Air			Oxygen or air				
				O_2	Air	O_2	Air	
	25 m	20 m	15 m	10 m		5 m		
6								4
10					5	–	5	10
15			5	–	–	–	15	20
20			5	5	–	20	–	30
25			5	5	–	35	–	45
30		5	–	5	–	50	–	60
35		5	5	10	–	60	–	80
40		5	5	15	–	60	–	85
45	5	–	5	20	5	60	5	100

RNPL AIR DIVING TABLES

Read pages 5 and 6

DEPTH NOT EXCEEDING: 60 m (approx.197 ft)								
Bottom time not exceeding (min)	Stoppages at different depths (min)							Total time for decompression (min)
	Air			Oxygen or air				
				O_2	Air	O_2	Air	
	25 m	20 m	15 m	10 m		5 m		
5								4
10					5	–	10	15
15			5	–	5	–	20	30
20			5	5	–	25	–	35
25		5	–	5	–	45	–	55
30		5	5	10	–	55	–	75
35	5	–	5	15	–	60	–	85
40	5	–	5	20	5	60	5	100
45	5	–	10	20	20	60	5	120

APPENDIX E: BUEHLMANN HIGH ALTITUDE TABLE
(2501-4500 m above sea level)

NO-DECOMPRESSION LIMITS. AIR DIVING DECOMPRESSION TABLE

2501 - 4500 m above sea level (24 hrs at altitude)

Depth m	BT min	Stops 9	6	4	2	RG
9	204				1	G
12	88				1	G
	100				5	G
	110				9	G
	120				13	G
15	50				1	E
	60				2	F
	70				8	G
	80				14	G
	90				20	G
18	32				1	D
	40				3	F
	50				7	F
	60			1	13	G
	70			3	17	G
21	22				1	D
	30				3	E
	35				6	F
	40			1	7	F
	45			3	10	F
	50			4	13	G
	55			6	15	G
	60			8	18	G
24	16				1	D
	25				4	E
	30			1	6	F
	35			3	8	F
	40			5	12	F
	45		1	6	15	F
	50		3	7	18	G

Depth m	BT min	Stops 9	6	4	2	RG
27	14				1	D
	20				4	E
	25			2	6	E
	30			5	7	F
	35		2	5	12	F
	40		4	6	15	G
30	11				1	D
	15				3	D
	20			2	5	E
	25		1	4	7	F
	30		3	5	11	F
	35	1	4	7	15	G
33	9				1	D
	12				2	D
	15			1	4	E
	18			3	5	F
	21		1	4	6	F
	24		3	5	7	F
	27	1	3	6	11	G
36	8				1	D
	12			1	3	D
	15			3	4	E
	18		1	4	6	F
	21		3	5	7	F
	24	1	4	6	11	F
	27	3	4	7	14	G
39	7				1	D
	12			2	4	E
	15		1	4	5	E
	18	1	2	5	6	F
	21	2	3	6	10	F
	24	3	5	6	14	G

NO-DECOMPRESSION LIMITS. AIR DIVING DECOMPRESSION TABLE

2501 - 4500 m above sea level (24 hrs at altitude)

Depth	BT	Stops					RG
m	min	12	9	6	4	2	
42	7					1	D
	9				1	3	E
	12			1	3	4	E
	15		1	2	4	6	F
	18		2	3	5	9	F
	21		4	4	6	13	F
	24	1	5	5	8	16	G
45	6					1	C
	9				2	3	E
	12			2	3	5	F
	15		2	3	4	7	F
	18		3	4	6	11	F
	21	1	5	5	7	15	G
48	6					1	C
	9			1	2	4	E
	12		1	2	4	6	F
	15		3	3	5	9	F
	18	1	4	5	6	14	G
51	5					1	C
	9			2	2	5	E
	12		2	3	4	6	F
	15	1	3	4	6	11	F
	18	2	5	5	7	16	G
54	6				1	2	E
	9		1	2	3	5	F
	12		3	3	5	7	F
	15	2	4	5	6	13	G

REPETITIVE DIVE TIME-TABLE 0 - 4500 m above sea level

Surface Interval Times

RG at start of surface interval

RG at start	G	F	E	D	C	B	A	"0"	✈
A								2	2
B							20	2	2
C						10	25	3	3
D					10	15	30	3	3
E				10	15	25	45	4	3
F			20	30	45	75	90	8	4
G		25	45	60	75	100	130	12	5
	G	F	E	D	C	B	A	hrs	hrs

RG at end of surface interval

Example:
Previous dive: 24 m, 35 min = Repetitive Group **(RG) = F**
- after 45 min at surface: **RG = C**
- after 90 min at surface: **RG = A** (intermediate time: use next **shorter** interval time)
- after 4 hrs: flying is permitted
- after 8 hrs: **RG = "0"**, no more Residual Nitrogen Time **(RNT)**

RG for No-Decompression Dives and RNT for Repetitive Dives

Repetitive dive depth m (intermediate depths: use next **shallower** depth)

RG	9	12	15	18	21	24	27	30	33	36	39	42	45	48	51	54	57
A	25	19	16	14	12	11	10	9	8	7	7	6	6	6	5	5	5
B	37	25	20	17	15	13	12	11	10	9	8	7	7	6	5	5	5
C	55	37	29	25	22	20	18	16	14	12	11	10	9	8	7	7	6
D	81	57	41	33	28	24	21	19	17	15	14	13	11	10	9	9	8
E	105	82	59	44	37	30	26	23	21	19	17	16	14	13	12	11	10
F	130	111	88	68	53	42	35	30	27	24	21	19	17	16	15	14	13

Example: RG = C at end of surface interval. Planned depth of repetitive dive = 27 m. **RNT = 18 min**, to be added to Bottom Time (BT) of repetitive dive.

APPENDIX F

KISMAN-MASUREL (KM) CODE FOR BUBBLE GRADING

Three parameters are used to describe the bubble signal. Each parameter is assigned a classification from 0 to 4. The first, frequency, represents the number of bubbles per cardiac period (Table F.1).

TABLE F.1

Frequency parameter	
Code	**Frequency (f)**
0	0
1	1 - 2
2	several 3 - 8
3	rolling drumbeat 9 - 40
4	continuous sound

For code 4, the bubbles are so numerous that they cannot be individually distinguished.

The second parameter differs for the two monitoring conditions - rest and movement (Table F.2). For the rest condition, it represents the percentage of cardiac periods having a specified bubble frequency. For the movement condition, it represents the percentage of cardiac periods having at least a specified bubble frequency (i.e. the first parameter) following the movement. The first such period must occur within 10 heart beats following the movement.

TABLE F.2

Percentage/duration parameter		
Code	**Rest Percentage (p)**	**Movement Duration (d)**
0	0	0
1	1 - 10	1 - 2
2	10 - 50	3 - 5
3	50 - 99	6 - 10
4	100	> 10

The third parameter is the amplitude of the bubble signal, which is compared to the amplitude of the normal cardiac sounds (Table F.3).

TABLE F.3

Amplitude parameter	
Grade	**Amplitude (a)**
0	no bubbles discernible
1	barely perceptible, $A_b << A_c$
2	moderate amplitude, $A_b < A_c$
3	loud, $A_b \simeq A_c$
4	maximal, $A_b > A_c$

The three parameters are combined in the form `fpa' for the rest case and `fda' for the movement case to give the KM code for each assessment. This KM code is reduced to a single Bubble Grade (g) according to Table F.4.

TABLE F.4

KM Code Bubble Grade

fpa fda	g	fpa fda	g	fpa fda	g	fpa fda	g
111	I-	211	I-	311	I-	411	II-
112	I	212	I	312	II-	412	II
113	I	213	I+	313	II	413	II+
114	I+	214	II-	314	II	414	III-
121	I+	221	II-	321	II	421	III-
122	II	222	II	322	II+	422	III
123	II	223	II+	323	III-	423	III
124	II	224	II+	324	III	424	III+
131	II	231	II	331	III-	431	III
132	II	232	III-	332	III	432	III+
133	III-	233	III	333	III	433	IV-
134	III-	234	III	334	III+	434	IV
141	II	241	III-	341	III	441	III+
142	III-	242	III	342	III+	442	IV
143	III	243	III	343	III+	443	IV
144	III	244	III+	344	IV-	444	IV

Reprinted from: Nishi, R. and Eatock, B., "The role of ultrasonic bubble detection in table validation". In: *Proceedings of the UHMS Workshop on "Validation of Decompression Schedules"*; 11-14 Feb 1987, Bethesda, MD.

APPENDIX G

U.S. NAVY RECOMPRESSION THERAPY TABLES 6 (Top) and 6A (Bottom)

WARNING: *The therapy tables reprinted in this appendix are incomplete as some of the rules accompanying the tables have been omitted.* These tables are only reprinted to give a general overview of a typical treatment regimen and they are not to be followed unless used in accordance with the appropriate directions for use.

OXYGEN TREATMENT OF TYPE II DECOMPRESSION SICKNESS

1. Treatment of Type II or Type I decompression sickness when symptoms are not relieved within 10 minutes at 60 feet.
2. Descent rate — 25 ft/min.
3. Ascent rate — 1 ft/min. Do not compensate for slower ascent rates. Compensate for faster rates by halting the ascent.
4. Time at 60 feet begins on arrival at 60 feet.
5. If oxygen breathing must be interrupted, allow 15 minutes after the reaction has entirely subsided and resume schedule at point of interruption.
6. Tender breathes air throughout unless he has had a hyperbaric exposure within the past 12 hours in which case he breathes oxygen at 30 feet in accordance with Section 8.12.5.7.
7. Table 6 can be lengthened up to 2 additional 25 minute oxygen breathing periods at 60 feet (20 minutes on oxygen and 5 minutes on air) or up to 2 additional 75 minute oxygen breathing periods at 30 feet (15 minutes on air and 60 minutes on oxygen), or both. If Table 6 is extended only once at either 60 or 30 feet, the tender breathes oxygen during the ascent from 30 feet to the surface. If more than one extension is done, the tender begins oxygen breathing for the last hour at 30 feet during ascent to the surface.

Depth (feet)	Time (minutes)	Breathing Media	Total Elapsed Time (hrs:min.)
60	20	Oxygen	0:20
60	5	Air	0:25
60	20	Oxygen	0:45
60	5	Air	0:50
60	20	Oxygen	1:10
60	5	Air	1:15
60 to 30	30	Oxygen	1:45
30	15	Air	2:00
30	60	Oxygen	3:00
30	15	Air	3:15
30	60	Oxygen	4:15
30 to 0	30	Oxygen	4:45

INITIAL AIR AND OXYGEN TREATMENT OF ARTERIAL GAS EMBOLISM

1. Treatment of arterial gas embolism where complete relief obtained within 30 min. at 165 feet. Use also when unable to determine whether symptoms are caused by gas embolism or severe decompression sickness.
2. Descent rate — as fast as possible.
3. Ascent rate — 1 ft/min. Do not compensate for slower ascent rates. Compensate for faster ascent rates by halting the ascent.
4. Time at 165 feet — includes time from the surface.
5. If oxygen breathing must be interrupted, allow 15 minutes after the reaction has entirely subsided and resume schedule at point of interruption (see Section 8.12.4.1).
6. Tender breathes oxygen during ascent from 30 feet to the surface unless he has had a hyperbaric exposure within the past 12 hours in which case he breathes oxygen at 30 feet in accordance with Section 8.12.5.7.
7. Table 6A can be lengthened up to 2 additional 25 minute oxygen breathing periods at 60 feet (20 minutes on oxygen and 5 minutes on air) or up to 2 additional 75 minute oxygen breathing periods at 30 feet (15 minutes on air and 60 minutes on oxygen), or both. If Table 6A is extended either at 60 or 30 feet the tender breathes oxygen during the last half at 30 feet and during ascent to the surface.
8. If complete relief not obtained within 30 min. at 165 feet, switch to Table 4. Consult with a Diving Medical Officer before switching if possible.

Depth (feet)	Time (minutes)	Breathing Media	Total Elapsed Time (hrs:min)
165	30	Air	0:30
165 to 60	4	Air	0:34
60	20	Oxygen	0:54
60	5	Air	0:59
60	20	Oxygen	1:19
60	5	Air	1:29
60	20	Oxygen	1:44
60	5	Air	1:49
60 to 30	30	Oxygen	2:19
30	15	Air	2:34
30	60	Oxygen	3:34
30	15	Air	3:49
30	60	Oxygen	4:49
30 to 0	30	Oxygen	5:19

APPENDIX H

ROYAL NAVY RECOMPRESSION THERAPY TABLE 62

WARNING:

The therapy tables reprinted in this appendix are incomplete as the rules accompanying the tables have been omitted. **These tables are only reprinted to give a general overview of a typical treatment regimen and they are not to be followed unless used in accordance with the appropriate directions for use.**

TABLE 62

OXYGEN RECOMPRESSION THERAPY

GAUGE DEPTH (*metres*)	STOPPAGES/ ASCENT (*minutes*)	ELAPSED TIME (*hours and minutes*)	RATE OF ASCENT (*metres/minute*)
18	20 (O_2)	0000–0020	—
18	5	0020–0025	—
18	20 (O_2)	0025–0045	—
18	5	0045–0050	—
18	20 (O_2)	0050–0110	—
18	5	0110–0115	—
18–9	30 (O_2)	0115–0145	3 m in 10 mins
9	15	0145–0200	—
9	60 (O_2)	0200–0300	—
9	15	0300–0315	—
9	60 (O_2)	0315–0415	—
9–0	30 (O_2)	0415–0445	3 m in 10 mins
Surface		0445	

INDEX

Adaptation
  to cold 135
  to DCS 110
  respiratory 36, 124
  underwater 3, 36, 124
After drop 138
Air consumption 528, 531
  calculation of 533
Air embolism 11, 65, 78
Alcohol 71, 167
  effects on DCS 71, 168
  effects on hypothermia 139, 168
  effects on narcosis 118
Altitude diving 70, 251, 273, 295, 320, 393
Alveoli 10, 15
Aorta 19
Anxiety 7, 71, 119
Arteries 18, 26
Arterial gas embolism 64, 78
Ascent
  indicator 97, 463
  line 97
  rate 61, 67, 93, 96, 188, 211, 231, 235, 252, 283, 308, 327, 352, 449, 463
Aspirn and DCS 72, 82, 111
Atrium 19, 20, 64, 70, 78

Balanced regulator 525
Bends, see
  decompression sickness
Blood
  composition 17
  donation and diving 112
Blue orb syndrome 7
Bone necrosis 84, 145
Bradycardia 37, 135, 140
Breathing
  capacity 7, 13
  resistance to 36, 123
Bronchi 10
Bronchioles 10
Bubble nuclei 49, 69
Buoyancy changes
  at depth 527
  at altitude 393
Buoyancy compensator 97, 528
Caisson workers 59, 69
Caloric effects 6
Capillary gauge 395
Carbon dioxide
  production 15, 123
  transport 15, 123
  build-up 123
  toxicity 125
Carbon monoxide 168
Cerebral decompression sickness 63, 65, 96
Chokes 62
Chamber, see
  Recompression chamber
Chemoreceptors 16
Cigarette smoking 62, 168
Cilia 10
Circulation 18
Cold, effect on bends 68, 210
Corneal lenses 111
Contamination of air supply 124
Contraceptive pill, see Pill
Convulsions 501, 518
Cylinders, SCUBA 518

Dalton's Law 41
DCS, see decompression sickness
Dead space (anatomical) 14
Decompression meter 444
Decompression computer,
  see dive computers
Decompression sickness
  Cause 60
  Signs/symptoms 61
  Predisposing factors 67
  Treatment 74
  First aid 78
  Implications 84
  Prevention 93
  Diving after 83
  Flying after 388

Decompression tables
History 177
Bassett 229
BS-AC 88 325
Buehlmann 253, 599
Buehlmann/Hahn 265
DCIEM 279, 560
Huggins 225
NAUI 237
PADI RDP 247
Royal Navy 304, 579
RNPL 304, 589
RNPL/BSAC 303
U.S. Navy
Standard 185, 196, 550
New 239
Decompression stop diving 105, 477
Decompression
line 477
stage 477
bar 103. 477
Decongestants 170
Depth gauge 106
Desaturation 43, 53, 459
Diffusion 15
Dive computers 106, 443, 388, 480
Dive profiles 106
Diving Reflex 37, 135
Doppler ultrasonic monitor 53, 95, 225, 280, 349
Drugs 72, 167
Dry suits 135
Dysbaric osteonecrosis
see, Bone necrosis

Emergency
Air supply 526
In-water recompression 517
Epiglottis 10
Equilibrium 41
Esophagus 10
Exercise, effects on bends 69
Expiration, see Breathing
Expired Air Resuscitation 15, 140
Eye damage 85, 154

Facial immersion 38, 135
Fast tissues 42, 61
Fatigue 71
Females, and diving 72, 153
FEV 1 14
Fitness for diving 70, 172, 173
Flying
before diving 389
after diving 70, 381
after DCS 388
Fetus, effect of
diving on 153
Foramen ovale
patent 20, 64, 78, 98, 154
Fresh water diving 393
Fudge factors, see
Safety factors

Gas density 36, 124
Gas diffusion, see diffusion
Gas embolism, see
Arterial gas embolism
Gas exchange 14
Gas uptake and elimination 41, 53, 68, 327, 459
Gastrointestinal decompression
sickness 66

Haldane 177, 185, 443
Half-time 248, 279, 348, 445, 460
Heat loss 131
Heart 19
Henry's Law 41
Helium 118, 75, 248
Hemoglobin 14
Hyperbaric oxygen 74, 500, 518
Hypercapnia 124
Hyperventilation 127
Hypothermia 136
Hypoxia 499

Immersion 37, 141
Inert gas narcosis 117
Inhalation 10
Inspiration 10
Inner ear decompression sickness 66
Insulation, thermal 134
Itch in bends 66

Joint bends 65, 67

Larynx 10
Light, underwater 4
Limiting line 305
Lung(s)
- Capacity 13
- Function 14
- Rupture 11, 12
- Structure 10

Lymphatic system 32

Maintenance of equipment 126, 527
Mammary implants 161
Masks 4
Medicine, see drugs
Medulla 16
Membrane, alveolar-capillary 11
Menstruation 161
Mental changes 7, 118
Motion sickness 171
Multi-day diving 105, 353, 459, 463
Multi-level diving 423, 443
Multiple ascents 67, 98
M-value 185, 225, 350
Necrosis, see
- Bone necrosis

Neutral buoyancy 528
Neurological
- decompression sickness 63, 65, 96

Nitrogen narcosis
- Cause 117
- Manifestations 118, 119
- Predisposing factors 120
- Prevention 120, 121

Nitrogen
- elimination 43, 53, 60, 68, 100, 459
- solubility 42
- uptake 41, 60, 68

Obesity, bends and 68
Octopus regulator 526
Omitted decompression 295, 355, 365, 463, 485
Oral contraceptives 161, 172
Osmosis 146
Oxygen
- effect on fetus 154
- equipment 504
- insufficiency 499
- therapy 74, 80, 501
- transport 14, 499
- toxicity 500, 518
- emergency recompression 518
- decompression 482

Oxyhemoglobin 14

Panic 7, 119, 527
Paralysis 63, 82, 84
Patent foramen ovale
- effect on DCS 20, 64, 70, 78

Perfusion 42
Pill, the 161, 172
Pharynx 10
Physiology
- Respiration 9
- Circulation 18
- Gas transport 14, 15, 41
- Respiratory control 16
- Diving physiology 36

Plasma 17, 27, 501
Pleura 10
Pneumothorax 12, 502
Psychological effects 7
Pregnancy, diving and, 153
Pulmonary barotrauma 168, 502
Pulmonary circulation 18, 62
Pulse 29, 37, 140

Rate of ascent,
  see ascent rate
  descent 282, 308
Recompression
  chamber 74
  in water 517
  therapy 74, 604, 605
Repetitive dives 68, 105, 192, 199, 205, 252, 258, 272, 287, 309, 339, 358, 368, 458
Regulator 123, 126, 525
Resistance to breathing 7, 36, 123
Respiration
  adaptation 37
  control of 16
  mechanism 10
Respiratory centre, see Medulla
Resuscitation 15, 140
Ringing in ears 66
RN Table 304, 579
RNPL Table 304, 589
RNPL/BSAC Table 303

Safety factors, for tables 94, 217, 218, 318
Saturation 41
Sea sickness 171
Shock 27, 63
Silent bubbles 53, 60, 85, 99, 381
Skip breathing 124
Slow tissues 42, 61, 100, 252, 381, 459
Smoking, see Cigarette smoking
Sound underwater 5
Spinal decompression sickness 63, 84
Supersaturation 47
Surface interval 105, 192
Surfactant 11
Systemic circulation 19

Tables, see Decompression tables
Tanks, see Cylinders
Temperature 42, 68, 131, 411
Thermocline 135, 412
Thoracic cavity 10
Tidal volume 14
Tissue half-time, see Half-time
Tissue compartment, see Half-time
Tolerance, to bends 110
Trachea 10

Ultrasonic monitoring
  of bubbles, see Doppler
Unconsiousness 63, 124, 137
U.S. Navy
  tables 185, 550
  diving practices 215

Vasodilation 27, 43, 126
Vasoconstriction 27, 43, 131
Veins 26
Ventilation 7, 36
Ventricular fibrillation 137
Ventricle 19
Vertigo 6, 66
Vision 4, 85, 111
Vital capacity 14

Weight-belt 393, 529
Wetsuit
  compression of 134, 527
Women in diving 72, 153

X-ray of long bones 148

Zero adjust 394

OTHER BOOKS BY JOHN LIPPMANN

"THE DIVING EMERGENCY HANDBOOK" by John Lippmann and Stan Bugg, J.L. Publications, Melbourne.

A guide to the identification of and first aid for SCUBA diving injuries.

Released in Austrália as **"The DES Emergency Handbook"** and available from J.L. Publications, P.O. Box 381, Carnegie, Victoria, 3163.

Released in the USA as **"The DAN Emergency Handbook"** and available from The Divers Alert Network (DAN), Box 3823, Duke University Medical Center, Durham, North Carolina 27710, and from Aqua Quest Publications Inc., P.O. Drawer A, Locust Valley, NY 11560-0495.

Released in the UK as **"The Diving Emergency Handbook"** and available from Eaton Publications, 55 High St, Teddington, Middlesex, TW11 8HA, London.

"THE ESSENTIALS OF DEEPER DIVING" by John Lippmann.

An overview of the theory and requirements of diving from 80-130 ft (24-39 m).

Published in Australia by The Federation of Australian Underwater Instructors (FAUI), P.O. Box 246, Tuart Hill, WA, 6060.

Published in the USA by Aqua Quest Publications Inc., P.O. Drawer A, Locust Valley, NY 11560-0495.